Language Perception and Production:

Relationships between Listening, Speaking, Reading and Writing

Cognitive Science Series

Collections

1. Reasoning and Discourse Processes   *T. Myers, K. Brown and B. McGonigle (eds), 1986*
2. New Directions in Semantics   *E. LePore (ed.), 1987*
3. Language Perception and Production: Relationships between listening, speaking, reading and writing   *A. Allport, D. G. MacKay, W. Prinz and E. Scheerer (eds), 1987*

Monographs

Agreement and Anaphora   *P. Bosch, 1983*

Language Perception and Production:

Relationships between Listening, Speaking, Reading and Writing

edited by

ALAN ALLPORT
University of Oxford, Oxford, England

DONALD G. MACKAY
University of California, Los Angeles, USA

WOLFGANG PRINZ
University of Bielefeld, Bielefeld, West Germany

and

ECKART SCHEERER
Universität Oldenberg, Oldenberg, West Germany

1987

ACADEMIC PRESS
Harcourt Brace Jovanovich, Publishers
London   Orlando   New York   San Diego   Austin
Boston   Sydney   Tokyo   Toronto

United States Edition published by
ACADEMIC PRESS INC.
Orlando, Florida 32887

Copyright © 1987 by
ACADEMIC PRESS INC. (LONDON) LTD.

British Library Cataloguing in Publication Data

Language perception and production:
relationships between listening, speaking,
reading and writing.
1. Communication—Psychological aspects
I. Allport, Alan
153   BF637.C45

ISBN 0-12-052750-2

Phototypeset by Katerprint Typesetting Services, Oxford
Printed by St Edmundsbury Press, Bury St Edmunds, Suffolk

Contributors

Alan Allport *Department of Experimental Psychology, University of Oxford, South Parks Road, Oxford OX1 3UD, U.K.*

Derek Besner *Department of Psychology, University of Waterloo, Waterloo, Ontario N2L 3G1, Canada*

Ruth Campbell *Department of Experimental Psychology, University of Oxford, South Parks Road, Oxford OX1 3UD, U.K.*

Max Coltheart *Department of Psychology, Birkbeck College, University of London, Malet Street, London WC1E 7HX, U.K.*

Anne Cutler *Applied Psychology Unit, 15 Chaucer Road, Cambridge CB2 2EF, U.K.*

Werner Deutsch *Max-Planck-Institut für Psycholinguistik, Wundtlaan, 6525 XD Nijmegen, The Netherlands*

Laurie B. Feldman *Department of Psychology, University of Delaware, 220 Wolf Hall, Newark, DE 19713, U.S.A.*

Sue Franklin *Department of Clinical Communication Studies, The City University, London, U.K.*

Elaine Funnell *Department of Psychology, Birkbeck College, Malet Street, London WC1E 7HX, U.K.*

Judith Goodman *Department of Education, University of Chicago, 5835 Kimbark Avenue, Chicago, Illinois 60637, U.S.A.*

Peter C. Gordon *Department of Psychology and Social Relations, William James Hall, 33 Kirkland Street, Cambridge, Massachusetts 02138, U.S.A.*

David Howard *Psychology Department, University College London, Gower Street, London WC1E 6BT, U.K.*

Janellen Huttenlocher *Department of Education, University of Chicago, 5835 Kimbark Avenue, Chicago, Illinois 60637, U.S.A.*

Robert J. Jarvella *Avdelningen för allmän sprakvetenskap, Umeå Universitet, 90187 Umeå, Sweden*

Remo Job *Istituto di Psicologia dell' Università di Padova, Padova, Italy*

Janice Kay *Department of Speech, The University, St Thomas' Street, Newcastle-upon-Tyne NE1 7RU, U.K.*

Steven Keele *Department of Psychology, University of Oregon, Eugene, Oregon 97403, U.S.A.*

Donald G. MacKay *Department of Psychology, University of California, Los Angeles, California 90024, U.S.A.*

Dominic Massaro *Program in Experimental Psychology, University of California, Santa Cruz, California 95064, U.S.A.*

David E. Meyer *Department of Psychology, The University of Michigan, Human Performance Center, 330 Packard Road, Ann Arbor, Michigan 48104, U.S.A.*

Stephen Monsell *Department of Experimental Psychology, University of Cambridge, Downing Street, Cambridge CB2 3EB, U.K.*

Robert J. Porter *Department of Psychology, University of New Orleans, Lakefront, New Orleans, Louisiana 70148, U.S.A.*

Wolfgang Prinz *Center for Interdisciplinary Research, University of Bielefeld, Wellenberg 1, 4800 Bielefeld, West Germany*

G. Sandström *Avdelningen för allmän sprakvetenskap, Umeå Universitet, 90187 Umeå, Sweden*

Eckart Scheerer *Institut für Kognitionsforschung, Fachbereich 5, Universität Oldenburg, Postfach 2503, 2900 Oldenburg, West Germany*

R. Schreuder *Interfaculty Research Unit for Language and Speech, University of Nijmegen, Nijmegen, The Netherlands*

Michael Studdert-Kennedy *Queens College and Graduate Center, City University of New York, New York, NY, U.S.A.*

Richard L. Venezky *Department of Educational Studies, University of Delaware, Newark, Delaware 19711, U.S.A.*

Preface

Recent years have seen a steadily increasing interest in the relations between perception and action as well as among their specialized subsystems, along with a growing awareness that the systems and subsystems for perception–action interact extensively and cannot be studied independently from one another. This volume provides an advanced level treatment of the most salient issues within this general concern as applied to the main systems and subsystems for language perception–production; listening, speaking, reading, and writing.

The chapters in this book received their impetus from a conference entitled 'Common processes in listening, speaking, reading, and writing' which took place at the Center for Interdisciplinary Research (ZiF), Bielefeld, West Germany in July 1985 as part of the Research Project on Perception and Action organized by Wolfgang Prinz. Like other books which grew out of the Perception and Action Project, the present volume carries an alphabetically determined order of editorship and reflects the interdisciplinary goals of the ZiF: though all but three of the conference participants were psychologists, the book contains information of interest not just to psycholinguists and linguists but also to cognitive psychologists, neurologists, neurolinguists, and kinesiologists.

The main thrust of the book is directed towards the uniquely human abilities and cognitive structures whereby adults perceive and produce language, whether written or spoken. The book also touches briefly on developmental issues—in children (*Studdert-Kennedy*), in the history of languages (*Cutler*), in the evolution of species-specific language abilities (*Studdert-Kennedy*), and in the evolutionary relationship between language and other types of perception–action (*Keele*). It touches on typewriting (*MacKay*, *Keele*) and handwriting, or at least the breakdown in writing ability known as dysgraphia (*Coltheart and Funnell*). The book also includes discussion of the relations between functional brain architecture and information processing (e.g., *Funnell and Allport*, *Keele*, *Monsell*).

Each chapter received at least two reviews, usually from fellow participants at the conference, but occasionally, when a review required special expertise, we called upon outsiders for help. The editors wish to express their special thanks to Deborah Burke (Pomona College, Claremont), Uli Frauenfelder (Max-Planck-Institut für Psycholinguistik), Hartmut Günther (Max-Planck-Institut für Psycholinguistik, Nijmegen), Leslie Henderson (Hatfield Polytechnical Institute), Herbert Heuer (University of Bielefeld), Jodi Kreiman (UCLA), Horst Mittelstaedt (Max-Planck-Institut für Verhaltensphysiologie, Seewiesen), David Rosenbaum (Hamshire College), and Diane Shapiro (UCLA), as well as to many other colleagues who served informally as outside consultants. Without their help, some of the conceptual butterflies in our chapters might still be caterpillars. Thanks are also due to Monika Niemann and Heike Stöver at the University of Oldenburg, who kindly assisted in compiling the subject index.

September, 1986

Donald G. MacKay
Alan Allport
Wolfgang Prinz
Eckart Scheerer

Contents

xi

Section 6.   Sequencing and timing in language perception and production

1 Relationships and modules within language perception and production: An introduction

Donald G. MacKay, Alan Allport, Wolfgang Prinz and Eckart Scheerer

The title of the present book reflects both a common interest of its contributors and a common approach which is emerging within the field at large. The approach treats perception and action as 'integrated-and-equal' rather than 'separate-and-unequal' and is part of a relatively small but rapidly growing tradition in psychology and related disciplines. Of the two, the separate-and-unequal tradition is by far the more prevalent approach to the relations between perception and action (see also Jarvella and Deutsch, Chap 3). Since the time of Descartes, most philosophers have viewed the afferent processes which mediate perception of the external world as separate from the efferent processes which mediate action in the external world. Philosophers have also viewed action as subordinate in importance to perception on functional, temporal, and evaluative grounds: functionally subordinate because they considered perception the sole means by which knowledge is acquired, temporally subordinate because they considered perception a necessary precursor to action, and evaluatively subordinate because they considered perception and contemplation as more important to life than action. Even when 'motor theories' had their heyday in psychology about a hundred years ago, and movement was thought to determine perceptual structure, theorizing remained solidly within the separate-and-unequal tradition (see Scheerer, 1984).

LANGUAGE PERCEPTION AND PRODUCTION
ISBN 0-12-052750-2

Of late, psychologists within the separate-and-unequal tradition, or as Jarvella and Deutsch prefer to call it in psycholinguistics, the apples-and-oranges approach to speaking and listening, have concentrated almost exclusively on perception, rather than on production or on the relation between the two, and often attribute quite different functions to these supposedly separate systems: perceptual systems are supposed to register and to construct a meaning for sensory events, whereas motor systems are supposed to translate goals into motor commands. As Turvey (1977) points out, perception and action have virtually no contact with one another within this framework: how a perceptual system perceives neither influences nor is influenced by how the motor system uses perception.

Psychologists within the separate-and-unequal tradition have explicitly attempted to study perception so far as possible in the *absence* of perception-related action, e.g., with tachistoscopic stimuli presented so briefly as to minimize the possibility of eye movements. As a result, two separate research areas, with little or no interaction between them, have developed in parallel within the separate-and-unequal tradition, one set specializing in afferent processes, the other in efferent processes. Theories of action have been constructed without reference to perception, and theories of perception have been constructed without reference to action, but as Howell and Harvey (1983) point out, virtually no theories have attempted to solve the problems of both perception and action at the same time.

There are of course exceptions, and at least two major theories of perception–production relationships (discussed below) have emerged in the study of language. Why has language been the focus of so much more interest in perception–production? Two reasons stand out. One concerns the obvious structural similarities between the units and products of language perception and production: Both make use of common or at least homomorphic units at the sentential and phonological levels, and one of the main goals of production is to duplicate in the listener the representational structure of the speaker.

The second reason is that language perception and production are intimately related and difficult to separate operationally. Every speaker is simultaneously a listener, and every listener is at least potentially a speaker. From an evolutionary perspective as well, language perception and production are virtually inseparable: The capacities for perceiving and producing speech could only have evolved simultaneously because if a series of mutations enabled a set of humans to understand language, their chances of surviving to transmit the mutation would only improve if a second (perhaps overlapping) set of humans underwent mutations which enabled them to speak (see Geschwind, 1983). Likewise, mutations which enabled a set of humans to speak would only improve *their* chances of survival if they had a language to speak and someone to understand them when they spoke. Like other communicative systems, speech perception and production are so closely intertwined as to require mutual adaptation or conjoint evolution.

Early theories of the perception–production relationship

Two early psycholinguistic theories explicitly attempted to relate speech perception and production: the 'classical' theory and the 'motor' theory of speech perception. Both theories exhibit the (perhaps unintended) influence of the separate-and-unequal tradition in philosophy: For example, both theories assume that components for speech perception and production are completely separate rather than shared.

The classical theory of perception–production

The 'classical theory' was motivated by Broca's and Wernicke's discovery of distinct types of aphasia arising from lesions at different cortical sites, and holds that the systems for perception and production at every level of processing employ separate components in anatomically separate areas of the brain (see Straight, 1980): Early studies of left hemisphere brain injuries seemed to suggest that production is localized in one area of the brain and perception in another, interconnected but separate area. However, recent studies using a variety of new and more sophisticated techniques suggest that the picture may be more complicated. Brain scan and cerebral blood flow studies indicate that Broca's area (which under the classical theory only becomes active during production) also becomes active during comprehension (Lassen and Larsen, 1980), and *vice versa*. Moreover, expressive and receptive deficits are usually commensurate in extent: with appropriate controls for lesion size, aphasics with severely impaired production also display severely impaired comprehension, and *vice versa* (Mateer, 1983). Finally, the distinctiveness of perception versus production deficits has recently become a topic of lively debate. Because aphasics can make up for comprehension deficits using non-linguistic cues, production deficits tend to be more obvious than perceptual deficits in everyday life, and Cooper and Zurif (1983) showed that appropriate tests of comprehension require controls for semantic and pragmatic cues. Using these more sophisticated tests, Cooper and Zurif (1983) argue that Broca's aphasics display comprehension deficits which parallel their more readily observed production deficits, and Wernicke's aphasics display production deficits which parallel their difficulty to demonstrate comprehension deficits. Interestingly, Wernicke was also aware of this parallel, but viewed the production deficits as secondary to and derivative of the perceptual deficits; by hypothesis, the production errors were induced by defective monitoring of self-produced feedback (see Geschwind, 1974, pp. 47–48). For Wernicke, production was both separate and subordinate, in complete agreement with the separate-and-unequal tradition in philosophy.

The early motor theory of speech perception

The early motor theory of speech perception (Liberman, Cooper, Harris and MacNeilage, 1962; Studdert-Kennedy, Liberman, Harris and Cooper, 1970) recognized the importance of interactions between the ability to perceive and to produce speech: motor units which are (necessarily) distinct from their corresponding perceptual units come to the aid of the perceptual units under the early motor theory. That is, speech perception and production employ separate components, but at least some speech sounds are perceived with the help of the components that are used for producing them. As in the separate-and-unequal tradition, perception and production also remain unequal in early motor theory: by making production more important than perception, only the sign of the inequality has been changed (see also Scheerer, 1984).

As Howell and Harvey (1983, p. 215) point out, 'Motor theory attempted to explain something about which very little was known (i.e., speech perception) in terms of something else about which even less was known (i.e., speech production). The problems associated with it are legion.' One of the problems concerned the logical basis of the theory. In order for a pattern of acoustic energy to call up its appropriate production components, a full-fledged perceptual analysis is necessary (see Morton and Broadbent, 1967; and Pick and Saltzman, 1978). This brings the basis for the theory into question because a full-fledged perceptual analysis prior to motor consultation means that perceptual components can accomplish speech recognition without help from the motor components. Later versions of the motor theory (see Studdert-Kennedy, Chap 4 and Porter, Chap 5) have attempted to overcome this and other problems, in part by adopting a subtly but at the same time significantly different framework, described below.

The integrated-and-equal approach to perception and production

The separate-and-unequal approach is not just unsuited (by definition) for studying the relation between perception and production: recent developments in many disciplines have contradicted its basic premise that perception and production are completely separate, and call for a new approach to the whole topic. A classical example is Karl Lashley's (1951, p. 186) observation that common components and mechanisms must underlie speech perception and production because 'the processes of comprehension and production of speech have too much in common to depend on wholly different mechanisms'. A more recent example is the neurolinguistic work of Ojemann (1983) and Mateer (1985) demonstrating cortical sites where electrical stimulation interferes with both the perception and the production of speech, as if identical sites play a role in both perception and production. Such observations suggest that the traditional anatomical separation between afferent versus efferent processes can no longer be usefully maintained, and are less consistent with separate-and-unequal theories than with the hypothesis of Lashley (1951), Miller, Galanter and Pribram (1960), MacKay (in press), and Studdert-Kennedy (Chap 4) that speech perception and production share some of their components.

Others have noted that functionally and temporally too, the relation between perception and action is generally interactive-supportive rather than dominant-subordinate. The main function of perceptual and cognitive systems is to guide purposeful actions, and to adjust ongoing actions to the situation at hand. As Allport (in press) points out, perceptual systems have evolved in all species of animals solely as a means of guiding and controlling action, either present or future. Perceptual systems are not primarily designed to describe and to classify the environment in answer to a question such as 'What is out there?', but to address the more general question 'What does it signify for me?: What must I *do* about what's out there?' (after MacKay, 1984). In short, the nature of the information required for the guidance of production ultimately determines how perceptual systems structure the sensory input: functionally, perception is as subordinate to action as action is to perception.

The integrated-and-equal approach therefore views perception and production as potentially equal and integrated, i.e., fundamentally interactive rather than separate, and takes as its main focus the *relations* between perception and production. Of course, the principles of the integrated-and-equal approach can be generalized to apply to *any* pair of heterogeneous systems, perception and production being only one highly salient pair. In particular, the integrated-and-equal approach extends also to the relations between different systems *within* language perception, or *within* language production. These within-domain relations crop up repeatedly in the book, especially relations between different types of perception, an example being Massaro's (Chap 6) demonstrations of low level interactions between the *auditory* mechanisms for hearing a syllable, and the *visual* mechanisms for seeing the speaker's moving lips.

One final point. As the above examples illustrate, the integrated-and-equal approach tends to criss-cross traditional disciplinary boundaries and approaches, and the present book contains information with origins in many different areas, not just psycholinguistics and linguistics, but mainstream psychology, neurology, and even kinesiology. The fact that the conference on which this book was based took place at the Center for interdisciplinary Research (ZiF) is anything but accidental.

Major themes of the book

Having reviewed the general approach represented in the book and its historical relations to the field at large, some signposts are in order regarding its chapters, their main lines of argument, and how they interconnect. The emphasis here is on what unites the chapters rather than on what differentiates them, which when not superfluous in a general introduction, tends to be premature. What holds the book together are two major themes which run throughout the book, and a set of minor themes which a smaller number of chapters share and which we used for organizing the book into sections.

Relationships within and between language perception and production

Relationships between the various systems and subsystems involved in language perception and production represent one of the main themes of the book (as its subtitle suggests), and the relationships taking part in this theme can be divided into four types (see also Marr and Poggio, 1977): (i). Relationships in the sense of influences, constraints, or mutual adaptations of one system or subsystem on another. (ii). Relationships in the sense of common and/or homologous representations or units shared by different systems or subsystems. (iii). Relationships in the sense of common and/or homologous processes, or functions shared by different systems or subsystems. (iv). Relationships in the sense of shared or separable cognitive structures or functional components. As will be seen, these four different types of relationships also weave their way into the fabric of the other main theme of the book (modularity).

Constraints, interactions, and mutual adaptations

Cutler (Chap 2), Massaro (Chap 6) and Studdert-Kennedy (Chap 4) deal with relations in the sense of constraints, interactions, or mutual adaptations between the systems and subsystems for language perception–production. Cutler argues that sentence production is adapted on-line to perception because speakers are constrained in their choice of syntax, words, and even phonology so that listeners can readily understand them. Massaro examines how perceptual information coming from different sources interacts and combines, as when we simultaneously hear a speech sound and see a speaker's moving lips. Studdert-Kennedy examines the constraints of perception on production seen when children imitate or reproduce utterances which are functionally equivalent to those heard.

Units of representation and their interrelations

Theoreticians are in general agreement that language perception and production employ identical distinctions, descriptive characteristics, or units of representation, at least for higher level units such as words and phrases. Studdert-Kennedy (Chap 4) and Porter (Chap 5) advance a much more radical proposal, namely that speech production and perception employ some of the same representational distinctions at very low, phonetic/articulatory levels. This 'units of representation' issue arises again at a slightly higher level in Campbell's (Chap 7) discussion of whether a common phonological code is accessed during speaking–hearing versus during mouthing–lipreading, i.e., producing silent lip-movements versus seeing a speaker's moving lips.

Essentially similar questions arise in the chapters on reading: Venezky and Massaro (Chap 8) ask a basically descriptive question about how the units of pronunciation in English are related to the units of orthography. Kay (Chap 9) asks a more process oriented question about whether visual word recognition and spoken production make use of the same phonological code, and Besner (Chap 11), Feldman (Chap 10) and Scheerer (Chap 12) take this question one step further by asking whether the involvement of phonological units in studies of visual word recognition is a language-specific effect of the writing systems studied, so that readers can proceed directly from letters to word meanings in some languages but not in other languages. The issue of relations between visual and phonological units of representation arises again when Besner and Feldman disagree about the extent to which lexical knowledge determines pronunciation in phonologically transparent writing systems, and also when Scheerer and

Kay ask whether letters which are visually undifferentiated sometime represent phonological-articulatory components which are fundamentally different, e.g., vowels versus consonants or syllable-final versus syllable initial consonants (see MacKay, 1982). Jarvella, Job, Sandström and Schreuder (Chap 13) add a further dimension by focussing on language specific effects of morphological structure during reading.

Shared and asymmetric processes

Several papers deal with relationships in the sense of processes which are either shared or asymmetric between language perception and production Gordon and Meyer (Chap 20), and Keele (Chap 21) argue that hierarchi processing plays a fundamentally similar role not just in the production and perception of speech and other skills, but in the acquisition, transfer, and flexibility of perception–production skills (see also MacKay, 1982). Keele (Chap 21), and MacKay (Chap 18) review evidence indicating that speech perception and production share some of the same timing mechanisms Gordon and Meyer argue for 'the common use of processing resources by speech perception and production'. However, Jarvella and Deutsch (Chap 3) show that speakers and listeners process descriptive statements differ ently at the sentential level: processing procedures are not completely identical for perception versus production. Huttenlocher and Goodman (Chap 19) come (implicitly) to a similar conclusion, showing that unlike speech production which proceeds of necessity from left-to-right at the phoneme level, identification of spoken words (and non-words) is not a strictly left-to-right process.

Shared, versus separate, cognitive structures

Relationships in the sense of shared versus separate cognitive structures for perception–production arise in many chapters, as the main focus in some implicitly or indirectly in others. The 'structures' referred to are identified in psychological or functional rather than neuroanatomical terms. For example, the memory system embodying the listener's lexicon of phono logical word forms — the phonological input lexicon (see e.g., Monsel (Chap 14), Howard and Franklin (Chap 16), Funnell and Allport (Chap 17), and Huttenlocher and Goodman (Chap 19)) — is one such postulated cognitive structure. In this example, one of the central questions at issue is whether the same structural component embodies both the listener's and the speaker's knowledge of lexical forms — that is, whether the phono logical input lexicon and the phonological output lexicon are one and the same, or whether they are separate structural components (Monsell). A similar question can be raised with respect to the orthographic lexicon (Coltheart and Funnell, Chap 15). While evidence from brain-injured patients may be used to address this kind of question, the identity of the postulated structural components is necessarily defined, at least initially, in terms of the psychological functions that they serve. The characteristic theoretical notation used by several of the contributors to represent their hypotheses is the structural 'box-and-arrow' diagram. Other contributors address questions of shared structural components, but without directly raising questions about the structural channels of communication between components, and so do not need such diagrams. For example, the evidence of Keele (Chap 21) and MacKay (Chap 18) implicates a shared structural component involved in the timing of speech perception–production and other skills without indicating how the timing, sequencing and content components are interconnected (but see MacKay, 1982; and in press).

Interestingly, closely related perception–production issues can arise as either a units-of-representation question or as a structural components question. For example, Monsell (Chap 14) and Coltheart and Funnell (Chap 15) examine the same basic relations between language perception versus production as Porter (Chap 5) and Studdert-Kennedy (Chap 4), but with a structural components focus. Porter and Studdert-Kennedy are concerned with what distinctions or descriptive units play a role in speech as it is perceived and speech as it is produced. What properties are abstracted out, and at what levels in speech perception–production? Monsell and Coltheart and Funnell ask whether or not the same specific cognitive structures are involved (in particular at the lexical level) in the perception and the production of spoken and written language.

Clearly, these two sorts of questions are closely related, and carry important implications for one another: If it turned out that language perception and production employed radically different distinctions or units of representation at all levels, then shared cognitive structures for perception–production would be out of the question. Similarly, unambiguous evidence for the existence of shared cognitive structures in language perception–production would seem to imply common units of representation for perception and production.

On the other hand, these closely related questions are not the same question in different guise. Common distinctions or representational units do not *necessarily* entail common cognitive structures (but see the earlier discussion for relevant data). Although the brains of different speakers of English represent say, phonemes, equivalently, this does not mean that they are one and the same brain in this respect; only that the individual, physically separate structures are in some way homomorphic. Likewise, as in Wernicke's theory, intimately interconnected but nevertheless distinct cognitive structures might represent the receptive and the expressive sides of language, even though these distinct cognitive structures encode equivalent properties or contrasts.

Modularity and the generality of language mechanisms

This second theme only comes to the surface in a relatively small number of papers (e.g., Monsell (Chap 14), Funnell and Allport (Chap 17), Keele (Chap 21), Gordon and Meyer (Chap 20), and MacKay (Chap 18)), but in fact flows quietly beneath every paper in the book. Modularity is central to the theme, but directed to the issue of what the true modules are, rather than to the idea of modularity *per se*, which is taken for granted. The common goal of this theme is to identify the *functionally separable subsystems* involved in language perception and production, and to show in detail how these different subsystems operate and communicate with one another.

One relatively homogenous set of papers (Monsell (Chap 14), Coltheart and Funnell (Chap 15), Howard and Franklin (Chap 16), and Funnell and Allport (Chap 17)) begins with a hypothesized module known as the lexicon, a system of word-specific mechanisms which is embodied somehow in the brain and which makes explicit the unique identity of each individual word-form by representing the otherwise arbitrary correspondences between the phonological, conceptual, syntactic and orthographic aspects of words (in so far as orthographic rules cannot uniquely specify the word's pronunciation). The goal of these chapters is to identify how many and what kinds of word-specific subsystems there are, and the nature of their connections to each other and to other, *non*-lexical systems, in short to provide a map of the lexical module and its relations to other modules for language perception–production. However, the modularity theme is more general than this 'cognitive architecture' approach: Other chapters, such as those by Scheerer (Chap 12), Kay (Chap 9) and Besner (Chap 11), take a different approach, but address the same questions about the separability of lexical and sublexical systems representing phonological and orthographic units.

Presupposed within the modularity theme as a rather strong working assumption is at least some degree of *specialization* of psychological mechanisms and their internal channels of communication. Not one chapter in the book deals with a 'general purpose' or non-modular mental mechanism capable of serving indifferently now this basic function and now that, without structural differentiation or specialization. Whether this modular bias reflects chance, artifact, or necessity is of course difficult to tell. After all, Fodor (1983) has argued that this approach may be the only viable one, and that we may as well give up hope of understanding cognitive processes in a 'general' or 'central' system where everything will interact with everything else in a way that no kind of experimental ingenuity or conceptual analysis can expect to disentangle. According to this somewhat pessimistic appraisal, the cumulative discovery of modules and the way they work is an essential precondition for any further progress in understanding cognitive processes.

However, if the idea of modularity is generally accepted in the book, Fodor's choice of specific modules and modular processes is not: For example, Fodor (1983) viewed perception and action, and language perception and production in particular, to be separate modules, whereas paper after paper in the present volume show that language perception and production have too much in common and are too interactive to be considered independent modules. Nor does the book adhere to the rigid 'encapsulation of processing' that Fodor (1983) considered essential to modularity. Indeed, modules may form a null set under this criterion, and MacKay (1982; and Chap 18) suggests a way of salvaging Fodor's concept of modularity by arguing for the 'partial encapsulation' of processing within modules, i.e., for the encapsulation of some but not all types of processing. Specifically, MacKay presents evidence indicating that 'processing' is an ambiguous term which must be further specified as either *priming* (which is unencapsulated, automatically crossing the boundaries between modules and systems within modules) or *activation* (which requires a module-specific activation mechanism and is therefore encapsulated or confined within particular modules or systems).

Closely related to the modularity theme is the issue of generality: whether language use shares some of the same underlying mechanisms as other behaviors. For example, Keele and MacKay review evidence indicating that speech and other action systems share the same timing mechanisms. Massaro likewise asks whether the mechanism responsible for integrating heterogeneous sources of information within language also plays a role in other (non-linguistic) perceptual systems. Finally, Keele, and Gordon and Meyer argue that the nested hierarchic organization so prevalent in language production also characterizes other complex behaviors such as piano playing, typing, gymnastics, and drawing. Indeed, Keele develops an intriguing functional argument for why evolution should favor hierarchic sequencing processes, and claims that the innate ability to learn and to modify hierarchic structures is most highly developed in humans, with language production and perception representing only a recent refinement of this more general genetic endowment. This view provides a clear challenge to current conceptions of how perception–action modules evolve, with particular perceptual devices emerging during evolution to provide information for particular actions, and Keele's challenge suggests that the modularity–generality issue will be with us for some time to come.

Minor themes and the structure of the book

Ordering of the chapters poses a major problem for a general book which resections and crossclassifies the field in a new way, and this was certainly true of the present volume. Traditionally, books on cognitive psychology move roughly from the peripheral to the central, starting with topics in perception, moving on to attention, and ending with memory, language, and thinking. If action or production is mentioned at all, it generally comes at the end, as an 'after-thought'. As editors, we were united in our opposition to this traditional organization, because neither perception–production relations nor language *per se* sit very well within a peripheral-to-central framework. After all, perception and production are closely related and central topics in the psychology of language, and language processing is virtually inextricable from a 'central' topic such as memory.

We therefore set about to determine what other themes or crossclassifying dimensions we could use to order our chapters. Six general dimensions stood out: experimental versus theoretical versus review chapters, lexical versus sublexical versus supralexical chapters, reading–writing versus listening–speaking chapters, perceptually oriented chapters versus production-oriented chapters versus perception–production chapters oriented towards the relation between the two, chapters oriented towards higher versus lower level processes, and finally, the four types of relationship (constraint-oriented chapters versus process-oriented chapters versus representation-oriented chapters versus chapters oriented toward cognitive structures).

In the end, after a great deal of soul searching, we decided on a compromise which took into consideration not just these six dimensions, but also our own special areas of expertise as editors. We divided the chapters into six sections and counting the book title as a seventh (phantom) section, we ordered adjacent sections and chapters on the basis of a 'greatest thematic overlap' principle. The result was complex but interesting, a sort of unity with a twist, not unlike a Möbius circle. The circle is readily traced along the higher- versus lower-level dimension, where the chapters flow down and then back up and join again in the end without actually intersecting. Section 1 (Constraints and asymmetries between language perception and production; Don MacKay, section editor) has very close ties with the book title and deals with input–output relationships in sentence production and comprehension. Stepping down from these relatively high level considerations, the reader soon encounters the lowest levels of perception–production in the sections entitled Perception and production of speech sounds, and Perceptual integration and common codes (Wolfgang Prinz, section editor), which examine the perception–production of articulatory-acoustic phonetics and phonology, including lip-reading of mouthed or silently articulated speech sounds. The next section switches to reading, beginning at roughly the same level (spelling-sound regularities and irregularities). This section, entitled Reading and ortho-graphies (Eckart Scheerer, section editor) begins the ascent of the Möbius circle, starting with phonologically 'shallow' writing systems (witness Serbo-Croatian) and ending with phonologically 'deep' writing systems (witness English) and the higher level morphological constraints on visual word recognition. This leads naturally to the section entitled Architecture of the mental lexicon (Alan Allport, section editor) which deals with the hypothesized lexical module, and raises issues about word-specific mech-anisms and their relationships to other, non-lexical mechanisms, both 'higher' and 'lower' in the system. Word meanings provide the predomi-nant focus, how they are expressed in speaking and writing, and how they are understood in listening and reading, and the functional relations between all four. The last section, entitled Sequencing and timing in language perception and production (Don MacKay, section editor), begins with the problem of sequencing and timing in perceiving and producing spoken words and syllables, and completes the return ascent to the highest level questions, ending with the relation between the evolution of mech-anisms for timing and sequencing in speech perception–production and other perception–action systems.

A similar unity-with-a-twist emerges for the four types of relationships (constraints-representations-cognitive structures-processes). The book be-gins with constraints that speakers take into consideration in order for listeners to understand them, and moves quickly into representations at the phonetic and phonological levels of speech production–perception, and at the grapheme and morpheme levels of reading. The next section (archi-tecture of the mental lexicon) deals with the shared (versus separate) cognitive structures for the perception–production of words, and the pro-cessing pathways linking print to meaning. The final section completes the Möbius circle: it begins with the processes and mechanisms underlying the timing and sequencing of speech sounds, syllables, words, and phrases in language perception–production, and returns again to the theme of con-straints, this time constraints on theories of sequencing and timing in speech perception–production.

References

Allport, D. A. (in press). Selection for action. In H. Heuer and A. Sanders (Eds) *Perspectives on perception and action*. Hillsdale, NJ: Erlbaum.

Cooper, W. E., and Zurif, E. B. (1983). Aphasia: Information-processing in language production and reception. In B. Butterworth (Ed.) *Language production* Vol. 2. London: Academic Press.

Fodor, J. A. (1983). *The modularity of mind*. Cambridge, MA: MIT Press.

Geschwind, N. (1974). *Selected papers on language and the brain*. Dordrecht: Reidel.

Geschwind, N. (1983). Comments on perceptual processing links. In M. Studdert-Kennedy (Ed.) *Psychobiology of language*. Cambridge, MA: MIT Press, p. 36.

Howell, P., and Harvey, N. (1983). Perceptual equivalence and motor equivalence in speech. In B. Butterworth (Ed.) *Language Production (Vol. 2): Development, Writing and Other Language Processes*. London: Academic Press, pp. 203–24.

Lashley, K. S. (1951). The problem of serial order in behavior. In L. A. Jeffress (Ed.) *Cerebral mechanisms in behavior*. New York: Wiley.

Lassen, N. A., and Larsen, B. (1980). Cortical activity in the left and right hemispheres during language-related brain functions. *Phonetica*, **37**, 27–37.

Liberman, A. M., Cooper, F. S., Harris, K. S., and MacNeilage, P. F. (1962). A motor theory of speech perception. In *Proceedings of the speech communication seminar*. Stockholm: Royal Institute of Technology.

MacKay, D. G. (1982). The problems of flexibility, fluency, and speed-accuracy trade-off in skilled behavior. *Psychological Review*, **89**, 483–506.

MacKay, D. G. (in press). The asymmetric relationship between the perception and production of speech. In H. Heuer and A. Sanders (Eds) *Perspectives on perception and action*. Hillsdale, NJ: Erlbaum.

MacKay, D. M. (1984). Evaluation: The missing link between cognition and action. In W. Prinz and A. Sanders (Eds) *Cognition and motor processes*. Berlin: Springer, pp. 175–84.

Marr, D., and Poggio, T. (1977). From understanding computation to understanding neural circuitry. *Neurosciences Research Program Bulletin*, **15**, 470–88.

Mateer, C. A. (1983). Motor and perceptual functions of the left hemisphere and their interaction. In S. J. Segalowitz (Ed.) *Language functions and brain organization*. New York: Academic Press.

Mateer, C. A. (1985). Common sites for oral motor sequencing and phoneme identification: Evidence from electrical stimulation of the language cortex. Paper presented to the Conference on 'Common Processes in Speaking, Listening, Reading, and Writing', at the Center for Interdisciplinary Research (ZiF), University of Bielefeld.

Miller, G. A., Galanter, E., and Pribram, K. H. (1960). *Plans and the structure of behavior*. New York: Holt.

Morton, J. and Broadbent, D. E. (1967). Passive versus active recognition models, or is your homunculus really necessary? In W. Wathen-Dunn (Ed.) *Models for the perception of speech and visual form*. Cambridge, MA: MIT Press, pp. 103–110.

Ojemann, G. A. (1983). Brain organization for language from the perspective of electrical stimulation mapping. *The Behavioral and Brain Sciences*, **6**, 189–230.

Pick, H. L., and Saltzman, E. (1978). Perception of communicative information. In

H. L. Pick, and E. Saltzman (Eds) *Modes of perceiving and processing inform-ation*. Hillsdale, NJ: Erlbaum.

Scheerer, E. (1984). Motor theories of cognitive structure: A historical review. In W. Prinz and A. Sanders (Eds) *Cognition and motor processes*. Berlin: Springer, pp. 77–97.

Straight, S. (1980). Auditory versus articulatory phonological processes and their development in children. In G. H. Yeni-Komshian, J. F. Kavanagh, and C. A. Ferguson (Eds) *Child phonology, Vol. 1: Production*. New York: Academic Press.

Studdert-Kennedy, M., Liberman, A. M., Harris, K. S., and Cooper F. S. (1970). The motor theory of speech perception: A reply to Lane's critical review. *Psychological Review*, **77**, 234–49.

Turvey, M. T. (1977). Preliminaries to a theory of action with reference to vision. In R. E. Shaw and J. Bransford (Eds) *Perceiving, acting and knowing*. Hillsdale, NJ: Erlbaum, pp. 211–65.

SECTION 1

Constraints and asymmetries between language perception and production

Introduction

Donald G. MacKay

Jarvella and Deutsch (Chap 3) note that psycholinguistic research has tended to concentrate on perception, rather than on production, or on relations between perception and production, so that neither the similarities nor the asymmetries between speaking and listening processes have attracted much attention (see also Fodor, Bever and Garrett, 1974). When theoreticians have taken note of the fact that at higher levels, language perception and production make use of the same units, content, and linguistic form, they have usually assumed that higher level perceptual processes are simply the reverse of the corresponding production processes, like the bidirectional reactions in chemical formulae. For example, Gordon and Meyer (1984, Figure 1) use a flow chart to summarize current theories of speech perception–production incorporating this 'symmetry assumption': arrows in one direction represent perceptual processes, while arrows in the opposite direction represent production processes.

Symmetry between the processes for perception and production has been a popular assumption (see Fodor, Bever and Garrett, 1974), perhaps in part because it enables researchers to devote all of their efforts to studying perception. If perception and production processes are symmetric, studies of production are redundant and unnecessary: solving the problem of perception also solves the problem of production. Like the separate-and-unequal tradition discussed in Chapter 1, the symmetry assumption subordinates action and encourages researchers to treat listening and speaking as independent systems.

The main point of Jarvella and Deutsch is that the symmetry assumption does not hold in general, and that perception and production processes are asymmetric: Using measures of processing time, Jarvella and

Deutsch show that speakers and listeners process the linguistic structure of a descriptive utterance in fundamentally different ways. This finding is important not just for current theories, but for the more general separate-and-unequal tradition whereby studies of perception-without-action are considered desirable and sufficient.

Whatever its underlying cause, the Jarvella–Deutsch asymmetry must be added to the growing list of asymmetries between perception versus production, which includes the effects of listening practice (see MacKay, 1984), and differences between recognition versus production vocabularies (the fact that children can usually recognize and understand a word long before they can use it in speech production; Clark and Hecht, 1983). Another companion in the list is the maximal rate asymmetry, the fact that speech perception can proceed much more quickly than speech production: Computer-compressed speech remains perceptually intelligible at 5 to 7 times the rate that people can produce speech of comparable intelligibility (Foulke and Sticht, 1969). This rate asymmetry reflects an inherent processing difference and cannot be completely explained in terms of the muscular or biomechanical factors involved in speech production (see MacKay, 1984). Nor does this complete the rapidly expanding list: a comparison of slips of the tongue versus slips of the ear reveals additional asymmetries which theories of perception–production must capture (see MacKay, 1984). As Jarvella and Deutsch point out, detailed theoretical analyses of the processes underlying listening and speaking are not just interesting and important, but necessary to capture the differences between them.

Cutler (Chap 2) takes a different and largely descriptive, rather than process oriented, approach to the relations between perception and production. Cutler argues that speakers make syntactic, lexical, and even phonological choices which are directed by the requirements of the listener for understanding an utterance, and that utterance production depends more on the nature of the listener's perceptual processes than on the production process itself, even in the articulation of phonological elisions and assimilations. Perhaps the producer takes the listener into account on-line in blocking certain phonological elisions, because the listener is there looking on and listening. Or perhaps elision-blocking rules, originally learned or invented for the sake of a listener, have become incorporated for automatic execution within the speaker's production system. Processing questions such as these remain to be answered, but are in principle subject to experimental test and disconfirmation. If speakers can be shown, say via videotape, to produce identical elisions and assimilations when talking aloud and on-line to a listener, and when silently mouthing to themselves (see Campbell (Chap 7)), one could conclude that an on-line listener is unnecessary for application of elision-blocking rules.

Cutler's paper stimulates another interesting question. Cutler argues that speakers creating new words avoid base-transforming derivations as difficult for listeners to perceive and comprehend (a hypothesis which suggests some easily-carried-out experiments for determining how listeners understand different types of neologism and perceive them under perceptually degraded conditions). The question is why the base forms in so many words undergo radical transformation in languages such as English, German and Russian. What opposing forces at the time of creation have enabled these perceptually problematic base-transforming derivatives to become accepted into the language?

Cutler's most interesting, or as she puts it, radical claim comes at the end of her paper and concerns an apparent exception to her 'perceptual constraint' hypothesis, the fact that speakers virtually camouflage word-boundary information which would seem to be extremely helpful for listeners to have. Her hypothesis is that rhythmic stress and intonation provide the missing boundary cues, but exactly what this 'beneficial organizing function of rhythm' is, and how listeners use this information to segment the speech signal into words remains to be determined.

References

Clark, E. V., and Hecht, B. F. (1983). Comprehension, production and language acquisition. *Annual Review of Psychology*, **34**, 325–49.

Fodor, J. A., Bever, T. G. and Garrett, M. F. (1974). *The psychology of language*. New York: McGraw-Hill.

Foulke, E., and Sticht, T. (1969). Review of research on the intelligibility and comprehension of accelerated speech. *Psychological Bulletin*, **72**, 50–62.

Gordon, P. C., and Meyer, D. E. (1984). Perceptual-motor processing of phonetic features in speech. *Journal of Experimental Psychology: Human Perception and Performance*, **10**, 153–78.

MacKay, D. G. (1984). The asymmetrical relationship between speech perception and production. *Perception and Action Report #8*, Center for interdisciplinary Research, University of Bielefeld, FRG. Also in press in H. Heuer and A. Sanders (Eds) *Tutorials in Perception and Action*. Hillsdale, NJ: Erlbaum.

2 Speaking for listening

Anne Cutler

Abstract

Speech production is constrained at all levels by the demands of speech perception. The speaker's primary aim is successful communication, and to this end semantic, syntactic and lexical choices are directed by the needs of the listener. Even at the articulatory level, some aspects of production appear to be perceptually constrained, for example the blocking of phonological distortions under certain conditions. An apparent exception to this pattern is word boundary information, which ought to be extremely useful to listeners, but which is not reliably coded in speech. It is argued that the solution to this apparent problem lies in rethinking the concept of the boundary of the lexical access unit. Speech rhythm provides clear information about the location of stressed syllables, and listeners do make use of this information. If stressed syllables can serve as the determinants of word lexical access codes, then once again speakers are providing precisely the necessary form of speech information to facilitate perception.

Introduction

The central argument of this chapter is that speech production is subject to perceptual constraints. Since speakers speak chiefly to communicate with listeners, it might seem quite unremarkable to claim that speakers construct their speech output so as to cater for listeners' needs. However, perceptually determined constraints on production turn out to be remarkably pervasive in the production process. Even at quite 'low' levels, i.e. relatively close to output, the production of an utterance is constrained by factors which have more to do with the nature of the listeners' perceptual process than with the nature of the production process itself. This chapter

LANGUAGE PERCEPTION AND PRODUCTION
ISBN 0-12-052750-2

will summarize evidence on the production of nonce-words, on the correction of slips of the tongue, and on the application of optional phoneme elision and assimilation rules, all of which shows sensitivity to perceptual factors constraining the production process. In the final sections it will be shown that even the task of word boundary detection, which is one of the chief difficulties of speech perception, appears to be facilitated by certain aspects of speech production: speakers provide rhythmic cues on which listeners can base a strategy of segmentation.

Speech as communication

A speaker's primary aim is to formulate a *message*. Thus what speakers say is, in most cases, what they want listeners to hear — not just what they want to utter to satisfy some purely internal articulatory need which could as easily be satisfied without a listener. The content of the message, that is, is determined by (the speaker's perception of) the characteristics of the listener. Likewise, listener characteristics can determine aspects of the message's form — speakers speak more simply to children, for instance, and to people with an imperfect grasp of the language in question. Some syntactic constructions are harder to process than others, as much psycholinguistic research has demonstrated; speakers replace harder constructions with easier ones when communication seems to be unsuccessful (Valian and Wales, 1976). Formal versus informal registers (with their consequent syntactic and lexical elaboration versus simplification) are chosen on the basis of the current relationship between speaker and listener. Speakers draw on their knowledge of what their listeners already know in choosing what to say and how exactly to express it. Consider Grice's four maxims of conversation: be brief, be relevant, be polite, be sincere. Rephrased, they exhort speakers to avoid boring, offending or deceiving their listeners.

If speech is to function effectively as the performance of a communicative act, the speaker must obviously cater to the listener's needs. Perhaps slightly less predictable, however, is the degree to which actual lexical selection can be subject to influences arising from the nature of the perception process. Choice of speech register, mentioned above, can of course have implications for lexical selection — determining a high frequency word rather than its low frequency synonym, choosing between a specific versus a more general term, using or avoiding the taboo adjective. But quite general perceptual constraints seem to apply even to lexical processes which do not involve social considerations. A case in point is the way speakers fill a momentarily felt lexical gap by making up a novel word, as described in the next section.

Perceptual constraints on word creation

When there is a choice between alternative word formations — e.g. for making a nonce verb out of a noun — the version which produces the more easily perceptible result is consistently preferred. In a series of experiments comparing speakers' preferences for different types of suffix (Cutler 1980a, 1981), for example, I found that suffixes which attach to an existing word without affecting its phonological structure (e.g. *-ness*, *-ish*) were chosen in preference to suffixes which resulted in a change in the base word's stress pattern or vowel quality. Thus in Table 1, the neologisms on the left in the upper portion of the table (all of which preserve without alteration the word to which they have attached) were preferred to those on the right, in which the original word is less perfectly preserved. *Incestuousness*, for instance, contains *incestuous* unaltered within it, whereas *incestuosity* changes the final vowel of *incestuous* and also shifts the primary stress from the second to the fourth syllable.

Table 1. Neologism preferences.

incestuousness	>	incestuosity
dowagerish	>	dowagerial
ambiguize	>	ambiguify
comprisement	>	comprision
but		
jejuneness	=	jejunity
auctioneerish	=	auctioneerial
splendidise	=	splendify
excusement	=	excusion

These results do not just reflect preference for some particular suffixes (e.g. *-ness*) over others (e.g. *-ity*); it is only whether or not the original form remains intact in the neologism which matters. This is clear from the further finding that no preference is shown between two suffix types if neither of them alters the phonology of the existing word to which they are attached. The pairs of neologisms in the bottom half of Table 1 exemplify this comparison. *Jejune*, for instance, is equally well preserved in *jejuneness* and *jejunity*; *auctioneer* in *auctioneerish* and *auctioneerial*. Speakers show equal preference for both members of such pairs.

The best neologism, then, is one in which the word on which it is based is transparently preserved. Neologisms, by definition, do not have entries in language users' mental lexicons; so the task of understanding a neologism must differ from the usual task of word identification. It can only be done, in fact, by dividing the neologistic affix from the rest of the form and processing the two parts separately.[1] A neologism which contains an intact known word, therefore, will easily separate into a lexically accessible word plus suffix; understanding it will be a simple matter of recognizing the existing word and combining it with the new (perhaps syntactically transforming) suffix to derive the novel meaning. If the known word is not transparently preserved, however, understanding the neologism will necessitate further procedures of undoing the phonological transformations before any available lexical entry can be accessed. The neologism preference data therefore seem to indicate that the determining factor in nonce word formation is how easily the new creation can be understood; i.e. speakers create neologisms with the listeners' needs in mind.

If simple transparency were the only issue in these results, however, it might be possible to construct an argument that transparent neologisms are preferred because they are easier to *produce* rather than because they are easier to *understand*: producing a new form involves using an existing lexical entry and adding a suffix to it, and it might be claimed that it is just easier to do this if an already available articulatory programme can simply be compiled with no alteration other than an added appendage in the form of a suffix. But the results of the acceptability experiments indicate that it is not necessary to preserve the entire known form for the new derived form to be functionally transparent; it is vitally important only that the initial portions of the known word be preserved intact, but the final segments may actually be distorted. Consider the last two examples in Table 1: *splendid* has lost its final segment in *splendify*, yet *splendify* is considered to be no less acceptable than *splendidise*; likewise *excusement* and *excusion* were rated equally acceptable, although only the first preserves the final [z] sound of the verb *excuse*. In each case it appears to be sufficient to preserve the first six phonetic segments of the known word — and as it happens in each case there is no other word in the English language beginning with those six segments. All words beginning [splɛnd] are part of the morphological family which includes *splendid*; only the verb and noun reading of *excuse* begin with [ɪkskju]. Thus what appears to be important in neologism formation is preserving just enough of a known word, going from left to right, to distinguish it from other words of the language — strong evidence that the transparency criterion is perceptual rather than productive.

The limits of perceptual constraints on production

Speakers cater to listeners' needs not only at the highest levels of the speech production process, such as message formulation and choice of style, but also at the lexical selection stage, even in the creation of novel word forms — as the previous section showed, a primary factor in this process is ensuring perceptibility. Yet we might expect that there would be limits on the degree to which perceptual constraints could operate in speech production. For instance, at the articulatory output level, it is reasonable to assume that it would be rather surprising to find perceptual constraints in operation. The way in which an articulatory programme is realized in muscle commands, jaw and tongue movements, and so on, is presumably not dependent on anything other than physiological factors concerned with the speaker's articulatory apparatus, plus accidental effects of the articulatory environment (e.g. the constraints imposed by trying to speak underwater, or with a mouth full of food, etc.). The actual execution of the motor programme once begun can therefore be considered immune from perceptual effects. However, it will be argued here that every conceptually prior level of speech production — that is, every level of the process up to and including compilation of the programme for articulation — is subject to constraints which derive ultimately from the communicative function of speech, and the constraints which the nature of the speech perception process places upon the successful realization of this function.

The preceding sections outlined some uncontroversial ways in which listener constraints affect higher levels of the production process, and some less obvious effects of perceptual factors upon lexical processes including augmentation of the lexical stock. The following sections concentrate upon levels of the production process which are rather closer to output — that is, those levels between word selection and articulation. In those intervening levels choices are made which will eventually constrain the details of the articulatory programme — i.e. precisely how the chosen words are to be uttered. One of the variables which can be manipulated at this level is prosodic structure; another is clarity of articulation of individual segments. Each of these will be briefly addressed in the immediately following sections, which summarize some cases in which speakers' articulatory choices appear to be rather surprisingly constrained by factors to do with the listener. The succeeding sections will then consider a case where it might seem that, again rather surprisingly, the listener is being denied assistance which the speaker could easily afford.

Some uses of accent

In the most general sense, the role of prosody in the production of an utterance is to assist in the communicative function — the speaker uses prosody to direct and control aspects of the listener's perception. Sentence

accent, for example, is used to highlight new information (that is, information which the speaker believes to be new to the listener, not information
which is new to the speaker). Although some linguists have devoted
considerable effort to describing sentence accent placement in terms of
syntactic structure, such descriptions are restricted to citation forms; in
practice, semantic factors tend to override syntactic factors in determining
which words receive accent (Cutler and Isard, 1980; Ladd, 1980). Speakers
adjust the relative prominence of the words they speak so as to communicate their message most efficiently. Moreover, this process is not necessarily a one-off assignment made at a relatively high-level utterance
planning stage. The speaker can be shown to be monitoring prosody and
adjusting it with the listener's comprehension in mind. This conclusion
arises from some recent work on the way slips of the tongue, once made
and detected by a speaker, are corrected.

Of course, not all slips of the tongue are detected by the speaker; and
not all slips which are detected are corrected. When a correction is issued,
however, the correction may have the same prosody as the original utterance, or it may be given a very different prosodic contour. This seems, on
the face of it, to be a trivially true observation; but it is not trivial. The
continuum of prosodic divergence between original utterance and correction is bimodal, not continuous. Goffman (1981) first noticed this phenomenon in radio announcers; some corrections hardly interrupt the flow of
speech at all, and in particular the prosodic pattern is not altered at all,
while others result in a radical change in the original prosody. Cutler
(1983) took pitch and amplitude measurements of a large corpus of error
corrections; each distribution of the difference between original and corrected utterance was clearly bimodal. For example, (1) is a typical
'unmarked' correction: the peak pitch reading for the error word (*Mike*) is
139 Hz, for the correction (*Martin*) also 139 Hz.

(1) and bowls the first ball to Mike — Martin Kent
(2) then he himself loses the chance, that is he risks the chance of dying

In (2), on the other hand, *loses* was again spoken with a peak pitch reading
of 139 Hz, but *risks*, the correction word, reached a peak of 217 Hz, a 56%
increase. (2) is a 'marked' correction.

Levelt and Cutler (1983) investigated the determinants of error correction marking, in a large corpus of corrections collected by Levelt (1983).
Firstly, they found that marking was only applied to corrections of real
errors, not to correction for appropriateness (such as replacing a correct
but general word by a more specific alternative). They argued that marking
a correction amounts to accenting it, in order to emphasize the contrast

between the correction and the original, incorrect utterance. This claim was further strengthened by the finding that the likelihood of marking a correction was a function of the *degree* of contrast between error and repair. The corpus in question consisted of speakers' descriptions of routes through a pattern of coloured dots, and word substitution errors were chiefly of two kinds: errors of direction, in which polar opposites were confused (e.g. *left* for *right*, *up* for *down*); and errors of colour, in which one of the eleven colour names in the pattern set was substituted for another. Levelt and Cutler argued that the degree of contrast was higher in direction errors than in colour errors, so that there should be a significantly greater probability of correction being marked with direction errors than with colour errors. Indeed, 72% of direction errors in the corpus were followed by marked corrections, but less than 50% of colour errors, a statistically significant difference. Levelt and Cutler concluded that how an error is corrected is determined by how the speaker perceives the error to have affected successful communication of the intended message. The more the actual utterance is at variance with the intended, the more likely it is that the speaker will adjust the prosodic structure to highlight the correction, thus drawing the listener's attention to the desired message.

The acceptability of segmental distortion

Further evidence from studies of slips of the tongue and the way they are corrected supports the general claim that speakers' repair actions are determined by how much the slips are likely to have disrupted perception. For example, errors of lexical stress, such as (3)–(6), are corrected only rarely:

(3) you think its sarCASm, but it's not.
(4) . . . we're still enTHUSiastic.
(5) from my PROsodic — proSODic colleagues.
(6) everyone knows that ecoNOMists — that eCONomists . . .

In the corpus of errors and corrections analysed by Cutler (1983), it was found that correction correlated strongly with the effect of the stress shift on the vowel which would have been stressed had the word been uttered correctly. When that vowel was reduced in the error utterance, the error was corrected in 61% of the cases — as in (5) and (6), in which the target word's stressed syllable (the second syllable of *prosodic* and *economists* respectively) was spoken with a reduced vowel. When the target word's stressed vowel was given the same full vowel quality in the error as it would have received in correct production, however, a correction was issued only

21% of the time. (3) and (4) are examples — in neither case was the target word's stressed syllable (the first syllable of *sarcasm*, the fourth of *enthusiastic*) reduced, and in neither case was the error corrected. That is, speakers seem to be particularly concerned to correct lexical stress errors when they have resulted in gross distortion of phonetic segments, such as changing a full vowel to a schwa.

Distortion of phonetic segments can also result from the application of certain phonological rules of elision and assimilation in casual speech. Cooper and Paccia-Cooper (1980) have studied these effects intensively, particularly the extent to which speakers will apply assimilations and elisions across word boundaries. For example, palatalization is the rule which produces, from a [d] or a [t] followed by the glide [j], an affricate [ʤ] or [ʧ]; it can apply across word boundaries such as in 'did you' and similar phrases. Cooper and Paccia-Cooper examined the likelihood of palatalization applying across a word boundary as a function of the informativeness of the words preceding and following this boundary. For example, they varied the frequency of these words, comparing '. . . rode your horse . . .' with '. . . goad your horse . . .', '. . . had utensils . . .' with '. . . had euglena . . .'. They found that varying the frequency of the [d] word (i.e. the word before the boundary) had absolutely no effect on the likelihood of speakers applying palatalization across the boundary; but varying the frequency of the [j] word had a dramatic effect: whereas with relatively high frequency phrases such as 'had utensils' over one-third of the productions were palatalized, with low frequency phrases such as 'had euglena' the frequency of palatalization dropped to 10%. The effect of contrastive stress was similar. Stressing the [d] word did not significantly inhibit palatalization; stressing the [j] word, however, almost completely suppressed it.

Cooper and Paccia-Cooper concluded that distorting the end of words does not concern the speaker greatly; speakers take pains, however, to avoid distorting the *onset* of words if the words are particularly informative (e.g. of low frequency; or contrastively stressed). It is difficult to conceive of an explanation for this effect in terms of demands of the production process alone. But again, the value to the perception process is quite obvious: the onsets of words are, for perception which takes place in time, the most crucial portions, and distortion of initial segments is likely to disrupt perception to a much greater extent than distortion of final segments.

Thus speakers' choices in on-line speech production — whether to correct a misplaced stress, whether to casually distort a word boundary — appear once again to be guided first and foremost by the requirements of their listeners' perceptual processes.

The curious case of word boundaries

The previous section discussed some circumstances under which casual speech processes may obscure word boundaries. In fact, word boundaries pose something of a problem for speech perception; in particular, they pose a problem for an account of speech production which invokes perceptual constraints.

Consider the current state of automatic speech recognition research. Isolated word recognizers are both feasible and available using current technology. Continuous speech recognizers, however, are simply still beyond current knowledge. The problem which so far has not been solved is that of segmentation. If speech recognizers could be supplied with reliable information about where each word in a continuous utterance began and ended, the successful construction of automatic continuous speech recognizers would be very close. But word boundary information is, at least, not reliably enough coded that speech scientists have as yet been able to make machines detect it.

The problem for the present argument is, therefore: despite all the examples cited above of speakers constraining their output in many and varied ways to make things easy for the listener, the one thing which speakers could do which would be particularly useful for listeners, namely provide precise information as to where one word ends and the next begins, they do not.

Why might it be particularly useful to know the boundaries of words? Strictly speaking, what is required is not boundaries between words (in the orthographic sense) but between whatever constitutes the units of lexical representation. Meaning must be represented in discrete units; it is impossible for listeners to carry around complete semantic representations for any sentence they might conceivably ever hear. The task of speech understanding consists of translating sound into meaning, i.e. locating the (discrete) lexical representations which correspond to the continuous stream of spoken sounds. If the listener knew exactly where the speech sounds representing one discrete meaning unit ended and those representing the next began, the task of locating lexical matches would be considerably facilitated. Why, given that speakers appear to strive to do so much else for listeners, do they not provide word boundary cues? Four possible answers, each logically distinct, suggest themselves:

(a) Speakers do in fact produce usable cues to word boundaries, although speech scientists and engineers have as yet failed to identify them.
(b) In the production process, constraints deriving from perceptual

systems may apply only up to a certain level; word boundaries are obscured by automatic processes operating beyond that level.

(c) There is a trade-off with the constraints imposed by characteristics of the production system, such that provision of word boundary cues could only be achieved at considerable cost in effort to the speaker.

(d) There is a trade-off with independent constraints imposed by characteristics of the perceptual system, such that marking of word boundaries would conflict with application of other perceptually determined effects.

The tentative answer which will be suggested in the following sections does not, however, correspond exactly to any of (a)–(d). It will be argued that both (a) and (d) are partly correct; but that, more importantly, it may be necessary to revise our conception of what the lexical unit is, or at least what the code for accessing it is. Word boundaries may not be what speech engineers think they are.

Stress patterns and segmentation

The processing of prosody is a somewhat neglected area of speech recognition research. It will be argued here that the problematic area of speech segmentation is one in which attention to the possible contributions of prosodic information could bring considerable advances, both in understanding human perception and in guiding automatic recognition.

Recent cross-linguistic work on segmentation in speech understanding has shown that the apparent units of segmentation may differ for speakers of different languages (Cutler, Mehler, Norris and Segui, 1983, 1986): the syllable appears to function as a segmentation unit for speakers of French but not for speakers of English. The search for units of perception has long exercised psycholinguistics, and this new evidence is rather disturbing, in that it suggests that aspects of the segmentation process may be language-specific, which in turn implies that the proper model of speech recognition may differ for different languages or speakers. This conclusion is disturbing simply because the aim of psycholinguistics is to model the general case of language perception and production, independently of language-specific variations. The perceptual unit model does not readily constitute a general model if the units in question may be vastly different.

Cutler and Norris (in press) have suggested a possible alternative model which is couched in more general terms and offers a potentially language independent framework for segmentation. This model draws a distinction between strong syllables (those with full vowels) and weak syllables (with reduced vowels, such as schwa). The basic claim is that the segmentation process treats the two types of syllable differently. Each full vowel, together with its syllabic onset, if any, is treated as a potential word onset. Reduced syllables are treated as unlikely word onset points.

In a stress language, like English, in which not all vowels are full, this means that strong syllables will be segmented in a way weak syllables are not. To demonstrate this, Cutler and Norris used a task requiring detection of a word embedded in a larger string. CVCC words such as *melt* were converted into non-words by having a VC string appended to them, so that the final consonant of the embedded word would then function as the onset of a second syllable. The vowel in this second syllable could be either full or reduced. Thus *melt* appeared in *meltive* (with strong second syllable: [mɛltajv] or *meltesh* (with reduced second syllable: [mɛltəʃ]). Subjects were required simply to listen to a string of such two syllable nonsense words and to respond whenever they detected one beginning with a real word. It was predicted that detection time would be longer for the *meltive* examples than for the *meltesh* since in the former case the second syllable, -*tive*, would be segmented and treated as a potential new word, thus disrupting the extraction of information from both the first and second syllables necessary for the successful detection of the embedded word *melt*. In *meltesh* the reduced vowel in the second syllable would not trigger the segmentation process, so detection of the word spread over both syllables should not be impeded.

Note that alternative word recognition models do not predict this difference. On a standard syllabification analysis the syllable boundary of both *meltive* and *meltesh* falls between the two medial consonants, so a syllabic segmentation unit model (e.g. Mehler, 1981; Segui, 1984) should predict that, because both strings will be segmented at the same place into two syllables, each string should make detection of the embedded word equally difficult. Similarly, a strictly left-to-right auditory word recognition model (e.g. Marslen-Wilson, 1980) should predict that the embedded word would be recognized as soon as it ended, irrespective of what sounds followed it; thus, again, such a model should predict no difference between the two conditions.

In fact, as predicted by the full vowel model, embedded words were detected significantly more slowly when they were followed by a full vowel than when they were followed by a reduced vowel. When the VC endings were edited off and the experiment rerun as a word detection task, no difference was found between the words which had had full vowels edited off and those which had had reduced vowels edited off. Thus the original difference was surely due to the nature of the following vowel.

Cutler and Norris argued that directing attention to strong syllables makes good perceptual sense. In a stress language, strong syllables are acoustically clearer than weak syllables. Moreover, as Huttenlocher (1984) has shown, strong syllables contain more phonetically useful information than weak syllables. Huttenlocher calculated the number of words potentially satisfied by a broad phonetic transcription such as 'stop-vowel-liquid-stop', and found that discarding information in weak syllables did not significantly increase the size of the set of words satisfied by a particular transcription, whereas discarding strong syllable information increased set size several-fold. Thus the phonetic content of strong syllables is more informative than that of weak syllables, as well as being more perceptible due to simple acoustic advantages of greater duration and intensity.

Moreover, there is independent evidence that English listeners treat strong syllables as potential word onsets. Taft (1984) found that listeners preferred to segment ambiguous bisyllabic strings at strong syllable onsets. For instance, whereas a one-word form was chosen more often for [lɛtəs], which could equally well be *lettuce* or *let us*, a two-word solution was chosen more often for [ɪnvɛsts], which could be either *invests* or *in vests*.

Thus the occurrence of strong syllables appears to be an important factor in segmentation. The rate of occurrence of strong syllables is the crucial ingredient in linguistic rhythm, be it stree-based in one language, syllable-based in another. This suggests that a key to understanding segmentation procedures in continuous speech recognition may lie in the processing of rhythm.

Rhythm in speech perception and production

There is a good deal of diverse evidence that rhythm provides useful information in speech perception. The disruption of rhythm certainly disrupts performance on many perceptual tasks. Martin (1979), for example, found that either lengthening or shortening a single vowel in a recorded utterance could cause a perceptible momentary alteration in tempo and increase listeners' reaction time to detect phoneme targets. Meltzer, Martin, Mills, Imhoff and Zohar (1976) similarly found that phoneme targets which were slightly displaced from their position in normal speech were detected more slowly. Buxton (1984) found that adding or removing a syllable on a word preceding a phoneme target also increased detection time.

These results suggest that listeners process a regular rhythm in a rather active way, using it to make predictions about temporal patterns; when manipulations of the speech signal cause these predictions to be proven wrong, perception is temporarily disrupted. There is yet further evidence which shows listeners to be actively following prosodic continuity. Wingfield and Klein (1971) demonstrated that prosodic breaks over-ride syntactic breaks in click location tasks — that is, more clicks are falsely reported to have been heard at the prosodic boundary, indicating that prosodic boundary marking is the most salient. Darwin (1975) similarly showed that prosodic continuity over-rides semantic continuity in shadowing.

The predictive use of prosody in speech understanding was particularly obvious in experiments in which phoneme targets on acoustically identical words were responded to faster when the target-bearing word was preceded by a prosodic contour indicative of sentence accent occurring at the target word's position (Cutler, 1976). Thus the target *d* was detected more rapidly in (7), in which the target-bearing word *dirt* is accented, than in (8), in which the accent falls on *rug* — even when tape-splicing had ensured that the word *dirt* was acoustically identical in both (7) and (8).

(7) She managed to remove the dirt from the rug, but not the grass stains.
(8) She managed to remove the dirt from the rug, but not from their clothes.

Since the only difference in the part of the sentence preceding the target was the prosody with which it was uttered, prosody must have been the source of the response time difference. It was argued that listeners were extracting from the prosodic pattern predictive cues as to where accent would fall, with a view to directing particular attention to the location of accent. Follow-up studies further investigated the components of the prosodic pattern contributing to this effect. When pitch variation was removed, i.e. the sentences were monotonized, acoustically identical targets were still responded to faster in sentences like (7) than in sentences like (8) (Cutler and Darwin, 1981). Thus intonational variation was not a necessary component of the predictive accent effect. In later experiments, however, sentence rhythm was manipulated, such that by the use of digital techniques the waveform was stretched or compressed and the temporal pattern of (7) imposed on (8) and vice versa, with all other components of the original prosody being left intact. In this case, the response time difference disappeared, which suggests that rhythmic factors are at least making a very strong contribution to the predictive value of prosodic contours.

Thus there is considerable converging evidence that listeners make active use of rhythmic structure in speech perception. Moreover, there is evidence that speakers are concerned to impose a regular rhythmic structure on their utterances where possible. Again, this evidence comes from research on slips of the tongue. Some slips of the tongue result in an alteration of the rhythm of the intended utterance — for example, slips in which a syllable is added or deleted, or in which stress placement is shifted. Analysis of such slips shows that the erroneous utterances are significantly more often more regular in comparison to the intended utterances than less regular (Cutler, 1980b). For example in (9) a syllable has been omitted from the intended word *interlocutor* to give the non-word *interlocker* (stressed on the first syllable):

(9) what the speaker thinks his interlocker knows

The resulting utterance clearly has a more regular rhythmic beat than the intended utterance, in that there is a constant number of weak syllables between any two strong syllables, whereas the intended utterance would have displayed a more varied pattern. Such regularization appears to show an underlying pressure towards rhythmicity in speech production, which occasionally expresses itself in the production of an error. A pressure towards rhythmicity may well admit of an explanation purely in terms of the demands of speech production itself; but on the other hand, given the evidence summarized in this section, it also accords very well with the notion of a speech production device closely attuned to the demands of the perceptual process.

Speaking for segmentation

The evidence of the preceding section suggests that rhythmic continuity is of very great importance to speech perception, since listeners use it so actively. Rhythmic continuity may be the main reason why speakers do not provide simple word boundary cues such as perceptible pauses between words. Words — or rather, units of lexical representation — can be of very differing lengths, so that marking the boundaries between them in some such prosodically sensitive way as pausing would of necessity result in a rather irregular and hence unpredictable rhythm. In this sense overt marking of word boundaries, on the face of it a great service to the perception process, could conflict with other perceptual demands — in this case, the demand for rhythmic continuity and regularity.

On the other hand, the very high degree to which perception is sensitive to rhythmic factors suggests that rhythm may perhaps offer an answer to the problem of segmentation. The essence of rhythm is the rate of occurrence of strong syllables. Listeners are very adept at computing speech rhythm, and using it predictively. It is not unreasonable to suggest that they may also be able to exploit it to generate word boundary information.

However, the word boundary information which they could extract would not be directly isomorphous with orthographic word boundary marking. Rhythm leads the listener to strong syllables. The results of the experiments described above suggest that strong syllables are indeed segmented in a way that weak syllables are not. Thus it may be that strong syllables are effectively the boundaries for lexical units. In some languages, all words begin with strong syllables; but in free stress languages, some words begin with weak syllables. The present proposal would imply that words beginning with weak syllables may not be accessed from the mental lexicon in strictly left-to-right order, but rather via their strong syllables. This is a radical proposal in terms of current models of word perception and speech recognition, since it violates the widely held assumption of 'sequential isomorphism', i.e. that the order of processing directly reflects the order of input.

However, it should be noted that independent arguments against the sequential isomorphism assumption have been offered by MacKay (Chap 18); and Huttenlocher and Goodman (Chap 19) have argued that a strictly left-to-right model of word recognition such as that of Marslen-Wilson (1980) cannot account for all word recognition performance. Therefore this proposal is in fact in line with other recent work. Moreover, the present proposal offers a solution to the word boundary problem which is directly in line with the other evidence on the relation between perception and production summarized above. Speakers accommodate their output to listeners' needs at all levels of the production process, including formulation of the details of the articulatory programme. Just as at other levels, speakers give listeners what they need at the word boundary level — and what they need at that level is prosody.

Conclusion

The evidence summarized in the preceding sections therefore presents a satisfyingly coherent picture. Throughout the speech production process, the demands of the perception process are operative, constraining word formation choices, blocking elisions and assimilations which might interfere with word recognition, prompting corrections of slips of the tongue only when comprehension is likely to be impaired. Even an apparent glaring exception to the pattern of perceptual sensitivity in production appears not to be an exception after all: although boundaries between orthographic words are not reliably marked in the speech signal, studies of the processing of rhythm suggest that listeners use rhythmic information to segment the speech signal into lexical units. There appears to be a strong pressure towards regularity of rhythm in the production of English, and regularity of rhythm is apparently just what listeners rely on to segment English. Thus the perceptual process is well served by the production process in all respects.

This is of course not to deny at all that production-internal factors constrain production. It would be extraordinary were perceptual exigencies to influence the production process in ways that were directly inimical to the needs of production. Regularity of rhythm, for instance, has an obvious role in facilitating speech production; indeed, Shaffer (1982) has argued that rhythm has a general beneficial organising function in all skilled motor performance. The background picture against which the present arguments should be considered is rather one in which production and perception processes co-operate at all levels. In fact, with respect to rhythmic processing, it has been argued that production and perception share an underlying timing mechanism (Keele, Pokorny, Corcos and Ivry, 1985). Speech production and perception play so important a role in our life that it should be no surprise to find that the two processes co-exist in cooperation rather than in competition. The present evidence of how speaking accommodates itself to listening is just further confirmation of this happy reciprocity.

Acknowledgment

The unpublished experiments described in the final two sections were supported by a grant from British Telecom. Jeffrey Bloom wrote the programs for temporal manipulation of speech waveforms, and Steve Bartram ran the experiments. Special thanks to Dennis Norris for many useful discussions.

Note

[1] Some researchers have claimed that normal identification of morphologically complex words also involves separation of affix and base (e.g. Taft and Forster, 1975; MacKay, 1976), although others have claimed that complex words have unanalysed lexical entries (e.g. Butterworth, 1982). Even if bases and affixes are always processed separately, the understanding of a neologism cannot be exactly the same process as the recognition of a known word, for the simple reason that we do notice when something we have heard is a made-up word. Therefore a model of the normal process based on recognition of the separate parts must allow for an additional process of recognition of the combination.

References

Butterworth, B. (1982). Lexical representation. In B. Butterworth (Ed.) *Language Production, Vol. 2: Development, Writing and Other Language Processes.* London: Academic Press.

Buxton, H. (1984). *Rhythm and Stress in Speech.* Unpublished PhD Thesis, University of Cambridge.

Cooper, W. E. and Paccia-Cooper, J. (1980). *Syntax and Speech.* Cambridge, MA: Harvard University Press.

Cutler, A. (1976). Phoneme-monitoring reaction time as a function of preceding intonation contour. *Perception and Psychophysics,* **20,** 55–60.

Cutler, A. (1980a). Productivity in word formation. *Papers from the Sixteenth Regional Meeting, Chicago Linguistic Society,* 45–51.

Cutler, A. (1980b). Syllable omission errors and isochrony. In H. W. Dechert and M. Raupach (Eds) *Temporal Variables in Speech.* The Hague: Mouton.

Cutler, A. (1981). Degrees of transparency in word formation. *Canadian Journal of Linguistics.,* **26,** 73–7.

Cutler, A. (1983). Speakers' conceptions of the functions of prosody. In A. Cutler and D. R. Ladd (Eds) *Prosody: Models and Measurements.* Heidelberg: Springer.

Cutler, A. and Darwin, C. J. (1981). Phoneme-monitoring reaction time and preceding prosody: effects of stop closure duration and of fundamental frequency. *Perception and Psychophysics,* **29,** 217–24.

Cutler, A. and Isard, S. D. (1980). The production of prosody. In B. Butterworth (Ed.) *Language Production.* London: Academic.

Cutler, A., Mehler, J., Norris, D. and Segui, J. (1983). A language-specific comprehension strategy. *Nature,* **304,** 159–60.

Cutler, A., Mehler, J., Norris, D. G. and Segui, J. (1986). The syllable's differing role in the segmentation of French and English. *Journal of Memory and Language,* **25,** 385–400.

Cutler, A. and Norris, D. G. (in press). The role of strong syllables in segmentation for lexical access. *Journal of Experimental Psychology: Human Perception & Performance.*

Darwin, C. J. (1975). On the dynamic use of prosody in speech perception. In A. Cohen and S. G. Nooteboom (Eds) *Structure and Process in Speech Perception.* Berlin: Springer.

Goffman, E. (1981). Radio talk. In E. Goffman (Ed.) *Forms of Talk.* Oxford: Blackwell.

Huttenlocher, D. P. (1984). *Acoustic-Phonetic and Lexical Constraints in Word Recognition: Lexical Access using Partial Information.* Unpublished M.Sc. thesis, MIT.

Keele, S. W., Pokorny, R. A., Corcos, D. M. and Ivry, R. (1985). Do perception and motor production share common timing mechanisms: a correlational analysis. *Acta Psychologica,* **60,** 173–91.

Ladd, D. R. (1980). *The Structure of Intonational Meaning.* Bloomington: Indiana University Press.

Levelt, W. J. M. (1983). Monitoring and self-repair in speech. *Cognition,* **14,** 41–104.

Levelt, W. J. M. and Cutler, A. (1983). Prosodic marking in speech repair. *Journal of Semantics*, **2**, 205–17.

MacKay, D. G. (1976). On the retrieval and lexical structure of verbs. *Journal of Verbal Learning and Verbal Behavior*, **15**, 169–82.

Marslen-Wilson, W. D. (1980). Speech understanding as a psychological process. In J. C. Simon (Ed.) *Spoken Language Generation and Understanding*. Dordrecht: Reidel.

Martin, J. G. (1979). Rhythmic and segmental perception are not independent. *Journal of the Acoustical Society of America*, **65**, 1286–97.

Mehler, J. (1981). The role of syllables in speech processing: infant and adult data. *Philosophical Transactions of the Royal Society*, B **295**, 333–52.

Meltzer, R. H., Martin, J. G., Mills, C. B., Imhoff, D. L. and Zohar, D. (1976). Reaction time to temporally displaced phoneme targets in continuous speech. *Journal of Experimental Psychology: Human Perception and Performance*, **2**, 277–90.

Segui, J. (1984). The syllable: a basic perceptual unit in speech processing? In H. Bouma and D. G. Bouwhuis (Eds) *Attention and Performance X: Control of Language Processes*. Hillsdale, NJ: Erlbaum.

Shaffer, L. H. (1982). Rhythm and timing in skill. *Psychological Review*, **89**, 109–22.

Taft, L. (1984). *Prosodic Constraints and Lexical Parsing Strategies*. Ph.D. Thesis, University of Massachusetts.

Taft, M. and Forster, K. I. (1975). Lexical storage and retrieval of prefixed words. *Journal of Verbal Learning and Verbal Behavior*, **14**, 638–47.

Valian, V. V. and Wales, R. J. (1976). What's what: talkers help listeners hear and understand by clarifying sentential relations. *Cognition*, **4**, 115–76.

Wingfield, A. and Klein, J. F. (1971). Syntactic structure and acoustic pattern in speech perception. *Perception and Psychophysics*, **9**, 23–5.

3   An asymmetry in producing versus understanding descriptions of visual arrays

Robert J. Jarvella and Werner Deutsch

Abstract

The speed of producing versus understanding descriptions of visual arrays is compared. The arrays contained three bars of all or only two different colors which subjects in preliminary research described using mainly S- versus mainly NP-conjunction. It is shown that array descriptions are initiated faster when each bar's position and color is named in turn (e.g., 'The left is red, the middle is blue, and the right is yellow'), but verified faster when two bars are named first in a single clause (e.g. 'The left and the right are red, and the middle is blue'). The findings suggest that an utterance's linguistic structure is processed by a speaker and listener in different ways, since the descriptions used were the same, and no corresponding difference arises when the arrays are used in a non-linguistic task.

Introduction

In ordinary use of language, spoken utterances are both produced and understood. Any utterance is thus processed twice: first by the speaker in producing the form and again by the listener (or listeners) in interpreting it. In principle, the language processing done in the two cases might range from being quite similar, or modality-independent, to being quite different, or modality-specific. This paper is concerned especially with how the processing done may differ. In the studies we report, this issue is taken up for the production versus verification of natural, spoken descriptions.

LANGUAGE PERCEPTION AND PRODUCTION
ISBN 0-12-052750-2

We begin by discussing why it is useful to compare acts of speaking and listening for the same linguistic form. An argument is given for exploring natural uses of utterances. Some views of how linguistic structure might be processed when language is produced and understood are then elaborated. Three experiments are reported. In Experiment 1, descriptions were elicited from speakers, in Experiment 2, they were verified by listeners, and in Experiment 3, subjects used equivalent stimulus material, but performed a non-linguistic task.

On comparing speaking and listening

The study of cognitive processes associated with using language usually is divided into two parts, one which is concerned with speaking and the other with understanding (see e.g., Fodor, Bever and Garrett, 1974; Clark and Clark, 1977). While recognizing that speakers and listeners usually both make use of the linguistic form and the corresponding content of utterances, most such work has attached no special significance to this correspondence, and studied the psychological processes involved as being separate and independent. Possible similarities, as well as asymmetries, between speaking and listening have as a result attracted relatively little attention, and even studies which have examined aspects of both activities for the same utterances are comparatively rare (e.g., Valian, 1971; Clark and Chase, 1974; Jarvella and Collas, 1974; Ford and Holmes, 1978; Deutsch and Jarvella, 1984; Deutsch, 1986).

There seem to be two reasons why little research has been aimed at revealing commonalities and differences between speaking and listening. The main reason is probably the obvious behavioral and sensory–motor differences between them. One could namely take the standpoint that, like apples and oranges, language production and perception must be so different that no direct comparison of the cognitive processes underlying them could be of much value. Even if this supposition were correct, however, a compelling argument can be given on methodological grounds for investigating speaking and listening in a yoked fashion. The problem is that language use and the language used by subjects in experiments are difficult to tell apart. A process comparison of several kinds of performance using the same utterances can serve as a means for seeing beyond language to the processes involved in its use.

A second related reason may explain the relative absence of comparative research on speaking and listening. Psycholinguistics has lost sight of linguistic structure as something which is processed from utterances. If one assumes that speakers and listeners use the same linguistic structure when they use language, but do so in different ways, however, a natural testing ground for theories of processing lies in observing different uses of the same linguistic forms. The 'apples and oranges' view of speaking and listening thus would have us draw an incorrect inference. Any rigorous attempt to delimit processes underlying language production or perception may require their experimental comparison (see also MacKay, forthcoming 1987).

Linguistic structure in speaking versus listening

Two views of the linguistic processing done in speaking and listening may be contrasted, one which embodies the idea of modality-independence, the other of modality-specificity.

Work in modern linguistics and psycholinguistics has been substantially influenced by the notion of 'linguistic competence' (Chomsky, 1965; see also Bresnan and Kaplan, 1982). Competence is usually taken to (a) correspond to the linguistic knowledge which an 'ideal' speaker–hearer has of his or her language, (b) be representable by a single formal system, or grammar, and (c) be involved in, or make up part of, linguistic performance. Without a theory of what else is involved in performance, points (a)–(c) might be interpreted as claiming that speakers and listeners use the same abstract system of grammatical rules and representations when they use language.

What about language use? By itself, the 'competence hypothesis' makes no predictions that human language processing will be a specific function of either variation in the form of natural utterances, or in the uses that are made of them. This is because it leaves undefined how a grammar (or linguistic form) will be used by speaker–listener. A theory of performance, however, might be defined which includes the assumption that speakers and listeners use grammar in the same way when they use language. Such a theory might seem to have little face validity, although, as Lashley (1951), Miller, Galanter, and Pribram (1960), Stevens and Halle (1967) and others have noted, the mechanisms underlying speaking and listening may overlap.

Taken as a theory of performance, an hypothesis of modality-independence makes both strong and testable claims. To reject the hypothesis, it would be sufficient to show, for example, that the structure-assigning process involved in speaking and listening is not the same. It need not actually be specified how language users use their grammar, or how given forms are processed. For this reason, we will not elaborate a specific theory of modality-independent processing. Any metric of complexity defined on sentence structure as such (i.e., independently of how it is processed) would qualify as such a theory.

In what ways does processing of the linguistic properties of utterances differ in speaking versus listening? Research in psycholinguistics has produced evidence that linguistic structure is relevant when language is used (see, e.g., Fodor, Bever and Garrett, 1974; Levelt, 1978) but has generally failed to show how such structure is processed.

In the present paper, we report a comparison of production and verification latencies for some spoken sentences which simply and naturally describe visual patterns. In planning the studies in which these data were gathered, it became apparent that realistic research into natural speaking and listening may often find itself somewhat at odds with traditional procedures and recipes for experimental design. Both the present studies' order (production, then perception), and the comparisons made within each experiment reported, were dictated by a concern to avoid artificial uses of the structures under observation. A preliminary study carried out to help identify form-content relations for the patterns' description, and the main production study conducted, significantly reduced the range of comparisons tested in the experiment performed on verification. Our principal aim in this work was to obtain and compare as near as possible to spontaneous performance on the same materials in speaking and listening tasks.

The linguistic domain of the present research was that of sentences in Dutch (but nearly equivalent in English) which simply and naturally describe several events by means of coordination. The situation studied was one in which a description attributed some common property to several parts of a visual stimulus, or different attributes to each part separately. In the experiments reported, subjects were presented a series of simple spatial arrays, each made up of three vertical bars of equal height. On some trials, two of the bars shown in an array were of one color, and the third bar of a different color, while on other trials, the colors of the three bars shown were all different.

The speaker's description of such stimuli might be expected to follow a certain principle of simplicity (cf. Clark and Chase, 1974), in this case based initially on color, and perhaps secondly location. Where both are described, for example, the natural tendency might be for the speaker to mention the colors from left to right and from many to few. Presupposing that what is being talked about are bars or colored lines not otherwise differing from each other, two parts having the same color at different locations might be described together, as in the beginning of (1).

(1) The middle one and the right one are red, and the left one is blue.

On the other hand, bars of different colors might best be described separately, as in (2).

(2) The left one is red, the middle one is blue, and the right one is yellow.

In fact, there does seem to be a close correspondence between arrays of the two types and structures such as those found in (1) and (2). When this pairing is not observed, as in 'The left one and the right one are red and yellow (respectively), and the middle one is blue', or followed only part way, as in 'The left one is blue, the middle one is red, and the right one is red', using the sentences in the context of such patterns seems less appropriate. In the preliminary experiment referred to above, we asked ten Dutch subjects to each describe four spatial arrays, three in which two parts were one color and the position of the third part of a different color was varied, and one in which three colors were present. The subjects were asked to first get an idea of how the patterns varied by sorting through a set of cards shown to them, and then to describe the arrays using their own words, one after the other. The following are examples of spontaneously produced descriptions:

'Aan de linker en aan de rechterkant van 't vlak 'n, eh, rooie vertikale lijn en in 't midden 'n groene vertikale lijn' ('On the left and on the right side of the area a, uh, red vertical line and in the middle a green vertical line')

'Drie verticale lijnen, de linkse twee zijn geel en de rechtse is groen' ('Three vertical lines, the left two are yellow and the right is green')

On the other hand, bars of different colors were described disjointly. This pattern is seen above, and also in other authentic examples given below:

'Drie vertikale lijnen, de linkse is groen, de middelste is rood, de rechte is blauw' ('Three vertical lines, the left is green, the middle is red, the right is blue')

'Aan de linkerkant 'n groene vertikale lijn, daartussenin is 't wit en dan 'n rooie vertikale lijn en daarna aan de rechterkant 'n blauwe vertikale lijn' ('On the left side a green vertical line, between them it's white, and then a red vertical line and after that on the right side a blue vertical line').

Although the utterances that were produced varied to some extent, with respect to the coordinate structures used different speakers agreed surprisingly well. There was a consistent pairing of an array's content with linguistic form. When the three bars seen in an array were different colors, coordination occurred almost exclusively at the level of full clauses, whereas coordination of noun phrases occurred only when two of the bars were colored the same.

The spoken descriptions we obtained are also consistent with data from experiments where subjects have shown some preference or a speed-accuracy advantage in using different coordinate structures in different contexts. Levelt and Maassen (1981, Experiment 3), for example, found that 78% of descriptions of movements by two objects in the same direction included some form of noun–phrase (NP) conjunction, whereas no such descriptions were produced when the objects made movements in opposite directions. In another study, Heeschen and Blomert (1982) found that adult aphasics make fewer errors when constructing arrays from descriptions like (1) and (2), and in verifying such descriptions when the array and linguistic form used to correspond. Levelt and Maassen speak of a congruence principle between percept and construction type, Heeschen and Blomert of 'better motivated' descriptions in the sense suggested by Saussure (1916).

Speed in task performance is perhaps the single most widely used index of a task's complexity. For speaking and understanding, an interesting case

---

Table 1. Overview of the sentence types used as descriptions in the experiments[a].

Three-event descriptions

(1) Sentence-initial NP conjunction
$((((de\ MIDDELSTE)_{NP}\ en\ (de\ RECHTSE)_{NP})_{NP}\ zijn\ ROOD)_S$
$en\ ((de\ LINKSE)_{NP}\ is\ BLAUW)_S)_S$

(2) Sentence conjunction only
$(((de\ LINKSE)_{NP}\ is\ ROOD)_S\ ((de\ MIDDELSTE)_{NP}\ is\ BLAUW)_S$
$en\ ((de\ RECHTSE)_{NP}\ is\ GEEL)_S)_S$

Elliptical answer to questions

(3) Compound NP
$(((de\ MIDDELSTE)_{NP}\ en\ (de\ RECHTSE)_{NP})_{NP})_S$

(4) Simple NP
$((de\ LINKSE)_{NP})_S$

Two-event descriptions

(5) NP conjunction
$(((de\ LINKSE)_{NP}\ en\ (de\ RECHTSE)_{NP})_{NP}\ zijn\ ROOD)_S$

(6) S conjunction
$(((de\ LINKSE)_{NP}\ is\ ROOD)_S\ en\ ((de\ RECHTSE)_{NP}\ is\ GEEL\ )_S)_S$

---

[a] Left and right parentheses mark noun phrase and sentence boundaries. Major lexical items (LINKSE MIDDELSTE RECHTSE, ROOD, BLAUW, GEEL = left/middle/right/red/blue/yellow) are capitalized, function words (de/zijn/is/en = the/are/is/and) are not. For explanation see text.

of possible cross-over in this respect would be one in which creating a particular description is relatively slow, but where, given the description, interpreting it in regard to its frame of reference can be relatively fast. Is there a plausible basis for predicting a shift in relative ease in this sense in producing and verifying Dutch sentences like (1) and (2) in Table 1? The differences between these structures arise principally from the fact that in (1) but not (2) there is a clause-internal coordination whereby two objects are described at once ('The middle one *and* the right one — are red'). Example (1) begins with an instance of noun phrase (NP) conjunction, whereas (2) contains only sentence (S) conjunction.

For example, suppose a phrasal structure is composed (e.g., Yngve, 1960; Johnson, 1966), and words are selected (e.g., Lindsley, 1975; Kempen and Huijbers, 1983). Starting an utterance with a compound NP then will require building more structure and choosing more words than starting an utterance beginning with a single NP.

It is plausible that elaboration of the first major linguistic segment in a spoken utterance will consume a significant proportion of the time needed for planning before speech is normally initiated (cf. Clark and Clark's (1977) 'skeleton plus constituent' model of speech production). For sentences of type (1), this initial constituent (3)

(3) The middle one and the right one

is more extensive than the initial constituent (4)

(4) The left one

of sentences of type (2).

Can we make the same prediction for the perceptual side? Probably not. In a verification task the listener has to compare the contents of a linguistic utterance with contents of a visually presented (set of) events. The linguistic form of an utterance may determine the nature of the comparison made, insofar as the listener treats the contents of each clause as a propositional object. But clause-internal structure will not influence the amount of time needed for making the comparisons, if the propositional contents of clauses have already been derived. If the number of clauses (propositional units) in a sentence determines verification time, then sentences of type (1) should be verified faster than sentences of type (2). Similarly, sentences of type (5)

(5) The left one and the right one are red

should be verified faster than sentences of type (6) with two clauses

(6) The left one is red and the right one is yellow.

Experiment 1: Production

The speakers in this study performed two related tasks. On some test trials, subjects were asked to describe a stimulus array in full (i.e., mentioning all three colored bars shown in it). On other trials, they were asked a question that required them to identify only one or two of the bars shown. The main prediction made was that utterances beginning with a compound NP would be slower to initiate. Pre-utterance latencies were also predicted to be shorter for the question answers than for the full descriptions.

Method

Materials and procedure. The utterances elicited were Dutch sentences corresponding to (1)–(4) in Table 1. Full descriptions of arrays began with a compound or only a simple NP. Sentences of the former type contained two clauses (e.g., 'De linkse en de rechtse zijn rood, en de middleste is blauw' — *The left (one)[2] and the right (one) are red, and the middle (one) is blue*), those of the latter kind three clauses (e.g., 'De linkse is rood, de middelste is blauw, en de rechtse is geel' — *The left (one) is red, the middle (one) is blue, and the right (one) is yellow*). Correspondingly, the sentences elicited by questions were simply noun phrases, again either compound (e.g., 'De linkse en de rechtse' — *The left (one) and the right (one)*) or simple (e.g., 'De linkse' — *The left (one)*). (For further details see Table 1.) On full description trials, the instruction 'Beschrijf de drie lijnen' (*Describe the three lines*) preceded presentation of the stimulus array. On question-answering trials, before the array was shown a question was asked ('Wat is/zijn de X lijn/en?' — *Which is/are the X line/s?* where X stands for a color name).

The arrays' colors were red, blue and yellow. On a given trial, any of the six permutations of these, or of two red bars and one blue bar and vice versa, could occur. Each possible array was presented only twice, once with an instruction to describe it and once following a question ('Which is' for three-color arrays, 'Which are' for those with just two colors). Order of presentation was randomized, with the limitation that two test trials of the same type (two or three colors, *and* description or question-answering) were never presented in succession. The arrays were constructed by marking three equidistant vertical lines across the face of empty 35 mm slides, and projected onto a 70 × 90 cm white translucent screen into a sound-attenuated test room. The bars appeared 3 cm wide, 40 cm high, and 20 cm apart. The subject sat facing the screen at a distance from it of about 1 m.

On a given trial, the subject being tested first heard a recorded instruction, was immediately shown the array, and as quickly as possible gave his or her response. The intertrial interval was 10 s. During this period, the experimenter prepared the playback tape recorder and slide projector used for the next item. The slide showing each array was triggered using a tachistoscopic shutter mounted on the projector. During each trial, the interval between slide onset and speech onset, and the duration of the subject's utterance, were determined on-line using a voice-operated relay and real-time clock interfaced to a PDP-11/55 computer. For checking response accuracy, a subject's utterances were also recorded. The test session, including instructions, lasted about 15 min.

Subjects and instructions. The subjects were 29 adult native speakers of Dutch with no history of speech or hearing disorders. Most subjects were students, and about half were male and half female. Subjects were tested individually. Two subjects were dismissed for failure to follow instructions. The data of four subjects tested had to be discarded because of equipment malfunctions during the experiment.

Subjects were told that they would be shown a number of visual displays, each of which they would need to describe or answer a question about. The colors present in arrays, and their composition were explained, and examples were given of appropriate responses for several samples slides and 'describe' or 'answer' type trials. Subjects were instructed by several practice trials to use the sentence forms which had been found to be the natural types of descriptions in the free description task. Subjects were told that they should respond as quickly as they could without making errors. General instructions and the recorded utterances starting each test trial were presented via a loudspeaker.

Results

Subjects' latencies to initiate speech and the duration of their utterances produced are shown for the four types of sentences in Table 2. In more than 95% of the cases, subjects produced an utterance beginning with a compound NP for two-color arrays, and an utterance beginning with only a simple NP for three-color arrays. No reliable tendency was found in any of the four main conditions for pre-utterance latencies to become faster with increasing position in the stimulus list. For utterance durations, such a trend ($p < 0.01$) was observed only for simple NPs used in question-answering. There was no tendency for either color names or positions named within conditions to affect either time measure recorded. Subjects did use a left-to-right and many-to-few order of mention in practically all cases.

The time measurements were analyzed using both raw scores and adjusted values, in which latencies more than two standard deviations from

Table 2. Speech-initiation Latencies, Utterance Durations (both in ms) and Error Rates in Experiment 1.

Response and Sentence Type	Pre-Utterance Latencies		Utterance Durations		Errors
	X̄	SD	X̄	SD	%
Full Descriptions of Arrays					
(1) Initial NP conjunction	1157	40	2680	133	4.3
(2) S conjunction only	930	40	2839	84	1.4
Elliptical Answers to Questions					
(3) Compound NP	984	48	1150	57	0.7
(4) Simple NP	730	29	621	64	1.4

Standard deviations are calculated for items per condition.

a subject's mean per condition were removed. The two methods gave highly similar results; the summary and test statistics reported are based on the latter. For both full descriptions of spatial arrays and elliptical answers to questions asked about them, more time was used to initiate an utterance beginning with a compound than with only a simple noun phrase. The corresponding differences, of 227 ms for complete descriptions, and 254 ms for question answers, are both reliable ($t(22) = 5.37$, $SE_{dif} = 42$ ms, and $t(22) = 8.79$, $SE_{dif} = 28$ ms respectively, $p < 0.001$ for each). Only two of 23 subjects, both in the description task, showed a partial cross-over against this trend. Pre-utterance latencies were, secondly, also longer for full descriptions than for question answers ($t(22) = 8.33$, $SE_{dif} = 57$ ms, $p < 0.001$). All 23 subjects followed this trend.

Third, when a full description began with a compound NP, it took on average 159 ms less time to produce once started than if it began with a simple NP($t(22) = 3.00$, $SE_{dif} = 55$ ms, $p < 0.01$ two-tailed). The data for 18 of the 23 subjects showed a tendency in this direction. Finally, as is obvious from table 2, utterance duration, for the two kinds of question answers also varied.

Discussion

Given a visual stimulus, latencies to begin a spoken utterance were significantly (*c.* 240 ms) longer when it started with a compound than with a simple noun phrase. The same general result was obtained for both full descriptions of three-event spatial arrays, and for elliptical answers to questions asked about such arrays and consisting of the respective NPs alone. Levelt and Maassen (1981) report a somewhat similar finding for descriptions of pairs of geometric figures which were seen beginning to move in the same versus opposite directions. There as well, pre-utterance latencies were longer when the figures were mentioned in a single clause than in separate clauses. Findings of this sort suggest that the planning and assembly for a within-clause coordination starting an utterance is more extensive, and that execution in speech may only follow this process.

The pattern of pre-utterance latencies found here is predicted by several linguistic features which arise out of the types of conjunction present in the sentences studied. These features include the number of simple predicate and argument terms underlying their initial clause and of major lexical items present there, the number of left branches in this clause which dominate the first word spoken, the number of constituents in the clause and sentence which incorporate the first word, and perhaps others (see, e.g., Miller and Chomsky, 1963). With the exception of the constituent (or equivalently the branching) parameter for *full* sentences produced, these features equally can predict a difference between NP and S conjunction in the direction obtained for sentences like 'The triangle moves up and the circle moves down' or 'The square and the crescent move up' by Levelt and Maassen.

The latter authors were able to rule out the *naming* difficulty of the second conjunct in an NP (e.g., 'crescent' in the last example) as the source of this difference. Perhaps similarly here, length of utterance in *words*, or in total *stress units*, does not appear to be a robust indicator of pre-utterance latencies, in contrast to more thoroughly prepared speech (cf. Sternberg, Monsell, Knoll and Wright, 1978). For both number of words produced and major stresses, one would predict longer pre-utterance latencies for fully S-conjoined structures, and not the shorter ones observed. Not surprisingly, utterance duration does seem to be related to sentence length in both these terms. However, constructing a natural utterance describing some disjunctively organized set of information and reproducing a well-learned list may represent basically different processes. In the one case, before speech is undertaken, an utterance's form may be filled in detail only for that part of the information to be expressed first. In the other, to be produced as a whole, the list may need to be retrieved or buffer-stored as such when it is programmed for articulation. A stress- or word-based model makes better predictions here for the pre-utterance interval if one limits the section of utterance concerned to its first major constituent. Levelt and Maassen's (1981) finding for name retrieval in NP conjuncts suggests that even this domain may sometimes be too wide for speech-level planning *per se*, however.

One remaining linguistic hypothesis — that subjects may have been indecisive about using compound NPs in full descriptions — runs counter to the strong natural relation noted between the types of array and respective sentence forms studied, the implicit instruction to follow this correspondence, and the generally fluent manner in which it was adhered to. The conceptual representations which subjects worked with in formulating their utterances, however, were probably full ones. To use the sentences appropriately, without frequent mis-starts, hesitations, or repairs, it would have been necessary in general to first determine what colors were in what positions in the arrays. Since little indication of such linguistic trouble, or of a strategy of self-terminating search, was to be found in the data, one might gather that all of the relevant stimulus information was analyzed as a pre-requisite to speaking.

Experiment 2: Verification

Experiment 2 studied verification of sentences against the same arrays used previously. The comparisons tested in the study were again restricted to normal uses of the sentences, and the number of trials was kept short and heterogeneous. Since the full descriptions of arrays given in Experiment 1 were usually both accurate and took the form suggested in our preliminary research, to obtain maximally comparable data, the critical 'true' judgements in the present study obtained for sentences of type (1) and (2) were also for full, appropriate descriptions.

Method

*Materials and procedure.*The sentences studied were the ones produced as full descriptions in Experiment 1 plus 12 Dutch sentences corresponding to (5) or (6). The latter sentences mentioned only two of the three positions in a stimulus array (e.g. 'De linkse en de rechtse zijn blauw' — *The left (one) and the right (one) are blue*, and 'De linkse is geel en de rechtse is rood' — *The left (one) is yellow and the right (one) is red*). For each of the four general sentence types studied, there were six main experimental items, one practice item and one filler item. Bars were mentioned from left to right and from many to few. Serial positions mentioned in sentences were balanced over items. The visual material was the same set of slides used in Experiment 1 plus four similar slides used for filler items.

The sentences presented were congruent with both arrays shown and parts mentioned in them. Experimental items of types (5) and (6) described a pair of positions having one color in common as sharing the opposite color or a pair of positions of different colors having the colors in the reversed order. Experimental items of type (1) and (2), as indicated, were true of their arrays. In the eight practice and filler items, this correspondence was reversed; sentences of type (1) and (2) were false and those of type (5) and (6) true. Stimulus order was randomized under the limitation that no two sentences of a single type and truth value directly succeeded one another. The test list was recorded by a native Dutch speaker who had also read the instructions accompanying test items in Experiment 1, and presented using the same apparatus. Onset of the stimulus array was triggered by an impulse recorded on the second channel of the stimulus tape co-synchronous with speech offset for each sentence. The intertrial interval was again 10 s. Subjects were tested individually and registered their responses by pressing one of two push buttons located on a table before them. Latency from slide onset to key press was measured using a computer-interfaced real-time clock, and recorded together with the key press made. The test session, including instructions, lasted about 15 min. Following the experiment, subjects were asked if they had noticed any tendency for particular sentences to be true or false. All subjects reported that they had not.

Instructions. Subjects were told that they would hear a series of spoken sentences, each followed by a slide related to the sentence. The picture presented might be accurately or inaccurately described by the sentence. Subjects were to indicate if the sentence agreed with the slide by pressing a push button marked 'goed' (*right*) and to indicate by pushing a button marked 'fout' (*wrong*) if it did not agree. They were told to make their decision quickly and accurately, and register them as soon as possible. One hand was used for recording each kind of response. Before the recorded items were presented, some examples of the kinds of sentences to be heard were presented together with a description of the slide types, and subjects were provided the opportunity to test the response keys.

Subjects. The subjects were 28 native speakers of Dutch without history of speech or hearing disorders. Most were students at the Dutch university in Nijmegen, and about half were male and half female. The subjects were tested individually. None of the subjects had taken part in Experiment 1.

Results

Subjects' response latencies for correct 'right'-'wrong' decisions are shown together with error rates obtained for the four types of sentences studied in Table 3. In all conditions, speed of response tended to increase somewhat across the stimulus list, but reached significance ($p < 0.01$) only for sentences of type (6). Neither colors within conditions nor left-to-right positions mentioned in them had any systematic effect on response latencies.

The data were analyzed using both raw scores and removing latencies more than two standard deviations from a subject's mean per condition. The same pattern of results was obtained; the summary and test statistics reported are based on the latter. For both full descriptions ('correct' responses) and partial ones ('false' responses), more time was used when the test sentence contained only sentence conjunction than when it contained some NP conjunction. The corresponding average differences, of 214 ms for three-event descriptions and 200 ms for two-event descriptions, are both reliable ($t(27) = 4.32$, $SE_{dif} = 43$ ms, and $t(27) = 4.61$, $SE_{dif} = 48$ ms respectively, $p < 0.001$ for each). In both cases, 23 of the 28 subjects followed in this pattern. Secondly, it can be noted that, between conditions, about the same average amount of time was used to respond to sentences of types (1) and (5), as for sentences of type (2) and (6).

Table 3. Latencies (ms) to correct responses and error rates in experiment 2.

Response and sentence type	Latencies		Errors (%)
	X	SD	
True descriptions (three events)			
(1) Initial NP conjunction	1117	86	6
(2) S conjunction only	1331	76	4
False Descriptions (two events)			
(5) NP conjunction	1123	86	5
(6) S conjunction	1323	108	5

Standard deviations are calculated for items per condition.

Discussion

In Experiment 2, subjects were asked to rapidly verify whether a description heard just before a visually presented array accurately described the array. If a sentence described two spatial positions together in one clause, whether or not the color identified in common for them was the one actually shared, decisions were registered about 200 ms faster than when a sentence referred naturally to each position mentioned in a separate clause, and the colors named matched the position or not. Verification of a sentence containing either NP or S conjunction and n clauses took almost the same average amount of time as falsification of a sentence with $n - 1$ clauses. These results by themselves do not suggest a notion of the number of clauses in an utterance being the determinant of verification time. However, false verification judgements on affirmative sentences are known to take longer than true judgements (Clark and Chase, 1972; Carpenter and Just, 1975, 1976).

Experiment 3: Pattern matching

The arrays and the sentences used in Experiment 1 and 2 were the same. The results of these two studies were different, however. Given appropriate arrays, speakers' latencies to initiate descriptions were greater when they began their utterances with conjoined noun phrases. But, given appropriate descriptions, listeners' latencies to tell whether they were true or not were greater when the utterances simply contained full clausal conjunctions. These divergent results cannot be attributed either to differences in linguistic structure or to differences among the arrays described. Rather, it seems likely that they stem from how the linguistic structures studied were processed, or how they were processed with respect to the arrays.

It may be worth asking, however, whether non-linguistic factors might have determined performance in *one* of the tasks (e.g., in verifying descriptions) and linguistic factors might have determined performance in the other task (e.g., in producing descriptions). This question can be posed experimentally by asking if there are any significant non-linguistic factors at play in the data. If this possibility can be dismissed, then the results of the two experiments should reflect the linguistic processing done in producing and in understanding the utterances.

Method

The non-linguistic task used was a same-different task. Subjects were shown 32 pairs of patterns in a random order. The patterns corresponded to those studied in Experiment 1 and 2, and consisted of three vertical bars, two of which might be colored the same, or all three colored differently. Within a pair, both patterns were of the same type, and were identical, with the bars in the same position, or different, with position of the two bars reversed. The patterns within a pair were displayed for 1 s each on a CRT with an interstimulus interval of 0.5 s. Subjects were tested from a similar population as used in the previous studies. The subjects' task was to quickly push one button if the patterns seen were identical and another button if they were different. Response time was measured from onset of the second pattern.

Table 4. Mean RT (ms) in pattern-matching task in experiment 3.

Contents of array	Correct responses		Grand mean
	Same	Different	
three different colours	757	868	813
two different colours	790	847	818
grand mean	773	857	

Results and discussion

The results obtained are summarized in Table 4. It can be seen in the table that response times overall were almost identical for patterns of the two major kinds: 818 ms on average when two of the bars shown were colored the same, and 813 ms when the 3 bars were all colored differently. Although 'same' responses were given faster than 'different' responses, ($F_{\text{same-dif}}(1,23) = 13.43$, $p < 0.005$), neither the number of different colors shown nor the interaction with same-different judgements approached significance. Thus, patterns of the two types are about equally easy to process in a non-linguistic task.

General discussion

When production and verification times for the same sentences used as natural descriptions were compared, completely asymmetrical patterns of latencies were discovered. For the two principal kinds of utterances studied, one, involving use of S coordination only, was found to be initiated about one fourth of a second faster on average in speaking, while the other, involving use of an initial NP conjunction, was found to be verified about one fifth of a second faster in listening. A control experiment showed that the patterns studied were about equally easy to process in a non-linguistic task. If one takes the results from Experiment 1 and 2 to index different amounts of processing normally performed for such utterances and their conceptual contents, the present findings serve to make a very general point: the psychological complexity of linguistic structures cannot be defined independently of the uses to which utterances are normally put. For the speaker, preparing to use one kind of structure may be relatively time-consuming. For the listener, interpreting the same structure with respect to the same reference domain may be relatively time-saving. The two types of descriptions studied appear to represent just such a case in point.

The time differences found here appear to reflect basically different processes at work, rather than some sampling error or bias associated with the choice of time intervals made for inferring these processes. It is a simple fact about speech communication that the cognitive activities underlying speaking and listening only partially overlap (i.e., *during* an utterance) in time. The time interval prior to an utterance is only relevant for speaking and may serve primarily for planning its form. The time interval following an utterance is relevant mainly for listening, and can serve to evaluate the contents of what is heard. We attribute the difference found in speech initiation times to the process of elaborating the *first* main constituent in an utterance on several interconnected levels. The difference found in verification times, on the other hand, seemed best explained by comparison process whereby a representation of an utterance's meaning fashioned from its (natural) clause structure is checked against knowledge of an array seen.

The explanation of the data offered above places the locus of the differences found in one place for speaking, and in another for listening. A coherent framework incorporating both results, however, might still be found. For example, technically speaking, relative slowness in producing compound NPs is predicted by stack depth needed by a push-down automaton to elaborate phrase structure from 'top to bottom' and 'left to right', and relative slowness in understanding more multiply branched S structures is predicted by the amount of memory correspondingly needed to build these structures from 'bottom to top' and 'left to right' (see Aho and Ullman, 1973). Here, one additional non-terminal node in both cases would need to be stored (the compound NP node sentence-initially in production, the additional S node sentence-finally in perception). Similar predictions can be derived from MacKay's node theory (MacKay, forth-coming 1987) according to which fewer nodes and sequential rules need to be activated to begin uttering a sentence of type (2) than to begin uttering a sentence of type (1). This means shorter production onset times for sentences of type (2), despite the fact that these sentences take consider-ably longer to complete.

One final general implication should perhaps be mentioned. Throughout the modern history of pyscholinguistics, a central problem has been the following: How can one relate structural regularities in language, and their abstract representation in the human mind, to the cognitive processes which are involved whenever language is ordinarily used? The kind of asymmetry illustrated here shows that a unitary conception of language structure in linguistic performance, or any view which pays insufficient attention to the specific pyschological properties of the speaking process on the one hand and the listening process on the other, will be inadequate, since it will fail to capture significant differences between them. Instead, it would seem necessary in actual language use to differentiate types or modes of linguistic processing.

Notes

[1] The present research was supported in part by a grant from the Stiftung Volks-wagenwerk to the Max-Planck Gesellschaft. We are indebted to Claus Heeschen, Stephanie Kelter, Wolfgang Prinz, Eva Ejerhed, and especially Don MacKay for valuable comments on earlier versions of the paper. The experiments were con-ducted with the aid of Bert van Deursen and Gerd Klaas.

[2] In the Dutch sentence corresponding to (1)–(6), the heads of the NPs are nominalized adjectives (cf. English 'the good, the bad, and the ugly') rather than pro-forms.

References

Aho, A. V. and Ullman, J. D. (1972). *Theory of parsing, translation, and compiling*, Vol 1. Englewood Cliffs, NJ: Prentice-Hall.

Bresnan, J. and Kaplan, R. M. (1982). Introduction: Grammars as mental representations of language. In J. Bresnan (Ed.) *The mental representation of grammatical relations*. Cambridge, MA: MIT Press.

Carpenter, P. A. and Just, M. A. (1975). Sentence comprehension: a psycholinguistic processing model of verification. *Psychological Review*, **82**, 45–73.

Carpenter, P. A. and Just, M. A. (1976). Models of sentence verification and linguistic comprehension. *Psychological Review*, **83**, 318–22.

Chomsky, N. (1965). *Aspects of the theory of syntax*. Cambridge, MA: MIT Press.

Clark, H. H. and Chase, W. G. (1974). Perceptual coding strategies in the formation and verification of descriptions. *Memory & Cognition*, **2**, 101–11.

Clark, H. H. and Clark, E. V. (1977). *Psychology and language*. New York: Harcourt Brace Jovanovich.

Deutsch, W. (1986). Sprechen und Verstehen: Zwei Seiten einer Medaille? In H.-G. Bosshardt (Ed.) *Perspektiven auf Sprache: Interdisziplinäre Beiträge zum Gedenken an Hans Hörmann*. Berlin: de Gruyter.

Deutsch, W. and Jarvella, R. J. (1984). Asymmetrien zwischen Sprachproduktion und Sprachverstehen. In C. F. Graumann and T. Herrmann (Eds) *Karl Bühlers Axiomatik*. Frankfurt: Klosterman.

Ford, M. and Holmes, V. M. (1978). Planning units and syntax in sentence production. *Cognition*, **6**, 35–53.

Fodor, J. A., Bever, T. G. and Garrett, M. (1974). *The psychology of language*. New York: McGraw-Hill.

Heeschen, C. and Blomert, L. (1982). Interaktion zwischen syntaktischer Komplexität und der Natürlichkeit des Ausdrucks beim Sprachverständnis von Aphasikern. Paper presented at the meeting of the Gesellschaft für Aphasieforschung und -therapie, Bonn.

Jarvella, R. J. and Collas, J. G. (1974). Memory for the intentions of sentences. *Memory & Cognition*, **2**, 185–88.

Johnson, N. F. (1966). On the relation between sentence structure and the latency in generating the sentence. *Journal of Verbal Learning and Verbal Behavior*, **5**, 375–80.

Kempen, G. A. M. and Huijbers, P. (1983). The lexicalization process in sentence production and naming: indirect election of words. *Cognition*, **14**, 185–209.

Lashley, K. S. (1951). The problem of serial order in behavior. In L. A. Jeffres (Ed.) *Cerebral mechanisms in behavior*. New York: Wiley.

Levelt, W. J. M. (1978). A survey of studies in sentence perception: 1970–1976. In W. J. M. Levelt and G. B. Flores d'Arcais (Eds) *Studies in the perception of language*. Chichester: Wiley.

Levelt, W. J. M. and Maassen, B. (1981). Lexical search and order of mention in sentence production. In W. Klein and W. J. M. Levelt (Eds) *Crossing the boundaries in linguistics*. Dordrecht: Reidel.

Lindsley, J. R. (1975). Producing simple utterances: how far ahead do we plan? *Cognitive Psychology*, **7**, 1–19.

MacKay, D. G. (forthcoming). The asymmetrical relationship between speech perception and production. In Heuer, H. (Ed.) *Issues in perception and action*. Hillsdale, NJ: Erlbaum.

MacKay, D. G. (1987). *The organization of perception and action: A theory for language and other cognitive skills*. New York: Springer Verlag.

Miller, G. A. and Chomsky, N. (1963). Finitary models of language users. In R. D. Luce, R. R. Bush and E. Galanter (Eds) *Handbook of mathematical psychology*, Vol 2. New York: Wiley.

Miller, G. A., Galanter, E. and Pribram, K. H. (1960). *Plans and the structure of behavior*. New York: Holt.

de Saussure, F. (1916). *Cours de linguistique générale*. Lausanne and Paris: Payot.

Stevens, K. N. and Halle, M. (1967). Remarks on analysis by synthesis and distinctive features. In W. Wathen-Dunn (Ed.) *Models for the perception of speech and visual form*. Cambridge, MA: MIT Press.

Sternberg, S., Monsell, S., Knoll, R. and Wright, C. E. (1978). The latency and duration of rapid movement sequences: comparison of speech and typewriting. In G. E. Stelmach (Ed.) *Information processing in motor control and learning*. New York: Academic Press.

Valian, V. (1971). Talking, listening and linguistic structure. Unpublished doctoral dissertation, Northeastern University.

Yngve, V. H. (1960). A model and an hypothesis for language structure. *Proceedings of the American Philosophical Society*, **104**, 444–66.

Section 2
Perception and production of speech sounds

Introduction

Wolfgang Prinz

How could a listener recover the phonetic pattern of a speaker's message? This is the central issue under debate in the two contributions to the second section. To be sure, the issue is not how the speaker's intended semantic message (which is certainly somehow conveyed by the speech sounds he/she produces) is received or reconstructed by the listener. Rather, the scope is limited to the phonetic aspects of communication by speech.

The contributions by Michael Studdert-Kennedy and Robert J. Porter consider a speaker and a listener. In a sense, both contributions elaborate a modern version of what used to be called a motor theory of speech perception, or, what we should perhaps more appropriately describe as a common-coding theory of speech perception and production. They share three basic assumptions.

Re-articulation. In a sense, the listener is considered a re-articulator of the sound pattern he/she is listening to. This is quite obvious and explicit in Studdert-Kennedy's account of speech imitation in infants, and somewhat less obvious (at least at first glance) in Porter's overview of some recent work in speech perception and production.

Specification. For the listener/re-articulator the information conveyed by the auditory sound pattern not only indicates *what* to do (in order to re-articulate) but also fully specifies *how* to do it. This implies that the auditory stimulus contains by itself all of the information needed for appropriate control of the articulators and that no further information (stimulus-derived or memory-retrieved) is required. This second assumption explains that the re-articulation hypothesis does not imply an unnecessary complication (which it looks like at first glance), but rather an

LANGUAGE PERCEPTION AND PRODUCTION
ISBN 0-12-052750-2

elegant idea for a theory of speech perception. This is because, under the specification hypothesis, re-articulation is regarded as an automatically available by-product of the auditory analysis of speech sounds.

Common coding. There are common codes (and, possibly, shared neural structures) suited for both the analysis of speech sounds and the control of articulator movements. This assumption is a natural consequence following from the first two hypotheses. Auditory specification of the listener's re-articulation cannot easily be conceived in a framework that separates perception entirely from action (or, sensation from motor control). Rather, it seems to require a common coding language for both and perhaps even a shared substrate for representing this language.

As is pointed out in both contributions one of the first methodological problems to be solved with these assumptions is how to give an appropriate descriptive account of sound patterns and patterns of articulatory gestures. With the above assumptions it is certainly not appropriate to describe articulator movements in terms of sequences of static segmental units like features or phonemes. Instead, one should consider the articulator movements themselves (or the motor structures that control them, respectively) to be the appropriate units of analysis. Studdert-Kennedy, after first criticizing the phoneme as a static linguistic unit, then re-introduces it as a perceptuomotor structure, consisting of a pattern of well-phased gestures of the articulators. In the same vein Porter makes a strong claim that what he calls 'the phonetic message' cannot be conveyed by articulator positions and vocal tract shapes but must be conveyed by the movements *per se*, i.e. in the changes of positions and shapes over time. The same applies to the stimulus information suited to unequivocally specify the pattern of articulator gestures. As Porter shows in some detail, the auditory system seems to be particularly sensitive to temporal modulations of acoustic signals and their phonetic relevance. Here, too, one is led to the conclusion that the 'static' description of speech sounds in terms of slices of acoustic spectra may be misleading.

Besides these commonalities some basic differences of the two approaches are too obvious to overlook. Studdert-Kennedy, in a search for functional units underlying speech and speech perception and in an attempt to trace their emergence in early language development, considers the phoneme the chief candidate for this function. In emphasizing the discrete nature of this perceptuo–motor control structure, he ends up with the unsolved issue of how these discrete units could generate continuous patterns of gesture. Porter, in an attempt to tackle the notorious many-to-one relationship between articulator positions and acoustic spectra, emphasizes the continuous character of both the ongoing analysis of temporal modulations of the acoustic signal in perception and the ongoing dynamic coordination of the articulators in production. With an approach like this which, on the action side, stresses coordination rather than control, no need is felt to introduce discrete functional units of perception and production.

4   The phoneme as a perceptuomotor structure

Michael Studdert-Kennedy

Abstract

Studies of speech and writing face a paradox: the discrete units of the written representation of an utterance cannot be isolated in its quasi-continuous articulatory and acoustic structure. We may resolve the paradox by positing that units of writing (ideographs, syllabic signs, alphabetic letters) are symbols for discrete, perceptuomotor, neural control structures, normally engaged in speaking and listening. Focussing on the phoneme, for which an alphabetic letter is a symbol, the paper traces its emergence in a child's speech through several stages: hemispheric specialization for speech perception at birth, early discriminative capacity followed by gradual loss of the capacity to discriminate among speech sounds not used in the surrounding language, babbling, and first words. The word, a unit of meaning that mediates the child's entry into language, is viewed as an articulatory routine, a sequence of a few variable gestures of lips, jaw, tongue, velum and larynx, and their acoustic correlates. Under pressure from an increasing vocabulary, recurrent patterns of sound and gesture crystallize into encapsulated phonemic control units. Once a full repertoire of phonemes has emerged, usually around the middle of the third year, an explosive growth of vocabulary begins, and the child is soon ready, at least in principle, for the metalinguistic task of learning to read.

Ever since I . . . started to read . . . there has never been a line that I didn't *hear*. As my eyes followed the sentence, a voice was saying it silently to me. It isn't my mother's voice, or the voice of any person I can identify, certainly not my own. It is human, and it is inwardly that I listen to it.

Eudora Welty (1983, p. 12).

LANGUAGE PERCEPTION AND PRODUCTION
ISBN 0-12-052750-2

Introduction

Any discussion of the relation between speech and writing faces a paradox: the most widespread and efficient system of writing, the alphabet, exploits a unit of speech, the phoneme, for the physical reality of which we have no evidence. To be sure, we have evidence of its psychological reality. But, ironically, that evidence depends on the alphabet itself. How are we to escape from this circle?

First, let me elaborate the terms of the paradox. Since the earliest spectrographic, cineradiographic and electromyographic studies, we have known that neither the articulatory nor the acoustic flow of speech can be divided into a sequence of segments corresponding to the invariant segments of linguistic description. Whether the segments are words, morphs, syllables, phones or features, the case is the same. The reason for this is simply that we do not normally speak phoneme by phoneme, syllable by syllable, or even word by word. At any instant, our articulators are executing a complex interleaved pattern of movements of which the spatiotemporal coordinates reflect the influence of several neighboring segments. The typical result is that any isolable articulatory or acoustic segment arises as a vector of forces from more than one linguistic segment, while any particular linguistic segment distributes its forces over several articulatory and acoustic segments. This lack of isomorphism between articulatory-acoustic and linguistic structure is the central unsolved problem of speech research (Liberman, Cooper, Shankweiler and Studdert-Kennedy, 1967; Pisoni, 1985). Its continued recalcitrance is reflected in the fact that (apart from a variety of technologically ingenious, but limited and brute force solutions) we are little closer to automatic speech recognition today than we were thirty years ago (Levinson and Liberman, 1981).

What then is the evidence for the psychological reality of linguistic segments? (I confine my discussion to the phoneme, although most of what follows would apply *mutatis mutandis* to all other levels of description.) First and foremost is the alphabet itself. Superficially, we might take the alphabet (or any other writing system) to be a system of movement notation analogous to those used by ethologists to describe, say, the mating behavior of Tasmanian devils (Golani, 1981). The difference lies in their modes of validation. The ethologist's units may or may not correspond to motor control structures in the devil's behavior; the units are sufficiently validated, if they lend order and insight to the ethologist's understanding of that behavior. By contrast, the alphabet (like music and dance notation) is validated by the fact that it serves not only to notate, but to control behavior: we both write and read. Surely, we could not do so with such ease, if alphabetic symbols did not correspond to units of perceptuomotor control. A writing system constructed from arbitrary units — phonemes and a half, quarter words — would be of limited utility. We infer then that lexical items (words, morphemes) are stored as sequences of abstract perceptuomotor units (phonemes) for which letters of an alphabet are symbols.

If this is so, those who finger the phoneme as a fictitious unit imposed on speech by linguists because they know the alphabet (e.g., Warren, 1976) have it backwards. Historically, the possibility of the alphabet was discovered, not invented. Just as the bicycle was a discovery of locomotor possibilities implicit in the cyclical motions of walking and running, so the alphabet was a discovery of linguistic possibilities implicit in patterns of speaking.

Of course, we do have other important sources of evidence that confirm the psychological reality of the phoneme: errors of perception (e.g., Browman, 1980) and production[1] (e.g., MacKay (Chap 18); Shattuck-Hufnagel, 1983), backward talking (Cowan, Leavitt, Massaro and Kent, 1982), aphasic deficit (e.g., Blumstein, 1981). But we can only collect such data because we have the metalinguistic awareness and notational system to record them. Illiterates may make speech errors (MacKay, 1970), and oral cultures certainly practise alliteration and rhyme in their poetry. But, like the illiterate child who relishes 'Hickory dickory dock', they probably do not know what they are doing (cf. Morais, Cary, Alegria and Bertelson, 1981). Thus, the data that confirm our inferences from the alphabet rest squarely on the alphabet itself.

The paradox I have outlined might be resolved, if we could conceptualize the relation between a letter of the alphabet (or a word) and the behavior that it symbolizes. Just how difficult this will be becomes apparent, if we compare the information conveyed by a spoken word with the information conveyed by its written counterpart. An experimenter may ask a willing subject either to repeat a spoken word or to read aloud its written form. The subject's utterances in the two cases will be indiscriminable, but the information that controlled the utterances will have been quite different. The distinction, due to Carello, Turvey, Kugler and Shaw (1984) (see also Turvey and Kugler, 1984) is between information that *specifies* and information that *indicates* or *instructs*. The information in a spoken word is not arbitrary: its acoustic structure is a lawful consequence of the articulatory gestures that shape it. In other words, its acoustic structure is *specific* to those gestures, so that the prepared listener can follow the specifications to organize his own articulation and reproduce the utterance. Of course, we do not need the full specification of an utterance, in all its phonetic detail, in order to perceive it correctly, as those who know a foreign language, yet speak it with an accent, demonstrate: capturing all the details calls for a subtle process of perceptuomotor attunement. But it is evident that the specification does suffice for accurate reproduction, given adequate perceptuomotor skill, both in the child who slowly comes to master a surrounding dialect and in the trained phonetician who precisely mimics that dialect.

By contrast, the form of a written word is an arbitrary convention, a string of symbols that *indicate* to a reader what he is to do, but do not tell him how to do it. What is important here is that indicational information cannot control action in the absence of information specific to the act to be performed. That is why we may find it easier to imitate the stroke of a tennis coach than to implement his verbal instructions. Similarly, we can only pronounce a written word, if we have information specifying the correspondences between the symbol string and the motor control structures that must be engaged for speaking. These are the correspondences that an illiterate has not discovered.

The question now is simply this: what is the relation between a discrete symbol and the continuous motor behavior that it controls? If a written symbol does indeed stand for a motor control structure, as argued above, we may put the question in a slightly more concrete form: What is the relation between a discrete motor control structure and the complex pattern of movements that it generates? The answer will certainly not come in short order. But perhaps we can clarify the question, and gain insight into possible lines of answer by examining how units of perceptuomotor control emerge, as a child begins to speak its first language.

Basic to this development is the child's capacity to imitate, that is, to reproduce utterances functionally equivalent to those of the adults around it. We have claimed above that an utterance specifies the articulation necessary to reproduce it. But until we spell out what specification entails, the claim amounts to little more than the observation that people can repeat the words they hear. At least three questions must be answered, if we are to put flesh on the bones.

First is the question of how a listener (or, in lipreading, a viewer) transduces a pattern of sound (or light) into a matching pattern of muscular controls, sufficient to reproduce the modeled event. We can say very little here other than that the acoustic/optic pattern must induce a neural structure isomorphic with itself. The pattern must be abstract in the sense that it no longer carries the marks of its sensory channel, but concrete in that it specifies (perhaps quite loosely, as we shall see below) the muscular systems to be engaged: no one attempts to reproduce a spoken utterance with his feet. The perceptuomotor structure is therefore specific to the speech system. Perhaps it is worth remarking that, in the matter of transduction, the puzzle of imitation seems to be a special case of the general puzzle of how an animal modulates its actions to fit the world it perceives.

The second question raised by imitation concerns the units into which the modeled action is parsed. Research in speech perception has been preoccupied with units of linguistic analysis: features and phonemes. These, as normally defined, are abstract units, unsuited to an account of imitation, because, whatever their ultimate function in the adult speaker, they do not correspond to primitives of motor control that a child might engage to imitate an utterance in a language that it does not yet know. The human vocal apparatus comprises several discrete, partially independent articulators (lips, jaw, tongue, velum, larynx) by which energy from the respiratory system is modulated. The perceptual units of imitation must therefore be structures that specify functional units of motor control, corresponding to actions of the articulators. Isolation of these units is a central task for future research. We will come back to this matter below.

A third issue for the study of speech imitation is the notorious many-to-one relation between articulation and the acoustic signal (Porter, Chap 5). Speakers who normally raise and then lower their jaws in producing, say, the word, 'Be!', may execute acoustically identical utterances with pipes clenched between their teeth. The rounded English vowel of, say, *coot* may be produced either with protruded lips and the tongue humped just in front of the velum, or with spread lips, the tongue further backed and the larynx lowered. Even more bizarre articulations are discovered by children, born without tongue blade and tip, who none the less achieve a surprisingly normal phonetic repertoire (MacKain, 1983). Thus, the claim that an utterance specifies its articulation cannot mean that it specifies precisely which articulators are to be engaged, and when. Rather, it must mean that the utterance specifies a range of functionally equivalent articulatory actions. Of course, functional (or motor) equivalence is not peculiar to speech and may be observed in animals as lowly as the mouse (Fentress, 1981, 1983; Golani, 1981). Solution of the problem is a pressing issue in general research on motor control. For speech (and for other forms of vocal imitation, in songbirds and marine mammals) we have an added twist: the arbiter of equivalence is not some effect on the external world — seizing prey, peeling fruit, closing a door — but a listener's judgment.

Early perceptual development

With all this in mind, let us turn to the infant. Perceptually, speech already has a unique status for the infant within a few hours or days of birth. Neonates discriminate speech from non-speech (Alegria and Noirot,

1982), and, perhaps as a result of intrauterine stimulation, prefer their mothers' voices to strangers' (DeCasper and Fifer, 1980). Studies of infants from one to six months of age, using a variety of habituation and conditioning techniques, have shown that infants can discriminate virtually any speech sound contrast on which they are tested, including contrasts not used in the surrounding language (see Eimas (1985) for review). However, similar results from lower animals (chinchillas, macaques) indicate that infants are here drawing on capacities of the general mammalian auditory system (see Kuhl (1986) for review).

Dissociation of left and right sides of the brain for speech and non-speech sounds respectively, measured by relative amplitude of auditory evoked response over left and right temporal lobes, may be detected within days of birth (Molfese, 1977). Left and right hemisphere short term memories for syllables and musical chords, respectively, measured by habituation and dishabituation of the cardiac orienting response to change, or lack of change, in dichotic stimulation, are developing by the third month (Best, Hoffman and Glanville, 1982). These and other similar results (see Best, *et al.* (1982) and Studdert-Kennedy (1986) for review) are important, because many descriptive and experimental studies have established that speech perceptuomotor capacity is vested in the left cerebral hemisphere of more than 90% of normal adults.

At the same time, we should not read these results as evidence of 'hard wiring'. At this stage of development not even the modality of language is fixed. If an infant is born deaf, it will learn to sign no less readily than its hearing peers learn to speak. Recent studies of 'aphasia' in native American Sign Language signers show striking parallels in forms of breakdown between signers and speakers with similar left hemisphere lesions (Bellugi, Poizner and Klima, 1983). Thus, the neural substrate is shaped by environmental contingencies, and the left hemisphere, despite its predisposition for speech, may be usurped by sign (Neville, 1980, 1985; Neville, Kutas and Schmidt, 1982). Given the diversity of human languages to which an infant may become attuned, such a process of epigenetic development is hardly surprising.

Early motor development

The development of motor capacity over the first year of life may be divided into a period before babbling (roughly, 0–6 months) and a period of babbling (7–12 months) (Oller, 1980). At birth, the larynx is set relatively high in the vocal tract, so that the tongue fills most of the oral cavity, limiting tongue movement and therefore both the possible points of intraoral constriction, or closure, and the spectral range of possible vocalic sounds. Accordingly, early sounds tend to be neutral, vowel-like phonations, often nasalized (produced with lowered velum), with little variation in degree or placement of oral constriction. As the larynx lowers, the variety of nonreflexive, nondistress sounds increases. By the second trimester, sounds include labial trills ('raspberries'), squeals and primitive syllabic patterns, formed by a consonant-like closure followed by a vowel-like resonance. These syllabic patterns lack the precise timing of closure, release and opening characteristic of mature syllables.

In fact, the onset of true or canonical babbling (often a quite sudden event around the seventh month) is marked by the emergence of syllables with the timing pattern (including closing to opening ratio), typical of natural languages (Oller, 1986). In the early months, syllables tend to be reduplicated (e.g., [bababa], [mamama], [dadada]); these give way in later months to sequences in which both consonant and vowel vary. Phonetic descriptions of babbled consonants (e.g., predominance of stops, glides, nasals, scarcity of fricatives, liquids, consonant clusters) tend to be similar across many language environments, including that of the deaf infant (Locke, 1983). We may therefore view these preferences as largely determined by universal anatomical, physiological and aerodynamic constraints on vocal action. At the same time, as we might expect in a behavior geared for environmental shaping, the repertoire is not rigid: individual infants vary widely both in how much they babble and in the relative frequency of their babbled sounds (MacNeilage, Hutchinson and Lasater, 1981).

We should emphasize that segmental phonetic descriptors are simply a convenient, approximate notation of what a child seems to be doing with its articulators — the only descriptors we have, in the absence of cineradiographic or other quantitative data. We should not infer that the child has independent, articulatory control over consonantal and vocalic portions of a syllable. The syllable, formed by rhythmically opening and closing the mouth, is a natural, cohesive unit of speech, with temporal properties that may be determined, in part, by the resonant frequency of the jaw. Its articulatory structure is perhaps related — at least by analogy, if not by homology — to the soft, tongue- or lip-modulated patterns of sound observed in the intimate interactions of Japanese macaque monkeys (Green, 1975; MacNeilage, personal communication).

Early perceptuomotor development

Imitation, long thought to be the outcome of a lengthy course of cognitive development (e.g., Piaget, 1962), is now known to be an innate capacity of the human infant. Meltzoff and Moore (1977, 1983) have shown, in a pair of meticulously controlled studies, that infants, within 72 hours of birth, can imitate arbitrary facial gestures (mouth opening, lip protrusion) and within 12–21 days (perhaps earlier, but we have no data) can also imitate tongue protrusion and sequential closing of the fingers (of particular interest for sign language acquisition). Of course, these are relatively crude gestures, far from the subtly interleaved patterns of movement, coordinated across several articulators, that are necessary for adult speech. The importance of the work lies in its implication that optically conveyed, facial gestures, already at birth, induce a neural structure isomorphic with the movements that produce them.

We should not expect speech sounds to induce an analogous neuromotor control structure at birth, not only because the sounds are complex, but because, as language diversity attests, speech is learned. Nonetheless, we might reasonably predict an early, amodal, *perceptual* representation of speech, since this must be the ground on which imitation is based. At present, we have to wait until 4–5 months for this, perhaps because appropriate studies have not yet been done on younger infants. Kuhl and Meltzoff (1982) showed that infants of this age looked longer at the videotaped face of a woman repeatedly articulating the vowel they were hearing (either [i] or [a]) than at the same face articulating the other vowel *in synchrony*. The preference disappeared when the signals were pure tones, matched in amplitude and duration to the vowels, so that infant preference was evidently for a match between a mouth shape and a particular spectral structure. Since spectral structure is directly determined by the resonant cavities of the vocal tract, and since the shape and volume of these cavities are determined by articulation (including pattern of mouth opening for [i] and [a]), the correspondence between mouth shape (optic) and spectral structure (acoustic) reflects their common source in articulation. Evidently, infants of 4–5 months, like adults in recent studies of lip-reading (e.g., McGurk and MacDonald, 1976; Summerfield, 1979, in press; Campbell, Chap 7) already have an amodal representation of speech, closely related to the articulatory structures that determine phonetic form.

Just how close this relation is we may judge from a second study similar to that of Kuhl and Meltzoff (1982). MacKain, Studdert-Kennedy, Spieker and Stern (1983) showed that 5–6 month old infants preferred to look at the videotaped face of a woman repeating the disyllable they were hearing (e.g. [zuzi]) than at the synchronized face of the same woman repeating another disyllable (e.g., [vava]). However, the two faces were presented to left and right of an infant's central gaze, and the preference for an acoustic-optic match was only significant when infants were looking at the right side display. We may interpret this result in light of studies by Kinsbourne and his colleagues (e.g., Kinsbourne, 1972; Lempert and Kinsbourne, 1982), demonstrating that attention to one side of the body facilitates processes for which the contralateral hemisphere is specialized. Infants might then be more sensitive to acoustic-optic correspondences in speech presented on their right sides than on their left. Thus, infants of 5–6 months may already have an amodal representation of speech in the hemisphere that will later coordinate the activity of their bilaterally inner-vated speech apparatus.

Signally absent from all of the foregoing is any indication that the infant is affected by the surrounding language. In fact, it has often been proposed (e.g., Brown, 1958) that the infant's phonetic repertoire drifts towards that of its native language during the babbling of the second half year, but, despite several studies, no firm evidence of babbling drift has been found (Locke, 1983). We do, however, have evidence of perceptual effects. Werker and her colleagues (Werker, 1982; Werker, Gilbert, Humphrey and Tees, 1981; Werker and Tees, 1984) have shown, in several cross-sectional and longitudinal studies, that, during the second half year, infants may gradually lose their capacity to distinguish sound contrasts not used in their native language. This is perhaps just the period when an infant is first attending to individual words and the situations in which they occur (Jusczyk, 1982; MacKain, 1982).

The general picture of perceptuomotor development over the first year, then, is of two parallel, independent processes, with production trailing perception. Doubtless, physiological changes in the left hemisphere are taking place, laying down neural networks that will later make contact. These processes may resemble those in songbirds, such as the marsh wren, in which the perceptual template of its species' song is laid down during a narrow sensitive period many weeks before it begins to sing (Kroodsma, 1981). The first behavioral evidence of a perceptuomotor link then appears with the bird's first song and, in the infant, with its first imitation of an adult sound.

First words and their component gestures

Up to this point we have talked easily of perceptual, or perceptuomotor, 'representations' without asking what is represented. During the 1970s, when intensive work on child phonology began, researchers quite reason-ably assumed that units of acquisition would be those that linguists had found useful in describing adult language: features and phonemes. Little attention was paid to the fact that these units, as defined by linguists, were abstract descriptors that could not be specified either articulatorily or acoustically, and were therefore of dubious utility to the child striving to talk like its companions. The oversight was perhaps encouraged by division of labor between students of perception and students of production whose mutual isolation absolved them from confronting what the child confronts: the puzzle of the relation between listening and speaking.

Over the past decade, child phonologists have come to recognize the fact, borne in also by pragmatic studies (e.g., Bates, 1979), that a child's entry into language is mediated by meaning; and meaning cannot be conveyed by isolated features or phonemes. The child's earliest unit of meaning is probably the prosodic contour: the rising pitch of question and surprise, the falling pitch of declaration, and so on, often observed in stretches of 'jargon' or intonated babble (Menn, 1978). The earliest *segmental* unit of meaning is the word (or formulaic phrase).

Evidence for the word as the basic unit of contrast in early language is rich and subtle (Moskowitz, 1973; Ferguson and Farwell, 1975; Ferguson, 1978; Macken, 1979; Menn, 1983a). Here I simply note three points. First is the observation that phonetic forms mastered in one word are not necessarily mastered in another. For example, a 15-month old child may execute [n] correctly in *no*, but substitute [m] for [n] in *night*, and [b] for [m] in *moo* (Ferguson and Farwell, 1975). Thus, the child does not contrast [b], [m] and [n], as in the adult language, but the three words with their insecurely grasped onsets.

A second point is that early speech is replete with instances of consonant harmony, that is, words in which one consonant assimilates the place or manner of articulation of another — even though the child may execute the assimilated consonant correctly in other words. Thus, a child may produce *daddy* and *egg* correctly, but offer [gɔg] for *dog* and [dʌt] for *duck* and *truck*: the child seems unable to switch place of articulation within a syllable. Such 'assimilation at a distance' suggests that the word is 'assembled before it is spoken' as a single prosodic unit (Menn, 1983a, p. 16).

The third point is that individual words may vary widely in their phonetic form from one occasion to another. A striking example comes from Ferguson and Farwell (1975). They report ten radically different attempts by a 15-month old girl, K, to say *pen* within one half-hour session: [mãˀ, ˇʌ, deᵈⁿ, hin, ᵐbõ, pʰɪn, tʰn̩tʰn̩tʰn̩, baʰ, dʰauᴺ, buã].[2] On the surface, these attempts seem almost incomprehensibly diverse one from another and from their model. But the authors shrewdly remark that 'K seems to be trying to sort out the features of nasality, bilabial closure, alveolar closure, and voicelessness' (Ferguson and Farwell, 1975, p. 14). An alternative description (to be preferred, in my view, for reasons that will appear shortly) would be to say that all the *gestures* of the model (lip closure, tongue raising and fronting, alveolar closure, velum lowering/raising, glottal opening/closing) are to be found in one or other of these utterances, but that the gestures are incorrectly phased with respect to one another. For example, lip closure for the initial [p], properly executed with an open glottis and raised velum, will yield [ᵐb], as in [ᵐbō], if glottal closure for [ɛn] and velum lowering for [n] are initiated at the same time as lip closure, tens of milliseconds earlier than in the correct utterance, [pɛn]. Thus, the adult model evidently specified for the child the required gestures, but not their relative timing. (Notice, incidentally, that the only gestures present in the child's attempts, but absent from the model, are tongue backing and tongue lowering for the sounds transcribed as [o], [a], and [u]. Four of these five 'errors' occur when the child has successfully executed initial lip closure, as though attention to the initial gesture had exhausted the child's capacity to assemble later gestures.)

One reason for preferring a gestural to a featural description of a child's — or for that matter of an adult's — speech is that it lends the description observable, physical content (Browman and Goldstein, 1986). We are then dealing with patterns of movement in space and time, accessible to treatment according to general principles of motor control (e.g., Kelso, Tuller and Harris, 1983; Saltzman and Kelso, 1987). For example, the problem of motor equivalence may become more tractable, because the gesture is a *functional* unit, an equivalence class of coordinated movements that achieve some end (closing the lips, raising the tongue, etc.) (Kelso, Saltzman and Tuller, 1986). Moreover, a gestural description may help us to explore the claim (based on the facts of imitation) that the speech percept is an amodal structure isomorphic with the speaker's articulation. Glottal, velic and labial gestures can already be isolated by standard techniques; tongue movements are more problematic, because they are often vectors of two or more concurrent gestures. Nonetheless, positing a concrete, observable event as the fundamental unit of production may help researchers to analyze articulatory vectors into their component forces, and to isolate the acoustic marks of those vectors in the signal.

Finally, to forestall misunderstanding, a gestural description is not simply a change of terminology. Gestures do not usually correspond one-to-one with either phonemes or features. The phoneme /m/, for example, comprises the precisely timed and coordinated gestures of bilabial closure, velum lowering and glottal closing. The gesture of bilabial closure corresponds to several features [− continuant], [+ anterior], [+ consonantal], etc. A gestural account of speech — that is, an account grounded in the anatomy and physiology of the speaker — will require extensive revision of standard featural or segmental descriptions (Browman and Goldstein, 1986).

From words to phonemes

To summarize the previous section, we have argued that: (1) an element of meaning, the word, is the initial segmental unit of contrast in early speech; (2) a word is a coordinated pattern of gestures; (3) an adult spoken word specifies for the child learning to speak, at least some of its component gestures, but often not their detailed temporal organization. (The third point does not imply that the child's perceptual representation is necessarily incomplete: the representation may be exact, and the child's difficulty solely in coordinating its articulators. The difference is not without theoretical interest, but, in the present context, our focus is on how a child comes to reorganize a holistic pattern of gestures into a sequence of phonetic segments, or phonemes. Whether the reorganization is perceptual, articulatory, or both need not concern us.)

What follows, then, is a sketch of the process by which phonemes seem to emerge as units of perceptuomotor control in a child's speech. I should emphasize that details of the process vary widely from child to child, but the general outline is becoming clear (Menn, 1983a, b).

We can illustrate the process by tracing how a child escapes from consonant harmony, that is, how it comes to execute a word (or syllable) with two different places (or manners) or articulation. Children vary in their initial attack on such words: Some children omit, others harmonize one or other of the discrepant consonants. For example, faced with the word *fish*, which calls for a shift from a labiodental to a palatal constriction, one child may offer [fɪ'], another [ɪʃ]; faced with *duck*, one child may try [gʌk], another [dʌt]. Menn (1983b) proposes a perspicuous account of such attempts: the child has '. . . learned an articulatory program of opening and closing her mouth that allows her to specify two things: the vowel and one point of oral closure' (p. 5). Reframing this in terms of gestures (an exercise that we need not repeat in later examples), we may say that the child has learned to coordinate glottal closing/opening and tongue positioning (back, front, up, down, in various degrees) with raising/lowering the jaw, in order to approximate an adult word. This description of a word as an articulatory program, or routine, composed of a few variable gestures, is a key to the child's phonological development.

Consider here a Spanish child, Si, studied by Macken (1979) from 1 year 7 months to 2 years 1 month of age. At a certain point, Si seemed only able to escape from consonant place harmony by producing a labial-vowel-dental-vowel disyllable, deleting any extra syllable in the adult model. Thus, *manzana* ('apple') became [manna]; *Fernando* became [mannə] or [wanno], with the initial [f] transduced as [m] or [w]; *pelota* ('ball') became [patda]. In some words, where the labial and dental were in the 'wrong' order, Si metathesized. Thus, *sopa* ('soup') became [pwæta], replacing [s] with [t], and *teléfono* became [fəntonno]. As Si's mastery increased, the class of words, subject to the labial–dental routine, narrowed: *manzana* became [tʃænna], *Fernando* became [tçɪnalto], and so on.

These examples make two important points: (1) the child brings adult words with similar patterns (e.g., *manzana, Fernando, pelota*) within the domain of a single articulatory routine, demonstrating use of the word as a unit; (2) at the same time, the child selects as models adult words that share certain gestural patterns, demonstrating an incipient grasp of their segmental structure.

We may view the developmental process as driven by the conflicting demands of articulatory 'ease' and lexical accumulation. As long as the child has only a few words, it needs only one or two articulatory routines. Initially, it exploits these routines by adding to its repertoire only words composed of gestural patterns similar to those it has already 'solved', and by avoiding words with markedly different patterns. (For evidence and discussion of avoidance and exploitation in early child phonology, see Menn, 1983a.) Once the initial routines have been consolidated, new routines begin to emerge under pressure from the child's accumulating vocabulary. New routines emerge either to handle a new class of adult words, not previously attempted, or to break up and redistribute the increasing cohort of words covered by an old articulatory routine.

Phonological development seems then to be a process of: (1) diversifying articulatory routines to encompass more and more different classes of adult model; (2) gradually narrowing the domain within a word to which an articulatory routine applies. The logical end of the process (usually reached during the third year of life, when the child has accumulated some 50–100 words) is a single articulatory routine for each phonetic segment. Development is far from complete at this point: there must ensue, at least, the systematic grouping of phonetic variants (allophones) into phoneme classes, and the discovery of language-specific regularities in their sequencing ('phonotactic rules'). But the emergence of the phonetic segment as a perceptuomotor unit brings the entire adult lexicon, insofar as it is cognitively available, within the child's phonetic reach. This signals the onset of the explosive vocabulary growth, at an average rate of some 5–7 words a day, that permits an average 6-year old American child to recognize an estimated 7000–11,000 root words, depending on family background (Templin, 1957; cf. Miller, 1977).

Conclusion

We began with a paradox: the apparent incommensurability of the quasi-continuous articulatory and acoustic structure of speech with the discrete units of its written representation. To resolve the paradox, we proposed that an alphabetic letter (or an element in a syllabary, or an ideograph) is a symbol for a discrete, perceptuomotor control structure. We then traced the emergence of such structures as encapsulated patterns of gesture in a child's speech. Implicit in their derivation is that a child, once possessed of them, is, at least in principle, ready for the metalinguistic task of learning to write and read (cf. Asbell, 1984).

What we have left unresolved is the relation between discrete motor control structures (word, syllable, phoneme) and the coordinated patterns of gesture that they generate. Perhaps we should regard the postulated structures as conceptual place-holders. Their functional analysis must await advances in neurophysiology and in the general theory of motor control.

Acknowledgement

My thanks to Björn Lindblom and Peter MacNeilage for critical comments, and discussion. The paper was written while the author was on sabbatical leave as a Fellow at the Center for Advanced Study in the Behavioral Sciences, Stanford, California. The financial support of the City University of New York and of the Spencer Foundation is gratefully acknowledged.

Notes

[1] Speech errors display a number of well-known biases. For example, word-initial errors are more common than word-medial and word-final errors; metathesis occurs only between segments that occupy the same position in the syllabic frame; and the phonetic form of an error is adjusted to the context in which the erroneous segment occurs, not to the context from which it was drawn. Thus, speech errors often reflect phonetic processes that follow access of a phonemically specified lexical item. An adequate account of speech errors must therefore accommodate not only the phoneme as the fundamental phonological unit of all spoken languages, but the processes of lexical access and phonetic execution that give rise to biases in speech error types and frequencies. For a model of speech errors within these constraints, see Shattuck-Hufnagel (1983); for fuller discussion of the issue, see Lindblom, MacNeilage and Studdert-Kennedy (forthcoming).

[2] The first two items listed were immediate imitations of an adult utterance. Later items were identified by their '. . . consistency in reference or accompanying

action' (Ferguson and Farwell, 1975, p. 9). Interobserver agreement in the study from which these transcriptions were drawn was over 90%. The validity of the assumed target, *pen*, is further attested by the many featural (or gestural) properties common to the target and each of the child's attempts. The attempts did not include, for example, [gog], in which only glottal closure would be shared with the presumed target.

References

Alegria, J., and Noirot, E. (1982). Oriented mouthing activity in neonates: Early development of differences related to feeding experience. In J. Mehler, E. C. T. Walker and M. Garrett (Eds) *Perspectives on Mental Representation*. Hillsdale, NJ: Erlbaum, pp. 389–97.

Asbell, B. (1984). Writer's workshop at age 5. *New York Times Magazine*, February 26th.

Bates, E. (1979). *The Emergence of Symbols*. New York: Academic Press.

Bellugi, U., Poizner, H. and Klima, E. S. (1983). Brain organization for language: clues from sign aphasia. *Human Neurobiology*, **2**, 155–70.

Best, C. T., Hoffman, H. and Glanville, B. R. (1982). Development of infant ear asymmetries for speech and music. *Perception and Psychophysics*, **31**, 75–85.

Blumstein, S. E. (1981). Phonological aspects of aphasia. In M. T. Sarno (Ed.) *Acquired Aphasia*. New York: Academic Press.

Browman, C. P. (1980). Perceptual processing: slips of the ear. In V. A. Fromkin (Ed.) *Errors in Linguistic Performance*. New York: Academic Press.

Browman, C. and Goldstein, L. (1986). *Towards an articulatory phonology*. *Phonology Yearbook*, **3**, 219–252.

Brown, R. (1958). *Words and Things*. Glencoe, IL: Free Press.

Carello, C., Turvey, M. T., Kugler, P. N. and Shaw, R. E. (1984). Inadequacies of the computer metaphor. In M. J. Gazzaniga (Ed.) *Handbook of Cognitive Neuroscience*. New York: Plenum.

Cowan, N., Leavitt, L. A., Massaro, D. W. and Kent, R. D. (1982). A fluent backward talker. *Journal of Speech and Hearing Research*, **25**, 48–53.

DeCasper, A. J. and Fifer, W. P. (1980). Of human bonding: Newborns prefer their mothers' voices. *Science*, **28**, 1174–6.

Eimas, P. D. (1985). The perception of speech in early infancy. *Scientific American*, **252**, 46–52.

Fentress, J. C. (1981). Order in ontogeny: relational dynamics. In K. Immelmann, G. W. Barlow, L. Petrinovich and M. Main (Ed.) *Behavioral Development*. New York: Cambridge University Press, pp. 338–71.

Fentress, J. C. (1983). Hierarchical motor control. In M. Studdert-Kennedy (Ed.) *Psychobiology of Language*. Cambridge, MA: MIT Press, pp. 40–61.

Ferguson, C. A. and Farwell, C. B. (1975). Words and sounds in early language acquisition: English initial consonants in the first fifty words. *Language*, **51**, 419–30.

Ferguson, C. A. (1978). Learning to pronounce: The earliest stages of phonological development in the child. In F. D. Minifie and L. L. Lloyd (Eds) *Communicative and Cognitive Abilities — Early Behavioral Assessment*. Baltimore, MD: University Park Press, pp. 273–97.

Golani, I. (1981). The search for invariants in motor behavior. In K. Immelmann, G. W. Barlow, L. Petrinovich and M. Main (Eds) *Behavioral Development*. New York: Cambridge University Press, pp. 372–90.

Green, S. (1975). Variation of vocal pattern with social situation in the Japanese monkey (Macaca fuscata): A field study. In L. A. Rosenblum (Ed.) *Primate Behavior*, Volume 4. New York: Academic Press, pp. 1–102.

Jusczyk, P. W. (1982). Auditory versus phonetic coding of speech signals during infancy. In J. Mehler, E. C. T. Walker, and M. Garrett (Eds) *Perspectives on Mental Representation*. Hillsdale, NJ: Erlbaum, pp. 361–87.

Kelso, J. A. S., Tuller, B. and Harris, K. S. (1983). A 'dynamic pattern' perspective on the control and coordination of movement. In P. F. MacNeilage (Ed.) *The Production of Speech*. New York: Springer, pp. 137–73.

Kelso, J. A. S., Saltzman, E. L. and Tuller, B. (1986). The dynamical perspective on speech production: Data and theory. *Journal of Phonetics*, **14**, 29–59.

Kinsbourne, M. (1972). Eye and head turning indicates cerebral lateralization. *Science*, **176**, 539–41.

Kroodsma, D. E. (1981). Ontogeny of bird song. In K. Immelmann, G. B. Barlow, L. Petrinovich and M. Main (Eds) *Behavioral Development*. New York: Cambridge University Press, pp. 518–32.

Kuhl, P. K. (1986). Infants' perception of speech: constraints on the characterizations of the initial state. In B. Lindblom and R. Zetterström (Eds) *Precursors of Early Speech*. Basingstoke, UK: MacMillan, pp. 219–44.

Kuhl, P. K. and Meltzoff, A. N. (1982). The bimodal perception of speech in infancy. *Science*, **218**, 1138–44.

Lempert, H. and Kinsbourne, M. (1982). Effect of laterality of orientation on verbal memory. *Neuropsychologia*, **20**, 211–14.

Levinson, S. E. and Liberman, M. Y. (1981). Speech recognition by computer. *Scientific American*, **244**, 64–86.

Liberman, A. M., Cooper, F. S., Shankweiler, D. P. and Studdert-Kennedy, M. (1967). Perception of the speech code. *Psychological Review*, **74**, 431–61.

Lindblom, B., MacNeilage, P. F., and Studdert-Kennedy, M. (forthcoming). *Evolution of Spoken Language*. Orlando, FL: Academic Press.

Locke, J. (1983). *Phonological acquisition and change*. New York: Academic.

MacKain, K. S. (1982). Assessing the role of experience in infant speech discrimination. *Journal of Child Language*, **9**, 527–42.

MacKain, K. S. (1983). Speaking without a tongue. *Journal of the National Student Speech Language Hearing Association*, **11**, 46–71.

MacKain, K. S., Studdert-Kennedy, M., Spieker, S. and Stern, D. (1983). Infant intermodal speech perception is a left hemisphere function. *Science*, **219**, 1347–9.

MacKay, D. G. (1970). Spoonerisms: The structure of errors in the serial order of speech. *Neuropsychologia*, **8**, 323–50.

Macken, M. A. (1979). Developmental reorganization of phonology: A hierarchy of basic units of acquisition. *Lingua*, **49**, 11–49.

MacNeilage, P. F., Hutchinson, J. and Lasater, S. (1981). The production of speech: Development and dissolution of motoric and premotoric processes. In J. Long and A. Baddeley (Eds) *Attention and Performance IX*. Hillsdale, NJ: Erlbaum.

McGurk, H. and MacDonald, J. (1976). Hearing lips and seeing voices. *Nature*, **264**, 746–8.

Meltzoff, A. N. and Moore, M. K. (1977). Imitation of facial and manual gestures by human neonates. *Science*, **198**, 175–8.

Meltzoff, A. N. and Moore, M. K. (1983). Newborn infants imitate adult facial gestures. *Child Development*, **54**, 702–9.

Menn, L. (1978). *Pattern, control, and contrast in beginning speech: A case study in the development of word form and word function.* Bloomington, IN: Indiana University Linguistics Club.

Menn, L. (1983a). Development of articulatory, phonetic, and phonological capabilities. In B. Butterworth (Ed.) *Language Production*, Vol 11. London: Academic Press.

Menn, L. (1983b). Language acquisition, Aphasia, and Phonotactic Universals. Paper presented at 12th Annual University of Wisconsin — Milwaukee Linguistics Symposium.

Miller, G. A. (1977). *Spontaneous Apprentices*. New York: The Seabury Press.

Molfese, D. L. (1977). Infant cerebral asymmetry. In S. J. Segalowitz and F. A. Gruber (Eds) *Language Development and Neurological Theory*. New York: Academic Press.

Morais, J., Cary, L., Alegria, J. and Bertelson, P. (1979). Does awareness of speech as a sequence of phones arise spontaneously? *Cognition*, **7**, 323–31.

Moskowitz, A. I. (1973). The acquisition of phonology and syntax. In K. K. J. Hintikka, J. M. E. Moravsik and P. Suppes (Eds) *Approaches to Natural Language*. Dordrecht, Netherlands: Reidel.

Neville, H. J. (1980). Event-related potentials in neuropsychological studies of language. *Brain and Language*, **11**, 300–18.

Neville, H. J. (1985). Effects of early sensory and language experience on the development of the human brain. In J. Mehler and R. Fox (Eds) *Neonate Cognition*. Hillsdale, NJ: Erlbaum, pp. 349–63.

Oller, D. K. (1980). The emergence of the sounds of speech in infancy. In G. H. Yeni-Komshian, J. F. Kavanagh and C. A. Ferguson (Eds) *Child Phonology, Vol 1: Production*, New York: Academic Press, pp. 93–112.

Oller, D. K. (1986). Metaphonology and infant vocalizations. In B. Lindblom and R. Zetterström (Eds) *Precursors of Early Speech*. Basingstoke, UK: MacMillan, pp. 21–35.

Piaget, J. (1962). *Plays, Dreams and Imitation in Childhood*. New York: Norton.

Pisoni, D. B. (1985). Speech perception: Some new directions in research and theory. *Journal of the Acoustical Society of America*, **78**, 381–8.

Saltzman, E. L. and Kelso, J. A. S. (1987). Skilled actions: a task dynamic approach. *Psychological Review*, **94**, 84–105.

Summerfield, Q. (1979). Use of visual information for phonetic perception. *Phonetica*, **36**, 314–31.

Summerfield, Q. (in press). Preliminaries to a comprehensive account of audio-visual speech perception. In B. Dodd and R. Campbell (Eds) *Hearing by Eye*. Hillsdale, NJ: Erlbaum.

Shattuck-Hufnagel, S. (1983). Sublexical units and suprasegmental structure in speech production planning. In P. F. MacNeilage (Ed.) *The Production of Speech*. New York: Springer, pp. 109–36.

Studdert-Kennedy, M. (1986). Sources of variability in early speech development. In J. S. Perkell and D. H. Klatt (Eds) *Invariance and Variability in Speech Processes*. Hillsdale, NJ: Erlbaum, pp. 58–76.

Templin, M. (1957). *Certain Language Skills of Children*. Minneapolis: University of Minnesota Press.

Turney, M. T. and Kugler, P. N. (1984). A comment on equating information with symbol strings. *American Journal of Physiology*, **246** (*Regulatory, Integrative, Comparative Physiology*, **15**) R925–7.

Warren, R. M. (1976). Auditory illusions and phonetic processes. In J. J. Lass (Ed.) *Contemporary Issues in Experimental Phonetics*. New York: Academic Press.

Welty, E. (1983). *One Writer's Beginnings*. New York: Warner Books.

Werker, J. F. (1982). *The development of cross-language speech perception: The effect of age, experience and context on perceptual organization*. Unpublished doctoral dissertation, University of British Columbia, Vancouver, BC.

Werker, J. and Tees, R. C. (1984). Cross-language speech perception: Evidence for perceptual reorganization during the first year of life. *Infant Behavior and Development*, **7**, 49–63.

5   What is the relation between speech production and speech perception?

Robert J. Porter Jr

Abstract

This chapter proposes a view of speech communication in which phonetic distinctions are realized in the rates and phases of vocal tract movements and in the rates and phases of the resulting modulations of acoustic energy. This view contrasts with the more traditional view in which vocal-tract shapes and the resulting spectra are emphasized. The new perspective is suggested by the success of recent work modeling speech production as a dynamic system in which movement 'periodicities' play an important role, and by psychoacoustic research which suggests an auditory sensitivity to acoustic modulations which may be perceptually independent of sensitivity to short-time spectral detail. Limited work exploring the phonetic relevance of movements and modulations provides encouraging support for the conclusion that the relations of speech messages in production and perception is parallel and direct, from the phonetic to the acoustic, and from the acoustic to the phonetic.

Introduction

What is the relation between speech perception and production? Because communication by speech requires the listener to recover the speaker's intended message, it may be said that one relation of production and perception involves listeners and speakers representing the abstract message in parallel ways.

But speech communication also involves the least–abstract sounds of speech themselves. To the extent that some aspect of the message is

LANGUAGE PERCEPTION AND PRODUCTION
ISBN 0-12-052750-2

conveyed by the sounds, perceivers and producers must also have logically parallel representations of speech sounds. What, however, is the nature of these basic representations, how do they map onto one another logically, and how do they relate functionally?

A commonly proposed basic representation is a phonetic one. Phonetic representations are usually described in terms of ordered sequences of segments which differ in terms of 'features' roughly corresponding to the articulatory events involved in production (e.g. Hockett, 1960). However, in spite of considerable evidence for its psychological reality in perception and production (recently, e.g., Soli, Arabie and Carroll, 1986; Shattuck-Hufnagel, 1983), the existence of a phonetic representation is not universally accepted.

One reason for the disenchantment with the concept of a phonetic representation is the problem of finding it in either of the two physical 'observables' in speech communication: Namely, vocal tract shapes and the speech spectra. Tract shapes and spectra do not typically reveal ordered segments corresponding to the ordered phonetic segments; neither are the, same shapes or acoustic spectra invariably associated with the same phonetic segment or features. In fact, similar shapes and acoustics appear to relate to different phonetic messages whereas different shapes and acoustics may relate to the same phonetic messages (Liberman, Cooper, Shankweiler and Studdert-Kennedy, 1967; Stevens and House, 1972). The relation becomes even more difficult to map when variations in speaker, speaking rate, and so forth, are considered. The opacity of the relation between the presumed phonetic representation, shapes, and spectra is referred to as the *speech invariance problem*.

The speech invariance problem suggests that speakers and listeners may represent speech messages in some non-parallel, non-phonetic, ways at the articulatory and auditory levels of description. In fact, several papers at the Bielefeld conference addressed the possibility that non-phonetic representations might be more appropriate for perceivers and producers of language by means *other* than speech (e.g. written language). If non-phonetic mediators could also be found for speech, the speech invariance problem might be solved. However, this paper will *not* directly explore that possibility. In fact, a phonetic-representation mediator is an explicit assumption of this presentation. What is explored, instead, is the possibility that the speech invariance problem may be, at least in part, a result of the way in which gestures and acoustics have been physically *described* by researchers rather than an inherent characteristic of speech communication. The traditional descriptions, it is argued, have led to a possibly erroneous conclusion about how phonetic information might be conveyed and, consequently, to the observation of the speech invariance problem.

This paper considers alternative descriptions of speech gestures and acoustics which may relate more directly to a phonetic representation. Importantly, these two logically complementary descriptions are closely tied to articulatory control and auditory analysis. This suggests speakers and listeners may have parallel representations of messages at *all* levels of production and perception.

The possible descriptive basis of the speech invariance problem

Physically speaking, speech production can be (and usually is) described as a process in which a sequence of spectral shapes is generated by a sequence of vocal tract shapes *via* the laws of physical acoustics. The speech invariance problem is observed when this analysis of gestures or sounds fails to reveal a clear relation between phonetic messages and either the sequence of vocal tract shapes or the sequence of spectral 'slices' which result: No single shape or spectrum, nor any particular sequence of shapes or spectra, can be found to map invariantly onto phonetic segments or their sequence. If it is assumed (as we said we will assume) that speech gestures and acoustics are vehicles for phonetic information, the only conclusion appears to be that the process of production itself somehow produces the lack of invariance by introducing message-irrelevant variations in shapes and acoustics.

Traditionally, message-irrelevant variation in shapes has been attributed to the physical and anatomical/physiological linkages between the articulators and between the cavities which produce the sounds (e.g. MacNeilage and DeClerk, 1969; Harris, 1974; Daniloff and Hammarberg, 1973; Kent and Minifie, 1977). During a speaker's realization of phonetic segments over time, it is supposed, the physical and physiological linkages constrain movement from one vocal tract shape to another and thus introduce movement-related 'co-articulation' of segments, and acoustic-cavity interactions, which delete, blur, or otherwise obscure representation of the phonetic information in vocal tract shape or acoustic spectrum (e.g. Fant, 1962; Stevens and House, 1961; Heinz, 1974). In this way the physical and physiological constraints on production are presumed to introduce *movement-relevant* but *message-irrelevant* acoustic ambiguity. Direct phonetic representation is, therefore, lost and is not directly available to the perceiver (or to the speech scientist) for analysis.[1]

The foregoing summary of speech communication includes two assumptions: First that phonetic representations participate in communication, and, second, that phonetic information, to the extent that it is manifest in speech at all, must be manifest in vocal-tract *shapes* (cavities) and the consequent spectral *shapes*. The first assumption we have chosen not to question. The latter assumption, in spite of its physical basis, is not the only possibility, however.

An alternative possibility

The *physical requirement* of acoustic-tube-to-spectrum mapping does not require articulator position, cavity shape, or the resulting spectral shapes to be, *per se*, the vehicles for phonetic information. Nor does that physical mapping require movement from one vocal tract configuration to the next to be physically necessary but message irrelevant. *A possible alternative is that the movements themselves are phonetically relevant and that articulator positions, vocal tract shapes, and spectral consequences are the vehicles for conveying the movement, not the other way around.*

In the alternative view, phonetic information could be manifest in, for example, *movements'* rates-of-change (velocities) and relative phases and these, in turn, could be represented in the rates and relative phases of changes in acoustic energy. This alternative possibility has consequences for the speech invariance problem in that invariance might be found in the relative or absolute rates and phases of *changes* in vocal tract shapes and spectra rather than in the absolute sizes or shapes of vocal tract cavities or the resulting spectral shapes. For expository purposes, these tract and spectrum changes will be referred to as movement 'periodicities' and acoustic 'modulations'.

The notion that periodicities and the resulting modulations may be the vehicles of phonetic information is suggested by: (1) the observation that speech motor control may be modeled as a process which coordinates sets of subsystems with periodic properties rather than one which controls articulator positions or cavity shapes, and (2) the observation that auditory perception appears particularly sensitive to acoustic modulations and to their phonetic relevance. The first of these observations is discussed extensively in the references noted below and will only be briefly reviewed here.

Speech motor control and periodic properties of gestures

Recent theoretical and empirical work suggests speech motor control may involve the dynamic coordination of the naturally oscillatory behavior of physiologically defined subsystems (Kelso, Vatikiotis-Bateson, Saltzman and Kay, 1985; Kelso and Tuller, 1984; Kelso, Saltzman and Tuller, 1986).

This orientation derives from parallel views concerning motor control in general (Gelfand and Tsetlin, 1962; Bernstein, 1967; Kugler, Kelso and Turvey, 1982; Saltzman and Kelso, 1983a, b; Haken, Kelso and Bunz, 1985), the organization of change in biological systems (Rashevsky, 1954; Rosen, 1970; Pattee, 1977; Iberall, 1978), and the organization of physical systems (Haken, 1983; Prigogine and Stengers, 1984). Detailed considerations of such systems are beyond the scope of this paper. An important characteristic of these dynamical systems, for the present discussion, is that their behavior is *intrinsically* periodic/oscillatory, with the rates and phases of the perodicities relating to the particular sets of subcomponents, and their coupling, involved in the behavior of the system. This characteristic of dynamic models of action has an important implication for understanding *any* form of action-based communication because it allows of two communicative options.

The first (and most commonly assumed) possibility is that the communicator opts to convey message distinctions by selecting action component systems and their coupling to produce distinct absolute space and time positions of actions: A non-speech example would be a symphony conductor's pointing at the violins and then to the horns to convey their order and moments of entry; in this case, absolute space–time positions of the gesture would be relevant to the musicians but not the movements themselves.

A second possibility is the communicator electing to convey message distinctions *via* the selection of action component systems and their coupling which produce periodic properties of the actions. In this case, message distinctions *may not be revealed in the absolute values of action positions in space and time.* This is because, physically speaking, both rate and relative phase of changes in position can be *independent* of absolute position and absolute time. An example of such communication would be the symphony conductor's two-handed gesture communication of interrelated rhythms; there the velocity and the relative phasing of the gestures, and not their absolute position in space or time, would be of relevance to the observing musicians.

To recapitulate the two possibilities. If communication is based in *absolute* position and time, then movements to and from those positions will be physically necessary but may be message irrelevant. On the other hand, if *movements themselves* are the basis of communication then absolute positions will be physically necessary but may be message irrelevant.

The importance of the dynamic model to the speech invariance problem is this: If a speaker's phonetic distinctions are manifest in the selection of a dynamic system's components and their coupling, then the message distinctions may be revealed more by descriptions of the periodic properties of vocal tract activity than by descriptions of the absolute vocal tract or articulator positions in space and time; in fact the latter may be arbitrarily related to the message. If this is the case, the speech invariance problem can be seen as arising from a focus on position rather than movement as the vehicle for phonetic information.

The dynamic model of production has a corresponding importance for perception: If speaker's messages are revealed in periodicities of articulations, then the listener's recovery of the speaker's message should be tied more to the discovery of acoustic 'modulations' which relate to the periodicities of movements than to the acoustic spectral profiles which relate to articulator absolute positions. That is, the *acoustic signal* should be seen to possess, and *perception* should be seen to detect, representations of the speech *movements* presumed to convey the phonetic message. The next sections review some aspects of the speech signal and of auditory processing which suggest this may, in fact, be the case.

Psychophysical dimensions of sounds

The least abstract description of sound is a simple frequency-by-time representation of physical energy. The three-dimensional (time × frequency × energy) sonagram is an example of such a representation. The perception of sound has traditionally been assumed to be based upon the auditory system's ability to provide a sensory mapping corresponding to these three fundamental dimensions of sounds. Psychophysical studies of the perceptual qualities of pitch, loudness and subjective duration have suggested that the auditory system may be able to provide such a mapping, although the relation of sensation to sound is quite complex and the three perceptual dimensions are not completely orthogonal.

Perceptual representations of time, frequency and energy are not the only sensory qualities sounds engender, however. For example, 'volume' (e.g. Gulick, 1971), and 'tonality' (e.g. Licklider, 1951), are psychophysically measurable 'complex' qualities which depend on relations among a sound's spectral attributes (e.g. spectral slope) rather than upon the absolute values of the spectral components.

Time-varying signals also yield 'complex' perceptual qualities which appear tied to the relational aspects (e.g. rate) of acoustic change rather than to the absolute values (i.e. duration) of signal components. For example, temporal variations in frequency (frequency modulation or FM) and amplitude (AM) subjectively yield a 'flutter' sensation (at modulations rates below approximately 5 Hz), and a qualitatively different modulation sensation of 'roughness' at higher rates[2] (e.g. Terhardt, 1968; Fastl, 1977).

Historically, the psychological qualities of 'complex' aspects of sounds have received less study than have the presumably more basic psychophysical mappings of pitch and frequency, loudness and level, and subjective- and objective-duration. This is due, in part, to the general success of reducing the basic psychophysical qualities to both physiological function and to absolute values of the physical dimensions. On the other hand, complex psychological qualities such as 'volume' and 'roughness' have seemed difficult to explicate physiologically, and have appeared difficult to relate in any direct, principled way to simple properties of the physical stimulus. This difficulty has biased reductionistic theories of audition away from considering the 'complex' psychological qualities.

The historic, reductionistic trend in auditory theory may be in the process of being supplanted. As will be discussed subsequently, recent work suggests that the so-called 'complex' psychophysical attributes may, in fact, be related to, for example, physical attributes of signals such as rates-of-change and the auditory system may be especially and biologically sensitive to these attributes. In this sense, the 'complex' perceptual attributes may be just as basic as other auditory qualities such as pitch or loudness and may, in fact, be even more fundamental.

It is important to note that a proposal of mechanisms particularly sensitive to, for example, the rate-of-change of signal spectrum or of energy over time need only complement, not supplant, those proposed to account for pitch, loudness and duration sensations. That is, auditory spectral resolution processes may indeed account for the pitch attributes of signals and some form of overall energy analysis may account for sensations of loudness and/or subjective duration. As noted previously, however, listening to spectrally and/or temporally complex signals can yield perceptions not only of pitch, duration, and loudness but also empirically measurable attributes which appear tied to the more relational aspects of temporal or spectral shapes. It is to be expected, consequently, that different acoustic signals might produce sensory experiences dominated by different psychological qualities (e.g., loudness instead of volume, or flutter instead of duration) depending upon the signals' structures and/or the task required of the listener. It is this observation which is particularly relevant in the case of speech. Speech is a complex signal which conveys its messages in ways which, indeed, seem related more to the relational properties of spectral and temporal shapes than to the absolute frequency, level, or duration of constituents. In addition, the timbre, loudness and subjective durations of acoustic segments of speech seem to be a minimal part of listeners' phenomenal experiences; experiences which are dominated, instead, by phonetic qualities. Might it be, then, that general auditory mechanisms directly sense the relational acoustic properties of speech signals and that these, rather than the other 'simpler' sensory qualities, convey phonetic information?

This question will be pursued by focusing on the perception of temporal modulations in acoustic energy because such variations might be found to relate to the periodicities of gestures which we have proposed to represent phonetic information. In this sense our proposal is in the spirit of Lindblom and others (e.g. Lindblom and Lubker, 1985; Fowler, in press; Ohala, 1981) who argue in favor of jointly examining production's and perception's natural capabilities when exploring the communicative role of speech.

Perception of temporal modulations

Perception of 'subaudible' temporal variations has not usually been viewed as a fundamental process in audition. This may be traceable to von Helmholtz, who reported his observations of the 'harp-like' structure of the inner ear and related these to listeners' sensitivity to tonal intervals; he proposed that audition was, essentially, 'phase deaf' regarding the tonal components of music. That is, spectral energies, but not relative phases, were detected at the first stage of auditory analysis by resonating portions of the organ of Corti. This formulation suggests fine temporal-grain spectral-descriptions to be the initial and, therefore, the most basic processes in hearing and implies that perception of other temporal changes in signals depend upon subsequent analysis of the resolved spectra with a time constant longer than that represented by phase differences among the spectral components.

Although von Helmholtz's physiological model has been displaced, the idea that hearing depends, at base, upon the analysis of temporally fine-grain spectral representations of sounds underlies many current theories of audition. As Goldstein (1967) points out, however, von Helmholtz may have intended his 'phase deafness' to be understood more in the context of musical abilities than in terms of the limits of human sensitivity. Von Helmholtz (1862) himself was aware that, as described in the previous section, some relatively short-time temporal variations, under some circumstances, do have perceptual consequences which appear independent of spectrum and pitch and of level and loudness. In fact, von Helmholtz (and others, including, for example, Stumpf (1883)) experimented with these 'modulation' sensations.

In more recent years, Goldstein (1967) and others (Feth, 1972; Coninx, 1978) have reported data and suggested explicit models for modulation sensitivity in terms of two stages of processing: The first stage is spectral extraction and the second is a non-linearity with an envelope-energy processor. Such models thus tie detection of temporal changes in signals to the combined operation of fine-grained spectral resolution followed by level-sensing mechanisms operating over relatively coarse time-periods. Consequently, these models maintain the traditional focus on the primacy of spectral descriptions of signals and provide, as 'output', only *qualitative* measures of the presence or absence of energy changes over time.

There are data, however, which suggest that the processing of acoustic change may be *quantitative* and may involve the operation of mechanisms directly sensitive to signal properties such as rates of change. We now turn to these data.

If general auditory mechanisms sensitive to temporal aspects of signals exist, then evidence from the perception of simple stimuli should show sensitivity to rates-of-change, phase, or other properties relatively independent of sensitivity to the presumably more basic properties of duration, frequency and level. Early studies of the perception of short duration, non-speech 'glide' signals (which varied in frequency) did show thresholds which varied with the property of modulation phase (i.e. glide direction). On the other hand, thresholds were also found to vary inversely with duration and bandwidth in a manner suggesting dependence on pitch and subjective duration sensitivity (Van Bergeijk, 1964; Nabelek, 1978; Collins and Cullen, 1978). However, these latter results did not speak directly to the issue of independent sensitivity to rate-of-change since changes in duration, range of frequency change, and rate-of-change of frequency were confounded. Cullen and Collins (1982) specifically investigated the independent effects of rate-of-change, controlling for duration and frequency extent. In addition to replicating earlier findings, their threshold data did reveal rate-of-change to account for results more adequately than either duration or frequency-extent alone.

Additional evidence suggesting the auditory system to be directly sensitive to phase and rate-of-change is provided by studies of the effects of AM or FM adaptation on the detectability of AM and FM. Much of this work has been recently, and extensively, reviewed by Kay (1982). For purposes of the present discussion, the work can be summarized as showing adaptation sensitivity for AM and FM in the 1 to 100 Hz modulation range (i.e., acoustic changes occurring with 1000 ms to 10 ms periods). In addition, spread of adaptation effects to non-adapted stimuli revealed adaptation effects to be 'tuned' with a 'bandwidth' of an octave or two (Kay and Matthews, 1972). Adaptation effects were also found to be at least partially independent of carrier level and frequency. Gardner and Wilson (1979) later confirmed phase dependence of adaptation for 8 Hz repeated sequences of rising or falling glides; these data thus complement the glide threshold results.

The results of the adaptation and glide studies together suggest the auditory system might possess mechanisms sensitive to 1 to 100 Hz variations in level or spectrum: That is, 'modulation sensors'. Perhaps importantly, this range is also that showing high FM and AM sensitivity (ΔI/I and ΔF/F) (Zwicker, 1952; Viemeister, 1979, Rodenburg, 1977). Modulation sensation may, then, be a component of the perceptual experience of time-varying signals which is independent of other dimensions of pitch, duration, etc.

If sensing of modulation is indeed a separate, independent dimension of audition, perceptions of modulations using different carriers but the same rates, or of AM and FM with the same rates, would be expected to be judged similar even though spectral detail and, consequently, other perceptual qualities such as pitch or loudness might be different. This appears to be the case. As noted above, rate-specific adaptation effects appear partly independent of carrier frequency, and cross-adaptation of FM and AM has also been demonstrated, although there are less effects of AM on FM (Regan and Tansley, 1979; Kay and Matthews, 1972). Von Bekesy suggested a direct experimental test of the possible perceived-modulation equivalence of AM and FM which was completed by Zwicker in 1962. Those results clearly demonstrated equivalent judgements of modulation for AM and FM for broadband noises at 2 to 10 Hz modulation rates, as well as other effects supportive of a common, underlying psychological dimension of 'modulation sensation' (e.g. subthreshold AM decreased the threshold of a simultaneous FM).

Investigation of the modulation sensation has also been pursued by Fastl, who extended observations made by Terhardt (1968). Terhardt psychophysically examined the 'roughness' quality of AM stimuli modulated at rates of from less than 10 Hz to as high as several hundred Hertz. To summarize briefly: For carriers above approximately 2 kHz, judgements of roughness tend to be maximum around a 70 Hz modulation rate, with roughness judged as very much less when modulation rates were lower than 20 Hz or higher than 200 Hz. Fastl (1977) used direct-magnitude-estimation methods and obtained similar results. Such findings suggest attribution of perceived roughness to the 'tuning' of a 1 or 2 octave 'modulation perception filter' to sensations produced by modulations in the 70 Hz region.

The notion that perception could be 'tuned' to select certain modulation sensations was further extended by Fastl (1982; 1983) who demonstrated reliable judgements when listeners were asked to comparatively rate what he called the 'modulation strength' (*Schwankungsstärke*) produced by various AMs and FMs at rates below those producing roughness (i.e. < 50 Hz). These results revealed a 1 or 2 octave bandpass-sensitivity in the

4 to 8 Hz modulation region similar to that seen for other rates in the roughness and adaptation studies.

The data discussed above support a conclusion that the auditory system contains mechanisms sensitive to the phase, extent and rate of frequency or amplitude modulation. Except for the glide studies, however, all of the experiments have used continuously modulated signals. In addition, the carriers have been sinusoids or broadband noises. If the modulation tuning suggested by those studies is to be related to speech perception, parallel examination of formant-like, harmonic, wideband signals, with single modulation-cycles, must also be attempted. A few preliminary studies of this type have been done in our laboratory using signals which consist of a steady-state formant in the 1200 to 1800 Hz region which is modulated in frequency, or amplitude, over 60 to 120 ms period. Results of these experiments suggest that Zwicker's observation of the perceived modulation equivalence of AM and FM, as well as judgements of the Fastl type, can be obtained with speech-like signals (Porter and Miller, 1983; Miller and Porter, 1983). Interestingly, such signals also have some phonetic qualities and pilot studies of listeners open-class judgements of the best phonetic identity of such sounds show systematic variations with the rate, extent and phase of AM and FM modulations which are consistent with the notion of perceptual tuning to modulation sensations (Porter and Miller, 1984).

The most extensive studies of the relation between (usually AM) modulation and phonetic judgements have been made at the Pavlov Institute of Physiology in Leningrad by L. Chistovich and her colleagues. A review of this work, in honor of Professor Chistovich, has recently been published (Porter, 1985a). These Russian investigators provide some important additional data regarding the notions of modulation sensation developed above.

Some of the Russian work is based on the observation that amplitude modulations of approximately 30 Hz can yield a perception which Russian-speaking listeners reliably label as '/r/-like'. (The 'r-like' sensation may be similar to the 'trilled' feature of /r/ or /l/ in some languages.) This perception seems to be of the same type as, yet qualitatively different than, either Fastl's modulation strength (which was observed at lower rates) and Terhardt's roughness (which appears at higher rates). Like perceived roughness and fluctuation strength, the /r/-sensation has also been shown to be a relatively stable quality of varying signals which is independent of carrier frequency and signal type (Chistovich *et al.* 1976).

Chistovich *et al.* proposed that /r/-like and other modulation qualities of the AM sounds reflect the operation of filter-like, change-detecting processes, which are tuned to different modulation rates. From this perspective, an /r/ sensation results from a tuning of a modulation filter to a center frequency of 25 Hz or so; in the case of the roughness filter the center frequency would be approximately 70 Hz; for fluctuation sensation the center frequency would be at about 4 Hz.

Stolyarova and Chistovich (1977) provided information on the characteristics of the postulated, tuned, modulation '/r/-filter' using two types of carrier (a 'harmonic complex' similar to a vowel, or a broadband noise). Results from both conditions revealed a 1-to-2 octave, filter-like, bandpass /r/-sensitivity to modulations at the 20 to 30 Hz rate. The observance of reliable /r/-judgements for both noise segments and harmonic complexes imply that general auditory 'modulation sensing' processes, tuned to specific rates, may be associated with phonetic quality judgements, just as they appear associated with roughness and modulation-strength judgements. In addition, the tuning of sensitivity within 1 to 2 octaves complements the roughness, modulation strength and adaptation results.

Additional Russian studies provided more information about possible modulation-detecting mechanisms and their relevance to speech. For example, real speech signals are characterized by several different changes in energy occurring in different frequency regions and at different times. The question arises, therefore, as to the way in which modulation detection mechanisms treat modulations occurring in different carrier regions. One Pavlov Institute study, done in collaboration with a French colleague, investigated this question by asking listeners to judge modulations occurring on different components of harmonic signals (0.5 + 1 + 1.5 + 2 + 2.5 kHz tone-complexes) (Rodionov, Carré and Kozhevnikov, 1976). The results revealed a tendency for modulations of different phases to 'cancel out' when the two modulated components were within 0.5 to 1 kHz but to 'amalgamate' to yield a larger perceived modulation if the carriers were more widely separated.

Later studies revealed additional subtleties of the interrelation of change-detecting mechanisms as a function of the relative timing of modulations in different components of harmonic signals. Lesogor and Chistovich (1978) used a 600 ms, two-tone (0.5 + 2.5 kHz) complex in which a single 6 dB ramp-like increment in level was introduced on one or both components. When a 5 ms step occurred in a single component, at a point 25 ms from the beginning of the signal, listeners reported a relatively categorical shift from a V to a CV percept, regardless of the component in which the change occurred. (The V was /i/-like and the consonant heard was /l/, /m/, or /n/ depending on the component modulated.) A similar shift occurred from CV to VCV when the step was placed at approximately 100 to 150 ms from signal onset. Introducing level variations in *both* components at *different* times were found to yield CVCV's when settings were made at appropriate times (i.e. one at 25 ms on one component and one at 150 ms on the other).

An additional observation of this Lesogor and Chistovich (1978) study was that the rise time of the step critically influenced the perceived syllabic structure: A slower 30 ms length ramp yielded VV's rather than the CV's and the VCV's produced with the 5 ms ramps. An important result was obtained when a 5 ms increment occurred at a delay of approximately 35 ms on one component and a 30 ms increment occurred at around 150 ms on the second. In this case, even though the signal's physical structure would suggest a CVV, listeners nearly equally often reported a VCV. This 'confusion' of the temporal order of events is consistent with a model of independent perceptual treatment of modulation and spectrum. That is, the detection of modulation itself is *independent* of the process of determination of the temporal sequence of spectrally distinct events. Because, in this experiment, there were no spectral variations, listeners could detect the modulations but could not reliably order them. In any case, the authors conclude that the CVV/VCV uncertainty '. . . is completely inexplicable on the basis of the very widely held assumption that the pattern of the signal recalled is equivalent to a section of the dynamic spectrogram covering the appropriate period of time, and that vowels and consonants correspond to different successive segments of this spectrogram' (Lesogor and Chistovich, 1978).

Modulation sensations and articulator motions

Results of the Russian studies complement those concerning the perception of AM, FM, glides, etc., in that all are consistent with the conclusion that the human auditory system is particularly sensitive to variations in the 2 to 70 Hz region and that perception can represent these modulations in terms of the 'sensory dimensions' of modulation rate, extent and phase. In addition, these dimensions seem at least partially independent of the other, 'simpler', sensory dimensions of pitch, loudness and duration. Studies of more speech-like signals reveal, furthermore, a possible association of phonetic distinctions and the modulation dimensions.

What might be, however, the basis of an association of phonetic messages and modulation sensations? It is this question which brings us back to the question of modulation's relation to gesture kinematics and which recalls the admonition to consider the possible complementarity of perception's and production's capabilities in speech communication. That is, it may be that an important aspect of the communicative relationship between perception and production lies in the relation between modulation sensations on the one hand, and the periodic properties of production kinematics on the other.[3]

This proposal has a certain direct appeal. After all, changes in speech acoustics are related to the movement of the articulators and it might be presumed that the velocities and phases of acoustic changes, as processed by a modulation-sensitive auditory system, could reveal those same aspects of articulatory gestures themselves. In that case, perception might proceed by relating the velocities and phases to the kinetics underlying the articulatory gestures involved and thus recover the 'articulatory features' of the speaker's phonetic representation.

The story cannot be this simple, however. Even if it is assumed that individual articulators have relatively fixed kinetic properties and, hence, usually stable and distinctive kinematic behaviors, even a dynamic model allows articulator behavior to vary with, for example, different 'driving forces' (e.g. perhaps articulatory 'effort' in the case of speech). It is also possible that some of what we might imagine are 'constants' of articulators' kinetics, like stiffness, may be scaled depending upon the context and/or the speaker. This means that *absolute* rates, extents, and phases of modulations of the same articulators, and of the resulting acoustics, could vary, and thus make more difficult the unambiguous recovery of the underlying kinetic aspects of the articulators and the phonetic representations we might presume to be tied to them.

Reconsideration of the dynamic approach to production may help here. Changes in such variables as the driving force or stiffness can change dynamical systems' behavior either quantitatively or qualitatively. Quantitative changes include variations in the absolute value of kinematic properties such as velocity. Dynamical systems naturally maintain a *relational* constancy among components of the action, however, and will thus tend to maintain, for example, constant phase relations among the action components even as they change in rate.

Qualitative changes in dynamical systems may also occur with variation in controlling variables. Such changes involve, however, a re-organization and/or re-selection of system subcomponents and their coupling. It is not always obvious at what point a qualitative change in dynamic system behavior will occur, and the nature of the re-organization can be extremely complex (e.g. Haken, 1983; Haken, Kelso and Bunz, 1985). For current purposes, however, it is sufficient to note that the qualitative changes may be distinguished from quantitative ones in terms of the former involving changes in the absolute values of kinematic properties with preservation of ratiometric constancy, whereas the latter involves changes in the relational (and, sometimes, absolute) values.

If such a formulation is to be applied to speech, it would mean phonetic distinctions map onto *relational* constancies in vocal tract kinematics rather than onto their absolute values. If this is the case, study of speech production should (and apparently does in some cases) reveal constancies in the *relations* between gestures' kinematics in coordinated utterances rather than in the absolute magnitudes of the variables (e.g. Tuller, Kelso and Harris, 1983). On the other hand, a consequence for speech *perception* should be that *the relations between* the rates, magnitudes and phases of modulation sensations, rather than their absolute values, should manifest phonetic invariances. Some data also support this conclusion in that phonetic decisions regarding temporally varying signals depend more upon the relative than on the absolute duration of acoustic segments (e.g. Summerfield, 1981; Pisoni, Carrell and Gans, 1983). Unfortunately these studies just barely explore the dynamic properties of production and their consequences for perception (but see, Kelso, *et al.*, 1986; Fowler, 1986), and considerable work needs to be done.

Conclusion

Speakers' phonetic representations appear to parallel those of listeners but the shapes produced and the spectra heard do not appear to reveal phonetic representations. As a result, theorists have been led to propose elaborate perception and production mechanisms to first produce and then overcome the apparent absence of phonetic representations in shapes and spectra. We have observed, however, that if control of articulation is viewed as the result of a dynamic system, we should not be surprised to find a rather opaque mapping of phonetic representations onto absolute space–time values of articulator positions or the vocal-tract shapes they produce. Nor should we be surprised to find that perceived phonetic distinctions fail to have clear representations in descriptions of speech acoustics as a sequence of frequency-by-amplitude slices. This paper argues that the characteristics of a dynamic control system which yield an ambiguous mapping in terms of absolute positions are also those which may *preserve* phonetic representations in the velocities and phasing of the coordinated movements involved in speech production.

Given the growing evidence in audition that the sensory system can directly detect the properties of acoustic modulations like those produced by speech movements, we further suppose that the sensing of such modulations map (rather directly) onto the phonetic representations of the listener.

That is, production-control subsystems' periodic properties map onto perceptually realized properties of acoustic modulations[4], and both map onto speakers' and listeners' phonetic representations.

Although the reviewed data tend to support our conclusion, there is far to go. In particular, it must be determined if the ranges of variation in the kinematics of the different coordinated subsystems in speech are sufficiently small to avoid ambiguity in the resulting modulations. It also remains to be determined if perception of modulations has sufficient resolution to allow recovery of the kinematic differences presumed relevant in speech.

Some data are beginning to suggest that the first of these conditions may be met, at least to the extent that gestures' velocities and phases appear relatively stable (Kelso, et al., 1985; Ostry, Keller and Parush, 1983; Fujimura, in press). As yet unreported, however (although in progress, Porter, Raphael and Ostry), are experiments examining the size and type of differences among different speech movements and the resulting acoustic modulations (see also Kelso, et al., 1986).

As regards the question as to whether the perceptual system can adequately resolve modulation differences, there are very little data. Only a few studies have specifically examined the *discriminability* of modulations of different rates, extents, or phases (e.g. Patterson, Johnson-Davies and Milroy, 1978). Of course, some estimate of the degree of sensitivity can be extracted from the work previously discussed which suggests tuning to within an octave or so in modulation rate. In addition, a few studies of the discrimination of rates of signal onset suggest a JND of within an octave for rates-of-change in the 10 to 50 Hz region (i.e. 20 to 100 ms durations, Van Heuven and Van den Broeck, 1979). Clearly, however, more direct study of modulation discrimination needs to be done, particularly with speech-like signals with both single and multiple cycles of amplitude and frequency variation. Our current work is directed along these lines.

Notes

[1] Few speech perception or production theories would completely embrace the characterization of communication presented here. For example, some might wish to minimize the role of phonetic representations (e.g. Elman and McClellen, 1983; Repp, 1981), others the role of vocal-tract shape or articulation representations (Cole and Scott, 1974). However, whereas some theorists may wish to place another emphasis or may decline explicitly incorporating aspects of the formulations as outlined, such theorists do implicitly acknowledge the principle outlined points. That is, *all* theories of speech perception and production must include an explication of the fact that listeners (usually) hear what speakers intend and that this is a result of one producing and one receiving an acoustic

signal. Since most (all?) extant theories would also accept the observation that a rather opaque relation appears to exist between the acoustic signal and the message intended or received; production, *in some way*, is presumed to *introduce* ambiguity and perception is presumed to *overcome* it. Thus, if communication is to be successful, perception must either implicitly or explicity take account of, or overcome, production's complicating tendencies. It is not a necessary condition, in such theories, that perception be said to actually *share*, or make reference to the processes involved in production (for example, perception might make use of non-speech context) but perception's processing must, at least *logically*, realize distinctions (acoustic or otherwise) which correspond to those the speaker respects.

[2] Both these sensations differ from those which occur at modulation rates above 300 Hz or so, where pitch-like sensations dominate. These pitch qualities appear related to the spectral properties of frequency spread produced by very rapid modulation.

[3] The suggestion that modulations of amplitude and frequency might play a rather important role in speech perception is a very old one (Fletcher, 1929; Dudley, 1940; see also discussion by Porter, 1985 a, b; Plomp, 1983; and Watson and Foyle, 1985). The proposed approach also bears some relation to suggestions that speech perception might be mediated by acoustic-change detectors (e.g. Stevens, 1973; Kewley-Port, 1983), spectral change (Stevens and Blumstein, 1981) and/or by processes which link perceptual decisions to motor abilities (e.g. Liberman *et al.*, 1967). The essential, contrastive features of the proposed approach are, however, that the perception of acoustic variation is a *general* auditory ability to detect and represent modulations of amplitude and frequency; that perceptual 'tuning' to the sensations yields the basis for (some) phonetic decisions; and that the nature of the relation of perception and production lies in a logical correspondence between the control of vocal tract movements and perception of the corresponding acoustic events and not (necessarily) a functional linkage. In the last regard, however, we note that we *are* inclined to view the 'output' of modulation perception to be directly and physiologically compatible with the 'input' to speech motor control (see Porter and Castellanos, 1980; Porter and Lubker, 1980).

[4] The proposal made here is, roughly, that the perception of speech actions, mediated by sound, involves the recovery of those (dynamic system) variables which characterize the equivalence of the same action manifest at different times in different contexts. The proposed perceptual activities may be said, in that case, to be inspired by, and analogous to, the research activities of action scientists who attempt to find descriptions of actions, and its control, which capture equifinality (e.g. see review by Saltzman, 1979; see also Saltzman and Kelso, 1983a, b). The current proposal also relates to (and in some cases is in debt to) that work which proposes a rather direct relation between perceptual events and the control of motor activity (e.g. Gibson, 1966; Turvey, 1977; Mace, 1977; Turvey, Fitch and Tuller, 1982; see also collections edited by Stelmach and Requin, 1980, and Kelso and Clark, 1982) as well as work concerning the perception of (non-speech) actions (e.g. Johansson, 1964; Runeson, 1977).

Acknowledgements

Preparation of this paper was supported, in part, by a Baylor Tutorial Fellowship to R. J. Porter to visit Haskins Laboratory in June/July 1984. The author extends thanks to Drs D. Rosenfield, J. A. S. Kelso, B. Tuller, E. Saltzman, C. Fowler, K. Harris, B. Lindblom and M. Turvey for their stimulating support; to two reviewers for their annoyingly correct criticisms; to A. Dadourian and S. Koroluk and the Haskins support staff for their help; and to V. Flax for aid with the manuscript. Special thanks to W Prinz for patience.

References

Bernstein, N. (1967). *The Coordination and Regulation of Movements*, Oxford: Pergamon.

Chistovich, L. A., Ventsov, A. V., Granstrem, M. P., Zhukov, S. Y., Zhukova, M. C., Karnitskaya, E. G., Kozhevnikov, V. A., Lisenko, D. M., Lyublinskaya, V. N., Mushnikov, V. N., Slepokurova, N. A., Fedorova N. A., Khaavel, R. Kh., Chistovich, I. A., and Shuplyakov, V. S. (1976). *Physiology of Speech: Human Speech and Perception* (in Russian). Leningrad: Nauka.

Cole, R. A., and Scott, B. (1974). Toward a theory of speech perception. *Psychological Review*, **81**, 348–74.

Collins, M. J., and Cullen, J. K. Jr. (1978). Temporal integration of tone glides. *Journal of the Acoustical Society of America*, **63**, 469–743.

Coninx, F. (1978). The detection of combined differences in frequency and intensity. *Acustica*, **39**, 137–50.

Cullen, J. K. Jr., and Collins, M. J. (1982). Audibility of short-duration tone-glides as a function of rate of frequency change. *Hearing Research*, **7**, 115–25.

Daniloff, R., and Hammarberg, R. (1973). On defining coarticulation. *Journal of Phonetics*, **1**, 239–48.

Dudley, H. (1940). The Carrier Nature of Speech. *Bell System Technical Journal*, **9**, 495–515.

Elman, J. L., and McClellan, J. J. (1983). *Exploiting lawful variability in the Speech Wave*. Draft for MIT Conference on Invariance and Variability in Speech Processes, October 8–10, 1–23.

Fant, G. (1962). Descriptive Analysis of the Acoustic Aspects of Speech. *Logos*, **5**, 3–17.

Fastl, H. (1977). Roughness and temporal masking patterns of sinusoidally amplitude modulated broadband noise. In Evans and Wilson (Eds) *Psychophysics and Physiology of Hearing*. London: Academic Press, pp. 403–14.

Fastl, H. (1982). Fluctuation strength and temporal masking patterns of amplitude-modulated broadband noise. *Hearing Research*, **8**, 59–69.

Fastl, H. (1983). Fluctuation strength of modulated tones and broadband noise. In R. Klinke and R. Hartmann (Eds) *Hearing–Physiological Bases and Psychophysics*. Frankfurt: Goethe Universitat Frankfurt, pp. 1–5.

Feth, L. L. (1972). Combinations of amplitude and frequency differences in auditory discrimination. *Acustica*, **26**, 67–77.

Fletcher, H. (1953). *Speech and Hearing in Communication*. Princeton, NJ: Van Nostrand. (First published as *Speech and Hearing* in 1929).

Fowler, C. A. (1986). An event approach to the study of speech perception from a direct-realist perspective. *Journal of Phonetics*, **14**, 1, 3–28.

Fujimura, O. A linear model of speech timing. In R. Channon and L. Shockey (Eds) *In Honor of Ilse Lehiste*, in press.

Gardner, R. B., and Wilson, J. P. (1979). Evidence for direction-specific channels in the processing of frequency modulation. *Journal of the Acoustical Society of America*, **66**, 704–9.

Gelfand, I. M., and Tsetlin, M. L. (1962). Some methods of control for complex systems. *Russian Mathematics Survey*, **17**, 95–116.

Gibson, J. J. (1966). *The Senses Considered as Perceptual Systems*. Boston, MA: Houghton-Mifflin.

Goldstein, J. L. (1967). Auditory spectral filtering and monaural phase perception. *Journal of the Acoustical Society of America*, **41**, 458–79.

Gulick, W. L. (1971). *Hearing: Physiology and Psychophysics*, Oxford: Oxford University Press.

Haken, H. (1983). *Synergetics: An Introduction* (3rd edn). Heidelberg: Springer.

Haken, H., Kelso, J. A. S., and Bunz, H. (1985). A theoretical model of phase transitions in human hand movements. *Biological Cybernetics*, **51**, 347–356.

Harris, K. S. (1974). Physiological aspects of articulatory behavior. In T. Sebeck (Ed.) *Current Trends in Linguistics* Vol 12 The Hague: Montin, 2281–302.

Heinz, J. (1974). Speech Acoustics in T. Sebeck (Ed.) *Current Trends in Linguistics*, Vol 12 The Hague: Montin, 2241–80.

Hockett, C. (1960). The Origin of Speech. *Scientific American*, **203**, 89–96.

Iberall, A. S. (1978). Cybernetics offers a (hydrodynamic) thermodynamic view of brain activities. An alternative to reflexology. In F. Brambilla, P. K. Bridges, E. Endroczi and C. Heusep (Eds) *Perspectives in Endocrine Psychobiology*. New York: Wiley.

Johansson, G. (1964). Perception of motion and changing form. *Scandanavian Journal of Psychology*, **5**, 181–208.

Kay, R. H. (1982). Hearing of modulation in sounds, *Physiological Review*, **62**, 894–975.

Kay, R. H., and Matthews, D. R. (1972). On the existence in human auditory pathways of channels selectively tuned to the modulation present in frequency-modulated tones. *Journal of Physiology*, **225**, 656–77.

Kelso, J. A. S., and Clark, J. E. (Eds) (1982). *The Development of Movement and Coordination and Control*. New York: Wiley.

Kelso, J. A. S., Saltzman, E. L., and Tuller B. (1986). Dynamical perspectives on speech production: Data and Theory, *Journal of Phonetics*, **14**, 29–59.

Kelso, J. A. S., and Tuller, B. (1984). Converging evidence in support of common dynamical principles for speech and movement coordination. *American Journal of Physiology*, **246**, R928–35 (Regulatory Integrative Comparitive Physiology, 15).

Kelso, J. A. S., Vatikiotis-Bateson, E., Saltzman, E. L., and Kay, B. (1985). A qualitative dynamic analysis of reiterant speech production: Phase portraits, kinematics and dynamic modeling. *Journal of the Acoustical Society of America*, **72**, 266–280.

Kent, R. D., and Minifie, F. (1977). Coarticulator in recent speech production models. *Journal of Phonetics*, **5**, 115–33.

Kewley-Port, D. (1983). Time-varying features as correlates of phase of articulation in stop consonants. *Journal of the Acoustical Society of America*, **73**, 322–35.

Kugler, P. N., Kelso, J. A. S., and Turvey, M. T. (1982). On the control and coordination of naturally developing systems. In J. A. S. Kelso and J. E. Clark (Eds) *The Development of Movement Control and Coordination*, New York: Academic, 5–78.

Lesogor, L. V., and Chistovich, L. A. (1978). Detection of a 'consonant' in a two-component complex sound stimulus and interpretation of the stimulus as a sequence of elements, *Fizilology Cheloveka*, **4**, 213–9.

Liberman, A. M., Cooper, F. S., Shankweiler, D. S., and Studdert-Kennedy, M. (1967). Perception of the speech code. *Psychology Review*, **74**, 431–61.

Licklider, J. C. R. (1951). Basic correlates of auditory stimulus. In S. S. Steven (Ed.) *Handbook of Experimental Psychology*. New York: Wiley.

Lindblom, B. and Lubker, J. (1985). The speech homunculus and a problem of phonetic linguistics. In V. A. Frompkin (Ed.) *Phonetic Linguistics*. Santran: Academic.

MacNeilage, P., and DeClerk, J. (1969). On the motor control of coarticulation in CVC monsyllables. *Journal of the Acoustical Society of America*, **45**, 1217–23.

Mace, W. (1977). James J. Gibson's strategy for perceiving: Ask not what's inside your head, but what your head's inside of. In R. E. Shaw and J. D. Bransford (Eds) *Perceiving, Acting and Knowing: Toward an Ecological Psychology*. Hillsdale, NJ: Erlbaum.

Miller, C. J., and Porter, R. J. Jr. (1983). Perception of 'modulation' in speech-like signals II: Discrimination of frequency extent as a function of spectral content and direction of change. *Journal of Acoustical Society of America*, **74**, S66.

Nabelek, I. V. (1978). Temporal summation of constant and gliding tones at masked auditory threshold. *Journal of the Acoustical Society of America*, **64**, 751–63.

Ohala, J. (1981). The listener as a source of sound change. In M. F. Miller (Ed.) *Papers from the parasession on language and behavior*. Chicago: Chicago Linguistics Society.

Ostry, D. J., Keller, E., and Parush, A. (1983). Similarities in the control of speech articulators and the limbs: Kinematics of tongue dorsum movement in speech. *Journal of Experimental Psychology, Human Perception and Performance*, **9**, 622–36.

Pattee, H. H. (1977). Dynamic and linguistic modes of complex systems. *International Journal of Genetic Systems*, **3**, 259–66.

Patterson, R. D., Johnson-Davies, D., and Milroy, R. (1978). Amplitude-modulated noise: The detection of modulation versus the detection of modulation rate. *Journal of the Acoustical Society of America*, **63**.

Pisoni, D. B., Carrell, T. D., and Gans, S. J. (1983). Perception of the duration of rapid spectrum changes in speech and nonspeech signals. *Perception and Psychophysics*, **34**, 314–22.

Plomp, R. (1983). The role of modulation in hearing. In R. Klinke and R. Hartmann *Hearing: Physiological Bases and Psychophysics*, Frankfurt: Zentrum der Physiologie, Universität Frankfurt.

Porter, R. J. (1985a). Pavlov Institute research in speech perception: Finding phonetic messages in modulations. *Speech Communication*, **4**, 31–9.

Porter, R. J. (1985b). Speech messages, modulations and motions. *Journal of Phonetics*, in press.

Porter, R. J. Jr., and Castellanos, F. X. (1980). Speech production measures of speech perception: Rapid shadowing of VCV syllables. *Journal of Acoustical Society of America*, **67**, 1349–56.

Porter, R. J. Jr., and Lubker, J. (1980). Rapid reproduction of vowel-vowel sequences: Evidence for a fast and direct acoustic–motoric linkage in speech. *Journal of Speech and Hearing Research*, **23**, 593–602.

Porter, R. J. Jr., and Miller, C. J. (1983). Perception of 'modulation' in speechlike signals I: Matching amplitude depth to frequency extent. *Journal of the Acoustical Society of America*, **72** (*Suppl.* 1) S3.

Porter, R. J. Jr., and Miller, C. J. (1984). Perception of 'modulation' in speechlike signals III: A psychoacoustic or phonetic dimension? *Journal of the Acoustical Society of America*, **75** (*Suppl.* 1).

Prigogine, I. and Stengers, I. (1984). *Order out of Chaos*. New York: Bantam Books.

Rashevsky, N. (1954). Topology and life: In search of general mathematical principles in biology and sociology. *Bulletin of Mathematical Biophysics*, **16**, 317–48.

Regan, D., and Tansley, B. W. (1979). Selective adaptation to frequency-modulated tones: Evidence for an information-processing channel selectively sensitive to frequency changes. *Journal of the Acoustical Society of America*, **65**, 1249–57.

Repp, B. H. (1981). On levels of description in speech research. *Journal of the Acoustical Society of America*, **69**, 1462–4.

Rodenburg, M. (1977). Investigation of temporal effects with amplitude modulated signals. In E. F. Evans and J. P. Wilson (Eds) *Psychophysics and Physiology of Hearing*. London: Academic, 429–47.

Rodionov, V. D., Carré, R., and Kozhevnikov, V. A. (1976). Consolidation of information on transient variations of signal envelopes in different channels of the auditory system. *Fiziology Cheloveka*, **2**, 1021–7.

Rosen, R. (1970). *Dynamical System Theory in Biology: Stability Theory and Its Application*. Vol 1, New York: Wiley.

Runeson, S. (1977). On the possibility of "smart" perceptual mechanisms. *Scandanavian Journal of Psychology*, **18**, 172–9.

Saltzman, E. (1979). Levels of sensorimotor representation. *Journal of Mathematical Psychology*, **20**, 91–163.

Saltzman, E., and Kelso, J. A. S. (1983a). *Skilled actions: A task dynamic approach*. Haskins Laboratories: Status Report on Speech Research, SR-76, 3–58.

Saltzman, E., and Kelso, J. A. S. (1983b). Toward a dynamical assessment of motor memory and control. In R. A Magill (Ed.) *Memory and Control of Action*. Amsterdam: North-Holland, pp. 17–38.

Shattuck-Hufnagel, S. (1983). Sublexical units and suprasegmental structure in speech production planning. In P. MacNeilage (Ed.) *The Production of Speech*. New York: Springer.

Soli, S. D., Arabie, P., and Carroll, J. D. (1986). Discrete representation of perceptual structure underlying consonant confusions. *Journal of the Acoustical Society of America*, **79**, 826–37.

Stelmach, G. E., and Requin, J. (Eds) *Tutorials in Motor Behavior*. Amsterdam: North-Holland.

Stevens, K. N. (1973). The potential role of property detectors in the perception of consonants. *MIT Electronics Laboratory QPR 110:* 155–68.

Stevens, K. N., and Blumstein, S. E. (1981). The search for invariant acoustic correlates of phonetic features. In P. D. Eimas and J. L. Miller (Eds) *Perspectives on the Study of Speech*. Hillsdale, NJ: Erlbaum.

Stevens, K. N., and House, A. (1961). An acoustical theory of vowel production and some of its implications. *Journal of Speech and Hearing Research*, **4**, 303–20.

Stevens, K. N., and House, A. S. (1972). Speech Perception. In J. Tobias (Ed.) *Foundations of Modern Auditory Theory* Vol 2. New York: Academic Press, 3–57.

Stolyarova, E. I., and Chistovich, I. A. (1977). Amplitude-frequency responses and threshold devices of a model of auditory envelope processing. *Fizilology Cheloveka*, **3**, 72–6.

Stumpf, C. (1983). *Tonpsychologie I*. Leipzig: Hirzel, 250.

Summerfield, Q. (1981). Articulatory rate and perceptual constancy in phonetic perception. *Journal of Experimental Psychology, Human Perception and Performance*, **7**, 1074–95.

Terhardt, E. (1968). Über akustische Rauhigkeit und Schwankungsstärke. *Acustica*, **20**, 215–24.

Tuller, B., Kelso, J. A. S., and Harris, K. S. (1983). Converging evidence for the role of relative timing in speech. *Journal of Experimental Psychology, Human Perception and Performance*, **9**, 829–33.

Turvey, M. T. (1977). Preliminaries to a theory of action with reference to vision. In R. E. Shaw and J. D. Bransford (Eds) *Perceiving, Acting, Knowing: Toward an Ecological Psychology*. Hillsdale, NJ: Erlbaum.

Turvey, M. T., Fitch, H. L., and Tuller, B. (1982). The problems of degrees of freedom and context-conditioned variability. In J. A. S. Kelso (Ed.) *Understanding Human Motor Control*. Champaign, IL: Human Kinetics, 239–52.

Van Bergeijk, W. S. (1964). Sonic pulse compression in bats and people: A comment. *Journal of the Acoustical Society of America*, **36**, 594–7.

Van Heuven, V. J. J. P., and Van den Broeck, M. P. R. (1979). Auditory discrimination of rise and decay times in tone and noise bursts. *Journal of the Acoustical Society of America*, **66**, 1308–15.

Viemeister, N. F. (1979). Temporal modulation transfer functions based upon modulation thresholds. *Journal of the Acoustical Society of America*, **66**, 1364–80.

Von Helmholtz, H. L. F. (1862). *On the Sensations of Tone*. New York: Dover. (Reprint of J. Ellis' 1885 English translation of the 4th, and last, German edition of 1877. Von Helmholtz completed the 1st edition of this work in 1862.)

Waston, C. S., and Foyle, D. C. (1985). Central factors in the discrimination and identification of complex sounds. *Journal of the Acoustical Society of America*, **78**, 375–80.

Zwicker, W. E. (1952). Die grenzen der Hörbarkeit der Amplitudenmodulation und der Frequenzmodulation eines Tones. *Acustica*, **1 & 2**, 125–33.

Zwicker, E. (1962). Direct comparisons between the sensations produced by frequency modulation and amplitude modulation. *Journal of the Acoustical Society of America*, **34**, 1425–30.

Section 3

Perceptual integration and common codes

Introduction

Wolfgang Prinz

The two contributions in this section consider various forms and modalities of language perception and of reproduction of linguistic materials. Unlike the contributions in section 2 that emphasize the issue of shared mechanisms and structures between perception and production, the main issue here is with common codes and shared mechanisms among various forms of language perception.

One of their common themes is to consider the skill of lip-reading and to elucidate the nature of the mechanisms involved in this particular form of language perception and its functional relationships to other forms of language perception. Dominic Massaro's chapter is concerned with understanding the mechanisms underlying the integration of information from different sources. He studies how various (logically) independent sources of information are combined when offered simultaneously. For instance, how are lip-read speech and heard speech integrated? Massaro offers a formalized model that accounts for the observed integration procedures and their products in terms of a mechanism that first continuously integrates the evidence from the independent information sources before it then categorizes the combined product as a particular phoneme. Moreover, he shows convincingly that the same model can also be applied to more complex levels of language processing (as well as to the processing of non-linguistic materials).

Clearly, the integration of information from different sources that are incommensurable by their nature, implies that these sources must somehow be coded in a common 'language' in which the information from the disparate sources becomes commensurable and serves as joint evidence for one or the other pre-established category.

LANGUAGE PERCEPTION AND PRODUCTION
ISBN 0-12-052750-2

In Ruth Campbell's contribution, the claim for commonalities between lip-reading and other forms of language perception is even stronger since she invokes a shared mechanism, rather than just a common language, for the coding of information from different sources. Starting from the well-established recency-effect in the serial recall of lip-read lists, she first presents evidence to show that lip-reading and silent articulation (mouthing) may not depend completely on a common coding system, as a strong theory of common coding of speech perception and production would claim. On the other hand, she then demonstrates a similar recency effect for pseudo-homophones of numbers (which is much weaker than for lip-read material, but stronger than for orthographically correct number words). On the basis of this and other evidence she argues that the underlying mechanism could be a shared coding system that translates various forms of linguistic inputs into a common abstract phonological (and still strictly pre-lexical) code. This common code can be accessed by heard, by lip-read, and, under conditions where sublexical phonological assembly is required, also by written input information.

6 Integrating multiple sources of information in listening and reading

Dominic W. Massaro

Abstract

Reading and listening are viewed as having analogous stages of language processing. In both domains, there are multiple sources of information supporting the identification and interpretation of the language input. The results from a wide variety of experiments are described within the framework of a fuzzy logical model. The assumptions central to the model are (1) each source of information is evaluated to give the degree to which that source specifies various alternatives, (2) the sources of information are evaluated independently of one another, (3) the sources are integrated to provide an overall degree of support for each alternative, and (4) perceptual identification and interpretation follows the relative degree of support among the alternatives. A formalization of these assumptions is applied to results of experiments studying (1) speech perception by ear and eye, (2) audible features in listening, (3) visible features in reading, (4) orthographic context in reading, (5) phonological context in listening, (6) lexical context, and (7) syntactic and semantic context. The adequate description of the results by the model indicates that the sources of support provide continuous rather than categorical information. The integration of the multiple sources results in the least ambiguous sources having the most impact on processing. The interpretation of these results provides major constraints to be met by potential theories of language processing.

Introduction

This paper focusses on the domains of reading and listening with regard to the question of common processes. Before beginning, it is necessary to distinguish between alternative meanings of common processes and the

LANGUAGE PERCEPTION AND PRODUCTION
ISBN 0-12-052750-2

meaning intended here. At a fundamental level common processes could imply identical processes or analogous processes. No one would make the claim that there are identical processes in speech perception and reading, certainly with regard to early stages of processing of the input. With regard to early stages then one can at most expect to uncover analogous processes in the two domains whereas identical processes may be functional at later stages of information processing. Thus, for example, we might look for analogous processes in processing segmental information in the sense that auditory segments of speech and visual segments of writing must be processed by the appropriate perceptual systems (Massaro, 1975a, 1975b). Given that speech and writing represent the same language, however, identical processes may begin to play a role once the more concrete characteristics of the language input are resolved. If it turns out that we have a single lexicon functional across these two domains, we can expect that phrase and sentence interpretation will behave similarly. Thus it is primarily an empirical question regarding first whether there are analogous processes functional in the early stages of information processing in listening and reading and secondly at what stages of processing do identical processes handle the comprehension of spoken and written messages.

Many processing domains can be viewed as providing multiple sources of information for appropriate perception and action. These domains include the visual perception of a three-dimensional world, the recognition of objects and concepts, and social judgement of people and actions. The goal of the present chapter is to consider evidence for the idea that a fundamental property of speech perception and reading is also the availability of multiple sources of information. Sources of information are defined as the features or attributes of the environment that are utilized in perception and action (Massaro, in press a d). The belief is that there are multiple sources of information available in language and a fundamental process is the evaluation and integration of these sources. Following the idea of analogous rather than common processes, we can expect that the sources of information available in the two domains will differ to a considerable degree. Some top-down sources might be similar, however, in the sense that they are common to both speech perception and reading. However, there can be no argument with the idea that the fundamental bottom-up sources of support in the two domains must be different. The question of interest with respect to the idea of analogous processes is whether the same procedures govern the evaluation and integration of the multiple sources across the two domains. This distinction might be considered in light of Fodor's (1983) concept of modularity. Even if we have different modules for reading and listening, these modules might share or have analogous processes.

Perhaps it is a truism that multiple sources of information are available to the language perceiver and yet few studies actually have addressed the important implications of this observation. These include the number and nature of the sources, how each source is processed, how the multiple sources are selected or integrated, and the nature of categorization resulting from these processes. I will first illustrate the approach I have taken to the integration issue by discussing audible and visible contributions to speech perception. The same approach will be extended to account for the range of domains involving language processing given multiple sources of information.

Although the visible mouth movements of the speaker are potentially informative and although perceivers have been shown to utilize some of this information given no or degraded auditory input, only within the last decade was it demonstrated that watching a speaker actually influences what the perceiver hears (McGurk and MacDonald, 1976). This phenomenon offers a potentially valuable paradigm for addressing the issues revolving around the conceptualization of multiple sources of information supporting language understanding. One reason is that it is easy to manipulate the audible and visible sources independently of one another. A second reason is the naturalness of the identification task given either just auditory or just visual or both sources of information. The goal of the experiment reported here is to demonstrate conclusively that the two sources are integrated in speech perception and to uncover the nature of the processes involved. Bimodal speech events were created by the combination of synthetic speech sounds along an auditory /ba/ to /da/ continuum paired with /ba/ or /da/ visual articulations. The single auditory and single visual cue conditions also were included. The analysis of the experiment provides a framework for conceptualizing this study and the description of more general problems in reading and listening. This framework will be applied to a variety of domains involving a comprehensive range of sources of information in language processing.

Integrating audible and visible speech

Method

Eight college students participated for one hour in the experiment. All test stimuli were recorded on color videotape, following the procedure of Massaro and Cohen (1983c). On each trial, a male speaker articulated /ba/, /da/, or nothing. The original audio track was replaced with synthetic speech consisting of a nine-step /ba/ to /da/ auditory continuum. Nine levels along the auditory /ba/ to /da/ continuum were factorially combined with two possible visual articulations, /ba/ and /da/. These 18 trials represent the bimodal condition. There were also auditory-alone and visual-alone conditions. In the auditory-alone condition one of the nine auditory stimuli was presented, but the speaker did not move his mouth. In the visual-alone condition the speaker's mouth articulated either /ba/ or /da/, but no auditory speech was presented. In every block of 54 trials, there were 18 bimodal conditions, 18 auditory-alone conditions, and 18 visual-alone conditions. Each subject was tested for a total 594 experimental trials.

Subjects were instructed to watch the speaker on the TV monitor and to listen to a possible speech sound coming from the TV. They were told of the three different kinds of trials: the bimodal trials, the auditory-alone trials, and the visual-alone trials. Subjects were asked to identify the speech event as one of eight alternatives by pressing one of eight buttons on the keyboard in front of them. The eight buttons corresponded to the alternatives /ba/, /da/, /bda/, /dba/, /ga/, /va/, /tha/, and 'other'. These alternatives were determined on the basis of pilot work and a previous experiment (Massaro and Cohen, 1983c). Subjects were instructed to use the identification category 'other' when none of the other seven response alternatives was appropriate. Subjects were told that although they might not be sure about what the speaker said, they should simply make the best decision that they could. Each trial was preceded by an auditory warning stimulus with a response interval of 2.75 s. Each subject was seated and viewed a 12 in color monitor, which presented both the video and audio. The subjects sat about two to three feet away from the TV with the loudness level of the speech at a comfortable listening level (70 dB-A).

Results

Figure 1 presents the observed proportion of each of the eight responses for the 29 unique speech events. Three separate analyses of variance were carried out across the three conditions. In all three analyses, the variables of interest were statistically significant. Subjects' judgements, as indicated by the proportion of responses, were influenced by the both visual and the auditory information. The interaction of the visual and auditory information with response was also significant in the bimodal condition.

The single modality conditions establish the contribution of both audible and visible sources, but it is more involved to determine that both sources simultaneously contribute to bimodal speech perception. Significant effects of both variables would occur if some subjects used one modality and other subjects used the other modality, or if a given subject used one modality on some trials and the other modality on other trials. On the other hand, the

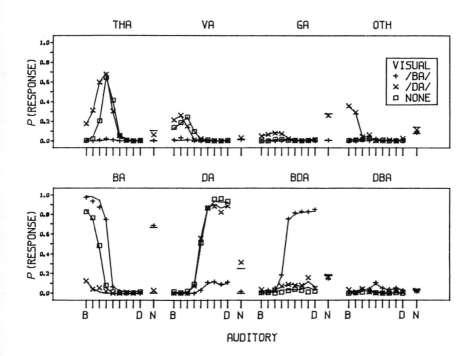

Figure 1. Observed (points) and predicted (lines) proportion of identifications for the eight response alternatives as a function of the auditory and visual dimensions for the auditory, visual, and bimodal syllables. The *x* abscissa gives the 9 levels along the auditory /ba/ to /da/ continuum and the N condition in which no auditory syllable was presented. The parameter of the graph gives whether the visual syllable was /ba/, /da/, or was not presented. The predictions are for the fuzzy-logical model of perception.

simultaneous contribution (integration) of both modalities can be established if the bimodal judgements can not be explained by a given subject using just a single dimension on each trial. Consider the three circled points in the right panel of Figure 2 for a typical subject. A visual /ba/ presented alone is identified as /ba/ about 90% of the time. The speech sound at the /ba/ end of the auditory continuum is heard as /ba/ about 82% of the time when presented alone. However, the same speech sound at the /ba/ end of the auditory continuum paired with a visual /ba/ is identified as /ba/ 100% of the time. Similar results exist for the other subjects as can be seen from the group results in the left panel of Figure 2. Thus, the visual

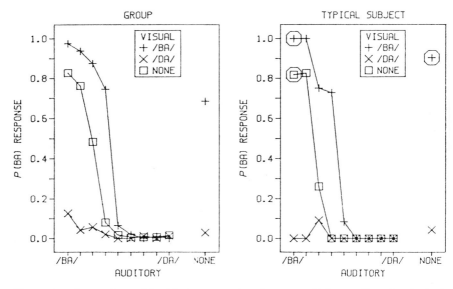

Figure 2. Proportion of /ba/ judgements for the group (left panel) and a typical subject (right panel) to the auditory, visual and bimodal speech events.

/ba/ contributes to the /ba/-ness of a syllable with an auditory /ba/ more than can be predicted by nonintegration.

The results of the experiment with open-ended response alternatives provide strong evidence for a true integration of the auditory and visual sources. In addition, the judgements given conflicting sources of information reveal a smart perceptual process. Given a visual /ba/ and an auditory /da/, subjects often reported /bda/. In contrast, a visual /da/ paired with an auditory /ba/ seldom produced /dba/ judgements. To explain the /bda/ judgements, the auditory and visual components must have been processed to a fairly deep level relatively independently of one another (i.e., without crosstalk). The process must also involve some assessment of the auditory and visual sources in terms of their compatibility with candidate categories. The alternative /bda/ given visual /ba/ and auditory /da/ is reasonable whereas the alternative /dba/ given visual /da/ and auditory /ba/ is not. A visual /ba/ is similar to a visual /bda/ whereas a visual /da/ is not at all similar to a visual /dba/. Thus, what seems as an unintuitive result makes good sense when we consider how well the two dimensions fit potential identification categories.

What model best describes the complex pattern of results? Two general classes of models can be contrasted on the basis of how the auditory and visual sources of information are evaluated and integrated in perceptual recognition. Before addressing this question, it is important to claim that the identification judgements represent direct indices of the perceptual experience of the speech event, not simply some *post hoc* judgement. Supporting evidence for this claim has been found using continuous rating judgements and reaction times (Massaro, in press b c d). One class of models assumes that the auditory and visual sources of information are categorized before integration, whereas the contrasting class assumes that categorization does not occur until integration is complete. These classes have been called categorical and continuous, respectively (Massaro, in press a b c; Massaro and Cohen, 1983 a b c). To test the alternatives against the present results, the categorical model formalized by Massaro and Cohen (1983c) was contrasted with a continuous model called a fuzzy logical model of perception (Oden and Massaro, 1978). It is reasonable to contrast these two models since there is no other testable categorical model in the literature and the fuzzy logical model has not yet been tested against an expanded factorial design with open-ended response alternatives. Furthermore, the two models require a similar number of free parameters to describe the results. Because of space limitations, the reader is referred to the other published descriptions of the models for their details (Massaro, in press a b c d; Massaro and Cohen, 1983 a b c).

The two models were fit to the results of each of the individual subjects using the program STEPIT (Chandler, 1969). The predictions of a model are determined by finding those parameter values that optimize the description of the results. Figure 1 gives the average predicted results for the fuzzy logical model. The root mean squared deviation (RMSD) between the predicted and observed values varied between 0.022 and 0.041 across the eight subjects with an average value of 0.030. This good description is very impressive since it is predicting an essentially open ended set of response alternatives with identical information for the unimodal and bimodal speech stimuli. Figure 3 gives the average predictions for the categorical model. The RMSD varied between 0.124 and 0.173 with an average value of 0.148. The results of each of the eight subjects were better described by the fuzzy logical model than the categorical model.

The evaluation and integration of multiple sources of information is proposed to be central in language processing, as it was in speech perception by ear and eye. The second section of the paper reviews a variety of domains in listening and reading supporting this proposal. In all cases, the fuzzy logical model provides a good description of the results whereas the categorical model would fail miserably. Given the constraints of the present chapter and the large number of different domains, the details of the experiments and the model fits can not be described fully. In many cases, however, this information is available in the literature. The goal of the

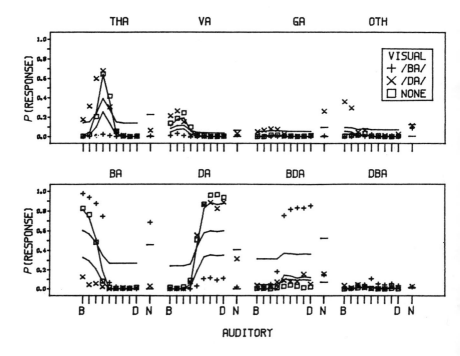

Figure 3. Observed (points) and predicted (lines) proportion of identifications for the eight response alternatives as a function of the auditory and visual dimensions for the auditory, visual, and bimodal syllables. The x abscissa gives the nine levels along the auditory /ba/ to /da/ continuum and the N condition in which no auditory syllable was presented. The parameter of the graph gives whether the visual syllable was /ba/, /da/, or was not presented. The predictions are for the categorical model of perception.

present summary is to highlight the generality of the principle of the important role of evaluating and integrating multiple and continuous sources of information in language processing.

Integrating audible features

One argument for the integration of multiple sources of auditory information in speech perception comes from the discovery of many different cues or features that contribute to the discriminable contrasts found in speech.

The perceived distinction between voiced and voiceless stop consonants in medial position such as /aga/ and /aka/ can be influenced by the preceding vowel duration, the silent closure interval, the voice-onset time, and the onset frequency of the fundamental (Massaro and Cohen, 1983b; Port and Dalby, 1982). The fuzzy logical model has survived tests across a wide variety of speech contrasts and acoustic features (Massaro, (1979b, 1984b, in press a; Massaro and Cohen, 1976; Massaro, Cohen and Tseng, 1985; Massaro and Oden, 1980 a b).

Integrating visual features

The study of letter recognition in reading has a different tradition from the study of speech recognition. Few studies have actually manipulated the signal in systematic ways and observed the consequences for recognition (Naus and Shillman, 1976). Oden (1979) was the first to use a factorial design to independently manipulate two characteristics of a letter. Rating judgements of these test items were well described by the fuzzy logical model. Consider a recent experiment carried out by Massaro and Hary

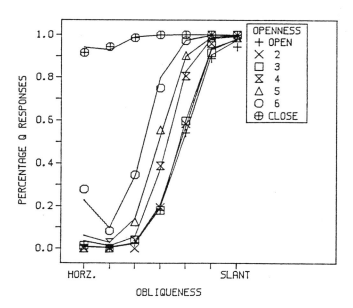

Figure 4. Observed (points) and predicted (lines) percentage of Q identifications as a function of the openness of the gap in the oval and the obliqueness of the straight line (from Massaro and Hary, submitted).

(in press). The uppercase letters Q and G served as test alternatives of two features varying in terms of the amount of gap on the right of the oval and the angle of the straight line. On each trial, the subject viewed a short presentation of one of the letters and indicated whether a G or a Q was presented. Figure 4 gives the proportion of Q responses as a function of the amount of gap in the oval and the angle of the straight line. Both variables influenced the judgements in the expected direction and the significant interaction between the two variables also reflect the larger contribution of one feature when the other feature is more ambiguous. The lines represent the predictions of the fuzzy logical model, which gave a good description of the results, the RMSD varied between 0.028 and 0.097 across the nine subjects and averaged 0.049.

Integrating orthographic context in letter recognition

It is well known that the orthographic (spelling) context of a letter influences its recognition. In the present framework, higher-order constraints operate independently of featural information about the letters. That is, featural analyses of letters are not modified by higher-order constraints. According to this view, the feature evaluation process makes available the same information independently of the higher-order constraints that are present.

It is possible to gradually transform the lowercase letter c into an e by extending the horizontal bar. To the extent the bar is long, there is good visual information for an e and poor visual information for a c. Now consider the letter presented as the first letter in the context -oin and the context -dit. Only c is orthographically admissible in the first context since the three consecutive vowels eoi violate English orthography. Only e is admissible in the second context since the initial cluster cd is an inadmissible English pattern. In this case, the context -oin favors c, whereas the context -dit favors e. The context -tsa and -ast can be considered to favor neither e or c. The first remains an inadmissible context whether e or c is present, and the second is orthographically admissible for both e and c.

The experiment factorially combined six levels of visual information with these four levels of orthographic context (Massaro, 1979a). The test string was presented for a short duration followed after one of four intervals by a masking stimulus composed of random letter features. The test letter also was presented at each of the four letter positions in each of the four contexts. The subject was asked to indicate whether an e or c was present in the test display. Subjects were instructed to make the best choice on the basis of what they saw.

Figure 5 gives the observed interaction of bar length and orthographic context across the four masking intervals, along with the predictions of the fuzzy logical model. The probability of an *e* response increased with increases in the bar length of the critical letter. The results also show a gradual resolution of the critical letter with increases in processing time before onset of the mask since the curves across bar length are steeper with longer masking intervals. An *e* identification was more probable for the context in which *e* but not *c* was orthographically admissible than for the context in which *c* but not *e* was admissible. The neutral contexts were intermediate. This context effect was larger at the more ambiguous levels of the bar length of the test letter. Context also had a larger impact on identification of the test letter at the extremes of the visual continuum to the extent the masking interval was short. These results are consistent with

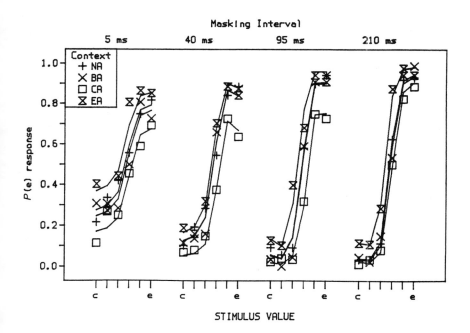

Figure 5. Observed (points) and predicted (lines) probability of an e identification response as a function of the bar length of the test letter (stimulus value), the orthographic context, and the masking interval before the onset of the mask. The context NA = neither *e* nor *c* admissible, BA = both admissible, CA = *c* admissible, and EA = *e* admissible (results from Massaro, 1979b).

the general premise that the contribution of context is larger with ambiguous relative to unambiguous bottom-up sources of information. The fuzzy logical model gave a good description of the average results with an RMSD of 0.039.

Integrating phonological context in syllable recognition

Massaro and Cohen (1983d) assessed how the information from the acoustic signal is combined or integrated with information from phonological constraints in English. Phonological constraints refer to the fact that languages are redundant in terms of the possible sequences of speech sounds. Listeners were asked to identify sounds along a continuum between /li/ and /ri/, which was made by varying the starting frequency of the third formant (F3) transition. These sounds were placed after each of four initial consonants: /t/, /s/, /p/, and /v/. When the sounds are placed after the initial consonant /s/, for example, /l/ is phonologically admissible in English, but /r/ is not. If phonological constraints influence perception, listeners should tend to hear /l/ following the sound /s/. Figure 6 gives the

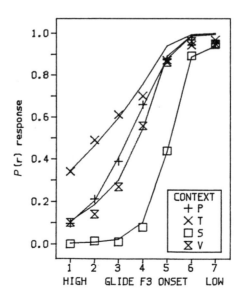

Figure 6. Observed (points) and predicted (lines) probability of an /r/ identification as a function of the F3 transition onset during the glide; the initial consonant is the curve parameter (from Massaro and Cohen, 1983d).

probability of /r/ identifications as a function of both F3 of the liquid and the initial consonant. As expected, the proportion of /r/ identifications increased with decreases in the starting value of F3 of the liquid. More importantly, an /r/ identification was more likely in the context of /t/ than in the context of /p/ or /v/ and least likely in the context of /s/. The effects of the initial context consonant were largest at the more ambiguous values of the liquid. The current model provides a good description of the results, the RMSD varying between 0.025 and 0.116 across the seven subjects and with an average RMSD of 0.055.

Integrating lexical information

Lexical constraints also might be expected to influence processing of written and spoken language. Ganong (1980) assessed the contribution of lexical context to the perception of stop consonants. The voice-onset time of an initial stop consonant was varied to create a continuum from a voiced to voiceless sound. The following context was varied so that either the voice or the voiceless stop would make a word. For example, subjects identified the initial stop as /d/ or /t/ with the following context *ash* (where /d/ makes a word and /t/ does not). Voiced (/d/) responses were more frequent when /d/ made a word than when /t/ made a word. The contribution of lexical context was largest at the more ambiguous levels of voice-onset time. These results have been described quantitatively by the fuzzy logical model with the standard assumption that acoustic featural information and lexical context make independent contributions to perceptual recognition (Massaro and Oden, 1980b).

Integrating sentential context in visible word recognition

One of the original studies of the combination of sentential context and stimulus information in word recognition were performed by Tulving, Mandler and Baumal (1964). Eight exposure durations were factorially combined with four sentential context lengths in a word recognition task. A tachistoscopic presentation of a test word followed the reading of the sentence context. Performance improved with increases in word duration and with sentential context. The outcome shows a larger contribution of sentential context when the exposure duration is intermediate and performance is neither very poor or very good. This result indicates that context is most effective when subjects have some but not relatively complete featural information about the test word. The fuzzy logical model provides a reasonably good description of the results, with a RMSD of 0.021 (Massaro, 1984a).

Integrating sentential context in audible word recognition

Analogous to the question of the utilization of context effects in reading, we can ask whether there is a similar contribution of sentential context in listening. A positive answer has been repeatedly found since Miller, Heise and Lichten's (1951) seminal study, but little quantitative work has been aimed at assessing how sentential context is integrated with the sensory information. In the present framework, sentential context provides an independent source of information made available to the word recognition process in perceiving continuous speech (Massaro, 1979b, 1984a, b; Massaro and Oden, 1980b).

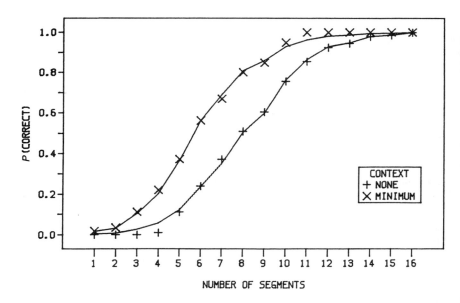

Figure 7. Observed (points) and predicted (lines) probability of identifying the test word correctly as a function of the nature of the sentential context and the number of segments of the test word. The Minimum context refers to minimum semantic and weak syntactic constraints. The None context refers to no semantic and weak syntactic constraints (after Tyler and Wessels, 1983).

Tyler and Wessels (1983) used the gating paradigm to assess the contribution of various forms of sentential context to word recognition. Subjects heard a sentence followed by the beginning of the test word (with the rest of the word gated out). The word was increased in duration by adding small segments of the word until correct recognition was achieved. The sentence contexts varied in syntactic and semantic constraints. Some sentence contexts had minimal semantic constraints in that the target word was not predictable in a cloze test given the sentence context and the first 100 ms of the target word. A positive effect of sentence context in this situation would be very impressive since it would illustrate a true integration of top-down and bottom-up information. That is, neither the context nor limited stimulus information would lead to word recognition, but when presented jointly word recognition is very good. Although the authors failed to report the actual proportion of times the target word could be guessed from the context presented alone, we can assume it was close to zero. Thus, the strong effect of minimum semantic context illustrated in Figure 7 can be considered to reflect true integration of top-down and bottom-up sources of information. Figure 7 also gives the predictions of the fuzzy logical model. The model captures the exact form of the integration of the two sources of information with a RMSD of 0.015.

Integrating syntactic, semantic and prosodic information in sentence interpretation

In the tasks described to this point, the language user had to perceive various surface forms such as identity of a particular word. The language user also faces the challenge of interpreting these surface forms in many instances (Oden, 1977). Presented with the statement, *the horse the bucket kicked*, it is necessary to determine whether the horse or the bucket did the kicking. Analogous to the description of determining the identity of spoken or written forms, the determination of interpretations should result from the evaluation and integration of multiple sources of information. These sources include syntactic variables such as word order, semantic variables such as animation, and prosodic information such as stress.

In the MacWhinney, Bates and Kliegl (1984) task, subjects are asked to interpret three-word phrases in terms of 'which one of the two nouns in the sentence is (the subject of the sentence), that is, (the one who does the action).' Thus, the task of the subject is to choose between the two noun alternatives based on the semantic/syntactic cues available. The authors manipulated word order, animacy, noun-verb agreement and stress in a factorial design. There were three possible word orders of the two nouns

(N) and verb (V) (NVN, NNV, and VNN); three levels of animacy (both nouns animate, the first noun animate and the second inanimate, and the first noun inanimate and the second animate); the verb would agree in number with the first noun, with both nouns, or with the second noun of the sentence; and three levels of stress (no stress, stress on first noun, and stress on second noun). Thus, there were 81 possible sentences and each subject judged each type of sentence only once. The dependent measure is the proportion of subjects choosing the first noun as subject/agent for each sentence type.

The application of the current model is relatively straightforward. Four independent sources of information are assumed to influence the choice between the first and the second noun as the subject or agent. These two

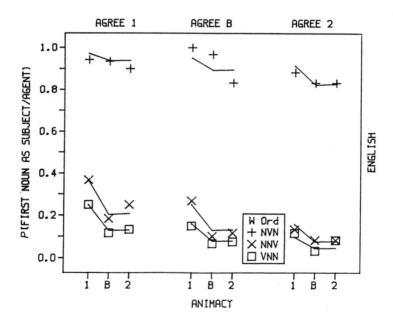

Figure 8. Observed (points) and predicted (lines) probability of identifying the first noun as subject/agent as a function of the animacy of the two nouns, (1 = first noun animate, 2 = both nouns animate, 2 = second noun animate) the word order, and the noun–verb agreement (Agree 1 = first noun and verb agree in number, Agree B = both nouns and verb agree in number, Agree 2 = second noun agrees in number) for the English listeners (after MacWhinney *et al.*, 1984).

interpretations can be defined as a function of the four sources. The second noun can be viewed as the subject or agent to the extent each of four sources are inappropriate for the first noun being subject or agent. Twelve free parameters are necessary to predict the 81 data points corresponding to the 81 unique sentence types.

Two forms of the model were fit to the results for the English subjects. In the first, four sources were assumed, whereas the second assumed no contribution of stress. The RMSD values were 0.044 and 0.046, respectively, showing that stress as manipulated in the study had very little, if any, cue value. This result is relevant to our definition of source of information. As manipulated in the MacWhinney *et al.* (1984) task, it can be concluded that stress does *not* function as a source of information in sentence interpretation for English listeners. Figure 8 gives the observed and predicted results for the 27 sentence types pooled over stress. The English subjects were influenced mostly by word order, but also by animacy and noun-verb agreement. These three variables can be considered to function as sources of information in sentence interpretation.

Concluding statement

The fuzzy logical model of information integration describes the results in a wide variety of domains of language processing, perhaps all of the domains studied to date. The general approach not only offers a theoretical framework, it provides an empirical technique for assessing potential sources of information supporting language processing. A remaining challenge for the present approach is whether similar processes might be functional in speaking and writing. Rather than evaluating and integrating multiple sources of information to achieve perceptual recognition or interpretation, the production of language involves conveying a message via multiple sources of information. To what extent analogous processes are functional across perception and production remains an unanswered question.

Acknowledgement

The writing of this paper and the author's research reported in the paper were supported, in part, by NINCDS Grant 20314 from the Public Health Service and Grant BNS-83-15192 from the National Science Foundation. The author gratefully acknowledges Brian MacWhinney for providing the results of their experiments.

References

Chandler, J. P. (1969). Subroutine STEPIT — Finds local minima of a smooth function of several parameters. *Behavioral Science*, **14**, 81–2.

Fodor, J. A. (1983). *Modularity of Mind*. Cambridge, MA: Bradford Books.

Ganong, W. F. III. (1980). Phonetic categorization in auditory word recognition. *Journal of Experimental Psychology: Human Perception and Performance*, **6**, 110–25.

MacWhinney, B., Bates, E., and Kliegl, R. (1984). Cue validity and sentence interpretation in English, German, and Italian. *Journal of Verbal Learning and Verbal Behavior*, **23**, 127–50.

Massaro, D. W. (1975a). *Experimental Psychology and Information Processing*. Chicago, IL: Rand-McNally.

Massaro, D. W. (Ed.) (1975b). *Understanding Language: An Information Processing Analysis of Speech Perception, Reading, and Psycholinguistics*. New York: Academic Press.

Massaro, D. W. (1979a). Letter information and orthographic context in word perception. *Journal of Experimental Psychology: Human Perception and Performance*, **5**, 595–609.

Massaro, D. W. (1979b). Reading and listening (Tutorial paper). In P. A. Kolers, M. Wrolstad, and H. Bouma (Eds) *Processing of Visible Language*, Vol 1. New York: Plenum, pp. 331–54.

Massaro, D. W. (1984a). Building and testing models of reading processes. In P. D. Pearson (Ed.) *Handbook of Reading Research*. New York: Longman, pp. 111–46.

Massaro, D. W. (1984b). Time's role for information, processing, and normalization. *Annals of the New York Academy of Sciences, Timing and Time Perception*, **423**, 372–84.

Massaro, D. W. (in press a). A fuzzy logical model of speech perception. In W. A. Lea (Ed.) *Towards Robustness in Speech Recognition*. Apple Valley, MN: Speech Science Publications.

Massaro, C. W. (in press b). Categorical partition: A fuzzy logical model of categorization behavior. In S. Harnad (Ed.) *Categorical Perception*, New York.

Massaro, D. W. (in press c). Information-processing theory and strong inference: A paradigm for psychological inquiry. In H. Heuer and A. F. Sanders (Eds) *Perspectives on Perception and Action*. Hillsdale, NJ: Erlbaum.

Massaro, D. W. (in press d). Speech perception by ear and eye. In B. Dodd and R. Campbell (Eds) *Hearing by Eye: Experimental studies in the psychology of lipreading*. Hillsdale, NJ: Erlbaum.

Massaro, D. W., and Cohen, M. M. (1976). The contribution of fundamental frequency and voice onset time to the /zi/-/si/ distinction. *Journal of the Acoustical Society of America*, **60**, 704–17.

Massaro, D. W., and Cohen, M. M. (1983a). Categorical or continuous speech perception: A new test, *Speech Communication*, **2**, 15–35.

Massaro, D. W., and Cohen, M. M. (1983b). Consonant-vowel ratio: An improbable cue in speech. *Perception and Psychophysics*, **33**, 501–5.

Massaro, D. W., and Cohen, M. M. (1983c). Evaluation and integration of visual and auditory information in speech perception. *Journal of Experimental Psychology: Human Perception and Performance*, **9**, 753–71.

Massaro, D. W. and Cohen, M. M. (1983d). Phonological context in speech perception. *Perception and Psychophysics*, **34**, 338–48.

Massaro, D. W., Cohen, M. M., and Tseng, C-Y. (1985). The evaluation and integration of pitch height and pitch contour in lexical tone perception in Mandarin Chinese. *Journal of Chinese Linguistics*, **13**, 267–89.

Massaro, D. W., and Hary, J. M. (in press). Addressing issues in letter recognition. Psychological Research.

Massaro, D. W., and Oden, G. C. (1980a). Evaluation and integration of acoustic features in speech perception. *Journal of the Acoustical Society of America*, **67**, 996–1013.

Massaro, D. W., and Oden, G. C. (1980b). Speech perception: A framework for research and theory. In N. J. Lass (Ed.) *Speech and Language: Advances in Basic Research and Practice*. Vol 3, New York: Academic Press, pp. 129–65.

McGurk, H., and MacDonald (1976). Hearing lips and seeing voices. *Nature*, **264**, 746–8.

Miller, G. A., Heise, G. A., and Lichten, W. (1951). The intelligibility of speech as a function of the context of the test materials. *Journal of Experimental Psychology*, **41**, 329–35.

Naus, M. J., and Shillman, R. J. (1976). Why a Y is not a V: A new look at the distinctive features of letters. *Journal of Experimental Psychology: Human Perception and Performance*, **2**, 394–400.

Oden, G. C. (1977). Integration of fuzzy logical information. *Journal of Experimental Psychology: Human Perception and Performance*, **3**, 565–75.

Oden, G. C. (1979). A fuzzy logical model of letter identification. *Journal of Experimental Psychology: Human Perception and Performance*. **5**, 336–52.

Oden, G. C., and Massaro, D. W. (1978). Integration of featural formation in speech perception. *Psychological Review*, **85**, 172–91.

Port, R. F., and Dalby, J. (1982). Consonant/vowel ratio as a cue for voicing in English. *Perception and Psychophysics*, **32**, 141–52.

Tulving, E., Mandler, G., and Baumal, R. (1964). Interactions of two sources of infirmation in tachistoscopic word recognition. *Canadian Journal of Psychology*, **18**, 62–71.

Tyler, L. K., and Wessels, J. (1983). Quantifying contextual contributions to word-recognition processes. *Perception and Psychophysics*, **34**, 409–20.

7   Common processes in immediate memory: Precategorical acoustic storage and some of its problems

Ruth Campbell

Abstract

Three aspects of a revised PAS theory (Crowder, 1983) are tested and found wanting. The assumption that lipread and silently articulated speech gestures map onto a common precategorical speech representation in immediate recall is weakened, because a mouthed suffix, unlike an auditory one, does not completely eliminate lipread recency. The system that gives rise to auditory recency and suffix effects (and those for lipreading and silent mouthing) is accessed (albeit weakly) by pseudo-homophones of number words: this vitiates the claim that only directly speech-related events such as lipreading, mouthing and listening can give rise to such effects. A young woman with perfect auditory speech comprehension and production fails to show auditory recency and suffix effects in immediate recall. This weakens claims that auditory registration must drive the PAS system automatically. Together, these results suggest that, far from having a necessary, auditory-derived sensory source, auditory recency and suffix effects in immediate serial recall reflect, in large part, activation of a linguistically more abstract system. This system, while still strictly pre-lexical, is yet relatively insensitive to modality of input, being accessed, variously, by heard, lipread, mouthed and written material that demands phonological assembly, and by combinations of these inputs.It could be equivalent to the phonological input buffer proposed by Monsell (Chap 14).

Introduction

In the immediate serial recall of heard lists there is a strong recency effect that is not apparent when written lists are recalled in order. This is the

LANGUAGE PERCEPTION AND PRODUCTION
ISBN 0-12-052750-2

modality specific recency effect. An elegant theory for this robust phenomenon was offered by Crowder and Morton (1969) who suggested that the
extra information that could be extracted from just-heard lists came from a
pre-categorical acoustic store (PAS). The essential qualities of PAS were
that its nature was essentially and deeply auditory/acoustic; that it would
be automatically activated by any acoustic speech event and that any
recently registered item in such storage would persist long enough to be
useful at some stage in recall. PAS reflected 'echoic' memory. For written
material, by contrast, no such persistent, precategorical trace existed; the
'icon', in the terms of those times, was of high capacity but extremely
limited duration.

The principle of automatic activation was supported by demonstrations
that an aftercoming auditory speech event, a suffix, interfered with auditory recency to the extent that the suffix shared auditory, rather than
lexical or semantic, qualities with the to-be-remembered list. There
appeared to be a gradient of such effects; the greater the auditory similarity
between list and suffix, the greater the diminution of auditory recency.
Thus, a suffix spoken in the same voice as a list has a more marked effect in
eliminating recency than a different voice suffix (Morton, Crowder and
Prussin, 1971).

The conjoint phenomenon of recency in immediate recall that is specifically eliminated by an auditory suffix is the signature of PAS.

The assumption that such effects could *only* be engendered by heard
lists, that they were truly 'echoic', was overturned when it became clear
that a silent lipread suffix could reduce auditory recency (Spoehr and
Corin, 1978); then it was shown that a lipread list could, itself, generate
recency that was specifically eliminated by an auditory suffix (Campbell
and Dodd, 1980, 1982, 1984; Gathercole, 1987; Greene and Crowder,
1984). Then, written lists, where each item was silently mouthed at presentation, were shown to generate recency, too. This recency was eliminated
by an auditory suffix (Nairne and Crowder, 1982; Nairne and Walters,
1983; Greene and Crowder, 1984). Clearly the necessary auditory-acoustic
base for PAS was eliminated by these data: PAS needed remodelling.
Crowder (1983) presents a remodelled PAS system, here called PAS 2,
which accommodates these new facts without too much difficulty. Its
principal differences from PAS are:

(1) PAS 2 is now conceived as a two-fold, possibly interactive, system in
which heard speech accesses the *grid* subcomponent, seen and mouthed
speech a *gestural* subcomponent. It is the common output from this two-
fold system that is reflected in auditory/lipread/mouthed/recency effects
that are eliminated by an auditory suffix.

(2) PAS can now be accessed by an internal feedback loop: that from written information, *when each item is mouthed at presentation*. The normal, articulatory-based rehearsal of written material does not usually use this loop, otherwise it, too, should show recency.

But is this necessarily the best way to model these effects? In the first place, are mouthing and lipreading really common processes, sharing a single 'box' in any processing system? On this hangs a potentially important distinction. Some theorists hold speech perception to be deeply amodal in the pre-lexical domain: lipread, mouthed, spoken and heard speech share a single common metric (Liberman and Mattingley, 1985). The extent to which this common metric is shared by written language is one of the crucial issues of this volume; the auditory/lipread/mouthed/recency/suffix effects suggest at least one distinction at this level. To the extent that PAS is remodelled by Crowder to accommodate a single mouthing-lipreading subcomponent it appears that Crowder here allies himself with such theorists of speech perception.

For others, however, who have long claimed auditory speech perception delivers a speech percept by computationally complex analysis of heard speech patterns and who already suspected PAS-type effects to occur at this stage of processing rather than more peripheral, sensorily-driven ones (Massaro, 1975), a real distinction may exist between the representation of perceived and produced speech; here, between lipreading and mouthing.

Without committing myself to any theoretical standpoint, our earlier findings suggest that lipreading is not just 'passive silent mouthing' (Crowder, 1983, p. 261). Firstly, saying 'ba-ba-ba. . .' while *lipreading* number lists has no more and no less effect on lipread recall than does saying 'ba-ba-ba. . .' while *listening* to lists and recalling those heard lists. (Campbell and Dodd, 1984; Experiments 1 and 2). If lipreading were 'passive silent mouthing', surely such overt speech actions should cause grave interference with lipreading? Then, in studies on serial recall of lipread lists in deaf children, we find no relation between articulatory fluency and lipread recency (Dodd, Hobson, Brasher and Campbell, 1983).

Of course, these are not direct tests of complete commonality between lipread and mouthed speech and Experiment 1 offers a first step in directly testing the proposal offered by PAS 2; namely that there is a substage of PAS where lipread and mouthed material are fully interactive. If this is so, a silent, lipread list that is followed by a silent mouthed suffix should fail to show recency. Lipread lists show recency that is completely abolished by a heard suffix (see e.g. Campbell and Dodd, 1982; 1984) and can be completely abolished by a lipread suffix, too (Gathercole, 1987). A strong

claim of commonality between mouthed and lipread processing for immediate recall, based on Crowder's PAS 2, must be that a mouthed suffix
should reduce lipread recency to the same extent as does a lipread or a
heard suffix.

Experiment 1: The effects of mouthing a suffix on lipread recall

Fifteen undergraduate subjects of the University of London lipread video-
tapes of seven-digit number lists for immediate, serial written recall.
Following fifteen practice trials, ten lists of each suffix type were seen to be
spoken in random order. The list types were: (1) list with no suffix; (2) list
with lipread suffix; — the word 'go' seen to be spoken; (3) a pure tone
signal to which the subject had been trained to mouth the word 'go' in
rhythm with the list. This last condition was particularly important since
disturbing the rhythm of the list can reduce suffix effects considerably. In a
control experiment, the same videotape was presented to ten subjects from
the same population who are instructed to *hum* the tone rather than mouth
the word 'go' in the tone-suffix condition. This was to ensure that any
effects of a mouthed suffix would be due solely to the mouthing of a speech
suffix and not to the processing of a tone signal and the effort and
production of a non-speech response. In this condition, too, subjects were
trained to hum in rhythm with list presentation.

Mean probability of error, averaged over the number of subjects in the
group, for each serial position, are shown separately for the experimental
and control groups in Figure 1.

Experimental group results

Analysis of individual subject means for each condition for each serial
position (repeated measures, 2-way ANOVA) gave significant F values
for main effects and their interaction. F for suffix type was 17.96 (2,28;
$p < 0.001$); F for serial position was 17.24; interaction F was 3.48 (12,68
$p < 0.001$).

Post hoc tests compared each suffix type against each of the others and
confirmed that the significant interaction held for all three suffix types.
Further *post hoc* tests showed that at serial positions 3, 6 and 7 there was a
significant difference between suffix types.

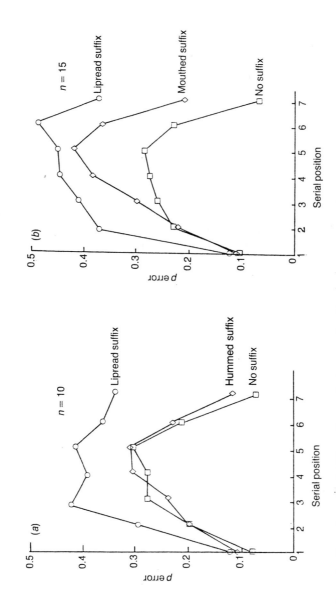

Figure 1. Experiment 1. (a) The effects of a hummed suffix on a lipread list. (b) The effects of mouthed suffix on a lipread list.

Control group results

Two-way, repeated measure ANOVA, with serial position and suffix type (silent, lipread or pure-tone-hummed) as the factors gave a significant effect of serial position ($F = 5.6$; 6,9; $p < 0.01$) and of suffix type ($F = 7.3$; 1,9, $p < 0.01$). The two-way interaction between these main effects was also significant. However, further ANOVAs showed no interaction between the no-suffix and the hummed-suffix condition ($F = 0.73$).

A mouthed suffix and a lipread suffix have effects that are significantly different both from each other and from a silent, no-suffix condition in the recall of a silent, lipread list. The control experiment shows that the effect of a mouthed suffix is not due to the processing of the pure tone in order to produce a non-speech output. Covert articulation of a suffix has an effect on lipread recall.

But this was not the crucial test of Crowder's 'common stage for lipread and mouthed processing' hypothesis. If lipreading and mouthing are aspects of a common system they should both reduce *recency* for lipread lists. One way to examine this, given the main effect of suffix type on recall accuracy, is to normalize list errors by plotting, within each condition, proportionate error for each serial position (and see Crowder, 1983; Nairne and Pusen, 1984, for the same rationale and manipulation).

When this is done (see Figure 2) the effect of a mouthed suffix on lipread recency is seen to be intermediate between that of a heard and a lipread suffix. Planned comparisons bear this out. At position 7 there is a significant difference ($t = 3.8$, $df = 14$, $p < 0.01$) between lipread and mouthed suffix proportionate errors and between no suffix and mouthed suffix proportionate errors ($t = 3.1$, $df = 14$, $p < 0.01$). However, the effect of a mouthed suffix cannot be claimed to be as effective as that of a lipread suffix. While a lipread suffix eliminates recency effectively (planned comparison of positions 6 and 7 gave $t = 0.8$, n.s.), comparison of positions 6 and 7 for the mouthed suffix condition gave $t = 5.8$ ($p < 0.01$). Recency was significantly present for the mouthed suffix, as for the no-suffix, condition.

It should be noted that the critical measure of recency (and of its elimination) in these experiments is to compare recall accuracy for the last with the penultimate item. The best statistical definition of recency is problematic: PAS theory *might* predict a quadratic function reflecting greater improvement of recall for recently heard parts of a heard than a written list. The best test of recency, if this were the case, would be a test of best-fit to the predicted function, rather than a test for sharp improvement in recall accuracy for the very last item. However, no precedent for such analysis has been set and so, since the main purpose of the present paper is

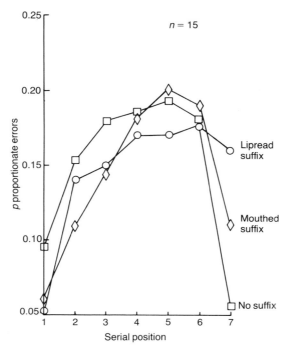

Figure 2.   Experiment 1. Means of normalized errors for the recall of a mouthed suffix on a lipread list.

to place these results in a context where they can be compared with others (Crowder, 1983; Greene and Crowder, 1984; Nairne and Walters, 1983 etc.), it would confuse, rather than clarify, were all data to be re-set into such analyses here.

Overall, this experiment shows that a mouthed suffix, made in rhythm with a lipread list, impairs lipread list recall, and that this impairment is not due to the tone cue or to making an oral (hummed) response to it. Yet the theoretically critical effect of a mouthing on lipread recency is ambiguous. While final item recall for a mouthed-suffix-list is impaired in contrast to final item recall for a list with no suffix, there is still a relative improvement in recall of the last, compared with the penultimate, item of the mouthed-suffix list. A mouthed suffix does not, then, eliminate lipread recency, though it can reduce it somewhat. Two facts are important with respect to this finding. Firstly, through-list effects, like those which the mouthed suffix produces here, seem to reflect attentional/strategic disruption of the memory trace (see Balota and Engle, 1981; and, for lipread lists, Campbell and Dodd, 1982; Gathercole, 1987). Secondly, the partial effect on recency of a mouthed suffix here should be contrasted with the very marked effect of both auditory and lipread suffixes in eliminating lipread recency (Campbell, 1987; Gathercole, 1987).

So, while a mouthed suffix can interfere with lipread recall and can even affect lipread recency a little, a strong theory of full commonality between lipread and mouthed suffix effects is not upheld by the results of this exploratory experiment. Further experiments will show to what extent this tentative rejection of a common substage for lipread and mouthed processing in immediate recall can be made more secure. Meanwhile, it should be noted that in one recent study, Gathercole (1986) finds that mouthed post-list distraction failed to affect the modality-specific recency effect, while spoken post-list distraction eliminated it. End-of-list mouthing (unlike mouthing list items as they are presented) does not appear to interact with audition in affecting the recall of the last item in immediate recall. These first explorations in teasing apart mouthing and lipreading effects suggest they can and should be differentiated. This is not encompassed by PAS 2.

Making written lists 'act auditory' — is mouthing the only way?

Mouthing written numbers as they appear, one at a time, is one way to make written lists 'act auditory' in immediate serial recall (as it can be in word recognition priming; Monsell, 1985; Chap 14). It would seem that this process can force a representation with something in common with the auditory/acoustic form of each number; a representation, which, since it is susceptible to auditory overwriting, satisfies the conditions for PAS processing (Nairne and Walters, 1983). Is there any other way to make this occur? Simply imagining the sounds of the numbers as they appear does not seem to do the trick (Nairne and Pusen, 1984). Crowder (1983) boldly asserts that

'graphemic information . . . would, of course, control categorical selection . . . but it would never contribute to auditory experience in the way that perceived speech gestures would . . .' (p. 260)

It is possible, however, to force readers to assemble the phonology of a number word by presenting it as a pseudo-homophone. While known words' phonology can be accessed by direct lexical means (THREE, FIVE, EIGHT) this cannot happen for unfamiliar forms which can sound like those words (THREA, FYVE, AIT). In order to recall lists of this sort as arabic numerals (3, 5, 8) two operations are necessary; first, a phonological form of the number word must be derived indirectly, by assembling the internal phonology corresponding to the letters in the string; secondly, this assembled representation (that should correspond to the phonology of a heard number word) must be transcoded into Arabic numeral notation.

Could such sub-lexical (a-lexical?) reading, since it requires phonological assembly to be effective, generate auditory-like effects in a serial recall task? That is, could the recall of such lists generate recency that is reduced by an auditory suffix? (Recency alone is an insufficient criterion for PAS; see Campbell, Dodd and Brasher, 1983, for several ways to make visual lists show recency.) If it did, we might have grounds for suspecting that PAS-like effects need not even be limited to direct, speech-related phenomena, but such effects may characterize *any* process that requires the serial assembly of phones to form a representation suitable for immediate, written recall. Normally, written words are not characterized by such processes, but since pseudo-homophones show evidence of such sub-, pre- or a-lexical assembly, this experiment asks whether pseudo-homophones of number words, when recalled as written digits, show recency and, if they do, is this affected by a heard suffix?

Experiment 2: Immediate recall of pseudo-homophone number lists and the effects on such recall of an auditory suffix

In this experiment sixteen undergraduates of the University of London were asked to recall, in strict serial order, using Arabic numeral notation, lists of eight digits which appeared on a VDU screen, one at a time, as lists of single number words (one, two, three, etc.) or as pseudo-homophones (wunn, tooe, threa . . .). The type of list varied unpredictably with each trial. Half of the lists were followed, pseudo-randomly, by an auditory suffix (the spoken word 'go'), heard just one second after last item offset, which subjects were asked to ignore. The suffix was pre-recorded in the voice of the experimenter and dubbed onto the audiotrack of the videotape which was used to present the test lists. The number lists themselves were generated by PET microcomputer which also controlled the time parameters of the display (0.75 s per item; 15 s between lists). The full experimental set of lists comprised forty word lists and forty pseudo-homophone lists. In each list any of the nine digits could be represented. Sampling from the nine numbers was random and without replacement within lists. Twenty lists (ten of each type) were presented with a heard suffix, twenty without. A practice list of ten lists, of each type, with and without auditory suffix preceded the presentation of the experimental list.

ANOVA (3-way, repeated measure) was performed on each subject's mean scores. The main effect of suffix type (absent or present) was not significant ($F = 0.34$); the main effect of list type (number word or pseudo-homophone) was highly significant ($F = 25.8$; 1,15; $p < 0.001$) and so was that of serial position ($F = 6.36$; 7,105; $p < 0.001$).

Also significant were three theoretically important interactions: that of position $\times$ suffix-type ($F = 3.99$; 7,105; $p < 0.001$); of position $\times$ list type ($F = 3.6$; 14,210; $p < 0.001$) and of suffix-type $\times$ list type $\times$ position ($F = 1.98$; 14,210; $p < 0.02$). *Post hoc* tests on this three-way interaction confirm that only on the pseudo-homophone lists did an auditory suffix have an effect confined to the last list item.

Thus the figure shows and the statistics confirm two important findings: (1) pseudo-homophone lists are better recalled than familiar number word lists and (2) pseudo-homophones show some recency that is specifically abolished by an aftercoming, to-be-ignored, spoken 'go'. There is less corresponding recency and no auditory suffix effect on the recall of familiar number words.

Regarding recency, this picture is further clarified when the data are normalized by deriving proportionate error scores for each condition for each serial position. The means of these data, which were derived for each subject, are also shown in Figure 3. Planned comparisons on the crucial recency effects re-iterate the story from the raw data; at position 8 only pseudo-homophones are significantly better recalled than any other list-type (t for pseudo-homophone without suffix versus with suffix was 3.85 ($df = 15$, $p < 0.01$). No other comparisons between conditions at this position reached significance. Comparing positions 7 and 8, pseudo-homophone lists gave $t = 5.6$ ($p < 0.01$), while no other comparisons reached significance except that of number words with suffix ($t = 4.7$). For number word lists, there is, if anything, more recency when an auditory suffix occurs than when it does not.

It appears then, that one way to make written lists 'act auditory' is to present them as pseudo-homophones of number words. Phonological assembly of the number word 'sounds' from the letter string may be sufficient to generate recency that can be eliminated by an auditory suffix. It remains to be established whether the pseudo-homophone decoding processes use the articulatory feedback loop needed for the mouthing of written material or whether other recursive systems, still pre-categorical (the interfering suffix was a speech sound of another semantic class than the to-be-remembered lists) are involved.

However, negative findings must also be pointed out. The recency effect for pseudo-homophone lists is not very marked. Silent pseudo-homophone

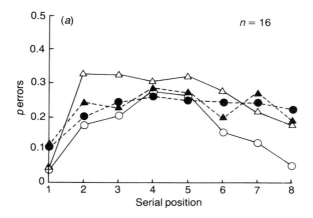

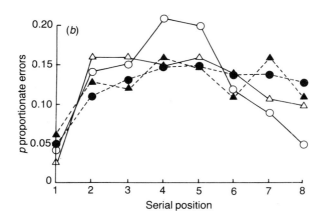

○——○ pseudo-homopone without suffix; ●--● pseudo-homophone with suffix; △——△ number words without suffix; ▲---▲ number words with suffix.

Figure 3. Experiment 2. The effect of an auditory suffix on number word and pseudo-homophone lists. (*a*) Mean raw errors. (*b*) Mean normalized errors

lists do not show very much more recency than silent word lists. *Post hoc* tests on the last serial position (raw scores) for each give $p = 0.06$. An auditory list would be expected to show a more marked effect than that generated by pseudo-homophones. One reason for this small recency may be the predictability of the pseudo-homophone spelling from trial to trial. After some exposure a reader might simply learn that THREA maps onto 3, rather than assemble 'three' from THREA by sub-lexical mapping procedures. If phonological spelling were forced on each trial by unpredictable spellings, the recall of such lists might look even more like that of heard lists.

The finding that pseudo-homophones of numbers are better recalled than are number words was confirmed in control studies with other list types. For instance, pseudo-homophones were better recalled than either familiar word spellings or roman numerals. If this is a robust finding it suggests that accessing the phonology of a word indirectly, rather than by direct lexical access, might give rise to a useful supportive memory code which has effects additive to those normally used in recalling written words. Such a secondary memory code is likely to be phonologically organized. Its precise characteristics await further investigation.

For the present, the important finding is that presenting written word lists as pseudo-homophones of number words generates a little recency in the recall of these numbers; recency which is specifically eliminated by an auditory suffix. Crowder's assertions about the impossibility of graphemic entry to PAS, except through mouthing, may be premature.

Is PAS automatically activated by heard speech?

One of the assumptions of both the classical and the revised versions of PAS is that it should be automatically activated by any auditory speech input. After all, the major piece of evidence for the theory was that an auditory suffix, which the subject is told to ignore, eliminates recency. It would seem to follow, therefore, that if auditory registration of speech sounds is intact, then auditory recency should be observed in serial list recall. If a case can be shown where this is not so, the theory will be weakened.

Such evidence is provided by RE, a university graduate in Psychology who appears to have normal speech input and output processing skills, yet who shows a range of associated problems in tasks concerned with the storage and manipulation of speech sounds (Campbell and Butterworth 1985; Butterworth, Campbell and Howard, 1986; Campbell, in press).

RE showed no developmental disability in acquiring speech; indeed she was advanced in the acquisition of an oral vocabulary. On testing as a young adult, moreover, RE categorized speech sounds normally (phonemic categorization testing) and detected oral mispronunciations with relish and accuracy (i.e. when 'Michael Heseltime' was said, she said 'No, it's Michael Heseltine'). As far as we can tell, her ability to register heard speech is perfect. Her speech output is fast, fluent and accurate. She can repeat rare multisyllabic words (up to 7 syllables) perfectly. However, RE shows a number of deficits on other tasks. In particular, her non-word reading and writing, in contrast to her reading and writing of known words, is very poor, and she has a digit span of 3–4 which is the same backwards and forwards. This span limitation occurs in all aspects of her verbal recall, including names and common nouns.

Of interest here, however, is the shape of her forward recall curve. Since her perception of speech is excellent and since PAS is organized in terms of such sensory features, PAS theory must predict that, however limited in span, RE should show auditory recency and suffix effects.

As Figure 4 shows, RE has no auditory recency in recalling digit lists that are just within span, and an auditory suffix has no effect on her recall.

RE's superior performance on written lists suggests that she uses an (optional?) orthographic recoding strategy in recalling auditory lists and other evidence converged on this conclusion. RE was worse at recalling heard lists with her eyes open than with her eyes shut (she improved from 50% performance on heard simple three-word lists to 80% accuracy). In a matching task where she was asked if two spoken lists sounded the same she affirmed that 'nought, zero, zero, one' and 'zero, zero, zero, one' sounded the same.

We have characterized RE's general debility as one of conscious phonemic awareness and manipulation. This affects other aspects of her recall.

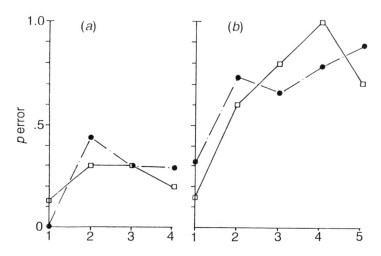

Figure 4. Immediate auditory digit recall in RE; effects of length of list and suffix. (a) four digits. (b) five digits. □———□ auditory lists with suffix; ●━━━● auditory lists without suffix.

She shows no phonemic confuseability effects in the recall of heard or written lists. Thus she recalls lists of rhyming letter names (B, V, T, G, E) as well as she does lists that do not rhyme (M, Z, O, R, F): this is not the case for normal subjects, whose recall of rhyming lists is much poorer than for non-rhyming lists.

It is at least feasible that RE's failure to show auditory recency and suffix effects and her failure to show phonemic confuseability effects in recall reflect one single impairment — an impairment in the activation of a phonologically structured representation which is usually activated by heard material and readily accessed in recall.

If this is so it suggests, quite strongly, that, for normal listener–speakers, the bulk of the auditory recency and suffix effect is not due to the establishment of an accessible sensory trace by auditory material, but rather, if there is automatic activation, it is of the 'Inner Voice' (Nairne and McNabb, 1985; Nairne and Pusen, 1984).

Discussion

Three aspects of PAS 2 have been tested in this paper. The first test suggested that mouthing and lipreading may not necessarily use the same processing substage in immediate recall, since mouthing, unlike hearing or lipreading, fails to eliminate lipread recency. The second test showed that written lists requiring phonological assembly for their recoding show more recency than written number names and that this recency is overwritten by an auditory suffix. Since this process did not use overt mouthing, the PAS 2 system, as presently specified, cannot admit it. The third test showed that, contrary to claims of automatic auditory activation in PAS, the ability to hear speech correctly need not predict auditory recency in immediate list recall.

Now each of these findings, individually, may be amenable to other explanations. It is possible that mouthing, since it reduces lipread recency a little, shares *some* processing with it at this early, precategorical stage. Only a very hard version of the 'shared gestural subcomponent' idea is invalidated by the failure to find full lipread recency elimination by a mouthed suffix. It is possible, moreover (though I think it unlikely) that the failure of a mouthed suffix to eliminate lipread recency was because the mouthed suffix may not always have been 'spoken', or planned to be spoken, in rhythm with the list. Other methodological factors may have diminished what might otherwise have been a more pronounced effect; null, or semi-null effects are always open to such criticisms. But it might well be that lipreading and mouthing are each, and independently, affected by audition. There is certainly an asymmetry of interference effects between audition, lipreading and mouthing: in general, hearing interferes badly with heard, lipread and mouthed list recency, while the effect of a lipread suffix on (say) an auditory list can be less pronounced (see Greene and Crowder, 1984; Gathercole, 1987). The issue of the exact amount of mutual interference between lipreading and mouthing in immediate recall will, however, only be resolved by further experiments; meanwhile, lipread recency is not eliminated by a mouthed suffix, while it is so eliminated by a lipread or by a heard suffix. Full commonality of lipreading and mouthing is, at least, unlikely.

The finding of recency for pseudo-homophone word lists was theoretically straightforward; recency was obtained which was eliminated by an auditory suffix. Yet it was experimentally slight. Recency for pseudo-homophone number words was not nearly as pronounced as that obtained for lipread, heard or mouthed lists. However, my suspicions that it is qualitatively a PAS-type effect are bolstered by a recent and completely independent replication (Crowder, personal communication). Again, only further experimentation will resolve the issue.

RE's idiosyncratic performance in recall, may, of course, be seen as just that: in other words, while PAS describes the normal state of affairs it does not necessarily claim to be universal in its application. But is this a useful counterattack? Surely any model of cognitive process *must* be posed, at least in the first instance, as a universal one, or problems concerning the precise conditions under which a proposed system operates will start to be more important than the process itself. What are we to do with the data provided by patients with cerebral/cognitive impairment, used so cogently in this volume (Howard and Franklin, Coltheart and Funnell; Funnell and Allport) to clarify theories of *normal* cognitive function? No, as a psychological heuristic, at the very least, we must assume that proposed models of cognitive function are universal in their application to people and that data from impaired function — even single cases — can illuminate normal processing. This is particularly important when the single case *disconfirms* received theory. Only one black swan is needed to disconfirm the hypothesis that all swans are white: the hypothesis that most swans are white is not what is under consideration; though it may become the crucial theory in the light of the one black swan.

So where does this three pronged attack on PAS lead us? While each, individual prong may have given PAS a pin-prick, does their combined action do more than scratch its integrity? The three-component (grid, gesture and phonetic feature extraction) development of PAS 2 was proposed in order to accommodate two sets of findings; the first was that phenomena in auditory speech perception may be reflected in immediate memory tasks (grid); the second, that certain classes of visual material (lipread and mouthed material — the gesture component) may access the PAS system. PAS 2 maintains as necessary the distinction between acoustic–auditory grid effects on the one hand and 'gestural' effects on the other. By showing that gestural effects may not be wholly interdependent and that non-gestural material; — written pseudo-homophones, can show PAS like effects the validity of the three sub-stage system is weakened. RE's recall functions compromise the sensory purity of the auditory 'grid' stage of PAS 2 more conclusively. Someone with good auditory speech registration should show PAS effects in recall. RE shows this is not so.

Together, these findings suggest that while there is a substage involved in the immediate recall of verbal material that is semantically pre-categorical and which shares many of the characteristics of heard speech, this storage mechanism is not particularly auditory. It might be more appropriately characterised as *phonetic*; as long as one in turn characterises phonetic as '*abstract* and *amodal*' (Studdert-Kennedy, personal communication; Liberman and Mattingley, 1985). This phonetic processing stage can be accessed by heard, lipread and mouthed information more independently than PAS 2 envisages, and also, if weakly, by written information that demands sublexical phonological assembly.

Is this stage best conceived as an input or an output stage? This depends, crucially and problematically, on exactly what one does when one tries to remember lists of written words: if the phonetic form of the word is activated in silent rehearsal we would expect written words to show recency; since they do not, this suggests either that the PAS-type stage is input located and that rehearsal is (solely) an output function or that written words (except when they are mouthed or assembled from odd spellings) are not usually recalled in terms of their strictly *phonetic* specifications.

One possibility is that such a phonetic processing stage is equivalent to the phonological input buffer proposed by Monsell (Chap 14) to account for analogous separations of auditory and mouthed-written from written effects in the priming of word recognition (see also Monsell, 1985). A somewhat similar idea, which is less specific about its location in the information processing of words and their sounds is proposed by Nairne (Nairne and Pusen, 1984; Nairne and McNabb, 1985), who suggests that the reason that written lists do not normally show recency in recall is because they are rehearsed in a phonological form and that it is this phonological rehearsal — the inner voice — that effectively eliminates recency that *should* occur for written lists. The reason that the inner voice does not eliminate heard, lipread, mouthed (and presumably pseudohomophone) recency is that these forms of input have additional, distinctive aspects that resist such overwriting. This nice idea suggests many interesting experimental investigations of such distinctiveness. One paradox, though is that RE, who would appear to have no 'inner voice' — indeed she tells us 'I don't hear words in my head' — ought to show recency for written lists, for her rehearsal is certainly not phonologically mediated. Possibly, though, RE does not even *encode* to-be-recalled material by the inner voice. If written (and auditory) material escapes such encoding no recency should ensue — however rehearsal is effected.

Wherever this stage is placed in a linear information processing model, and whatever one calls it, it would seem to have the following characteristics: RE does not have one; it is therefore (potentially at least) dissociable from overt speech and from speech comprehension mechanisms. It is not particularly sensitive to modality of input, unlike earlier, sensory-based stores, but is phonetic in its organization and character. It is not necessarily input driven, as Crowder (1983) has pointed out. Both mouthing and assembling the pronunciation of written words from their unusual spellings require feedback loops, as suggested by PAS 2 and, in this volume, by Monsell. Whether one loop will suffice is another, experimental question. Since lipreading and mouthing do not, here, show completely interactive effects I am doubtful that a single deeply amodal phonetic representation will suffice to explain these effects. Lipreading may yet access the inner voice somewhat independently of mouthing.

A further aspect of this system should be noted. It is likely that auditory speech inputs can take preemptive control of the phonetic processing stage. Auditory suffixes affect lipread and mouthed recency more than vice versa (see, for instance, Greene and Crowder's data and also Campbell and Dodd, 1982). Moreover the effect of a heard suffix on such lists can be very powerful. For instance, in one experiment (Campbell and Dodd, 1984; Experiment 3), we found that a heard suffix in a man's voice and a heard suffix in a woman's voice had equally disastrous effects on the accuracy of last-item recall of a lipread list where a familiar woman (the author) was seen to be the speaker. This is quite unlike the effect of same and different-voice heard suffixes on heard lists; these characteristically show a reduction of recency as the voice of the list and the voice of the suffix speaker are made more different (Morton, Crowder and Prussin, 1971).

This leads to an unresolved question; where do such effects of sensory specificity in the recall of heard lists come from? They cannot be accounted for in a more abstract, more central phonetic processing stage. In PAS 2 they are accounted to take place in the grid; a substage designed to reflect the similarities between speech perception and speech memory. But one possibility, in line with Nairne's speculations on 'distinctiveness' in auditory traces, is that these effects are best conceived as sensory episodic traces, logically independent of precategorical phonetic processing. So, too, may be some part of lipread and of mouthed same-modality effects. Kolers in numerous ways (for example, Kolers, 1976) has shown recall to be surprisingly sensitive to the precise sensorial format in which to-be-remembered material is presented. A characteristic of this sensitivity seems to be that it often emerges without subjective awareness. Recency phneomena in immediate recall, and their elimination by appropriate suffixes, may constitute just such a class of relatively automatic phenomena. One mechanism for the establishment of such useful episodic memory traces at recall may be provided by distributed memory networks. Such systems (see Allport, 1985 and this volume) are flexible enough to let sensory format impinge on the processing system and to be reactivated at recall in a powerful, automated, yet fully pre-lexical manner.

The gist of this story then, is that, for all its elegance, PAS 2 may not be the best model to account for the phenomenon, robust and well replicated, that it set out to explain. Recency and suffix effects in immediate recall are not a function of modality sensitive systems; if they are to be characterized in a common metric, this metric appears to be phonetic and can be activated by a number of inputs. Such a phonetically organized process could be identical with the processing stage identified by Monsell (Chap 14) in the recognition of heard and mouthed words. Acoustic purity is not a necessary, nor even a sufficient (see RE) component of such a system: acoustic purity can be dropped with impunity. Whether as pretty (and as testable) a model as PAS can be constructed from these pieces is another matter.

Acknowledgements

This work was funded by a Medical Research Council (UK), grant. I am indebted to Derek Besner, David Howard, Barbara Dodd and John Morton for their critical advice on the experiments reported here. A special debt is owed to Max Coltheart who suggested Experiment 2 to Barbara Dodd and myself in 1981. Dominic Massaro and Michael Studdert-Kennedy forced me to examine my own preconceptions in invigorating and critical ways. I am particularly grateful to them for helping to clarify several of the issues that underly this paper; confusions that remain are all my own work.

References

Allport, D. A. (1985). Distributed Memory, Modular subsystems and Dysphasia. In S. Newman and R. Epstein (Eds) *Current Perspectives in Dysphasia*. London: Churchill-Livingstone, pp. 32–61.

Balota, D. A. and Engle, R. W. (1981). Structural and Strategic Effects in the Stimulus Suffix Effect. *Journal of Verbal Learning and Verbal Behavior*, **20**, 346–57.

Butterworth, B., Campbell, R. and Howard, D. (1986). The uses of short-term memory: a case study. *Quarterly Journal of Experimental Psychology*, **38A**, 705–738.

Campbell, R. (in press). Some Uses and Abuses of Short Term Memory: evidence from a single case study. In G. Cossu (Ed.) *Studi Neurolinguistici dei disturbi di lettura*.

Campbell, R. (1987). Lipreading and Immediate Memory Processes. In B. Dodd and R. Campbell (Eds) *Hearing by Eye*. London: Erlbaum.

Campbell, R. and Butterworth, B. (1985). Phonological Dyslexia and Dysgraphia in a Highly Literate Subject: a Developmental Case with Associated Deficits of Phonemic Processing and Awareness. *Quarterly Journal of Experimental Psychology*, **37A**, 435–75.

Campbell, R. and Dodd, B. (1980). Hearing by Eye. *Quarterly Journal of Experimental Psychology*, **32**, 85–99.

Campbell, R. and Dodd, B. (1982). Some Suffix Effects on Lipread Lists. *Canadian Journal of Psychology*, **36**, 509–15.

Campbell, R. and Dodd, B. (1984). Aspects of Hearing by Eye. In H. Bouma and D. Bouwhuis (Eds) *Attention and Performance*, Vol 10, Hillsdale, NJ: Erlbaum, pp. 299–312.

Campbell, R., Dodd, B. and Brasher, J. (1983). The Sources of Visual Recency. *Quarterly Journal of Experimental Psychology*, **35A**, 571–87.

Crowder, R. G. (1983). The Purity of Auditory Memory. *Philosophical Transactions of the Royal Society of London, B*, **302**, 251–65.

Crowder, R. and Morton, J. (1969). Precategorical Acoustic Storage (PAS). *Perception and Psychophysics*, **6**, 41–60.

Gathercole, S. (1986). The Modality Effect and Articulation. *Quarterly Journal of Experimental Psychology*, **38A**, 461–74

Gathercole, S. (1987). Lipreading: Implications for Theories of Short Term Memory. In B. Dodd and R. Campbell (Eds) *Hearing by Eye*. London: Erlbaum, 227–241.

Greene, R. L. and Crowder, R. G. (1984). Modality and Suffix Effects in the Absence of Auditory Stimulation. *Journal of Verbal Learning and Verbal Behavior*, **23**, 371–82.

Kolers, P. (1976). Reading One Year Later. *Journal of Experimental Psychology: Human Learning and Memory*, **2**, 554–64.

Liberman, A. L. and Mattingley, I. Q. (1985). The Motor Theory of Speech Perception Revised. *Cognition*, **21**, 1–34.

Massaro, D. (1975). *Understanding Language: An Information Processing Analysis of Speech Perception, Reading and Psycholinguistics*. New York: Academic Press.

Massaro, D. (1987). Speech Perception by Ear and Eye. In B. Dodd and R. Campbell (Eds) *Hearing by Eye*. London: Erlbaum, 53–81.

Monsell, D. (1985). Repetition and the Lexicon. In A. W. Ellis (Ed.) *Progress in the Psychology of Language*, Vol 2. London: Erlbaum.

Morton, J., Crowder, R. G. and Prussin, H. A. (1971). Experiments with the Stimulus Suffix Effect. *Journal of Experimental Psychology*, **91**, 161–80.

Nairne, J. S. and Crowder, R. G. (1982). On the Locus of the Stimulus Suffix Effect. *Memory and Cognition*, **10**, 350–7.

Nairne, J. S. and Pusen, C. (1984). Serial Recall of Imagined Voices. *Journal of Verbal Learning and Verbal Behavior*, **23**, 331–42.

Nairne, J. S. and Walters, V. (1983). Silent Mouthing produces Modality and Suffix-like Effects. *Journal of Verbal Learning and Verbal Behavior*, **22**, 475–83.

Nairne, J. and McNabb, W. L. (1985). More Modality Effects in the Absence of Sound. *Journal of Experimental Psychol., Learning, Memory and Cognition*, **11**, 596–604.

Section 4
Reading and orthographies

Introduction

Eckart Scheerer

The present section is concerned with the processing of written language up to and including the word level. The discussion relates predominantly to data from two experimental paradigms: the *pronunciation task* and the *lexical decision* task. The two tasks have very different *formal* require-ments: language production need not be involved in lexical decision, and the mental lexicon need not be accessed in pronunciation. *Functionally*, the processing resources tapped by the two tasks may have much more in common: decisions on the lexical status of letter strings may be influenced by their phonological representations, and the pronunciation of words (perhaps even of non-words) may rely on the activation of entries in the mental lexicon. The functional analysis of the two tasks, both considered in isolation and in comparison to each other, provides most of the evidence concerning various questions about the relation of visual word recognition to the perception and production of spoken language. At what point in the processing sequence does the organization of spoken language impose itself on the organization of written language? Are sublexical units involved in recognizing and pronouncing words? If yes, what are they? Are they derived from spoken language, or are there autonomous sublexi-cal units of written language? Given that some phonological code inter-venes between perception and production, what is its nature: acoustical or articulatory? Questions that have been posed, in the present volume, not for English only, but for a variety of languages — seven in all — with a view to finding out to what extent the processing of written words is influenced by a given language's orthography (or writing system[1]); with the

LANGUAGE PERCEPTION AND PRODUCTION
ISBN 0-12-052750-2

result that an additional question arises: Are there any mechanisms of word processing that are invariant across orthographies?

Answers to these questions are often given in terms of a broad dichotomy between two classes of theories. It concerns the locus of 'translation' from written to spoken language in word processing. One school of thought opts for a prelexical or nonlexical locus: pronunciation is 'assembled', on the basis of grapheme–phoneme conversion rules, and 'phonological recoding' serves as the basis for reaching a decision concerning the lexical status of a letter string. At the other extreme, there have been theoreticians denying any prelexical involvement of phonology; lexical entries are accessed on the basis of graphemic information alone, the pronunciation of words is stored with their entries in the mental lexicon and retrieved for the entire word, while the pronunciation of non-words or unfamilar words is 'derived' from analogies to words or by means of an interactive 'spreading activation' process. As almost always in the history of science, extreme positions have proven difficult to defend, and various compromise solutions are being sought for. *Dual-route* theory supplements the prelexical phonological recoding route by a direct-access route that in fact bears most of the burden in word recognition and pronunciation. *Analogy* and *spreading activation* theories look for ways to accommodate the pronunciation of letter strings for which analogies are not available.

The contributions in this section are a good reflection of the present state of the art concerning the prelexical versus postlexical phonology issue. Much theorizing in the field suffers from two drawbacks. One of them is the tendency to think in linear stage terms, without allowing for interactions between stages; the other is that most existing theories are notoriously underspecified in that they do not generate predictions which are sufficiently precise for deciding between alternative theories. In Kay's and Venezky and Massaro's chapters advances towards overcoming such drawbacks are made. Kay argues for a multi-level, interactive account in which grapheme–phoneme conversion is supplemented by various lexical and sublexical sources of information. Venezky and Massaro emphasize multiple independent sources of information; their model is spelled out in more detail in Massaro's contribution to another section of this book.

The chapters by Besner, Feldman and Scheerer deal with the influence of different orthographies on word processing. Languages with an alphabetic orthography are often classified according to whether they represent phonology at the graphemic surface structure or at the deep structure, e.g., of morphemes. Among Indo-European languages, English and Serbo-Croatian represent two extremes of a phonologically deep and a phonologically shallow orthography. The Japanese *kana* syllabaries are phonologically shallow. As witnessed by English and German, phonologically deep orthographies can exhibit various degrees of regularity, with German, at least as far as native words are concerned, being more regular than English. The deep/shallow dimension has attracted the interest of researchers because of the intuitive notion that the strong lexical component of word processing in English might result from the complicated nature of grapheme–phoneme conversion in that language, and that prelexical conversion to phonology might still be a viable route in languages with shallow orthographies. The strong version of this claim denies lexical involvement in assembling the pronunciation of *katakana* and of Serbo-Croatian. Feldman, who reiterates the view that 'skilled readers of Serbo-Croatian analyse words phonologically', presents data arguing for the involvement of morphological analysis working at a postlexical level. On the other hand, Besner maintains that lexical knowledge is involved in pronouncing *katakana* and Serbo-Croatian; he bases his argument partly on his own experiments and partly on a re-analysis of earlier data by Feldman and her associates. Scheerer shows the utilization of grapheme–phoneme conversion rules by readers of German, not only in pronunciation tasks but also in lexical decision, where many authorities on English are inclined to deny their involvement. In addition, he draws attention to what he calls 'graphotactic structure' and Venezky and Massaro prefer to call 'scribal constraints'.

While Feldman raises a dissenting voice, Besner and Scheerer seem to agree that the deep-shallow dichotomy does not entail a totally different organization of word processing. Both sublexical and lexical contributions are implicated in both types of orthography. The nature and measurement of sublexical and lexical orthographic structure in *English* is discussed in Venezky and Massaro's chapter. Highlights of their discussion are (a) the distinction between statistical and rule-governed measures, (b) the distinction between phonological and scribal constraints, (c) the development of spelling-to-sound metrics at various fluency levels, and (d) the fruitful application of their metrics to the data of an experimental series in the literature — an effective procedure for promoting interaction among investigators. Kay also takes up the issue of sublexical constraints, particularly with reference to phonology. She shows that grapheme–phoneme conversion rules are not utilized in a deterministic but rather in a probabilistic fashion, that their use is determined by type rather than by token frequency, and that some ordinarily neglected determinants such as the difference between initial and final segments and the difference between vowel correspondence and rhyming need to be considered.

Research on *morphological structure* as a determinant of word processing is reported by Feldman and by Jarvella, Job, Sandström and Schreuder. In contrast to Feldman, Jarvella and his co-workers reach the conclusion that full forms are not represented in the mental lexicon, neither in Italian nor in Dutch. Apart from this general similarity, Italian and Dutch seem to differ in that Italian relies on stem plus inflection, and Dutch on individual morphemes; moreover, the processing involved in constructing a word from subword lexical entries is different: left-to-right in Italian, non-deterministic in Dutch. These are intriguing results, especially because they have been obtained by applying an identical method (introducing brief signal asynchronies between word parts) to two different languages. In Feldman's work, on the other hand, another method (repetition priming) was used. It remains to be seen whether the discrepancy between Feldman's and Jarvella's results are due to differences of method or to a real difference between the mental structures and/or processes activated by different languages.

Granted that a phonological code is involved, not only in word pronunciation but also in lexical access, the question poses itself whether or not this code is invariant across orthographies. Besner has a provocative suggestion: we can be reasonably certain that the code is articulatory in Japanese *kana*, while in English its tie to articulation seems to be much less close. By implication, we may suppose that, once demands on working memory and on phoneme deletion are removed, the phonological code in English has a strong *auditory* component. One way to test this assumption is to look for parallels between visual word recognition on the one hand and auditory recognition and short-term storage of speech sounds on the other hand. Given that vowels have a special status in auditory short-term storage (Crowder, 1971) and in auditory recognition (Pisoni, 1973), one is tempted to speculate that they might enjoy a similar privilege in visual word recognition. In fact, some scattered results reported in chapters of this section may be taken to support such a speculation; e.g., Kay's finding concerning the importance of the vowel correspondence, or Scheerer's result that the amount of delay in lexical decision produced by pseudo-homophones depends on the type of homophony, with vowel-based homophony being much more effective than consonant-based homophony. In another section of this book, Campbell presents evidence that pseudo-homophones activate a phonological code which shares certain functional attributes of auditory short-term storage, such as the recency and the suffix effect.

Looking back at the contributions to this section, the reader might wish for a more integrated and uniform picture of visual word processing, especially with respect to the comparison among different orthographies. But it should be noted that direct comparisons are often rendered impossible by the very structural factors that are being investigated. For instance, in a language with a bidirectional one-to-one mapping between graphemes and phonemes, there can be neither homophony nor orthographic irregularity. As a result, investigators have been forced to resort to such techniques as alphabet mixing in Serbo-Croatian or exploiting the apostrophe in Italian. In view of these difficulties, it is in fact amazing that certain orthography-invariant similarities in word reading have been demonstrated. Employing common methodologies where this is possible, and re-analysing each other's data, might promote still better comparability.

Note

[1] For reasons given in my own chapter, I prefer to make a distinction between the terms 'writing system' and 'orthography', applying the former to the classification of basic principles involved in the representation of spoken language by written language, and the latter to the set of rules which is employed in a language with a given writing system. According to this terminological convention, some of the studies contained in this section are concerned with writing systems rather than orthographies. In order to maintain terminological uniformity, I have preferred to retain the vocabulary employed by most contributors to this section.

References

Crowder, R. G. (1971). The sound of vowels and consonants in immediate memory. *Journal of Verbal Learning and Verbal Behavior*, **10**, 587–96.

Pisoni, D. B. (1973). Auditory and phonetic memory codes in the discrimination of consonants and vowels. *Perception & Psychophysics*, **13**, 253–60.

8 Orthographic structure and spelling–sound regularity in reading English words

Richard L. Venezky and Dominic W. Massaro

Abstract

This chapter is a logical/empirical exploration of lexical and sublexical information that is potentially utilized in reading printed words. It assumes a single recognition process for words wherein information from different sources is integrated over time to yield a recognition decision, based on the relative degrees of support for the various word alternatives. Two of the sources of information that are of particular interest here are orthographic structure and spelling-to-sound correspondences. Among the approaches to quantifying orthographic structure, statistical redundancy and rule-governed measures have been the most often utilized for empirical studies over the past 30 years. These, along with spelling-to-sound mapping, are discussed and their limitations noted. Finally, three classes of metrics for scaling letter strings based on their spelling–sound correspondences are proposed: membership, exertion and fluency. For fluency, different orders of scalings are derived, using a mean fluency score for each word. Then an exertion measure and one of the fluency measures are compared to other lexical and sublexical metrics as predictors for reaction times in pronunciation and lexical decision tasks. The fluency measure accounted for a significant percentage of the variance in these studies, as did word frequency and orthographic structure. These results support the assumption that multiple sources of information contribute to printed word recognition in reading and pronunciation.

LANGUAGE PERCEPTION AND PRODUCTION
ISBN 0-12-052750-2

Framework

The pursuit of mechanisms for word recognition in reading has occupied a central role in experimental psychology since Wundt opened the doors of his Leipzig laboratory in the 1880s. Word shape, determining letters and sound were the focal points of the earliest speculations and experiments, but spelling constraints (i.e., orthographic structure) were also probed in at least one experiment before 1910 (Dearborn, 1906; see Venezky, 1984, for a review). Since the revival of cognitive psychology in the 1950s, however, the primary focus of word recognition studies has been first on statistically defined and now linguistically defined units. In the past two decades, research on sublexical units has shifted back and forth, often like desert sand, across single-letter positional frequency, bigrams, trigrams, structural regularity, spelling–sound regularity, analogically defined phonological regularity, and even regularity defined by an edition of the Oxford English Dictionary (Parkin, 1982, 1984). Several major attempts at synthesizing this area have appeared in the last five years (Gough, 1984; Henderson, 1982), along with several notable collections of papers that touch on the subject (Kavanagh and Venezky, 1980; Lesgold and Perfetti, 1981; Tzeng and Singer, 1981).

In none of these works, however, have the sublexical properties of printed English words been carefully examined. In this chapter we focus narrowly on two different forms of sublexical information in printed words: orthographic structure and spelling-to-sound regularity. The former refers to information at the level of the letters themselves while the latter refers to information obtained by mapping letters into sounds. The motivation for this work is in part natural curiosity about orthography, but it also derives in part from the disagreements, misconceptions and occasional confusions that we often see in the stimuli selected for word recognition experiments. Our intention, however, is not to make folly or to criticize, but to delineate issues in stimulus selection that have not been attended to sufficiently in the past.

Before addressing this problem, we propose a framework for conceptualizing word recognition in reading. Such a framework, we believe, focuses the field on significant issues and inoculates us to some degree from pseudo-issues and false dichotomies. A literate person faced with a written word is captured by it and seems to have no choice but to read it. Our phenomenal experience attests to this fact, as does experimental demonstrations of the Stroop (1935) effect and its variants (Jonides, Naveh-Benjamin and Palmer, 1985). Adult readers are clearly experts rather than novices in the reading domain of pattern recognition, in the same sense that experts are differentiated from novices in chess or radiography (Chase and

Simon, 1973; Lesgold, 1984). Although we do not accept a binary distinction between automatic and voluntary skills, the former more adequately represents word recognition for the adult reader (van der Heijden, Hagenaar and Bloem, 1985). Thus, we envision word recognition as a highly automatic, fast and efficient skill, but one analogous to other domains of pattern recognition such as speech and shape perception.

Following Massaro (1979; Chap 6), we assume that a single recognition process exists for printed words whereby information from various sources (e.g., features of the graphic image, letters, letter combinations and linguistic and non-linguistic context) are integrated over time to yield (usually) a recognition decision. These multiple sources of information are evaluated, and then integrated to determine what degree of support is given to alternative word candidates. The different sources are evaluated relatively independently of one another without crosstalk, and each has its own time course for becoming available. Integration involves conjoining the various sources and has the consequence that the least ambiguous sources available will have the most impact on the outcome. A decision is based on the relative degrees of support among the various word alternatives.

Consider a word being recognized in the context of a sentence. Sentential constraints might facilitate recognition (e.g., decrease naming time) even though the nature of the letter and word processing did not change. A highly constraining context would contribute much more than a less constraining context, again without modifying letter and word processing. That is, featural analysis and letter resolution would occur independently of context, but information derived from context and information derived from the word would be conjoined to give faster recognition relative to the case of either context or word information being presented alone (see Massaro, Chap 6, for a more complete presentation of this model). Depending upon the relative qualities of these inputs and the reader's prior experience, any one will be more or less important to a specific recognition task.

There is an emerging consensus among some researchers that for English highly familiar words are accessed from visual information of the letters with relatively small contributions from morphemic structure, spelling-to-sound correspondences and context. For less familiar words, poorer readers, or reduced stimulus quality, these other types of information appear to play significant roles (Becker and Killian, 1977; Gernsbacher, 1984; McConkie and Zola, 1981; Perfetti, Goldman and Hogaboam, 1979; Rosson, 1985; Waters, Seidenberg and Bruck, 1984; West and Stanovich, 1978). In terms of the present framework, the different results merely reflect differences in the relative ambiguity of the various sources of information. The contribution of sublexical sources is inversely related to the contribution (information value) of the lexical source. Within the metaphor of horse-race models, all horses are always in the race, but the contribution of any one horse is a function of the speed of other horses. Lest the reader be misled by the metaphor, however, the outcome of the race reflects the contribution of several horses, not just the winner.

Orthographic structure

Statistical redundancy I — ordered approximations

Ordered approximations to English were the first measures of orthographic structure utilized in modern (i.e., post-behaviorism) reading studies. Using algorithms proposed by Shannon (1948, 1951), nth-order approximations to English were generated and used in free recall tasks (e.g., Gilmore and Egeth, 1976; Miller, Bruner and Postman, 1954). As recently as nine years ago ordered approximations were advocated as psychologically relevant descriptions of orthographic structure (Mewhort and Beal, 1977). Since ordered approximations are left-context and not right-context sensitive, however, the probability of recall of any letter in a letter string would (in this theory) be unaffected by succeeding letter context. Thus, the predicted probability of correctly reporting the *a* in a highly constraining context like *state* would be the same as for less constraining contexts like *stack* (cf. *stick*, *stuck*). In addition, the possibility that real words, pseudo-homophones, and structurally illegal strings could be generated with higher ordered approximations has led to a general abandoning of this definition of orthographic structure. There is simply too much variability *within a given order* of approximation to qualify it as a meaningful index of orthographic structure.

Statistical redundancy II — letter counts

A second approach to statistical measures of English orthography was developed from frequency counts of letters and letter sequences. Underwood and Schulz (1960), for example, tabulated bigrams and trigrams from a sample of the Thorndike and Lorge (1944) word list. These position-free token counts were used in word recognition studies, with mixed results, by Anisfeld (1964), Gibson, Shurcliff and Yonas (1970), and others. A serious drawback to these counts, their lack of position sensitivity, was overcome by Mayzner and Tresselt (1965) and Mayzner, Tresselt and

Wolin (1965a, 1965b), who derived position-sensitive single-letter, bigram and trigram counts for words three to seven letters in length. (Position sensitive single letter and bigram counts from a larger corpus have been published in Massaro *et al.*, 1980 and Solso, 1979.)

The Mayzner *et al.* tables have been used by Mason (1975, 1978) to explore single-letter positional frequency effects in good and poor readers. Using a target search task, Mason (1975) found that good readers (6th grade level) were significantly more sensitive to single letter positional frequency than poor readers of the same grade level. Although Mason (1975) confounded rule-governed orthographic structure with positional frequency, a small but significant positional frequency effect remains when structure is removed (Massaro, Venezky and Taylor, 1979).

Both single-letter and bigram frequencies have continued to be used in studies of word recognition (e.g., Bouwhuis, 1979; Krueger, 1979; Massaro, Jastrzembski and Lucas, 1981; McClelland and Johnston, 1977; Rice and Robinson, 1975.) However, Gernsbacher (1984) observed that the effect of bigram frequency was often confounded with word familiarity, as measured by subjective familiarity ratings of subjects. She demonstrated that when familiarity is controlled in a lexical-decision task, the bigram effects found in several earlier studies disappear. This result, plus the high intercorrelations among pronounceability, rule-governed orthographic structure, single-letter frequency, bigram frequency and word frequency make it difficult to choose among these measures.

Rule-governed measures

Rule-governed regularity describes the predictable structure of the orthography in terms of phonological and scribal constrains. However, a critical feature of this description is that the predictable structure of letter occurrences can be utilized without any mediation of the spoken language. In contrast to the spelling-to-sound descriptions in the next section, utilization of orthographic structure in perceptual recognition is assumed to occur independently of how the printed pattern is translated to sound. Although much of the structure of a written alphabetic language necessarily follows its phonology, access to the phonology is not necessary for utilization of the orthographic structure. Direct evidence for this assumption comes from the utilization of orthographic structure by deaf readers (Gibson, Shurcliff and Yonas, 1970; Hanson, 1986). In addition, Singer (1980) found that a phonological rendering of words presented in an artificial alphabet was not necessary for learning and utilizing orthographic structure. In the sections which follow, both the phonological and the scribal constraints of English spellings are outlined.

Phonological constraints

The primary constraints on English orthography derive from the allowable sequences of sounds in English words. Thus, /sk/ is an allowable initial consonant cluster and therefore spellings for it exist (e.g., *sk*, *sc*, *sch*); on the other hand, /tl/ and /dl/ do not occur and never did occur initially in English words, and therefore no spellings for these sequences occur in English words (but they do in Tlingit and several other languages in which initial /tl/ and /dl/ occur). Complicating this relationship between sound and spelling, however, are several factors, including scribal pedantry, which leave us with spellings for (1) sound sequences which once occurred, but have since been dropped from the language (e.g., *wr-*, *kn-*, *gn*), or for (2) sound sequences that were presumed to have occurred in the language from which a word was borrowed (e.g., for *psychology*, this assumption is supportable; for *ptarmigan* it is clearly based on mistaken etymology; and for *debt* (and various others), it is only partially true, in that /b/ and /t/ occurred in the Latin ancestor of *debt* (*debitum*), but not as a final cluster). A further complication is the deviation in serial order of several spellings from the order of sounds which they represent. Chief among these is *wh*, a spelling for which some English speakers have retained /hw/, and *-le*, as in *bottle*, etc., which spells (in deliberate speech) /əl/ (*wh-* and *-le* are scribal reversals of earlier *hw-* and *-el*).

But even with these deviations from expected practice, most English sounds are represented in a moderately rational fashion in the orthography (Venezky, 1970). However, since English possesses more than one potential spelling for almost every sound, a second set of constraints, here called scribal constraints, enter into rule-governed orthographic structure.

Scribal constraints

These constraints have resulted in English spelling from 1300 years of sound change, lexical borrowings, scribal tampering and occasional attempts at standardization. While no complete codification exists, Venezky (1970) summarizes from a linguistic standpoint the major and minor scribal patterns of English. These patterns are divided into four groups: (1) gemination; (2) distribution of u and w, i and y; (3) vowels before geminates and pseudo-geminates; and (4) the distribution of c, j, k, and v, and q. In group one are the rules that regulate the doubling of graphemes in different word positions and the single rule that outlaws tripling of graphemes.[1] English does not allow a, h, i, j, k, q, u, w, x, and y to double (geminate), and restricts the doubling of *v* to a small group of words (e.g., navvy, savvy). For doubled *k*, *g* (pronounced /j/) and *ch* English scribes of the seventeenth century adopted *ck*, *dg*, and *tch*, respectively. These *pseudo-geminates* obey the same distribution rules as true geminates. A few exceptions to the gemination rules exist, such as *aard-vark, skiing, trekked,* but these are rare. In general, doubled consonants (and the pseudo-geminates) can not occur in initial position, and those freely admitted in final position are restricted to ff, ss, and ll,[2] plus the pseudo-geminates (but *dg* must always be followed by *e*). Based on these rules, pseudo-words like *taaf, ooming, brihh, ssoch, ckip, and swodg* would be pronounceable, but scribally irregular.

In the second group of scribal rules are those that control the distribution of *u/w* and *i/y* as second elements of digraph vowels, and which restrict *u* and *i* to initial and medial positions. These two graphemes alternate as second elements of diagraph vowels: *u* occurs before consonants while *w* is used before vowels and in word final position (e.g., *sound, lower, cow*).[3] Less frequent are a small group of French borrowings: *caribou, tableau,* etc. Similarly, with ai/ay, ei/ey, oi/oy and ui/uy, the *i* form occurs before consonants while the *y* form occurs before vowels and in word final position. (The words that admit *i* in final position are Latin plurals like *radii,* which is also irregular for having a doubled *i*; Italian plurals like *ravioli* and *macaroni*; and a handful of others of various origins: *magi, yogi, rabbi, ski, khaki,* etc.) The u/w distribution rule has a relatively large number of exceptions where the *w* form occurs before a consonant (e.g., *howl, town, owl, newter, pewter*). Exceptions to the i/y distribution are rarer (e.g., *oyster*). By these rules, pseudo words like *stou, tawp* and *nayb* are scribally irregular.

The third group of rules outlaws digraph vowels before doubled consonants and before the pseudo-geminates *ck, dg* and *tch*.[4] Thus, pseudo-words like *soick, treedge* and *teaffer* are also illegal. In the last group are the distribution rules for *c* (not allowed in final position except in the ending *-ic*), *j* (allowed only in initial position), *k* (generally restricted initially and medially to occurring before e, i, and y, and finally only after diagraph vowels), *q* (must be followed by *u*) and *v* (not allowed in final position). Exceptions to these rules are rare, consisting mainly of a handful of French borrowings that end in *c* (*cognac, zodiac, lilac*), plus a few others (e.g., *zinc, talc, bloc, arc*).

Pseudowords that violate these rules include forms like *blec, pojer, kriff, qwaft* and *trev*. Massaro *et al.* (1980) showed through subjective ratings and two-alternative forced-choice tasks that subjects utilize both rule-governed information and statistical information in discriminating among pseudowords. Hart (1980) obtained familiarity ratings (closeness to English words) for grapheme strings that incorporated or violated 12 different types of scribal regularity, holding phonological regularity constant. The lowest ratings (least word-like) were obtained for *dg, tch* and *ck* in initial position (e.g., *tchean*) and doubled consonants in initial position (e.g., *mmish*). In a related lexical decision task, Hart (1980) found no pseudo-homophone effect for pronounceable but scribally irregular pseudo-words (e.g., *ckode*), a result replicated by Venezky (1981).[5] Finally, Massaro and Hestand (1983) showed that primary school children improve grade by grade from first through third grade in their ability to utilize rule-governed information.

Spelling–Sound regularity

The second form of sublexical information of interest here is spelling–sound regularity, which is based on the consistency with which graphemes can be mapped into phonemes. E. Gibson and colleagues attempted to define a dichotomous pronounceability (i.e., regularity) measure which they then employed in a full recall task (see Gibson and Levin, 1975, for a review). Besides confounding recognition with memory for unfamiliar letter strings (Baddeley, 1964), the Gibson studies also confounded structural regularity with pronounceability, as was found by Gibson, Shurcliff and Yonas (1970) using deaf subjects who also showed a pronounceability effect. This possibility had been demonstrated earlier with primary school children by Thomas (1968), who showed that pronounceable and unpronounceable CCVs (e.g., dri, rdi) were equally inferior to pronounceable CVCs (e.g., dir) in an oral recall (spelling) task. A number of researchers have attempted to show that lexical access in reading English is mediated by phonology generated by rule from graphemic input (e.g., Baron and Strawson, 1976; Coltheart *et al.*, 1977; McCusker, Hillinger, and Bias, 1981; Rosson, 1985; Rubenstein, Lewis, and Rubenstein, 1971; Stanovich and Bauer, 1978). Henderson (1982) discusses in depth the complex and often contradictory empirical evidence for phonological mediation and the theories proposed to account for these data (see also Humphreys and Evett, 1985; and Venezky, 1981).

Since Henderson's (1982) text, a number of studies have, through improved stimulus control, shown that phonological effects are confined to low familiarity words (e.g., Rosson, 1985; Waters and Seidenberg, 1985; Waters, Seidenberg and Bruck, 1984). In a recent study, Seidenberg (1985) showed that in a naming task, not only was the spelling–sound effect restricted to the low frequency words, but was also absent in the fastest one-third of the subjects as defined by mean naming latency. Phonological effects have been obtained primarily with pseudowords (e.g., Rubenstein, Lewis, and Rubenstein, 1971); those from real words tend to be relatively small (e.g., Gough, 1984; Stanovich and Bauer, 1978). This latter observation applies whether spelling–sound rules, lexical analogies (Glushko,

1979), or sound-to-spelling tabulations (Rosson, 1985) have been utilized. Nevertheless, phonological effects have been found consistently in lexical access for Serbo-Croatian readers (e.g., Feldman and Turvey, 1980) and in categorization tasks for Japanese kana (e.g., Kimura, 1984) and Chinese (see Hung and Tzeng, 1981 for a review).

Issues in rule derivation

Most studies that use a rule-governed approach to spelling–sound regularity draw on linguistic descriptions of English orthography for rules. However, several issues remain unresolved in the derivation of spelling–sound correspondences. The first relates to the context to consider in rule derivation. For example, if the *d* in *Indian* is viewed only in the context of other *d* pronunciations, we would assign it to the *regular* category. But in relation to the following vowel context and word stress pattern, *d* in *Indian* is irregular because it does not palatalize to /ǰ/ as in *cordial* and *educate* (cf. *ss* in *issue, z* in *azure* and *t* in *bastion*). In the next section we propose a series of levels or orders for describing increasingly more sophisticated spelling–sound rules such as these.

A second issue relates to the corpus of words from which rules are derived. Venezky (1970) is based, with some editing, upon a corpus from the 1930s that includes many inflectional and derivational forms, plus proper names. A more recent corpus, or one restricted to base forms might alter some of the rule statistics. Then, the notion of *rule* itself must be questioned. Venezky (1970) bases rules on recognizable word features, including stress and morpheme boundaries, but excluding etymology. The latter feature, which figures prominently in Chomsky and Halle (1968), raises issues of validity and reliability. While some words contain foreign spellings (e.g., *ph*), many carry no obvious clues to their origins. Furthermore, origin itself is often insufficient for predicting spelling–sound correspondences. For example, both *chief* and *chef* are derived from the same French word, yet *chef*, which was borrowed relatively recently, exhibits a modern French pronunciation of *ch*, while *chief*, which was borrowed before French initial /tš/ changed to /š/, retains the earlier French form. Similar dichotomies can be found in *ch* words from Greek (e.g., *machine, machination*), many of which were borrowed via Latin or French.

Exactly what makes a rule is beyond the coverage of this chapter. We will, nevertheless, offer one example of the complexity of this issue. *Bush* and *push* both contain what most people would classify as irregular pronunciations of *u* (cf. *flush, rush, crush, dull, hull*). However, after a non-nasal bilabial, *u* corresponds regularly to /ʊ/ in some following consonant environments (e.g., *full, pull, bull, bushel, butcher, fulsome*). Does this make the *u* in *bush* and *push* regular? Semi-regular?

Given a set of rules from whatever source, an issue remains in how to use the rules to scale regularity. While most experimenters have treated regularity as a binary variable, at least one (Rosson, 1985) has tried to create a continuous regularity scale by extracting the log of the weakest (i.e., least common) correspondence in a word. This measure, unfortunately, confounds spelling–sound regularity and grapheme frequency of occurrence. By this measure, a highly regular but relatively infrequent correspondence (e.g., *qu* — /kw/ would be scaled lower than a common but irregular correspondence (e.g., ea — /ɛ/). As the next section shows, these two approaches do not exhaust the possible scaling techniques for spelling–sound regularity.

Lexical analogies

One of the more serious drawbacks to rule-based systems is their clumsiness in accounting for rule change. Developmental studies of letter–sound learning show, for example, that children change from an invariant /k/ pronunciation for *c* in initial position, to a /k/-/s/ differentiation in initial position, to a full differentiation across all word positions (Venezky, 1974, Venezky and Johnson, 1973). If we assume that at each stage only the currently active rules are accessible, then the construction of new rules requires either deductive learning, which is unlikely, or re-exposure to the corpus of *c* words, with attention now to the graphemes immediately following *c*. A more attractive alternative utilizes active access and re-organization of words stored in a mental lexicon.

A step in this direction has been proposed by Glushko (1979), who suggested that both real word and pseudoword pronunciations can be accounted for by reference to the set of real words activated by a stimulus's ending. For real words, lexical access is made on a holistic basis. However, at the same time that a word's pronunciation is activated, so are the pronunciations of all similar words (i.e., neighbors). If any of these have ending pronunciations that differ from the ending pronunciation of the stimulus, response delay occurs. For pseudowords, a similar process is hypothesized, with uniform pronunciation neighbors producing faster and more accurate pronunciations than neighbors with variant pronunciations.

As a first step, the model is appealing, but it leaves many issues unresolved. For example, by the strict criteria Glushko used for selecting neighbors (same length, same spelling after initial grapheme), many pseudowords can be constructed that have no real word neighbors (e.g., *tebe, fibe, lufe, soge*). The Glushko model cannot account for the pronunciations that subjects give to these, nor can it account for initial grapheme pronunciations or pronunciations of most multi-syllabic words.

Bauer and Stanovich (1980) attempted to utilize the Glushko model, but altered the neighborhood criteria to include variable lengths and chaining via pronunciation to alternate spellings. Thus, *site* might activate (via its pronunciation) *sight* which would activate (also via pronunciation) *height*, which activates (by spelling) *weight*, which activates *fate* and *great*, and so on through an unmanageably large corpus. It is not clear how a subject would arrive at a pronunciation via this model. Because of these extensions to the neighborhood criteria, Bauer and Stanovich (1980) is not an accurate replication of Glushko (1979). For example, in their second experiment, five of the nine words which they label 'regular, inconsistent' are 'regular, consistent' by Glushko (1979).[6]

Henderson (1982) has proposed several alterations to Glushko's criteria, including the marking of spelling units and vowel–consonant status, and activation by regions of visually related forms, including those in initial position. These suggestions move the activation model towards the rule-based model, while retaining the ability to account for change. But little empirical evidence has been gathered to test these ideas. In the next section we propose a sequence of increasingly more sophisticated linguistic metrics for scaling spelling–sound regularity, taking into account different scaling techniques and different approaches to defining spelling–sound rules. Our only claim for these is that they offer a systematic approach to exploring the psychological relevance of spelling–sound translation systems.

Spelling–sound metrics

For the present we consider the generation of a pronunciation from the spelling of a visually presented stimulus. Furthermore, we consider only those generation procedures that operate on spelling–sound correspondences. That other approaches to arriving at a pronunciation have been suggested, or that spelling–sound models have been subjected to various criticisms is not at issue here in that our primary concern is to explicate those stimulus properties that need to be considered in testing spelling–sound models. Following the ideas presented at the beginning of this chapter on processing of information from different sources, we are not assigning any particular level of importance to spelling–sound information over other sources such as orthographic structure. The goal of the current exploration is to derive a metric for scaling letter strings such that assumptions about pronunciation via spelling–sound translation can be tested.

Three classes of metrics are considered: *membership, exertion* and *fluency*, corresponding to dichotomous, interval and continuous scaling.

Membership

This class of metrics assigns letter strings to regular and irregular classes upon the basis of some canonization of spelling–sound rules. Besides the criticisms mentioned above of spelling–sound rule systems, this class also suffers from low resolving power; it can not make differential predictions within either the regular or irregular class. For example, the mapping of *i* to silence in *business*, which is a unique irregularity, must be treated the same as the more common irregularity of *i* in *triple*.

Exertion

Exertion metrics attempt to scale spelling–sound regularity along an integer scale, utilizing the number of different pronunciations for each spelling unit in a word as a basis for scaling. Consider, for example, the spelling *heir*. Initial *h* has a highly common pronunciation (/h/), and a rarer one as in American English *herb* (ϕ). *ei* has six 'common' pronunciations, as exemplified by the words *feint, either* (/i/), *height, albeit, counterfeit* and *heir*, of which the first five occur more often (by type counts) than the *ei* pronunciation in *heir*. For *r*, the pronunciation in *heir* represents the most common mapping. For scaling, we can assign a count of zero to each correspondence that is the most common for the spelling involved, a one if it is the second most common, and so on. These separate counts can then be combined as a sum for the entire word. By starting the counts at zero, some degree of independence from the number of spelling units in a word is achieved (for *heir*, the process would yield a score of six.) This is labeled an *exertion* metric because it corresponds (roughly) to the number of different pronunciations that would need to be generated before the correct one is produced, assuming that the order of testing proceeds from more common to less common correspondences.

Fluency

A fluency score utilizes the actual frequencies of occurrence for correspondences to create a continuous scale. One approach to this metric has been tried by Rosson (1985), who utilized the lowest frequency correspondence, based on sound-to-spelling type counts. Besides confounding spelling unit frequency with spelling–sound frequency, as discussed earlier, this measure assumes a parallel assignment of correspondences such that the slowest single correspondence controls reaction time. While there is insufficient evidence to reject this hypothesis, we prefer at this early stage in the development of metrics to propose alternative approaches for comparison to each other.

Therefore, as one alternative to a weakest rule fluency metric, we propose a mean fluency metric. The *fluency score* assigned to a particular spelling–sound correspondence is based on the occurrences of that correspondence relative to the sum of all correspondences for that same grapheme. That is, for a complete set of correspondences $f_1, f_2 \ldots, f_n$ of a spelling, the fluency score of any f_i is $(f_i / \sum_i f_i) \times 100$, where multiplication by 100 transforms the distribution from a 0–1 scale to a 0–100 scale. This approach ensures that consistent but infrequent correspondences like $z \rightarrow$ /z/ will have higher fluency scores than inconsistent but frequently occurring correspondences like $ea \rightarrow$ /ɛ/. For the *c* pronunciations shown in Table 1, the fluency scores are: /k/ = 74.32; /s/ = 21.98; /š/ = 3.67; and /č/ = 0.03. The total fluency score assigned to a word is the mean of its grapheme fluency scores.

Table 1. Correspondences for *c*.

Pronunciation	Word position			
	total	initial	medial	final
/k/	2431	1336	718	377
/s/	719	150	569	0
/š/	120	0	120	0
/č/	1	1	0	0

Rule systems

Fluency scores, like membership and exertion scores, derive from a base set of spelling–sound rules. But the notion of *rule* in this domain is not well-formed, thus allowing different rule sets, depending upon the features which are admitted for rule formation. For the computation of mean fluency scores we define four levels or types of spelling–sound rules, here called *orders*. These are also applicable, *mutatis mutandis*, to membership and exertion scalings, although because of space limitations we apply them here only to mean fluency scores. A zero order spelling–sound scaling is based upon single grapheme counts without regard for position of letters within words or any higher order contextual or linguistic considerations. Notice that this definition leads to treating digraphs and trigraphs as sequences of single graphemes rather than as separate units. Thus, the fluency score for *chin* would be derived from the separate scores for *c, h, i* and *n* at the zero order. (In this case, we treat the correspondences of *ch* as c → /č/ and h → /ɸ/.) From both a psychological and a linguistic standpoint, the zero-order metric is uninteresting, and will not be pursued further.

A first-order scaling takes into account functional units,[7] so that *chin* is now treated as a sequence of three units: *ch, i, n*. Position of graphemes within words, however, is still ignored. This means, for example, that the fluency score for final *e* in words like *flame* and *take* is based on all possible correspondences for *e* rather than just those for *e* in final position. For a second-order measure, we take into account grapheme positions within the word; namely, initial, final and medial, where medial is everything left after the first (initial) and last (final) units are removed. For the *c* correspondences given in Table 1, we now have fluency scores for each word position as shown in Table 2. For final *e*, the fluency score for *e* → /ɸ/ as in *flame* is now 100 rather than 15 for first order *e* → /ɸ/.

Table 2.   Second-order fluency. Scores for c pronunciations.

Pronunciation	Word position		
	initial	medial	final
/k/	89.84	51.03	100.00
/s/	10.09	40.44	0.00
/š/	0.00	8.53	0.00
/č/	0.07	0.00	0.00

Third-order scalings admit the more general linguistic rules; namely, the long–short vowel rule (including the final *e* pattern);[8] the *c* rule[9] palatalization of /s/ /z/, /t/, /d/; the phonotactics of consonant clusters, and *w*-influence.[10] For the pronunciations of *c*, rules at this level render almost all of them totally regular, the exceptions being words like *arcing, facade* and *cello*. At this level, the correspondences for *c* are divided into three classes as represented by the following word groups: (1) *coal, picnic, secret*; (2) *ceiling, ocelot, society*; (3) *ocean, social*. Fluency scores are then computed separately for correspondences within each of these groups. The fourth and highest level of scaling takes into account all of the minor spelling–

Table 3.   Fluency measures.

Word	Order of scaling				
	0	1	2	3	4
chin	47.6	83.1	85.8	85.8	85.8
shape	33.4	65.5	81.0	99.7	99.7
cent	57.8	57.8	62.4	77.0	99.3

sound rules that have potential psychological reality. This includes, for example, a rule for initial *th* based on form class (functors versus content words), but excludes rules based on etymology. Shown in Table 3 are fluency measures for three words: *chin, shape* and *cent*, at five levels or orders of scaling.

For *chin*, the step from zero to first order scalings yields a large increase in the fluency score because at the zero order *ch* is treated as a sequence of two units with *c* mapped into /č/ and *h* into silence. But higher-order rules have only a marginal effect thereafter because neither position nor context have a major influence over the mappings involved. For *shape* large increases occur in metrics 1, 2 and 3 because of (1) the change from treating *sh* as two separate units at the zero order to treating it as one at order one; (2) the change at order two to considering position in the correspondences for *e*; and (3) the addition of the long–short vowel rule at order three. The fourth-order scaling, on the other hand, produces no further increase in the score for *shape*. *Cent* differs from *chin* and *shape* in that the zero and first-order scalings yield identical fluency scores while the second-, third-, and fourth-order scalings produce increasingly higher scores. The largest increases derive from the long–short rule (third order) and the *c* rule (fourth order).

Testing psychological reality

One test of the psychological reality of the various metrics proposed here could be based on English words that discriminate clearly among the different predictions made. Another possibility is to evaluate how well these metrics predict performance on individual words in pronunciation and lexical decision tasks. Following this latter suggestion, we evaluated these new metrics against a recent series of experiments by Waters and Seidenberg (1985). The authors sytematically varied word frequency, spelling-to-sound correspondences, and orthographic regularity in six pronunciation and lexical-decision tasks. Although a relatively small number of words was used in each experiment and each task, RT differences between certain stimulus sets were significant and revealed that a systematic analysis was warranted. To overcome the limitations with correlations based on small sample sizes and to simplify the analysis, the results were modified to allow three grand analyses. First, for each word in a given task in a given study, the dependent measure for that word was its RT minus the mean RT across all words in that task and study. This was done for every word in every task in every study except for words that did not occur in the Kučera and Francis (1967) word list. In addition, only words between four and seven letters in length were included because of certain constraints of assigning measures of orthographic structure.[11] This gave a total of 505 cases for the analysis. Since some words were used in several tasks, there were not 505 unique words although there were 505 unique dependent measures.

Six independent variables were included in the analysis. Log word frequency was based on log to the base 10 of the Kučera and Francis (1967) corpus. The orthographic measures were average position sensitive log bigram and trigram counts based on the Massaro *et al.* (1980) sublexical counts of the Kučera and Francis word list. To provide a measure independent of word length, only initial, medial and final positions were included. The counts were based on all words between four and seven letters in length. Thus, each test word, regardless of word length, could be assigned a bigram count from a single table and analogously for the trigram count. The exertion measure and the second-order fluency measure were included as measures of spelling-to-sound correspondences. Finally, number of neighbors was computed for each word by counting the number of words that differed by a single letter from each test word (again based on Kučera and Francis, 1967).

Partial correlations are given in Table 4, reflecting the correlation of each independent variable, with the dependent variable, with the variance of all other variables pulled out. As can be seen in the table, both orthographic structure and spelling-to-sound correspondences account for some of the variance. Word frequency also is an important variable although number of neighbors is not. Given the findings of Waters and Seidenberg (1985) that differences were found for only words of low word frequency, the analysis was repeated for high and low frequency words

Table 4.   Partial correlations between RTs and six predictor variables for Waters and Seidenberg (1985).

Predictor	All words	Low frequency	High frequency
log word freq	−0.293*	−0.418*	0.058
fluency	−0.137*	−0.219*	0.033
log bigram	−0.146*	−0.145*	−0.097
neighbours	−0.028	−0.020	0.024
exertion	0.026	−0.027	−0.139*
log trigram	0.082	0.002*	0.069

Number of cases is 505, 280 and 225 for all words, low frequency words, and high frequency words, respectively.

* Significant ($p \leq 0.05$) and in the appropriate direction.

analysed separately. These partial correlations are also given in Table 4. Replicating the conclusions based on group comparisons, the item analysis shows no significant effect of spelling-to-sound correspondences for high-frequency words. However, the effect of orthographic regularity is marginally significant ($p \leq 0.10$) for these same words.

Conclusions

The new metrics proposed here for spelling–sound regularity reflect some of the uncertainty that remains to be resolved in visual word recognition. Testing of orthographic structure and spelling–sound regularity represents a maturing process that has occurred over the past decade. By contrasting simultaneously different metrics for orthographic structure and spelling–sound regularity, we have the potential of describing the multiple sources of information that are functional in reading printed words.

Notes

[1] Following Venezky (1970), we use *grapheme* to refer to the alphabetic units a . . . z, corresponding to Henderson's (in press) *sense I*. For compatibility with a highly diverse literature, however, we will continue to use the term *letter* (and its hyphenates) when it is the label commonly employed in the work under discussion.

[2] Exceptions exist for b(ebb), d(add, odd), g(egg), and n(inn).

[3] Two common exceptions to this latter rule are *you* and *thou*.

[4] Almost all exceptions to this rule are French borrowings like *chauffeur*.

[5] cf. Scheerer, Chap 12.

[6] Base, duel, tooth, strewn, throng.

[7] Functional units for English are (a) those graphemes or grapheme sequences whose phonological correspondences can not be predicted from the correspondences of their separate components (e.g., ch, tch, a, b, ee) or (b) graphemes whose primary function is to indicate the pronunciation of another functional unit or preserve a graphotactical or morphological pattern (e.g., *e* in *rage* and *nurse*, *u* and *e* in *catalogue*). The often employed 'grapheme-phoneme rule' is actually inconsistent, in that mappings are often not between a grapheme and phoneme but between a functional unit and one or more phonemes (e.g., ch-/č/).

[8] A single-letter vowel spelling is short (checked) before a compound consonant (e.g., *x*, *ck*) or a consonant cluster; otherwise it is long (free).

[9] *c* is soft (/s/) before *e, i, or y*; otherwise it is hard (/k/). (Palatalization of /s/ to /š/ as in *ocean* is covered by the next rule.)

[10] For these three rules, see Venezky, 1970.

[11] With these constraints, only 6 of 224 words were dropped.

References

Ainsfeld, M. A. (1964). Comment on "The role of grapheme-phoneme correspondence in the perception of words." *American Journal of Psychology*, **77**, 320–6.

Baddeley, A. D. (1964). Immediate memory and the "perception" of letter sequences. *Quarterly Journal of Experimental Psychology*, **16**, 364–7.

Baron, J., and Strawson, C. (1976). Use of orthographic and word specific knowledge in reading words aloud. *Journal of Experimental Psychology: Human Perception and Performance*, **2**, 386–93.

Bauer, D. W., and Stanovich, K. E. (1980). Lexical access and the spelling-to-sound regularity effect. *Memory and Cognition*, **8**, 424–32.

Becker, C. A., and Killian, T. H. (1977). Interaction of visual and cognitive effects in word recognition. *Journal of Experimental Psychology: Human Perception and Performance*, **3**, 389–401.

Bouwhuis, D. G. (1979). *Visual recognition of words*. Unpublished doctoral dissertation, Katholieke Universiteit, Nijmegen, Holland.

Chase, W. G., and Simon, H. A. (1973). Perception in chess. *Cognitive Psychology*, **4**, 55–81.

Chomsky, N., and Halle, M. (1968). *The sound pattern of English*. New York: Harper & Row.

Coltheart, M., Davelaar, E., Jonasson, J. T., and Besner, D. (1977). Access to the internal lexicon. In S. Dornic (Ed.) *Attention and Performance VI*. Hillsdale, NJ: Erlbaum.

Feldman, L. B., and Turvey, M. T. (1980). Words written in kana are named faster than the same words written in kanji. *Language and Speech*, **23**, 141–7.

Gernsbacher, M. A. (1984). Resolving 20 years of inconsistent interactions between lexical familarity and orthography, concreteness, and polysemy. *Journal of Experimental Psychology: General*, **113**, 253–81.

Gibson, E. J., and Levin, H. (1975). *The psychology of reading*. Cambridge, MA: MIT Press.

Gibson, E. J., Shurcliff, A., and Yonas, A. (1970). Utilization of spelling patterns by deaf and hearing subjects. In H. Levin and J. P. Williams (Eds) *Basic studies on reading*. New York: Basic Books.

Gilmore, G. C., and Egeth, H. E. (1976). When are nonwords easy to see? *Memory and Cognition*, **4**, 519–24.

Glushko, R. J. (1979). The organization and activation of orthographic knowledge in reading aloud. *Journal of Experimental Psychology: Human Perception and Performance*, **5**, 674–91.

Gough, P. (1984). Word recognition. In P. D. Pearson, R. Barr, M. L. Kamil, and P. Mosenthal (Eds) *Handbook of reading research*. New York: Longman.

Hanson, V. L. (1986). Access to spoken language and the acquisition of orthographic structure: Evidence from deaf readers. *Quarterly Journal of Experimental Psychology*, **38A**, 193–212.

Hart, J. (1980). The psychological reality of different spelling patterns. Unpublished doctoral dissertation, University of Delaware.

Henderson, L. (1982). *Orthography and word recognition in reading*. London: Academic Press.

Henderson, L. (in press). On the use of the term "grapheme." *Language and Cognitive Processes*.

Humphreys, G. W., and Evett, L. J. (1985). Are there independent lexical and nonlexical routes in word processing? An evaluation of the dual-route theory of reading. *The Behavioral and Brain Sciences*, **8**, 689–740.

Hung, D. L., and Tzeng, O. J. L. (1981). Orthographic variations and visual information processing. *Psychological Bulletin*, **90**, 377–414.

Jonides, J., Naveh-Benjamin, M., and Palmer, J. (1985). Assessing automaticity. *Acta Psychologica*, **60**, 157–71.

Kavanagh, J. F., and Venezky, R. L. (Eds) (1980). *Orthography, reading, and dyslexia*. Baltimore, MD: University Park Press.

Kimura, Y. (1984). Concurrent vocal interference: Its effects on kana and kanji. *Quarterly Journal of Experimental Psychology*, **36A**, 117–131.

Krueger, L. E. (1979). Features versus redundancy: Comments on Massaro, Venezky, and Taylor's "orthographic regularity, positional frequency, and visual processing of letter strings". *Journal of Experimental Psychology: General*, **108**, 125–30.

Kučera, H., and Francis, W. N. (1967). *Computational analysis of present-day American English*. Providence, R.I.: Brown University Press.

Lesgold, A. M. (1984). Human skill in a computerized society: Complex skills and their acquisition. *Behavior Research Methods, Instruments, & Computers*, **16**, 79–87.

Lesgold, A. M., and Perfetti, C. A. (Eds) (1981). *Interactive Processes in Reading*. Hillsdale, NJ: Erlbaum.

Mason, M. (1975). Reading ability and letter search time. Effects of orthographic structure defined by single-letter positional frequency. *Journal of Experimental Psychology: General*, **104**, 146–66.

Mason, M. (1978). From print to sound in mature readers as a function of reader ability and two forms of orthographic regularity. *Memory & Cognition*, **6**, 568–81.

Massaro, D. W. (1979). Letter information and orthographic context in word perception. *Journal of Experimental Psychology: Human Perception and Performance*, **5**, 595–609.

Massaro, D. W., and Hestand, J. (1983). Development of relations between reading ability and knowledge of orthographic structure. *Contemporary Educational Psychology*, **8**, 174–80.

Massaro, D. W., Jastrzembski, J. E., and Lucas, P. A. (1981). Frequency, orthographic regularity, and lexical status in letter and word perception. In G. H. Bower (Ed.) *The psychology of learning and motivation*, **15**, 163–200.

Massaro, D. W., Taylor, G. A., Venezky, R. L., Jastrzembski, J. E., and Lucas, P. A. (1980). *Letter and word perception: Orthographic structure and visual processing in reading*. Amsterdam: North-Holland.

Massaro, D. W., Venezky, R. L., and Taylor, G. A. (1979). Orthographic regularity, positional frequency, and visual processing of letter strings. *Journal of Experimental Pscyhology: General*, **108**, 107–24.

Mayzner, M. S., and Tresselt, M. E. (1965). Tables of single-letter and digram frequency counts for various word-length and letter-position combinations. *Psychonomic Monograph Supplements*, **1**, 13–32.

Mayzner, M. S., Tresselt, M. E., and Wolin, B.R. (1965a) Tables of tetragram frequency counts for various word-length and letter-position combinations. *Psychonomic Monograph Supplements*, **1**, 79–143.

Mayzner, M. S., Tresselt, M. E., and Wolin, B. R. (1965b). Tables of trigram frequency counts for various word-length and letter-position combinations. *Psychonomic Monograph Supplements*, **1**, 33–78.

McClelland, J. L., and Johnston, J. C. (1977). The role of familiar units in perception of words and nonwords. *Perception & Psychophysics*, **22**, 249–61.

McConkie, G. W., and Zola, D. (1981). Language constraints and the functional stimulus in reading. In A. Lesgold and C. A. Perfetti (Eds) *Interactive processes in reading*. Hillsdale, NJ: Erlbaum.

McCusker, L. X., Hillinger, M. L., and Bias, R. G. (1981). Phonological recoding and reading. *Psychological Bulletin*, **89**, 217–45.

Mewhort, D. J. K., and Beal, A. L. (1977). Mechanisms of word identification. *Journal of Experimental Psychology: Human Perception and Performance*, **3**, 629–40.

Miller, G. A., Bruner, J. S., and Postman, L. (1954). Familiarity of letter sequences and tachistoscopic identification. *Journal of General Psychology*, **50**, 129–39.

Parkin, A. J. (1982). Phonological recoding in lexical decision: Effects of spelling-to-sound regularity depend upon how regularity is defined. *Memory and Cognition*, **10**, 43–53.

Parkin, A. J. (1984). Redefining the regularity effect. *Memory & Cognition*, **12**, 287–92.

Perfetti, C. A., Goldman, S. R., and Hogaboam, T. W. (1979). Reading skill and the identification of words in discourse context. *Memory & Cognition*, **7**, 273–82.

Rice, G. A., and Robinson, D. O. (1975). The role of bigram frequency in perception of words and nonwords. *Memory & Cognition*, **3**, 513–18.

Rosson, M. B. (1985). The interaction of pronunciation rules and lexical representation in reading aloud. *Memory and Cognition*, **13**, 90–8.

Rubenstein, H., Lewis, S. S., and Rubenstein, M. (1971). Evidence for phonemic recoding in visual word recognition. *Journal of Verbal Learning and Verbal Behavior*, **10**, 645–57.

Seidenberg, M. S. (1985). The time course of phonological code activation in two writing systems. *Cognition*, **19**, 1–30.

Shannon, C. E. (1948). A mathematical theory of communication. *Bell System Technical Journal*, **27**, 379–423, 623–56.

Shannon, C. E. (1951). Prediction and entropy of printed English. *Bell System Technical Journal*, **30**, 50–64.

Singer, M. H. (1980). The primacy of visual information in the analysis of letter strings. *Perception and Psychophysics*, **27**, 153–62.

Solso, R. L. (1979). Positional frequency and versatility of letters for six-, seven-, and eight-letter English words. *Behavior Research Methods and Instrumentation*, **11**, 355–358.

Stanovich, K. E., and Bauer, D. N. (1978). Experiments on the spelling-to-sound regularity effect in word recognition. *Memory & Cognition*, **6**, 410–15.

Stroop, J. R. (1935). Studies of interference in serial verbal reactions. *Journal of Experimental Psychology*, **18**, 643–62.

Thomas, H. (1968). Children's tachistoscopic recognition of words and pseudowords varying in pronounceability and consonant-vowel sequence. *Journal of Experimental Psychology*, **77**, 511–13.

Thorndike, E. L., and Lorge, I. (1944). *The teacher's wordbook of 30,000 words*. New York: Bureau of Publications, Teachers College, Columbia University.

Tzeng, O. J. L., and Singer H. (Eds) (1981). *Perception of print: Reading research in experimental psychology*, Hillsdale, NJ: Erlbaum.

Underwood, B. J., and Schulz, R. W. (1960). *Meaningfulness and verbal learning.* New York: Academic Press.

van der Heijden, A. H. C., Hagenaar, R., and Bloem, W. (1984). Two stages in postcategorical filtering and selection. *Memory & Cognition*, **12**, 458–69.

Venezky, R. L. (1970). *The structure of English orthography.* The Hague: Mouton.

Venezky, R. L. (1974). Theoretical and experimental bases for teaching reading. In T. A. Sebeok (Ed), *Current trends in linguistics* (Vol. 12). The Hague: Mouton.

Venezky, R. L. (1981). Letter-sound regularity and orthographic structure. In M. L. Kamil (Ed) *Directions in reading: Research and instruction.* (Thirtieth Yearbook of the National Reading Conference.) Washington, DC: NRC.

Venezky, R. L. (1984). The history of reading research. In P. D. Pearson, R. Barr, M. L. Kamil and P. Mosenthal (Eds) *Handbook of reading research.* New York: Longman.

Venezky, R. L., and Johnson, D. (1973). The development of two letter-sound patterns in grades 1–3. *Journal of Educational Psychology*, **64**, 109–115.

Waters, G. S., and Seidenberg, M. S. (1985). Spelling-sound effects in reading: Time-course and decision criteria. *Memory & Cognition*, **13**, 557–72.

Waters, G. S., Seidenberg, M. S., and Bruck, M. (1984). Children's and adults' use of spelling-sound information in three reading tasks. *Memory & Cognition*, **12**, 293–305.

West, R. F., and Stanovich, K. E. (1978). Automatic contextual facilitation in readers of three ages. *Child Development*, **49**, 717–27.

9 Phonological codes in reading: Assignment of sub-word phonology

Janice Kay

Abstract

Since we can pronounce nonsense letter strings like *pream* rapidly and accurately, there must be a mechanism which allows us to translate spelling patterns smaller than a word into their corresponding sounds. Using findings from speeded naming of nonwords, the following work attempts to establish the sizes of orthographic and phonological units that can be used in sub-lexical phonological recoding. In summary, the evidence appears to rule out simple mechanisms of grapheme–phoneme conversion, but suggests that this source of knowledge must be supplemented by higher-order units such as the letter-cluster: initial and rhyme segment. Sub-lexical effects in word processing and lexical effects in sub-word processing are briefly reviewed. Finally, principles underpinning the assignment of sub-word phonology are considered.

Introduction

We may be forgiven for thinking that the ability to read single words is a basic skill (at least in literate communities) which is relatively simple to explain. Things are rarely as simple as they seem, however, and psychologists have long attempted to model the processes which are involved. In the past, investigation focused on the claim that written words are automatically recoded into a speech code prior to recognition in a mental lexicon (e.g. Rubenstein, Lewis and Rubenstein, 1971; Gough, 1972), and phonological recoding was assumed to take place using non-lexical spelling–sound rules. Such rules had a double function: they also allowed the

LANGUAGE PERCEPTION AND PRODUCTION
ISBN 0-12-052750-2

pronunciation of new words. It soon became clear, however, that word recognition can also be based on visual information and *dual-route models* were proposed, in which both sources of information can be used in recognition and production (Meyer, Schvaneveldt and Ruddy, 1974; Coltheart, 1980; Morton and Patterson, 1980). More recently, debate has shifted to the question of whether rule-governed knowledge used in translating print into pronunciation actually exists, or whether analogical knowledge based on visual and phonological properties of words, does the work of rules (see Henderson, 1985a; Humphreys and Evett, 1985; Kay, 1985; and Patterson and Morton, 1985 for critical reviews). However, many would now argue that this debate has generated more heat than light and that the dual-route-versus-analogy distinction will prove to be sterile (Norris and Brown, 1985).

The most damaging criticism that can be levelled at the recent form of the debate is the one that is most readily apparent (as many of the collection of commentaries that follow Humphreys and Evett's (1985) review have observed). Both dual-route and lexical analogy theories have remained stubbornly underspecified. At present, amendments and elaborations forced by a gradual accumulation of new data are being incorporated into both types of model, but it is becoming clearer that after a final honing and polishing, the two models may appear gleaming and sharp, but theoretically and empirically indistinguishable. Therefore, rather than concentrating on a comparison between dual-route and lexical analogy models, examining how they can each be accommodated to the various experimental effects, I have chosen in this chapter to focus on the nature of orthographic and phonological codes that appear to be available in translation from print to sound. In particular, I will look at the size of units that can be used and the principles for assigning phonology.

First let us consider a few facts. In the English orthography, certain linguistic and socio-linguistic factors have conspired over centuries to produce a percentage of words in the language whose pronunciation cannot be predicted from their spelling because the relationship between their constituent graphemes and corresponding phonemes is unpredictable: compare, for example, *couch* and *touch*, or *sworn* and *sword*. Irregular words like *touch* and *sword*, menaces to the foreigner learning the language and the beginning reader alike, can only be pronounced correctly if their pronunciation is known. This fact requires that *word-specific* (or morpheme-specific) information about spelling and pronunciation must be available for readers of English to recognize and pronounce words such as these correctly. On the other hand, we can readily pronounce word-like written letter strings like *pream* that we have never seen before and which cannot have complete lexical representations. Some sort of alternative mechanism is therefore also needed which allows us to construct pronunciations for *sub-word* letter strings. It is to this mechanism that I will now turn.

Single-level models of sub-lexical translation

One way of evaluating models of sub-lexical translation is to examine how they account for evidence about how written *nonwords* are pronounced. For the time being, I will concentrate on evidence from this source, leaving the consideration of data from normal word identification and naming for a later section.[1]

Until recently, the most favoured candidate for a mechanism of sub-lexical phonological recoding was a system of algorithmic grapheme–phoneme correspondence (GPC) rules (Coltheart, 1978). According to this proposal, written letter strings are segmented into graphemes (letters or letter groups)[2] which are then assigned phonemic correspondences by rule. Such rules are believed to be psychological realizations of linguistic rules for the pronunciation of English orthography such as those distinguished by Venezky (1970). A pronunciation is then assembled with the aid of co-articulation rules.

The task of identifying individual graphemes in a letter string and then assigning corresponding phonemic values is, however, considerably complicated by the lack of isomorphism between English orthography and phonology that results in a degree of ambiguity in both graphemic segmentation and phonemic assignment. Thus, there is no necessary one-to-one relationship between letters and graphemes: component letters of a string can correspond with a single grapheme on one occasion but with two or more graphemes on another (take the example of *th* which occurs as a single unit in *brother*, but as two units *t* and *h* in *hothead*). Moreover, many graphemes, especially vowels, can have a range of possible phonemic values (e.g. the vowel *a* may represent at least five separate sounds, as in *land, name, was, calm* and *sofa*) (see Henderson, 1982, for an excellent, comprehensive discussion of associated difficulties).

Predictability between spelling and sound patterns that comes from higher-order information about morphological structure, form class and stress is not open to this mechanism since it does not deal directly with specific knowledge about words. Some of the ambiguity at each stage may, however, be resolved by taking the surrounding graphemic context into account, and it has been assumed that such context-sensitivity is incorporated into the mechanism. But in cases in which there are a number of legitimate ways to pronounce a particular grapheme, it has been proposed that the most frequent correspondence (based on a *type count* of the number of words in the language containing a particular correspondence) is *invariably* applied (Coltheart, 1978). The grapheme *ea*, for example, can be pronounced in at least three different ways in words: /i/, /ɛ/ and /ei/. According to this *deterministic* mechanism, the most frequent correspondence, /i/, will always be assigned to the phonologically recoded string. Nonwords like *pream* and *preat* will invariably be pronounced as /prim/ and /prit/.

It is easy to demonstrate experimentally that a system of GPC rules that operate deterministically cannot work as a mechanism of phonological recoding (at least, not without some other system operating in tandem). Thus, Glushko (1979) showed that, in a speeded naming task, skilled readers sometimes pronounced nonwords like *preat*, which resembled visually similar irregular words (e.g. *great, sweat*) so as to rhyme with their word neighbours (that is, with an irregular GPC rule). These nonwords, which he called *inconsistent*, also took significantly longer to name than *consistent* nonwords like *pream*, which has the same ending as a set of words which all rhyme (e.g. *dream, beam, seam* etc.)

One loses nothing, however, by suggesting that the system of GPC rules operates probabilistically rather than on an 'all-or-none' basis. One could assume that the most frequent GPCs are not always applied; less frequent correspondences (e.g., *-ea-* → /ɛ/ or /ei/) are also sometimes produced (Kay and Lesser, 1985, show how phonological alternatives may be assigned probabilistically). This assumption still cannot account for Glushko's findings, however, since consistent and inconsistent nonwords shared the same vowel. A probabilistic GPC mechanism would produce approximately the same ratios of each type of pronunciation for both sets of nonwords.

Glushko's findings apparently point to a mechanism of phonological recoding that can operate on orthographic and phonological units larger than graphemes and phonemes: clusters of vowel and consonant like *-eat* and *-eam*. Inconsistent letter clusters like *-ead* might be associated with phonological alternatives (e.g. /id/ and /ɛd/) and might take longer to invoke than consistent letter clusters like *-eam* that have only a single phonological correspondence. Several authors (e.g. Kay and Marcel, 1981; Shallice, Warrington and McCarthy, 1983) have suggested that the *strength* of alternative phonological correspondences may be determined by their incidence in orthographic word neighbours (in much the same way as regularity of grapheme-phoneme correspondences is assumed to be gauged; cf. Rosson, 1985).

In a recent study (described in Kay, 1985), I reported that which pronunciation is assigned to an inconsistent nonword is indeed influenced by the incidence of each type of pronunciation of the letter cluster (see

Table 1). Let me illustrate the findings briefly with three nonword examples: *pook, doot* and *tave*. Most words ending in *-ook* are pronounced as /ɒk/ rather than /uk/ (*book, cook, rook*). On the other hand, most words ending in *-oot* are pronounced /ut/ (*boot, coot, root*). (Note that the commonest phonemic correspondence of the grapheme *oo* is /u/.) Accordingly, there was a tendency for the vowel of an inconsistent nonword like *pook* to be pronounced /ɒ/, common in word neighbours, which was absent in the case of a nonword like *doot*. On the other hand, individual word frequencies seemed to have no effect on the choice of nonword pronunciation. Thus, most words ending in *-ave* rhyme with /eiv/; *have* is an exception. It is also a very frequent word, but, none the less, the nonword *tave* was generally pronounced /teiv/.

Table 1. Mean percentages of regular and irregular pronunciations of non-words with either a regular bias†, irregular bias or no bias of the rhyme segment.

	Regular bias e.g. *tave* (N = 150)	No bias e.g. *rull* (N = 150)	Irregular bias e.g. *jook* (N = 150)
Irregular pronunciation e.g. /rɒl/	1.4	11.3	21.3
Regular pronunciation e.g. /rʌl/	91.3	77.3	69.3
Erroneous pronunciation e.g. /rul/	7.4	11.3	9.3

† Bias is measured by counting the number of visually similar words with each type of pronunciation. In the 'No Bias' condition, neither the regular nor the irregular pronunciation predominates in words.

However, the results of Table 1 also indicate that even when the word-final letter cluster is overwhelmingly pronounced with an irregular GPC pronunciation in words (e.g., -ook in *book* and *cook*), the *majority* of nonword pronunciations corresponded with the (GPC) regular pronunciation. This finding may be explained in a number of ways. One possibility is that only word-final letter clusters (rhymes) were varied in this experiment and no account was taken of a possible influence of word-initial clusters (e.g. *poo-* in *pook, doo-* in *doot*) which may have corresponded with regular phonology.[3] That rhymes may be more important in determining pronunciation than other units of sub-lexical phonology has been justified on somewhat *ad hoc* grounds: 'the salience of rhyme for adults and the primacy with which this develops in children' (Glushko, 1980). However, empirical support for this view has been provided by Treiman (1983). She showed that adults playing novel word games found it easier to learn rules that kept the rhyme intact than others that divided this unit.

In a recent speeded naming experiment, I investigated whether an influence of word-initial (CV) clusters would also be found in pronouncing nonwords. Take the example of our old friend *pook*. The consonant–vowel unit is always pronounced /pu/ in words like *poodle* or *pool*, corresponding with the regular pronunciation of the vowel. This is not the case for *wook*; words beginning with *woo-* are usually pronounced /wɔ/ (*wool, wood* etc.). Sixteen pairs of nonwords like *pook* and *wook*, sharing the same ending but differing in the *inherent bias* of the initial segments, were constructed for the experiment (each member of a pair was seen by different subjects). The results are briefly summarized in Table 2.

Table 2. Mean percentages of regular and irregular pronunciations of non-words with either a regular bias† or an irregular bias of the initial consonant–vowel.

	Regular bias e.g. *pook* (N = 160)	Irregular bias e.g. *wook* (N = 160)
Irregular pronunciation e.g. /wɔk/	11.9	23.1
Regular pronunciation e.g. /wuk/	82.5	66.3
Erroneous pronunciation e.g. /mul/	5.6	10.6

† Bias is measured by counting the number of visually similar words with each type of pronunciation.

Nonwords like *wook* with an inherent bias towards the irregular pronunciation were pronounced irregularly more often than their 'regular bias' counterparts like *pook*, but, yet again, the percentage of irregular pronunciations was still low (around 25%). Of course, in constructing nonword pairs, it was difficult also to take account of the bias in the way the rhyme segments are pronounced in words. It did seem that those nonwords that happened also to have an 'in-built' bias of the rhyme towards the irregular pronunciation (e.g. *wook, holl, nind, clow, wough, homb*) were more likely to be pronounced in this way than those with no such bias, but it appears likely that an orthographic–phonological unit *other* than the initial letter cluster and the rhyme is having an influence on sub-word pronunciations. This can be illustrated with the nonword *wook*. We have seen that the letter clusters *woo-* and *-ook* both have a bias towards the /ɒ/ pronunciation of the vowel. If a phonological recoding mechanism were operating only with units of this size, then we would expect this nonword *always* to be pronounced /wɒk/, to rhyme with *book* and *cook*. The nonword was given to 60 people who were simply asked to pronounce it. Just under two-thirds of the sample (37/60) said /wɒk/, but far short of the projected 100%. This finding implies that information supplied by grapheme–phoneme correspondences (of the form, '-oo- is most often pronounced /u/') is also contributing to the letter string's pronunciation.

Rosson (1985) has also provided data from speeded naming experiments which appear to demand a role for GPCs, as well as higher-level knowledge in spelling–sound translation. Moreover, as several researchers have recently pointed out (e.g. Marcel, 1980; Balota, 1985; Coltheart, 1985; Mitchell, 1985, Parkin, 1985), nonwords like *joov* consist of initial letter clusters and rhymes that are not represented in word exemplars (*joo-* and *-oov* are never found at the beginnings and ends of English words). Yet they are readily pronounceable. This must be because of GPC knowledge. So, it seems that processes of spelling–sound translation can use information about grapheme-phoneme and letter cluster correspondences (this is not to say, however, that the information is stored in the form of rules; I will return to this point in a later section).

Multi-level models of sub-lexical translation

Patterson and Morton (1985) have put forward a model of pronunciation assembly which incorporates both grapheme–phoneme correspondences and rhyme segments (called *bodies*). With more than one sub-lexical level at each stage of the translation process, orthographic segmentation and phonological assignment procedures become considerably more complicated than in single-level models, to say nothing of the way in which a final decision on pronunciation is reached. However, Patterson and Morton are quite explicit about how they think phonological assignment procedures operate and how a final decision is made between phonological information specified by the two types of unit. This makes their model relatively straightforward to implement computationally and to test (Bishop and Kay, in preparation).

Patterson and Morton suggest that GPCs operate deterministically (in that single, most frequent correspondences are produced), whilst some letter cluster rhymes operate deterministically and others probabilistically.

The latter statement perhaps requires more explanation. Rhyme segments which have an inherent bias towards either the regular pronunciation (e.g. *-ool* → /ul/, as in *cool*), or the irregular pronunciation (e.g. *-ook* → /ɒk/, as in *cook*), only have one stored phonological correspondence. Other rhyme segments in which regular and irregular pronunciations are approximately equally represented in words (e.g. -eaf in *deaf* and *leaf*) will have both pronunciations stored, with a choice between them being made on a probabilistic basis.[4]

The proposal put forward by Patterson and Morton, concerning the method in which phonological assignment is organized in GPC and rhyme components of sub-word translation, is based on the data collected by Kay (1982) and briefly reported above (Table 1). These data also led Patterson and Morton to consider how information from GPCs and rhymes interact in arriving at sub-lexical pronunciations. In fact, they propose that there is *no* interaction between the two levels: it is suggested that the lion's share of pronunciations (around 70%) are produced by GPCs (this accounts for the preponderance of regular pronunciations of nonwords in Kay's data). On a remaining 30% of occasions, pronunciation is determined by relevant rhyme segments. This means that, in theory, irregular nonword pronunciations should not exceed 30% of the database in speeded naming experiments such as those described above. It is perhaps important to point out, however, that the weightings assigned to the separate sub-lexical systems provide 'a first-approximation fit' of available data (Patterson and Morton, p. 348). They do not crucially affect the operating characteristics of the model. Nor, if the 70–30% ratio is shown to be incorrect, could this finding be said to endanger the basic assumptions of the model. However, one possible difficulty for the Patterson and Morton model is the finding (illustrated in Table 2) that initial letter cluster segments can influence nonword pronunciations. Incorporating this unit into the model would seem to require some modifications, particularly with regard to the decision rule between sub-word phonological components, and would make elaboration of orthographic segmentation procedures even more pressing.

The initial letter cluster is only one of the orthographic and phonological units that can contribute to sub-word pronunciations in the model put forward by Shallice and his colleagues (Shallice, Warrington and McCarthy, 1983; Shallice and McCarthy, 1985). In this model, orthographic and phonological units of a number of different sizes (graphemes and phonemes, letter-clusters, syllables and morphemes) are stored as separate items alongside each other in an orthographic and a phonological lexicon. Shallice and McCarthy (1985) have elaborated a parsing mechanism based on 'relaxation' procedures derived from scene recognition programs in computer vision (e.g. Hinton and Anderson, 1981), which they claim can surmount segmentation difficulties. Shallice, Warrington and McCarthy (1983) also suggest that alternative pronunciations of individual letter groups may be selected on the basis of strength of correspondence (see above). But the authors are less specific about how phonological specifications from between levels of representation (which may or may not conflict), are reconciled to produce a unitary (prearticulatory) response. However, this question and, indeed, the question of how sub-word phonology is assigned, must be dealt with by any multi-level model (including the lexical analogy or parallel activation models put forward by Marcel (1980, Kay and Marcel, 1981); Henderson, 1982; Seidenberg, 1985).

Using findings from speeded naming of nonwords, I have attempted, in this and the previous section, to establish the size of orthographic and phonological unit that can be used in sub-lexical spelling–sound translation. In summary, the evidence appears to rule out simple mechanisms of grapheme–phoneme conversion, but suggests that this source of knowledge must be supplemented by higher-order units such as the letter cluster; initial and rhyme segment. I have briefly described two multi-level models of pronunciation assembly; I have dealt with how lexical analogy models may incorporate this knowledge elsewhere (Kay, 1985).

Sub-lexical effects in word processing

In this section I want briefly to review empirical evidence for the influence of sub-word-sized segments on word identification and production. For a comprehensive review of this topic, the reader is directed to Humphreys and Evett (1985) and associated commentaries.

It has long been claimed that effects of phonological recoding, operating with grapheme–phoneme correspondences, can be measured in speeded naming tasks (Baron and Strawson, 1976; Gough and Cosky, 1977; Stanovich and Bauer, 1978). Thus, exception words yield significantly longer latencies than regular words and are more often mispronounced. The interest aroused by Glushko's (1979) findings, again using a speeded naming procedure, was therefore due primarily to the demonstration that certain words like *beat*, that can be regarded as regular according to GPC rules, take significantly longer to pronounce than other words with the same regular vowel (e.g. *beam*). Unlike *beam*, *beat* has word neighbours with conflicting, irregular pronunciations (e.g. *great, sweat*), and it seems that the reaction-time cost for such words can be ascribed to a lack of consistency of pronunciation of the *rhyme* (in whichever form it is represented).[5] This result parallels consistency effects in nonword pronunciation described above.

It is clear, however, that the influence of these effects is not as broad as initial findings would suggest. For example, Parkin (1985) has recently reported the details of an unpublished re-analysis of the response data in Glushko's experiments. He claims that an effect of consistency on naming latencies is only evident for regular words which have irregular neighbours in approximately equal number. The same pattern is also found for the nonword set. The value of these results, and similar findings using nonwords reported above (and Kay, 1982), is that they serve to inform about the way in which phonological correspondences of sub-word units may be represented. But more importantly, perhaps, work pursuing effects of consistency (and, indeed, regularity) in word naming has suggested that these factors do not affect speeded naming of *high-frequency* words (Andrews, 1982; Seidenberg, Waters, Barnes and Tanenhaus, 1984). For these words at least, it appears that whole-word phonology can be derived *without* influence from sub-word components. However, both effects of consistency (*beat* being slower to name than *beam*) and regularity (*great* being slower to name than *beat*) have been observed in naming low-frequency words (Seidenberg *et al.*, 1984).

Effects of regularity and consistency are not reliably found when subjects are required to decide whether the stimulus is a word (even when the same experimental stimuli precipitate effects in word *naming*). Thus, using lexical decision measures, some researchers have failed to observe effects of regularity (Coltheart, Besner, Jonasson and Davelaar, 1979; Andrews, 1982) and consistency, even with low frequency words (Seidenberg *et al.*, 1984) whilst others have reported effects (albeit smaller in magnitude than in speeded naming) (Bauer and Stanovich, 1980; Parkin, 1982; Parkin and Underwood, 1984). The confusion generated by conflicting findings using lexical decision procedures highlights differences in cognitive processes employed in lexical decision and speeded naming tasks (cf. Balota and Chumbley, 1984), not least of which is the variability with which people apparently use phonology (word or sub-word) to guide their lexical decisions. A related argument, recently put forward, holds that lexical decision and pronunciation tasks may tap different periods in the time course of phonological activation of word and sub-word processing (Seidenberg, 1985; Waters and Seidenberg, 1985).

To make clear the main points of this section: effects of sub-lexical phonology can be observed in speeded naming of words (if less often in lexical decision). They tend to be confined to words low in frequency, however. None the less, they must be accounted for in considering the interaction between lexical and sub-lexical knowledge in spelling–sound translation.

Lexical effects in sub-word processing

Kay and Marcel (1981) have demonstrated that an irregular word like *head* can significantly prime the irregular pronunciation of an inconsistent non-word like *jead*, presented immediately afterwards. Kay (in preparation) has extended this finding to show that an irregular word sharing the initial letter cluster with a subsequent nonword (e.g. *head-heaf*) can also prime irregular sub-word pronunciations to a significant extent.

An even more interesting finding has been described by Rosson (1983). She reported that the pronunciation of a nonword can be influenced by that of an irregular word, even when the word itself has not been presented, but a *semantic associate* of the word has been presented instead. Thus, the word *brush*, a close semantic associate of *comb*, can bias the regular pronunciation of the nonword *jomb* (/ʤoɒm/), without the mediation of *comb*. Although Rosson's study may be criticized on a number of metho-dological grounds (cf. Patterson and Morton, 1985), this result has been replicated by the present author (Kay, in preparation). In a similar vein, Campbell and Besner (1981) demonstrated that specifically *syntactic* knowledge can be brought to bear on how a nonword is pronounced. They showed that whether the voiced or voiceless pronunciation was given to *th-* at the beginning of a nonword was dependent, in large measure, to the position the nonword occupied in a sentence (replacing either a grammati-cal word or content word). For the unit *th-*, form class is an infallible guide to voicing.

It is clear from the experiments of Kay and Marcel (1981) and Rosson (1983) that word primes significantly raise the probability of a particular nonword pronunciation being produced, compared with a baseline condi-tion in which the nonword remains unprimed. Priming is far from being 100% effective, however. It is therefore perhaps worth considering why it sometimes fails to work. I have an observation that bears on this point. It seems to be the case that some nonwords are easier to prime than others (either preceded by an orthographically similar word or by a semantic associate of that word). It appears that these are letter strings in which there is an *inherent bias* towards the pronunciation that is being primed. Thus, our old friend *wook*, which has, as we have seen, an in-built bias towards the irregular pronunciation of both the initial segment and rhyme, is relatively easy to prime using a word which shares the rhyme (e.g. *book-wook*) or the initial segment (e.g. *wool-wook*). This also applies to a semantic associate prime (e.g. *cotton-wook*), in which *cotton* is used as an associate of *wool*. Conversely, the irregular pronunciations of nonwords like *doot* and *fave*, which have a bias in all segments towards the regular pronunciation, are difficult to prime with a visually similar irregular word, or semantic associate of that word.

The representation of sub-word phonology

Early work in this area claimed that: (1) a system of grapheme–phoneme correspondence rules is used to supplement specific knowledge about the spelling and pronunciation of words; (2) that rules for the pronunciation of individual graphemes are derived from the frequency of phonemic correspondences in words (based on the frequency of each *type* of pronunciation); and (3) that such rules are deterministic; that is, the most frequent correspondence is always applied (Coltheart, 1978). It is quite clear that the first claim is incorrect, or at least only partially true, since there is evidence from speeded word and nonword naming that higher-level correspondences must also be incorporated into a model of pronunciation assembly. Findings which indicate that GPCs do play some part in determining pronunciation suggest that the third claim is also incorrect; they are not applied in an 'all-or-none' fashion. Thus, the nonword *fouch* is sometimes pronounced /fooʧ/, a pronunciation that is not found in words ending in *-ouch* (Kay, 1982). This finding indicates that it is the vowel correspondence, rather than the rhyme, that is responsible for this particular pronunciation. However, the correspondence *-ou-* → /oʊ/, although legitimate (e.g. *soul, dough*), is not the most frequent pronunciation of the unit (this honour falls to *-ou-* → /aʊ/).

On the other hand, the second claim may be correct. Recent evidence suggests that assignment of grapheme–phoneme correspondences is governed by type frequency (Rosson, 1985). I have claimed that higher-level correspondences, such as those of the initial segment and rhyme, are also governed by type frequency, both in primed and unprimed pronunciations of nonwords (see above). There are also data from Parkin's (1985) reanalysis of consistency effects in words (see above), which may be interpreted as demonstrating an influence of type frequency on sub-word components in word pronunciation. However, it remains to be seen whether this influence is limited to low-frequency words.

Type frequency is a general principle which drives the notion of rule assignment in linguistics: *regularity* is governed by the number of instances of a particular feature (cf. Hockett, 1958, p. 280). However, I certainly do not wish to argue that sub-word correspondences are stored in the form of rule-based knowledge. I simply want to claim that this property underpins the concept of *strength* of sub-word phonological correspondences, however they are stored. At the same time, though, it is well established that individual word-frequencies (*token frequency*) are important in the production of whole-word phonology (e.g. Fredriksen and Kroll, 1976). It appears that both properties may be important in determining the pronunciation of written letter strings: one which exerts its influence mainly in the pronunciation of words, the other in the pronunciation of sub-word components.

Acknowledgements

I would like to thank Derek Besner, Laurie Feldman, Leslie Henderson and Eckart Scheerer for their helpful criticisms of an original version of this chapter. The work is funded by an MRC Project Grant.

Notes

[1] Limitations on space make it difficult also to consider findings from acquired reading disorders. The reader is directed to Shallice and McCarthy (1985) and Humphreys and Evett (1985; and associated commentaries) for discussion of how they may bear on the dual-route-versus-lexical analogy debate.

[2] Coltheart's proposal treats graphemes as those units which correspond with phonemes. Henderson (1985b) discusses an alternative (and preferred) formulation in which graphemes have a function in the written language that is 'parallel to and broadly equivalent with the role assigned to phonemes in the spoken language', rather than being defined purely in terms of reflectors of speech sounds.

[3] Note that this is also true of speeded naming and lexical decision experiments looking for sub-lexical effects in word processing (e.g. Glushko, 1979; Seidenberg, Waters, Barnes and Tanenhaus, 1984).

[4] The system is slightly more complicated than this. In fact, there are at least four, and possibly five, types of rhyme segment distinguished by Patterson and Morton (1985, p. 346–7).

[5] Whether as parts of word analogies or as separately-stored sub-word units.

References

Andrews, S. (1982). Phonological recoding: Is the regularity effect consistent? *Memory & Cognition*, **10**, 565–75.

Balota, D. A. (1985). Bringing together some old and new concerns about dual-route theory. *The Behavioral and Brain Sciences*, **8**, 705–6.

Balota, D. A. and Chumbley, J. I. (1984). Are lexical decisions a good measure of lexical access? The role of word frequency in the neglected decision stage.

Journal of Experimental Psychology: Human Perception and Performance, **10**, 340–57.

Baron, J. and Strawson, C. (1976). Use of orthographic and word-specific knowledge in reading words aloud. *Journal of Experimental Psychology: Human Perception and Performance*, **2**, 386–93.

Bauer, D. W. and Stanovich, K. E. (1980). Lexical access and the spelling-to-sound regularity effect. *Memory & Cognition*, **8**, 424–32.

Campbell, R. and Besner, D. (1981). This and thap — Constraints on the pronunciation of new written words. *Quarterly Journal of Experimental Psychology*, **33A**, 375–96.

Coltheart, M. (1978). Lexical access in simple reading tasks. In *Strategies of Information Processing*, ed. G. Underwood. London: Academic Press.

Coltheart, M. (1980). Reading, phonological recoding and deep dyslexia. In M. Coltheart, K. E. Patterson and J. C. Marshall (Eds) *Deep Dyslexia*. London: Routledge and Kegan Paul.

Coltheart, M. (1985). In defence of dual-route models of reading. *The Behavioral and Brain Sciences*, **8**, 709–10.

Coltheart, M., Besner, D., Jonasson J-T. and Davelaar, E. (1979). Phonological encoding and the lexical decision task. *Quarterly Journal of Experimental Psychology*, **31**, 489–507.

Fredriksen, J. and Kroll, J. (1976). Spelling and sound. Approaches to the internal lexicon. *Journal of Experimental Psychology: Human Perception and Performance*, **2**, 361–79.

Glushko, R. J. (1979). The organization and activation of orthographic knowledge in reading aloud. *Journal of Experimental Psychology: Human Perception and Performance*, **5**, 674–91.

Glushko, R. J. (1980). Principles for pronouncing print: The psychology of phonography. In A. M. Lesgold and C. A. Perfetti (Eds) *Interactive Processes in Reading*. Hillsdale, NJ: Erlbaum.

Gough, P. B. (1972). One second of reading. In J. F. Kavanagh and I. G. Mattingley (Eds) *Language by Ear and by Eye*. Cambridge, MA: MIT Press.

Gough, P. B. and Cosky, M. J. (1977). One second of reading again. In N. J. Castellan, D. B. Pisoni and G. H. Potts (Eds) *Cognitive Theory II*. Hillsdale, NJ: Erlbaum.

Henderson, L. (1982). *Orthography and Word Recognition in Reading*. London: Academic Press.

Henderson, L. (1985). Issues in the modelling of pronunciation assembly in normal reading. In K. E. Patterson, J. C. Marshall and M. Coltheart (Eds) *Surface Dyslexia: Neuropsychological and Cognitive Studies of Phonological Reading*. London: Erlbaum.

Henderson, L. (1985b). On the use of the term 'grapheme'. *Language and Cognitive Processes*, **1**, 135–48.

Hinton, G. and Anderson, J. (1981). *Parallel Models of Associative Memory*. Hillsdale, NJ: Erlbaum.

Hockett, C. F. (1958). *A course in modern linguistics*. New York: Macmillan.

Humphreys, G. W. and Evett, L. J. (1985). Are there independent lexical and non-lexical routes in word processing? An evaluation of the dual-route theory of reading. *The Behavioral and Brain Sciences*, **8**, 689–705.

Kay, J. (1982). Psychological mechanisms involved in oral reading. Unpublished Doctoral Dissertation. University of Cambridge.

Kay, J. (1982). Mechanisms of oral reading: a critical appraisal of cognitive models. In A. W. Ellis (Ed.) *Progress in the Psychology of Language*, **Vol 2**. London: Erlbaum.

Kay, J. and Lesser, R. (1985). Phonological processes in reading: Evidence from Surface Dyslexia. *Quarterly Journal of Experimental Psychology*, **37A**, 39–81.

Kay, J. and Marcel, A. J. (1981). One process, not two, in reading aloud: Lexical analogies do the work of non-lexical rules. *Quarterly Journal of Experimental Psychology*, **33A**, 397–414.

Marcel, A. J. (1980). Surface dyslexia and beginning reading: A revised hypothesis of the pronunciation of print and its impairments. In M. Coltheart, K. E. Patterson and J. C. Marshall (Eds) *Deep Dyslexia*. London: Routledge and Kegan Paul.

Meyer, D. E., Schvaneveldt, R. W. and Ruddy, M. G. (1974). Functions of graphemic and phonemic codes in visual word recognition. *Memory & Cognition*, **2**, 309–21.

Mitchell, D. C. (1985). Access to the lexicon. Are there three routes? *The Behavioral and Brain Sciences*, **8**, 717–18.

Morton, J. and Patterson, K. E. (1980). A new attempt at an interpretation, or, an attempt at a new interpretation. In M. Coltheart, K. E. Patterson and J. C. Marshall (Eds) *Deep Dyslexia*. London: Routledge and Kegan Paul.

Norris, D. and Brown, G. (1985). Race models and analogy theories: A dead heat? A Reply to Seidenberg. *Cognition*, **20**, 155–68.

Parkin, A. J. (1982). Phonological recoding in lexical decision: Effects of spelling-to-sound regularity depend on how regularity is defined. *Memory & Cognition*, **10**, 43–53.

Parkin, A. J. (1985). Dual route theory and the consistency effect. *The Behavioral and Brain Sciences*, **8**, 720–1.

Parkin, A. J. and Underwood, G. (1983). Orthographic versus phonological irregularity in lexical decision. *Memory & Cognition*, **11**, 351–5.

Patterson, K. E. and Morton, J. (1985). From orthography to phonology: An attempt at an old interpretation. In K. E. Patterson, J. C. Marshall and M. Coltheart (Eds) *Surface Dyslexia*. London: Erlbaum.

Rosson, M. B. (1983). From SOFA to LOUCH: Lexical contributions to pseudo-word pronunciation. *Memory & Cognition*, **11**, 152–60.

Rosson, M. B. (1985). The interaction of pronunciation rules and lexical representations in reading aloud. *Memory & Cognition*, **13**, 90–9.

Rubenstein, H., Lewis, S. S. and Rubenstein, M. A. (1971). Evidence for phonemic recoding in visual word recognition. *Journal of Verbal Learning and Verbal Behaviour*, **10**, 645–58.

Seidenberg, M. S. (1985). The time course of phonological code activation in two writing systems. *Cognition*, **19**, 1–30.

Seidenberg, M. S., Waters, G. S., Barnes, M. A. and Tanenhaus, M. K. (1984). When does irregular spelling or pronunciation influence word recognition? *Journal of Verbal Learning and Verbal Behaviour*, **23**, 383–404.

Shallice, T., Warrington, E. and McCarthy, R. (1983). Reading without semantics. *Quarterly Journal of Experimental Psychology*, **35A**, 111–38.

Shallice, T. and McCarthy, R. (1985). Phonological reading: from patterns of impairment to possible procedures. In K. E. Patterson, J. C. Marshall and M. Coltheart (Eds) *Surface Dyslexia*. London: Erlbaum.

Stanovich, K. E. and Bauer, D. W. (1978). Experiments on the spelling-to-sound regularity effect in word recognition. *Memory & Cognition*, **6**, 410–15.

Treiman, R. (1983). The structure of spoken syllables: Evidence from novel word games. *Cognition*, **15**, 49–74.

Venezky, R. L. (1970). *The Structure of English Orthography*. The Hague: Mouton.

10 Phonological and morphological analysis by skilled readers of Serbo-Croatian

Laurie B. Feldman

Abstract

Special properties of Serbo-Croatian were exploited in order to investigate the ability of skilled readers to appreciate the phonological and morphological components of Serbo-Croatian words. In the first experiment bivalent letter strings (namely, those composed exclusively of characters that appear in both the Roman and Cyrillic alphabet) were presented in a lexical decision task. Latencies were prolonged relative to unique alphabet transcriptions of those same words and the outcome was interpreted as a phonological effect. In the second experiment, decision latencies to phonologically bivalent root morphemes with alphabetically bivalent and unique inflectional affixes were compared. Results of ambiguity obtained only when the affix as well as the base morpheme were bivalent suggesting that recognition of the base morpheme alone does not govern decision latencies. In the third experiment, phonologically bivalent words and their unique alphabet controls were presented in the context of semantic associates which were printed in an alphabet that was either congruent or incongruent with the target. For bivalent words, semantic association and alphabetic congruency facilitated in an additive fashion but for unique alphabet controls semantic association but not alphabetic congruency was significant. Results indicate distinct loci for associative and alphabetic effects. Finally, in the fourth experiment, facilitation due to repetition of a base morpheme was observed but repetition of the same orthographic pattern in unrelated words produced no facilitation. Collectively, the studies provide evidence for phonological and morphological analysis by skilled readers of Serbo-Croatian.

Serbo-Croatian, the major language of Yugoslavia, possesses two distinctive properties that have been exploited as tools in the study of reading.

LANGUAGE PERCEPTION AND PRODUCTION
ISBN 0-12-052750-2

First, most literate speakers of Serbo-Croatian are facile in two alphabets, Roman and Cyrillic. The two alphabet sets intersect and words composed exclusively from the subset of characters that occur in both alphabets can be assigned two phonological interpretations — one by treating the characters as Roman graphemes and one by treating the characters as Cyrillic graphemes. By exploiting the availability of two overlapping alphabets, the nature of phonological codes and how they figure in lexical access has been explored. Second, the inflectional and derivational morphology is complex in Serbo-Croatian and extensive families of morphologically-related words exist. The complex morphology permits one to investigate how morphological structure is appreciated by the proficient language user. In the present report, results of a series of experiments that investigated phonological and morphological analysis in word recognition tasks by adult readers of Serbo-Croatian are summarized and discussed in terms of a characterization of skilled reading in Serbo-Croatian. To anticipate, the skilled reader of Serbo-Croatian appears to appreciate both phonological and morphological components of words.

The bi-alphabetic environment

Serbo-Croatian is written in two different alphabets, Roman and Cyrillic. The two alphabets transcribe one language and their graphemes map simply and directly onto the same set of phonemes. These two sets of graphemes are, with certain exceptions, mutually exclusive. Most of the Roman and Cyrillic letters occur only in their respective alphabets. These are referred to as *unique* letters. There are, however, a limited number of letters that are shared by the two alphabets. In some cases, the phonemic interpretation of a shared letter is the same whether it is read as Cyrillic or as Roman; these are referred to as *common* letters. In other cases, a shared letter has two phonemic interpretations, one by the Roman reading and one by the Cyrillic reading, these are referred to as *ambiguous* letters[1] (see Figure 1). Whatever their category, the individual letters of the two alphabets have phonemic interpretations (classifically defined) that are virtually invariant over letter contexts. (This reflects the phonologically shallow nature of the Serbo-Croatian orthography.) Moreover, all the individual letters in a string of letters, be it a word or nonsense, are pronounced — there are no letters made silent by context (see Feldman and Turvey, 1983; Lukatela, Popadić, Ognjenović and Turvey, 1980; Lukatela, Savić, Gligorević, Ognjenović and Turvey, 1978).[2]

Given the relation between the two Serbo-Croatian alphabets, it is possible to construct a variety of types of letter strings. A letter string that

Serbo-Croatian Alphabet
— Uppercase —

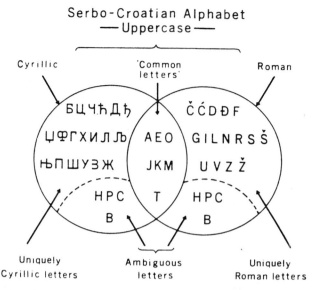

Figure 1. The characters of the Roman and Cyrillic alphabets (printed from Feldman and Turvey, 1983, with permission from the American Psychological Association).

contains at least one uniquely Roman character in addition to shared characters would be read in only one way and it could be either a word or meaningless. A letter string composed entirely of common and ambiguous letters is bivalent. That is, it could be pronounced in one way if read as Roman and pronounced in a distinctly different way if read as Cyrillic; moreover, it could be a word when read in one alphabet and meaningless when read in the other or it could represent two different words, one in one alphabet and one in the other, or finally it could be meaningless in both alphabets (see Table 1).

Consider the word that means WIND. As with any word in Serbo-Croatian, it can be written in either Roman characters or Cyrillic characters. In its Roman transcription (i.e., VETAR), the word includes unique and common characters and is phonologically unequivocal. By contrast, in its Cyrillic transcription (i.e., BETAP), the word includes only ambiguous and common characters and is therefore phonologically bivalent. By its Cyrillic reading it is a word. By its Roman reading it is meaningless. In the present series of experiments, two forms of the same word are compared where one is phonologically bivalent and the other is phonologically unequivocal. Notice that by comparing two printed forms of the same

Table 1. Types of letter strings and their lexical status.

Composition of letter string	Phonemic interpretation		Meaning
Ambiguous and common[1]			
BETAP	Roman	/betap/	meaningless
	Cyrillic	/vetar/	wind
POP	Roman	/pop/	priest
	Cyrillic	/ror/	meaningless
POTOP	Roman	/potop/	flood
	Cyrillic	/rotor/	motor
PAJOC	Roman	/pajotc/	meaningless
	Cyrillic	/rajos/	meaningless
Common			
MAMA	Roman	/mama/	mother
	Cyrillic	/mama/	mother
TAKA	Roman	/taka/	meaningless
	Cyrillic	/taka/	meaningless
Unique and common[2]			
VETAR	Roman	/vetar/	wind
	Cyrillic	impossible	
ПОП	Roman	impossible	
	Cyrillic	/pop/	priest
ROTOR	Roman	/rotor/	motor
	Cyrillic	impossible	
ПОТОП	Roman	impossible	
	Cyrillic	/potop/	flood
RAJOS	Roman	/rajos/	meaningless
	Cyrillic	impossible	
ПАЈО П	Roman	impossible	
	Cyrillic	/pajots/	meaningless

[1] Phonologically bivalent letter strings.

[2] Phonologically unequivocal controls.

Adapted with permission of the American Psychological Association from Feldman and Turvey, 1983.

word, problems of equating familiarity, richness of meaning, length and number of syllables are eliminated.[3] To reiterate, the letter strings exemplified by BETAP and VETAR are the same word and, therefore, identical in all respects but one, namely, the number of phonological interpretations.

Phonological analysis in skilled readers

When bi-alphabetic adult readers of Serbo-Croatian performed a lexical decision task (i.e., Is this letter string a word by either a Roman or a

Cyrillic reading?), single letter strings composed of ambiguous and common characters (i.e., those letter strings that could be assigned both a Roman and a Cyrillic alphabet reading) typically incur longer latencies than the phonologically unequivocal alphabet transcription of the same word. This outcome has been reported both in a mixed alphabet context where the lexical interpretation of a letter string was sometimes in Roman and sometimes in Cyrillic (Feldman and Turvey, 1983; Lukatela *et al.*, 1980) and a pure alphabet context where the lexical interpretation was always in Roman (Feldman, 1983; Lukatela *et al.*, 1978). The effect of phonological ambiguity is significant both for bivalent words and pseudo-words but it is more robust for words. In characterizing the effect of ambiguity in lexical decision, several outcomes prove essential. First, the effect of phonological ambiguity did not vary as a function of word familiarity. For each word, decision latency to its phonologically unequivocal form was used as an index of familiarity and was correlated with the difference in decision latency between the bivalent and unequivocal forms of the word. In lexical decision, that correlation approached zero (Feldman and Turvey, 1983).[4] Second, words composed entirely of common letters (with no ambiguous or unique letters) such as MAMA were accepted as words no more slowly than letter strings that included common and unique letters. Likewise, pseudowords composed entirely of common letters such as TAKA were rejected as words no more slowly than letter strings that included common and unique letters. Note that the distinction between common and ambiguous letters derives from their phonology: each type of letter occurs in both alphabets but only the latter have two phonemic interpretations. The foregoing discrepancy of outcomes suggest that it is *phonological* bivalence rather than a visually based alphabetic bivalence that governs the slowing of decision latencies (see Lukatela *et al.*, 1978, 1980, for a complete discussion). Third, lexical decision latencies to letter strings composed entirely of ambiguous and common letters were always slowed whether both alphabet readings yielded a positive response such as 'POTOP' (Lukatela *et al.*, 1980) or a negative response such as 'PAJOC' (Feldman, 1981; Lukatela *et al.*, 1978, 1980) or the Cyrillic reading and the Roman reading yielded opposite responses such as 'BETAP' or 'POP' (Feldman and Turvey, 1983; Lukatela *et al.*, 1978, 1980). This outcome invalidates a decision stage account of the detriment due to bivalence that posits some type of post-lexical interference between conflicting lexical judgments. Moreover, insofar as lexical decision is alleged to be susceptible to decision-stage influences in a way that naming is not (Balota and Chumbley, 1984; Seidenberg, Waters, Sanders and Langer, 1984) it is noteworthy that the detriment due to bivalence is generally enhanced in naming relative to lexical decision. Finally, the difference in decision latency between the bivalent and unequivocal forms of a word increased as the number of ambiguous (but not common) characters increased (Feldman and Turvey, 1983). It was eliminated, however, by the presence of a single unique letter (Feldman, Kostić, Lukatela and Turvey, 1983). These findings imply that a segmental phonology is assembled from an analysis of a letter string's component orthographic structure and that sometimes (multiple) phonological interpretations are generated. The foregoing results of lexical decision experiments with phonologically bivalent letter strings provide evidence that access to the lexicon in Serbo-Croatian necessarily involves an analysis that is (1) sensitive to phonology and component orthographic structure; (2) is not sensitive to the lexical status of the various alphabetic readings. These results have been interpreted as evidence for an assembled segmental phonology in Serbo-Croatian.

In an attempt to understand conditions under which phonological codes and lexical knowledge do interact in Serbo-Croatian, we have begun to explore associative priming of phonologically bivalent words (Feldman, Lukatela, Katz and Turvey, forthcoming). In this procedure, target words are sometimes presented in the context of another word that is associated with it and decision latencies to the target with and without its associate are compared. Phonologically bivalent words and the unequivocal alphabet transcription of those same words were presented as targets in a lexical decision task. Half of the bivalent targets were words by the Cyrillic reading and half were words by their Roman reading. On some proportion of trials, target words were presented in the context of another word that was associatively related to it and preceded it by 700 ms. Sometimes, the alphabet of the associate was congruent with the alphabet in which the target reading was a word. Sometimes the associate and the target reading were alphabetically incongruent. Results showed significant facilitation in the context of associates, evidence of lexical mediation. More interestingly, decision latencies for bivalent letter strings that are words by one of their alphabet readings were reduced less when those words are preceded by an associate printed in the other, incongruent alphabet than when the associate was printed in the same alphabet as the word reading of the target. This outcome suggests alphabetic congruency as a second source of facilitation. For example, bivalent BETAP which means WIND when read as Cyrillic was preceded by the word for STORM. Inspection of word means in Table 2 reveals that target decision latencies for BETAP type words were 64 ms faster when it was preceded by the Cyrillic form of the word for STORM than by the Roman form of the same word. By contrast, target decision latencies for the same words written in their phonologically unequivocal form were facilitated equally by the prior presentation of an associated word printed in either the congruent or incongruent alphabet.

For example, WIND written in Roman, namely VETAR, is phonologically unequivocal and decision latencies were not significantly different when the word for STORM appeared in its Cyrillic or Roman form. Likewise for pseudowords, alphabet congruency had no effect (see Table 2).

Table 2. Lexical Decision (ms) to bivalent words and their unequivocal controls in the context of alphabetically congruent and alphabetically incongruent associates.

	Bivalent (BETAP)	Unequivocal (VETAR)
Alphabet of associate:		
Congruent	709	672
Incongruent	775	685
(No associate)	845	765

From Feldman, Lukatela, Katz, and Turvey (in preparation).

In summary, lexical decision latencies for phonologically bivalent letter strings are reduced significantly more when preceded by associates that are alphabetically congruent with the word reading of the letter string, than by associates that are not congruent. By contrast, decision latencies for phonologically unequivocal letter strings are not influenced by the alphabet of the associate. Associative and alphabetic sources of facilitation can be identified. Whereas facilitation by association occurs for all the words and is assumed to be lexical in origin, facilitation by alphabet congruency of associate and target was important *only* for bivalent letter strings. The special dependency of alphabetic congruency on ambiguity suggests that alphabetic priming and phonological ambiguity have a common origin.

In summary, studies of phonological ambiguity indicate that skilled readers of Serbo-Croatian analyse words phonologically. In judging letter strings composed exclusively of ambiguous and common letters for a lexical decision, adult readers appear to assign a phonological interpretation (or several) to each character (Feldman and Turvey, 1983). At the same time, the alphabet in which a prior occurring associate is printed appears to bias the generation or the evaluation of various phonological interpretations of a bivalent letter string. An analogous effect is absent in phonologically unequivocal words and in all pseudowords.

Morphological analysis in skilled readers

The effect of phonological ambiguity has provided a means to evaluate the analytic skills of readers with respect to morphological components. As

noted above, the Serbo-Croatian language, in a manner that is characteristic of Slavic languages generally, makes extensive use of inflectional and
derivational morphology. A noun can appear in any of seven cases in the
singular and in the plural where the inflectional affix varies according to its
gender, number, and case. For example, the words STAN and KORA
which mean 'apartment' and 'crust' respectively in nominative case can be
inflected into six other cases in the singular and in the plural and different
inflectional affixes mark each case (with some redundancy of affixes).
Similarly, derived forms for 'little apartment' or 'thin crust' can be generated by adding one of the diminutive affixes (namely, ČIĆ, ICA, ENCE,
AK) to the base word to produce STANČIĆ and KORICA respectively.
The prevalence of inflectional and derivational formations in Serbo-Croatian are evidence of its productiveness (see Table 3).

Table 3. Examples of morphologically-related words formed with the base morpheme 'PIS' meaning 'write'.

Example	Derivational prefix	Base morpheme	Derivational suffix	Inflectional suffix	Meaning
OPIS	O	PIS			description
OPISI	O	PIS		I	descriptions (nom. plural)
PIŠEM	PIŠ			EM	I write (1p. sing)
PIŠETE		PIŠ		ETE	you write (2p. plural)
PISAC		PIS	AC		writer
PISCIMA		PIS	C	IMA	writers (dat. plural)
PISMO		PIS	MO		letter
POPIS	PO	PIS			inventory
POTPIS	POT	PIS			signature
SPISAK	S	PIS	AK		list

† All words are in nominative singular unless otherwise noted.

One way in which sensitivity to morphological constituents is construed
is in terms of a morphological parser that operates prior to lexical access
such that affixes are stripped from a multimorphemic word and the base
morpheme serves as the primary unit for lexical search (see Caramazza,
Miceli, Silveri and Laudanna, 1985). Frequency of the base unit and the
whole word as well as the difficulty of segmenting the appropriate base unit
figure significantly in decision latency (Taft, 1979; Taft and Forster, 1975).
In one experiment (Feldman, Kostić, Lukatela and Turvey, 1983) the
effect of phonological ambiguity was exploited to assess whether the base
morpheme or the whole word serves as the unit for lexical access of

inflected words in Serbo-Croatian. Words were presented in nominative and dative case for a lexical decision. Words were selected so that the nominative case and the base morpheme (i.e., nominative minus inflectional affix for most singular nouns) were phonologically bivalent in the Cyrillic alphabet and phonological unequivocal in Roman. For example, the nominative case of the word meaning VEIN is composed entirely of ambiguous and common letters when printed in Cyrillic (i.e., BEHA) and is therefore phonologically bivalent. In Roman, by contrast, it comprises unique and common letters (i.e., VENA) and is, therefore, phonologically unequivocal. Importantly, in the dative case, neither alphabet rendition is bivalent because the inflectional affixes for words of its class are the phonemes /u/ and /i/ both of which are represented by a unique letter in each alphabet, although the base morpheme of the Cyrillic form (i.e., BEH) is still bivalent.

The major outcome of that experiment was a significant interaction of alphabet and case. The difference in latency between dative nouns presented in Cyrillic and Roman was -28 ms which was not significant whereas the difference between nominative nouns was 304 ms which was significant. In that dative nouns always included a unique letter, it appears that the effects of phonological bivalence do not occur if letter strings composed of ambiguous and common characters contain even one unique character. Importantly, in that experiment, the unique character always constituted an inflectional morpheme. Stated in terms of morphological units, the outcome of that experiment was that an inflectional affix composed of a unique character and appended to a bivalent base morpheme cancelled the detriment due to ambiguity. Evidently, the reader could use the alphabet designation of the inflectional affix to assign a reading to the base morpheme. In conclusion, bivalence defined on the word but not on the base morpheme alone slowed performance on a lexical decision task. This outcome indicates that lexical access of inflected nouns is not restricted to information in the base morpheme unit. Rather, it encompasses the *entire* word.

An alternative perspective on a reader's appreciation of morphology assumes that lexical entries are accessed from whole word units and that the principle of organization among lexical entries or the lexical representations themselves capture morphological structure. The final experiment (Feldman and Moskovljević, in press) exploits the complex derivational morphology of Serbo-Croatian to provide further evidence that whereas the morphological structure of words is accessible to the skilled reader, lexical entries are not accessed from base morphemes. The experiment incorporated a comparison of three types of nouns all in nominative case: First, base forms (e.g., STAN, KORA). Second, the diminutive form of those same nouns which, as described above, is formed (productively) by adding one of the suffixes ČIĆ, ICA, ENCE, AK to the base form (e.g, STANČIĆ, KORICA) where choice of suffix is constrained by gender of the noun. And third, an unrelated monomorphemic word whose construction inappropriately suggests that it contains the same base form and a diminutive affix (e.g., STANICA, KORAK). The latter are referred to as pseudodiminutive nouns. The examples mean 'station' and 'step' respectively.

The experimental design was a variation on the primed lexical decision task borrowed from Stanners and his colleagues (Stanners, Neiser, Hernon and Hall, 1979) and known as repetition priming. In the present adaptation of the task, base forms appeared as target words and they were preceded 7 to 13 items earlier in the list by a prime which was either the identical word again in its base form, its diminutive or a pseudodiminutive form. Decision latency to the target as a function of which type of prime preceded it was examined. In addition, decision latencies to the first presentation of the word in its base, diminutive, and pseudodiminutive forms were compared. Results are summarized in Table 4.

Table 4.   Lexical Decision (ms) to target words preceded by identity, diminutive, or pseudodiminutive primes.

Prime		Target		Type of prime
STAN	610	STAN	563	Identity
STANČIĆ	754	STAN	585	Diminutive
STANICA	718	STAN	609	Pseudodiminutive

From Feldman and Moskovljević (in press).

Decision latencies on primes were fastest for base forms, followed by pseudodiminutives and lastly, diminutives. The pattern corresponded with that predicted by frequency and provided no evidence that monomorphemic pseudodiminutive forms were slowed by an inappropriate parsing of morphemic structure. In addition, latencies for base and diminutive forms correlated significantly and neither correlated with pseudodiminutive forms. An examination of target latencies provided further evidence that pseudodiminutive words are not associated with an inappropriate base morpheme (and affix) whereas true morphological relationships are appreciated. Decision latencies to target words that were preceded by pseudodiminutive words were as slow as target words presented for the first time. In contrast, both base word and diminutive primes significantly reduced target decision latencies. In summary, results in the repetition priming variation of lexical decision showed significant facilitation for morphological relatives and no facilitation for unrelated pseudodiminutive words. In light of the claim that semantic relatedness of prime to target does not facilitate target decision latencies at lags as long as those introduced in the present task (Dannenbring and Briand, 1982; Henderson, Wallis and Knight, 1984), the foregoing results are interpreted as morphological in nature. In conclusion, the present experiment showed that the skilled reader of Serbo-Croatian is sensitive to morphological structure as evidenced by the results in repetition priming but offered no evidence that morphological analysis entails decomposition to a base morpheme prior to lexical access.

In summary, an examination of results from lexical decision and naming tasks that take advantage of the bi-alphabetic condition in Serbo-Croatian provides evidence that skilled reading in Serbo-Croatian proceeds with reference to phonology. Specifically: (1) Skilled readers are slowed when a letter string is phonologically bivalent relative to when it is phonologically unequivocal. (2) The alphabet congruency of a prior-occurring associate can speed decision latencies for phonologically bivalent (but not unequivocal) words. Moreover, it appears that phonological bivalence is defined on the entire word, not in the base morpheme alone which suggests that (3) Skilled readers do not attempt lexical access from an isolated base morpheme. Concurrently, they consider its affix. Failure to find evidence that base morphemes are the units for lexical access should not be construed as a claim against morphological analysis by the reader, however. The results from repetition priming indicate that prior presentation of a morphological relative but not of a visually similar word facilitates decision latency to a target. The foregoing results support the claim that the skilled reader of Serbo-Croatian analyses words both phonologically and morphologically.

Acknowledgements

This research was supported by funds from the National Academy of Sciences and the Serbian Academy of Sciences to Laurie B. Feldman; by NICHD Grant HD-01994 to Haskins Laboratories and by NICHD Grant HD-08495 to the University of Belgrade.

Notes

[1] The introduction of two alphabets into Yugoslavia reflects the influence of the Orthodox Church in the Eastern regions and the Catholic Church in the Western regions. The Cyrillic script is probably an adaptation of the Greek uncial alphabet of the 9th century AD and the Roman script is a variation of the Latin alphabet which was also derived from the Greek, probably via Etruscan (Diringer, 1948). In both cases, the scripts had to be adjusted to represent sounds not

present in the Greek language and several mechanisms have been identified. (1) Combining two or more characters to represent a single phoneme such as DZ and, arguably, LJ and NJ. (2) Adding a diacritical mark to an existing letter to form a new letter such as Č, Ć, Š. The creation of new letters by inclusion of a diacritic is particularly prevalent in the adaptation of Roman script to languages whose repertoire of phonemes differs greatly from the Latin. Palatal-alveolar fricatives and affricates are represented in this fashion in many Slavic languages, including Serbo-Croatian (Wellisch, 1978). (3) Taking an existing symbol which was not used in the new language to represent a phoneme not present (or represented by multiple symbols) in the old language. For example, Roman C became /ts/ and Roman K remained /k/. (4) Borrowing characters from other scripts. Insofar as particular adaptations were made independently in each alphabet and the shape of some letters (e.g., D, S, R) were modified slightly in the transition to Latin (Diringer, 1948) the intersection of the two alphabet sets represents a complex of factors.

[2] One consequence of the consistent mapping of grapheme to phoneme is that many dialectal variations are represented in writing such that spelling as well as pronunciation can vary from region to region. For example, the word that means MILK is MLEJKO in the dialects near Belgrade and is MLIKO in dialects along the Dalmatian Coast. It is important to note that the orthography fully specifies segmental phonology but that accent (rising/falling; long/short) is not represented. While vowel accent may differentiate between two semantic interpretations of a written letter string, this distinction is often ignored especially in the dialects of the larger cities, however (Magner and Matejka, 1971).

[3] By law, all elementary school students must demonstrate competence to read and write in both alphabets. With the exception of liturgical text, which is relatively uncommon, the choice of alphabet is not systematic across genres of printed material. Therefore, it can be assumed that the Roman and Cyrillic forms of a word are equally familiar to the skilled reader.

[4] In naming, however, more familiar words showed smaller effects of phonological ambiguity (Feldman, 1981). Analogous to claims made from studies with English materials (Seidenberg, 1985; Stanovich and Bauer, 1978), those words that are recognized more slowly and are presumably less familiar are more susceptible to phonological effects in a naming task than are less-familiar words.

References

Balota, D. A. and Chumbley, J. I. (1984). Are lexical decisions a good measure of lexical access? The role of word frequency in the neglected decision stage. *Journal of Experimental Psychology: Human Perception and Performance*, **10**, 340–57.

Caramazza, A., Miceli, G., Silveri, C. and Laudanna, A. (1985). Reading mechanisms and the organisation of the lexicon: Evidence from acquired dyslexia. *Cognitive Neuropsychology*, **2**, 81–114.

Dannenbring, G. L. and Briand, K. (1982). Semantic priming and the word repetition effect in a lexical decision task. *Canadian Journal of Psychology*, **36**, 435–44.

Diringer, D. (1948). *The alphabet: A key to the history of mankind*. London: The Fleet Street Press.

Feldman, L. B. (1981). Visual word recognition in Serbo-Croatian is necessarily phonological. *Haskins Laboratories Status Report on Speech Research*, **SR-66**, 167–202.

Feldman, L. B. (1983). Bi-alphabetism and word recognition. In D. Rogers and J. A. Sloboda (Eds) *The acquisition of symbolic skills*. New York: Plenum.

Feldman, L. B., Kostić, A., Lukatela, G. and Turvey, M. T. (1983). An evaluation of the "Basic Orthographic Syllabic Structure" in a phonologically shallow orthography. *Psychological Research*, **45**, 55–72.

Feldman, L. B., Lukatela, G., Katz, L. and Turvey, M. T. (in preparation). Alphabetic and associative priming of phonologically ambiguous words.

Feldman, L. B. and Moskovljević, J. (in press). Repetition priming is not purely episodic in origin. *Journal of Experimental Psychology*: Learning, Memory and Cognition.

Feldman, L. B. and Turvey, M. T. (1983). Visual word recognition in Serbo-Croatian is phonologically analytic. *Journal of Experimental Psychology: Human Perception and Performance*, **9**, 288–98.

Henderson, L., Wallis J. and Knight, D. (1984). Morphemic structure and lexical access. In H. Bouma and D. Bouwhuis (Eds) *Attention and performance X*. London: Erlbaum.

Lukatela, G., Popadić, D., Ognjenović, P. and Turvey, M. T. (1980). Lexical decision in a phonologically shallow orthography. *Memory & Cognition*, **8**, 124–32.

Lukatela, G., Savić, M., Gligorijević, B., Ognjenović, P. and Turvey, M. T. (1978). Bi-alphabetical lexical decision. *Language and Speech*, **21**, 142–65.

Magner, T. F. and Matejka, L. (1971). *Word accent in Serbo-Croatian*. University Park, PA: Pennsylvania State University Press.

Seidenberg, M. S. (1985). The time course of phonological code activation in two writing systems. *Cognition*, **19**, 1–30.

Seidenberg, M. S., Waters, G. S., Sanders, M. and Langer, P. (1984). Pre- and post-lexical loci of contextual effects on word recognition. *Memory & Cognition*, **12**, 315–28.

Stanners, R. F., Neiser, J. J., Hernon, W. P. and Hall, R. (1979). Memory representation for morphologically related words. *Journal of Verbal Learning and Verbal Behavior*, **18**, 399–412.

Stanovich, K. E. and Bauer, D. W. (1978). Experiments on the spelling-to-sound regularity effects in word recognition. *Memory & Cognition*, **6**, 410–15.

Taft, M. (1979). Recognition of affixed words and the word frequency effect. *Memory & Cognition*, **9**, 263–72.

Taft, M. and Forster, K. (1975). Lexical storage and retrieval of prefixed words. *Journal of Verbal Learning and Verbal Behavior*, **14**, 638–647.

Wellisch, H. H. (1978). *The conversion of scripts — its nature, history, and utilization*. New York: Wiley.

11 On the relationship between orthographies and phonologies in visual word recognition

Derek Besner

Abstract

A common view in the literature is that the nature of the code that subserves lexical access in different orthographies is a function of the directness of the mappings between orthography and phonology. Lexical access is held to be necessarily based upon phonology in shallow orthographies, and a graphemic code in deep orthographies. A selective review of evidence from dyslexic, aphasic, dysarthric and intact subjects suggests that this view is incorrect. It is suggested instead that both graphemic and phonological codes subserve lexical access in both deep and shallow orthographies. There are also clear differences in the nature of the phonological code that can be used for lexical access as a function of orthography. This code appears more closely tied to articulatory mechanisms in shallow orthographies than in deep ones.

Background: Is reading alphabetic English ever parasitic on some form of speech code?

It used to be a common view that reading English is like listening; what the reader must do is translate print into sound.

> "In order to read alphabetic languages one must have an ingrained habit of producing the sounds of one's language when one sees the written words which conventionally represent the phonemes."
>
> (Bloomfield, 1942)

"The heart of (reading skill) is surely the process of decoding the written symbols to speech."

(Gibson, 1970)

"A word to be recognized is recoded phonemically even when it is presented visually."

(Rubenstein, Lewis and Rubenstein, 1971)

"The printed word is mapped onto a phonemic representation by the reader."

(Gough, 1972)

"So while we cannot see how to show that the process is ubiquitous, we tentatively cling to the view that the reader automatically converts letters in to phonological form, and then searches the lexicon for an entry headed by this form."

(Gough and Cosky, 1977)

More recent work shows that the translation of print into phonology can not be a *necessary* condition for lexical access. Numerous studies of acquired dyslexics with severely impaired ability to assemble phonology none the less retain considerable ability to read aloud and make lexical decision and synonym judgements of printed words (e.g. Coltheart, Patterson and Marshall, 1980). For such individuals, a graphemic code clearly provides a sufficient basis for lexical access.

The pendulum of opinion then swung the other way. It is often claimed that, at least in college level readers, phonology is *never* utilized in the recognition of single, visually presented content words when the task does not require overt naming (e.g. lexical decision, semantic categorization).

"In sum we think the hypothesis that speech recoding is used normally by mature readers to determine the meaning of words in text should be laid to rest."

(Banks, Oka and Shugarman, 1981)

"To the extent to which lexical access, as defined by the requirements of the YES response in lexical decision, corresponds to lexical access as the first step in comprehending single printed words during normal reading, our results suggest that pre-lexical phonological recoding is not used in normal reading."

(Coltheart, Besner, Jonasson and Davelaar, 1979)

"The failure to demonstrate any effect of regularity on lexical access times (in lexical decision and semantic categorization tasks) implies that lexical access in skilled readers relies *exclusively* on a visual code, even though phonological encoding is occurring."

(Coltheart, 1980)

Phonological influences on visual word recognition

The conclusion that phonological processing *never* influences visual word recognition in college level readers is too strong. A number of counterexamples are evident in the literature.

One approach has been to compare lexical decision times to single words whose correspondence between spelling and sound is *regular* (e.g. BRIBE, TRIBE) with words where the correspondence is *irregular* (e.g. FREAK, BREAK). A number of investigators have reported that 'regularity' influences performances in this task (Andrews, 1984; Barron, 1985; Parkin, 1982; Parkin and Underwood, 1984; Stanovich and Bauer, 1978; Bauer and Stanovich, 1980; Waters and Seidenberg, 1985). Two observations appear important (cf. Waters and Seidenberg, 1985). First, unusual *spelling* (operationalized in terms of bigram frequency) is a separable component of 'regularity'. Secondly, regularity effects are (a) most likely to be seen with low frequency words, and (b) most easily obtained when a large proportion of words with unusual spelling patterns (e.g. aisle, fuel) are included in the list. Waters and Seidenberg's argument is that inclusion of such items increases the difficulty of discriminating words from nonwords, thus retarding overall latency and giving a slow acting phonological code a chance to influence performance (but see Barron, 1985).

Related findings implicating the importance of context have been reported by Shulman, Hornak and Sanders (1978) who showed that lexical decision to the simultaneous presentation of pairs of words are faster when the words are pronounced the same way as compared to when they are not (e.g. BRIBE–TRIBE versus FREAK–BREAK) provided that the nonwords are 'legal' ones (see also Meyer, Schvaneveldt and Ruddy 1974). This effect is not obtained when the nonwords are composed of consonants or random letters (but see Barron, 1981; 1985).

Another approach has used pseudohomophones (nonwords which sound like real words but are spelled differently, e.g. BRANE) and examined their influence upon the processing of homophones. When the background contains pseudohomophones there is no difference between homophones (rain/reign) and nonhomophones (Coltheart, Davelaar, Jonasson and Besner, 1977; Davelaar, Coltheart, Besner and Jonasson, 1978). However, if there are no pseudohomophones in the list then the low frequency member of a homophone pair is slower than a frequency matched non-homophone control (Davelaar *et al.*, 1978). The simplest story is that both graphemic and phonemic encoding co-occur; naive subjects tend to rely on the outcome of the phonological route. However, when such reliance produces a high error rate (i.e. when the nonwords sound like English words) these subjects are able to abandon relying upon the output of a phonological code and rely on the graphemic code instead.

A reciprocal influence of homophones upon pseudohomophones in lexical decision has been reported by Dennis, Besner and Davelaar (1985) who showed that the pseudohomophone effect (slower responses to BRANE type items than to FRANE type items) is reduced or eliminated when the list is devoid of homophones. It should be noted, however, that the absence of an effect is not necessarily evidence against the operation of some process thought to be associated with that effect. Thus, Besner, Dennis and Davelaar (1985) found that despite the absence of a pseudo-homophone effect, phonological properties of these pseudohomophones nonetheless primed responses to their real word counterparts on a subsequent trial (e.g. BRANE→brain) over and above any effects attributable to mere graphemic similarity.

The conclusion seems clear; context matters. It is not the case that, for skilled readers of alphabetic English, phonology either *always* or *never* influences visual word recognition. The truth lies somewhere in between; phonology is *sometimes* influential.

A remaining difficulty is that much of the evidence on this point comes from the lexical decision task; the relevance of this task to 'normal' reading is obscure. It is thus somewhat reassuring to see effects attributed to the use of assembled phonology appearing (but sometimes not, see Cohen, 1980) in various forms of sentence reading tasks (e.g. Doctor and Coltheart, 1980; Coltheart *et al.*, 1986; Treiman, Baron and Fryd, 1984; Waters, Seidenberg and Bruck, 1984), and in semantic categorization (Van Orden, 1986).

Word recognition in orthographies with consistent spelling–sound correspondence

A contrasting, widely held view is that when orthgraphies have highly regular symbol–sound correspondences, lexical access relies *exclusively* upon phonological recoding (e.g. Feldman, Kostić, Lukatela and Turvey 1983; Turvey, Feldman and Lukatela, 1984; Morton and Sasanuma, 1984; Sasanuma, 1980; 1984). This claim is examined in more detail in the context of Kana, the Japanese syllabic script, and Serbo-Croatian.

Lexical access in Kana

Written Japanese is composed of two distinct orthographies; Kanji, the logographic script used to represent content words, and Kana, the syllabic script. Kana is further divided into two; Katakana is the character set used to represent foreign loan words (e.g. computer, telephone) while the Hiragana character set is used to represent grammatical morphemes. Kana is also a regular writing system in the sense that each character has an invariant pronunciation; each character roughly corresponds to a syllable (Morton and Sasanuma, 1984).

Kana, unlike English, is completely regular. It could in principle always be understood by first translating the spelling into sound and then listening to the sounds. How do Japanese readers actually recognize words written in Kana?

The standard answer is based in large part on the results of neuropsychological investigations of patients with acquired reading disorders due to cerebral insult.

". . . it appears that each script, Kana and Kanji, calls for the application of a specific strategy which is most suitable for its efficient processing in a particular task, i.e. . . . a phonologically mediated strategy, or a strategy of script to phonology (and then to meaning, as in a comprehension task) for Kana."

(Sasanuma, 1980)

". . . each script is read by the mediating internal representation appropriate to it. The syllabic Kana characters are read via a phonological representation, whereas the ideographic Kanji characters are not."

(McCusker, Hillinger and Bias, 1981)

"The best data available for helping us to decide on the organization of reading processes in Japanese appear to be neuropsychological. The general conclusion is that Kana is read phonetically and Kanji is read visually."

(Morton and Sasanuma, 1984)

These conclusions rest on clinical observations (c.f. see Sasanuma, 1980). When patients are unable to deal with *nonwords* written in Kana (oral reading, rhyming and lexical decision) their performance on *words* written in Kana is extremely poor (oral reading, lexical decision and comprehension as measured by written word/picture matching adapted from the Peabody Picture Vocabulary Test). Since oral reading, rhyming and lexical decisions to nonwords written in Kana are presumed to be based on preliminary phonological recoding, the deficits seen with *words* written in Kana are taken to mean that, in contrast to English, lexical access of Kana is always preceded by phonological recoding.[1]

What are we to make of this interpretation? Perhaps the most important consideration is to note that the conclusion is based upon an argument by association. If nonword processing in Kana is impaired, then word processing in Kana is impaired; it is simply *assumed* that the deficit is a common one. The difficulty is that conclusions about identity of mechanism based upon the observation of associated deficits seen in neuropsychological investigations are simply not compelling since tomorrow may provide a patient with *dissociated* deficits (see Sasanuma, 1985 for suggestive evidence).

An alternative approach to the question of whether Kana can be read on the basis of access to a graphemic lexicon is to pursue experiments analogous to those done on intact, English reading subjects. A common finding in English is that words are named faster than nonwords (e.g. Forster and Chambers, 1973; Fredriksen and Kroll, 1976). The received explanation is that words have lexical representations which can be *addressed* graphemically and a whole word pronunciation retrieved from the lexical entry. The pronunciation for a nonword is *assembled* by reference to 'rules', analogies, or some combination of both (e.g. see Henderson 1982, 1985 for reviews). The former route may be faster than the latter.[2]

By analogy with English then, if Japanese Kana affords lexical access upon the basis of a graphemic code then words ought to be named faster than nonwords. The results of such an experiment by Besner and Hildebrandt (1986) can be seen in Table 1. Nine native speakers of Japanese named a mixed set of words normally printed in Katakana, Kanji words transcribed into Katakana, and nonwords printed in Katakana which were displayed one at a time on a CRT. The words and nonwords were matched for number of characters, and initial syllable. The nonwords consisted of words transformed into nonwords by altering one or two characters. Subjects took part in an 'immediate' condition in which the

Table 1. Mean RT's (ms) and error rates for naming words and non-words printed in Katakana.

	Words normally printed in Katakana		Kanji words transcribed into Katakana		Non-words printed in Katakana	
	RT	%E	RT	%E	RT	%E
Immediate	614	1.2	678	2.5	760	7.9
Delay	297	0.0	318	1.5	384	2.0

subject named the stimulus when it appeared on the screen and a 'delayed' condition in which the stimulus appeared on the screen and the subject named it upon the presentation of an auditory signal which occurred approximately 1 s after the onset of the display.

The results from the immediate condition show quite clearly that words normally written in Katakana are named more quickly and accurately than both Kanji words transcribed into Katakana and nonwords printed in Katakana. The delay condition shows that only some of the difference between words and nonwords can be attributed to differences in ease of articulation. Subtracting the delay condition times from the immediate condition times still leaves a significant difference between words normally seen in Katakana on the one hand, and Kanji transcribed into Katakana, and Katakana nonwords on the other. Note also that the advantage for words normally written in Katakana in the immediate condition cannot be totally accounted for by simply assuming that it is a process of phonological assembly which is easier for words than nonwords, since these words are also faster than Kanji words transcribed into Katakana.

The results from this experiment are most easily explained by the suggestion that subjects name words normally written in Katakana by reference to an orthographic lexicon at least some of the time. It would thus appear that while linguistic descriptions of alphabetic English and Japanese Kana are quite different, the psychological processes involved in their oral reading have more in common than previously thought.

Lexical access in Serbo-Croatian

The Serbo-Croatian orthography is somewhat complex; a clear summary can be found in Turvey *et al.* (1984) (see also Feldman, Chap 10). For present purposes, the important point is that the Serbo-Croatian language is written in two alphabets (Roman and Cyrillic) and its orthography is phonologically shallow; the spelling–sound correspondences are simple and direct in both of the alphabets. The claim in the literature is that skilled readers access the lexicon in a manner that must include an analysis of phonological components.

". . . lexical decision in Serbo-Croatian necessarily involves a phonologically analytic strategy."

(Feldman and Turvey, 1983)

". . . interpretation of the data suggests that a phonological recognition strategy in Serbo-Croatian is not optional."

(Turvey, Feldman and Lukatela, 1984)

"How then does a reader determine that a string of letters is a word? For the Serbo-Croatian orthography we wish to conclude that he or she does so by encoding the written word into a phonological form."

(Feldman, Kostić, Lukatela and Turvey, 1983)

"To conclude, the Serbo-Croatian orthography is phonologically very regular (permitting a valid prediction of how a word sounds solely on the basis of the letters comprising the word) and as such encourages neither the development of options for accessing the lexicon, nor, relatedly, a sensitivity to the linguistic situations in which one option fares better than another."

(Turvey, Feldman and Lukatela, 1984)

I would not like to suggest that a phonological code is never used as a basis for lexical access in Serbo-Croatian; the data reviewed by Turvey *et al.* suggests that it is. More questionable is the claim that a graphemic code is never a sufficient basis for lexical access. Indeed, if the logic underlying the interpretation of Besner and Hildebrandt's Katakana experiment is accepted, and can be extended to Serbo-Croatian, then Katz and Feldman's (1983) own data suggest that a graphemic code is sometimes used in the recognition of Serbo-Croatian. Table 2 shows data which represents naming time for words and nonwords printed in Serbo-Croatian.

Table 2. Mean RT (ms) for naming words and non-words printed in Serbo-Croatian.

Words		Non-words	
RT	%E	RT	%E
612	3.5	690	5.0

The source is Katz and Feldman, 1983, Figure 1 and Table 1. The RT data are estimated from the figure and collapsed across related and unrelated conditions.

Words are named substantially faster than nonwords,[3] just as Forster and Chambers (1973) and Frederiksen and Kroll (1976) observed for English, and Besner and Hildebrandt (1986) found for Japanese Kana. It is difficult to see why the standard interpretation given to the English and Japanese findings should not also apply to the Serbo-Croatian data. Namely, words can access a lexical entry upon the basis of a graphemic code and a whole word pronunciation retrieved from the lexical entry. The pronunciation for a nonword, in contrast, must be *assembled* upon the basis of spelling–sound correspondence 'rules', analogies, or some combination of both.

If this interpretation of the naming latency advantage for words over nonwords is accepted, then it establishes a basis for the claim that word recognition in Serbo-Croatian involves the use of a graphemic code for lexical access at least some of the time.

As an empirical claim then, the proposition that, in college level readers, both graphemic and phonological codes influence visual word recognition in English, German (see Scheerer, Chap 12), Kana and Serbo-Croatian can be defended. As a general *assumption* it is not obvious why the use of such codes should not also apply to *all* orthographies, with the possible exception of logographic scripts like Chinese (but see Seidenberg, 1985).

Nature of the 'graphemic' code used as a basis for lexical access as a function of script type

It has been argued here that some form of 'graphemic' code serves as a basis for lexical access in a number of orthographies. What is not known is the extent to which, if any, these codes resemble each other across scripts. For example, it is often supposed that the 'graphemic' code used for lexical access of alphabetic English is based upon preliminary letter recognition rather than outline shape, transletter features, or features smaller than letters (Henderson, 1982; Allport, 1979; Adams, 1979; McClelland, 1976; Paap *et al.*, 1984; Besner, 1983; Besner, Davelaar, Alcott and Parry, 1984). There is little in the way of evidence or speculation about the nature of graphemic access codes in the other scripts discussed in this chapter. The exception, perhaps, is the claim that mixing Roman and Cyrillic scripts within a word in Serbo-Croatian fails to impair naming latency or lexical decision relative to a script-consistent word, provided that each of the characters has an unambiguous phonemic realization (Turvey *et al.*, 1984). This observation is remarkable in that it runs counter to what would be expected on the basis of a skills approach to word recognition (e.g. Kolers, 1985) and because it contrasts with the observation that case alternation impairs naming latency performance in English, despite the fact that words retain in full their advantage over nonwords (Besner, 1983). These results suggest that the nature of the graphemic code which can be used for lexical access varies as a function of script type. An explanation for these differences remains to be articulated.

Nature of the 'phonological' code used for lexical access as a function of script type

A frequently investigated question concerns whether skilled readers can translate from print to a phonological form without reference to an articulatory code. The general view in the literature is that it is not possible (e.g. Kleiman, 1975; Barron and Baron, 1977; Levy, 1981; Bryant and Bradley, 1985; Allport, 1979; Wilding and White, 1985). The conclusion to be reached here is that a more careful consideration of tasks suggests circumstances in which such a conversion is possible without recourse to an articulatory level. For present purposes the more interesting claim is that scripts vary with respect to *the degree* to which phonological recoding is tied to articulatory mechanisms for the purpose of lexical access.

One approach to this issue has been to look at the selective nature of reading disorders in Japanese. Sasanuma and Fujimura (1971) examined two groups of aphasics equated for their ability to comprehend spoken speech; one of the groups also exhibited overt speech production difficulties. Both groups were tested on a picture-word matching task. The group with no articulatory disorder was *equally* impaired, relative to control subjects, in their ability to understand both the logographic (Kanji) and syllabic (Kana) scripts. Particular interest resides in the group with a speech production deficit. These patients did not differ from the other group on this task when the words were written in Kanji, but were selectively and severely impaired when the words were written in Kana.[4] These and other results have lead Allport, among others, to the conclusion that

". . . visually presented words can only be transformed into a phonological representation via the mechanisms responsible for the organization of articulatory motor acts. To restate this more directly, there appears to be no direct conversion from a graphemic to an auditory code, but only into a code of articulatory instructions.

(Allport, 1979)

Similar conclusions can be drawn from experiments in which intact subjects read Japanese. Kimura (1984) and[5] Kimura and Bryant (1983) found that semantic judgements of pairs of Kana words, and picture–word matching tasks involving Kana were severely impaired by a concurrent task which engaged speech production mechanisms (counting aloud). This contrasted with minimal impairment when the matching task used logographic Kanji instead of Kana.

Experiments with alphabetic English have been given a similar interpretation. For example, Baddeley, Thomson and Buchanan (1975) have shown that concurrent articulation completely eliminates word length and phonemic similarity effects seen in serial order recall tasks under conditions of visual presentation. They concluded that

". . . suppression stops the translation of a visual stimulus into a phonemic code."

(Baddeley, Thomson and Buchanan, 1975)

A finer grained analysis suggests that the latter conclusion is too strong. Translation from print into phonological form without mediation by an articulatory level is implied by the findings that (a) intact subject's performance on phonological lexical decision (does this letter string sound like a real word — e.g. PALLIS — yes) can be unaffected by suppression (e.g. Besner, Davies and Daniels, 1981) (b) the pseudohomophone effect in lexical decision can be unaffected by suppression (Besner, 1986) (c) homophone judgements of printed material can be unaffected by suppression (e.g. Baddeley and Lewis, 1981) (d) the superior performance of pseudohomophones over controls in a serial order recall task with *visual* presentation survives the imposition of suppression while word length and phonemic similarity effects are completely eliminated (Besner and Davelaar, 1982) (e) dysarthric subjects are just as good at homophone judgements of printed words as nondysarthric controls (Bishop, 1985).[6]

It can thus be suggested that there is a dissociation between reading Japanese Kana and alphabetic English. When subjects are forced to rely on phonology because the words have never been seen in Kana before, patients with speech production difficulties and intact subjects engaged in concurrent articulation are impaired at reading Kana. In contrast, when subjects are forced to rely on phonology when reading alphabetic English, there are a number of tasks in which either dysarthria or concurrent articulation fails to impair performance. The 'phonological' codes involved in reading these scripts are therefore manifestly different; phonological reading of Kana would appear to be more closely tied to articulatory mechanisms than is phonological processing of English.

What happens in other scripts? There are occasional references to the assertion that the 'phonological' code involved in reading Serbo-Croatian is actually *articulatory* in nature (cf. Katz and Feldman, 1983) but there is as yet no empirical basis for this claim. I am unaware of any evidence from other orthographies that bears directly on the nature of the phonological code which can be used for lexical access. It would be interesting to learn whether suppression or speech production difficulties produce word recognition deficits in Serbo-Croatian or other scripts.

General conclusion

We are as yet remarkably ignorant about the relationship between orthography and phonology as a function of script type but at least two interim claims can be made. (1) While linguistic descriptions of various orthographies are quite different, the psychological operations applied in aid of their recognition appear more similar than previously thought. More specifically, both 'graphemic' and 'phonological' codes are involved in lexical access across a number of orthographies. (2) On the other hand, while the psychological *operations* applied to various scripts for the purpose of lexical access appear similar, the nature of the *representations* underlying these codes appears, in some instances, quite different. Evidence regarding similarities or differences in the nature of the graphemic code as a function of script type is almost nonexistent. In contrast, it is clear that different forms of phonology are involved in lexical access across orthographies.

Acknowledgements

Supported by Grant no. A0998 from the Natural Sciences and Engineering Research Council of Canada. I am particularly grateful to Leslie Henderson, Janice Kay, Eckart Scheerer, Muriel Vogel-Sprott, Eileen Davelaar, Robert McCann and Gary Waller for constructive criticism.

Notes

[1] It is not a matter of the patients being unable to read *anything* since Kanji reading is often quite well preserved.

[2] Note it is not critical that addressed phonology be inherently faster. If words can be named via either route (most of them, anyway) while nonwords can only be named via the use of assembled phonology, then words will be faster than nonwords because of the redundancy gain associated with a response based upon the faster of two processors on any single trial, provided that processing in these two routes is not perfectly correlated.

[3] It would be useful to have data from a pseudohomophone condition consisting of words written in a mixture of Roman and Cyrillic scripts and from a delay condition so as to rule out phonological assembly and ease of articulation as accounting for all of the difference between word and nonword naming times.

[4] This was particularly true of content words normally written in Kanji that were presented in Kana, and were hence orthographically unfamiliar, forcing reliance upon phonological recoding for purposes of lexical access.

[5] All of the Kana words in the Kimura studies are normally seen only in Kanji.

[6] In contrast, *rhyming* is clearly impaired by suppression (Besner, 1986; Besner *et al.*, 1981; Barron and Baron, 1977; Kleiman, 1975; Wilding and White, 1985; Johnston and McDermott, 1986). I have suggested that the homphony/rhyme distinction results from either (a) more reliance on working memory for rhyme judgements; (b) a phoneme deletion operation necessary for rhyme judgements but not homophone judgements; (c) both (a) and (b) (Besner, 1986).

References

Adams, M. J. (1979). Models of word recognition.*Cognitive Psychology*, **11**, 133–76.

Allport, D. A. (1979). Word recognition in reading (Tutorial paper). In P. A. Kolers, M. E. Wrolstad, and H. Bouma (Eds) *Processing of Visible Language*. New York: Plenum.

Andrews, S. (1984). Phonological recoding: Is the regularity effect consistent? *Memory & Cognition*, **10**, 565–75.

Baddeley, A. D. and Lewis, V. (1981). Inner active processes in reading: The inner voice, the inner ear and the inner eye. In A. M. Lesgold and C. A. Perfetti (Eds) *Interactive processes in reading*. Hillsdale, NJ: Erlbaum.

Baddeley, A. D., Thomson, N. and Buchanan, M. (1975). Word length and the structure of short term memory. *Journal of Verbal Learning and Verbal Behavior*, **14**, 575–89.

Banks, W. P., Oka, E. and Shugarman, S. (1981). Recoding of printed words to internal speech: Does recoding come before lexical access. In O. J. L. Tzeng and H. Singer (Eds) *Perception of Print: Reading Research in Experimental Psychology*. Hillsdale, NJ: Erlbaum.

Barron, R. W. (1981). Reading skill and reading strategies. In A. M. Lesgold and C. A. Perfetti (Eds) *Interactive processes in reading*. Hillsdale, NJ: Erlbaum.

Barron, R. W. (1985). Interactions between spelling and sound in literacy. In D. R. Olsen, N. Torrance and A. Hildyard (Eds) *Literacy, Language and Learning*. Cambridge: Cambridge University Press.

Barron, R. W. and Baron, J. (1977). How children get meaning from printed words. *Child Development*, **48**, 587–94.

Bauer, D. W. and Stanovich, K. E. (1980). Lexical access and the spelling to sound regularity effect. *Memory & Cognition*, **8**, 424–32.

Besner, D. (1986). Phonology, lexical access in reading and articulatory suppression: a critical review. *Quarterly Journal of Experimental Psychology* (in press).

Besner, D. (1983). Basic decoding components in reading: Two dissociable feature extraction processes. *Canadian Journal of Psychology*, **37**, 429–38.

Besner, D. and Davelaar, E. (1982). Basic processes in reading: Two phonological codes. *Canadian Journal of Psychology*, **36**, 701–11.

Besner, D., Davelaar, E., Alcott, D. and Parry, P. (1984). Wholistic reading of alphabetic print: Evidence from the FDM and the FBI. In L. Henderson (Ed.) *Orthographies and Reading*. Hillsdale, NJ: Erlbaum.

Besner, D., Davies, J. and Daniels, S. (1981). Reading for meaning: The effects of concurrent articulation. *Quarterly Journal of Experimental Psychology*, **33A**, 415–38.

Besner, D., Dennis, I. and Davelaar, E. (1985). Reading without phonology? *Quarterly Journal of Psychology*, **37A**, 477–91.

Besner, D., Hildebrandt, N. (1986). Visual and phonological codes in oral reading of Japanese Kana. *Journal of Experimental Psychology: Learning, Memory and Cognition* (in press).

Bishop, D. V. M. (1985). Spelling ability in congenital dysarthria: Evidence against articulatory coding in translating between phonemes and graphemes. *Cognitive Neuropsychology*, **2**, 229–51.

Bloomfield, L. (1942). Linguistics and Reading. *Elementary English Review*, **19**, 125–30.

Bryant, P. and Bradley, L. (1985). *Children's Reading Problems*. Oxford: Blackwell.

Cohen, G. (1980). Reading and searching for spelling errors. In U. Frith (Ed.) *Cognitive processes in spelling*. London: Academic.

Coltheart, M. (1980). Reading, phonological recoding and deep dyslexia. In M. Coltheart, K. E. Patterson and J. C. Marshall (Eds) *Deep Dyslexia*. London: Routledge and Kegan Paul.

Coltheart, M., Besner, D., Jonasson, J. T. and Davelaar, E. (1979). Phonological recoding in the lexical decision task. *Quarterly Journal of Experimental Psychology*, **31**, 489–507.

Coltheart, M., Davelaar, E., Jonasson, J. T., and Besner, D. (1977). Access to the internal lexicon. In S. Dornic (Eds.) *Attention and performance VI*. Hillsdale, NJ: Erlbaum.

Coltheart, M., Patterson, K. E. and Marshall, J. C. (1980). *Deep Dyslexia*. London: Routledge and Kegan Paul.

Coltheart, V., Laxon, V., Rickard, M. and Elton, C. (1986). Phonological recoding in reading for meaning. Paper presented to the Joint Conference of Experimental Psychology Society and Divisions "Ricerca di base" (SIPs) Padova, Italy.

Davelaar, E., Coltheart, M., Besner, D. and Jonasson, J. T. (1978). Phonological recoding and lexical access. *Memory & Cognition*, **6**, 391–402.

Dennis, I., Besner, D. and Davelaar, E. (1985). Phonology in visual word recognition: Their is more to this than meets the I. In D. Besner, T. G. Waller and E. MacKinnon (Eds) *Reading Research: Advances in Theory and Practice*. London: Academic.

Doctor, E. A. and Coltheart, M. (1980). Children's use of phonological encoding when reading for meaning. *Memory & Cognition*, **8**, 195–209.

Feldman, L. B., Kostić, A., Lukatela, G. and Turvey, M. T. (1983). An evaluation of the "Basic Orthographic Syllabic Structure" in a phonologically shallow orthography. *Psychological Research*, **45**, 55–72.

Feldman, L. B. and Turvey, M. T. (1983). Word recognition in Serbo-Croatian is phonologically analytic. *Journal of Experimental Psychology: Human Perception and Performances*, **9**, 288–98.

Forster, K. I. and Chambers, S. M. (1973). Lexical access and naming time. *Journal of Verbal Learning and Verbal Behavior*, **12**, 627–35.

Fredriksen, J. R. and Kroll, J. F. (1976). Spelling and sound: approaches to the internal lexicon. *Journal of Experimental Psychology: Human Perception and Performance*, **2**, 361–79.

Gibson, E. (1970). The ontogeny of reading. *American Psychologist*, **25**, 136–43.

Gough, P. B. (1972). One second of reading. In J. F. Kavanagh and I. T. Mattingly (Eds) *Language by ear and by eye*. Cambridge, MA: MIT Press.

Gough, P. B. and Cosky, N. J. (1977). One second of reading again. In N. J. Castellan, D. B. Pisoni and G. R. Potts (Eds) *Cognitive Theory Vol 2*. Hillsdale, NJ: Erlbaum.

Henderson, L. (1985). Issues in the Modelling of Pronunciation Assembly in Normal Reading. In K. E. Patterson, J. C. Marshall and M. Coltheart (Eds) *Surface Dyslexia*. Hillsdale, NJ: Erlbaum.

Henderson, L. (1982). *Orthography and Word Recognition in Reading*. London: Academic.

Johnston, R. S. and McDermott, E. A. (1986). Suppression effects in rhyme judgment tasks. *Quarterly Journal of Experimental Psychology*, **38A**, 111–24.

Katz, L. and Feldman, L. B. (1983). Relation between pronunciation and recognition of printed words in deep and shallow orthographies. *Journal of Experimental Psychology: Learning, Memory and Cognition*, **9**, 157–66.

Kimura, Y. (1984). Concurrent vocal interferences: Its effects on Kana and Kanji. *Quarterly Journal of Experimental Psychology*, **36A**, 117–32.

Kimura, Y. and Bryant, P. (1983). Reading and writing in English and Japanese: A cross-cultural study of young children. *British Journal of Developmental Psychology*, **1**, 143–54.

Kleiman, G. M. (1975). Speech recoding in reading. *Journal of Verbal Learning and Verbal Behavior*, **14**, 323–29.

Kolers, P. A. (1985). Skill in reading and memory. *Canadian Journal of Psychology*, **39**, 323–9.

Levy, B. A. (1981). Interactive processing during reading. In A. M. Lesgold and C. A. Perfetti (Eds) *Interactive processes in reading*. Hillsdale, NJ: Erlbaum.

McClelland, J. L. (1976). Preliminary letter identification in the perception of words and nonwords. *Journal of Experimental Psychology: Human Perception and Performance*, **2**, 80–91.

McCusker, L. X., Hillinger, M. L. and Bias, R. G. (1981). Phonological recoding and reading. *Psychological Bulletin*, **89**, 217–45.

Meyer, D. E., Schvaneveldt, R. W. and Ruddy, M. G. (1974). Functions of graphemic and phonemic codes in visual word recognition. *Memory & Cognition*, **2**, 309–21.

Morton, J. and Sasanuma, E. (1984). Lexical access in Japanese. In L. Henderson (Ed) *Orthographies and Reading*. Hillsdale, NJ: Erlbaum.

Parkin, A. J. (1982). Phonological recoding in lexical decision: Effects of spelling to sound regularity depend upon how regularity is defined. *Memory & Cognition*, **10**, 43–53.

Parkin, A. J. and Underwood, G. (1984). Orthographic versus phonological irregularity in lexical decision. *Memory and Cognition*, **11**, 351–5.

Rubenstein, H., Lewis, S. S. and Rubenstein, M. A. (1971). Evidence for phonemic recoding in visual word recognition. *Journal of Verbal Learning and Verbal Behavior*, **10**, 645–57.

Sasanuma, S. (1985). Surface dyslexia and dysgraphia: How are they manifested in Japanese? In K. E. Patterson, J. C. Marshall and M. Coltheart (Eds) *Surface Dyslexia*. Hillsdale, NJ: Erlbaum.

Sasanuma, S. (1984). Can surface dyslexia occur in Japanese? In L. Henderson (Ed) *Orthographies and Reading*. Hillsdale, NJ: Erlbaum.

Sasanuma, S. (1980). Acquired dyslexia in Japanese: clinical features and underlying mechanisms. In M. Coltheart, K. E. Patterson and J. C. Marshall (Eds) *Deep Dyslexia*. London: Routledge and Kegan Paul.

Sasanuma, S. and Fujimura, O. (1971). Selective impairment of phonetic and nonphonetic transcriptions of words in Japanese aphasic patients: Kana versus Kanji in visual recognition and writing. *Cortex*, **7**, 1–18.

Seidenberg, M. S. (1985). The time-course of phonological code activation in two writing systems. *Cognition*, **19**, 1–30.

Shulman, H. G., Hornak, R. and Sanders, E. (1978). The effects of graphemic, phonemic, and semantic relationships on access to lexical structure. *Memory & Cognition*, **6**, 115–23.

Stanovich, K. E. and Bauer, D. W. (1978). Experiments on the spelling to sound regularity effect in word recognition. *Memory & Cognition*, **6**, 410–5.

Treiman, R. Freyd, J. J. and Baron, J. (1984). Phonological recoding and use of spelling–sound rules in reading sentences. *Journal of Verbal Learning and Verbal Behavior*, **22**, 682–700.

Turvey, M. T., Feldman, L. B. and Lukatela, G. (1984). The Serbo-Croatian orthography constrains the reader to a phonologically analytic strategy. In L. Henderson (Ed.) *Orthography and Reading*. Hillsdale, NJ: Erlbaum.

Van Orden, G. C. (1986) A ROWS is a ROSE: Spelling, sound and reading. *Memory & Cognition* (in press).

Waters, G. S. and Seidenberg, M. S. (1985). Spelling–sound effects in reading: time-course and decision criteria. *Memory & Cognition*, **13**, 557–72.

Waters, G. S., Seidenberg, M. S. and Bruck, M. (1984). Children's and adults' use of spelling–sound information in three reading tasks. *Memory & Cognition*, **12**, 293–305.

Wilding, J. and White, W. (1985). Impairment of rhyme judgments by silent and overt articulatory suppression. *Quarterly Journal of Experimental Psychology*, **37A**, 95–107.

12 Visual word recognition in German

Eckart Scheerer

Abstract

Word recognition was studied in German, a language with a phonologically deep writing system but relatively consistent spelling-to-sound rules. Pseudohomophony and graphotactic regularity had additive effects on lexical decisions for nonwords. The pseudohomophone effect was not an artifact of lexical neighborhood size. It was concluded that nonword rejection involves the conjunctive combination of graphotactical and phonological criteria. The magnitude of the pseudohomophone effect was different for two types of homophony-generating rules; lexical decision was slowed down when nonwords were auditorily similar but not homophonic to words. Using loan words as an equivalent of 'irregular words' in other languages, evidence for phonological recoding of words was sought. Both decision latency and pronunciation latency were longer for loan words than for native words, independent of lexical variables such as frequency or neighborhood size. The effect was essentially restricted to those loan words violating German grapheme–phoneme mappings. Nonwords derived from loan words were rejected faster than nonwords derived from native words. Most aspects of the data can be explained by a revised version of dual route theory.

'Writing system' and 'orthography'

The present chapter is concerned with visual word recognition in German, a language with a phonologically deep writing system but a (relatively) regular orthography. A distinction is made between 'writing system' and 'orthography', where 'writing system' refers to the basic principles involved in the representation of spoken language by written language, and

LANGUAGE PERCEPTION AND PRODUCTION
ISBN 0-12-052750-2

'orthography' to the set of rules or regularities governing the correct use of the characters associated with a writing system (Scheerer, 1986). Writing systems are either logographic or phonographic; the latter are either syllabaries or alphabets. In many languages, the pronunciation of morphemes varies in a context–dependent fashion. *Phonologically deep* writing systems apply the principle of *graphemic morpheme constancy*, i.e., the spelling of morphemes is kept constant in spite of context-induced changes in their pronunciation. In *phonologically shallow* writing systems, such pronunciation changes are expressed in spelling. Conceptually, the 'deep versus shallow' dimension of writing systems does not coincide with the 'regular/irregular' dimension of orthographies. If the context-sensitive pronunciation rules for graphemically constant morphemes work in a strictly deterministic way, a phonologically deep writing system may be said to have a completely regular orthography. On the other hand, phonologically shallow writing systems need not exhibit perfectly regular orthographies; exceptions may be introduced by loan words. Nevertheless, overall there will be a rough correlation between writing system (shallow/deep) and orthography (regular/irregular).

Our approach to orthography is similar to the one taken by Venezky and Massaro (Chap 8). We assume that the correct use of graphemes is governed by three types of constraints: (1) the permissible sequence of sounds, (2) the permissible sequence of graphemes, and (3) the mapping of graphemes into phonemes. Thus, we have *phonotactic, graphotactic* and *grapheme–phoneme constraints*; they are equivalent to Venezky and Massaro's phonological constraints, scribal constraints and spelling–sound regularity. Venezky and Massaro contrast phonological and scribal constraints, as measures of 'orthographic structure', to spelling–sound regularity. However, it is only on the basis of spelling–sound rules that phonological constraints can affect the correct use of graphemes. As a consequence, it seems more convenient to distinguish between two sources of constraints on grapheme use: those that are autonomous to written language, and those that derive from the relationship between written language and spoken language. The term 'orthography' is often restricted to the former type of constraint, but this usage rests on the assumption that a purely distributional analysis of written language, disregarding its relation to spoken language, is sufficient to define graphemes (Eisenberg, 1983; Henderson, 1985). It would also imply that languages with a bidirectional one-to-one mapping between graphemes and phonemes do not have an orthography. Such implications are better avoided. Therefore, the generic term 'orthography' will be applied to all types of constraints on grapheme use.

The main focus of this chapter is on the relative contributions of grapho-tactic and grapheme–phoneme regularity to word recognition in German. Sublexical sources of constraints are stressed, in line with Venezky and Massaro, and an attempt is made to assess the relative merits of rule-based and frequency-based approaches to orthographic regularity. In addition, sublexical and lexical contributions to word recognition are pitted against each other. Word recognition is investigated by measuring lexical decision time and pronunciation latency. In English, two 'effects' have often been used for drawing inferences on the organization of word recognition. First: in lexical decision, nonwords that are homophonic with words (pseudoho-mophones) take longer to reject than pseudowords, i.e. pronounceable nonwords that are not homophonic with words (the *pseudohomophone effect*, Rubenstein, Lewis and Rubenstein, 1971). Second: regularly spelled words produce briefer decision and/or pronunciation latencies than irregularly spelled words: the *regularity effect* (Baron and Strawson, 1976). Modern work on word recognition in German is scarce, and our first task is to establish the existence and the determinants of the two effects in German. This, in turn, requires a brief discussion of some basic features of the German writing system.

Some features of the German writing system

A writing system is phonologically deep if it adheres to the principle of morpheme constancy. The German writing system satisfies this criterion. On the other hand, contextual variations in the pronunciation of mor-phemes are much more restricted than they are in English. The best known context-dependent pronunciation rule is that voiced consonants at the end of a word or in front of an unvoiced consonant get unvoiced. Thus, *Werk* and *Werg* are homophonic, while *Sark* is a pseudohomophone of *Sarg*. Morpheme constancy overrides graphotactics. For instance, there is a rule that geminated consonants do not occur in front of another consonant but this rule is suppressed when it comes into conflict with morpheme con-stancy. Consequently, the geminated *l* in *fallen* is not suppressed in the third-person form *fällt*.

Before looking at graphotactic and grapheme–phoneme constraints of German orthography, it must be said that the German writing system, properly speaking, is defined for German native words only. *Loan words* often deviate from German graphotactics and/or grapheme–phoneme rules. Violations of graphotactics are also found in some proper names and geographical terms of German origin.

According to Sommerfeldt, Starke and Nerius (1981), about one quarter of German graphemes are mapped on more than one phoneme, and about two thirds of the phonemes are mapped on more than one grapheme. Some of the violations of one-to-one mapping are caused by the morphemic constancy principle. Occasionally, more than one letter is used to express a phoneme; there is one trigraph (*sch*, corresponding to /ʃ/) and some digraphs (e.g. *ch*, corresponding to /x/ or /ç/, which are allophonic). The exact sound value of a grapheme is often marked by the graphemes following it; in particular, the short vowels are marked not by the vowels themselves, but by the consonants following them, subject to some graphotactic regularities. While these context-dependent rules may pose problems for *spelling*, in *reading* they do not prevent the non-lexical assembly of a word's correct pronunciation. However, in some polymorphemic words morpheme parsing is needed for correct pronunciation; for instance, the trigraph *sch* is pronounced /sç/ if it results from the combination of morphemes (e.g. in *Häuschen*). Mentrup (1971) lists 279 homophones, but many of these pertain to derived forms rather than base forms of words (for instance, the verb form *fällt* is homophonic to the noun *Feld*). Homographic heterophones (e.g. written words or word forms with more than one pronunciation) are very rare and in most cases distinguished by the initial capitalization rule for nouns (e.g. the noun *Rast*, pronounced with a short vowel, versus the verb form *rast*, pronounced with a long vowel).

There is no very obvious way to measure a language's overall orthographic regularity; but the commonsense notion that German has a 'more regular' orthography than English is not totally misleading, especially with respect to the assignment of phonemes to graphemes.

German has a complicated set of *graphotactic regularities*. Two examples will be given. (1) *Vowel length* is marked either by putting *h* after a vowel, or by vowel gemination (including *ie*), or it is left unmarked. The three cases do not occur at random. *u* is never geminated, *ih* occurs only in some personal pronoun forms. Lengthening by *h* is much more frequent than gemination, but occurs only in front of liquid consonants. Vowel length is never marked in front of *b, d, f* and *g*. These constraints are graphotactic and have no foundation in phonotactics. One additional constraint, namely, that *k, p* and *z* never follow a vowel in ungeminated form, has phonotactic reasons. (2) *Consonant gemination* is used to mark brief vowels preceding consonants. But some consonants are never geminated (*c, h, j, v, w, x*), some geminates occur in medial position only (*bb, dd, gg*), and two geminates are produced by combining two different letters (*ck* and *tz*). Consonant gemination is suppressed after another consonant or after a diphthong. Spellings such as *Hertz* or *Quartz*, which may be familiar to English readers, do not conform to German graphotactics; the first is derived from a proper name, the second got the redundant *t* in the process of borrowing from German (where it is spelled *Quarz*) into English.

What implications do the properties of the German writing system have for the construction or selection of material to be used for research on word recognition?

Pseudohomophones for native German words can be constructed by applying a limited number of rules. Finding pseudohomophones can be relegated to a computer program that does not need *lexical* knowledge about pronunciation but only has to exclude the few lexical homophones arising in the process. Depending on the graphemic context, application of these rules results in pseudohomophones that either conform or do not conform to the graphotactic rules of the German orthography. For instance, *Parg* is a graphotactically regular pseudohomophone of *Park*, while *derp* is a graphotactically irregular pseudohomophone of *derb*. Moreover, pseudowords as well as pseudohomophones may be either graphotactically regular (e.g. *Parn*) or irregular (e.g. *derv*). Graphotactically irregular pseudohomophones and pseudowords conform to the German writing system, as evidenced by the fact that their pronunciation is transparent to a competent user of German. In sum, it is possible, among German non-lexical letter strings, to vary homophony/non-homophony to words and graphotactic irregularity/regularity in an orthogonal fashion.

By definition, all letter combinations occurring in native German words (with the exception of some proper names) are graphotactically legal. It follows, tautologically, that there are no native German words that are graphotactically irregular. As a result, the *regularity* effect cannot be investigated in native words. Loan words can be used for the purpose, though. In German, recently borrowed loan words are spelled *and* pronounced as in the language from which they were borrowed. As a result, many (but by no means all) loan words violate the orthographic rules for native words. All combinations of grapheme–phoneme and graphotactic regularity and irregularity can and in fact do occur among loan words, although the number of cases in each category is very different. Moreover, some loan words are 'phonologically irregular', that is, they contain sounds that either do not occur in German or violate German phonotactics. *Jazz* is a good example; /ʤ/ is not a German phoneme, and /z/ does not occur in final position. Some speakers use the correct pronunciation, but assimilation to German phonology is more usual, *jazz* being pronounced like *chess* (which is not a loan word in German).

Phonological recoding and the dual route theory

In the lexical decision task, the subject is presented with a string of letters and has to decide whether it spells a word. Reaction time is the principal dependent variable, although error rate sometimes provides useful information, too.

This task has been used for a variety of purposes, but mainly for studying access to the 'mental lexicon'. The mental lexicon is a hypothesized structure in people's minds (or brains); a minimal formulation is that it contains at least three components: orthographic and phonological addresses and semantic descriptions (see the section on the 'Architecture of the mental lexicon' for more sophisticated discussions). In order to be recognized as a word, a letter string must activate the lexical entry corresponding to the word in question. How does this activation occur?

The initial position (Rubenstein, *et al.*, 1971; Stanners, Forbach and Headley, 1971) was that lexical access is mediated only by *phonological recoding*: by means of rules governing grapheme–phoneme correspondences and/or the parsing of words into sublexical units such as syllables or spelling patterns, a letter string is converted into a phonological representation, which is compared (either serially or in parallel) to the phonological addresses in the lexicon. Accordingly, all pseudohomophones should be misclassified as words. However, this is not true; most pseudohomophones are rejected, but with longer latency than pseudowords. Rubenstein *et al.* therefore assumed that a 'spelling recheck' was done for pseudohomophones, a procedure that requires graphemic addresses in the mental lexicon.

For the English language, phonological recoding is no longer accepted as the only mechanism involved in lexical access. Grapheme–phoneme conversion will not lead to correct lexical decisions about orthographically irregular words. It was therefore suggested that such words are accessed directly from their graphemic representations (Baron and Strawson, 1976). In *dual route theory* (Coltheart, 1978), it is assumed that upon representation of a letter string the direct and the indirect (phonologically mediated) access routes are used in parallel, and that lexical decision is based on whichever route first provides sufficient evidence about the lexical status of a letter string. In the theory, phonological recoding is reduced to a merely subsidiary principle. The direct route is assumed to operate more quickly, and it will 'win the race to the lexicon' except for infrequent regular words; as shown by the pseudohomophone effect, the rejection of nonwords may also be based on the indirect route.

More recently, the existence of 'independent lexical and nonlexical routes in word processing' has been put into question (Humphreys and

Evett, 1985). One aspect of the criticism concerns the pseudohomophone effect. It has been argued that the effect is a misnomer because it can be reduced to a graphemic similarity effect (Martin, 1982; Taft, 1982). However, even if pseudohomophones and pseudowords are matched for graphemic similarity to words, the pseudohomophone effect occurs, but only when homophonic words are present (Dennis, Besner and Davelaar, 1985). Another restriction is that the effect obtains only when no more than 25% of the nonwords are pseudohomophones (McQuade, 1981). Data of this type seem to indicate that phonological recoding is under strategic control and is abandoned when it interferes with rapid lexical decision.

Why does the phonological recoding route play such a minor role in lexical decision? All of the studies mentioned so far have been done on English, a language with a phonologically deep writing system and a very complicated set of grapheme–phoneme rules. In a language with bidirectional one-to-one mapping between graphemes and phonemes, there can be no pseudohomophones. Lukatela and his group (e.g. Lukatela, Popadić, Ogćjenovin and Turvey, 1981) exploited the fact that Serbo-Croatian, a language with these characteristics, is written in two alphabets comprising a subset of letters common to both but pronounced differently in both alphabets. Pronunciation ambiguity arising from this feature leads to a lengthening of lexical decision times, a result that is interpreted as implying obligatory phonological recoding (see Feldman, Chap 10). However, as pointed out by Besner (Chap 11), even in languages with shallow writing systems pronunciation may have a lexical component; by implication, a direct route to the mental lexicon would exist in such languages. When grapheme–phoneme conversion is not complicated by context effects and parsing problems do not arise, the phonological route need not be slower than the direct route. Phonological recoding effects in languages with a shallow writing system are therefore compatible with dual route theory.

The pseudohomophone effect in German

Owing to its writing system, German is well suited to test dual route theory. On the one hand, the grapheme–phoneme conversion rules are sufficiently transparent to allow the prelexical assembly of phonology. On the other hand, it is likely that autonomous graphotactic regularities will be used in lexical decision. Up to now, only two studies on the pseudohomophone effect in German have been reported. Gfroerer, Günther and Weiss (1984) found that the effect was restricted to nonword lists containing no more than 25% pseudohomophones. Schilling (1985) failed to find the effect altogether. Neither of these investigators controlled for graphotactic irregularity as a potential confounding factor.

Let it be assumed that pronounceable nonwords (pseudowords) are rejected because they violate graphotactics and/or because they do not activate an appropriate phonological address in the mental lexicon. Let it further be assumed that graphotactic analysis takes less time than grapheme–phoneme conversion and searching for phonological addresses, and that once a phonological address is activated, a spelling-recheck is done, allowing the rejection of pseudohomophones. Consider now an experiment in which lexical decisions are required for (graphotactically) regular pseudohomophones, irregular pseudohomophones, regular pseudowords and irregular pseudowords. In generating predictions about decision latencies, two ways of combining evidence from graphotactic analysis and phonological recoding must be distinguished. In the *disjunctive* mode, lexical decision is based on whichever evidence is available first. Consequently, irregular items will be rejected faster than regular items, irrespective of pseudohomophony, and a pseudohomophone effect will occur for regular items only. In the *conjunctive* mode (Koriat, 1984), lexical decision is completed when evidence from *both* sources is available. Again, irregular items will be rejected faster than regular items, but a pseudohomophone effect will occur for both types of items.

These predictions were tested in an experiment[1] in which graphotactic regularity and pseudohomophony were varied orthogonally to each other. All items had four letters. Graphotactic regularity was assessed by means of the grapheme-distributional information given by Philipp (1974) and checked with a standard (Duden, 1980) and a reverse alphabetic dictionary (Mater, 1970). The graphotactically irregular items contained one trigram that does not occur at the beginning or at the end of German native words. All irregular items were pronounceable according to German grapheme–phoneme rules. All nonwords differed by one letter from German words; the pseudohomophones were derived from their word mates by applying

Table 1. Decision latencies (in ms) and percentage of errors (in parentheses) as a function of graphotactic regularity and pseudohomophony.

	pseudohomophone	pseudoword	mean
graphotactically regular	812 (7.2)	767 (3.1)	789 (5.2)
graphotactically irregular	776 (2.8)	724 (0.9)	750 (1.9)
mean	794 (5.0)	746 (2.0)	

homophony-generating rules that result, depending on the context, in graphotactic regularity or irregularity. The word list did not contain homophonic words, words from which a pseudohomophone was derived, or loan words violating German grapheme–phoneme rules. Pseudohomophones comprised 25% of the nonword list.

The data of interest are the latencies of '*no*' responses for the four categories of nonwords (see Table 1). The results form a very clear-cut pattern. Pseudowords were rejected 48 ms faster than pseudohomophones, and irregular nonwords were rejected 39 ms faster than regular nonwords. Both effects were significant by items and subjects analyses, but their interaction was not ($F < 1$). Pseudohomophony and regularity were perfectly additive.

Thus, nonwords were rejected on the basis of a conjunctive combination of graphotactic and phonological criteria; graphotactic violations alone did not prevent use of phonological information. Hart (as reported by Venezky and Massaro, Chap 8) found no pseudohomophone effect for graphotactically irregular English pseudowords. However, it is unlikely that this divergence from the present results reflects a greater reliance of English readers on graphotactic criteria. Hart apparently used quite drastic violations of graphotactics (e.g. *ckode*). In the present study, most irregular trigrams contained bigrams that were permissible in the relevant positions; letter patterns that never occur in German (e.g. *zz*) or letters that never occur in a given position (e.g. *w* in the end position) were not used. It is conceivable that in German, too, the pseudohomophone effect vanishes if violations of this type are used.

In one sense, however, the pseudohomophone effect may be more 'robust' in German than in English. Summarizing all available studies in English, Dennis, *et al.* (1985, p. 191) state that 'the pseudohomophone effect is difficult to obtain when homophones are absent'. Homophones were absent in the present study, but the effect was obtained, and its size was comparable to the typical size found for English pseudohomophones when 50% of the words are homophones (Dennis, *et al.*, 1985, Table V).

Despite its robustness, the pseudohomophone effect could have been an artifact of pseudohomophones being graphemically more similar to words. A convenient way to measure graphemic similarity of a given nonword to words is the number of 'neighbors' it has, i.e., the number of words differing by one letter from the nonword. When Martin (1982) controlled the number of neighbors across pseudohomophones and nonwords, the pseudohomophone effect disappeared, a result that could not be replicated by Besner and Davelaar (1983). In our study, the average number of neighbors was 4.18 for pseudohomophones and 4.06 for pseudowords. Across all nonwords, the correlation between number of neighbors and decision latency was 0.368; for pseudohomophones alone it was 0.309, and for pseudowords 0.490. All correlations were significant. The regression of latency on number of neighbors was linear; the slopes for pseudowords and for pseudohomophones were virtually parallel to each other. We conclude that the pseudohomophone effect was not an artifact of greater graphemic similarity to words. In this respect, our data are comparable to those of Besner and Davelaar (1983), but the latter authors did not find significant correlations between neighborhood size and decision latency. One explanation for this discrepancy is that in our study neighborhood size and graphotactic regularity were very highly correlated; on the average, irregular letter strings had 2.57 and regular letter strings 5.67 neighbors.

The effect of neighborhood size and its confound with graphotactic regularity raises a theoretical problem. Up to now we have assumed that as far as graphemics is concerned the rejection of nonwords does not arise from the negative outcome of a search through the mental lexicon, but from the evaluation of sublexical units (graphotactically permissible letter combinations) in the input string. The graphemic lexicon was implicated in pseudohomophones only, as a means to perform the 'spelling check' necessary for their evaluation. In McClelland and Rumelhart's (1981) and other 'lexical pooling' models (Henderson, 1982), it is assumed that the graphemic code subserving word recognition consists of all letters making up a word, and no provision is made for any supraletter but sublexical units. Accordingly, lexical addresses are activated not only by words, but also by nonwords provided that they share letters with words. Neighborhood size could be taken as a measure of the number of lexical addresses activated by a given nonword. In a model of this type, the phonological representation of a letter string would not be *assembled* on the basis of grapheme–phoneme conversion rules, but *derived* from the phonological entries connected to the graphemic addresses activated by the letter string. The pseudohomophone effect would then result from the *automatic* (or obligatory) coactivation of phonological addresses by graphemic addresses.

The case for prelexical assembly of phonology in lexical decision could be strengthened by showing that the size of the pseudohomophone effect depends on the *rules used for generating pseudohomophones*. In our data, there was some indication that the various rules generating homophony were not equally effective. Accordingly, two rules were selected for further study in another experiment: (1) Equivalence of unmarked long vowel and long vowel marked by *h* (e.g. *Tal/Tahl*, *Kohle/Kole* and (2) transformation of voiced into voiceless consonants at the end position (e.g. *Burg/Burk*, *Wort/Word*). For the former rule, the pseudohomophone effect amounted to 85 ms, and for the latter, to 41 ms.

These data are open to at least two interpretations. One of them relates to the different *transparency* of the two rules. Though vowel lengthening by *h* is subject to some graphotactic constraints, in some graphemic contexts the decision whether a word is spelled with a 'lengthening *h*' can be made on the basis of lexical knowledge only. To ascertain whether a word with an unvoiced end consonant is spelled with a letter corresponding to a voiced or a voiceless consonant, one only needs to append a vowel to it, as happens naturally in the case of grammatical suffixes; the end consonants then regain their 'proper' sound values. Thus, while *Burk* is a pseudohomophone of *Burg*, *Burken* is not a pseudohomophone of *Burgen*. While *Tahl* can only be rejected by means of a spelling check, *Burk* could be rejected without recourse to the graphemic entry for *Burg*. So far, this interpretation has not been tested by us.

Another explanation relates to the actual *use* of homophony-generating rules; perhaps pseudohomophones are not homophones but rather 'homoiophones', that is, phonologically *similar* but not *exactly equal* to their word mates. This possibility was tested for pseudowords that differed from words in their beginning consonants according to the voiced/voiceless contrast (e.g. *Gras/Kras*). In standard pronunciation, such pairs are not homophonic. Yet to reject them took 40 ms longer than to reject pseudowords differing from words on the place of articulation dimension (*Gras/Dras*), a delay which was almost equal to the pseudohomophone effect contingent on the voiced–voiceless transition. Speech spectrogram measurements are currently under way to test whether there are any pronunciation differences between presumed pseudohomophones and their word mates.

Kras and *Dras* differ from *Gras* by one letter and one articulatory feature; nonwords of both types had the same average number of graphemic word neighbors. Yet they produced a sizeable and significant difference in rejection latency, an effect which is not explicable by graphemic factors and seems to require a nonlexically assembled phonological representation. To a German listener, *Kras* sounds much more similar to *Gras* than *Dras* does. Perhaps, as suggested by Besner (Chap 11), the phonological representation is auditory rather than articulatory. The suggestion is plausible, but more research is needed to substantiate it.

The processing of loan words

The evidence presented so far was based on the *rejection of nonwords*. It remains to be shown that phonological recoding is involved in the *acceptance of words*. Another as yet undecided point is the nature of graphotactic effects. Do they arise from differential activation of graphemic addresses in the mental lexicon or from the evaluation of graphotactic regularities? These questions were dealt with in two experiments on lexical decision and pronunciation latency for loan words and pseudowords derived from them.

So far the processing of loan words in German has not been studied. Consequently, the first step in research is to find out whether there are any differences between loan words and native German words which are not related to orthographic factors yet influence lexical decision time and pronunciation latency. There are two likely factors of that sort. First, loan words may on the average be used less often than native words; and second, loan words may have fewer graphemic neighbors than native words. Accordingly, these factors were kept constant across both classes of words.

A *word list* was compiled in the following way. Six groups of native words and of loan words were selected by means of a dictionary of loan words (Duden, 1982), such that the words in each group had 0, 1, 2, 3, 4–5, or 6–10 neighbors. Within each group, loan words and native words were matched with respect to frequency. All had four letters.

A list of 256 *nonwords* was selected from a corpus of all four-letter strings that can be formed by concatenating bigrams occurring in German 4-letter words. For each of the approximately 32 000 letter strings, the summed positional bigram frequency (computed on a type basis) and the number of neighbors were determined. The corpus was then divided into pseudo native words and pseudo loan words; every letter string containing at least one bigram occurring in loan words only was considered to be a pseudo loan word. Four groups of pseudo native words and pseudo loan words were selected, such that the strings in each group had 0, 1, 2–3 and 4–6 neighbors. Within each group, half of the strings had high and the other half low positional bigram frequency. Thus, we have two measures of regularity: a rule-based (derivation from native words versus from loan words) and a statistical measure (positional bigram frequency); both are varied independently from each other and from the number of neighbors.

Consider *nonwords* first. In *lexical decision*, pseudo loan words were rejected a significant 32 ms more quickly than pseudo native words, but positional bigram frequency did not have an effect. On the other hand, rejection latencies were again positively correlated with neighborhood size, and the regression lines for the two types of nonword were parallel to each other. Thus, while rejection of nonwords obviously had a lexical component, there was also an effect of orthographic regularity which could not be reduced to the mere frequency of sublexical letter patterns. A hint as to the nature of this rule-based orthographic effect can be obtained by considering *pronunciation latency*. Pseudo loan words were named 51 ms slower than pseudo native words. Neighborhood size did not have a significant effect, though there was some indication of a curvilinear relation, with nonwords having one neighbor only taking longest to pronounce. Almost half (49.2%) of the pseudo loan words elicited more than one pronunciation from our subjects; typically, these consisted in the application of either French or English pronunciation rules (for instance, *ou* was pronounced either /u:/ or /au/. Even 14.1% of the pseudo native words elicited more than one pronunciation, and the second pronunciation typically reflected lexical assimilation to a loan word (for instance, the *g* in *boge* was pronounced /ʒ/ instead of /g/). Pronunciation uncertainty (measured by Shannon's information statistic *H*) correlated 0.497 with pronunciation latency. Across all nonwords, lexical decision time correlated neither with pronunciation latency nor with pronunciation uncertainty. However, *pseudo native words* receiving more than one pronunciation were rejected 40 ms slower than those with unique pronunciation. Among *pseudo loan words*, pronunciation uncertainty did not have a significant effect; if at all, ambiguous pronunciation was associated with somewhat faster rejection than unique pronunciation. Apparently, if a graphotactic pattern specifies that German grapheme–phoneme rules are not applicable, then lexical decision is not based on a phonological representation.

Neighborhood size did not have a significant effect on decision latency for *words*, but its effect on pronunciation latency was marginally significant. Words having more neighbors were pronounced somewhat faster, more so for loan words than for native words. Both decision and pronunciation latency correlated negatively with log word frequency, but to a different extent (decision latency: −0.421; pronunciation latency: −0.212). Decision latency and pronunciation latency were positively correlated (0.536), even after log word frequency was partialled out (0.504). Thus, the two dependent measures were affected by common factors not related to word frequency.

Mean decision and pronunciation latencies are displayed in Table 2. There was a 'loan word effect' for both: loan words were accepted 41 ms and pronounced 24 ms more slowly than native words. The loan words used in the experiment were not selected for orthographic criteria, but they could be classified, *post hoc*, according to such criteria. A first, 'regular' group does not contain any violations of German orthography (e.g. *Film, Test, Oper*). *Graphotactically irregular* loan words contain at least one bigram that does not occur, in a given position, among native words (e.g. *Skat, Taxi, Type*). When the pronunciation of a loan word is listed in a standard German dictionary (Duden, 1980) it belongs to the group with *irregular grapheme–phoneme correspondence* (e.g. *Baby, Chef, Team*).

This group includes some words that were graphotactically regular and had neighbors with regular German pronunciation (e.g. *Volt, Page, Loge*), but the subgroup was too small to warrant separate analysis. The validity of the classification was supported by the frequency of pronunciation errors (see Table 2): almost 20% of the pronunciations assigned to words with irregular grapheme–phoneme correspondence were wrong, while for all other words virtually no mispronunciations were made.

Table 2. Latencies (in ms) and percentage of errors (in parentheses) for lexical decision and pronunciation.

	Lexical decision	Pronunciation
Native words (96[a])	639 (3.7)	573 (0.3)
All loan words (96)	680 (6.7)	597 (7.5)
Regular loan words (35)	649 (5.8)	566 (0.9)
Loan words with irregular graphotactics (28)	663 (5.8)	591 (1.6)
Loan words with irregular grapheme-phoneme correspondence (33)	727 (8.4)	634 (19.5)

[a] Numbers in parentheses refer to the number of cases in each category.

For both lexical decision and pronunciation, there was a progressive increase of latency across the three groups of loan words. However, when the loan word groups were tested against native words, a significant effect was obtained for one group only, namely, for those with irregular grapheme–phoneme correspondence. Supplementary analyses on the loan word data by means of biserial correlation coefficients showed that grapheme–phoneme irregularity still had significant effects on both latency measures when frequency was partialled out. When the correlation between decision and pronunciation latency was partialled out in addition, there was no longer a significant effect on decision latency. Pronunciation latency alone was affected by two variables: pronunciation uncertainty (measured again by the Shannon information statistic) and presence versus absence of an initial consonant cluster.

If it is assumed that effects common to lexical decision and pronunciation are located at the lexical access stage (see Lorch, Balota and Stamm, 1986), then it can be concluded that the grapheme–phoneme regularity effects observed in the experiments arose during lexical access rather than, for instance, at some post-lexical decision stage. Considering that effects of neighborhood size and frequency were controlled, the most parsimonious assumption is that lexical access was in part mediated by phonological recoding involving the application of German grapheme–phoneme conversion rules. For loan words with deviant grapheme–phoneme correspondence, the phonological recoding route comes into conflict with the direct route. Occasionally, this conflict could be observed *in statu nascendi*: sometimes a subject would begin pronouncing a loan word according to German grapheme–phoneme rules and then switch, *during pronunciation*, to the appropriate (non-German) pronunciation; e.g. *Baby* was pronounced /ba.. be:bi/. The process could also work the other way round: *Juli*: /ʤ.. ju:li/.

Our data on lexical decision come into conflict with a major trend emerging from research on the regularity effect in English, a trend which is aptly summarized in the title of a recent paper: 'Spelling-to-sound regularity affects pronunciation latency but not lexical decision' (Parkin, McMullen, and Graystone, 1986). At most, lexical decision seems to be affected by graphotactic irregularity. as for instance with the 'strange words' employed by Seidenberg, Waters and Barnes (1984). In our loan word experiments, graphotactic irregularity *per se* had no effect, but only when it was correlated with deviations from German grapheme–phoneme rules. In the pseudohomophone experiments, graphotactic regularity did have an effect, but there it was confounded with neighborhood size; moreover, it could be used as one criterion for distinguishing words from nonwords, while in the present experiments both words and nonwords contained graphotactic violations. It remains to be seen whether lexical decision for graphotactically irregular loan words is slowed down when they are embedded in a list of graphotactically regular nonwords.

In a language like German, which is characterized by a dichotomy between a native, 'regular' vocabulary and a loan word vocabulary which in part violates spelling-to-sound rules, graphotactic violations may serve the useful function of signalling the language from which a loan word has been borrowed. For instance, all German words ending in *w* and *y* or beginning with *sh* are borrowed from English. Some elementary knowledge of English grapheme–phoneme rules can be assumed even for people with little formal instruction in English, owing to the immense avalanche of recent borrowings from that language. Newly arriving loan words encountered in print may therefore be pronounced correctly on a non-lexical basis. As suggested by Kay (Chap 9), the process of sublexical spelling–sound translation requires higher-order units such as letter clusters or initial segments. Evidence for this was provided by our pseudo loan words, for instance, by those containing a middle *ou*, which does not occur in native German words. *Wouf*, suggesting English origin, was most often pronounced /wauf/; *souf*, carrying no obvious clue as to its origin, produced an almost chaotic variety of pronunciations. Venezky and Massaro (Chap 8) doubt the reliability and validity of the etymological principle in the assignment of pronunciation, but graphotactics may very well be a means to increase its usefulness.

Concluding remarks

In studies on speech recognition, recent work on the different status of the syllable in French and English has opened the perspective 'that the proper model of speech recognition may differ for different languages and speakers'. Cutler (Chap 2), from whom this quotation is taken, finds such a perspective disturbing and prefers an alternative, more general model capable of accommodating language-specific effects as special cases. We are sympathetic to such an approach. No claim is made that the processing of German words requires a model which is totally different from those that have been developed for English. If certain amendments are made to it, *dual route theory* (Coltheart, 1978) is a viable candidate for an orthography-invariant model of visual word processing. First, the *relative processing rates* on the direct and the indirect route should be allowed to vary according to the overall regularity of a language's orthography, in order to account for the emergence of more stable phonological recoding effects in languages with consistent grapheme–phoneme mappings. Second, various ways of *combining evidence* from the two routes should be considered. When graphemic and phonological criteria for lexical status are highly but not perfectly correlated, conjunctive combination as advocated here is more plausible than the competition implied by the horse-race model. Third, parsing of the input string should involve *graphotactically defined units*, in order to allow for the selection of appropriate grapheme–phoneme conversion rules.

Acknowledgements

This report is based, in part, on the MA theses by Gudrun Berger and Jutta Torinus. The help of Arno Schilling and Bettina Kewitz is gratefully acknowledged. Portions of the data analyses and the preparation of the chapter were done during my stay at the Zentrum für Interdisziplinäre Forschung, Universität Bielefeld. Alan Allport, Derek Besner, Leslie Henderson and Richard Venezky helped to improve a first version of the manuscript; remaining faults are mine, not theirs. Some passages of this chapter are taken from an earlier publication (Scheerer, 1986).

Note

[1] Space limitations prevent the reporting of the experiments in full detail. Prior to the publication of an extended report in a professional journal, lists of all stimulus items and detailed data analyses may be obtained from the author.

References

Baron, J. and Strawson, C. (1976). Use of orthographic and word-specific knowledge in reading words aloud. *Journal of Experimental Psychology: Human Perception and Performance*, **2**, 386–93.

Besner, D. and Davelaar, E. (1983). Suedohomofoan effects in visual word recognition: Evidence for phonological processing. *Canadian Journal of Psychology*, **37**, 300–5.

Coltheart, M. (1978). Lexical access in simple reading tasks. In G. Underwood (Ed.) *Strategies of Information Processing*. London: Academic, pp. 151–216.

Dennis, I., Besner, D. and Davelaar, E. (1985). Phonology in visual word recognition: Their is more two this than meats the I. In D. Besner, T. G. Waller and E. McKinnon (Eds) *Reading Research: Advances in Theory and Practice*. London: Academic, pp. 167–97.

Duden: Rechtschreibung der deutschen Sprache und der Fremdwörter (1980). 18th edn Mannheim: Bibliographisches Institut.

Duden: Fremdwörterbuch (1982). 4th edn Mannheim: Bibliographisches Institut.

Eisenberg, P. (1983). Orthografie und Schriftsystem. In K. B. Günther and H. Günther (Eds) *Schrift, Schreiben, Schriftlichkeit*. Tubingen: Niemeyer, pp. 41–68.

Gfroerer, S., Günther, H. and Weiss, L. (1984). Zur Frage des visuellen und phonologischen Zugangs zum mentalen Lexikon. *Phonetica*, **41**, 41–9.

Henderson, L. (1982). *Orthography and Word Recognition in Reading*, London: Academic Press.

Henderson, L. (1985). On the use of the term 'grapheme'. *Language and Cognitive Processes*, **1**, 135–48.

Humphreys, G. W. and Evett, L. J. (1985). Are there independent lexical and nonlexical routes in word processing? An evaluation of the dual-route theory in reading. *The Behavioural and Brain Sciences*, **8**, 689–740.

Koriat, A. (1984). Reading without vowels: lexical access in Hebrew. In H. Bouma and D. Bouwhuis (Eds) *Attention and Performance X*. Hillsdale, NJ: Erlbaum, pp. 227–42.

Lorch, R. F. Jr., Balota, D. A. and Stamm, E. G. (1986). Locus of inhibition effects in the priming of lexical decision: Pre- or postlexical access? *Memory & Cognition*, **14**, 95–103.

Lukatela, G., Popadić, D., Ogćjenovin, P. and Turvey, M. T. (1980). Lexical decisions in a phonologically shallow orthography. *Memory & Cognition*, **8**, 124–32.

Martin, R. C. (1982). The pseudohomophone effect: The role of visual similarity in non-word decisions. *Quarterly Journal of Experimental Psychology*, **34A**, 394–409.

Mater, E. (1970). *Rückläufiges Wörterbuch der deutschen Gegenwartssprache*. Leipzig: VEB Verlag Enzyklopädie.

McClelland, J. L. and Rumelhart, D. E. (1981). An interactive activation model of context effects in letter perception: Part 1. An account of basic findings. *Psychological Review*, **88**, 375–407.

McQuade, D. V. (1981). Variable reliance on phonological information in visual word recognition. *Language and Speech*, **24**, 99–109.

Mentrup, W. (1971). *Mahlen oder malen? Gleichklingende, aber verschieden geschriebene Wörter*. Mannheim: Bibliographisches Institut.

Parkin, A. J., McMullen, M. and Graystone, D. (1986). Spelling-to-sound regularity affects pronunciation latency but not lexical decision. *Psychological Research*, **48**, 87–92.

Philipp, M. (1974). *Phonologie des Deutschen*. Stuttgart: Kohlhammer.

Rubenstein, H., Lewis, S. S. and Rubenstein, M. A. (1971). Evidence for phonemic recoding in visual word recognition. *Journal of Verbal Learning and Verbal Behavior*, **10**, 645–57.

Scheerer, E. (1986). Orthography and lexical access. In G. Augst (Ed.) *New Trends in Graphemics and Orthography*. Berlin: De Gruyter, pp. 262–86.

Schilling, A. (1985). *Simulation des Worterkennens*. Frankfurt: Peter Lang.

Seidenberg, M. S., Waters, G. S. and Barnes, M. A. (1984). When does irregular spelling or pronunciation influence word recognition? *Journal of Verbal Learning and Verbal Behavior*, **23**, 383–404.

Sommerfeldt, K.-E., Starke, G. and Nerius, D. (1981). *Einführung in die Grammatik und Orthographie der deutschen Gegenwartssprache*. Leipzig: Bibliographisches Institut.

Stanners, R. R., Forbach, G. B. and Headley, D. B. (1971). Decision and search processes in word-nonword classification. *Journal of Experimental Psychology*, **90**, 45–50.

Taft, M. (1982). An alternative to grapheme–phoneme conversion rules? *Memory & Cognition*, **10**, 465–74.

13   Morphological constraints on word recognition

Robert J. Jarvella, Remo Job, Görel Sandström and
Robert Schreuder

Abstract

A stimulus onset asynchrony (SOA) technique was used to determine what
(linguistically defined) part of a visually presented word is utilized to trigger the
process of identifying word forms. Naming latencies and lexical decision latencies
obtained for Italian verb forms suggest that the information initially required
corresponds to a portion of a word containing its root and sufficient to determine its
stem. Initially seeing only this portion resulted in response latencies not significantly slower than those obtained when whole words were made available at once.
Root-visibility alone, stem-decidability alone, as well as root-visibility plus root-
. decidability led to latencies slower than obtained in a full-word condition. Naming
latencies for Dutch verb forms were more consistent with a morpheme-based
lexicon. In Dutch, initially seeing a morphologically defined part of a stimulus word
contributed to speed in naming the word. Further results from Dutch indicate that
the word identification process can begin using fewer word-initial letters than
necessary to determine a word's root.

Word recognition is a cognitive process in which a sensory event is
mapped over time onto an internal representation. The event may be
auditory, visual, or (in reading Braille) tactile. The internal representation
can be viewed as an object which is retrieved from or constructed using our
mental lexicon. Research in word recognition is concerned largely with
learning (a) what lexical elements are stored in memory, (b) how information from a stimulus word is used to identify lexical elements in memory,

LANGUAGE PERCEPTION AND PRODUCTION
ISBN 0-12-052750-2

and (c) how an internal representation is constructed from the lexical elements identified. These are three different, though clearly related, issues. In this paper, we will refer to the first issue as the lexical entry problem, to the second issue as the stimulus mapping problem, and to the third issue as the word construction problem.

The paper is organized as follows. We first introduce a framework for viewing recent research in word recognition, and consider several existing theories from this perspective. In the main part of the paper, we then review results from our research concerned with recognition of printed words shown 'normally', with all letters in a word made available at once, and recognition of the same words shown with small, nearly undetectable, stimulus-onset asynchronies. Data reported for two languages — Dutch and Italian — will be seen to argue against a hypothesis that, in word recognition, words are stored and retrieved from the internal lexicon as full forms.[1] In a concluding section, we evaluate the results with respect to the three issues identified.

The conceptual framework

Words and sentences are two types of linguistic structures. Both are made up of smaller elements, and have meanings which are in part predictable from the meanings of those elements. Various views of how words and sentences are processed when language is used might be taken. One way of thinking about linguistic structures as processing units is as objects which are built up by combining smaller pieces. An alternative way is to think of structures as being stored and retrieved as wholes, i.e., as being permanently in memory. In the psychology of language, it has probably been more common to regard processing done above the level of words as involving the combination of pieces into larger wholes, but of processing done at the word level as involving storage and retrieval of full (unitary) forms.

In linguistics, two arguments which have been suggested against a 'full listing hypothesis' at the level of sentences are (1) the set of sentences in any natural language is an infinite and hence, unlistable, set, and (2) people produce and understand utterances of novel sentences, i.e., sentences unlistable on the basis of their previous life experience. In most human languages, however, the number of different word forms is potentially so large that, for practical purposes, it may also be considered unlimited.[2] As in the case of sentences, people produce and understand forms of words which they have not experienced previously, and hence are unlikely to have stored on any internal list.

Table 1. Some English words formed with the root morpheme 'read'.

	Full word form			
	Stem			Inflectional affix
Example	Derivational prefix	Root	Derivational suffix	
read		read		∅
reads		read		-s
reader		read	-er	∅
readers		read	-er	-s
reread	re-	read		∅
rereads	re-	read		-s

Consider a little more closely some facts about the internal structure of words. Word forms are structurally analyzable into minimal parts carrying independent meaning, called morphemes. That the meaning carried by morphemes is 'independent' can be taken to mean simply that some 'kernel' part of their meaning is the same, irrespective of context. In English, the verb form 'reads', for example, can be said to contain two morphemes: the verb root 'read' (or, phonetically, [ri:d]), which carries some meaning we can represent as 'READ' and the suffix '-s' ([z]), carrying some meaning like 'THIRD PERSON SINGULAR PRESENT TENSE'. The form 'rereads' could, similarly, be said to contain three morphemes, the same pair as in 'reads' plus a prefix 're-', carrying some meaning like 'DO AGAIN'. And the noun 'readers' also can be said to contain three morphemes: the same verb root as in 'reads' and 'rereads', a nominal-forming suffix '-er', meaning something like 'PERSON WHO DOES X', where 'X' stands for the verb with which the suffix occurs, and the suffix '-s', this time having a meaning 'PLURAL'.[3]

Besides distinguishing roots from non-roots, linguists often divide the latter into two subcategories: inflectional and derivational affixes. Inflectional affixes tend to apply to all members of a major grammatical class, and are generally word-final.[4] Derivational affixes, on the other hand, tend to be used less productively (in a smaller, less predictable set of word forms) than inflections, and often include both prefixes and suffixes.

The arrangement of roots and affixes in words suggests that word forms — like sentences — have a kind of internal constituent structure. Consider Figure 1 and Table 1. First, a word form has a 'stem' portion. The stem portion of a word may be morphologically simple and consist of only a root morpheme (e.g., in 'read'). Or the stem may be morphologically complex and consist of a root plus one or more derivational affixes (e.g., in 'reread' and 'reader'). Secondly, in addition to a stem, full word forms in some

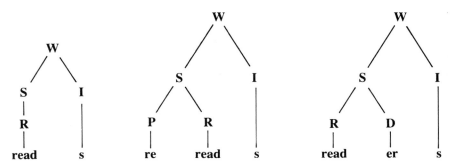

Figure 1. Constituent diagrams for some English words. W = word, S = stem, P = derivational prefix, D = derivational suffix, I = inflection.

word classes, such as nouns, verbs, and adjectives, may contain an inflection. As suggested above, inflectional affixes in most languages are word-final, and tend to apply to all the word stems — both simple and complex — in a given word class (e.g., in 'reads', 'writes', 'rereads', 'rewrites', etc.).

Let us relate this sketch of morphological structure to the initial set of issues (a)–(c). Does the description given tell us anything about what linguistic units might be stored in the mental lexicon, what information from a word token might be used to identify these forms, or how the forms, once identified, might be integrated into a larger lexical representation?

As far as problem (a) is concerned, Table 1 suggests that lexical elements in memory might be defined at one of three morphological levels: the forms of words which are stored in memory might be full word forms; the forms might be the stems of words together with sets of inflections; or the forms might be the individual roots and affixes from words.[5] As for problem (b), stimulus mapping could be done correspondingly on the basis of information identifying a full orthographic form, a word's stem and inflection, or a word's root and other affix morphemes. Thus, the same three morphological levels — the full word level, the level of word stems plus inflections, and the level of individual morphemes in words — could provide the basis for an answer to both the lexical entry and stimulus mapping problems. It seems natural to expect that the same morphological level should provide the key to answering both questions. Third, consider the word construction problem (c). The construction of a larger internal form should not be needed if a word is identified as a single, unanalyzed whole. However, if memory elements are not identified for full words as such, but rather for a word's stem and inflection, or for its set of individual morphemes, lexical lookup for more than one entry per word form will tend to be needed, and perhaps some further process in which the parts are combined.

Consider now two recent treatments of word recognition in light of this analysis: Marslen-Wilson's (1980) 'cohort' theory, and Forster's (1976) search theory. The cohort theory claims that stimulus (and other) information is used from the beginning of a word onwards to reduce uncertainty, and that a spoken word is recognized when only a single word remains as a candidate. A word spoken in isolation 'is recognized at that point, starting from the beginning of the word, at which the word in question becomes uniquely distinguishable from all of the other words in the language beginning with the same sound sequence' (Marslen-Wilson, 1980, p. 54).

In the cohort model, the morphological level for the processes making up word recognition is not explicitly defined. Without stating some linguistic level for lexical entries, however, or a corresponding level for mapping a word token onto lexical entries, the amount of stimulus information needed for recognition to occur cannot be predicted. In particular, for words which are morphologically complex, as one passes from the level of full forms to word stems to that of root and other morphemes, a decreasing amount of word-initial information will tend to be distinctive, and an increasing amount of word-final information will tend to be redundant. The cohort model appears to make clear predictions only for words which consist of a single root morpheme, where a word's root, stem, and full form coincide.

Marslen-Wilson and Tyler (1980) showed that listeners can make word-monitoring responses within a few hundred milliseconds of a spoken word's onset, and well before its offset, in a one- or two-sentence linguistic context. However, since inflections on words are crucial for distinguishing related word forms, if full word forms are not looked up directly in memory, some further process must be postulated to deal with inflections. The cohort theory excludes further analysis of the speech signal, forcing the feature to be obtained, e.g., syntactically. (For further discussion of the cohort theory, see Huttenlocher and Goodman, Chap 19.)

In Forster's (1976) 'search' model of lexical access, the linguistic level at which (printed) words are taken to be looked up in memory is also left undefined but is implied to be that of full forms. The stimulus mapping process is taken to work in several steps. First, the initial letters in a word form are used to identify a 'bin' containing the beginnings of similarly spelled words, and the bin is searched for an element which is sufficiently 'similar' to the stimulus word. (The criterion of similarity needed is left unspecified). A pointer associated with that particular element is then used to identify the corresponding entry in a 'central' memory file. Finally, the entry identified there is compared with the properties of the stimulus word (see Forster, 1976, pp. 269–270). The final step in the model amounts to a post-access-check' and allows for end-of-word information to play a role in word recognition.

The search model predicts that the first few letters from a printed word, or perhaps its first syllable, generally will be effective in beginning to access the mental lexicon (perhaps unless the word starts with a prefix — see Taft and Forster, 1975). This prediction apparently was not upheld in work by Forster himself (1976, p. 282). English words were shown to subjects with a 62.5 ms onset asynchrony in a lexical decision task, and their beginning portion failed to have any effect on reaction time. This result might be explained in two ways: (1) Word-initial information is not sufficient to initiate lexical look-up. (2) Word-initial information is sufficient, but the beginning portion of the words studied for some reason failed to suffi- ciently narrow the search process. Suppose, for example, that word-initial information is useful in recognizing words just in case the information has some further status in the mental lexicon. Using the same task and a 90 ms stimulus-onset asynchrony, significant priming effects were obtained with full but not partial root information for English by Lima and Pollatsek (1983).

Both the cohort and the search models fail to specify what lexical elements are stored in memory, and consequently, what stimulus inform- ation would be useful for identifying them. Let us thus consider the linguistic status of lexical entries and stimulus mapping a little further.

In all but the morphologically most simple words, the information needed to identify a word's root, its stem, and its full form would conceiv- ably be different. At any of these levels, identification of lexical elements might be made from stimulus information nondeterministically or determi- nistically. One possibility is that substrings of letters (or, for speech, phones) would be used which correspond exactly to the parts of a word's overt form. Another possibility is that only minimal substrings needed to uniquely determine one lexical element at a particular level would be used.

We stated earlier that it is natural to expect that the linguistic level of lexical entries and that used in identifying entries from stimulus inform- ation will be the same. If a lower linguistic level than that corresponding to memory elements were used to identify lexical entries, the mapping would generally fail to individuate single entries. In many cases, sets including morphologically unrelated words would be picked out. For instance, the letters corresponding to the first possible morpheme in English 'pathos' would also identify the words 'pa', 'pat', and 'path', and 'pathology'. In other cases, reduction to a set of related words might occur, but again no single lexical element would tend to be identifiable (e.g., the string 'read' would map onto 'reading', 'readings', 'reader', 'readers', 'readable', etc.).

Similarly, if a higher linguistic level than that of memory elements were used to identify entries, again no single entry would often be identifiable. For example, if lexical entries were defined at the level of stems or morphemes, and a full word was used in identification, in many cases, the word would fail to distinguish among several actual stems or roots. For example, the stimulus string 'pathos' would map onto 'pa', 'pat', and 'path' as well as 'pathos', and the string 'readers' would map onto 'read' as well as 'reader'.

When the linguistic level defined for stimulus mapping and lexical entries is the same, such ambiguities would be substantially reduced but might not be eliminated entirely. In cases where stimulus information used still identified more than one element in memory (because, for example, one word or stem falls within another word or stem), further analysis would be needed to make a choice between them.

In our own research, a working assumption has been that a reader looks up a lexical form in memory on detecting a string of letters which corresponds to it, or on detecting an initial substring of the letters, if that is sufficient to distinguish the item from other stored lexical entries. We further have assumed that only one mental lexicon is used in reading printed words: a full form lexicon, a lexicon containing the set of word stems plus inflections in a language, or one containing its set of elementary morphemes. Especially the latter assumption may prove to be untenable eventually (see, e.g., Koskenniemi, 1983; Bybee, 1985; Caramazza, Miceli, Silveri and Laudanna, 1985; Ejerhed and Bromley, 1986). However, because it allows a word to be looked up in memory only on one level, making this assumption allows theories to be formulated and tested which may be more easily falsified.

General method

The research summarized here uses a method of stimulus presentation in which only some of the letters from a printed word may be made visible at the very onset of stimulation, the remainder being momentarily withheld (Eriksen and Eriksen, 1974). The logic behind the method is that the letter information in a printed word can be divided into different functional parts, and that withholding some parts will affect the word recognition process more than withholding other parts. The data obtained were latencies in naming words and in deciding whether letter strings were words.

There are two principal ways in which one can evaluate results obtained in such tasks. First, one can look for the appearance of processing slow-downs. It can be asked whether speed of response is reduced when one part of a word form is initially withheld than when other parts, or no part, is withheld. Secondly, one can look for possible facilitative effects of seeing different parts of a word before the word as a whole is seen. In this case, the early information presented is viewed as a kind of priming stimulus. For small stimulus-onset-asynchronies (SOAs), the two methods can be combined. Initially seeing only part of a word may delay the word's recognition when measured from stimulus onset, but measured from presentation of the whole word, it may still produce facilitation.

The languages studied here were Italian and Dutch. The stimulus-onset asynchronies used varied between 30 and 60 ms. Such time asynchronies verge on being subliminal in tasks of the present kind, and may be brief enough such that only the front end of the word recognition process is affected, without disrupting processing downstream.

Results from Italian

Two kinds of studies have been conducted in Italian using a 40 ms SOA and no SOA. A lexical decision task was used in a total of 10 experiments (Jarvella and Job, 1985; to appear), and a naming task in a similar set of experiments (Job and Jarvella, in preparation). The primary data we will review come from parallel studies using the two tasks to study two samples of verbs, one made up of forms of 45 high frequency verbs, and the other made up of the corresponding forms of 45 lower frequency verbs. The high frequency verbs were among the 500 most frequent lexical items in Italian, based on a corpus of 500 000 printed words (Bortolini, Tagliavini and Zampolli, 1972). Italian verbs have about 40 inflected forms which distinguish tense, mood, person and number. The same 12 forms of verbs were included in both word samples, with one form assigned randomly to each verb.

The words were displayed on a computer-controlled CRT in three principal ways: without any SOA, i.e., with all letters shown at once (ALL), and with only some word-initial (BEG) or word-final (END) substring initially made visible and the remaining letters added after 40 ms. Response time was measured from stimulus onset until a button was pressed, or until a voice-key was triggered. Forty-five subjects were tested on the verb samples in lexical decision, and 36 subjects in naming. Within subjects, one third of the items seen were presented in ALL, one third in BEG, and one third in END. In the lexical decision task, to ensure that subjects would access their mental lexicon, non word filler items were used which observed phonotactic constraints. These nonword items were shown with the same onset asynchrony as the words, and were formed by substituting one letter in an existing word, with the position of the changed letter varied between the beginning and end of the word to discourage *ad hoc* strategies.

The verb stimuli were selected such that, for a given word, the stem could be determined from an initial substring of the word's letters, but the full form could not, because the word's ending distinguished its inflected form. The word forms had a mean length of 9.5 characters, and, based on a 40 000 entry Italian dictionary, became stem-decidable after 5.8, or 61%, of their letters. The words were segmented to define BEG and END substrings by dividing each word at the earliest point at which its stem could be determined (after the minimal stem-decidable substring). For example, 'ricorderemo', meaning 'we will remember', was divided into 'ricorde' (BEG) and 'remo' (END); 'eluderemo', meaning 'we will elude', was divided into 'elud' (BEG) and 'eremo' (END). In practice, the word-initial BEG portion always included a verb form's full root, plus any additional letters needed to determine the word's stem (and hence what particular verb was involved).[6]

Table 2. Mean lexical decision and naming latencies (ms) for printed Italian words shown all at once (ALL) and with a small stimulus-onset asynchrony (BEG or END portion alone visible for the first 40 ms).

Sample	High frequency verbs			Low frequency verbs		
condition	ALL	BEG	END	ALL	BEG	END
Task						
Lexical decision	1191	1205	1269	1264	1273	1344
Naming	676	684	719	710	727	742

Mean latencies are shown in Table 2 for the two word samples and tasks used. As can be seen, responses were faster and more accurate in naming. It can also be seen that the differences between the beginning-of-word (BEG) and whole-word (ALL) conditions are small across both word samples and tasks, though in BEG nearly half of the words' letters were withheld for the first 40 ms. The overall difference between BEG and ALL is only 12 ms, and too small to reject the null hypothesis that briefly withholding the final portion of the words had any effect on their recognition ($t(89) = 0.90$). This suggests that the BEG stimuli used were functionally equivalent at stimulus onset to full words. The effect is not limited to verbs, moreover. Across a set of 104 nouns and adjectives studied under the same three stimulus conditions, Jarvella and Job (1985) found a mean difference of -3 ms between latencies in corresponding BEG and ALL conditions.[7]

These results argue against lexical lookup of full word forms, since withholding letter information needed to determine full forms failed to delay subjects' responses. The data are consistent, however, with both mapping of stimulus properties onto words' stems and also — since the root of the word was part of the information shown in BEG — identification and lookup of words' roots. A root-alone hypothesis is possible to reject, however, as is a theory claiming that it is the raw amount and not the quality of stimulus information made initially available which determines performance. Jarvella and Job (1985; to appear) report lexical decision data for Italian verbs which further tests the root hypothesis. Two samples of verbs were studied, with the BEG portion defined as only a word's full root, or as a root-decidable portion including the full root. Again, the SOA used was 40 ms. In these cases, response latencies were 21 ms slower in BEG than in the ALL condition for the same words, showing that seeing the root morpheme had only a partial effect. The BEG portions corresponded to 59% of words' letters, but yielded only 19 ms of 'facilitation'. In the present study, stem-decidable BEG portions corresponded to 61% of the words' letters and yielded 28 ms of facilitation. Thus, with almost the same proportion of beginning-of-word letters shown, there was about 50% more effect in BEG when the stem of a verb form was decidable and its root was visible than if the root was visible alone, or both visible and decidable. Further analyses showing that the amount *per se* of word-initial stimulus information shown fails to predict the stem-superiority effect are presented in Jarvella and Job (1985; to appear).

Now consider latencies in the END condition, also shown in Table 2. The effect of withholding the beginning of a word initially ranges from having virtually no consequence in naming to having a significant inhibitory effect in lexical decision. In the latter case, latencies were 79 ms slower than in ALL, or 39 ms slower than would be expected if no information had initially been presented ($t(89) = 2.34$, $p < 0.025$ two-tailed). This finding might be expected if inflections normally are processed only after the stems of words are identified. For the lexical decision data reported by Jarvella and Job (to appear), the number of letters in an inflection predicted more than 60% of the variance in response time between words. We interpret this as indicating that inflections are processed and not merely retrieved.

Results from Dutch

Two sets of studies have also been conducted in Dutch, in both cases using two SOAs (30 and 60 ms) and no SOA. In both instances, the word forms studied were verb forms, and the task was naming.

In one set of studies, Jarvella, Schreuder and Puthli (to appear) studied seven forms of verbs shown in Table 3. The verbs included weak and strong verbs, and verbs with lexical stressed and unstressed prefixes. A total of 250 word forms from 142 medium frequency verbs with different roots were used as stimuli. (For a short summary of Dutch verb morphology, see Jarvella and Meijers 1983.)

Table 3.   Morphological structure of Dutch verb forms studied (from Jarvella, *et al.*, to appear).

Verb type	Full form	Stem		Inflection
		Prefix	Root	
Unprefixed verbs				
Weak verbs				
(1) past singular	werkte		werk	-te
(2) past participle	gewerkt	ge-	werk	-t
Strong verbs				
(3) present plural/ infinitive	zingen		zing	-en
(4) past plural	zongen		zong	-en
(5) past participle	gezongen	ge-	zong	-en
Prefixed verbs				
Unstressed prefix				
(6) past singular	verdiende	ver-	dien	-de
Stressed prefix				
(7) present plural/ infinitive	aannemen	aan-	nem	-en

Each stimulus word was presented without an SOA (with all letters shown at once) and, depending on its linguistic structure, in up to four conditions where part of the word was shown initially and the rest was initially withheld. Sixty subjects were tested. Subjects were presented a set of 142 test words twice, once with stimuli not in the ALL condition shown with a 30 ms SOA, and once with a 60 ms SOA. Analysis of the data showed no effects of presentation order. The data summarized below are averaged across the two SOAs (average SOA of 45 ms in all part-of-word conditions).

The full-word and part-of-word conditions studied were selected to answer the following questions: Is a word named faster when it is shown all at once (ALL) than when its stem is shown and its inflection is initially withheld? Is a word named faster when its stem is seen all at once than when its root is shown but a prefix initially withheld? Is a word named faster when its root alone is shown initially than when its non-root portion is?

As can be seen in Table 4, the answer to each of the three questions tended to be 'yes'. First, across the two SOAs studied, latencies in ALL were faster than those when only a word's stem was initially made visible. The differences were 13, 16, 17, 18 and 24 ms for forms exemplified by 'werkte', 'zongen', 'verdiende', 'aannemen', and 'zingen' respectively. In each case, the least significant difference was smaller than the observed difference ($\alpha = 0.05$, items analysis).

Secondly, latencies in the stem-first condition tended to be faster than in a corresponding root-first condition. Comparison within prefixed word forms like 'verdiende' and 'aannemen' showed that, when only a word's full stem was made visible initially, naming latencies were 11 ms faster than when its root, or root plus suffix, was made visible and its prefix initially withheld ($t(69) = 3.47$, $p < 0.005$).

This tendency is further confirmed by latencies for nonlexically prefixed verbs. For past tense forms like 'werkte' and 'zongen', in which the stem and root coincide, responses were 15 ms slower than in the ALL condition when only the root was initially presented. For past participles of the same words, which begin with the prefix 'ge-' (e.g., 'gewerkt', 'gezongen'), responses were 30 ms slower than in the ALL condition when only the root was initially presented ($t(71) = 1.96$, $p < 0.05$ for the difference of the differences).

Table 4. Mean naming latencies for Dutch verbs shown all at once (whole word = ALL condition) or with only part of the full form shown at first (mean SOA = 45 ms) (from Jarvella et al., to appear).

	Whole Word	Stem	Root	Prefix	Inflection	Root + Inflection	Prefix + Inflection
(1) werkte	586	599	(=stem)	—	620	(=word)	—
(2) gewerkt	616	n.a	644	n.a	n.a	n.a	652
(3) zingen	591	615	(=stem)	—	n.a	(=word)	—
(4) zongen	611	627	(=stem)	—	n.a	(=word)	—
(5) gezongen	634	n.a	665	n.a	n.a	n.a	n.a
(6) verdiende	583	600	608	620	n.a	611	n.a
(7) aannemen	551	569	583	580	n.a	580	n.a

n.a = not available.

Third, naming latencies tended to be faster when the root of a word was presented initially than when it was withheld initially. Presenting only the root of words like 'werkte' and 'gewerkt' at first led to responses 21 and 8 ms faster than when the rest of the word was presented initially, and the root withheld. Similarly, responses were 12 ms faster when only the root of words like 'verdiende' initially was presented than when only the prefix was. On the other hand, for words like 'aannemen', which begin with a separable particle, initially presenting this element alone led to responses 3 ms faster than initially showing only the verb root.

The above results can be interpreted as evidence for full forms, stems, and roots of words all playing some role early in the perception of printed Dutch words. And if the part-of-word data are viewed in a slightly different way, what this role is can be made somewhat clearer. As suggested above, a response facilitation measure can be defined by counting the latency of responses from appearance of the full stimulus versus the appearance of any stimulus. The measure of facilitation can be obtained from the measure of inhibition by subtracting the amount of inhibition from the SOA. For example, withholding the inflection on forms like 'werkte' initially retarded response latencies by 13 ms *vis-à-vis* the whole word condition. Since the average SOA was 45 ms, for the same stimulus, presenting the rest of the word 'facilitated' response latencies by $45 - 13 = 32$ ms. Considering the results above in these terms, it can be seen that word stems tended to produce more facilitation on latencies than words' roots alone, and roots to produce more facilitation than nonroots.

Jarvella *et al.* discovered an interesting tendency for the amount of facilitation defined in this way to be additive for different parts of a word shown which form a hypothetical constituent, but not otherwise. The facilitation for the stem of forms like 'werkte', i.e., 'werk-' (32 ms), plus that for the inflection, i.e., '-te' (11 ms), summed nearly to the 45 ms average SOA, which is the expected effect of seeing the whole word. Similarly, for verbs with unstressed prefixes like 'verdiende', the facilitation for the prefix 'ver-' (8 ms), plus that for the verb's root '-dien-' (20 ms), summed to that for the word form's stem 'verdien-' (28 ms). And for stressed prefix verbs like 'aannemen', the facilitation for the prefix 'aan-' (16 ms) plus that for the verb root '-nem-' (13 ms) also approximated that for the full stem 'aannem-' (27 ms).

In other, 'nonconstituent' cases, the effect on naming latencies produced by different pieces of a word separately is less than obtained when the pieces are presented as a whole. Thus, for forms like 'gewerkt', facilitation of the root alone (17 ms) plus that for the two affixes alone (9 ms) sums to less than the 45 ms average SOA. For forms like 'verdiende', it was found that presenting the verb root plus inflection initially actually led to response times which were slower than when the root portion alone was first made visible. This kind of data shows that the morphological effects found for Dutch, like those for Italian, are not to be explained by length factors.

In another set of studies, Sandström, Schreuder and Jarvella (to appear) studied present plural-infinitive forms and past participal forms of Dutch verbs. A total of 144 verbs of six types were studied, with no overlap among the words' roots. The words were presented in four conditions: (a) in an ALL condition, with all letters shown at once; (b) with only a word's stem initially made visible; (c) with the smallest initial substring of the word sufficient to determine its root made visible first; (d) with the smallest initial root-decidable substring minus one letter made visible first. Root-decidability was defined from a standard reference list of Dutch words, supported by word completion data. The stimuli were presented to 48 subjects. As before, each subject named the words in a list twice, once with words not in the ALL condition shown with a 30 ms SOA, and once with a 60 ms SOA. The data showed no effects of presentation order, and are presented averaged across the two SOAs below.

The present study differed from the previous Dutch experiments mentioned in that the beginning of words were used to define a root-decidable and a root-nondecidable condition. In most cases, words' verb roots were fully visible initially only in the stem and ALL conditions. The study also differed from the Italian naming studies discussed, in that the stems of words investigated were not decidable from partial stimulus information.

Table 5. Mean naming latencies for Dutch verbs shown all at once and with only part of the full form shown at first (mean SOA = 45 ms) measures from stimulus onset (from Sandström *et al.*, to appear).

| Whole | Initial stimulus shown | | |
	Stem	root decidable point	root decidable point − 1 letter
579	592	599	600

Overall mean naming latencies for the four conditions studied are shown in Table 5. With respect to the ALL condition, the three part-of-word conditions delayed responses from a minimum of 13 ms for words' stems up to 21 ms where the initial stimulus was one character less than root-decidable. (Least significant difference by items = 5.2 ms with $\alpha = 0.01$.) For all six types of verbs studied, the ALL condition led to significantly faster responses than in both the root-decidable condition and the root-decidable minus one letter condition. Latencies in the ALL condition also tended to be faster than in the stem condition, and in the stem condition than in the root-decidable and the root-decidable minus one letter conditions, though not all the differences found were reliable. The latter two conditions did not differ significantly in any experiment. Thus, root-nondecidable strings produced a significant effect on naming latencies, and one not different from that produced by minimal root-decidable ones.

Discussion

In the introduction, we identified three issues in word recognition: the problem of lexical entries, the problem of stimulus mapping, and the problem of word construction in case lexical entries looked up are not full words. In this section, we interpret the results summarized above with respect to these issues, and consider whether the same theory of the lexicon is supported in both Dutch and Italian.

On the lexical entry issue, the data reported for both Italian and Dutch seem to argue against a full form lexicon. In the case of Italian, briefly withholding end-of-word information which distinguishes one full word form from other forms of the same word failed to have any effect on either lexical decision or naming latencies. In the case of Dutch, the pattern of naming latencies found in various part-of-word presentation conditions tended more to support the lexical status of roots and derivational prefixes, as well as word stems and inflections.

With reference to the stimulus mapping issue, stimulus information initially triggering the form identification process in Italian seems to correspond to that needed to determine a word's stem. No difference in response latencies was found for words shown in a whole-word (ALL) condition and the same words shown in a beginning-of-word (BEG) condition which included only a word's root plus a minimum of letters needed to distinguish the word's stem from forms of other words. Neither stem decidability, nor full root visibility alone, nor root visibility and root decidability, led to such an effect.

For Dutch, initially seeing less than a full stimulus word does slow naming latencies. However, initial presentation of only a word's root or stem portion leads to faster latencies than initial presentation of only affix portions of the word, and full stem substrings tend to lead to faster latencies than smaller word-initial substrings, even if these include enough information in principle to determine a word's root. A simple all-or-none criterion of root decidability in Dutch does not seem to make good predictions for the amount of facilitation observed.

The data reported also bear on the word-construction issue. If whole words were the units stored and looked up in the mental lexicon, we should not expect any representation to be constructed from a word's morphological parts. However, the Italian data strongly suggest that inflections are processed and not simply looked up: length of inflections was found to predict the majority of variance in lexical decision latencies for words. The data suggest, moreover, that inflections are processed after lexical lookup. The Dutch data, on the other hand, suggest that sub-wordforms stored in the lexicon may be looked up and bound together into a hierarchical structure in which two levels are represented: one at which a word's root plus derivational affixes form a constituent, and another at which the word's stem plus its inflection form a constituent.

Readers of Italian and Dutch thus may have mental lexicons organized in somewhat different ways. It is probably premature, for either language, to claim that internal lexical entries correspond only to words' roots and affixes, or only to their stems plus inflections (see also Jarvella and Meijers, 1983; Job and Sartori, 1984). However, the results reported here using stimulus-onset asynchronies suggest that in Italian the mental dictionary may contain stem representations, looked up in a deterministic, left-to-right way, plus inflectional systems specific to particular word classes (or subclasses). In Dutch, the main forms stored and looked up in memory could well be individual morphemes.

Acknowledgement

The work reported here was supported by research grants from CNR (Rome) and HSFR (Stockholm). This paper was written during a period when Remo Job was a visiting scholar in Sweden supported by the Swedish Institute. A grant from the Dutch Organization for the Advancement of Pure Research (ZVO) to Robert Schreuder also helped bring the authors to Umeå to work together. We would like to thank Eva Ejerhed and Kimmo Koskenniemi for valuable discussions about language processing.

Notes

[1] Some evidence against retrieval of full forms in speaking can be found in speech production errors (see, e.g., Fromkin, 1973; Garrett, 1980).

[2] A third argument against a full listing hypothesis is that, for any sentence, it is possible to construct a longer one, i.e., there is no longest sentence. Whether there is a longest word can also be doubted, especially if all compounding is taken to form words. Orthographically, compounding is treated differently even in languages as closely related as English versus other Germanic languages. We do not take a stand here on whether it can be better described as a lexical or a syntactic phenomenon.

[3] This passage is necessarily over-simplified. The validity of the morpheme-concept, and the meaningfulness of using it to try to segment linguistic units, can be disputed. This, however, is only partly what is at issue here. What should be noted is simply that productive morphological processes in a language like

English utilize recurring units to arrive at word-forms whose semantics can be regarded as compositional in rather the same way as sentence semantics can. The fact that different kinds of allomorphy complicate the concept of 'recurring units' need not concern us here.

[4] 'Word-extreme' might be a better term. In prefixing languages, inflections tend to be word-initial rather than word final.

[5] The question of the level of 'abstractness' of lexical entries is one we do not address here. That is, we take no standpoint on whether different allomorphs such as, for instance, [s], [z] or [iz] for the third person singular present tense in English verbs, are listed in their surface forms, or are represented as a non-alternating underlying form (or in some other way).

[6] By operationally defining stem-decidability in this way, it is unnecessary to posit a particular analysis of where the stem of an Italian verb form ends and its inflection begins.

[7] The approximation of lexical decision latencies in BEG to those in ALL is not significantly closer for nouns and adjectives than for verbs, nor does it depend on whether stem-redundant letters not part of a word's root are withheld. Thus, for words with a monomorphemic stem (e.g. 'giraff-a'), the full stem is needed to get the effect, but for a word with a polymorphemic stem (e.g. 'usabil-e'), less than the full stem may be needed.

References

Bortonlini, U., Tagliavini, C. and Zampolli, A. (1972). *Lessico di frequenza della lingua italiana contemporanea*. Pisa: Garzanti.

Bybee, J. L. (1985). *Morphology. A study on the relation between meaning and form*. Amsterdam: John Benjamins.

Caramazza, A., Miceli, G., Silveri, M. C. and Laudanna, A. (1985). Reading mechanisms and the organization of the lexicon: Evidence from acquired dyslexia. *Cognitive Neuropsychology*, **2**, 81–114.

Ejerhed, E. and Bromley, H. B. (1986). A self-extending lexicon. In F. Karlsson (Ed.) *Papers from the Fifth Scandinavian Conference on Computational Linguistics*. Helsinki: University of Helsinki Department of Linguistics, Publications no. 15.

Eriksen, B. A. and Eriksen, C. W. (1974). The importance of being first: A tachistoscopic study of the recognition of four-letter words. *Perception & Psychophysics*, **15**, 66–72.

Forster, K. (1976). Accessing the mental lexicon. In R. J. Wales and E. Walker (Eds) *New approaches to language mechanisms*. Amsterdam: North-Holland.

Fromkin, V. (1973). *Speech errors as linguistic evidence*. The Hague: Mouton.

Garrett, M. F. (1980). Levels of processing in sentence production. In B. Butterworth (Ed.) *Language production*, vol 1. London: Academic Press.

Jarvella, R. J. and Job, R. (1985). La percezione delle parole scritte. In T. de Mauro (Ed.) *Proceedings of the Italian Linguistic Society*. Rome: S.L.I.

Jarvella, R. J. and Job, R. (to appear). Asynchronous perception of printed words. Manuscript submitted for publication.

Jarvella, R. J. and Meijers, G. (1983). Recognizing morphemes in spoken words: Some evidence for a stem-organized mental lexicon. In G. B. Flores d'Arcais and

R. J. Jarvella (Eds) *The process of language understanding*. New York: Wiley.

Jarvella, R. J., Schreuder, R. and Puthli, V. (to appear). Hierarchical structure in word perception. Manuscript submitted for publication.

Job, R. and Jarvella, R. J. (in preparation). Word structure and naming latencies in Italian.

Job, R. and Sartori, G. (1984). Morphological decomposition: Evidence from crossed phonological dyslexia. *Quarterly Journal of Experimental Psychology*, **36A**, 435–58.

Koskenniemi, K. (1983). A two-level model for morphological analysis. In A. Bundy (Ed.) *Proceedings of the Eighth International Joint Conference on Artificial Intelligence*, Karlsruhe, Germany, vol 2. Los Altos, CA: Kaufmann.

Lima, S. and Pollatsek, A. (1983). Lexical access via an orthographic code? The basic orthographic syllable structure (BOSS) reconsidered. *Journal of Verbal Learning and Verbal Behavior*, **22**, 310–22.

Marslen-Wilson, W. (1980). Speech understanding as a psychological process. In J. C. Simon (Ed.) *Spoken language generation and production*. Dordrecht: Reidel.

Marslen-Wilson, W. and Tyler, L. (1980). The temporal structure of spoken language understanding. *Cognition*, **8**, 1–71.

Sandström, G., Schreuder, R. and Jarvella, R. J. (to appear). Root decidability and naming latencies in Dutch. Manuscript submitted for publication.

Taft, M. and Forster, K. I. (1975). Lexical storage and retrieval of prefixed words. *Journal of Verbal Learning and Verbal Behavior*, **14**, 638–47.

Section 5

Architecture of the mental lexicon

Introduction

Alan Allport

The four chapters in this section deal with psychological processes that are central, in more than one sense, to the perception and production of language — that is, the encoding and decoding of *word-forms* and of *word-meanings* and the intercommunication between their respective domains.

The 'mental lexicon'. One of the most striking and obvious features of natural language is that the relationship between its surface *forms* — specifically, the sounds or written marks of words — and their *meaning* is, in very large measure, arbitrary.[1] Thus there are simply no evident, systematic relationships of *meaning* among words (that is, root morphemes) in English that happen to rhyme, or that have similar initial sounds, or the same number of syllables, etc. As a consequence, it is only through the intermediary of a system that in some way codes the identity of each individual word-form, and that also, in some way, binds or links each word-form uniquely to appropriate representations of its word senses (or 'meaning'), that the psychological transactions between linguistic utterances (ultimately as acoustic or visible forms) and the cognitive processes of thought and understanding can occur.

Such a system of *lexical* (i.e. *word-specific*) mappings between the domains of phonology (and orthography) and the domain or domains of semantic or conceptual representation must, of course, be implemented in some specific psychological mechanisms. Further, in so far as the corresponding spoken and written forms of a given word cannot be uniquely identified by orthographic rule (cf. Section 4 of this volume), then again a psychological system that links lexical (word-specific) forms between the phonological and the orthographic domains is also needed. Moreover, in

LANGUAGE PERCEPTION AND PRODUCTION
ISBN 0-12-052750-2

so far as lexical forms themselves enjoy a functionally privileged status within either the phonological or the orthographic domain (as suggested, for example, by the 'word superiority effects' seen in tachistoscopic perception, in immediate recall and repetition tasks, etc.) it seems plausible to infer that there are also in some way word-specific functional units embodied *within* each of these coding domains. Together, the psychological mechanisms embodying these different forms of word-specific or 'lexical' knowledge can be referred to collectively as the *'mental lexicon'*.

Functional architecture. Some writers refer to the mental lexicon as one 'module' within the cognitive system. Certainly its different components appear tightly coupled. Nevertheless, it is possible to tease apart the behavioural contributions of different functional components within this tightly knit system, and to chart both the functional identity of these components and the channels or pathways that link them — that is to chart their *'functional architecture'* (or 'functional anatomy'). The contributors to this section of the book share not only their focus on the specifically *lexical* mechanisms of language; they also have the same, shared goal of establishing empirically the detailed functional architecture of the various lexical subsystems, the structure of their interconnections, and their relations to other, *non*-lexical systems.

These four chapters are concerned with a wide range of intricately interconnected issues. Among them, three principal, broad lines of questioning predominate:

(1) How many and what different kinds of separable *lexical* components can be identified?

(2) How are the lexical and sublexical coding systems of *spoken* and of *written* language interconnected?

(3) What is the nature of conceptual or semantic coding of word meanings, and how is it functionally interrelated to the coding of unique word-forms, in either modality?

These three broad themes appear and reappear throughout the following four chapters in a variety of ways. In Chapter 14, Monsell begins by opening up some fundamental, theoretical questions about 'functional architecture' in relation to the mental lexicon. His chapter provides an essential introduction to the issues grouped under the first of the three broad headings, above.

How should we conceptualize a subject's knowledge of word-forms? Is this purely *'procedural'* knowledge, in the form of neuropsychological 'pathways' that transcode from one neural pattern to another? Or is our stored knowledge of individual word-forms realized, in some sense, as specific *'representations'* of those forms? (My own view is that, at some level or levels of analysis, *both* forms of knowledge are appropriate and necessary; nevertheless, we should be exceptionally, logically circumspect about attributing explicit, 'declarative' knowledge to individual neuropsychological components. It is worth emphasizing that, in connectionist terms at least (Feldman and Ballard, 1982; Rumelhart and McClelland, 1986), the traditional procedural/declarative distinction becomes difficult to sustain in any clear way. In so far as any particular activity-pattern in a network of active elements can be said to 'represent', then what is represented must depend on the entire structure of network interconnections). Monsell raises these, and other, very hard theoretical issues in an exceptionally lucid manner; he challenges all of us to make explicit in our theorizing — in our box-and-arrow diagrams or whatever — what our fundamental and generally unexpressed assumptions on these questions are. What (in this sense) is a *logogen* system? Is it a store of explicit 'representations', a purely procedural transcoding device, or what? What kind of device (in the same sense) is the so-called 'articulatory loop'? And so on.

The substantive focus of Monsell's chapter is the (currently highly controversial) issue of the relationship between the lexical knowledge that is used in spoken word *recognition* (and comprehension) and the lexical knowledge used in spoken word *production*. What (if anything) is shared between them? Monsell sets out a spectrum of theoretical alternatives, as possible answers to this question, and reviews a wide range of data pertinent to it. He tentatively concludes in favour of *functionally separate* lexica (and separate *sub*lexical coding systems) for perception and production, but with strong (sublexical) channels of communication between them, in both directions.

In the subsequent chapter, Coltheart and Funnell address themselves to the parallel question about shared versus separate lexica in the perception and production (respectively) of *written* language. 'Is the orthographic lexical entry which must be accessed if *yacht* is to be read correctly the same lexical entry that must be accessed if 'yacht' is to be spelled correctly?' In addressing this question, Coltheart and Funnell explore the possibilities of a hitherto little-used approach to single-case, neuropsychological data. Their chapter provides an invaluable guide to the complexities of answering this kind of question, from neuropsychological data, and to some of the techniques for overcoming them. (Of their methodology, more anon.) Their analyses lead them to the tentative conclusion that there is a *single* 'orthographic lexicon' — a single store of knowledge concerning written word-forms — that is used *both* in reading and in spelling. Their conclusion, as regards written language, is thus in direct contrast with Monsell's as regards spoken language. No doubt it is possible that the psychological mechanisms respectively of spoken and of written language just are radically differently organized in this respect. There are many important differences between language in its spoken and written forms, and this possibility should by no means be excluded. Equally, it must be recognized that their conclusions, in both cases, are put forward tentatively, as the best available interpretation of the data under review. The reader should be in no doubt that controversy on this issue is liable to continue, both on the spoken and the written side. In the meanwhile these two chapters will serve as indispensable reference points in any future discussion of these issues.

Traditionally, one of the most powerful methods available to us for identifying functionally separable subsystems is the discovery of 'double dissociations' between the residual abilities of contrasting neuropsychological patients. (One patient, that is, exhibits an impairment of psychological function A, but not of function B; another patient shows an impairment of function B, but not of A. The inference is that *independent* psychological systems or components, A' and B', are responsible for these psychological functions A and B.) The research described here by Howard and Franklin (Chap 17) provides a classic illustration of this approach, directed towards the second and the third of our problem areas: the functional communication between coding systems of written and spoken words, and their access to semantic encoding systems.

The behavioural identification of a unique underlying psychological function is no simple matter. It is worth emphasizing that specialized, cognitive subsystems are seldom to be identified, simply and uniquely, with any one behavioural task, surely not, at least, with the sorts of lexical and sublexical tasks examined here. To take an example discussed extensively in the preceding section of this book as well as in the present one, the behavioural task of reading-aloud-isolated-words-from-print can be shown to depend on a number of different specialized cognitive subsystems. None of these subsystems, on its own, is sufficient for performance of the task; and none of them is *uniquely* concerned with the task of reading aloud and with no other behavioural or linguistic task. Some of the *same* subsystems that are used in reading aloud can contribute also to the behavioural task of silent reading *comprehension*, as the elegant task analyses by Howard and Franklin abundantly illustrate. Furthermore, the *same* overt task, at least loosely defined (e.g. 'understanding written words') may sometimes be performed in several alternative ways, by means of different combinations of subsystems and their interconnections — what Howard and Franklin call different 'routines' — so that only the detailed experimental manipulation of contrasting task demands is capable of teasing apart their separate contributions.

Howard and Franklin discuss the properties of *three* distinct 'routines' — sequences of psychological recoding procedures — that can be used in understanding written words and pseudowords (BOTE). Their data provide further, very powerful evidence for the neuropsychological separability of two of their routines, though the third distinction, requiring the double-dissociability of *lexical* versus *sublexical* systems for recoding from print to sound, is yet to be demonstrated, and is still the subject of hot controversy. Their results also offer new and compelling evidence of feedback pathways from sublexical 'output phonology' back to coding systems that handle normal speech input and thence, by this roundabout route, to comprehension. In so doing, their data also strongly support the conclusion, advanced by Monsell, of functionally separable, *sublexical* coding systems capable, on the one hand, of representing phonological sequences — syllables, word-fragments — in a form needed for the control of overt articulation ('output phonology') and, on the other hand, a system or systems specialized for sublexical coding of speech input ('input phonology'). Such a conclusion, it may be pointed out, is without prejudice to the further question of whether or not there is a common phonological *lexicon*, shared between the processing of speech comprehension and speech production. Their results are of course highly pertinent, on the other hand, to the issues discussed earlier in this volume by Porter and by Studdert-Kennedy (Chaps 4 and 5), and by Campbell (Chap 7).

While Howard and Franklin make use of the classic methodology of 'double' dissociations, Coltheart and Funnell exploit a different approach, based on the detailed investigation of a single dyslexic and dysgraphic subject. Their argument is this. Suppose the same source of lexical, orthographic knowledge is used both in spelling production and in written word recognition. If this were the case, and if, furthermore, a subject's lexical orthographic knowledge could be shown to be (at least partially) impaired, in tasks of written word recognition, for a *specific subset* of words, then the *same* subset of words should be found to be impaired also in tasks of spelling production. This was the prediction that they set out to test, and their chapter provides both a fascinating account of the difficulties involved and an exemplary guide to how they may be overcome.

Of the three broad groupings of issues that I listed earlier, the third — concerned with the nature of semantic or conceptual encoding of word-meanings and the functional communication between this conceptual/semantic domain (or domains) and the coding of *word-forms* — is by far the least explored and the least well understood, at least from the point of view of 'functional architecture', although these are manifestly issues of the greatest centrality and importance for understanding human cognition. The chapter here that attempts, as its main goal, a foray into this relatively uncharted area — that by Funnell and Allport — is thus inevitably something of an exploratory venture. Its principle antecedents are the investigations of 'semantic errors' in those brain-damaged patients characterized as deep dyslexic and/or deep dysgraphic (e.g. Coltheart, Patterson and Marshall, 1980). Like these studies, it attempts to exploit the 'privileged view' of a given, cognitive subsystem, that becomes accessible when other, related subsystems are no longer functional. The two patients described by Funnell and Allport are neither deep dyslexic nor deep dysgraphic, in that they do not commonly make 'semantic' errors in their written–spoken transcoding of individual words. Nevertheless, like those patients, they have a profound disability in transcoding 'directly' between the written and the spoken forms, so that their residual performance at such tasks (e.g. reading aloud, writing to dictation) depends, as Funnell and Allport set out to show, on the mediation of a conceptual/semantic coding of the words. Characteristics of this conceptual/semantic mediation thus become accessible to rather direct behavioural investigation.

As regards questions of functional architecture, the principal issue to which Funnell and Allport's chapter is addressed is the following. The existence of modality- (or domain-) specific lexical coding systems, respectively within the phonological and the orthographic domains, is comparatively well established. Is there also, in addition to these, some more abstract, modality- or domain-independent lexicon? And/or, phrased in somewhat different terms, are there *word-specific* (hence strictly 'lexical') coding units within the conceptual/semantic domain? The answer to both these questions, Funnell and Allport contend, is 'No'. The brain's representation of referential word-meanings, they argue, is not parceled up in functional coding units that correspond neatly, one-for-one, with the individual lexical units of a particular language. Cognitive or conceptual/semantic representation is thus, in a very fundamental sense, language independent.

Note

[1] This is not to say that such relationships are, necessarily, arbitrary. In English and many other languages, derivational and inflexional morphology encodes certain systematic relationships of meaning. In general, the arbitrariness is most apparent, and most nearly complete, in the correspondences between unaffixed word-stems (root morphemes) and meaning. The discussion here, and throughout the chapters in this section, is largely confined to the coding — the perception, comprehension and production — of free, root morphemes. Issues of lexical morphology, or of syntactic processes, are touched on in these chapters, but they are not the focus.

References

Coltheart, M., Patterson, K. and Marshall, J. C. (Eds) (1980). *Deep Dyslexia.* London: Routledge and Kegan Paul.

Feldman, J. S. and Ballard, D. H. (1982). Connectionist models and their properties. *Cognitive Science*, **6**, 205–54.

Rumelhart, D. E., McClelland, J. L. and the PDP research group. (1986). *Parallel Distributed Processing: Explorations in the Microstructure of Cognition. Volume 1: Foundations.* Cambridge, MA: Bradford Books/MIT Press.

14 On the relation between lexical input and output pathways for speech

Stephen Monsell

Abstract

There evidently exists in the brain a processing pathway for the generation of spoken words from meaning, and a pathway for identifying and accessing the associated properties of spoken words during comprehension. This chapter addresses the relationship between these two pathways, especially with respect to the lexical level of processing.

A spectrum of logically possible relations between speech input and output pathways is first outlined, then available data are brought to bear. Several effects of production processes, even though silent, on later processing of speech input, imply either the sharing of common mechanisms by the two pathways, or separate pathways reciprocally interconnected at a sub-lexical level or levels. Some features of these data tentatively favour the latter alternative, as do data on simultaneous talking and listening. Little can be concluded from available neuropsychological and speech error data. Data on short-term retention of word sequence are argued to require two 'phonological buffers', linked but possibly located in separate input and output pathways.

The data thus seem compatible with separate input and output pathways, with reciprocal sub-lexical links. Observations that silent mouthing has more auditory-like effects than other silent phonology-generation tasks suggest (at least) two levels of sub-lexical output → input linkage. The possibility of a lexical but non-semantic input → output link, in addition to sub-lexical linkages, is considered.

Introduction

This chapter explores some questions about the 'functional anatomy' of the lexicon. It discusses the relationship between the processing pathway(s)

LANGUAGE PERCEPTION AND PRODUCTION
ISBN 0-12-052750-2

used to identify an auditory word and access its associated properties, and the pathway(s) used to generate the articulatory properties for a word.

Lexical domains

Words participate in, and are a vehicle for translation between, several distinct representational *domains*. Each word we know corresponds to, or addresses, some set of attributes in the *Conceptual/Functional* (to be abbreviated CF) domain — semantic properties, syntactic class, usage conventions, etc. It is undoubtedly an oversimplification to treat these attributes as constituting a single domain (see Shallice, 1987 and Funnell and Allport, Chap 17) but it is for the present convenient. Next, we have some capacity for representing, in a relatively abstract way, the sound structure of a chunk of speech input, be it one or more words, or word-like forms, or word fragments. By 'abstract' I mean that the same word spoken in different contexts and by different speakers, and even in different dialects, must be in some sense reduced to the 'same' description. This I will term the domain(s) of *input Phonology* (abbreviated iP). I use the term 'phonology' informally, with no commitment to the phonological units (e.g. phonemes) favoured by any particular linguistic theory. We must similarly represent the articulatory structure of speech output — the domain(s) of *output Phonology* (oP). One of the issues at the heart of this chapter will be whether there exists in our heads (as opposed to in linguistic phonological theory) a representational domain so abstract that — like the linguists' phonemes — it is indifferent to whether it is representing speech input or output. If there is, my terminology will permit us simply to call it the common *Phonology* (P) domain. (Similar considerations lead us to define *input Orthography* (iO) and *output orthography* (oO) domains — representing abstractly the identity and ordering of orthographic units, be they letters, graphemes, transgraphemic features, etc., in textual input and output, respectively, and to contemplate the possibility of a common O domain.)

Lexical pathways

Comprehension of a spoken word must involve, minimally:

• the formation of a temporary description of the sound structure of the auditory input — i.e. a representation of it in the iP domain;

- the comparison (in some sense) of this temporary description to an array or 'lexicon' of permanently stored iP forms corresponding to all the words we know, and a determination of the best match;

- the retrieval, or activation, of the CF attributes associated with the best-matched iP form.

The processing pathway that carries out these logically distinct and successive (though possibly temporally overlapping) operations must be a *lexical* pathway: the iP → CF mapping it accomplishes is *word-specific* (or morpheme-specific), rather than dependent upon some rule-governed relationship between sub-morphemic chunks of sound and CF attributes. (In contrast, some transcodings between domains can be *non-lexical* — i.e. indifferent to whether the descriptions they transcode are of whole words, non-words, or word fragments. These include the pathways that enable us to transcribe single graphemes (iO → oO), to shadow single speech sounds (iP → oP), to interpret grunts, hesitation noises and onomatopæic neologisms like 'ZAP!' (iP → CF), and, possibly, to pronounce regularly spelled visual words 'by rule' (iO → oP) or write such words to dictation (iP → oO). See the chapters in Section 4 of this book on phonological factors in the processing of orthography.)

There must also exist a lexical pathway that generates a spoken word to convey meaning, i.e. accomplishes CF → oP transcoding. Presumably this takes as its input a specification of the desired word in terms of form class, semantic attributes, langue, emotional force etc., attempts to find a match in its lexicon, and, if successful, generates an oP description suitable for controlling articulatory activity.

In a purely formal sense the CF → oP pathway may be said to accomplish the inverse of the transcoding performed by the iP → CF pathway. However, the 'functional anatomy' question that will occupy us in the major part of the paper is: what is the relationship between the processing mechanisms comprising the iP → CF and the CF → oP pathways? Are they quite separate? If so, how are they linked? Or do they share common components? If so, what components do they share? A common 'lexicon' of P word-forms? Common mechanisms for sub-lexical representation and/or processing? Both? I set out some broad classes of model below, and then review what seem to me the most promising categories of evidence for distinguishing them. As much as possible, I want to address these questions while making only minimal assumptions about the nature of the lexical access processes accomplished by these pathways. To what extent is this possible?

Lexical access

Many questions about the nature of lexical access processes have been raised in the literature in recent years. Illustrated with respect to the identification and comprehension of spoken words, they include the following:

- Is the matching process serial (e.g. Forster, 1976) or parallel (e.g. Morton, 1969; Marslen-Wilson and Tyler, 1980; McClelland and Elman, 1986)?

- Is there direct influence of prior sentential context on the process of finding the best match (e.g. Marslen-Wilson and Tyler, 1980; Marslen-Wilson, in press, versus Forster, 1981), or of activating the relevant meaning or 'word-sense' (Glucksberg, Kreuz and Rho, 1986, McClelland, in press, versus Swinney, 1979).

- Do the iP forms to which input is matched correspond to morphemes or to words (e.g. Taft, Hambly and Kinoshita's, 1986, assertion of prefix-stripping)?

- Is the formation of the temporary sub-lexical iP description of the input to be viewed as taking place at a processing level distinct from the processing level defined by the activation of permanent word representations? This is the case in models like that of McClelland and Elman (1986) and its antecedents, in which distinct levels of 'feature', 'phoneme' and 'word' units are postulated. An alternative idea is that phonological word-forms are permanently encoded only by the formation of 'auto-associative' interconnections among large arrays of nodes each representing a phonological micro-attribute (Allport, 1985; Funnell and Allport, Chap 17). According to this conception, sub-lexical and lexical iP representation is all accomplished at the same 'level' of encoding, but by different-sized networks of connectivity, within the iP domain.

- Are we to take a 'declarative' or a 'procedural' view of the representation of word-forms?

I hope to demonstrate in the rest of the chapter that we can make progress on the question of the relation between input and output pathways without taking a position on the answer to these questions, though I shall not be able to avoid indicating points at which the two kinds of question interact. The 'declarative' versus 'procedural' question in particular deserves preliminary exegesis.

Declarative versus procedural conceptions of a 'lexicon'

Suppose we require someone on one occasion to comprehend and on the other to write down a spoken word. The former requires a lexical iP → CF pathway, the latter a lexical iP → oO pathway (given that sound → spelling correspondences are irregular or unpredictable in English). The default assumption among most contemporary cognitive neuropsychologists is first to draw a box labelled something like 'auditory input lexicon' (e.g. Howard and Franklin, Chap 16) or 'phonological (lexical) codes' (e.g. Funnell and Allport, Chap 17), and then draw (at least) two pathways projecting from it, one to meaning representation and the other to orthography. The implicit assumption is that both these tasks use the *same* lexicon, and that it contains phonological representations of words *independent of the transcoding to which they contribute*. Various deficits are then attributed to impairment at one or more functional loci in the diagram: (a) access *to* the lexicon, (b) the *lexicon* itself, or (c) access *from* it to (e.g.) meaning. For example, Allport (1984a), discussing Bramwell's (1897/1984) celebrated case of 'word meaning deafness', noted that, although the patient could not comprehend the spoken words 'Edinburgh' and 'come', she could nevertheless write them to dictation. Because these are irregularly spelled words, he concluded that *the* phonological input lexicon must have been intact and the patient had suffered a *disconnection* between it and conceptual representation. (The latter must have been intact because she could read these and most other words with comprehension.)

This conception of the lexicon is fundamentally 'declarative'. It depends on the idea that the words we know are explicitly represented *as such* — in a lexicon of 'auditory input logogens', 'word-detectors', 'phonological word-forms', 'phonological lexical entries' (or whatever), independently of the particular transcodings to which the lexicon may (or may not) contribute.

An alternative, 'procedural', view of lexical representation is possible. A lexical pathway may be viewed as a processing module specialized for the performance of (word-specific) transcoding from one particular input domain to one particular output domain. Such a module could be organized as an encapsulated 'production system' — a set of condition → action 'demons' inspecting the input for their condition, e.g., a particular iP pattern, and, if they detect it (with sufficient confidence), producing appropriate activation in the output domain. (See Allport (1980a) for a general introduction to production-type psychological models.) From this perspective, the representation of words is not explicit and separate from what is done to those words, but is embodied in the potential for, and performance of, *particular inter-domain transcodings*. On this account, Bramwell's patient had lost her iP → CF lexical pathway while her iP → oO pathway remained functional. In the intact language user we might therefore posit not one function-independent and explicit iP lexicon but (if at all) two iP lexica, one embodied in an iP → CF transcoding module and one in an iP → oO module.

Now, I know of no *data* which can distinguish these perspectives, and I may seem to the reader to be making a tedious fuss about two logically different but pragmatically equivalent ways of saying the same thing. However, precommitment to one perspective *or* the other can have consequences for the possible relationships between input and output pathways one is prepared to contemplate, the techniques one uses to test hypotheses, and the functional anatomy diagrams one draws to present one's conclusions.[1] (Cf. the distinction betwen wave and particle representations of electromagnetic radiation?) For example:

• To view words as explicitly represented by word-detectors, or logogens, permits one to contemplate the possibility that iP → CF transcoding and CF → oP transcoding are accomplished via the *same* set of logogens or word-detectors (see Models 5 and 6 below). Within a strict procedural conception, however, this possibility seems *inexpressible* since procedures, or productions, are inherently unidirectional; their 'conditions' and 'actions' cannot be exchanged.

• Proponents of recent versions of the logogen model, such as Morton (1979), Patterson and Shewell (1987), and Howard and Franklin (Chap 16) posit separate iP input and oP output logogens, directly coupled by a 'wire' leading from each logogen in the input lexicon to the corresponding logogen in the output domain. Such a coupling can be expressed only within a declarative conception of the lexicon, and would appear to embody a view of logogens as in themselves a domain of representation rather than (as is sometimes claimed) mere transcoders.

• To explore the relation between lexical pathways empirically, we must give subjects tasks which exercise a particular lexical pathway. In the declarative framework, *any* transcoding task requiring identification of an auditory word must be *assumed* to activate *the* iP lexicon (or its equivalent).[2] From the procedural perspective, it remains an open question as to whether activation of the iP → CF pathway to accomplish comprehension will also, automatically, result in activation of the iP → oO pathway required for writing irregularly spelled words to dictation without comprehension.

• One of the most popular, but least well understood, psycholinguistic tasks is lexical decision. Within the declarative framework, this task tends to be seen as requiring lexical *identification* — matching to a word form in *the* input lexicon, without necessarily requiring lexical *retrieval* — activation of a description in any particular output domain. However, James' (1975) observation that concreteness/abstractness can influence lexical decision time is often cited as problematic for this assumption (see Gernsbacher, 1984, for further discussion), and it seems clear that interactions of retrieved meaning with context ('post-lexical congruence effects') may account for components of semantic priming of LDT under some circumstances (e.g. Forster, 1981, de Groot, 1984). The nature of lexical decision is no less ambiguous within the procedural framework. For example, visual LDT could be accomplished using either the iO → CF pathway, or the iO → P pathway, or both. If we want to use LDT to measure the accomplishment of processing by an input pathway, it would be nice to know which. But we do not.

I have said enough, I hope, to show that there are important and unresolved questions concerning not only the details of lexical mechanisms, but also how best to conceive of them. All this said, I propose in the remainder of this paper to evade or gloss these difficulties as much as possible. I start by setting out a logically possible range of classes of model for the relation between iP → CF and CF → oP pathways in terms that are as neutral as I can manage with respect to different perspectives and views of lexical access. I will try to indicate points at which this neutrality is compromised.

Possible relationships between phonological input and output pathways

Model 1

A convenient starting point is the idea that the iP → CF and CF → oP pathways are completely separate, except that the input pathway terminates in the same CF domain of representation with which the output pathway begins. (I suppose that even the assumption of a conceptual code common to input and output processing could logically be challenged, but I shall not weary the reader by doing so; see Funnell and Allport's chapter for a discussion of conceptual codes.)

Two simple observations render this model unrealistic. We can readily shadow nonsense speech, and there are patients who can repeat spoken words of which they appear to have no comprehension (Bramwell, 1897/ 1984; Symonds, 1953; Warrington, 1975). So there must be a route from speech input to speech output bypassing the CF domain.

1. SEPARATE PATHWAYS

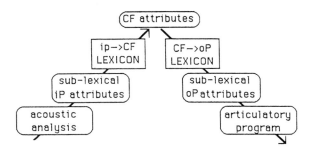

2. SEPARATE PATHWAYS + SUB-LEXICAL i—>o LINKS

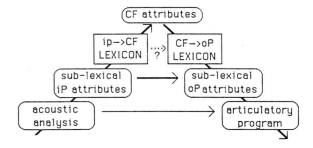

3. SEPARATE PATHWAYS + SUB-LEXICAL i—>o AND o—>i LINKS

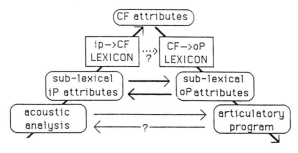

Figure 1. A spectrum of possible relationships between lexical input and output pathways for speech.

4. COMMON SUB-LEXICAL REPRESENTATION OR MECHANISM

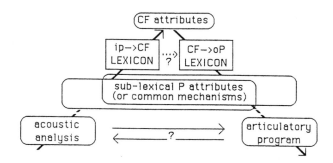

5. COMMON LEXICAL "REPRESENTATIONS"

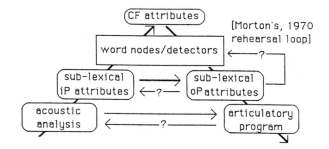

6. COMMON LEXICAL AND SUB-LEXICAL REPRESENTATION / MECHANISM

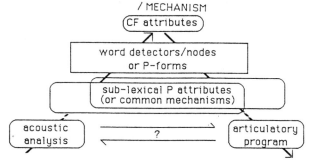

Figure 1. (continued)

Model 2

The next class of model therefore adds a non-semantic bypass, giving us something very like the classical Wernicke–Lichtheim model of the aphasias — by no means a historical relic (Cf. McCarthy and Warrington, 1984). This route must include a non-lexical component, because we can easily shadow non-lexical gibberish, provided that it observes phonotactic constraints with which we are familiar, and single speech sounds. Such shadowing is relatively easy; for single speech sounds it can have a remarkably short latency (e.g. Porter and Castellanos, 1980; Porter and Lubker, 1980, on shadowing of single consonant closures and vowel transitions). In comparison, copying non-speech sounds or speech with an unfamiliar phonology seems both hard and slow, though I know of no formal data on this point. This contrast argues for a (fast) phonology-specific but non-semantic iP → oP route in addition to any more general (but, in most people, slow and effortful) capability for mimicry of sound.

Is it possible that the non-semantic iP → oP pathway includes a *lexical* component? In the Wernicke-Lichtheim model, there was a direct connection between the 'sound-images' of words and their 'motor images', which could be construed as lexical. Recent versions of the logogen model (e.g. Patterson and Shewell, 1986; Howard and Franklin, Chap 16) also posit direct links between input logogens and output logogens bypassing meaning. I shall return in a later section to the possibility of a word-specific component in the non-semantic iP → oP route.

Model 3

The next step, as we contemplate decreasing degrees of independence between input and output pathways, is to posit one or more non-lexical oP → iP pathways: i.e. pathways carrying information to speech *perception* mechanisms about the current status of the speech *production* system. Gordon and Meyer (1984, p. 172) provide an example of such a proposal, motivated by the discovery that preparation to speak can influence auditory speech discrimination (see below). Even in the absence of specific data, there are several arguments for the reasonableness of this idea.

Sub-vocal rehearsal. One role for such a pathway would be to allow us to rehearse and/or to edit (cf. Baars, Motley and Mackay, 1975) a planned utterance prior to production. For example, McCarthy and Warrington (1984), in their otherwise faithful revival of the Wernicke–Lichtheim model, add an oP → iP pathway, apparently just to provide a route for rehearsal. Some sort of sub-vocal speech rehearsal loop is, of course, a standard and central constituent of models of working memory (e.g.

Baddeley, 1983) and, indeed, cognition in general. Yet there has been a curious reluctance to specify with any precision what the stations on this vital Inner Circle Line of the mind might be in relation to ideas about the lexicon. In an honourable exception to this generalization, Morton's (1979) version of the logogen model (see Model 5 below) explicitly incorporated a rehearsal loop. However, Morton's (1979) revision of the logogen model transformed it into a version of Model 2, and left the arrow depicting rehearsal pointing from the 'response buffer' into empty theoretical space! This curious deficit has not, I believe, been remedied in later variants until Howard and Franklin's chapter (Chap 16) which adds a route from response buffer to auditory input logogens, thus making it an instance of Model 3. We shall return below to the anatomy of sub-vocal rehearsal.

Monitoring of one's own speech. It is clear from spontaneous corrections of speech errors, from the deterioration of speech with the onset of deafness, and from the effects of delayed auditory feedback that we monitor our own speech output. One strategy for doing so would be to listen to it and analyse it completely *de novo*, as if it were someone else's speech. But a rather more efficient strategy, given that we 'know' what we are about to say, is the one familiar from the postulate in models of visual movement perception of 'efference copy' (Held, 1965), or 'corollary discharge' (Sperry, 1950), namely to 'feed forward' a description of planned action to relevant sensory processing modules. Higher-level analysis and correction need be embarked upon only if the sensory input does not then match the anticipated consequences of planned or executed speech output (cf. Morton, 1968). Lackner (1974) makes a somewhat different suggestion: that articulatory corollary discharge is used somehow to stabilize perceptual analysis mechanisms against perceptual adaptation to the characteristics of one's own voice (see below) rather than of one's interlocutor.

Language learning. Given separate iP → CF and CF → oP pathways, learning to produce a particular P pattern in response to a CF description involves the formation of different associations from those learned to access those CF attributes on the basis of P input. This may be one rationale for the dissociations observed, early in spoken language development, between receptive and productive vocabulary (Menn, 1983). However, such dissociations are not a striking property of adult speech. Within the 'separate pathways' framework, this could be because children develop, or develop control over, a sub-lexical oP → iP route, whereby the phonological products of the output lexicon can be checked against entries in the input lexicon and reinforced, or modified, as necessary, to bring the systems into closer correspondence.

Model 4

The fourth class of model assumes that there are separate iP → CF and CF → oP lexical pathways, but that some sub-lexical component of the processing system is shared between the pathways.

As one variant of this idea, consider the claim (e.g. Baddeley, 1983) that one component of working memory is a 'buffer' which maintains, in some form of sub-lexical speech code, the identity and order of a short sequence of syllables or words, and may be probed by (among others) a 'span' task, i.e. immediate serial recall of a short sequence of visual or auditory words. In the earliest theories, this buffer was typically conceived of as involving an 'acoustic' code (e.g. Conrad, 1964; Sperling and Speelman, 1970): i.e. it was specialized for the representation of speech *input*. Later, in response to findings on errors made in span tasks by the congenitally deaf (Conrad, 1970), and data on the interacting effects on span performance of word length and articulatory suppression, Baddeley, Thomson and Buchanan (1975) attributed temporary storage of sequence to an 'articulatory loop', a system specialized for the representation and maintenance of articulatory *output*. However, in Baddeley *et al*'s most recent treatment of the articulatory loop (e.g. Vallar and Baddeley, 1984; Baddeley, Lewis and Vallar, 1984), the *storage* component of the articulatory loop is now described as an *input* buffer, because of the finding that irrelevant speech input interferes with performance of a visual span task (Colle and Welsh, 1976; Salame and Baddeley, 1982). Seen words are assumed to be entered into this input buffer by the generation (presumably lexically mediated) of their phonological patterns, and it is only this *process* that is 'articulatory'.

Now, regardless of the data (to which I will return anon), it should be clear that the proponent of a theory in which there is but one (sub-lexical) 'phonological buffer' has three options about where to put it. It can be (as Baddeley *et al*. now appear to assume[3]) a component of the speech *input* processing mechanism, but one to which an articulatory output code can gain access — presumably via an oP → iP pathway, as in Model 3. Or it can be an articulatory *output* buffer, but one to which speech input is automatically transmitted via a sublexical iP → oP link, as in Models 2 and 3. Or it can be a *common* P-buffer, shared by input and output processes, but 'belonging' to neither. The last of these would be an instance of Model 4.

Gordon and Meyer (1984) provide a second example of Model 4. An alternative explanation they consider for the interaction they observe between articulatory preparation and auditory discrimination (see below) is that both speech input and speech output processes call upon a common 'clock' mechanism for timing voicing onset time in consonants.

Models 5 and 6

The classes of model sketched so far assume separate lexica for speech input and output. The alternative possibility is that the same lexicon mediates both iP → CF and CF → oP transcoding. However, what this means depends critically on one's conception of a 'lexicon' (unlike Models 1–4). Some specific examples follow:

'Word-detector' models. In the pre-1977 version of Morton's logogen model (Morton, 1969, 1970), a common set of logogens was activated by input both *from* a precategorical acoustic system (iP), and *from* the 'cognitive system' (CF), and sent output either *to* the cognitive system, or *to* an articulatory 'response buffer' (oP). Hence the same logogens mediated iP → CF and CF → oP transcoding (and also an oP → oP recycling process assumed to underly sub-vocal rehearsal). Since there were no common mechanisms below the lexical level, we may depict this as Model 5 (in Figure 1). MacKay (in preparation) has recently argued that though there are undoubted asymmetries between speech perception and production (Chap 18), words, syllables and phonemes are represented by the same 'mental nodes' for perception and production. Since this is to assume common representation at both lexical and sub-lexical levels, we may depict this as Model 6.

Allport's distributed representation model. Allport (1984a) argues, for reasons we shall examine below, in favour of a common lexicon of phonological word-forms used both for matching speech input to, and for the generation of speech output. According to Allport (1985; see also Funnell and Allport, Chap 17), the phonological form of a word comes, through repeated exposure, to be represented as a matrix of interconnections among the micro-attributes of the word *within* the P domain. There are also matrices of interconnections *between* the P and CF domains which mediate word-specific transcoding. In fact since the inter-connections are unidirectional, there are *two* sets of between-domain interconnective matrices, one for P → CF and one for CF → P mapping. Thus, according to Allport, phonological representation at both a lexical and a sub-lexical level is shared by speech input and speech output processes although there are separate inter-domain mapping structures. We may therefore consider Allport to be represented by Model 6. However, the lexical and sub-lexical boxes are to be read in this case not as separate levels but as separate phases in the access process: something like before and after the settling of the P-system into the stable state that results from successful recruitment of mutual activation by attributes interconnected to represent a word-form. It is also worth noting that it would be equally possible to frame a separate-pathways model in terms of distributed representations: in this case there would be matrices of interconnections within and between iP, oP and CF systems.

Liberman, Cooper, Shankweiler and Studdert-Kennedy's (1967) motor theory of special perception was the most extreme common-mechanisms theory. Speech input was analysed by synthesis: using production mechanisms to generate a relatively peripheral code to which input was then matched. However, proponents of this view have generally retreated to the more modest claim (see Liberman and Mattingly, 1985, and Studdert-Kennedy, Chap 4) that what the listener recovers from speech input is a specification of the articulatory gestures of the speaker. This allows for a particularly natural and intimate linkage from speech input to articulatory output, but does not require gesture–recovery and gesture–production mechanisms to be identical.

That concludes my attempt to define and illustrate a basic spectrum of possible models for the relationship between lexical iP → CF and CF → oP pathways. Doubtless the space of possible models could be partitioned in different ways, but we will find the present ordering, in terms of increasingly intimate relations between the two pathways a useful one as we undertake our next task, which is to consider how particular categories of evidence might discriminate among these classes of model.

Data on the relation between input and output pathways

I will first review several kinds of data indicating that speech production processes, even when they do not result in audible output, influence the later processing of heard speech. That requires a relationship between input and output pathways at least as intimate as that depicted in Models 3–6. Next I will argue against 'common lexicon' models — i.e. Models 5 and 6. Then I will consider arguments against the 'common buffer' variant of Model 4. This will leave me tentatively advocating Model 3, though it will be apparent that as the field of candidates narrows, so the evidence and arguments become progressively weaker! Finally, I will elaborate upon the sub-lexical linkages between the separate pathways of Model 3.

Influences of phonological production on perceptual identification

Repetition priming
Various measures of word identification, such as lexical decision time (LDT), or perceptual accuracy for degraded stimuli, show facilitation from

a prior perceptual encounter with the word, in the same sensory modality, earlier in the experiment. This is the phenomenon of *repetition priming*. Let us call the task whose performance is facilitated the *probe* task, and the earlier encounter that produces the facilitation the *priming* encounter. The following properties of repetition priming (documented at length by Monsell, 1985) are critical. The facilitation occurs over long lags between priming and probe encounters (e.g. an hour). It does not depend on the subject expecting a repetition. It occurs when the priming and probe tasks are different. For example, Monsell and Banich (in preparation) found that LDT for a printed word was facilitated just as much by prior naming of that word as by making a lexical decision to it. Facilitation that transfers across tasks cannot be attributed to task-specific learning of a response (or decision) association of the form: 'When I see letter string X I press button B (or reach a positive decision)', but must somehow be associated with a process preceding task-specific decision processes and common to the prime and probe tasks. Moreover, under the conditions with which we will be concerned, a long-lasting repetition effect is observed for words, but not for non-words. But, repetition of the word's meaning alone is insufficient; the phonological or orthographic form must be repeated (though variations in the realization of that form, such as voice or typeface, have little effect). In combination, these properties locate the effect in access to a *lexical* level of representation in an input pathway: i.e. with finding a lexical match for a particular word and/or retrieving its (non-task-specific) properties.

Now suppose that we take a probe task requiring access to a lexicon of iP forms, such as auditory lexical decision. Probe trials are preceded by one of two kinds of priming encounter with the word. In one case, the subject has heard the word and been required to access its meaning; this we expect to produce a within-modality repetition priming effect of the usual kind (as assessed in comparison to probe trials not preceded by any priming encounter). In the other case, the subject has been required silently to generate the word's phonology in response to a description of its meaning; i.e. exercise his CF → oP lexicon. Do we now observe a priming effect?

- If we do not, then we would have a case for rejecting a common-lexicon model (i.e. Models 5 or 6), because access to the single lexical representation of phonological form proposed by such models should be required to accomplish both the auditory lexical decision task and the CF → oP task.
- If we do observe a priming of lexical decision by silent production then there are two possible interpretations:
    (a) Models 5 or 6 are correct, and the CF → oP priming task involves access to the same lexical representation as the lexical decision task, or

(b) Models 3 or 4 are correct, in that different lexica are involved for input and output, but the phonological code generated by access to the CF → oP lexicon is fed back via either a common sub-lexical P-system (Model 4) or via a sub-lexical oP → iP route (Model 3) to prime entries in the iP lexicon mediating the lexical decision task.

If priming of identification by production is observed, can interpretations (a) and (b) be distinguished? Perhaps. Interpretation (b) admits the possibility that, under *some* conditions, the sub-lexical oP → iP linkage will be inoperative or at least reduced in effectiveness. Hence (b) allows priming of identification by phonology-generation to occur under some conditions, but be absent or weak under others. In contrast, according to interpretation (a), if priming ever occurs, it ought always to occur, at least for conditions under which both prime and probe tasks require access to the common P-lexicon.

Comparison between the priming effects of a *perceptual* encounter with a word and *generation* of the word's phonology was the focus of a series of experiments I carried out in collaboration with Marie Banich (see Monsell and Banich, in prep., and Monsell, 1985 for fuller description). One constraint upon our choice of priming tasks was the need to ensure that the *context* of the two kinds of priming encounters was as similar as possible. We knew from earlier work that the priming produced by a perceptual encounter with an isolated word could be attenuated when the word is encountered in the context of a sentence (Monsell and Banich, Exp. 1) or a related word (Jacoby, 1983). It would thus be inappropriate to contrast the priming effect of a generation task involving (e.g.) presentation of a definition *sentence* with that of a perceptual task involving presentation of the word *in isolation*. For this reason, all priming trials began with the visual presentation of a sentence missing one word that (as determined by pre-testing) an average subject could supply quickly and reliably: e.g. 'Swan Lake is a famous —'. On the generation priming encounters, subjects indicated — as will be described — what the missing word was. On the perceptual priming encounters, a candidate word was presented one second after the sentence (approximately the minimum generation latency) and the subject indicated with a key press whether it belonged in the sentence or not; only words which did belong were later probed.

In two experiments (Experiments 3 and 4 of Monsell and Banich, in prep.), the probe task was auditory lexical decision. The interval between priming encounter and probe trial was between half a minute and six minutes, filled with other priming or probe trials. We examined the effect of the following priming tasks:

(1) Deciding whether an auditory word fit the sentence frame.

(2) Speaking the missing word aloud.

(3) Silently mouthing the missing word.

(4) Deciding whether the missing word contained the same vowel sound as a monosyllabic test word displayed after the sentence — 'phonological matching'.

(5) Writing the missing word blind (i.e. without seeing one's hand or script).

(6) Deciding whether a printed word fit the sentence frame.

Task 1 provides the within-modality repetition condition to which priming observed in other conditions can be compared. Tasks 2, 3 and 4 require the generation of phonology. Task 2 also results in auditory input corresponding to that phonology, while Tasks 3 and 4 do not. Tasks 5 and 6 might be expected to result in, but do not logically require, activation of a phonological code. It should be noted that though non-word repetition effects were observed in these experiments, they were labile and of short persistence in comparison to the stable and non-decaying effect on words, and that the priming effects observed for words did not depend on active

Table 1. Data from Monsell and Banich (in preparation).

(A) Probe task is auditory lexical decision

Prime encounter	Mean RT (ms)	(error) (%)	Facilitation relative to Task 1 (%)	Priming effect (ms)
Exp 3 Control (unprimed)	857	(5.2)		
1. Hear the word	793	(1.5)	(100)	64 (p<0.01)
2. Say the word (aloud)	808	(2.1)	77	49 (p<0.01)
5. Write the word (blind)	830	(2.0)	42	27 (p<0.05)
6. See the word	821	(1.6)	57	46 (p<0.01)
Exp 4 Control (unprimed)	882	(5.5)		
1. Hear the word	814	(1.6)	(100)	68 (p<0.01)
3. Mouth the word (silently)	830	(2.2)	76	52 (p<0.01)
4. Generate for phonological match	851	(3.7)	46	31 (p<0.01)
5. Write the word (blind)	842	(3.1)	59	40 (p<0.01)
(B) Probe task is visual lexical decision				
Exp 2 Control (unprimed)	637	(4.8)		
1. See the word	610	(1.6)	(100)	27 (p< 0.01)
2. Write the word (blind)	632	(2.5)	18	5 (n.s.)
3. Say the word (aloud)	635	(1.1)	7	2 (n.s.)
4. Hear the word	636	(2.3)	4	1 (n.s.)

expectation of repetitions. (These and other details are discussed in full by Monsell and Banich, in preparation.)

The results are summarized in Table 1A. The first point to notice is that all forms of priming encounter produced significant facilitation of auditory lexical decision. Assuming that repetition priming under these conditions is indeed associated with lexical access, we can conclude that *generation* of a phonological word-form activates entries in whatever lexicon is used for auditory lexical decision. As argued above, this could be either because a common P-lexicon is involved (Models 5 and 6) or because output from the CF $\rightarrow$ oP lexicon is fed into an iP analysis pathway (as in Models 3 and 4).

The other interesting feature of these data was that Task 3 — silently mouthing the word — facilitated later auditory LD just as much as Task 2 — saying the word out loud, while Tasks 4, 5 and 6, although apparently resulting in phonological activation, had a significantly weaker effect. In the case of Tasks 5 and 6, one might speculate that since they could be accomplished on the basis of orthographic processing alone, generation of a phonological code is an option sometimes not exercised. However, this account will not work for Task 4 as we were careful to ensure that the vowel-sound matches could not be made on the basis of orthographic criteria. An alternative idea, which will be elaborated below, is that generation of a relatively *peripheral* articulatory code produces a qualitatively different and more substantial activation of the input pathway than mere activation of phonology.

Corroboration of our finding that silent phonological generation primes later auditory identification is available from recent work by Gipson (1984, 1986). In Gipson's experiments encounters with words in several priming tasks were followed after a few minutes by the task of identifying spoken words in noise. There may be some problems with the exact comparability of Gipson's auditory and phonology-generation priming tasks in terms of task repetition, delay and context, but it is nonetheless clear from his data that the following tasks — requiring generation of a word's phonology without the subject hearing it — facilitated accuracy of later auditory identification:

● Pointing to the referent of a printed pseudohomophone (e.g. PHOCKS) in a picture

● Evaluating the association between a pseudohomophone and several pictures

● Pointing to the non-word member of a pseudohomophone + non-word pair.

However, Gipson also found that saying the number of syllables either in a printed word, or in the name of a pictured object, did not significantly prime later auditory recognition of the word. (Subjects could not count syllables on the basis of orthographic criteria alone.) I have already suggested that the existence of a few conditions in which phonological generation does not prime identification sits more comfortably with Models 3 and 4 than with Models 5 and 6. In this case, it seems quite plausible that the requirement to speak a word (denoting the number of syllables) *other than* the target word might block activation, via a sub-lexical oP → iP link, of the target word's entry in an input lexicon. A common lexicon account provides no obvious account of why this condition, but not our phonology-generation tasks, fails to prime auditory recognition.[4]

Sub-lexical influences of production on perception

Meyer, Gordon and Benson (in preparation; see Gordon and Meyer, 1984) had subjects prepare to produce a specified CV syllable. On half the trials they were cued to produce the prepared syllable. On the other half, they had to classify a heard CV syllable as one of four alternatives: classification RT was retarded if the auditory syllable and the syllable prepared for production differed in the voicing feature. (A comparable result was not obtained for place of articulation.) As Gordon and Meyer (1984) point out, this indicates either 'cross-talk', at a relatively peripheral level, from the production pathway to the perceptual pathway, or competition between perceptual and production processes for a common mechanism, such as a voice-onset timing 'clock'. Cooper (1979) appears to favour the common mechanism idea to explain an observation of 'motor → perceptual' adaptation. He found that repeated whispered production of a CV syllable, which the subject was allegedly prevented from hearing by white noise, could nevertheless shift the corresponding perceptual phoneme category boundary. Unfortunately, this effect was not reliably observed in all his subjects, and no evidence is available on the completeness of the auditory masking.

Arguments against 'common lexicon' models

So far we seem to have good evidence for ruling out Model 2. It provides no mechanism for silent speech production processes to influence identification of auditory words or phonemes, yet that is what is observed. I have also argued that details of the repetition priming data — Monsell and Banich's observation of stronger priming from mouthing than from other phonology-generation tasks, Gipson's failure to get priming from syllable counting — are more compatible with separate-but-linked pathways (Models 3 and 4) than with the idea of a common P lexicon (Models 5 and

6). The most straightforward expectation to which a separate pathways model gives rise is that the iP $\rightarrow$ CF and CF $\rightarrow$ oP pathways, though linked, should be under some conditions empirically dissociable. For example, they might be able to process different words at the same time. Or, they might be anatomically distinct enough to be dissociated by localized brain injury. Let us examine these possibilities in turn, and then consider an argument for a common lexicon from speech errors.

Dual task studies

If the same set of 'word-detectors', or 'word-nodes' or 'phonological word-forms' is used for generating phonological patterns as for identifying them, then one might expect that attempts simultaneously to generate one stream of phonological word-forms while identifying an unrelated stream would result in difficulties.

What kind of interference should we expect? We know from the work of Ostry, Moray and Marks (1976) and others that, under some circumstances, two auditory streams of words can be monitored for a semantic target almost as accurately as one. However, this ability to process lexically two input streams at a time with little or no cost seems limited to an extremely constrained set of circumstances: targets must not occur simultaneously in the two streams; the action taken in response to a target in either stream must be of the same kind; subjects must be thoroughly practised with the mapping of target onto response (see Allport, 1980b, for review). We might then conclude that even if word representations in a common lexicon can be activated for production and recognition simultaneously and without cost, it would be hard to *connect* each activated representation to, or *route* activation to, articulation or comprehension processes, appropriately and exclusively. The nearest analogue in the existing attentional literature would seem to be the Stroop task. Here it seems that both the orthographic and the colour attributes of the stimulus simultaneously activate colour–name lexical representations; the problem is to ensure that the appropriate lexical representation controls articulatory output. As is well known, when the ink colour and the orthography conflict, massive interference is observed. Thus a common-lexicon view would appear to predict that simultaneous generation and identification of different phonological forms should lead to considerable cross-talk between the tasks (i.e. intrusions of words from one stream into the other) or to major interference due to 'executive overhead' incurred in keeping separate the products of two separate sources of lexical activation.

It is worthy of remark, then, that professional simultaneous translators typically spend two-thirds of their translating time speaking simultaneously with the speaker whose speech they are translating. Yet input and output rates are rapid, output is produced in well-formed and long phonemic clauses, often concurrently with the comprehension of syntactically complex and/or degraded input, and cross-talk errors are very rare (see Gerver, 1976, and Gerver and Sinaiko, 1978). However, there is typically a lag of 2 to 10 s between input and output, which permits the hypothesis of rapid switching of common mechanisms between servicing the input and output streams. The sensitivity of translators to environmental noise also bespeaks the allocation of unusual cognitive effort.

What is needed, of course, is formal experimentation on the simultaneous processing of different speech input and output streams, ideally without the complication of different languages. Shallice, McLeod and Lewis (1985) have recently reported a pioneering study. In their basic condition, the primary task was to name a stream of visual words, presented just slower than a 'breakdown' rate determined individually for each subject, and the secondary task was to monitor an auditory stream of words (presented at approx. 2.5 words per s) for a semantically defined target (a proper name among other nouns). They observed relatively little interference in the dual task condition. Nor were reading errors associated with successful auditory detections, as a simple switching account would predict. In contrast, simultaneous performance of two allegedly comparable tasks that both require lexical input processing (shadowing plus the auditory semantic monitoring task) or two tasks that arguably require lexical output processing (naming visual words plus phoneme monitoring) produced massive interference. (Other task combinations were also tested in an attempt to demonstrate that the various auditory tasks were indeed comparable in general 'difficulty'.)

There are undoubtedly problems interpreting Shallice *et al*'s data. Performance was at ceiling in the single task conditions, making the true size of the dual task decrement hard to estimate. It is not obvious that it is lexical generation of phonological patterns that limited processing rate in the reading task. There may have been auditory masking difficulties in the dual input task. It is not clear that the phoneme-monitoring task used in the dual 'output' task is exclusively an output task. Difficulty levels were not perfectly matched between the basic and control conditions, even by the authors' own criteria. (It could even be argued — somewhat implausibly, given all the evidence on 'automatic' activation of meaning by printed words — that the reading task exercised only an O → P lexicon, and the auditory monitoring task a P → CF lexicon, leaving open the possibility that one common lexicon of phonological word forms would be used for P → CF and CF → P transcodings, and a different one for O → P and P → O transcoding).

These problems, largely to do with the adequacy of the control conditions, are serious, and will doubtless be addressed in further research.
Nevertheless, I believe that a strong argument can be founded simply on
the absence of a serious cross-talk problem in Shallice *et al*'s basic dual-task
condition. The Stroop-like difficulty that I argued this condition should, at
these presentation rates, impose upon a system with a common lexicon,
simply did not occur.

Neuropsychological evidence

This is perhaps the most obvious kind of evidence to look for. If there are
separate lexical iP → CF and CF → oP pathways, then we might expect to
observe cases of impaired auditory word comprehension with preserved
generation of speech, and vice versa. Perusal of the neurological literature
might lead one to believe that both patterns are observed. However, as
Allport (1984a) has persuasively argued, unambiguous support for either
pattern of dissociation is wanting. Patients can certainly be found who
appear to have difficulties in generating appropriate phonological word
forms, but succeed in conventional clinical tests of auditory word recognition. However, Allport notes that these tests of recognition involve a very
restricted set of alternatives, compared to the large set implicit in confrontation naming. In support of his critique, Allport was able to show that
three such patients were all impaired in an auditory lexical decision test —
a test of word recognition more comparable in difficulty to confrontation
naming. The possibility therefore exists that all such patients reported have
been thus impaired.

What of the other half of the hoped-for dissociation? Cases of alleged
'word-meaning deafness' — preservation of word production with loss of
auditory word comprehension other than that attributable merely to loss in
prelexical iP processing — are, according to Allport (1984a), both rare and
when reported, inadequately described to evaluate properly, or not pure
enough. For example, cases reported by Symonds (1953) and Yamadori
and Albert (1973) both have associated anomia, and/or reading deficits
suggesting a general CF representational deficit, rather than just difficulty
in access to CF attributes from iP codes. The most striking case available
still seems to be the patient reported by Bramwell (1897/1984).[5] Though
apparently deaf to the meaning of anything that was said to her, this
patient had good spontaneous speech and could repeat verbatim and write
whole sentences said to her, and, having once written them, understand
them by reading, since her reading skills were well preserved. This certainly appears to be a deficit specific to the iP → CF pathway. However, as
noted in my preliminary discussion of declarative versus procedural views
of the lexicon, Allport can interpret this patient's deficit as a disconnection

of meaning from — rather than loss of — a (declarative) P lexicon normally used for comprehension, and is not thus obliged to abandon his view that this lexicon serves both comprehension and production.

It seems that we must, for the present, simply suspend judgement and wait for neuropsychologists to seek out suitable patients and, on the basis of Allport's critique, apply more exacting tests. What if no cases of dissociation are ever found? Then we can conclude only that iP → CF and CF → oP lexical pathways are not *anatomically* dissociable by gross damage; they may still be functionally distinct.

An alternative to beating the bushes for cases of all-or-none dissociation between comprehension and production is detailed comparison of the *pattern* of receptive and productive loss in the same patient, as attempted by Coltheart and Funnell (Chap 15) in the orthographic domain. The basic idea is that if the same set of words, or (perhaps) word types, is impaired in comprehension as in production, this would be prima-facie evidence for a common lexicon. As their paper illustrates, this strategy is trickier than it may appear, and it is hard to get the comparison off the ground at all unless there is marked consistency from test to test in the pattern of loss within comprehension, or within production.[6]

Phonological influences on production errors

In some sense CF → P transcoding must involve formation of a CF description, matching of it to available word-senses, and retrieval of the corresponding phonology. Thus it is not surprising to observe instances, in both normal and brain-damaged subjects, of semantic paraphasias of the mother → 'daughter' type, presumably due to corruption of a semantic feature or two. But there also occur paraphasias phonologically similar, but semantically unrelated, to the target (e.g. gory → 'gaudy') — 'malapropisms' in Fay and Cutler's (1977) terminology. These seem puzzling: surely there is no phonology available until lexical selection has been accomplished. How can phonologically similar but semantically unrelated words get substituted?

Fay and Cutler (1977) interpret malapropisms, as does Allport (1984a), as evidence for a common lexicon. Violently paraphrased, their argument is as follows. If word A is produced instead of word B, then A and B must be 'neighbours' in the lexicon. That A and B are sometimes phonologically related indicates that the lexicon used for production is organized in terms of phonological neighbourhoods. This only makes any sense if it is also the lexicon used for identification of phonological input.

One problem with this argument is that it relies entirely on the metaphor of the lexicon as a (quasi-spatial) array and lexical selection errors as errors of 'aiming' at a target in the array. But there are at least two alternative accounts of malapropisms and related phenomena which do not depend on assuming a common lexicon. Nor are they mutually exclusive.

Following the example of McClelland and Rumelhart's (1981) interactive activation model for visual word recognition, Dell (1985) and Stemberger (1985) have recently developed interactive activation models for the generation of phonology. Among the critical properties of these models are (a) word and phoneme nodes are reciprocally interconnected, so that not only do partially activated word nodes activate the nodes of their constituent phonemes, but activated phoneme nodes also activate the nodes for words with those phonemes in the appropriate position, and (b) within each level nodes inhibit each other, so that the eventual result is the outcome of a competition for dominance at each level among a cohort of partially activated nodes. The process starts with a semantic specification, and hence the initial cohort of partially activated word nodes will tend to be semantically related words, whence derive semantic substitution errors and blends. But, as the activation process evolves, the phoneme → word links will tend to cause words phonologically related to the target to enter the activated cohort. A malapropism occurs on those (rare) occasions when such a word ends up winning the competition, presumably through weakness of the appropriate word → phoneme connections, or a higher initial activation level for the substituted word or its constituents, or just random noise (see Ellis, 1985, for a more extended discussion). The positive feedback loops that develop between each activated word node and its constituent phoneme nodes also account for other properties of speech errors, such as the bias against non-lexical productions in errors of phoneme sequencing (Dell, 1985, Stemberger, 1985).

An alternative account of malapropisms and other interactions between phonological form and lexical selection relies on assuming separate iP → CF and CF → oP pathways linked either by a common sub-lexical P-buffer (Model 4), or by a sublexical oP → iP → oP loop (Model 3), in which phonological patterns, once generated, are often maintained for a second or two prior to articulation. If one assumes that the iP → CF lexicon is sometimes used to refresh and/or repair the contents of the buffer/loop, perhaps when partial forgetting of phonological attributes has occurred, then a malapropism may arise as a result of a *recognition* error. In addition, if one uses a separate input lexicon to *check* the contents of the buffer/loop (cf. Baars *et al*'s, 1975, 'prearticulatory editing' process) then post-lexical losses or exchanges in phonological attributes will be less likely to be detected when the result is a word than when it is a non-word: a rationale both for malapropisms, and for the general lexical bias effect.

In short, there is nothing in the speech error data that requires a common lexicon.

The phonological representation of word sequences

So far there seems to be no evidence positively favouring a common-lexicon model, but several fragments favouring separate pathways. If we take them seriously, that narrows the original theoretical spectrum to Models 3 and 4. The difficulty with testing Model 4 is that it requires us to be specific about what the sublexical mechanism shared by the two pathways might be. In this section, I shall examine just one candidate for the role: the phonological 'buffer' store implicated in span-type tasks. I have already noted that proponents of a single P-buffer can, and to some extent have, treated it as an input buffer, an output buffer, or a common buffer. I want now to argue that the span data are in fact better accounted for by two 'buffer' stores, each with substantial capacity for the representation of phonological sequence, that one is an iP buffer and one an oP buffer, and that they and the iP → oP and oP → iP pathways linking them comprise a sub-vocal rehearsal loop with storage capacity.

Let us begin with the data on which Baddeley, Lewis and Vallar (1984) base their recent characterization of the 'articulatory loop'.

With *visual presentation*, span for ordered recall is reduced by increasing either the phonological similarity or the spoken length of the words. Irrelevant concurrent articulation ('suppression') during presentation also impairs recall and eliminates the effects of similarity and word length. Recall is also somewhat impaired by irrelevant auditory input, especially of words phonologically similar to the to-be-remembered sequence.

With *auditory presentation*, suppression has little effect if concurrent with presentation only. But when maintained throughout recall as well, it more dramatically impairs recall, and eliminates an effect of word length. The effect of phonological similarity on recall is, however, not eliminated by suppression throughout presentation and recall.

Baddeley *et al.* (1984) interpret this pattern in terms of a single phonological buffer (or 'P-buffer', as I am calling it). Phonological similarity effects reflect the form of coding in the buffer. Information enters the P-buffer either *directly* (i.e. without lexical mediation) and *automatically* from auditory input or, via an *optional* 'articulatory' *translation* process (presumably part-lexical), from visual input. Information in the P-buffer can also be refreshed or recycled by means of an optional 'articulatory' *rehearsal* process. This is what makes the P-buffer part of an articulatory *loop*. Loss of information in the P-buffer is assumed to be sufficiently rapid relative to standard rates of presentation and recall that normal performance in span tasks depends heavily on maintenance rehearsal via the articulatory loop. A 'suppression' task preempts both the articulatory rehearsal process and the articulatory translation process. (Indeed, these appear to be conceived of as identical, in a sense unclear to me, as they involve different transcodings.) The effect of suppression on a visual sequence is to deny it significant representation in the P-buffer, so that the residual level of recall is largely mediated by non-phonological mechanisms (see Monsell, 1984, for discussion of these) immune to the influence of phonological similarity and word length. An auditory sequence automatically gets represented in the P-buffer (and hence always exhibits P-similarity effects), but is denied the benefits of rehearsal via the loop as long as suppression continues. This is supposed to explain the difference between the effects of suppression during presentation only and throughout presentation and recall. (It is, however, unclear to me how the sequence is assumed to be maintained during presentation without rehearsal if it cannot be adequately maintained during recall without rehearsal, given that presentation rate is typically comparable to the rate of recall.) Word length effects arise during the articulatory rehearsal process — because the longer it takes to 'articulate' words internally, the fewer can be rehearsed in unit time. They are thus abolished by suppression.

A two-buffer interpretation of the same data

Though iP and oP buffers represent information in codes specialized for speech input and speech output respectively, 'phonologically similar' items will have similar codes in either buffer. Hence similarity effects can arise from deterioration of information in either buffer. What about word length and suppression effects?

Version 1. This follows Baddeley *et al*'s account in attributing word-length effects to the rate of rehearsal, though now in an iP → oP → iP loop, and suppression effects to the preempting of this process. However, when 'suppression' is required during auditory presentation but not recall, the sequence can be held in the iP buffer (to which it has automatic access) until the end of the list, and is then cycled through the iP → oP → iP loop for maintenance during recall, which produces a word length effect. The effects of irrelevant auditory input on visual span are due to the injection of irrelevant information into the rehearsal loop via its automatic access to the iP buffer.

Version 2. In this version the effect of word length is attributed purely to the oP buffer, whose capacity is assumed to depend on the phonological complexity of the words,[7] (whereas the capacity of the iP buffer might, like a tape loop, be more a matter of auditory elapsed time). The suppression task preempts much of the capacity of the oP pathway, including the oP buffer, and thus interacts with word length, as well as blocking use of the oP ↔ iP loop for rehearsal. Hence word length effects will be attenuated by suppression, as will recall, except in the case of an auditory sequence held in the iP buffer during presentation and then transferred to the oP buffer after suppression stops prior to recall. According to this version, the effects of irrelevant speech input on visual recall (Salame and Baddeley, 1982) must be attributed to a relatively automatic iP → oP link. However, surely with practice one could learn to decouple this link. Recall how well simultaneous translators seem to deal with simultaneous input and output sequences.

So far I have argued that a two-buffer model can deal with Baddeley *et al*'s data at least as well as their model. Now I want to argue that the two-buffer model has a distinct advantage when one examines data from other sources. The most important observation is that neurological impairment of short-term memory for sequence seems to come in a variety of forms difficult to explain with a single buffer, but interpretable in terms of coupled input and output buffers.

Allport (1984b) reports a patient (RC) who, though severely impaired in repetition span (zero recall of a 4 digit list) and markedly dysfluent in spontaneous speech, exhibits much better performance on a 'matching-span' task. In this task, an auditory sequence of words is presented, at about one word a second, followed after two seconds by a second sequence either in the same order or with two words reversed. Subjects must decide which, and normal span is around 6 digits; RC achieved error-free performance up to at least 4 digits, suggestive of preservation of an input buffer, coupled with impairment of an output system.[8]

In contrast, Shallice and Butterworth's (1977) JB, Allport's (1984b) JD, and Caramazza *et al*'s (1981) MC all exhibit relatively fluent spontaneous production, i.e. relatively well-ordered phonemic clauses of normal length, coupled with a dramatic impairment in repetition span and word-order deficits in comprehension. Allport (1984b) found that in JD, at least, this was accompanied by marked impairment of matching span and unusually marked effects of articulatory suppression on repetition span, even when suppression was required only during presentation. This is compatible with an impaired input system, from which information can only be retained if transferred immediately to an intact oP system, unless the latter is pre-empted by the suppression task.

It is also worthy of note that, according to Allport (personal communication), matching span, which I assume to be mediated largely by the iP buffer, is not influenced by word length in normal subjects, even though the retention intervals are comparable to repetition span. For the two-buffer account, this suggests that effects of word length are to be attributed to use of the oP buffer *per se* (as in Version 2 above) rather than to the subject needing to use the iP ↔ oP loop for maintenance via a duration-dependent rehearsal process (as in Version 1). Another observation more easily interpretable in terms of separate iP and oP buffers is that of Cheng (1974). He had subjects recall visual letter sequences using names different from the (equally appropriate) names they simultaneously heard ('bee', 'kay' 'gee' versus 'bah' 'kah', 'gah') and obtained dissociable effects of both 'auditory' and 'articulatory' similarity.

My conclusion is that the data on repetition and matching span tasks can now only be accommodated by a model with at least two sub-lexical 'phonological buffers'. The most natural interpretation of these, though not the only one (see Footnote 8) is as separate but linked capacities for the representation of phonological sequence in speech input and output processing pathways respectively. To that extent, these data are compatible with Model 3, elaborated to permit representation of *sequences* of syllables or words within the separate input and output pathways. Let us now consider in more detail the nature of the iP → oP and oP → iP linkages in Model 3.

The nature of the oP → iP link

Recall that in Monsell and Banich's priming experiments, silently mouthing a word primed later identification of it just as much as saying it aloud, while other phonology-generation tasks had a somewhat weaker effect. There is at least one other situation in which mouthed output has been found to have an effect mimicking auditory input. It involves modality and suffix effects in immediate serial recall. Typically, the last item (or two) of an auditory sequence is better recalled than the corresponding items of a visual sequence (the modality effect) and this advantage is eliminated by an irrelevant spoken suffix (the suffix effect). This pattern has traditionally been attributed to recovery of the last item of the spoken sequence from a sensory, modality-specific auditory store (PAS) with a long trace persistend compared to its analogue in the visual system. (See Crowder, 1983, for review).

This picture has been complicated by a number of findings (see Campbell, Chap 7, for discussion). Among them is the discovery by Nairne and Walters (1983) and by Greene and Crowder (1984) that lists and suffixes visually presented, but *actively, though silently, mouthed* by the subject, yield auditory-like recency and suffix effects just like those obtained if the subject says them aloud. On the other hand, Nairne and Pusen (1984) found that merely imagining the experimenter saying the items had no such effect. In a recent experiment in my laboratory,[9] a similar contrast was observed. Subjects recalled a list of words which they had also to monitor for a rhyming pair. Though phonological coding was thus enforced, an auditory-like recency effect was observed only when the subjects were also required to mouth the words silently as they were presented.

To accommodate his and Nairne's results, Crowder (1983) has suggested that there may be two internal pathways sending information from speech production to input processing modules: an inner pathway transmitting a relatively abstract phonological code, and an outer pathway sending information from processes determining articulatory gestures to a more peripheral mechanism for the perceptual analysis of articulatory gestures (whether heard or seen). The precategorical 'auditory' store is thus replaced by a store specific to 'speech input' features and located in the input pathway between the points at which the inner and outer loops make contact with it. I propose to adopt Crowder's proposal as an elaboration of Model 3 (see Figure 2). The inner oP → iP link would constitute one half of the iP ↔ oP rehearsal loop tapped by span-type tasks and discussed in the previous section. It may be activated by any task requiring generation of an oP code, and does not require generation of articulatory gestures *per se*. It may be relevant that Baddeley and Wilson (1985) have observed the word-length effect they believe to be diagnostic of the 'articulatory loop', together with normal span and phonological similarity effects, in dysarthric patients incapable of articulation. Activation of the outer link, in contrast,

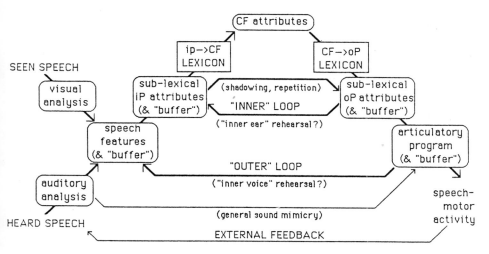

Figure 2. A tentative conclusion: Model 3 elaborated to show 'inner' and 'outer' oP → iP routes, and 'buffer' stores. (For discussion of the articulatory program buffer, not discussed in this chapter, see Monsell, 1986.)

requires generation of commands for articulatory gestures (as in silent mouthing) not merely the generation of an oP code. Presumably many tasks prompting 'phonological' processing of iO or CF input (e.g. reading, writing, syllable counting, phoneme monitoring, rhyme judgements and, perhaps, 'auditory imagining') do not usually generate articulatory commands in skilled literate language users. It is possible that the difference between activating and not activating the 'outer' loop corresponds to the phenomenal distinction between the 'inner voice' and the 'inner ear', to which Baddeley and Lewis (1981) have drawn attention, experienced during internal processing of phonology.

The nature of the iP → oP link

Model 3 assumes (as do all of Models 2–6) a non-semantic but phonology-specific link from speech input to output processes, an iP → oP link. Presumably it is this link that is impaired in (at least one type of) conduction aphasia, and preserved in the absence of the semantic link in the transcortical aphasias (McCarthy and Warrington, 1984). One question about this link is to what extent it includes a lexical, or word-specific, component. Two phenomena seem especially relevant to this question.

Selective impairment of non-word repetition

It is frequently observed that patients with speech repetition difficulties have considerably more difficulty in repeating non-words than words of equivalent phonological complexity (e.g. McCarthy and Warrington, 1984; Caramazza, Miceli and Villa, 1986; Caplan, Vanier and Baker, 1986). By itself this is unsurprising, since for words, semantic mediation between input and output is presumably available to support production of an oP code. But if semantic mediation were the only difference, one might then expect this pattern to be invariably associated with the occurrence of semantic paraphasias, which sometimes it is not (Carammaza et al., 1986; Caplan et al., 1986). Moreover, Warrington (1975) has reported patients with a greater auditory repetition span for words than for non-words, even though these were words they could neither comprehend nor discriminate from non-words.

Given separate iP → CF and CF → oP pathways, one interpretation (e.g. Patterson, 1986) is that words are better repeated because of the existence of a *lexical* (but non-semantic) iP → oP link, in addition to any sublexical iP → oP mapping. In recent versions of the logogen model, this lexical route assumes the form of direct connections between auditory input logogens and phonological output logogens (e.g. Patterson and

Shewell, 1987; Howard and Franklin, Chap 16). (As I have already noted, this depiction turns logogens into declarative representors of phonological word-form, rather than, as in earlier conceptions, mere inter-domain 'switches', or evidence-accumulators.) One may restate this interpretation more 'procedurally' by saying that — just as O → P transcoding appears to involve both lexical and sub-lexical mappings (Coltheart, 1985), so the direct iP → oP link involves both lexical and sub-lexical mappings.

There is an alternative possibility. Suppose that the architecture of the CF → oP pathway is as hypothesised in the interactive activation models of Dell (1985) and Stemberger (1985), with word (or morpheme) nodes activated not only top-down, by CF nodes, but bottom-up by oP sub-lexical (e.g. phoneme) nodes. We now add to this architecture links from sub-lexical iP to sub-lexical oP nodes. Activation arriving over this route will recruit activation from oP word nodes if the pattern of activation matches the phonological form of words available in the CF → oP pathway. If iP → oP transmission is degraded, this recruitment will give an advantage to words (much as it produces a lexical bias in errors) even with no direct link between iP word nodes and oP word nodes. In other words, lexical superiority in repetition does not necessarily require a direct lexical but non-semantic link between iP and oP codes.

Phonemic cueing

The naming of a picture or completion of a definition can be helped by cueing with the initial sound of the word or a phonemically similar word in both normals (e.g. Bowles and Poon, 1985) and anomic patients (Howard and Orchard-Lisle, 1984). It has been suggested, by Butterworth (1983) for example, that this is problematic for a model assuming separate iP → CF and CF → oP lexical routes: how can iP and CF information *combine* to select an oP word candidate? But there are at least three possible accounts within the framework of Model 3.

(1) Partial activation of a lexical iP → oP link. One account relies on a lexical component of the iP → oP link, as proposed above. Stated in logogen-terminology: partial activation of input logogens resonating to a particular onset sound is assumed to result in partial activation of the linked output logogens, such activation combining with the otherwise inadequate activation due to CF input.

(2) Partial activation via the iP → CF → oP route. It could be argued that the phonemic cue partially activates matching lexical entries in the iP → CF pathway, and this in turn further constrains the CF code so that a more accurate semantic representation is transmitted to the CF → oP pathway. This proposal may excite scepticism because it requires a model of word identification in which it is assumed that activation of *meanings*

occurs at a point during the identification process when a large cohort of lexical candidates still remains in contention. However, early semantic activation of this kind is an assumption of current versions of the 'cohort' model for spoken word recognition for reasons unrelated to phonemic cueing. Sceptics are referred to forthcoming evidence on semantic priming by cohort members discussed by Marslen-Wilson (in press).

(3) The Dell/Stemberger interactive account. The extension to phonemic cueing is straightforward (see also Ellis, 1985): presentation of a cue such as the initial sound partially activates corresponding sublexical nodes in the output pathway via a strictly non-lexical iP → oP link: such activation reinforces positive feedback loops within the production network favouring word candidates containing that phoneme in word-initial position; as a result the activation level of the appropriate word node will rise more rapidly, giving it an advantage in the competition.

Hence both the word repetition advantage and phonemic cueing *can* be explained by assuming a lexical component to the iP → oP link, but they need not be if processing in the CF → oP pathway is assumed to be interactive.

Summary of the argument

Silent generation, or preparation for generation, of phonology influences later auditory identification of words. This rejects models with less intimate connections between speech input and output processing than Model 3. The common-lexicon models (5 and 6) offer no account of why such priming differs in degree for different phonology-generation conditions, or sometimes fails. They also appear to predict more interference between concurrent speaking and listening than is actually observed. More data on both points is sorely needed, but the present balance of evidence favours Models 3 or 4. Suitable evidence on neuropsychological dissociation of word production and comprehension, though potentially powerful, has yet to be published. Nor are speech errors as informative as some have thought.[10]

Can we discriminate between Models 3 and 4? Data on short-term retention of word sequences cannot be accommodated by a single phonological buffer shared by input and output processes, but are compatible with separate (but linked) capacities for sequence representation in the input and the output pathways. Model 3 is thus the tentative victor, though it certainly remains possible that there are other shared sub-lexical mechanisms, such as those to do with timing (see Keele, Chap 21).

The last issue considered is the nature of the non-CF connection between output and input pathways required by Model 3 and perhaps Model 4. The auditory-like effects of silent mouthing suggest two levels of connection ('inner' and 'outer') from the output pathway to the input pathway. Phonemic cueing and the advantage of words over non-words in repetition deficits require either a lexical but non-semantic component to the connection from the input to the output pathway, or the attribution of an 'interactive' architecture to the output pathway.

A brief coda on orthographic input and output pathways

Much the same spectrum of possible relations as we have contemplated for the relation between iP → CF and CF → oP pathways may be applied, *mutatis mutandis*, to the relationship between iO → CF and CF → oO pathways. There is additional complexity because of the availability of phonologically mediated iO → P → CF and CF → P → cF routes (at least for regular words in alphabetic or syllabic scripts). Allowing for this, empirical tests may in principle be developed analagous to those I have reviewed for speech.

At present, the evidence is thin. Coltheart and Funnell (Chap 15) carefully examine data on the relationship between patterns of surface dyslexia and surface dysgraphia, and tentatively argue in favour of a common lexicon for orthographic input and output. On the other hand, Monsell and Banich (in preparation) and Monsell (in press) have carried out orthographic variants of the repetition priming experiment discussed earlier in this chapter. They tested for priming of visual lexical decision by prior blind writing of the word in response to a definition and/or dictation. The results have been mixed, but in one experiment using the same words, priming tasks and design as their auditory LDT experiments Monsell and Banich (Experiment 2) found that blind writing produced no significant priming of visual LDT (see Table 1b). I have therefore argued (no less tentatively than Coltheart and Funnell!) in favour of separate pathways with either no, or a much weaker, oO → iO link than the phonological analogue. Such a conclusion also seems to be favoured by a fragment of evidence from Tenney (1980) supporting the common intuition that writing and inspecting a word of whose spelling one is unsure improves one's probability of ending up with the correct spelling, something that should not happen if the visual input merely provides access to the same store of orthographic knowledge as provided the candidate spelling in the first place.

Acknowledgements

Drafts of this paper evoked (provoked?) more words of commentary from Alan Allport, Max Coltheart, Karalyn Patterson, and an anonymous referee than there are in the paper. I am very grateful to them for their efforts (even if not entirely successful) to preserve me from inconsistency, ignorance and folly.

Notes

[1] This point was brought forcibly home to me by the comments of Alan Allport, Max Coltheart, Karalyn Patterson and Tim Shallice on the first draft of this chapter, in which I used a diagrammatic notation (see Monsell, 1985) that I alleged was neutral with respect to the 'lexical access' issues mentioned above. Mature reflection has forced me to concede that it leant in the direction of the 'procedural' conception of the lexicon *almost* as much as their own diagrams embody a 'declarative' conception.

[2] Of course, it is perfectly *possible*, within the declarative framework, to contemplate one iP lexicon used for and activated by iP → CF transcoding, and another for iP → oO transcoding. But no-one does.

[3] 'The phonological store appears involved in short-term tasks such as auditory verbal span, and is useful in comprehension of spoken speech. This system does not seem to play an important role in the production of speech.' (Vallar and Baddeley, 1984, p. 160.)

[4] For example, Gipson interprets his finding in terms of a common lexicon, arguing that repetition priming is associated with a process, required for perceptual identification, called 'verification', that 'integrates' the accessed P word-form with active auditory codes. Verification is assumed not to occur during articulatory generation from the same word form. The problem is that this provides no account of why Monsell and Banich's phonology-generation tasks did prime auditory identification.

[5] A similar case (HN) has now been reported in more detail by Kohn and Friedman (1986), whose account of him also provides an excellent illustration of the 'declarative' conception of the phonological input lexicon discussed earlier. However, since HN is impaired in some naming tasks, he evidently does not

[6] Howard (personal communication) has recently obtained evidence that one of the patients whom he describes elsewhere in this volume may be an instance of *dissociation* between patterns of receptive and productive loss for spoken words.

[7] This assumption is at odds with Baddeley, Thomson and Buchanan's (1975) claim that the word-length effect is a function of the words' spoken duration not the number of syllables or phonemes, and their estimate, on this basis, from measures of overt rehearsal rate, that the capacity of the articulatory loop is about 1.5 seconds' worth of speech. However, their claim depends critically upon one experiment: Baddeley *et al.*'s Exp IV, which used a vocabulary of only ten (rather odd) words. The status of their speech rate measure also seems problematic: people *can* speak at about twice the rate they measure (Landauer, 1962). If what they measure is not maximum speech rate, what is it?

[8] Allport (1984b), although offering a two-buffer interpretation, prefers to interpret what I describe as an iP buffer, as part of a common P-system. That even JB exhibits frequent phonemic paraphasias argues, says Allport, for a disturbance of phonological representation common to both input and output. An alternative possibility is that JB's production system is in itself unimpaired, but her speech suffers from a loss of the support normally provided by the oP → iP → oP rehearsal loop, because of damage to the iP component.

[9] An undergraduate project carried out by Mellany Ambrose and Emma Weisblatt.

[10] It goes without saying that other sources of evidence may prove to be useful. For instance, we might find that word recognition and word production operate with different units. It is possible, for example, that while a process of morphological composition occurs during the production of regularly affixed forms, auditory input is matched to a lexicon of lexemes without decomposition (see Butterworth, 1983, for further discussion).

References

Allport, D. A. (1980a). Patterns and actions. In G. Claxton (Ed.) *Cognitive Psychology: New Directions*. London: Routledge and Kegan Paul, pp. 26–64.

Allport, D. A. (1980b). Attention and performance. In G. Claxton (Ed.) *Cognitive Psychology: New Directions*. London: Routledge and Kegan Paul, pp. 112–53.

Allport, D. A. (1984a). Speech production and comprehension: one lexicon or two? In W. Prinz and A. F. Sanders (Eds) *Cognition and motor processes*. Berlin: Springer, pp. 209–28.

Allport, D. A. (1984b). Auditory-verbal short-term memory and conduction aphasia. In H. Bouma and D. G. Bouwhuis (Eds) *Attention and performance*, Vol 10. London: Erlbaum, pp. 313–25.

Allport, D. A. (1985). Distributed memory, modular sub-systems and dysphasia. In S. Newman and R. Epstein (Eds) *Current perspectives in dysphasia*. Edinburgh: Churchill Livingstone.

Baars, B. J., Motley, M. T. and MacKay, D. G. (1975). Output editing for lexical status in artificially elicited slips of the tongue. *Journal of Verbal Learning and Verbal Behavior*, **14**, 382–91.

Baddeley, A. D. (1983). Working memory. *Philosophical Transactions of the Royal Society of London*, **B302**, 311–24.

Baddeley, A. D., Thomson, N. and Buchanan, M. (1975). Word length and the structure of short-term memory. *Journal of Verbal Learning and Verbal Behavior*, **14**, 575–89.

Baddeley, A. D. and Lewis, V. (1981). Inner active processes in reading: the inner voice, the inner ear, and the inner eye. In A. M. Lesgold and C. A. Perfetti (Eds) *Interactive processes in reading*. Hillsdale, NJ: Erlbaum, pp. 107–29.

Baddeley, A. D., Lewis, V. J. and Vallar, G. (1984). Exploring the articulatory loop. *Quarterly Journal of Experimental Psychology*, **36A**, 233–52.

Baddeley, A. D. and Wilson, B. (1985). Phonological coding and short-term memory in patients without speech. *Journal of Memory and Language*, **24**, 490–502.

Bramwell (1897/1984) Illustrative cases of aphasia. *Lancet*, No. 1, 1256–9 (reprinted in *Cognitive Neuropsychology*, **1**, 249–58).

Bowles, N. L. and Poon, L. W. (1985). Effects of priming on word retrieval. *Journal of Experimental Psychology: Learning, Memory and Cognition*, **11**, 272–83.

Butterworth, B. (1983). Lexical representation. In B. Butterworth (Ed.) *Language production*, Vol 2. London: Academic Press, pp. 257–94.

Caplan, D., Vanier, M. and Baker, C. (1986). A case-study of reproduction conduction aphasia. *Cognitive Neuropsychology*, **3**, 99–128.

Caramazza, A., Basili, A. G., Koller, J. J. and Berndt, R. S. (1981). An investigation of repetition and language processing in a case of conduction aphasia. *Brain and Language*, **14**, 235–71.

Caramazza, A., Miceli, G. and Villa, G. (1986). The role of the (output) phonological buffer in reading, writing and repetition. *Cognitive Neuropsychology*, **3**, 37–76.

Cheng (1974). Different roles of acoustic and articulatory information in short-term memory. *Journal of Experimental Psychology*, **103**, 614–18.

Colle, H. A. and Welsh, A. (1976). Acoustic masking in primary memory. *Journal of Verbal Learning and Verbal Behavior*, **15**, 17–32.

Coltheart, M. (1985). Cognitive neuropsychology and the study of reading. In M. I. Posner and O. Marin (Eds) *Attention and Performance XI*. Hillsdale, NJ: Erlbaum, pp. 3–37.

Conrad, R. (1964). Acoustic confusions in immediate memory. *British Journal of Psychology*, **55**, 75–84.

Conrad, R. (1970). Short-term memory processes in the deaf. *British Journal of Psychology*, **61**, 179–95.

Cooper, W. E. (1979). *Speech perception and production: studies in selective adaptation*. Norwood, NJ: Ablex.

Crowder, R. G. (1983). The purity of auditory memory. *Philosophical Transactions of the Royal Society of London*, **B302**, 251–65.

De Groot, A. M. (1984). Primed lexical decision: combined effects of the proportion of related prime-target pairs and the stimulus-onset asynchrony of prime and target. *Quarterly Journal of Experimental Psychology*, **36A**, 253–80.

Dell, G. S. (1985). Positive feedback in hierarchical connectionist models: applications to language production. *Cognitive Science*, **9**, 3–23.

Ellis, A. W. (1985). The production of spoken words: a cognitive neuropsychological perspective. In A. W. Ellis (Ed.) *Progress in the psychology of language*, Vol 2, London: Erlbaum, pp. 107–45.

Fay, D. A. and Cutler, A. (1977). Malapropisms and the structure of the mental lexicon. *Linguistic Inquiry*, **8**, 505–20.

Forster, K. I. (1976). Accessing the mental lexicon. In R. J. Wales and E. Walker (Eds) *New approaches to language mechanisms*. Amsterdam: North-Holland, pp. 257–87.

Forster, K. I. (1981). Priming and the effects of sentence and lexical constraints on naming time: evidence for autonomous lexical processing. *Quarterly Journal of Experimental Psychology*, **33A**, 465–95.

Gernsbacher, M. A. (1984). Resolving 20 years of inconsistent interactions between lexical familiarity and orthography, concreteness and polysemy. *Journal of Experimental Psychology: General*, **113**, 256–81.

Gerver, D. (1976). Empirical studies of simultaneous translation. In R. W. Brislin (Ed.) *Translation: applications and research*. New York: Gardner Press, pp. 165–207.

Gerver, D. and Sinaiko, H. W. (Eds) (1978). *Language interpretation and communication.* New York: Plenum.

Gipson, P. (1984). A study of the long term priming of auditory word recognition. Unpublished Ph.D dissertation, University of Cambridge.

Gipson, P. (1986). The production of phonology and auditory priming. *British Journal of Psychology*, **77**, 359–375.

Glucksberg, S., Kreuz, R. J. and Rho S. (1986). Context can constrain lexical access: implications for models of language comprehension. *Journal of Experimental Psychology: Learning, Memory and Cognition*, **12**, 323–355.

Gordon, P. and Meyer, D. E. (1984). Perceptual-motor processing of phonetic features. *Journal of Experimental Psychology: Human Perception and Performance*, **10**, 153–78.

Greene, R. L. and Crowder, R. G. (1984). Modality and suffix effects in the absence of auditory stimulation. *Journal of Verbal Learning and Verbal Behavior*, **23**, 371–82.

Held, R. (1965). Plasticity in sensorimotor systems. *Scientific American*, **213**, (Nov), 84–94.

Howard, D. and Orchard-Lisle, V. (1984). On the origin of semantic errors in naming: evidence from the case of a global aphasic. *Cognitive Neuropsychology*, **1**, 163–90.

Jacoby, L. L. (1983). Remembering the data: analyzing interactive processes in reading. *Journal of Verbal Learning and Verbal Behavior*, **22**, 485–508.

James, C. T. (1975). The role of semantic information in lexical decisions. *Journal of Experimental Psychology: Human Perception and Performance*, **104**, 130–6.

Kohn, S. E. and Friedman, R. B. (1986). Word meaning deafness: a phonological-semantic dissociation. *Cognitive Neuropsychology*, **3**, 291–308.

Lackner, J. R. (1974). Speech production: evidence for corollary discharge stabilization of perceptual mechanisms. *Perceptual and Motor Skills*, **39**, 899–902.

Landauer, T. K. (1962). Rate of implicit speech. *Perceptual and Motor Skills*, **15**, 646.

Liberman, A. M., Cooper, F. S., Shankweiler, D. P. and Studdert-Kennedy, M. (1967). Perception of the speech code. *Psychological Review*, **74**, 431–61.

Liberman, A. M. and Mattingly, I. G. (1985). The motor theory of speech revisited. *Cognition*, **21**, 1–36.

Marslen-Wilson, W. (in press). Parallel processing in spoken word recognition. *Cognition*.

Marslen-Wilson, W. and Tyler, L. K. (1980). The temporal structure of spoken language understanding. *Cognition*, **8**, 1–71.

McCarthy, R. and Warrington, E. K. (1984). A two-route model of speech production: evidence from aphasia. *Brain*, **107**, 463–85.

McClelland, J. L. (in press). How we use what we know in reading. In M. Coltheart (Ed.) *Attention and Performance XII.*

McClelland, J. L. and Elman, J. L. (1986). The TRACE model of speech perception. *Cognitive Psychology*, **18**, 1–86.

McClelland, J. L. and Rumelhart, D. E. (1981). An interactive activation model of context effects in letter perception. *Psychological Review*, **88**, 375–407.

Menn, L. (1983). Development of articulatory, phonetic, and phonological abilities. In B. Butterworth (Ed.) *Language production*, Vol 2. London: Academic Press, pp. 3–50.

Meyer, D. E., Gordon, P. C. and Benson, P. (in preparation). Inhibitory effects of articulatory motor programming on speech perception.

Monsell, S. (1984). Components of working memory underlying verbal skills: a 'distributed capacities' view. In H. Bouma and D. G. Bouwhuis (Eds) *Attention and Performance*, Vol 10. London: Erlbaum, pp. 327–50.

Monsell, S. (1985). Repetition and the lexicon. In A. W. Ellis (Ed.) *Progress in the psychology of language*, Vol 2. London: Erlbaum, pp. 147–95.

Monsell, S. (1986). Programming of complex sequences: evidence from the timing of rapid speech and other productions. In H. Heuer and C. Fromm (Eds) *Generation and modulation of action patterns*. Experimental Brain Research Series 15. Berlin: Springer, pp. 72–86.

Monsell S. (in press). Non-visual orthographic processing and the orthographic input lexicon. In M. Coltheart (Ed.) *Attention and Performance XII*. London: Erlbaum.

Monsell, S. and Banich, M. T. (in preparation). Repetition priming across input and output modalities: implications for the functional anatomy of the lexicon.

Morton, J. (1968). Considerations of grammar and computation in language behaviour. In J. C. Catford (Ed.) *Studies in language and language behavior*. Progress Report IV, US Dept. of Education.

Morton, J. (1969). Interaction of information in word recognition. *Psychological Review*, **76**, 165–78.

Morton, J. (1970). A functional model for memory. In D. A. Norman (Ed.) *Models of human memory*. New York: Academic Press, pp. 203–54.

Morton, J. (1979). Facilitation in word recognition: experiments causing change in the logogen model. In P. A. Kolers, M. Wrolstad and H. Bouma (Eds) *Processing of visible language*. New York: Plenum.

Nairne, J. S. and Walters V. L. (1983). Silent mouthing produces modality- and suffix-like effects. *Journal of Verbal Learning and Verbal Behavior*, **22**, 475–83.

Nairne, J. S. and Pusen, C. (1984). Serial recall of imagined voices. *Journal of Verbal Learning and Verbal Behavior*, **23**, 331–42.

Ostry, D., Moray, N. and Marks, G. (1976). Attention, practice and semantic targets. *Journal of Experimental Psychology: Human Perception and Performance*, **2**, 326–36.

Patterson, K. E. and Shewell, C. (1987). Speak and spell: dissociations and word-class effects. In M. Coltheart, R. Job and G. Sartori (Eds) *The cognitive neuropsychology of language*. Hillsdale, NJ: Erlbaum.

Patterson, K. E. (1986). Lexical but non-semantic spelling? *Cognitive Neuropsychology*, **3**, 341–67.

Porter, R. J. and Castellanos, F. X. (1980). Speech production measures of speech perception: rapid shadowing of VCV syllables. *Journal of the Acoustical Society of America*, **67**, 1349–56.

Porter, R. J. and Lubker, J. F. (1980). Rapid reproduction of vowel–vowel sequences: evidence for a fast and direct acoustic-motor linkage in speech. *Journal of Speech and Hearing Research*, **23**, 593–602.

Salame, P. and Baddeley, A. D. (1982). Disruption of short-term memory by unattended speech: implications for the structure of working memory. *Journal of Verbal Learning and Verbal Behavior*, **21**, 150–64.

Shallice, T. (1987). Impairments of semantic processing: multiple dissociations. In M. Coltheart, R. Job and G. Sartori (Eds) *The cognitive neuropsychology of language*. Hillsdale, NJ: Erlbaum, pp. 111–127.

Shallice, T. and Butterworth, B. (1977). Short-term memory impairment and spontaneous speech. *Neuropsychologia*, **15**, 729–35.

Shallice, T., McLeod, P. and Lewis, K. (1985). Isolating cognitive modules with the dual-task paradigm: Are speech perception and production separate process. *Quarterly Journal of Experimental Psychology*, **37A**, 507–32.

Sperling, G. and Speelman, R. G. (1970). Acoustic similarity and auditory STM. In D. A. Norman (Ed.) *Models of human memory*. New York: Academic Press, pp. 151–202.

Sperry, R. W. (1950). Neural basis of the optokinetic response produced by visual inversion. *Journal of Comparative and Physiological Psychology*, **43**, 482–9.

Stemberger, J. P. (1985). An interactive-activation model of language production. In A. W. Ellis (Ed.) *Progress in the Psychology of Language*, Vol 1. London: Erlbaum, pp. 143–86.

Swinney, D. A. (1979). Lexical access during sentence comprehension. (Re)consideration of context effects. *Journal of Verbal Learning and Verbal Behavior*, **18**, 645–59.

Symonds, C. Aphasia. *Journal of Neurology, Neurosurgery and Psychiatry*, **16**, 1–6.

Taft, M., Hambly, G. and Kinoshita, S. (1986). Visual and auditory recognition of prefixed words. *Quarterly Journal of Experimental Psychology*, **38A**, 351–66.

Tenney, Y. J. (1980). Visual factors in spelling. In U. Frith (Ed.) *Cognitive factors in spelling*. London: Academic Press, pp. 215–29.

Vallar, G. and Baddeley, A. D. (1984). Fractionation of working memory: neuropsychological evidence for a phonological short-term store. *Journal of Verbal Learning and Verbal Behavior*, **23**, 151–61.

Warrington, E. K. (1975). The selective impairment of semantic memory. *Quarterly Journal of Experimental Psychology*, **27**, 635–57.

Yamadori, A. and Albert M. L. (1973). Word category aphasia. *Cortex*, **9**, 112–125.

15   Reading and writing: One lexicon or two?

Max Coltheart and Elaine Funnell

Abstract

In order for irregular words to be read or spelled correctly, it is argued that lexical codes must exist which specify exactly the orthographic components of individual words. The question with which this chapter is concerned is whether or not such codes are stored in independent orthographic lexicons for reading and spelling, or whether a single orthographic lexicon subserves both tasks.

An apparently straightforward prediction from a theory which postulates a single orthographic lexicon for reading and spelling is that equivalent impairments should be found in reading and spelling tasks in patients with acquired dyslexia and dysgraphia. We outline some basic problems inherent in this approach. First, only impairments in reading and spelling which arise within the orthographic lexical codes themselves provide evidence for adjudicating between the two theories. Second, the degree of consistency in performance across different tasks is difficult to assess if there is a non zero chance of guessing correctly, and if other variables such as word frequency affect performance.

Bearing these problems in mind, we studied the performance of a patient (HG) with acquired difficulties in reading and spelling. It was established first that HG's difficulties in reading and spelling originate within the orthographic lexical codes required by these tasks. Then, evidence was found which favoured the existence of a single lexicon of orthographic codes for reading and spelling: first an equivalent effect of word frequency in reading and spelling, and second, a set of words which showed consistent effects in reading and spelling, independent of word frequency.

LANGUAGE PERCEPTION AND PRODUCTION
ISBN 0-12-052750-2

Introduction

Many people concerned with modelling the mental processes employed in normal reading have proposed that, at least for reading aloud, two different processing procedures are available. Current conceptions of these so-called 'dual-route' models of oral reading are reviewed by, for example, Coltheart (1985), Henderson (1985) and Patterson and Morton (1985). The terms 'lexical' and 'non-lexical' are often used to refer to the two processing procedures. The non-lexical procedure for reading aloud depends upon the use of general rules specifying relationships between orthographic segments and their corresponding phonological forms. This system of rules has been viewed (e.g. by Coltheart, 1978) as operating solely at the level of phonemes (so that the correspondences used are between individual phonemes and their written representations) but it has become clear that larger units need also to be postulated (for review see, e.g. Coltheart, 1985 and Patterson and Morton, 1985). A crucial feature of the non-lexical procedure is that it will produce *incorrect* phonological forms when applied to 'irregular' or 'exception' words — those words which disobey the prevalent letter–sound relationships of the language. Thus, in English the application of standard rules would cause *pint* to be mispronounced as /pɪnt/ and *yacht* to be mispronounced as /jætʃt/.

Words such as these contain unique mappings from orthography to phonology — that is, mappings which are specific to the particular word. Since normal readers will succeed when asked to read aloud irregular words, they must have available a *word-specific* procedure for converting print to pronunciation — the lexical procedure, which depends upon access to word-specific information in a system of orthographic knowledge, an orthographic lexicon for reading. The lexical procedure can be used for reading all words (regular or irregular) but not for reading non-words, simply because non-words do not have lexical representations. The non-lexical procedure will produce correct responses when used with non-words or regular words, but will wrongly recode irregular words.

When an impaired reader reads *pint* as /pɪnt/ and *yacht* as /jætʃt/, as some do (for review see Patterson, Marshall and Coltheart, 1985), it is natural to suppose that the reader's impairment has led to failure to gain access to the orthographic lexicon for reading. Such failure prevents the use of the lexical procedure for reading, so there is no alternative but to use the non-lexical procedure — which, of course, yields errors when applied to irregular words. Thus, the distinction between lexical and non-lexical procedures for reading aloud may be used to describe not only intact but also disordered reading.

Precisely the same arguments apply to spelling. A non-lexical procedure for spelling, depending upon general rules specifying relationships between phonological segments and their corresponding orthographic forms, is postulated to account for the normal speller's ability to write non-words to dictation. This procedure would also yield correct spellings for some words, but would fail for words such as 'pint' or 'yacht'. Since normal spellers succeed in writing such words to dictation, a lexical (that is, word-specific) procedure for spelling is also postulated, and hence dual-route models for spelling have been developed (see, e.g. Ellis, 1982). Here the lexical procedure for spelling depends upon access to word-specific information in a system of orthographic knowledge, an orthographic lexicon for spelling.

When an impaired speller writes 'pint' as PYNTE or 'yacht' as YOT, as some do (see, e.g. Hatfield and Patterson, 1983; Coltheart, Masterson, Byng, Prior and Riddoch, 1983) it is natural to suppose that the speller's impairment has led to failure to gain access to the orthographic lexicon for spelling. Hence, just as for reading, the distinction between lexical and non-lexical procedures may be used to describe not only intact but also disordered spelling.

Thus, an orthographic lexicon for reading has been postulated, and also an orthographic lexicon for spelling. The question with which our chapter is concerned is whether or not these two lexicons are really only one. Is the orthographic lexical entry which must be accessed if *yacht* is to be read correctly the same entry that must be accessed if 'yacht' is to be spelled correctly (as proposed, for example, by Funnell, 1983a)? Or should we distinguish between an orthographic *input* lexicon used for reading printed words and an orthographic *output* lexicon used for producing printed words (as proposed, for example, by Coltheart, 1981)?

Figure 1 presents examples of both types of model. According to Model 1 (from Funnell, 1983a), a single set of orthographic codes is used for lexical reading and lexical spelling. In contrast, Model 2 (from Patterson and Shewell, 1987) distinguishes between an orthographic input lexicon (upon which lexical reading depends) and an orthographic output lexicon (upon which lexical spelling depends). The same contrast between the two models exists in the domain of phonology: Model 1 postulates a single set of phonological codes used both for recognizing and producing spoken words, whilst Model 2 distinguishes a phonological input lexicon from a phonological output lexicon.

How might one set about the task of empirical adjudication between these two radically different conceptions of the lexical representation of orthographic knowledge? There are various ways in which studies of

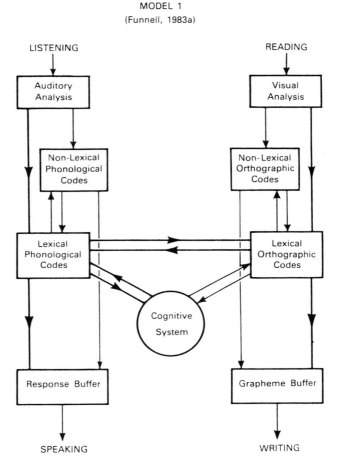

Figure 1. Two models of lexical organization. Model 1 is from Funnell (1983b). Model 2 is from Patterson and Shewell (1987).

reading and spelling in normal subjects might be of use here: some of these are discussed in detail in the chapter by Monsell. A second approach is to use neuropsychological evidence: it is this approach with which our chapter is concerned. The examples we have given earlier make it clear that, for some dyslexic patients, it is appropriate to characterise their impairment as specifically affecting lexical orthographic processing for reading. Equally, in some dysgraphic patients the impairment is one of lexical orthographic processing for spelling. What can we learn about the lexical representation

MODEL 2
(Patterson and Shewell, 1986)

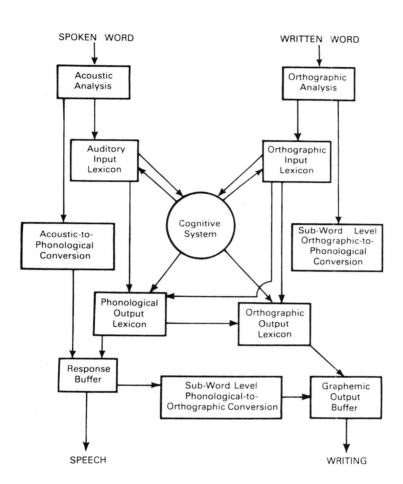

of orthographic knowledge by studying these forms of acquired dyslexia and dysgraphia? If it is suggested that there is a single source of knowledge subserving both lexical reading and lexical spelling (as is the case for Model 1), one might expect to see extremely close relationships between characteristics of reading and characteristics of spelling in patients with this form of dyslexia and this form of dysgraphia. In the extreme case, for example, if the reason why a patient fails to read certain words is because the orthographic entries needed for reading them have been destroyed, then on Model 1 (but not on Model 2), lexical spelling of precisely these words will necessarily also be impossible.

However, Model 1 does not require that impairments of lexical reading must *always* be associated with impairments of lexical spelling and vice versa: let us consider why not.

Surface dyslexia and surface dysgraphia as syndromes

We began by arguing that when a patient reads *pint* as /pɪnt/ or *yacht* as /jæʧt/, it is reasonable to interpret this as evidence of a failure of lexical orthographic processing for reading; and the term usually used to describe this kind of acquired dyslexia is 'surface dyslexia'. However, for any adequately detailed model of reading — and certainly for both Model 1 and Model 2 — there will be several very different ways in which lexical orthographic processing for reading can be impaired so as to yield regularization errors such as the ones we have just mentioned. Here, for example, are seven different patterns of impairment to lexical processes of Model 1, *any of which would result in dependence upon sub-lexical processes and so cause regularization errors in the reading aloud of irregular words*:

(1) Pathway from Visual Analysis to Lexical Orthographic codes impaired;

(2) Entries within Lexical Orthographic Codes inaccessible or deleted;

(3) Pathway from Lexical Orthographic Codes to Lexical Phonological Codes *and* pathway from Lexical Orthographic Codes to Cognitive System both impaired;

(4) Pathway from Lexical Orthographic Codes to Lexical Phonological Codes impaired *and* entries within the Cognitive System inaccessible or deleted;

(5) Pathway from Lexical Orthographic Codes to Lexical Phonological Codes *and* pathway from Cognitive System to Lexical Phonological Codes both impaired;

(6) Entries within Lexical Phonological Codes inaccessible or deleted;

(7) Pathway from Lexical Phonological Codes to Response Buffer impaired.

If surface dyslexia is defined as that form of acquired dyslexia in which regularization errors occur in reading aloud irregular words, then all seven of these patterns of impairment qualify as surface dyslexia. This would obviously be a peculiar stance to adopt. Why should one use a single syndrome label for patterns as diverse as (1), which is a visual input problem, and (6), which is an anomia not affecting any component of the language-processing system that directly concerns orthographic processing? But a more trenchant point can be made: to give all seven of these patterns the syndrome label 'surface dyslexia' is self-contradictory because, if one does so, surface dyslexia is no longer a syndrome, in the sense of a collection of two or more symptoms which invariable co-occur. There is *no* second symptom which will be seen in all seven variants of surface dyslexia. Anomic difficulties will be seen in variants (5), (6) and (7), but can be absent in the other variants; a defect of auditory comprehension will be present in variant (4) but can be absent in all other variants; and so on. The only thing all seven variants have in common is a single symptom, the regularization error. So if we use the term 'surface dyslexia' in all seven instances, the term no longer refers to a syndrome: it is referring only to a single symptom.

Exactly the same point can be made concerning surface dysgraphia. There are various loci within Model 1 at which impairments will produce such phonologically correct misspellings as 'yacht' → *yot*. No other symptom will be consistently present across these various impairment patterns; so surface dysgraphia will not be a syndrome, just a symptom.

Furthermore, precisely the same arguments can be made in relation to Model 2, concerning both surface dyslexia and surface dysgraphia. For each disorder, there are several different underlying patterns of impairment which are sufficient to produce the same reading or spelling symptom.

The general implication for cognitive neuropsychology of this line of reasoning is that we have probably gone as far as we can usefully go in thinking about language disorders in terms of syndromes, and that the time has come to replace this approach by one based on relating individual patients' patterns of symptoms to particular models of the language processing system. This issue is discussed further by Ellis (1987) and Coltheart (1987).

This issue is of central importance to our chapter. Earlier we made the point that Model 1 inclines one to expect to see close similarities in the reading and spelling patterns of patients with surface dyslexia and surface dysgraphia (because of the postulation of a common orthographic lexicon for reading and spelling). We also argued that the model does not require that these similarities always be observed. Consider the seven different patterns of impairment of Model 1 that would be expected to cause regularization errors in reading aloud. Of these seven, only *one* should have any effect on spelling: the second. Therefore, whether Model 1 predicts that a patient with surface dyslexia will exhibit surface dysgraphia depends upon the source of the surface dyslexia. If it is because at least some entries within the system of Lexical Orthographic Codes are inaccessible or deleted, then spelling must suffer too, because lexical spelling requires use of these entries. If, instead, the surface dyslexia corresponds to any of the other six patterns we identified earlier then, on Model 1, spelling can be intact.

Hence, for neuropsychological attempts to adjudicate between Model 1 and Model 2, it is not sufficient simply to study the spelling performance of any surface dyslexic, nor to study the reading performance of any surface dysgraphic. What one needs is to identify a surface dyslexic patient whose reading difficulties are at least sometimes caused by inability to access entries within an orthographic lexicon (rather than by any of the other six possible causes). If this patient's spelling were normal, this would be evidence against Model 1 and for Model 2. If, on the other hand, the patient were surface dysgraphic, this would favour Model 1 in the sense that this result is *required* by the model. However, the result is also compatible with Model 2: the patient may simply have two separate impairments, one affecting reading and the other spelling. The way forward here would be to try to determine whether or not there are detailed similarities between the way the patient reads and the way he spells, similarities of a kind that Model 1 predicts, but which are merely fortuitous given Model 2. For example, if it turned out that the set of words the patient cannot read is the same as the set of words he cannot spell, this would count strongly in favour of Model 1.

So identifying a patient as surface dyslexic will not suffice: we must go further and pinpoint the source of the surface dyslexia before we will know whether studies of this patient will be relevant to attempts to adjudicate between the two types of model of orthographic knowledge.

Differential diagnosis of subvarieties of surface dyslexia

Suppose one determines that a surface dyslexic has no anomia (for example, has intact picture naming and no word-finding problems in spontaneous speech). This is evidence against the presence of variants (5), (6) and (7) (all of which ought to be accompanied by anomia); and if spontaneous speech is in fact normal in all ways, that is evidence against the presence of variant (4). Here we would be left only with variants (1), (2) and (3) as possible interpretations of the patient's acquired dyslexia. One can do exactly the same kind of thing with Model 2: define all the variant patterns that will generate regularization errors, and then eliminate that subset in which anomia must be an accompanying symptom.

A second approach is to study reading *comprehension* rather than oral reading. Studies of reading comprehension in 'surface dyslexia' have revealed the existence of *homophone comprehension* errors. The patient, asked to give the meaning of single printed words, might define *brews* as 'an injury' (see, e.g. Coltheart *et al.*, 1983; Howard and Franklin, Chap 16). Here the patient has not fully negotiated the route from Visual Analysis to Cognitive System, and has had no alternative but to attempt to comprehend the *phonological form* yielded by non-lexical (or perhaps lexical) orthographic processing. This phonological form is, of course, ambiguous when the stimulus is a homophone. This symptom, the homophone confusion in reading comprehension, will not occur in variants (4), (5), (6) and (7), but will occur in variants (1), (2) and (3).

Suppose a patient does make homophone confusions of this kind. What can one do further, to distinguish which of variants 1, 2 and 3 is an appropriate characterization of the patient? A little. Consider the homophone confusion *bury* → 'it's a fruit on a tree' (Coltheart *et al.*, 1983). Here the patient evidently has the correct phonology of the stimulus but incorrect semantics. Now, *bury* is an irregular word so, whether one adopts Model 1 or Model 2, its phonology can only be obtained *lexically*. Therefore correct access to an orthographic lexicon (followed by correct communication from orthographic lexicon to phonological lexicon) has occurred. Yet access from orthographic lexicon to semantics has failed. Thus if homophone confusions *with irregular homophones* are a frequent occurrence, this is indicative of variant 3.[1] For the other two variants, a failure of orthographic processing affecting access to semantics would similarly affect access to lexical phonology, so the only phonological code available would be non-lexically derived (and so would be incorrect for irregular words).

A second way of distinguishing 3 from 2 and 1 is to use visual lexical decision tests. If lexical decisions depend upon intact access to Lexical Orthographic Codes, good lexical decision performance implies variant 3, whilst poor performance implies 1 or 2.

Finally, can one distinguish variant (1) from variant (2)? The distinction here is a vital one, so we will discuss it in a little more detail. What we meant by variant (2) is that entries in the Lexical Orthographic Codes systems are in such a state that access to some of them, or access to them sometimes, cannot be achieved, regardless of the task the patient is trying to perform. This is represented by viewing the difficulty as one *internal* to the system of Lexical Orthographic Codes. What we mean by variant (1) is that access to this system itself sometimes cannot be achieved when the patient is trying to read. This is represented by viewing the difficulty as one affecting the *pathway* from Visual Analysis to Lexical Orthographic Codes.

This distinction is sometimes referred to using the terms 'representation deficit' (here, because of the state of a particular representation, it is inaccessible) and 'access deficit' (here the problem is that the procedure by which access to representations is achieved is malfunctioning).

Shallice (1987) discusses methods which might be used to study whether a particular impairment corresponds to a representation deficit or an access deficit. To begin by putting Shallice's claim crudely: if the reason a patient failed to process an item correctly was because of a representation deficit, one would expect continued failures on subsequent presentations of that item. Thus representational deficits imply that there will be consistency across occasions in which items can be processed and which cannot. If, instead, the impairment is an access deficit, item-specific consistency across occasions would not be expected.

It must be acknowledged that this way of drawing inferences from neuropsychological data is to a considerable degree model-specific. It applies only to models whose characterization of access procedures is such that item-specific effects cannot arise during access. Many models are of this kind, but not all. For example, suppose one viewed access from Visual Analysis to Lexical Orthographic Codes as using a network of pathways linking individual letter-level units to word-level units. Damage to a set of these pathways would by definition constitute an access deficit; yet item-specific consistency across occasions would be observed. Those words to which each damaged input pathway was linked would be consistently poorly processed; all other words would be consistently successfully processed (for further discussion of this point see Riddoch, Humphreys, Coltheart and Funnell, in press). Nevertheless, Shallice's criteria remain useful, since they help to constrain models.

More generally, consistency effects are intrinsically important anyway. If it is found that impairments of the use of a particular representational system exhibit item-specific consistency, then that system must in some sense contain individual representations of those items. Not all theories of visual word recognition posit the existence of independent orthographic representations of individual words. Even fewer theories of semantics posit independent semantic representations of individual words.

Problems in studying item-specific consistency across occasions

Successful lexical orthographic processing is required if correct comprehension of printed homophones is always to be achieved. Successful lexical orthographic processing is also required if correct spelling of homophones is always to be achieved. So why not look to see whether the homophones a patient does not comprehend are precisely those he cannot spell (strong evidence for Model 1) or whether, alternatively, the two sets of words have no relationships (may led to strong evidence for Model 2)? We did this. What we achieved was not adjudication between the models, but instead a deeper understanding of the problems that need to be solved before investigations of consistency can be made to yield acceptable evidence pro or con particular models. There are two major problems. The first has to do with using tasks where 'chance level' is not zero: that is, although the task may require lexical processing to *ensure* correct response, the responses yielded by non-lexical processing may sometimes be correct. Comprehending printed regularly spelled homophones is an example: if, when lexical orthographic processing fails, the patient uses a phonological representation derived by non-lexical rules relating orthography to phonology, the probability of correct comprehension is reduced only to 0.5. In contrast, reading aloud a highly irregular word like *quay* or *yacht* would never succeed if lexical orthographic processing fails.

The second problem is how to determine whether any observed correspondence between performance on one occasion and performance on another is due (1) to item-specific consistency or (2) to the effect of some variable — word frequency, for example — which would introduce a correlation between performances on different occasions even when item-specific consistency is entirely absent.

Chance levels

Suppose there is a task which requires correct lexical processing to ensure perfect performance and for which non-lexical processing would yield a percent correct ('chance level') of 0.50. With a single set of words, the task is given twice to a particular patient. One wishes to know whether item-specific consistency effects are present.

For any item, four possible outcomes are possible (both occasions right, both wrong, right/wrong, and wrong/right: 11, 00, 10 and 01). If there is perfect consistency, a certain probability distribution of these outcomes, emphasizing 11 and 00, is calculable. If there is zero consistency, a different distribution is calculable. The results of the calculations depend on p (overall probability of success) and the chance level. Table 1 compares, for various values of p, the distribution predicted by perfect consistency and the distribution predicted by zero consistency. It is obvious that these distributions are so similar that empirical distinction between them is not a reasonable prospect. Further calculations show that only when the 'chance level' (probability of correct response without lexical processing) approaches zero do the distributions diverge sufficiently to make empirical studies viable: and even here the sensitivity of such studies will be higher when the overall probability of successful lexical processing is around 0.4 to 0.6 than when it is much higher or lower than this. Table 2 illustrates this.

Table 1.

$p=$	0.8		0.6		0.4		0.2		0.1		0.05	
	C	I	C	I	C	I	C	I	C	I	C	I
11	0.85	0.81	0.70	0.64	0.55	0.49	0.40	0.36	0.33	0.30	0.29	0.28
10	0.05	0.09	0.10	0.16	0.15	0.21	0.20	0.24	0.23	0.25	0.24	0.25
01	0.05	0.09	0.10	0.16	0.15	0.21	0.20	0.24	0.23	0.25	0.24	0.25
00	0.05	0.01	0.10	0.04	0.15	0.09	0.20	0.16	0.23	0.20	0.25	0.23

p = overall probability of success
C = hypothesis of perfect consistency
I = hypothesis of zero consistency
Assumed 'chance rate' = 0.5.

Table 2.

$p=$	0.8		0.6		0.4		0.2		0.1		0.05	
	C	I	C	I	C	I	C	I	C	I	C	I
11	0.80	0.64	0.60	0.36	0.40	0.16	0.20	0.04	0.10	0.01	0.05	0.00
10	0.00	0.16	0.00	0.24	0.00	0.24	0.00	0.16	0.00	0.09	0.00	0.05
01	0.00	0.16	0.00	0.24	0.00	0.24	0.00	0.16	0.00	0.09	0.00	0.05
00	0.20	0.04	0.40	0.16	0.60	0.36	0.80	0.64	0.90	0.81	0.95	0.90

p = overall probability of success
C = hypothesis of perfect consistency
I = hypothesis of zero consistency
Assumed 'chance rate' = 0.00.

Allowing for retest concordance not due to item-specific consistency

Suppose one selects a set of 100 items and a task where the 'chance level' is essentially zero. These items are presented twice, on different occasions, to investigate whether item-specific consistency effects are present. Suppose also that the stimuli represent a range of frequency and that probability correct is positively related to frequency. To simplify, assume that there are just two levels of frequency, corresponding to probabilities correct of 0.9 and 0.3. If there is *zero* item-specific consistency (that is, the probability of an item being correct on the second occasion is dependent only on its frequency and is independent of the result on the first occasion), the contingency coefficient is nevertheless highly significant in this example: C = 0.342, χ^2 = 13.25. It follows that a significant contingency coefficient does not imply that item-specific consistency effects are present, unless one takes account of effects of such associated variables as frequency. Those who have inferred consistency from contingency (Warrington and Shallice, 1984; Howard and Franklin, Chap 16) have not yet attempted to do this. There is a method of trying to take account of frequency effects when investigating item-specific consistency: we describe this method when analysing our own data below.

So far this chapter has been devoted to setting out some of the basic problems which need to be dealt with if one wishes to use neuropsychological data in pursuing the question of whether there is one orthographic lexicon or two. In the remainder of the chapter we will summarize some of our efforts to grapple with these complexities in studying a dyslexic and dysgraphic patient, HG. We intend to report the results of this study in full elsewhere: only those aspects of it especially germane to the question of how orthographic information is lexically represented will be referred to here.

Case report

HG, a retired accountant born in 1914, was admitted to hospital on 20 April 1984 after a 36 h history of severe headache, dysphasia, alexia and inability to recognize his wife. At admission he was found to have severe receptive and nominal dysphasia, inability to recognize faces or to read, colour agnosia, sensory neglect on the right side and a right homonymous hemianopia extending twenty degrees across the mid-line. CT scan showed large haemorrhages in the posterior left temporal lobe and in the right calcarine cortex.

Many of these difficulties became less severe in the months after the initial episode. He received speech therapy twice weekly from May 1984 to September 1984. Re-assessed on 7 September 1984, he presented with a mild anomia, good auditory comprehension and oral expression, and impairments of reading and spelling.

In July 1984, his acquired dyslexia took the form of letter-by-letter reading (Patterson and Kay, 1982) since, when unable to recognize a single word immediately, he frequently named the letters of the word aloud, left to right, and was then able to identify the word. However, this mode of responding soon became very rare, and by the time our detailed investigations began, his reading was characteristic of surface dyslexia, and his spelling characteristic of surface dysgraphia. We have seen numerous samples of his premorbid writing: spelling was excellent, and it is certain that HG was previously a highly literate man.

We studied his reading and spelling from August 1984, to the end of 1985. At that time he suffered a further stroke: this severely affected his visuospatial processing and resulted in visual agnosia, prosopagnosia and neglect of left-sided visual space.

Reading aloud

In three sessions in November–December, 1984, HG was asked to read aloud 34 irregular words selected from the 39 irregular words in Coltheart, Besner, Jonasson and Davelaar (1979). All were read correctly. This surprised us, in view of the pervasive co-occurrence of surface dyslexia and surface dysgraphia and the fact that HG's spelling at that time was profoundly surface dysgraphic. Similar results were obtained when HG was asked to read aloud the 40 words listed by Shallice, Warrington and McCarthy (1983) as highly irregular: he performed surprisingly well, scoring 36/40. His errors were *chaos* → "/kɔz/", *suede* → '/su:d/", *litre* → "/lɪtə/", and *borough* → '/bɒroʊ/".

These errors are instructive. Firstly, the last three are perfect regularization errors, as would be expected from a surface dyslexic. Secondly, the responses in all four cases are themselves words. This suggested to us that HG may have been using a lexicalization strategy to overcome difficulties in reading irregular words. There may have been occasions when HG was having difficulty in accessing a word's representation in an orthographic lexicon. On such occasions he might also have attempted to read it via rules relating letters to sounds. Such attempts, when the stimulus is an irregular word, may have been abandoned because they generally yield phonological forms which are not words. *Suede*, *litre* and *borough* are unusual irregular words, in that their regularizations are themselves words; so with these irregular words HG's strategy could not be used to detect the occurrent of regularization errors.

This conjecture was tested directly by giving HG the 40 highly irregular words (Shallice *et al.*, 1983) to read again, randomly interspersed with an equal number of pronounceable non-words. He was told that some of the stimuli were words and others were non-words. Under these circumstances, rejection of attempts at reading when they yielded phonological forms which were not words would not be a particularly useful strategy, since half the time the correct phonological form is not a word. Here HG's performance declined to 28/40, significantly worse than the performance when only words were present (McNemar's Test = 6.125, $p < 0.02$). The twelve errors made were *nought* — /tʌft/, *chaos* → /ʃoɑz/, *borough* → /bɒrɒf/, *quay* → /kweɪ/, *sieve* → /siːv/, *bouquet* → /biːkuːt/, *litre* → /lɪtə/, *suede* → /suːd/, *colonel* → /kɒlɒnəl/, *aisle* → /eɪl/, *suite* → /suːt/, and *trough* → /truːg/. These errors are virtually all regularization errors. It seems very clear, then, that HG is surface dyslexic in the sense that he frequently must use non-lexical processing to read words aloud, but can use a lexicalization strategy to avoid many errors that he would otherwise make.

His ability to read words lexically — that is, to read irregular words aloud correctly — depends strongly upon word frequency, as illustrated in Figure 2.

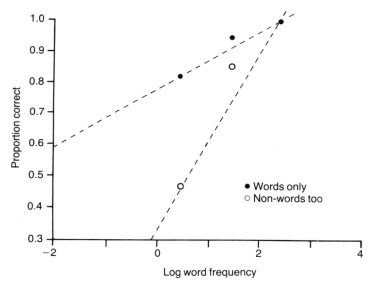

Figure 2. HG reading aloud highly irregular words as a function of word frequency, with (O) or without (●) accompanying non-words.

In the condition where only words are presented, the word-frequency effect is not significant (Kendall $S = 55$, $Z = 1.39$, $p = 0.32$). When both words and non-words are presented, the word-frequency effect is highly significant (Kendall $S = 165$, $Z = 2.73$, $p = 0.003$).

Shallice *et al.* (1983) provided two other lists of 40 words, a regular list and a mildly irregular list. These were given to HG to read aloud, intermingled with non-words. Degree of regularity exerted a highly significant effect (Regular 39/40, Mildly Irregular 35/40 and Highly Irregular 28/40: Kendall $S = 880$, $Z = 3.43$, $p = 0.0004$).

In toto, 149 non-words were presented to HG for reading aloud. He read these stimuli very well, scoring 91% correct. We regard this performance as sufficiently good to propose that HG, like HTR (Shallice *et al.*, 1983) and MP (Bub, Cancelliere and Kertesz, 1985), but not other reported cases of surface dyslexia, has intact use of the non-lexical procedure for reading aloud; as Masterson (1985) shows, normal subjects read non-words at about this level.

We show below that, when single-word reading comprehension of homophones is tested, HG frequently makes homophone confusion errors. Hence his lexical reading system is impaired at some point prior to semantic access — of the seven patterns of impairment we defined earlier, his is variant (1), (2) or (3) (or any combination of these). Variant (4) is excluded because his auditory comprehension, and his comprehension of regular non-homophonic printed words, was very good.

How are we to account for the finding that his success in using the lexical reading procedure (as indexed by success in reading aloud irregular words) is less when non-words are present in the test than when all the stimuli for oral reading are words? We suggest that for him it is very difficult (rather than simply sometimes impossible) to process print lexically, especially for low-frequency words. In tests of oral reading, high frequency words require little processing so their lexical identification is rapid. However, he does not attempt the extensive processing needed to identify low-frequency words lexically when this processing may turn out to be fruitless (i.e. when the stimulus is often a non-word). When, in contrast, all the stimuli can be read correctly by the lexical procedure, he is prepared to put greater effort into applying this procedure.

An alternative suggestion is that he uses a strategy of *phonological lexicalization*: application of spelling–sound rules to an irregular word produces a phonological representation which is not a word but which is not entirely unlike the correct pronunciation of the stimulus, so HG searches a phonological lexicon for a word whose pronunciation is similar to the non-word pronunciation yielded by the application of spelling–sound rules. We regard this as unlikely for two reasons. Firstly, no process of successive phonological approximation was evident during HG's attempts at reading irregular words. Secondly, some of the irregular words he read correctly (in the absence of non-words) are so irregular that application of spelling–sound rules would produce a pronunciation too deviant from the correct one to make correct word identification via phonological lexicalization feasible: examples are *colonel, aisle, bouquet* and *quay*.

Reading comprehension

As mentioned above, we carried out tests of reading comprehension with homophones. There were 107 pairs of homophones, 214 words in all: for all 107 pairs, he had previously provided, in response to the *spoken* form, appropriate definitions of *both* members of the homophone pair. In the reading task, 46 of the 214 words were wrongly defined: 42 of these responses were homophone confusions such as *frays* → 'music, sentence' and *brews* → 'to fall and hurt'. Subsequently, this 214 word test was entirely repeated, with similar results. As Figure 3 shows, the probability that a homophone will be correctly understood is a linear function of log word frequency.

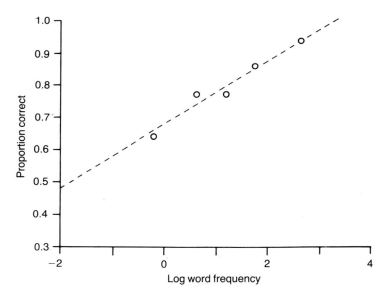

Figure 3. HG's comprehension of printed homophones, as a function of word frequency.

Each of these 214 words was classified as regular or irregular in spelling-to-sound correspondence, and homophone comprehension performance examined separately for the two sets of words. The results are shown in Figure 4. Very few irregular words, even low-frequency ones, were wrongly comprehended. Homophone confusions were common with regu-

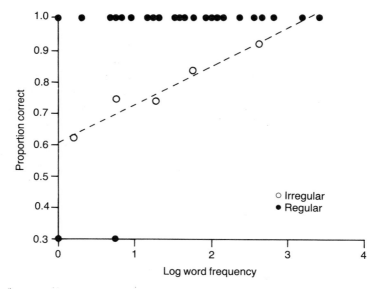

Figure 4. HG's comprehension of printed homophones as a function of regularity of spelling-to-sound correspondence. ●, irregular; ○, regular.

lar words; with these words, comprehension accuracy increased linearly as a function of log word frequency, the regression equation being:

$$\text{pr (correct)} = 0.761 + 0.053 \log F$$

Comprehension was significantly better with irregular than with regular homophones (Mann–Whitney Test: $z = 3.318$, $p < 0.001$). This is the first report of a surface dyslexic performing *more* accurately with irregular than with regular words. We offer the following explanation, which follows directly from the account we have already given of the effects of the presence versus absence of non-words upon HG's reading of irregular words.

In attempting to comprehend a printed word, HG makes an attempt at lexical orthographic processing. Low frequency words require more orthographic processing than high frequency words if they are to be lexically identified. For HG this is true in an exaggerated form. Phonological codes, on the other hand, he can readily derive non-lexically from print. For regularly spelled homophones, such phonological codes will be words, and so HG can rationally produce comprehension responses, based on such codes: these responses will either be correct or will be homophone confusions.

If the stimulus is an irregular homophone, the non-lexically derived phonological code will generally be a non-word, so cannot yield a comprehension response. Here all HG can rationally do is to make every attempt to succeed in lexical orthographic processing. Thus, just as the degree to which he attempts such processing in oral reading depends upon whether non-words are present or not, so the degree to which he attempts it in reading comprehension depends upon whether the stimulus is a regular word or an irregular word.

We have described two studies of lexical orthographic processing in reading so far, one involving the oral reading of irregular words and the other the comprehension of printed homophones. A third method for studying lexical orthographic processing is visual lexical decision. To ensure that visual lexical decision had to be orthographic, we used as non-word stimuli pseudohomophones (which when phonologically recoded become words).

In a forced-choice version of this task, where HG was asked to choose which was the word from a simultaneously presented word and non-word pair, he performed well, scoring 38/41. In a Yes/No version, involving two replications of a random sequence of 41 words and 41 non-words, his hit rate was high (79/82) but he also produced numerous false alarms (34/82). These data are presented in Table 3, broken down by frequency. In the case of non-words the frequency is the frequency of the word with which the non-word was pseudohomophonic. Also included in Table 3 are data from HG's spelling-to-dictation of the words from which the non-words were derived.

Table 3. Lexical decision performance (non-words are all pseudohomophones) plus spelling-to-dictation accuracy for the words from which the non-words were derived.

	Word frequency		
	⩾100	10–99	<10
Hit rate	1.00	0.97	0.95
Correct rejection rate	0.80	0.59	0.50
Spelling to dictation	0.80	0.59	0.48

A first point to make about these results is that the correct rejection rates show a very nearly significant frequency effect (Kendall $S = 306$, $Z = 1.58$, $p < 0.06$). The higher the frequency of the word from which a pseudohomophone was derived, the more likely HG is to correctly reject the pseudohomophone. Spelling accuracy is significantly related to word frequency ($S = 348$, $Z = 1.79$, $p < 0.05$).

A second point to note is the extremely close similarity between the percent correct responses for the three groups of pseudohomophones and the accuracy of spelling for these three groups.

We suggest the following interpretation of these various findings. In lexical decision with pseudohomophonic non-words, non-lexical recoding from print to phonology is futile: lexical orthographic processing is required, even if, for low-frequency words, the processing necessary is abnormally extensive for HG (though ultimately successful). The result is that hit rate is very high. When the stimulus is a (pseudohomophonic) non-word, of course access to an orthographic lexicon does not occur, but HG has no way of being sure whether this failure of access is due to his impaired lexical reading processing or to the fact that the stimulus is a non-word. So, as a check, he uses the non-lexically derived phonological form of the non-word and attempts to retrieve the correct *spelling* of that non-word, to check this against the stimulus. When this retrieval succeeds, the retrieved spelling will not match the stimulus, so HG can respond 'No'. But we know that retrieval of spellings is imperfect in HG, and when a spelling cannot be retrieved, HG decides to respond 'Yes' (make a false alarm) because, after all, the phonological form of the stimulus is a word.

This account explains (a) the very good performance in forced-choice lexical decisions, (b) the very high hit rate in Yes/No lexical decision, (c) the relationship between frequency and correct rejection rate in Yes/No lexical decision.

Of course, on this account a high hit rate in lexical decision with regular words does not necessarily indicate a high degree of success in achieving access to an orthographic lexicon. It could be that such access often fails for words, but HG still responds YES, either because of a successful match from the spelling check, or because his default response when all lexical access fails is YES. But this predicts that when highly irregular words are used with pseudohomophonic non-words in a lexical decision task, hit rate will be reduced, and this was not so: with the 40 Highly Irregular words of Shallice *et al.* (1983) randomly intermixed with forty pseudo-homophones, hit rate was 0.93. False alarm rate was 0.20, with more false alarms made to pseudohomophones when they were derived from low-frequency words, a trend consistent with the results of Table 3. We therefore prefer the interpretation that we advanced two paragraphs above.

Summary of interpretation of HG's reading defect

HG comprehends nearly all printed homophones when they are irregular (though producing many homophone confusions to regular words of the same frequency, length and other characteristics); therefore he is *capable* of effective use of the pathway Visual Analysis → Lexical Orthographic Codes → Cognitive System, even for low frequency words.

HG reads aloud correctly nearly all highly irregular words, even when they are low in frequency, when he knows all the stimuli in an oral reading test are words. This again shows he is capable of correctly accessing Lexical Orthographic Codes from Lexical Phonological Codes.

A third demonstration that access to Lexical Orthographic Codes can be effective is HG's high hit rate in lexical decision, even when the word stimuli are highly irregular and the non-words are pseudohomophones.

What his neurological damage has done is not so much to prevent lexical orthographic processing for reading as to make the processing required for successful lexical-orthographic identification abnormally extensive, especially for low-frequency words. Consequently, if in any reading task a reasonable level of performance can be achieved by using non-lexical recoding from print to phonology, this line of least resistance is adopted. Hence in reading comprehension tasks regular homophones, especially if of low frequency, are often comprehended via non-lexical conversion of orthography to phonology. The resulting phonological form is a word, so *auditory* comprehension will be possible. Even if HG notices that this form is homophonic and so ambiguous, he still has a 50/50 chance of responding correctly.

And in oral reading, when irregular words are accompanied by regular words and non-words, non-lexical conversion of orthography to phonology will produce correct responses much of the time — at the cost of making regularization errors to those irregular words which fail to be processed lexically with ease.

Finally, if our view that HG uses retrieved spellings as a checking mechanism in visual lexical decision is correct, the frequency effect upon accuracy of rejection of pseudohomophones implies that lexical orthographic processing for spelling is not intact: the less frequent a word, the less likely its correct spelling can be accessed from phonology. Hence we report now some direct investigations of HG's spelling.

Spelling to dictation

Each of the 214 homophones which were presented to HG for reading comprehension were also presented to him auditorily, accompanied by a disambiguating phrase: his task was to write down the target word. Of his 68 errors, virtually all were phonologically correct: examples are 'blew' → *bloo*, 'mane' → *main*, 'guessed' → *guest* and 'moan' → *mone*.

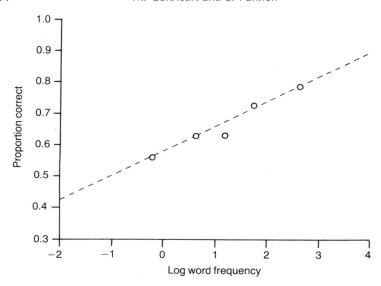

Figure 5. HG's spelling-to-dictation of disambiguated homophones, as a function of word frequency.

Once again, accuracy was linear with log word frequency. Figure 5 shows the results of this spelling test, plus the results of a complete replication of it, with percent correct plotted against log word frequencies. The linear regression equation from the pooled data was: percent correct = 0.5801 + 0.0772 log F. The frequency effect in Figure 5 is significant: the 98.33% confidence interval for the slope of the function is 0 to 0.18 (i.e. the hypothesis that the slope is not positive can be rejected, the associated p-value being < 0.05). This confirms the conclusion we drew from our interpretation of the Table 3 data: HG sometimes fails to retrieve spellings from an orthographic lexicon, with the probability of correct retrieval being a (linear) function of log word frequency.

These failures to retrieve spellings are by no means always complete. Examples such as 'bury' → *burry*, 'none' → *non*, 'damned' → *dambed*, 'knows' → *knos*, 'Mayor' → *mayre*, 'mayor' → *mayer*, 'some' → *som*, 'sighed' → *sighd*, and 'which' → *whitch* represent instances where some but not all of the orthographic information from a word's entry in an orthographic lexicon has been retrieved. These are errors of 'partial lexical knowledge' (Ellis, 1982); it appears, strikingly often, that the responses are a composite of the two possible spellings of the homophone. Sometimes HG retrieved the target's homophone from the orthographic lexicon ('aisle' → *isle*, 'sole' → *soul*, 'gilt' → *guilt*, 'quay' → *key*, 'nun' → *none*, 'taut' → *taught*) and sometimes errors of partial lexical knowledge occurred here too ('sum' → *som*, 'taut' → *taht*). A natural interpretation of these homophone substitutions is a failure of direct communication from the Cognitive System to the Lexical Orthographic Codes.

If HG, in attempts to access an entry in an orthographic lexicon, sometimes accesses only part of this entry, this would not only explain the kinds of spelling errors just mentioned, but also, given Model 1, might explain why homophones are more accurately comprehended in reading than they are spelled. Partial orthographic information would more often uniquely identify a printed word than be useable to generate the word's precise spelling. PLA-CE must be the fish — but in spelling should the missing letter be I or Y — or even E?

Comparison of reading with spelling

When HG tries to access orthographic representations during reading, he fails abnormally often. This is also true for spelling. We began this chapter by asking whether the systems of orthographic representations involved in reading and spelling are the same or different. Can HG's difficulties tell us anything about this?

The answer would certainly be affirmative if it were the case that the words for which lexical orthographic processing failed in reading were shown to be the same as the words for which lexical orthographic processing failed in spelling. We have, however, already discussed the problems that arise for efforts to demonstrate the existence of this kind of item-specific consistency between reading and spelling.

We have provided various reasons for claiming that HG's difficulties in lexical reading and spelling are genuinely *orthographic*. His auditory comprehension of the homophones he is liable to misspell is intact, and his reading difficulties are not anomic in origin since reading comprehension as well as oral reading is affected. Thus, the first obstacle we discussed has been surmounted: the spelling and reading problems are due to genuinely orthographic impairments.

However, we cannot profitably study the relationship between the words HG can comprehend from print and the words he can spell to dictation by analysing the relative frequencies of the four possible response patterns for a word when it is given in a reading and a spelling test. The probabilities of succeeding in each task even when lexical orthographic processing fails are well above zero (0.50 for reading comprehension of regular homophones; about 0.38, we estimate,[2] for spelling our homophones to dictation) and so, as we mentioned earlier, the predictions concerning relative frequencies of the four possible response patterns are too similar for the two hypotheses concerned (perfect item-specific consistency; zero item-specific consistency) to be empirically distinguishable.

Nor is the contingency coefficient useful, since HG's success in reading *and* his success in spelling are both positively correlated with word frequency, and this is enough to produce a significant contingency coefficient even if there is no item-specific consistency at all.

So we have tried a different tack. Let us suppose that there is a single orthographic lexicon, whose entries mediate both lexical reading and lexical spelling. Some of these entries are, because of HG's neurological damage, in such a state that they cannot be properly or fully accessed on every occasion; the probability of any entry having this property is inversely related to word frequency. The remaining entries are in a normal state: that is, at least, they can always be accessed correctly.

We cannot identify any entry as being in a normal state simply on the ground that the word corresponding to it is read correctly or spelled correctly, since, as we have pointed out, there are non-zero probabilities of correct homophone comprehension and of writing to dictation even if lexical orthographic processing fails. But suppose we adminster a test of lexical orthographic processing for reading twice (homophone comprehension, for example). This partitions words into two sets: Set A (words always correctly understood) and Set B (words for which at least one error occurs). It must be the case that words with impaired lexical entries will mostly be in Set B (not all: some will be in Set A because two correct guesses have occurred). Words with normal lexical entries will all be in Set A.

It follows that, on Model 1, Set B words will be spelled less accurately than Set A words *even when differences in word frequency are taken into account*. On Model 2, associations between reading and spelling are due to the independent effects of word frequency upon the dyslexia and the dysgraphia: once such effects are extracted, there should be no link between whether a particular word can be spelled correctly and whether it can be read correctly.

We focused our attention on the 171 of our 214 homophones that were regular in spelling–sound correspondence, because HG, we argue, used a strategy for overcoming deficient lexical–orthographic processing in reading when homophones were irregular. We divided these 171 homophones into two sets. Set B ($N = 64$) were words defined incorrectly at least once in the two homophone–comprehension tests. How well were they spelled? Spelling accuracy averaged over the two spelling session was a linear function of log word frequency. The regression equation was:

$Y = 0.4911 + 0.0892 \log F$ and the slope of this equation was significant (the 98.333% confidence interval for the slope was 0 to 0.272).

For Set A words ($N = 107$), those always defined correctly, the equation relating spelling to word frequency was $Y = 0.6703 + 0.0117 \lg F$. The slope of the equation does not approach significance: even the 64.129% confidence limit includes negative values (-0.026 to $+0.067$). The two functions are plotted in Figure 6. The regression analyses confirm the impression given by this function. Spelling performance is better for words perfectly read than for words imperfectly read, even when word frequency is taken into account. Indeed, for words perfectly read, spelling accuracy is not significantly related to word frequency, whilst for words imperfectly read spelling accuracy is linearly related to log word frequency.

Hence there is to a significant degree a set of words for which both spelling and reading is difficult for HG and another set for which both reading and spelling are easy. It is not clear, on Model 2, how this might arise. Model 1 offers a natural interpretation: there is a single orthographic lexicon, used both for reading and spelling, and the entry for each of these words in this lexicon has been impaired. Our chapter thus offers some support for Model 1,[3] and so contrasts with the chapter by Monsell — where the reader will find some support for Model 2.

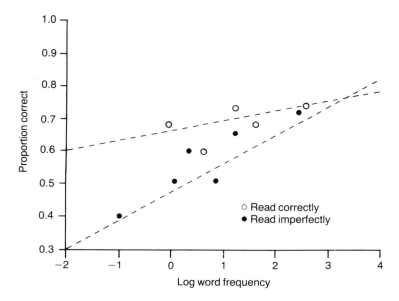

Figure 6. HG's spelling of homophones as a function of how well he reads them.

Acknowledgements

This work was supported by a research grant from the Economic and Social Research Council. We thank David Howard for his dismantling of an earlier draft, and Stephen Monsell and Alan Allport for valuable comments.

Notes

[1] The argument here, to be more precise, is that the two impairments defining Variant 3 operate at least partly independently. Homophone confusions with irregular words arise when the patient's route from Lexical Orthographic Codes to Cognitive System fails to function correctly. Regularization errors occur when the patient's route from Lexical Orthographic Codes to Lexical Phonological Codes malfunctions.

[2] We arrived at this estimate by using the system of non-lexical phoneme to grapheme rules assembled by Hanna, Hanna, Hodges and Rudolf (1966). This system correctly spelled 38% of our words.

[3] Our analysis has allowed us to claim that the link between spelling performance and reading performance is not mediated solely by the effects of a confounding variable (word frequency). It might be argued, however, that some other confounding variable of which we are unaware is responsible for the similarities between spelling and reading performance. This variable would have to be one which affects reading and spelling in the same way. The more variables one can identify which have the same effect on reading as on spelling, the more evidence one is accumulating for Model 1.

References

Bub, D., Cancelliere, A. and Kertesz, A. (1985). In K. E. Patterson, J. C. Marshall and M. Coltheart (Eds) *Surface Dyslexia: Neuropsychological and Cognitive Studies of Phonological Reading*. London: Erlbaum.

Coltheart, M. (1978). Lexical access in simple reading tasks. In G. Underwood (Ed.) *Strategies of Informating Processing*. London: Academic Press.

Coltheart, M. (1981). Disorders of reading and their implications for models of normal reading. *Visible Language*, **XV(2)**, 245–86.

Coltheart, M. (1987). Functional architecture of the language-processing system. In M. Coltheart, G. Sartori and R. Job (Eds) *The Cognitive Neuropsychology of Language*. London: Erlbaum.

Coltheart, M. (1985). Cognitive neuropsychology and the study of reading. In M. I. Posner and O. S. M. Marin (Eds) *Attention and Performance XI*. Hillsdale, NJ: Erlbaum.

Coltheart, M., Besner, D., Jonasson, J. T. and Davelaar, E. (1979). Phonological recoding in the lexical decision task. *Quarterly Journal of Experimental Psychology*, **31**, 489–508.

Coltheart, M., Masterson, J., Byng, S., Prior, M. and Riddoch, J. (1983). Surface dyslexia. *Quarterly Journal of Experimental Psychology*, **35A**, 469–95.

Ellis, A. W. (1982). Spelling and writing (and reading and speaking). In A. W. Ellis (Ed.) *Normality and Pathology in Cognitive Functions*. London: Academic Press.

Ellis, A. W. (1987). Intimations of modularity, or, the modelarity of mind: doing cognitive neuropsychology without syndromes. In M. Coltheart, G. Sartori and R. Job (Eds) *The Cognitive Neuropsychology of Language*. London: Erlbaum.

Funnell, E. (1983). Ideographic Communication and Word-Class Differences in Aphasia. Unpublished Ph.D. thesis, University of Reading, U.K.

Hanna, P. R., Hanna, J. S., Hodges, R. E. and Rudolf, E. H., Jnr. (1966). *Phoneme-grapheme Correspondences as Cues to Spelling Improvement*. Washington, DC: US Government Printing Office.

Hatfield, F. M. and Patterson, K. E. (1983). Phonological spelling. *Quarterly Journal of Experimental Psychology*. **35A**, 451–68.

Henderson, L. (1985). In K. E. Patterson, J. C. Marshall, and M. Coltheart (Eds) *Surface Dyslexia: Neuropsychological and Cognitive Studies of Phonological Reading*. London: Erlbaum.

Masterson, J. (1985). On how we read non-words: data from different populations. In K. E. Patterson, J. C. Marshall and M. Coltheart (Eds) *Surface Dyslexia: Neuropsychological and Cognitive Studies of Phonological Reading*. London: Erlbaum.

Patterson, K. E. and Kay, J. (1982). Letter-by-letter reading: psychological descriptions of a neurological syndrome. *Quarterly Journal of Experimental Psychology*, **34A**, 411–42.

Patterson, K. E., Marshall, J. C. and Coltheart, M. (Eds) (1985). *Surface Dyslexia: Neuropsychological and Cognitive Studies of Phonological Reading*. London: Erlbaum.

Patterson, K. E., and Morton, J. (1985). From orthography to phonology: an attempt at an old interpretation. In K. E. Patterson, J. C. Marshall and M. Coltheart (Eds) *Surface Dyslexia: Neuropsychological and Cognitive Studies of Phonological Reading*. London: Erlbaum.

Patterson, K. E. and Shewell, C. (1987). In M. Coltheart, G. Sartori and R. Job (Eds) *Cognitive Neuropsychology of Language*. London: Erlbaum.

Riddoch, M. J., Humphreys, G. W., Coltheart, M. and Funnell, E. (in press). *Cognitive Neuropsychology*.

Shallice, T. (1987). Impairments of semantic processing: multiple dissociations. In M. Coltheart, G. Sartori and R. Job (Eds) *The Cognitive Psychology of Language*. London: Erlbaum.

Shallice, T., Warrington, E. K. and McCarthy, R. (1983). Reading without semantics. *Quarterly Journal of Experimental Psychology*, **35A**, 111–38.

Warrington, E. K. and Shallice, T. (1984). Category-specific semantic impairment. *Brain*, **107**, 829–54.

16   Three ways for understanding written words, and their use in two contrasting cases of surface dyslexia (together with an odd routine for making 'orthographic' errors in oral word production)

David Howard and Sue Franklin

Abstract

This chapter identifies the properties of three distinct routines that can be used for written word comprehension. These are (i) 'direct' lexical access to semantics; (ii) semantic access on the basis of a lexically derived phonological code; and (iii) semantic access on the basis of a phonological code assembled by a 'sub-lexical reading routine'. The written word comprehension of two surface dyslexic patients is analysed in terms of these three routines. There is a double dissociation between the patients: one, MK, relies exclusively on 'direct' lexical access, and cannot phonologically recode for semantic access. The other patient, EE, relies mainly on phonological recoding via the 'sub-lexical reading routine'. The role of processes that recode written material into phonological form for semantic access are considered in the light of the performance of the patients. A final section presents evidence, from MK's picture naming, for another routine for using orthographic information in spoken word production, resulting in apparent orthographic 'regularization' errors in oral speech.

LANGUAGE PERCEPTION AND PRODUCTION
ISBN 0-12-052750-2

Introduction

This chapter is concerned with the relationship between the procedures used for written word comprehension and those used to understand spoken words. The empirical evidence is drawn from the contrasting patterns of performance of two patients with acquired reading disabilities, both of whom can be described as 'surface dyslexics'. Coltheart and Funnell (Chap 15) provide a detailed discussion of the range of problems that can occur in surface dyslexics; like them we will use the term to describe patients who show two characteristic features in their oral reading of single words. First, 'surface dyslexics' show particular difficulty in reading aloud 'irregular' English words — those whose pronunciation is not deducible from their spelling (e.g. SEW, PINT, COLONEL) — compared to regularly spelled words (FEW, HINT, KERNEL; cf. Venezky, this volume). Second, when words are misread, many of the readings produced are phonologically plausible renderings of the letter string — for example, reading BURY as '/bjʊrɪ/', MOVE as 'mauve' or YACHT as '/jæʧt/'.

The occurrence of these two features in oral word reading demonstrates that these patients are not always able to use lexically specific information to derive pronunciations for written words; instead they use some kind of 'sub-lexical' reading routine (SLRR) in oral word reading, when lexically-specific knowledge is not available. The SLRR can be used for reading real words or non-words, but will only give the correct phonology consistently for regularly spelled real words (for a discusssion of how the SLRR might operate see Kay, Chap 9). We use the term 'routine' to describe any information processing procedure, or sequence of procedures that can be used to perform some task — in this case oral word (and non-word) reading.

Early investigations of surface dyslexic patients tried to identify the features of a dyslexic 'syndrome' (e.g. Marshall, 1976; Coltheart, Masterson, Byng, Prior and Riddoch, 1983). Among the set of features proposed was one relating to word comprehension: 'semantic reading of the visual stimulus is determined by the (frequently erroneous) phonology of the response' (Marshall, 1976, p. 114; see also Coltheart *et al.*, 1983, p. 486). So words are understood as they are (mis)pronounced; semantic access depends on prior phonological recoding. Thus JC, the first 'surface dyslexic' described by Marshall and Newcombe (1973) read LISTEN as 'Liston . . . that's the boxer' (Sonny Liston was world heavyweight champion in the early 1960s). Given that these patients often derive the phonology of words via a SLRR, we would predict that 'surface dyslexics' will have particular difficulty in understanding words that they mispronounce. Thus, just as such patients are worse at *pronouncing* irregularly spelled words, they are also worse at *understanding* them, when compared with matched regular words. Regular words with homophones will also cause these patients difficulty in comprehension: while the written word WINE has a recognizably different meaning from its (heterographic) homophone WHINE, semantic access which is based only on a phonological code (i.e. '/waɪn/') will be unable to distinguish between the two meanings. 'Surface dyslexics', when basing semantic access on phonological recodings will have no principled way of deciding whether WINE means 'a fermented grape drink' or 'a high, complaining cry', and will be forced to choose between these interpretations on the basis of their relative frequency or some other kind of feature. (See Coltheart and Funnell, Chap 15, for a discussion of ways of making this decision.) When 'surface dyslexic' patients are given regular words with homophones to understand, the predicted homophone confusion errors do occur: with JC, Newcombe and Marshall (1981) found errors such as BEE glossed as 'to be or not to be, that is the question', and BILLED defined as 'to build up, buildings'.

Newcombe and Marshall (1981) and Coltheart *et al.* (1983) noticed that homophone errors could occur not only with regular words, but also with irregular words: for example, CD, described by Coltheart *et al.* (1983), defined BURY as 'a fruit on a tree'. If CD had been using a phonological code derived by a SLRR to read the word, she would have generated a non-word (probably '/bjʊrɪ/'). Instead she made a homophone error to the *correct* pronounciation. Because the word BURY is irregular, this phonology must be lexically derived. Coltheart *et al.* argue that there must therefore be two distinct routines for obtaining a phonological code from a written word which then can be used for semantic access: in one of these the phonological code is generated by a sub-lexical reading routine; in the other the phonological code is generated using a lexical (but non-semantic) routine.

The initial attempts to define 'surface dyslexia' as a homogeneous syndrome have not proved successful; qualitative differences among patients have become clear in a number of respects (cf. Patterson, Marshall and Coltheart, 1986). For example, analysis of oral word reading by 'surface dyslexic' patients shows that different patients may pronounce words via the SLRR using very different sizes of orthographic unit (cf. Shallice, Warrington and McCarthy, 1983; Kay and Lesser, 1985; Newcombe and Marshall, 1986).

In terms of word comprehension, a number of reports show that some patients sometimes understand words correctly even where they fail to retrieve the correct phonology. In these patients, semantic access cannot always be on the basis of a phonological code (cf. Deloche, Andreewsky and Desi, 1982; Kay and Patterson, 1986; Goldblum, 1986; Kremin, 1986).

For GAUGE Kay and Patterson's patient, EST, said 'that is something about a railway . . . that's as much as I've got, train . . . /gɔʤ/ [gorge].[1] On these occasions, the patient must be accessing the word meaning 'directly' without prior phonological recoding (assuming, that is, that the phonological word form that EST produced is the only one on which he could have based lexical access). Note also that all these subjects misunderstood irregular words and made homophone errors showing that, on other occasions, semantic access did depend on phonological recoding. In many of these patients none of the word comprehension routines was working well; with regular words (where any of the three comprehension routines should yield the correct answer), EST was only 58% correct in word definition.

The data from word comprehension in surface dyslexics demonstrate that three different routines are available for written word comprehension:

(1) Direct semantic access without phonological recoding; whole, familiar words are recognized by a 'visual input lexicon' which then accesses the corresponding central semantic representation.

(2) Semantic access on the basis of a phonological code which is lexically derived.

(3) Semantic access on the basis of a lexical code which is generated by a SLRR.

The distinction between routines 2 and 3 may not be entirely clear cut. As Kay and Patterson (1986) point out, according to some theories of the operation of the SLRR, it may sometimes yield the correct pronunciation for some irregular words. If, for example, the SLRR operates using analogies with lexically-represented words, it might give the correct pronunciation for WARN, by using analogies with WAR, WART or WARP. For the purposes of this discussion, we will assume that there is a lexical, and non-semantic routine for accessing the phonological representations of familiar words (cf. Funnell, 1983; Coltheart, 1985) and that, as a consequence routines 2 and 3 are distinct.

It is easy to demonstrate that all three of these written word comprehension routines are available to normal, non-brain-damaged subjects: the 'direct', non-phonological route must exist to account for our ability to distinguish between the different senses of words with homophones. The availability of the other two routines can be demonstrated with stimuli that *require* phonological recoding for semantic access: we can readily perform tasks involving pseudohomophones (i.e. non-words which when pronounced sound like real words). Normal people can decide that a PHOCKS is an animal, or that BRANE (and not PRANE) sounds like a word, and that YOO NEAD TO WOSH THOZE PHILTHIE TROW-ZAS is a well-formed sentence. All these tasks require lexical access on the basis of a phonological code derived from a SLRR.

Evidence for the existence of a routine that uses lexically-derived phonology to access the semantic system can only come from miscomprehension of irregularly-spelled words with homophones: it is possible to understand AISLE TELL YEW WEAR THE SUITES ARE; THEIR UNDER LOCK AND QUAY. Because AISLE, WEAR, SUITES and QUAY are irregular words their phonology used for lexical access must be lexically derived.

The properties of these three word comprehension routines are summarized in Table 1. The only feature that has not been mentioned already is comprehension of pseudohomophones by the 'direct access' route. In the absence of phonological recoding by a SLRR, pseudohomophones will not generally be understood correctly. However, a wholly lexical routine might be able to use information based on approximate visual access; it could accept, as a best approximation, a visually similar word. This might yield correct comprehension of visually similar pseudohomophones such s SKOOL or BRANE, but not of dissimilar ones such as PHOCKS or KWYER. Deep dyslexic patients who seem to have no information from a SLRR, use this kind of routine when asked to read non-words aloud (Saffran and Marin, 1977).

Table 1.   The properties of three routines for understanding written words.

Word types	Examples	Routine 1 Direct semantic access	Routine 2 Semantic access after *lexical* phonological recoding	Routine 3 Semantic access after phonological recoding via a SLRR
Regular real words (without homophones)	BOAT COUNTY	Correct	Correct	Correct
Irregular real words (without homophones)	YACHT MORTGAGE	Correct	Correct	Incorrect
Regular real words with homophones	BERRY KERNEL	Correct	Sometimes correct	Sometimes correct
Irregular real words with homophones	BURY COLONEL	Correct	Sometimes correct	Incorrect
Pseudohomophones visually similar to target	STREEM SKOOL	Sometimes correct	Sometimes correct	Correct
Pseudohomophones visually dissimilar to target	PHOCKS KWYER	Incorrect	Incorrect	Correct

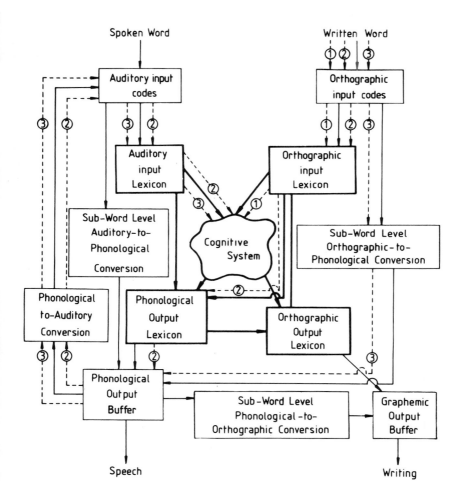

Figure 1. A modified version of the 'logogen model' adapted from Patterson and Shewell (1987). The three routines available for written word comprehension are marked: 1. 'Direct' semantic access, 2. Semantic access on the basis of a lexically derived phonological code, and 3. Semantic access on the basis of a phonological code generated via the sub-lexical reading routine.

Most current lexical theories can incorporate these three routines for comprehension; most theorists have assumed that lexical access on the basis of phonological recoding (routines 2 and 3) depends on auditory word recognition devices which can recognize phonologically coded material. Current versions of the 'logogen model' need modification to accommodate semantic access on the basis of phonological recoding. They need a routine to convert output phonology at the level of the (output) response buffer into input auditory codes — the process of 'phonological-to-auditory conversion'. In Figure 1 the three routines are shown mapped into a modified version of Patterson and Shewell's (1987) update of the logogen model. They can equally easily be mapped onto the model adopted by Monsell (this volume). Routine 1 is directly from iO to CF by a lexical mapping; routine 2 is from $iO \rightarrow oP \rightarrow iP \rightarrow CF$, where the $iO \rightarrow oP$ mapping is lexical. Routine 3 is identical to routine 2 except that it involves a non-lexical mapping from iO to oP.

This chapter presents data from word comprehension tasks of two 'surface dyslexics'. Their oral word reading is very similar; the information that they can use in word comprehension is very different. MK relies exclusively on routine 1 — direct semantic access — and there is no evidence that he can ever use either of the routines which depend on phonological recoding. Despite adequate ability to read aloud short pseudohomophones (e.g. BOTE), MK is quite unable to understand them. This, we will argue, is because he lacks any routine for converting output phonology into an input form (i.e. in the logogen model, 'phonological to auditory conversion', or in Monsell's notation $oP \rightarrow iP$). Data from EE are presented to contrast with MK; like many other 'surface dyslexics' he relies principally on phonological recoding via the SLRR for word comprehension, although he occasionally uses either of the other two routines (1 or 2). In terms of their word comprehension processes there is a double dissociation between these two patients: MK is significantly better than EE on all comprehension tasks requiring direct lexical access, while EE is significantly better than MK in all comprehension tasks that *require* phonological recoding.

Case reports

Patient EE (see also Byng and Coltheart, 1986; Coltheart, 1982; Campbell, 1983)

EE is a 46 year old left-handed postman, who suffered a head injury when falling from a ladder in September 1980. He was initially aphasic showing, according to the notes, 'moderate nominal dysphasia' and 'moderate receptive dysphasia'. The experiments reported here were done between August 1984 and July 1985 (i.e. 4–5 years post-onset). At this point his spontaneous speech was fluent with occasional word finding difficulty. Auditory comprehension of single words was reasonably good: he scored 107 on the Peabody Picture Vocabulary Test (PPVT: Dunn, 1965) — a normal score for a seventeen year old. Written word comprehension was somewhat worse: on the PPVT with written presentation he scored 94 (normal for a fourteen year old). Single word repetition was excellent (100/100), and he had a digit span of over four items forwards and three backwards. His reading was typically 'surface dyslexic' (see below) and in writing single words to dictation he was a 'surface dysgraphic'. Writing the Coltheart word lists to dictation he managed 26/39 on regular words and 12/39 on irregular words; many of his errors were plausible spellings (e.g. 'biscuit' → BISKET, 'treat' → TREET). Picture naming was severely disturbed: he scored 15 on the first (and easiest) 45 items from the Boston Naming Test (BNT; Kaplan, Goodglass and Weintraub, 1976), and he failed to name any of the thirty items in the Graded Naming Test (GNT; Warrington and McKenna, 1983). His errors are typically descriptions — e.g. THIMBLE → 'for sewing; it stops the needle going into your finger'; SUNDIAL → 'for the time . . . sun time . . . a sun timer'. Picture recognition is, however, intact: he scores 49/52 on the picture version of the Pyramids and Palm Trees test (Howard and Patterson, unpublished).

Patient MK

MK is a 68 year old retired oil company executive. In September 1982 he suffered a left hemisphere CVA which left him with a Wernicke's aphasia. The experiments reported in this paper were done between January 1984 and July 1985 (i.e. 15–33 months post onset). MK's spontaneous speech is fluent and he uses a variety of grammatical constructions, but he has some word retrieval difficulty and makes phonologically related word selection errors and some errors which are semantically related to the (presumed) targets. His auditory word comprehension is somewhat impaired relative to his likely pre-morbid level — on the PPVT with auditory word presentation he scored 112/150; his auditory comprehension is worse with low imageability words than high imageability words (word definition: low imageability words 27/1000, high imageability 65/100; word sets matched for phoneme length and word frequency). Single word repetition is severely impaired; he makes a variety of different types of errors, including semantic errors (e.g. 'teach' → 'learn'; 'pint' → 'beer'). Repetition is better for high imageability words (61/100) than low imageability words (29/100), and better for 'content words' (15/60) than 'function words' (4/40; sets of high frequency words matched across word class for imageability). He cannot repeat any non-words. In writing to dictation MK is a 'deep dysgraphic' (cf. Bub and Kertesz, 1982; Hatfield and Patterson, 1984). He cannot write non-words to dictation; he is better at writing high imageability words (47/100) than low imageability words (26/100), and better at 'content words' (14/60) than 'function words' (6/40). He makes semantic errors (e.g. 'penny' → MONEY; 'lady' → GIRL). Picture naming is relatively well preserved, with scores at, or just below the bottom edge of the normal range: on the BNT he was correct with 34/60 in spoken naming and 37/60 written naming. On the GNT he scored 11/30 spoken, and 12/30 written. Comprehension of written words was superior to comprehension of spoken words: on the PPVT with written word presentation he scored 123/150. MK's oral word reading, which will be described in more detail below, was 'surface dyslexic'.

Oral word reading

The effects of word regularity

Table 2 shows the accuracy of these two patients in reading three different lists of 'regular' and 'irregular' words; both patients are consistently significantly worse at reading 'irregular' words. On the Parkin lists both patients are particularly poor at reading the 'very irregular' words, defined by Parkin (1982) as those whose pronunciation is given in the Oxford Paperback Dictionary.

Non-word reading

The two patients read 60 orthographically possible non-words, mixed with real words, on two occasions; there were equal numbers of one and two syllable words with 3–6 phonemes. Neither patient showed any effect of syllable length, but MK showed a significant effect of non-word phoneme length (Table 2). Neither patient reads non-words flawlessly. MK is considerably more accurate than EE with short non-words.

Reading errors

A complete listing of errors on the Coltheart lists are given in Table 3. It can be seen that, for both patients, the difference between 'regular' and 'irregular' words is accounted for by phonologically plausible errors; other errors distribute (approximately) equally between the two word types.

Table 2. (i) The effects of word 'regularity' on oral reading.

a. Word lists from Coltheart *et al.* (1979).

	Regular words n=39	Irregular words n=39	Fisher exact test
EE	0.87	0.69	z=1.63, p<0.06
MK	0.90	0.67	z=2.18, p<0.02

b. Word lists from Bauer and Stanovich (1980)

	Regular words n=100	Irregular words n=100	Fisher exact test
EE	0.85	0.60	z=3.79, p<0.001
MK	0.85	0.72	z=2.06, p<0.02

c. Word lists from Parkin (1982).

	Regular words n=33	Mildly irregular words n=33	Very irregular words n=33	Jonckheere trend test
EE	0.82	0.73	0.30	z=4.16, p<0.001
MK	0.91	0.82	0.52	z=3.52, p<0.001

(ii) Oral reading of non-words; relationship between accuracy and phoneme length (60 non-words presented twice)

	Phoneme length 3 n=9	4 n=31	5–6 n=20	Jonckheere trend test
EE	0.67	0.53	0.68	z=0.75, n.s.
MK	0.94	0.87	0.70	z=2.42, p<0.01

It is clear that, in terms of the definition given in the introduction, both patients are 'surface dyslexics'; they often assemble pronunciations for words using a sub-lexical reading routine.

Tasks requiring direct lexical access

Lexical decision with irregular words and pseudohomophones

In lexical decision tasks, normal subjects are generally (slightly) slower at deciding that pseudohomophones (e.g. BRANE) are not real words than control non-words, which are equally word-like but which, when pronounced, do not sound like words (e.g. PRANE; Coltheart, Davelaar, Jonasson and Besner, 1977; Besner and Davelaar, 1983). That is, lexical information produced by routine 3 can interfere with rejection of non-words. Relying on a phonological code (produced via the SLRR — i.e. routine 3) for the lexical decision will cause problems both with pseudoho-

Table 3. Errors in oral word reading. Complete corpus from the Coltheart *et al.*
(1979) word lists.

	Regular words	Irregular words
Patient EE		
1. Phonologically plausible errors		GROSS → '/grɒs/' [gross]
		SUBTLE → '/'sʌbtəl/' [subbtle]
		BURY → '/bʌrɪ/' [burry]
		BOWL → '/baʊl/' [bowel]
		SWORD → '/swɔd/' [swored]
		MOVE → '/məʊv/' [mauve]
2. Other errors	THRONG → 'thorough'	GAUGE → 'garage'
	BARGE → '/breɪdʒ/' [brage]	BOROUGH → 'through'
	STREWN → 'stern'	LOSE → 'loss'
	PLUG → 'plough'	CIRCUIT → 'not biscuit'
	COUNTY → 'country'	TROUGH → 'tough'
		FLOOD → '/fuld/' [fooled]
Patient MK		
1. Phonologically plausible errors	SPEAR → '/spɛə/' [spare]	AUNT → '/ɒnt/' [ornt]
		GONE → '/gəʊn/' [goen]
		SEW → '/su/' [soo]
		LOSE → '/ləʊz/' [loze]
		MORTGAGE → '/'mɔtgeɪdʒ/' [morttgage]
2. Other errors	TEETH → 'tooth'	ANSWER → '/ɒnsə/' [ornser)
	PROTEIN → '/prʊ'teɪn/' [prutane]	THOROUGH → '/θəʊmɒn/' [thomon]
	CAPSULE → '/'kɒpsjul/' [copsule]	SCARCE → '/spɑs . . slɑs/' [sparce . . slarce)
		SUBTLE → 'sublet'
		BUILD → '/hɪld/' [hilled]

mophones (because the phonology generated by the SLRR *does* sound like
a word), and irregular words (because their SLRR phonology does *not*
sound like a word).

The two patients were given a lexical decision task: the real words were
the 39 regular words and the 39 irregular words from Coltheart *et al.*
(1979); the non-words were adapted from the set used by Besner and
Davelaar (1983). There were 39 pseudohomophones and 39 control non-
words: the two lists were matched for length and N-ness (the number of
different real words that could be made by changing just one letter in each
of the non-words) — the two lists were therefore equal in visual similarity
to real words.

The results (Table 4) show that MK performs respectably, with an
overall error rate of 2.5%. In both accuracy and response latency, differ-

ences between irregular words and regular words, and differences between pseudohomophones and control non-words do not approach statistical significance. There is no evidence that MK uses any phonological information in this task.

Table 4. Lexical decision with irregular words and pseudohomophones.

Examples	Regular words SPEND TAKE n= 39	Irregular words PROVE COME n=39	Pseudo-homophones CHUZE KORD n=39	Control non-words THUZE KORP n=39
Patient EE				
Probability of error	0.10	0.10	0.41	0.13
Mean correct RT (secs)	1.86	1.85	3.29	3.17
(standard deviation)	(1.04)	(1.53)	(2.24)	(2.26)
Patient MK				
Probability of error	0.00	0.05	0.05	0.00
Mean correct RT (secs)	2.04	2.13	1.96	1.74
(standard deviation)	(1.09)	(0.88)	(0.97)	(0.86)

By contrast, EE performs poorly: his mean error rate is 19%. While he is relatively fast and accurate with both irregular and regular real words, he accepts 41% of pseudohomophones. It is clear that, with non-words, he often bases his decision on the phonology generated by the SLRR; it is also clear that he does not always do this with real words — although he is less likely to read irregular words than regular words correctly, he is equally able to accept the two classes in lexical decision. The failure to find a difference with real words suggests that EE has representations of these in an input lexicon; like HG, the patient described by Coltheart and Funnell (Chap 15), EE's difficulty in rejecting pseudohomophones is probably due to his use of the SLRR in checking 'no' responses. Like HG, the pseudohomophones EE incorrectly accepts correspond to real words of lower frequency than the ones he rejects (log transformed frequencies, t (37) = 2.01; $p < 0.05$ one tailed). The checking procedure only works reliably with high frequency items.

Definition of regular and irregular words

Both of these patients have difficulty in reading irregular words aloud. Because they often rely on a SLRR to generate phonology, they make reading responses which do not correspond to any real English word. If they base semantic access on this phonological code (i.e. use routine 3 for comprehension), they will often fail to find any meaning for irregular words. The two patients were therefore given the words from Parkin's (1982) lists to define. We accepted as 'correct' definitions any response which indicated that the appropriate meaning had been accessed, and did not try to assess whether the semantic representations were complete or in some way degraded. Thus, for BEAR we would accept any of 'animal', 'grizzly, 'fierce', 'koala'.

Table 5. Definition of regular and irregular words from Parkin (1982).

	Regular words $n=33$	Mildly irregular words $n=33$	Very irregular words $n=33$	Jonckheere trend test
EE	0.82	0.70	0.30	$z=4.16, p<0.001$
MK	0.94	0.91	0.88	$z=0.64$, ns

Although eleven months had intervened between the time when EE read this list aloud (see Table 2) and when he defined the words (see Table 5), his oral reading performance is an accurate predictor of his ability to define the words; the proportion correctly defined in each category is almost exactly the same as the proportion read correctly. He even shows consistency item-by-item: of the 61 words read correctly in August 1984, 50 (82%) were defined correctly in July 1985, while only 10 (26%) of the words that had been misread were given an appropriate definition. This degree of consistency is highly significant (contingency coefficient $C = 0.470, p < 0.001$).[2]

MK, on the other hand, can define irregular words just as well as regular words, even though he is much worse at reading (very) irregular words aloud. He cannot therefore be relying on a phonological code for semantic access, so he must be using the 'direct' routine (1).

Definition of real words with homophones

Where semantic access depends on a phonological code, homophones will be difficult to understand. While BREAK and BRAKE are orthographically distinct, their phonology — /breɪk/ — is identical and so ambiguous. A patient using routine 3 should sometimes make 'homophone errors' with regular words (e.g. defining BRAKE as meaning 'to destroy') and *not* with irregular words, and a patient who uses routine 2 will sometimes make homophone errors with irregular words (e.g. BREAK means 'to slow down'), as well as with regular words. The patients were given 25 regular words with homophones and 25 irregular words with homophones for definition.

As the results in Table 6 show, MK performs with reasonable accuracy in this task; he made no homophone errors with either regular or irregular words, nor has he made any such errors on any other occasion. This is consistent with the conclusion from the previous two experiments: MK relies on routine 1 for the comprehension of real, familiar words, and there is no evidence that he ever uses an internally generated phonological code for lexical access.

Table 6. Defining written words with homophones (proportions of responses of each type).

	Patient EE	Patient MK
Regular words (n=25)		
Correct responses	0.52	0.96
Homophone errors	0.12	0.00
Other definitions	0.08	0.04
No definition	0.28	0.00
Irregular words (n=25)		
Correct responses	0.48	0.92
Homophone errors	0.08	0.00
Other definitions	0.04	0.08
No definition	0.40	0.00

EE, in contrast, is very much worse than MK in defining these words. He makes homophone errors with both regular words (e.g. DOE → 'something you cook with'), and irregular words (e.g. KNOW → 'no money — not got anything'). He must therefore be using routine 2 for semantic access on some occasions. That he is much better than chance in choosing between the correct meaning and the meaning of the homophone demonstrates that he cannot be using *only* a phonological code for semantic access: one additional source of information that he tries to use is his knowledge of a word's spelling. So, for example, STAKE → 'that's not how you spell steak you eat'; unfortunately his spelling is poor, so he sometimes comes to the correct conclusion for the wrong reasons: HERE → 'Its not when you hear something — that's H-E-I-R'; PLANE → 'Its spelled like a plane you fly not a plane you cut wood with'. On other occasions his attempts to use spelling mislead him: BREAK → 'To break something. B-R-A-K — there should be an E on it. I guess its on a car', PASTE → 'not something you put on wall paper; its not spelled like that'.

EE does not rely exclusively on phonological codes for semantic access; there are (very) occasional responses where he defines a word correctly that he cannot read aloud. For example, QUAY → '/kjʊə/ . . . /kjʊə/ [cure . . . cure] — I can't say it. Its something in the sea and ships tie onto it', LOAN → '/əʊən/ [lowen] — not to borrow something'. He can, therefore, occasionally use routine 1.

Tasks requiring a phonological code for lexical access

On all the tasks that required 'direct' lexical access without phonological recoding MK performed very much better than EE: MK had no difficulty in accepting irregular words in lexical decision, he had no difficulty in defining irregular words, and made no 'homophone' comprehension errors. Only EE ever made responses that demonstrated that he was using a phonological code, by accepting pseudohomophones in lexical decision, and having difficulty in defining irregular words and words with homophones. In this section, we report the results on a set of tests that *require* the subjects to use a phonological code to perform well. In these experiments, which all involve pseudohomophones, the previous pattern is reversed; EE is very much better than MK at accessing lexical information from pseudohomophones.

Choosing the pseudohomophone

The patients were presented with 39 pairs of non-words: of each pair one was a pseudohomophone and the other a control non-word. The two words differed in a single letter; they were in fact the non-words from the lexical decision task, where the two sets of non-words were matched for their visual similarity to real words. With each pair the subjects were asked to 'choose the one that would sound like a real word', but they were not allowed to say the words aloud. Examples of pairs of non-words are STAWN – STAWK, FLOO – FROO, JATE – WATE. A chance level of performance is 50% correct.

EE managed 81% correct: this is significantly better than chance (Binomial test, $p < 0.001$). MK, on the other hand, was only 62% correct, which is not significantly better than chance ($p > 0.10$). On this task, which requires the use of routine 3, EE performed significantly more accurately than MK (McNemar's test, $p < 0.05$).

Defining pseudohomophones

The two patients were given a list of 80 pseudohomophones to define such as BOTE, TODE, TIAL and KWENE. On separate occasions they also defined the corresponding written real words (BOAT, TOAD, TILE, QUEEN . . .) and read the pseudohomophones aloud. Any response which demonstrated some knowledge of the meaning of the appropriate real word was counted correct.

Table 7. Defining written pseudohomophones, written real words and reading the pseudohomophones aloud (proportions correct; n=80 in each cell).

	Pseudo-homophone definition	Real word definition	Pseudo-homophone reading
EE	0.58	0.71	0.55
MK	0.38	0.89	0.83

The results (Table 7) show that EE is significantly better than MK at defining pseudohomophones ($p < 0.01$). As MK is significantly better than EE at defining the real written words ($p < 0.01$), this cannot be because of a specific difficulty in the task of definition. As MK is significantly better than EE at reading the pseudohomophones aloud correctly, his difficulty in pseudohomophone definition cannot be located in the process of accessing a phonological code. By elimination,therefore, MK's difficulty in this task must lie in the processes of access to the semantic system from an output phonological code. In terms of the model outlined in Figure 1, the problem must be either in the process of 'phonological-to-auditory conversion' or in the process of semantic access from an auditory input code. The next experiment examines which of these two processes is responsible for MK's difficulty.

The effects of word imageability on pseudohomophone definition

This experiment takes advantage of the fact that MK is better at defining *auditorily* presented words when they have high rather than low imageability ratings. Thus on a set of 100 auditorily presented words of each type (matched for frequency and length), he defined 65% of the high imageability and only 27% of the low imageability words. With written words, his performance was very much better (high imageability 99%, low 67%); this relatively good performance demonstrates that (i) the difficulty with low imageability words with auditory presentation is not only because low imageability words are harder to define, and (ii) that the auditory comprehension problem is (at least partly) in the process of semantic access, and not in defective central semantic representations.

A list of 25 high imageability words and 25 low imageability words was prepared. The lists were matched for word length and word frequency. From these words pseudohomophones were generated, and the lists matched for the degree of visual similarity between the real word and the pseudohomophones. (Visual similarity was assessed as follows: each letter that was identical and in the same ordinal position, counting from either beginning or end, scored 1, an each shared letter in a different position scored 0.5. These scores, totalled, were then divided by the total number of letters in the real word. Thus PRUFE/PROOF scores 2.5/5 = 0.5, STYOODENT/STUDENT 6/7 = 0.86, PHITE/FIGHT 1.5/5 = 0.3.)

MK was given the written pseudohomophones to define. He was also asked to define the auditorily presented real words, and to read the pseudohomophones aloud. The results (Table 8) show that, consistent with other results, MK is much better at defining spoken words of high imageability, but, surprisingly, his ability to define their written pseudohomophones is unaffected by their imageability. From this we can infer that he does not use his auditory semantic access system in comprehending pseudohomophones.

Table 8. Patient MK's performance in defining high and low imageability written pseudohomophones, spoken real words and reading the pseudohomophones aloud.

Task	High imageability words $n=25$	Low imageability words $n=25$	Fisher exact test
Written pseudohomophone definition	0.40	0.36	$z=0.00$, ns
Auditory real word definition	0.88	0.40	$z=3.21$, $p<0.001$
Reading written pseudohomophones aloud	0.56	0.68	$z=0.58$, ns

Table 9. The effects of word length on oral reading and definition of written pseudohomophones (patient MK).

Phoneme length	n	Pseudohomophone definition	Pseudohomophone reading
6–7	8	0.38	0.25
5	11	0.27	0.64
4	25	0.44	0.64
2–3	6	0.33	1.00

Table 10. The effects of visual similarity between pseudohomophones and the corresponding real words on oral reading and definition of written pseudo-homophones (patient MK; for definition of the measure of 'visual similarity' see text).

'Visual similarity'	*n*	Pseudohomophone definition	Pseudohomophone reading
0.86–0.70	15	0.53	0.60
0.67–0.57	18	0.33	0.44
0.50–0.30	17	0.29	0.82

MK is clearly not using the (normal) routine 3 for understanding pseudo-homophones. *Post hoc* analyses allow us to identify how he does do it. The effects of word length on oral pseudohomophone reading and pseudohomophone definition are shown in Table 9; the non-words he reads aloud correctly are significantly shorter than those on which he makes errors (Mann-Whitney, $p < 0.025$). Thus his sub-lexical reading routine is more likely to work correctly with shorter non-words. In contrast, his definition of these pseudohomophones is unaffected by their length. This demonstrates that MK cannot be using the SLRR in the task of pseudohomophone definition.

MK manages to produce appropriate definitions for nearly 40% of pseudohomophones; how does he do it? Table 10 shows the influence of the visual similarity between pseudohomophone and the corresponding real word on his ability to define it. It transpires that the non-words he defines correctly are more visually similar to their real-word homophones than those that he fails to define (Mann-Whitney, $p < 0.05$). Analysis of MK's performance in the previous experiment (see Table 7) shows that there too visual similarity was an important factor; on pseudohomophones with a similarity of more than 0.70 he defined 0.67 correctly; on those with similarity <0.5 he was 0.28 correct. Thus MK appears to be using the technique of 'approximate visual access' in pseudohomophone definition. He is in fact using exactly the same approach as 'deep dyslexic' patients when confronted by non-words (Saffran and Marin, 1977; Patterson, 1978). While MK uses visual similarity in understanding non-words, unlike the deep dyslexics he does not use this technique to pronounce them. The effect of word length on reading pseudohomophones aloud suggests that, like normal people, he uses a SLRR for this task, but that it is (mildly) defective.

The pattern of errors supports this view. In definition, many of MK's responses seem to be related to highly visually similar real words:

KONSURT → 'bride' (consort?)
PALISS → 'bed' (palliasse?)
CHARE → 'stockbroker' (share?)

PHITE → 'pale' (white?)
RASHEN → 'bacon' (rasher?)
NIGHF → 'twilight' (night?)

The errors in oral reading of these pseudohomophones, on the other hand, reflect mistakes in the operation of a sub-lexical reading routine. Of these six examples he read all but one correctly aloud. His error was:

KONSURT → /ˈkɒsɔt/ [kossort].

Errors with other items include:

TRETE → /tret/ [trett]
EKSIBBIT → /ɛkˈsæbit/ [exabbit]
PHORLT → /fɔt/ [fort]
PORSHEN → /ˈpɜʃən/ [persian]
KULCHER → /ˈkɜtʃə/ [kercher]
SKAIRCE → /skɑs/ [skarce]

Conclusions from the comprehension tasks

In terms of their oral word reading both these patients are clearly 'surface dyslexics'. They read regular words better than irregular words, and when they misread words, many of their errors are phonologically plausible renderings of the letter string. Clearly they lack (some) of the lexically-specific knowledge that is needed to deal with the irregularities of English orthography; faced with letter strings for which they have no lexical source of the phonology, they have to generate a spoken word form using a sub-lexical reading routine. The existence of phonologically plausible reading errors demonstrates that the patients use the SLRR; with neither patient, though, is the SLRR working perfectly. Given single syllable non-words to pronounce, MK does rather better than EE, but both patients make errors, and MK makes less errors with short non-words than longer ones.

The similarity that the patients exhibit in oral reading breaks down when we consider word comprehension tasks. Here their performance, which is summarized in Table 11, shows a classic *double dissociation*. In all tasks where reliance on phonological recoding would lead to errors (i.e. tasks 4, 5, 6, in Table 11) EE performs significantly *worse* than MK. In all tasks with pseudohomophones that require phonological recoding before lexical access (i.e. tasks 7 and 9 in Table 11), EE performs significantly *better* than MK. This double dissociation, therefore, provides conclusive proof that there are at least two independent routines for semantic access: a 'direct' route (1) and routes that rely on phonological recoding (2 and 3). Earlier studies of 'surface dyslexics' demonstrated that there can be occasional responses where a patient can understand a word that s/he cannot pro-

Table 11. Summary of performance of the patients on different experimental tasks.

	Patient EE	Patient MK
Oral reading		
1. Regular versus irregular words: Errors:	Regular⟩irregular; Phonologically plausible errors.	Regular⟩irregular; Phonologically plausible errors.
2. Non-word reading	Moderate	Better than EE, with short non-words
	Short=long.	Short⟩⟩long.
Visual lexical decision		
3. Regular versus irregular words	No difference.	No difference.
4. Pseudohomophones versus control non-words	Pseudohomophones ⟨⟨controls.	No effect.
Written word comprehension		
5. Regular versus irregular words	Regular⟩irregular.	No difference.
6. Defining written words with homophones	Poor performance; Homophone errors.	Good performance; No homophone errors.
7. Defining pseudo-homophones	Definition as good as oral reading.	Definition ⟨⟨ oral reading for short words.
8. Visual similarity effect		Visually similar⟩⟩ dissimilar.
Forced choice pseudohomophone selection		
9. Accuracy	Reasonable	At chance

nounce (e.g. Kay and Patterson, 1986); EE follows that pattern. But the evidence presented above shows that, for EE, such responses are exceptional; he usually understands a word as he pronounces it. MK provides the first clear empirical demonstration of a very different pattern of comprehension in a 'surface dyslexic' patient: (i) he has good comprehension of irregular words which he mispronounces, and (ii) he *never* (mis)understands a word as his (mis)pronunciation of it. His typical comprehension response given the word STEAK is 'nice beef /stik/'; EE given the same word might say 'that's not a word, /stik/'.

This double dissociation demonstrates that direct semantic access and semantic access via phonological recoding depend on different and partially independent routines. On the other hand, there are no grounds, in MK or EE's performance here, for differentiating between routines 2 and 3 — that is between two different semantic access routines which depend on phonological recoding, respectively, of lexically derived phonology or of phonology generated by a SLRR. Depending on the nature of the routine that is used to read non-words, and the levels of correspondence between orthography and phonology which it employs, a SLRR might derive the correct phonology for a substantial proportion of non-words (cf. Henderson, 1986; Kay, Chap 9). The existence of a further double dissociation between two dyslexic patients, each relying exclusively on one of the two routines (2 and 3) would demonstrate that there really are two independent non-semantic routes to phonology.

For MK, correct comprehension is not contingent on achieving the correct phonology. The final experiment makes clear why this is. Even in the task of defining pseudohomophones (which *requires* the use of an internally-generated phonological code for lexical access) MK cannot use this kind of routine. He has to fall back on the (inefficient) routine of approximate visual access, known from the non-word reading of deep dyslexics. The reason for his failure in these tasks with pseudohomophones can be pinpointed with some accuracy. His SLRR is working reasonably well; he has only marginal difficulty in generating a phonological code when reading short non-words aloud (although his performance is worse with longer items). Auditory semantic access, while not perfect, is reasonably intact at least for concrete words. The reason why he does not use routine 3 in *understanding* pseudohomophones is that the process of 'phonological-to-auditory conversion' appears entirely abolished. This is why he never makes homophone confusion errors in word definition; why he is unaffected by the presence of pseudohomophones in a lexical decision task; and why he cannot distinguish a pseudohomophone from a control non-word.

MK clearly has a defective routine for using output phonological representations to access input phonology. His performance pattern allows us to put some constraints on the possible functional architecture of the lexical system. First it demonstrates that output phonological codes cannot access auditory word recognition devices directly; in Monsell's notation, input phonological codes (iP) must be distinct from the output phonological codes (oP). Second, to account for oral reading of non-words, there must be a non-lexical routine that allows input orthography (iO) to be converted eventually into output phonology (oP). As Monsell points out in this volume, this routine has conventionally been drawn as a direct connection from iO to oP, but there is no real evidence against a routine that goes via input phonology (i.e. $iO \rightarrow iP \rightarrow oP$). As MK can read (short) non-words aloud with tolerable accuracy he must have a functioning sub-lexical $iO \rightarrow oP$ routine. MK cannot repeat non-words at all, so he has no sub-lexical $iP \rightarrow oP$ routine. His sub-lexical reading cannot therefore depend on a routine $iO \rightarrow iP \rightarrow oP$. There must, therefore, be a non-lexical routine which converts *directly* from input orthography to output phonology.

Intriguingly MK has both an impaired non-lexical $iP \to oP$ routine, and an impaired $oP \to iP$ routine. Evidence from the association of impairments in brain-damaged patients is notoriously weak, but there is a possibility that there is a single $iP \leftrightarrow oP$ routine which can convert, sub-lexically, in either direction.

We have tried to demonstrate in this chapter that brain-damaged patients can have selective patterns of impairment in their word comprehension routines, and that these patterns can motivate particular forms of lexical theory. In the final section we use MK's picture naming performance to demonstrate that there must be a routine for converting output orthography into an input orthographic code.

On another 'feedback' routine in lexical processing

In testing MK's oral picture naming, we notice that he made occasional errors which showed a striking resemblance to his errors in oral word reading. These included occasional responses where he 'sounded' a silent letter in the written word, 'regularizations', and some errors in stress assignment.

ACORN → '/'ækɔn/' [accorn]
NOOSE → '/nuz/' [nooze]
COMB → '/kəʊmb . . . kɒm/' [combb com]
CANOE (kayak) → '/kiæk . . . kænəʊ/' [keeack kanno]
SCROLL → '/skrɒl/' [skroll]
HAT (toque) → '/təʊkeɪ/' [toekay]
MOUSTACHE → '/mʌstætʃiəʊ/' [mustatchio]
CUSHION → '/kʌʃnz/' [kushens]
VOLCANO → '/vɒlkænəʊ . . . vɒlkɒnəʊ/' [volcanno volcarno]
WREATH → '/rɛθ/' [reth]
PALETTE → '/pæ'let/' [paLET]
TUTU (crinoline) → '/krenəʊlaɪn/' [krenolyne].

Examination of the data from single word repetition tasks revealed more errors of (apparently) the same kind. Thus:
'palm' → '/pælmə/' [pal-mer]
'move' → '/məʊv/' [mauve]
'mortgage' → '/mɔtgeɪdʒ/' [morttgage].

We investigated this phenomenon more formally by assembling a set of 45 pictures of items with 'irregularly' spelled names; we borrowed a second set of 20 such pictures from Sally Byng and Max Coltheart. MK named the pictures orally, and, in a separate session one week later, read their names aloud. The results are shown in Table 12.

Table 12. Naming pictures of objects with irregularly spelled names, and reading the written words aloud. (Patient MK.)

	Oral picture naming	Oral word reading
(a) Coltheart–Byng set (n=20)		
Proportion correct	0.75	0.75
Errors:	COMB → '/kɒmb/ [komb]	COMB → '/kəʊmb/' [combb]
	BEAR → '/bɪə/' [beer]	BEAR → '/bɪə/' [beer]
	CANOE → '/kænəʊ/' [kannoe]	PEAR → '/pɪə/' [peer]
	MONEY → 'monkey, pounds, cash'	LEOPARD → '/'lɛməd/' [lemmed]
	FOOT → 'shoes ankles soles'	BOWL → '/baʊl/' [bowel]
(b) Howard–Franklin set (n=45)		
Proportion correct	0.91	0.84
Errors:	COMB → '/kəʊmb, kɒm/' [combb, kom)	COMB → '/kɒmb/' [komb]
	BLOUSE → 'smocks, /pɪənəʊfə/' [peeanofer: cf PINAFORE]	RAZOR → '/raɪzə/' [riser]
		ACORN → '/əkɒn/' [ukorn]
		BEAR → '/bɪə/' [beer]
	SCISSORS → 'scissor'	HEART → '/hɜːt/' [hurt]
	SEWING → '/su/ [soo]	SEWING → '/suɪŋ/ [sooing]
	MACHINE machine'	MACHINE machine
		TRIANGLE → '/tri'æŋgəl/' [treeangle]

There are several examples here of 'phonologically plausible errors' in oral picture naming of just the same kind as MK makes in oral word reading. We have to conclude that he occasionally uses orthographic information in naming, and (probably) in word repetition. In effect, he writes the word down in his head and then reads it aloud using his SLRR. The precise mechanism for this in terms of our modification of the Patterson and Shewell (1987) version of the logogen model is given in Figure 2. In this figure a new routine has been added allowing spelling specifications in the 'graphemic output buffer' to access orthographic input codes. In Monsell's notation (Chap 14), this routine goes: $CF \rightarrow oO \rightarrow iO \rightarrow oP$, and the iO and oP mapping is sub-lexical. The existence of these 'orthographic' naming errors by MK confirms that a feedback routine from oO to iO does exist.

There is at least one other neuropsychological case study that suggests that there is a feedback connection from the 'graphemic output buffer' to the visual input system. Morton (1980) provides a brief sketch of a patient,

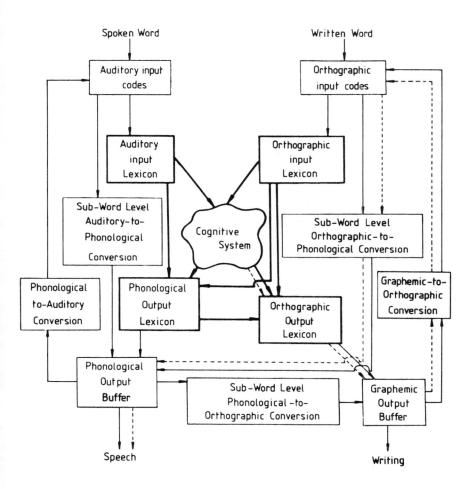

Figure 2. The 'logogen model' adapted to allow for 'orthographic' errors in oral speech production. The dotted line marks the routine which is responsible for these errors.

Gail, who had difficulty in accessing the meanings of auditorily presented words; she appeared to have a moderate degree of word deafness. When trying to understand auditorily presented words she would often write them down, and use the written word for semantic access:

> She was being asked to define the spoken word PLOUGH. She had no idea of its meaning but then wrote it down correctly — not as PLOW, which would have been the obvious result of a simple phoneme–grapheme conversion. She still had no idea of what it meant and then said, 'I've forgotten what it is — (pause) see it in a field — using some sort of machine — something to do with soil . . .'
>
> (Morton, 1980, p. 131).

On this occasion Gail wrote the word down on paper, so only an external feedback loop was involved. When Gail was prevented from writing words down (by denying her paper and pencil), she would report that this did not worry her as she 'wrote them down in her head' (Hatfield, personal communication). If her self-report is accurate, Gail was using, as a strategy in word comprehension, effectively the same routine that MK sometimes uses in retrieving picture names: the graphemic-to-orthographic feedback routine. Quite what role a routine of this kind plays in normal subjects is unclear. One possibility is that it is involved in an editing system used to eliminate non-word spelling errors. What is clear from MK's performance is that a lexical routine of this kind must exist.

Acknowledgements

We thank Dr R. Zeegan for permission to report these investigations on MK; we thank Sally Byng and Max Coltheart for arranging for us to see EE, and for loaning us materials. Alan Allport, Derek Besner, Stephen Monsell and Karalyn Patterson made useful comments on a draft of the manuscript. David Howard was supported by a grant from the Medical Research Council, and Sue Franklin by North West Thames Regional Health Authority.

Notes

[1] Where we present responses in phonemic transcription, we also provide an alphabetic approximation to the pronunciation in square brackets — [].
[2] After word frequency effects have been taken into account, there is still a statistically significant degree of consistency.

References

Bauer, D. W. and Stanovich, K. E. (1980). Lexical access and the spelling-to-sound regularity effect. *Memory and Cognition*, **8**, 424–32.

Besner, D. and Davelaar, E. (1983). Suedohomofoan effects in visual word recognition: evidence for phonological processing. *Canadian Journal of Psychology*, **37**, 300–5.

Bub, D. and Kertesz, A. (1982). Deep agraphia. *Brain and Language*, **17**, 146–65.

Byng, S. and Coltheart, M. (1986). Aphasia therapy research: methodological requirements and illustrative results. In E. Hjelmquist and L. B. Nilsson (Eds) *Communication and handicap*. Amsterdam; North Holland, Elsevier.

Campbell, R. (1983). Writing non-words to dictation. *Brain and Language*, **19**, 153–78.

Coltheart, M. (1982). The psycholinguistic analysis of acquired dyslexia: some illustrations. *Philosophical Proceedings of the Royal Society of London*, **B298**, 151–64.

Coltheart, M. (1985). Cognitive neuropsychology and the study of reading. In M. I. Posner and O. S. M. Marin (Eds) *Attention and performance, XI*. Hillsdale, NJ: Erlbaum.

Coltheart, M., Davelaar, E., Jonasson, J. T. and Besner, D. (1977). Access to the internal lexicon. In S. Dornic (Ed.) *Attention and performance, VI*. Hillsdale, NJ: Erlbaum.

Coltheart, M., Besner, D., Jonasson, J. T. and Davelaar, E. (1979). Phonological encoding in the lexical decision task. *Quarterly Journal of Experimental Psychology*, **31**, 489–507.

Coltheart, M., Masterson, J., Byng, S., Prior, M. and Riddoch, J. (1983). Surface dyslexia. *Quarterly Journal of Experimental Psychology*, **35A**, 469–96.

Dunn, A. (1965). *The Peabody Picture Vocabulary Test*, Minneapolis: American Guidance Service.

Funnell, E. (1983). Phonological processes in reading: new evidence from acquired dyslexia. *British Journal of Psychology*, **74**, 159–80.

Goldblum, M. C. (1986). Word comprehension in surface dyslexia. In K. E. Patterson, J. C. Marshall and M. Coltheart (Eds) *Surface dyslexia: neuropsychological and cognitive analyses of phonological reading*. London: Erlbaum.

Hatfield, F. M. and Patterson, K. E. (1984). Interpretation of spelling disorders in aphasia: impact of recent developments in cognitive psychology. In F. C. Rose (Ed.) *Advances in neurology 42; progress in aphasiology*. New York: Raven.

Henderson, L. (1986). Issues in the modelling of pronunciation assembly in normal reading. In K. E. Patterson, J. C. Marshall and M. Coltheart (Eds) *Surface dyslexia: neuropsychological and cognitive analyses of phonological reading*. London: Erlbaum.

Kaplan, E., Goodglass, H. and Weintraub, S. (1976). *The Boston Naming Test*. Boston: Veteran's Administration.

Kay, J. and Lesser, R. (1985). The nature of phonological processing in oral reading: evidence from surface dyslexia. *Quarterly Journal of Experimental Psychology*, **37A**, 39–81.

Kay, J. and Patterson, K. E. (1986). Routes to meaning in surface dyslexia. In K. E. Patterson, J. C. Marshall and M. Coltheart (Eds) *Surface dyslexia: neuropsychological and cognitive analyses of phonological reading*. London: Erlbaum.

Kremin, H. (1986). Routes and strategies in surface dyslexia and dysgraphia. In K. E. Patterson, J. C. Marshall and M. Coltheart (Eds) *Surface dyslexia: neuropsychological and cognitive analyses of phonological reading*. London: Erlbaum.

Marshall, J. C. (1976). Neuropsychological aspects of orthographic representation. In R. J. Wales and E. Walker (Eds) *New approaches to language mechanisms*. Amsterdam: North-Holland.

Marshall, J. C. and Newcombe, F. (1973). Patterns of paralexia. *Journal of Psycholinguistic Research*, **2**, 175–99.

Morton, J. (1980). The logogen model and orthographic structure. In U. Frith (Ed.) *Cognitive processes in spelling*. London: Academic.

Newcombe, F. and Marshall, J. C. (1981). On the psycholinguistic classifications of the acquired dyslexias. *Bulletin of the Orton Society*, **31**, 29–46.

Newcombe, F. and Marshall, J. C. (1986). Reading and writing by letter sounds. In K. E. Patterson, J. C. Marshall and M. Coltheart (Eds) *Surface dyslexia: neuropsychological and cognitive analyses of phonological reading*. London: Erlbaum.

Parkin, A. J. (1982). Phonological recoding in lexical decision: effects of spelling-to-sound regularity depend on how regularity is defined. *Memory and Cognition*, **10**, 43–53.

Patterson, K. E. (1978). Phonemic dyslexia: errors of meaning and the meaning of errors. *Quarterly Journal of Experimental Psychology*, **30**, 587–607.

Patterson, K. E. and Shewell, C. (1987). Speak and spell: dissociations and word class effects. In M. Coltheart, R. Job and G. Sartori (Eds) *The cognitive neuropsychology of language*. London: Erlbaum. In press.

Patterson, K. E., Marshall, J. C. and Coltheart, M. (1986). *Surface dyslexia: neuropsychological and cognitive analyses of phonological reading*. London: Erlbaum.

Saffran, E. M. and Marin, O. S. M. (1977). Reading without phonology: evidence from aphasia. *Quarterly Journal of Experimental Psychology*, **29**, 515–25.

Shallice, T., Warrington, E. K. and McCarthy, R. (1983). Reading without semantics. *Quarterly Journal of Experimental Psychology*, **35A**, 111–38.

Warrington, E. K. and McKenna, P. (1983). *The Graded Naming Test*. London: NFER.

17 Non-linguistic cognition and word meanings: Neuropsychological exploration of common mechanisms

Elaine Funnell and Alan Allport

Abstract

We report the investigation of two, contrasting dysphasic patients (fluent and non-fluent) who, we showed, were unable to transcode from written to spoken, or from spoken to written linguistic forms, except via the encoding of referential word meaning. Their impairments thus exposed to 'privileged view' systems involved in representing referential word meanings and their mappings to and from language-specific forms.

In three different, cross-modal transcoding tasks (reading aloud, writing to dictation, and aural-visual matching), the patients' performance revealed a steep gradient across different classes of words, according to the words' specific, concrete reference or 'conceptual independence'. This gradient was not found in within-modality tasks. The pattern of performance was investigated further in a variety of related tasks. The data appear at odds with the theoretical construct of unitary 'word-concepts', employed in certain semantic memory models; in particular our observations appear incompatible with the existence of modality-independent (but language specific) word units or 'concept nodes', mediating word comprehension and production. We discuss alternative conceptions of non-linguistic, cognitive codes and the representation of word meaning.

Introduction

This book is concerned with shared, or 'common', mechanisms in the principal receptive and expressive modalities of language: listening, speak-

LANGUAGE PERCEPTION AND PRODUCTION
ISBN 0-12-052750-2

ing, reading and writing. Our contribution is directed towards what we take to be the most central of all such commonalities — central, that is, to all intelligent, communicative uses of language — namely the underlying, cognitive representation of meaning, and the transactions between this cognitive domain and the domain of spoken and written linguistic forms.

Current neuropsychological models of the mental lexicon share the strong assumption that transcribing between spoken and written forms of the same word — in reading aloud or in writing to aural dictation — is mediated by (at least) two radically distinct functional routes or recoding systems in the brain (Allport and Funnell, 1981). On the one hand there are systems that provide relatively 'direct' recoding between the phonological and the orthographic domains (systems which, in some models, are further subdivided into lexical and sublexical components). On the other hand there are functionally quite distinct 'semantic' procedures for transcoding between spoken and written language, mediated via the cognitive representation of word meaning. Further evidence of the functional separability of 'semantic' and 'non-semantic' transcoding between spoken and written word-forms is amply illustrated in the three preceding chapters.

In some neurological patients, however, such 'direct' transcoding between spoken and written word-forms can be impaired or even abolished. In such cases, communication between spoken and written language appears to depend on the mediation of a system of representation that is itself independent of the surface forms of words. In this paper we describe the residual abilities of two such patients to transcode, in various ways, between written and spoken forms. (The experiments we describe here are, for the most part, limited to the transcoding of individual, isolated words.) The results of these experiments enable us to infer some important features of the non-linguistic cognitive codes mediating their performance, and of their relation to different classes of spoken and written words.

The subjects

Our investigation concerns two, contrasting dysphasic patients, whose remaining language abilities, as seen in their spontaneous speech, represent one of the most striking, and commonly observed dissociations in aphasia. We can illustrate these contrasting dysphasic types with the patients' spoken descriptions of the 'Cookie Theft' Picture (Goodglass and Kaplan, 1972). First, for comparison, here is a description of this picture, given by a non brain-damaged subject:

'A boy is taking a cookie from a cookie jar. He is standing on a stool to reach the cupboard and he is handing it to — presumably — his sister, who is standing with an outstretched arm waiting for it. The stool is overbalanced and about to fall over. A lady, presumably his mother, is standing in front of the sink with an open window in front of her, drying a plate, whilst the sink overflows with water onto the floor.'

The speech pattern of the first patient (RC) is extremely hesistant. Long pauses ranging from ten to forty seconds separate each short utterance.

'Water . . . man . . . no . . . woman . . . child, no man, . . . and girl . . . cupboard . . . man . . . falling . . . jar . . . cakes . . . head . . . face . . . window . . . tap.'

RC was able to name many items in the picture, but, unlike the normal subject, was unable to describe it in syntactically connected phrases. This pattern of grossly dysfluent speech, confined almost exclusively to specific words (here predominantly nouns) and devoid of syntactic construction, conforms with the classic pattern of severe Broca's aphasia, as described in the Boston Classification of Aphasic Types (Goodglass and Kaplan, 1972).

The picture description produced by our second patient (AL) was very different. His speech was prosodic and fluent, but marked by frequent hesitations and repetitions in which he appeared to be trying, generally unsuccessfully, to produce the name of a specific object or event in the picture:

'Well, it's a, it's a . . . place and its a g-girl and a boy . . . and they've got obviously something which is is made . . . some made, made, made. Well, it's just beginning to go and be rather unpleasant . . . um . . . and this is -mm- the . . . this is the the woman, and she's put putting some stuff, and the . . . it's, it's . . . that's being really too big t to do, and nobody seems to have got anything there at all at all, and er it's . . . I'm rather surprised at that, but there you are. This, this . . . er this stuff, this . . . is coming. They were both being one and another . . . er put here and er . . . um um . . . I suppose the idea is that the . . . er two people should be fairly good . . . but I think its going to go somewhere; and as I say its . . . down again . . . Let's see what else has gone . . . er . . . The the . . . this is just . . . I don't know how she did, how they did this, but it must have been fairly hard when they did it and er . . . I think there isn't v very much there, I think'

In comparison with the account given by the normal subject, the paucity of specific referential words leaves AL's account curiously empty of meaning. Very common 'general purpose' words have replaced words with specific reference: nouns such as *place, stuff, thing* and verbs such as *go, do, put* and *make* predominate. In a sample of more than 4000 words taken from AL's description of a variety of pictures and from recorded conversations, only 10% of the noun and 3% of the verb instances could be considered to be specific in reference.

This characteristic of anomic speech, the loss of *specific* reference and its replacement by *non*-specific referring terms has been described many times before (e.g. Geschwind, 1967; Goodglass, 1980; Caramazza and Berndt, 1978). Contrary to some reports of anomia, in which a predominant loss of nouns is noted (e.g. Lesser, 1978, p. 16), AL has not lost the ability to produce particular grammatical word-classes; there are plentiful examples of all the grammatical classes in his speech, including nouns. In a simple naming test of 36 pictured, common objects, AL correctly named only 8, while RC named 30/36. When AL is directly challenged to produce specific referential words, his speech production becomes extremely laboured and hesitant, and his attempted approximations to the target word, when he can be persuaded to attempt them, exhibit marked phonemic distortions. AL also has a severe deficit of oral and written repetition, with a digit-span of only two items, again with abundant phonological errors and effortful production. However, unlike some patients of this kind, the probability of AL's successful word-production appears unaffected by word-length. Thus, for example, the probability of his correct repetition of isolated words, of one and three syllables, was 0.52 and 0.49 respectively. The combined pattern of fluent, anomic speech and marked repetition deficit, with phonological errors in naming, is characteristic of so-called 'conduction aphasia' (Green and Howes, 1977; see also Allport, 1984a).

It is worth emphasizing that, despite their severe language disability, neither RC nor AL exhibited any other obvious cognitive impairment. Their understanding of events, of personal and causal interactions, as reflected in their non-linguistic behaviour appears entirely normal.

Cross modality (spoken–written) transcoding tasks: single words

RC and AL differ dramatically in the word-classes that are available to them in their spontaneous speech. In order to investigate further their abilities with these different word classes, in *other* language tasks, we selected a sample ($n = 245$) of what we have called *specific* and *non-specific* words. 'Specific' words were drawn from those word-classes notably absent from AL's spontaneous speech, whereas the 'non-specific' words occurred there plentifully. (We should emphasize that this initial classification into 'specific' and 'non-specific' words was directly and empirically based on the corpus of AL's recorded, spontaneous utterances (Funnell, 1983).) These two word-groups were further subdivided according to grammatical class and, in the case of 'specific' nouns, into additional subcategories of concrete, abstract, and superordinate nouns. 'Concrete' nouns were the names of basic level objects (Rosch, 1978); following Rosch *et al.* (1976), biological category names such as 'tree' and 'fish' were included as basic level, concrete nouns rather than as 'superordinates'. Table 1 provides further details and examples.

Table 1. Words grouped according to specificity. Median word-frequency (Kucera and Francis, 1967) and median ratings of imageability (range 0–7).

Word category	Examples	Frequency (medians)	Imageability
'Specific' word classes			
Concrete nouns	apple, canoe, pistol	21	6.3
Superordinate nouns	fruit, vehicle, weapon	35	5.4
Abstract nouns	proof, skill, pride, theme	54	2.4
Specific adjectives	hot, loud, shiny, sour	49	4.3
Specific verbs	bake, write, sing, knit	34	4.3
'Non-specific' word classes			
Generic nouns	place, thing, idea, stuff	264	2.4
Non-specific adjectives	same, next, few	1,095	2.3
Non-specific verbs	go, take, want, use	683	1.7
Pronouns	he, they, it	3,286	3.1
Spatial prepositions	in, below, under	895	2.7
Functors	and, but, for	2,292	0.6

The patients' performance with these different word-classes was tested in three cross-modality transcoding tasks: *reading aloud, writing to dictation*, and *aural–visual matching*. In the first two of these tasks, a single word was presented to the patient, either orally or in written (lower-case, printed) form, and the patient was requested to write down or, respectively, to read the word aloud. No time limit was given. In aural–visual matching a printed list of words, drawn from the same word-category, was provided. One of the words in the list was spoken to the patient, who was asked to point to its written version in the list. Unlike reading aloud and writing to dictation this task in principle requires only recognition of the corresponding word form, rather than its overt recall. No doubt this matching task can be performed by more than one method or 'strategy'. Some experimental data, that allows us to identify the strategy adopted by our patients, is described later.

Between them, these three tasks tap all four modalities of language performance that are the subject of this volume: reading, writing, listening and speaking.

Table 2. Proportion of correct responses in three tasks of transcoding between spoken and written language. (Words having 'specific' reference are those that appear unavailable in AL's spontaneous speech.)

Subject	Word class	Reading aloud	Writing to dictation		Aural–Visual matching
			(Initial letter)	(Whole word)	
AL	'Specific'	0.42	0.75	0.07	0.47
	'Non-Specific'	0.10**	0.25*	0.03	0.19**
RC	'Specific'	0.81	0.88	0.11	0.71
	'Non-Specific'	0.35**	0.48**	0.08	0.17**

Significance level of specific/non-specific difference: $* = p<0.01$; $** = p<0.001$.

Table 2 summarizes the patients' overall level of accuracy at each of these three tasks. (In the task of writing to dictation, performance was so poor that, for the present analysis, only the scores for the initial letter of each word will be used. For both patients, accuracy of writing to dictation declined monotonically from left to right within a word, such that, for many words, only the initial letter was correct. In some cases they were unwilling to attempt to write more than the first one, or possibly two, letters of a word.) In striking contrast to their very different patterns of spontaneous speech, *both* patients were significantly more successful in transcoding 'specific' than 'non-specific' words in each of the three transcoding tasks ($p < 0.001$ for each of the six comparisons, except for AL in writing to dictation, $p < 0.01$).

Error Analysis

In reading aloud, the large majority of errors were simple omissions, i.e. failures to respond at all. In writing to dictation, the majority of errors were similarly either a failure to respond altogether, or the production of only a single letter or incomplete word. The frequency of these and the remaining error types are listed in Table 3.

Table 3. Proportion of different types of error observed in reading aloud and in writing to dictation.

Error type	Reading aloud		Writing to dictation	
	AL	RC	AL	RC
Omission	0.68	0.71	0.27	0.44
Unrelated word	0.14	0.15	0.03	0.00
Perseveration	0.12	0.00	0.00	0.00
Semantic	0.01	0.00	0.01	0.01
Derivational	0.01	0.03	—	—
Visual	0.02	0.01	—	—
Incomplete word	0.01	0.04	0.26	0.11
Single letter	—	—	0.39	0.41
One deviant letter	—	—	0.04	0.03

Table 4 provides a more detailed summary of accuracy for each of the eleven word-categories. It is clear from this table that what we have classified as 'specific' and 'non-specific' word-categories do not simply fall into two dichotomous groups, as regards performance on these tasks. Rather, their performance shows a continuous decline across word-sets, with a considerable degree of concordance across the three tasks. The difference in the level of performance between the most and the least successful word class *within* either the 'specific' or the 'non-specific' group is greater than the overall difference between these two groups. Nevertheless, across all tasks, the best performances are obtained consistently to specific word classes and the poorest to non-specific. With the exception of generic nouns, there is relatively little overlap between the two groups.

It is worth noting that the '*non*-specific' words are nearly all of very high frequency of occurrence in normal language (Table 1). If this were the sole (or even major) factor in successful performance, then the expected ordering of the different word-classes would of course be almost completely the reverse of what we actually find. If there is an effect of word frequency in our data, it is masked by the effects of other and clearly much more powerful factors.

Grammatical class, as such, also appears to play relatively little part in determining the superiority of 'specific' over 'non-specific' words, at least as regards the major grammatical categories of nouns, verbs and adjectives. Thus, for example, *specific* verbs and adjectives produce consistently better performances than *non*-specific verbs and adjectives; concrete nouns are transcoded much more successfully than abstract nouns, across all three tasks, etc. We also note in passing that effects which have sometimes been attributed to grammatical class are rather easily confounded with other *semantic*, or non-linguistic variables (Allport and Funnell, 1981).

E. Funnell and A. Allport

Table 4. Reading aloud and aural–visual matching: proportion of words correctly transcoded. (Writing to dictation: proportion of correctly written initial letters.) Words categorised according to specific reference and grammatical word class.

Reading aloud		Writing to dictation		Aural–visual matching	
		RC			
specific adjs.	**0.93**	**superord. nouns**	**0.88**	**superord. nouns**	**1.00**
specific verbs	**0.90**	**concr. nouns**	**0.73**	**specific verbs**	**1.00**
concr. nouns	**0.88**	**specific verbs**	**0.71**	generic nouns	0.92
generic nouns	0.66	**specific adjs.**	**0.60**	**concr. nouns**	**0.90**
superord. nouns	**0.58**	**abstract nouns**	**0.50**	**specific adjs.**	**0.85**
abstract nouns	**0.50**	pronouns	0.29	**abstract nouns**	**0.63**
non-spec.verbs	0.40	functors	0.20	pronouns	0.57
non-spec. adjs.	0.40	spatial preps.	0.00	spatial preps.	0.44
functors	0.36	non-spec. verbs	0.00	non-spec. adjs.	0.29
spatial preps.	0.22	generic nouns	0.00	functors	0.28
pronouns	0.20			non-spec. verbs	0.20
		AL			
concr. nouns	**0.65**	**concr. nouns**	**0.65**	**concr. nouns**	**1.00**
generic nouns	0.33	**specific verbs**	**0.43**	**superord. nouns**	**0.88**
specific verbs	**0.30**	**superord. nouns**	**0.38**	**specific verbs**	**0.75**
specific adjs.	**0.29**	spatial pres.	0.37	generic nouns	0.67
abstract bouns	**0.25**	**abstract nouns**	**0.25**	**specific adjs.**	**0.61**
prounouns	0.20	non-spec. verbs	0.22	**abstract nouns**	**0.54**
non-spec. verbs	0.20	**specific adjs.**	**0.20**	functors	0.50
superord. nouns	**0.17**	pronouns	0.14	pronouns	0.43
non-spec. adjs.	0.00	functors	0.10	non-spec. verbs	0.30
spatial preps.	0.00	generic nouns	0.00	spatial preps.	0.22
functors	0.00			non-spec. adjs.	0.17

It will scarcely have escaped notice that, while RC is most successful, generally, in transcoding those word-classes that are also present in her spontaneous speech, for AL the reverse appears to be the case. AL's spontaneous speech contains virtually no specific referring words; yet, like RC, he is much more successful at transcoding these specific word-categories than the non-specific words which appear prolifically and fluently in his spontaneous utterances. The explanation of this very striking reversal will occupy a considerable part of our discussion later in this chapter. For the present we simply note that two patients who show sharply contrasting patterns of dysphasia, according to classifications based on their spontaneous expression — amounting to an apparent 'double dissociation' with respect to their usage of 'specific' and 'non-specific' words — perform qualitatively quite similarly in these tasks of cross-modal transcoding.

Direction of transcoding in aural–visual matching

Unlike the other two transcoding tasks, in aural–visual matching the direction of the transcoding process is open to question. On the one hand the strategy may be similar in some respects to the task of writing to dictation: i.e. based on the auditorily presented word the patient endeavours to *generate an orthographic code* and then compares this with each of the visually presented letter-strings until a match is found. Secondly, the patients might rely on their partial ability to read aloud, generating a *phonological* representation from the written words in the list to match with the auditorily presented word. As a third possibility they might attempt to compare 'receptively' both spoken and written words in terms of their meaning. Of course, they might also use a combination of these strategies.

The following simple experiment was designed to exclude the second and the third (the 'reading' strategy and the 'meaning comparison' strategy).

Experiment 1: Aural–visual matching to single letters

In this experiment, in place of a list of written words, the subjects were presented with a row of three *letters*, one of which formed the initial letter of the (single) auditorily presented word. The idea was that, by presenting only initial letters for aural–visual matching, the potential 'reading' strategy and the semantic matching strategies could be excluded. (Table 6, below, shows that these patients were completely unable to transcode isolated letters overtly into phonological form.) For Experiment 1a, two sets of 30 words were selected for auditory presentation. One set consisted of 'specific', concrete nouns (median frequency 83 per million); the other set was composed of 'non-specific' words, including verbs, adjectives and functors (median frequency 872 per million). Each 'specific' word was paired with a 'non-specific' word that shared the same initial letter; thus 'nose' was paired with 'next', 'girl' with 'get', 'hand' with 'how', etc. On a

Table 5. Aural–visual matching of spoken words to initial letter: proportion correct.

	Experiment 1a			Experiment 1b		
	spec.	non-spec.	(diff.)	spec.	non-spec.	(diff.)
RC	0.96	0.36	**	0.78	0.44	*
AL	0.80	0.53	*	0.67	0.44	

Significance level of specific/non-specific difference:
*$p<0.05$ **$p<0.001$.

given trial the subject saw three letters (e.g. j k n) and heard a single word
(e.g. 'nose'). The non-target letters in each trial were chosen so that their
phonemic equivalents differed from the target letter by, on average, 3.3
distinctive features (Chomsky and Halle, 1968). For Experiment 1b, a new
set of 18 'specific' and 18 'non-specific' words was constructed, for which
the initial letters could not be derived by simple grapheme–phoneme (or
phoneme–grapheme) correspondences (e.g. 'knife'–'know'; 'wrist'–'who,
etc.). The procedure was otherwise identical to that for Experiment 1a.
Thus, even if the patient had been able to derive an implicit pronunciation
from the initial letters, this would not enable them to perform successfully
in Experiment 1b.

The results of this experiment are shown in Table 5. As in the previous
(word-to-word) aural–visual matching task (Table 2) we found a clear
superiority of 'specific' over 'non-specific' words. (The higher overall
accuracy in the present task may be attributed to the smaller number of
alternatives.) The implication seems clear, that for these patients aural–
visual matching performance does not depend on an implicit 'reading
aloud' strategy. Neither can it depend on the purely 'receptive' encoding
and comparison of word meanings, since isolated initial letters presumably
do not lend themselves to semantic encoding. It seems possible, therefore,
that even when they were doing aural–visual matching of complete words,
AL and RC depended predominantly on the strategy of implicitly generating the written form of the word (or at least its initial letter) and comparing
this against the visually presented alternatives. It seems equally clear (from
Experiment 1b) that their performance depends on a *lexical* transcoding
process rather than on the use of any phoneme–grapheme correspondences. The issue of non-lexical transcoding is explored further in the
following section.

Non-lexical, written-spoken transcoding

We constructed a set of pronounceable, one-syllable pseudowords (e.g.
kulp, tife, peem), on which the patients, AL and RC, were asked to
perform each of the three transcoding tasks, as for real words. They also
carried out the same three tasks (reading aloud, writing to dictation, and
aural–visual matching) with single written letters and their spoken phonetic
counterparts (e.g. the letter p and the spoken syllable /pə/). As can be seen
from Table 6, the patients were unable to read these stimuli aloud correctly
or to write them to dictation. In the matching task where no spoken or
written output is required, AL's performance was still not significantly
better than chance, but RC was able to score around 50% correct. It seems

clear from these results that the patients' remaining ability to transcode meaningful words correctly between written and spoken form — in particular in reading aloud and in writing to dictation — cannot depend on the preservation of *sub*-lexical processes of graphemic–phonetic recoding, even as regards the initial-letter score in writing words to dictation (Table 2). (In the case of RC's performance at aural–visual matching, however, though not in the other two tasks, scores at or below 50% with real words may be difficult to interpret and *could* depend on residual, sublexical recoding.)

Table 6. Non-lexical transcoding tasks: proportion correct.

Task	Subject	Non-words	Stimuli Letters/phonemes	
		Whole item correct	Initial letter correct	
Reading aloud	AL	0.00	0.00	0.00
	RC	0.00	0.10	0.00
Writing to dictation	AL	0.00	0.13	0.00
	RC	0.00	0.00	0.16
Aural–visual matching	AL	0.06	0.38*	0.25
	RC	0.54*	0.54*	0.50*

* above chance (* $p < 0.01$)

Normal, literate individuals are clearly able to recode written language into speech — and *vice versa* — 'directly', that is in terms solely of phonetic and orthographic *form*, without mediation of semantic recoding. Several of the chapters in this volume are explicitly concerned with these direct kinds of recoding processes. RC and AL, however, suffer from a radical inability to generate the spoken form of words directly from their written form, or their written form directly from speech. Nevertheless even minimal, direct information-transmission between orthographic and phonological coding domains might be sufficient to cue the patients when an *incorrect, semantically mediated* response was generated sufficient perhaps to enable them to veto its production, even though 'direct' transcoding of this kind was altogether insufficient, in their case, to specify what the correct response should be. If the patients retained some such residual 'direct' transcoding ability, as seems apparent from their aural–visual matching performance, this could account for the more or less complete absence of synonym or other 'semantic' errors in their reading aloud and in their written dictation (Table 3).

Within-modality lexical tasks

The evidence we have presented shows that, for these patients, translation between the spoken and written forms of familiar words was very much better for 'specific' than for 'non-specific' words. What we have not yet established is whether this difference extends to *within*-modality operations on the word-forms themselves. For example, is it possible that, in these dysphasic patients, the systems underlying knowledge of individual word-forms (*'logogen* units'?) are themselves differentially impaired or differentially accessible, as regards 'specific' and 'non-specific' words? We endeavoured to test this possibility by means of three different, within-modality tasks: auditory–vocal repetition, written copying, and a lexical decision task.

Auditory–vocal repetition

Single monosyllabic words were spoken, once only, in full view of the patient, who was asked to repeat the stimuli aloud. Twenty 'specific' words were taken from the set of concrete nouns ($n = 10$) and specific verbs ($n = 10$) used in the cross-modal transcoding tasks; twenty 'non-specific' words were drawn from the set of non-specific verbs ($n = 10$) and syntactic functors ($n = 10$) used in the same tasks. Twenty pseudo-words (as used above) were also presented for oral repetition. Table 7 summarizes the results. Three points can be made. First, both patients show some impairment (AL considerably so) on what is, for normal speakers, an extremely easy task. For both patients, and particularly in the case of AL, spoken production in these tasks appears intensely effortful and laboured. Both patients, we infer, suffer from a low-level impairment in the motor production of speech, which affects 'specific' and 'non-specific' words indifferently. The same impairment arguably accounts for the relatively poor performance of both patients in spoken production tasks (including reading aloud) even for highly specific referential words. Second, their repetition performance is at least partly mediated by word-specific, lexical knowledge; auditory-vocal repetition of pseudowords, for both patients, is

Table 7. Auditory–vocal repetition of single words according to word class (specific words, non-specific words and matched non-words). Proportion correct.

Word category	AL	RC
specific words ($n=20$)	0.74	0.85
non-specific words ($n=20$)	0.75	0.90
non-words ($n=20$)	0.55	0.70

Word/non-word advantage: AL $d=2.27$, $p<0.05$; RC $d=2.30$, $p<0.05$.

significantly inferior to the repetition of real words. Third, there is no sign of the superiority of 'specific' over 'non-specific' word-classes that was so marked a feature of the cross-modal tasks.

Written copying

Sets of 'specific' and 'non-specific' words were selected in the same way as for auditory–vocal repetition, with the constraint that every item had just four letters. Pseudowords, differing from real words by just one letter, were similarly constructed. Each written stimulus was exposed, one at a time, for three seconds. As soon as it was removed the patient attempted to write it down. A fresh sheet of paper was provided for each response. Their performance was extremely poor. AL averaged only 0.30 correct, while RC scored no better than 0.25, for word stimuli. Both patients performed even less accurately with pseudowords: AL scored 0.20, while RC scored zero. As with auditory–vocal repetition, there was no significant difference between their performance on the 'specific' and 'non-specific' word-sets. Again, we are led to infer an impairment in the retrieval of orthographic codes for written production, which affects all classes of letter-strings indifferently.

Lexical decision

Better performance with words than with pseudowords on the preceding repetition tasks is an indication that the performance, depends, in part at least on word-specific representations. That is, the difference between word and pseudoword performance, at the least, must depend upon word-level representations. A more direct approach to the status of the spoken and written word-forms in these patients' internal representation might be offered by a lexical decision task. Sets of 'specific' (concrete nouns) and 'non-specific' words (functors) were selected. Each written word was altered by one letter to form a corresponding, orthographically legal pseudoword. For the spoken version of the task, the pseudowords always differed by at least two articulatory distinctive features from their corresponding real word. The patients were asked to classify each item as a real English word or not. Table 8 shows the results. In contrast to the preceding two production tasks, the level of accuracy was high. So far as this evidence goes, there is again no indication of any impairment selectively affecting the internal representation of *non*-specific, spoken or written word-forms. (Of course, performance at or near ceiling, as here, may obscure more subtle differences, but these could scarcely be such as to account for the very large effects seen in cross-modality transcoding.)

Table 8. Lexical decision with written and spoken words and matched non-words (twenty items in each set). Proportion correct.

	AL		RC	
	Words	Non-words	Words	Non-words
Visual presentation				
Concrete nouns	1.0	0.9	1.0	0.9
Functors	1.0	1.0	1.0	1.0
Auditory presentation				
Concrete nouns	1.0	1.0	1.0	1.0
Functors	1.0	0.9	1.0	0.9

From the evidence of these three, within-modality tasks it seems clear that the specificity effect seen in transcoding *between* spoken and written word-forms is not the result of *differential* impairment in the coding systems ('*logogen*' units'?) that encode the spoken and written forms of the words themselves. However, our evidence indicates some impairment in the retrieval from both the orthographic and the phonological domains. Manifestly, a word's specificity of reference is a matter of its semantic representation, and our hypothesis is that in order to perform the cross-modal transcoding tasks these subjects are forced to rely on a 'semantic' or conceptual recoding of the word's meaning, from which its form is then retrieved in the other modality. We can represent this hypothesis diagrammatically as in Figure 1 (cf. Allport and Funnell, 1981).

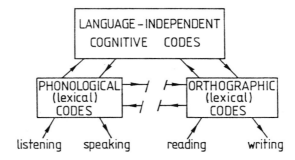

Figure 1. Diagram illustrating minimal components of the mental lexicon and postulated functional disconnection manifested in performance of subjects AL and RC.

(*Note*: there is a continuing debate concerning the question of whether the *same* lexical memory mechanisms are involved both in the reception and in the expression of language, or whether perception and production access different, functionally separable lexical codes ('*logogen* units'); e.g. Allport, 1984b; Shallice, McLeod and Lewis, 1985. The debate is energetically pursued by Monsell (Chap 14) and Coltheart and Funnell (Chap 15). Fortunately for us, we shall not have to wait for this issue to be resolved before our discussion, in this chapter, can be continued. Since the specificity effect evidently does not extend to the lexical (word-form) codes themselves, the arguments that we put forward here regarding the relations between words and non-linguistic, conceptual codes are essentially neutral *vis-à-vis* the question of shared, or separate input- and output-logogen systems.)

Semantic recoding

The hypothesis of non-linguistic, conceptual mediation, as the primary means by which our dysphasic subjects were able to translate, in either direction, between written and spoken word-forms is obviously related to current interpretations of the linguistic impairments in patients classified as 'deep dyslexic' and 'deep dysgraphic' (e.g. Morton and Patterson, 1980a; Bub and Kertesz, 1982). Unlike these patients, however, AL and RC seldom if ever produced responses that were clearly semantically related to the target word ('semantic' errors), either in reading aloud or in writing to dictation. Responses which could be classified in this way constituted no more than 1% of all their responses, in either task. Most of their errors either took the form of an inability to respond at all, or occurred as fragmentary, incomplete or apparently unrelated words (Table 3). This contrasts sharply with the pattern of responses reported in patients classified as deep dyslexic or deep dysgraphic, in which 'semantic' errors are the criterial feature (Coltheart, 1980). Granted that in AL and RC, as in the deep dyslexics/dysgraphics, there is a basic inability to recode -'directly'- between the spoken and written surface-forms of language, the contrasting distribution of error-types in these groups is further confirmation that the 'semantic' errors, which are the most immediately dramatic indices of deep dyslexia and deep dysgraphia, are not a direct or necessary consequence of the surface-recoding impairment, but reflect further, multi-component impairments in the so-called 'semantic' routines (cf. Shallice and Warrington, 1980; Patterson, 1981).

AL's and RC's dependence on 'semantic' mediation for cross-modal transcoding is further illustrated as follows. The experiment used two versions of an aural–visual matching task, in which the semantic similarity between non-matching, distractor items and the correct, target item was manipulated. In the forced-choice version of this task, the subject heard a spoken word and was confronted with two written words; his or her task was to point to the written word named by the experimenter. The two written words were either similar in meaning (e.g. *hut* and *shed, bush* and *shrub*) or were essentially unrelated (e.g. *hut* and *bush*). In the second version of the test, a single written word was exposed that was either identical, related in meaning, or unrelated to the spoken word. The subject's task was then to indicate whether written and spoken words were identical. Each task was performed twice, once with the spoken word presented *before* the written word(s) were uncovered (A → V); and, on another occasion (separated by at least two weeks), with the written word(s) set out in front of the subject in advance, before the auditory word was presented (V → A). Table 9 summarizes the results.

When the distractors were semantically unrelated to the target, then, regardless of the order of presentation, there were almost no errors. The same was true with semantically similar words, provided the patients heard the auditory word *before* the written stimuli were exposed (A → V). When the written stimuli were shown first (V → A), on the other hand, AL and RC frequently judged words that were related in meaning — though with no particular similarity of *form* — (e.g. dress–frock, pot–jar, rug–mat, etc.) to be literally identical.

Table 9. Two tasks of aural–visual matching: (i) two-alternative, forced choice, (ii) same/different 'verification'. The tasks were repeated in two different presentation orders: written stimuli presented first (V→A), or auditory word presented first (A→V). In each case a single spoken word is to be matched to a written word. The number of correct decisions is shown.

(i) *Forced choice*		AL	RC	(ii) *Verification*		AL	RC
unrelated pairs	A→V	32	32	unrelated (*n*=8)	A→V	8	8
(*n*=32)	V→A	32	31	e.g. hut/bush	V→A	8	8
e.g. hut/bush							
related pairs	A→V	32	32	related (*n*=8)	A→V	6	8
(*n*=32)	V→A	22	26	e.g. hut/shed	V→A	2	5
e.g. hut/shed							
				identical (*n*=8)	A→V	7	8
				e.g. hut/hut	V→A	8	8

We interpret these results as follows. First, the semantic confusion between rather approximate synonyms, in the V → A condition, is a clear indication that the patients depended on a semantic code for the cross-modal comparison of word-forms. Second, their essentially error-free performance, even with words having related referents, at least in the A → V condition, provides evidence that AL and RC were able to encode relatively subtle conceptual distinctions between word-meanings. (It is not entirely clear why the V → A sequence was more difficult for them. Possibly it resulted from the activation of a combined semantic field, representing the overlap of meaning of the simultaneously present, written words, before the auditory word arrived.)

Dimensions of word meaning

In deep dyslexic patients, success in reading aloud (and in deep dysgraphic patients, success in writing to dictation) is greater for words rated by normal subjects as highly imageable in meaning (e.g. Patterson, 1981; Bub and Kertesz, 1982). We obtained ratings (by 10 normal subjects) of all the words used in the cross-modal transcoding tasks, on a number of scales, including *Imageability, Concreteness* and conceptual *Independence*. As can be seen from inspection of Tables 1 and 4, RC's and AL's transcoding performance, as in deep dyslexia, is strongly correlated with Imageability, as it is also with ratings of Concreteness and of conceptual Independence. (See Table 10 for details.)

(Conceptual *Independence* is a measure of the degree to which the meaning of a word can be thought of independently of the meaning of other, associated words. For example, if the meaning of the word *heavy* can be conceptualized only in relation to some particular object or kind of object, then the word is rated low in Independence, whereas if it can be conceptualized independently of any such relationship, it is to be rated high on this scale.)

We also asked subjects to rate the words according to the ease with which they could be verbally defined. This *Verbal Definition* measure, however (which would appear similar to the 'ease-of-predication' scale used by Jones, 1985), was considerably *less* predictive of transcoding performance by our patients than were the preceding three measures. (See Table 10 again[1].)

Finally, as a major undertaking, the entire word-set was rated according to eight further '*Sensory Dimensions*': colour, shape, sound, smell, taste, touch, weight and movement. For each word, on each of these sensory

Table 10. A.   Pearson correlation coefficients between ratings on four global variables and performance in aural–visual matching. Two comparisons are made: (i) between mean scores across 11 word categories, (ii) between scores on individual words (n=161).

Patient			Major variables			
			Image-ability	Concrete-ness	Indepen-dence	Verbal definition
AL	(i)	word categories	0.75	0.80	0.85	0.61
	(ii)	individual words	0.51	0.52	0.55	0.36
RC	(i)	word categories	0.77	0.79	0.82	0.63
	(ii)	individual words	0.60	0.54	0.57	0.40

Table 10. B.   Inter-correlations between ratings on the four global variables, across 11 word categories.

	Concreteness	Independence	Verbal definition
Imageability	0.94	0.91	0.92
Concreteness		0.98	0.80
Independence			0.76

dimensions, the subjects judged to what degree the word evoked an idea or image in which that sensory dimension was represented. Subjects rated the words on a scale from zero to seven: zero indicated that the relevant dimension had no part in the representation that was evoked; one indicated a low level, seven a very salient level of representation. We also obtained ratings, in a similar way, of two dimensions of '*Subjective Response*' to the words: a measure of emotional response, and a measure of subjective motor involvement or interaction, evoked by the words.

The purpose of all this was to look for possible interrelations between constituent dimensions of specific sensory reference and the success or failure of semantically mediated transcoding. First, it is noteworthy that all eight individual sensory dimensions correlated positively and significantly with transcoding performance. In contrast, the two measures of subjective response failed to produce significant correlations. (See Table 11A.) This pattern is repeated in correlations with the three global measures of Imageability, Concreteness and Independence (Table 11B).[1]

Table 12 gives examples of the rated values, on the eight sensory dimensions, for a sample of ten individual words. The word *dog*, for example, has relatively high ratings on all the Sensory Dimensions except taste (reassuringly for dog-lovers), while the word *and* scores near zero on

Table 11. A. Pearson correlation coefficients between rated salience of sensory dimensions (and subjective response) and performance on aural–visual matching, across 11 word categories.

	Sensory dimensions								Subjective response	
Subject	*colour*	*shape*	*sound*	*taste*	*smell*	*touch*	*weight*	*movt.*	*emot.*	*self movt.*
AL	0.83	0.78	0.82	0.72	0.79	0.72	0.68	0.69	0.31 ns	0.30 ns
RC	0.77	0.66	0.81	0.78	0.76	0.74	0.62	0.66	0.52 ns	0.37 ns

Table 11. B. Pearson correlation coefficients between ratings on the four global scales and on individual sensory dimensions, across 11 word categories.

	Sensory dimensions								Subjective response	
Global rating scales	*colour*	*shape*	*sound*	*taste*	*smell*	*touch*	*weight*	*movt.*	*emot.*	*self movt.*
Imageability	0.96	0.88	0.95	0.90	0.92	0.96	0.83	0.86	0.52 ns	0.51 ns
Concreteness	0.97	0.97	0.87	0.87	0.95	0.92	0.95	0.85	0.46 ns	0.36 ns
Independence	0.94	0.95	0.87	0.83	0.90	0.90	0.89	0.86	0.45 ns	0.38 ns
Verbal definition	0.82	0.77	0.89	0.74	0.80	0.88	0.74	0.86	0.26 ns	0.64

all eight dimensions. Further down Table 12 it can be seen that pairs of words with intuitively similar meanings (as employed in the demonstration experiment, above) also produce very similar profiles across these eight dimensions.

Interestingly, it appears that a word's ability to evoke a range of different sensory dimensions is not needed for its successful semantic transcoding, provided that at least one sensory dimension is strongly evoked. Certain classes of words score highly on only a few, or on only one sensory dimension. Colour names (e.g. *red*) and adjectives that refer predominantly to one sensory modality (e.g. *loud, sour, shiny, cold*) are typical of these. (See examples, Table 12.) However, salient representation on many sensory dimensions is evidently not a necessary condition of successful semantic transcoding, nor for high ratings of Imageability: colour names are rated as very highly imageable (mean score 6.1 in our ratings); so are modality-specialized adjectives (Funnell, 1983). Colour names, for example, were transcoded as efficiently as other word classes that scored

Table 12. Examples of mean rating scores on the sensory dimensions for ten individual words (means of 10 subjects).

	Sensory dimensions							
	colour	shape	sound	smell	taste	touch	weight	movement
dog	4.6	**5.9**	**5.8**	**5.6**	2.0	**5.5**	**5.0**	**5.8**
and	0.2	0.5	0.2	0.4	0.1	0.4	0.3	0.7
red	**7.0**	0.6	1.4	1.6	1.2	1.5	0.8	0.8
loud	1.5	0.6	**6.5**	0.6	0.4	0.7	1.3	1.7
sour	2.8	1.0	1.3	**5.4**	**6.4**	1.7	0.7	0.6
arm	3.8	**5.5**	1.8	2.5	1.8	4.4	**4.9**	**5.0**
leg	3.8	**5.6**	1.8	2.3	2.1	4.6	**5.0**	**4.9**
tulip	**5.9**	**6.1**	0.8	**5.2**	1.5	4.3	3.4	2.5
daffodil	**6.3**	**6.4**	1.0	**5.8**	2.7	4.8	4.1	3.1

highly across many different sensory dimensions: (RC reading aloud colour names 0.9, aural visual matching 1.0; AL reading 0.5, matching 0.9). That is, 'breadth' or 'richness' of encoding across many different properties does not appear to be, as analogy with the ease of retrieval in certain episodic memory tasks might suggest (e.g. Tulving, 1984), an important factor in semantic transcoding, for our patients. This conclusion also runs counter to recent proposals by Jones (1985), addressed to the reading performance of deep dyslexics.

Impaired syntactic processing

Evidently AL's and RC's linguistic deficits were not confined to their inability to recode directly between spoken and written words. Both patients were selected for study initially on the basis of their profound, but also complementary patterns of aphasic impairments in spontaneous speech. Specifically, while RC's expressive language was essentially devoid of phrase- or sentence-structure,[2] AL's speech consisted of colloquially well-formed, syntactic phrases. Nevertheless, in our written-spoken transcoding tasks the pattern of performance of both these patients was strikingly similar. In particular, the *specific* open-class, referring words, conspicuously absent in AL's spontaneous speech, were none the less those with which he was *most* successful (as was RC) at cross-modal transcoding;

at the other end of the range, the 'little words' — syntactic functors, connectives, pronouns, prepositions — word-classes that were almost totally absent in RC's speech but abundant in AL's, were the *least* successfully transcoded by *both* patients. Thus, for AL, but not for RC, there was a startling discrepancy — amounting to a complete reversal — between the word-classes present, and apparently appropriately used, in his spontaneous speech, and those which, when presented in isolation, he could correctly transcode cross-modally.

Purely descriptive analyses of spontaneous speech, however, can be very misleading. Thus the distribution of (appropriately used) word-classes, or the syntactic well-formedness of phrases in spontaneous speech is, in itself, a weak criterion of underlying syntactic abilities. (Any simple dialogue system like ELIZA (Weizenbaum, 1966) that depends on a repertoire of canned phrases and a minimal lexical substitution procedure, can satisfy this sort of criterion with very limited syntactic processing abilities.) In fact, when AL was given formal syntactic tasks that could not be performed on the basis of some sort of phrasal lexicon, he was generally at a loss. For example, asked to point to one of two pictures that matched a semantically reversible phrase (e.g., 'a hat in a box' versus 'a box in a hat') AL did no better than chance (7/14 written, 8/14 spoken). RC (less surprisingly) was also completely unable to do this word-order task at above chance level (again, 7/14 written, 8/14 spoken). In expressive tasks, for example when AL was requested to produce the appropriate spatial preposition ('in', 'on', 'beside', etc.) inserted in a phrase such as 'It is *on* the thing', to describe the relation between two objects in front of him (a toy animal and a box), he was likewise completely unable to comply, even though such phrases were typical of his own spontaneous utterances. The best he could do was to produce oblique phrases, not containing the desired preposition, such as 'It's this way' (plus appropriate gesture) or 'It's the other side'. RC was, of course, unable to perform this task.

In contrast, the ability of both AL and RC to understand the *reference* of the individual words used in their syntactic comprehension tasks appeared to be virtually intact. Both were able to select one of two pictures representing unrelated objects, such as 'box' and 'hat', given either written or spoken object names, without error. Similarly, given a single spatial preposition, such as 'in' or 'under', both AL and RC could point correctly to one or two scenes showing objects in different spatial relations, for example 'a cow in a box', 'a cow under a box', etc. (AL, 19/20 written, 19/20 spoken; RC, 18/20 written, 18/20 spoken).

There is thus a remarkable dissociation between (i) the production of closed-class words, either inserted into a given phrase on request, or even in isolation — which was completely beyond these patients' capabilities — and (ii) the production of these same words as part of a *previously assembled, referring noun-phrase*, at which AL, but not RC, was dramatically successful.

This contrast was apparent also in written production. Thus, for example, AL was totally unable to write the word *the*, on dictation, either alone or as part of one of the phrases that he characteristically produced in spontaneous speech (e.g. *the other place*). As an experiment, we took a subset of such phrases ('The other place', 'The horrible mess', and so on) and taught them to AL as the names of a set of fictitious public houses. That is, AL was asked to match each phrase, spoken by the experimenter, to a picture of a particular pub. When he could do this matching task without error, we then asked him to *write down* the name of each public house, given the picture. In each case he then wrote, correctly and readily, the written word *The*, followed by some (or all) of the remainder of the name. He could do the same, as well, given only the spoken pub name. However, given *other* phrases, equally current in his spontaneous speech, also beginning with *The*, but not associated in this way as the names of particular places or objects, he was unable to write a single letter. (Note that at no time during the training process had the written form of any of the phrases been presented.) It appears that the written (and/or spoken) form of the word 'the' could be retrieved when it formed part of a pre-assembled phrase with definite reference. The pre-assembly, however, did not have to have taken place in the modality of output. There are a number of similar examples, in the literature, of the facilitation of word production when a word acquires more specific, restricted reference (e.g. Saffran, Schwartz and Marin, 1976). An adequate explanation of the phenomenon is another matter.

Detailed analysis of these patients' syntactic deficits belongs in another paper. Suffice it here to say that, despite the impressive differences in their spontaneous speech, on formal testing *both* patients showed major syntactic impairments. Undoubtedly, this syntactic disability also contributed in a major way to the word-class differences in written–spoken transcoding that we have observed. (Note, however, that many of the contrasts that we observed — for example, between 'concrete', 'superordinate', and 'abstract' nouns — are hardly to be accounted for in terms of purely syntactic impairment.) That is, (i) these patients are unable to transcode words between the written and spoken modalities *in terms of their forms alone*; (ii) they must thus do so, if at all, in terms of other, non-formal, domains of representation, i.e., presumably, in terms of semantic and syntactic properties of the words; (iii) to the extent that our patients are unable to interpret or use a variety of syntactic contrasts, then of course only words that have some non-syntactic, *referential* meaning will be successfully transcoded (cf. Morton and Patterson, 1980b).[3]

Discussion: words and meanings

In the following discussion we shall accept what appears to be a minimal, and in some respects inescapable, assumption: that transcoding between spoken and written words was mediated, in these patients, by some system of cognitive representation that is wholly independent of the *forms* of words.

'Sensory' and 'non-sensory' cognitive systems

Given this assumption, one hypothesis that is rather readily suggested is that the cognitive system, through which transcoding occurred, is a system specifically concerned with representing *sensory or perceptible* properties of the external world.

Several authors have postulated the existence of two (or more) functionally distinct conceptual (or 'semantic') systems: typically, one system concerned with sensory (or 'concrete' or 'imageable') concepts or properties, and another system that represents non-sensory ('abstract' or 'functional' or 'non-imageable') concepts (e.g. Warrington, 1975; Warrington and Shallice, 1984; Morton and Patterson, 1980a). A related view, sometimes not very clearly distinguished from this one, postulates independent '*verbal*' and '*visual*' semantic systems (e.g. Beauvois, 1982), a view that, in turn, is sometimes referred back to Paivio's (1971) distinction between what he called 'non-verbal' and 'verbal symbolic processes'. Some authors, notably Warrington and Shallice (1984), Hart, Berndt and Caramazza (1985), and Shallice (1987), have argued for further functional separation of categories and even modality-specific semantic systems. A somewhat different perspective, but also arguing for a high degree of modularity in the representation of non-linguistic knowledge is offered by Allport (1985).

Suppose that some such functional separation (at least) of 'sensory' and 'non-sensory' conceptual representation does indeed exist. Then one of two possible further assumptions are needed to account for our results. Either:

(i) RC and AL have a very severe (almost total?) loss of the non-sensory cognitive systems; or

(ii) their non-sensory cognitive abilities remain essentially intact but are: (a) selectively inaccessible from, and/or (b) they are selectively unable to access, either spoken or written language.

A number of considerations, however, argue against the first of these (naively formulated) alternatives. To begin with, neither RC nor AL showed any obvious impairment of non-linguistic, conceptual abilities. AL, for example, is a craftsman who makes highly skilled use of precision and power tools in metalwork and woodwork; both patients show what appears as a full and entirely normal range of emotional response. Their behaviour, both in formal testing and in everyday practical activity, appears completely inconsistent with the sort of functional loss — amounting to a major dementia — that would be entailed by hypothesis (i).

Further, it may be questioned whether the transcoding data is consistent, in detail, with a simple dichotomy between access to 'sensory' versus 'non-sensory' *concepts*, as such. The effects of rated Imageability, Concreteness, and conceptual 'Independence' show a steady gradation in cross-modal transcoding performance, across the different word-classes, ranging continuously from zero to 100% (Table 4). There seems no indication here that individual 'word-concepts' might be simply *partitioned* into two sets, one set of 'sensory' word-concepts which is essentially intact, and another set of 'non-sensory' concepts that is severely impaired.

As a third consideration, which argues against alternative (ii) (a), both patients gave evidence of a relatively high level of comprehension, as seen in word-to-picture matching, in respect of word classes (spatial prepositions, logical connectives — see below) on which the cross-modal transcoding tasks yielded some of their lowest scores. In certain circumstances, at least, it appears that spoken and written language *is* able to access 'non-sensory' (and 'non-specific') word meanings in these patients.

The particular difficulty of cross-modal transcoding of 'non-specific' words, for these patients, may be not so much in the demands such tasks make on the *receptive* encoding of word meanings, as in the subsequent *generation*, or retrieval, of an appropriate word-form, in the other modality, based on that conceptual encoding. That is, a critical difference between 'sensory' and 'non-sensory' (or, for that matter, between more or less 'imageable' or more or less 'conceptually independent') word meanings here may have to do with differences between these cognitive representations in the process of language *production*, as suggested by alternative (ii) (b), above. The following demonstration further illustrates AL and RC's ability to show comprehension, under certain conditions, of word categories which they could not effectively transcode from one modality to another.

Understanding logical connectives

We selected a set of nine 'non-specific' words: the connectives *and, not, only, both, with, without, just, together, alone*. Presented in isolation, without a specific context or scenario to which the words could be referred, the patients were simply unable to transcode these words at all between the spoken and written modalities; at best, that is (in aural–visual matching) no better than their performance with single letters or nonsense words. The test words were now combined with two proper nouns, *Peter* and *Mary*, to make phrases of from one to three words: e.g. *Peter without Mary; not Peter; Mary and Peter; just Mary; together*; etc. Three line-drawings were present throughout the experiment: a boy alone, a girl alone, and a boy and a girl together. The characters in these drawings were introduced to the patients as 'Peter' and 'Mary'.

Twenty-two phrases were then presented to the patient, and he or she was asked to point to a corresponding picture. If the patients responded solely on the basis of the number and identity of the proper nouns in each phrase, ignoring the connectives, then, given the construction of the set of phrases, they should score 12/22. The test was completed twice: once with spoken and once with written presentation of the phrases. In the spoken version, AL made no errors, RC scored 20/22 correct; in the written version, both patients made just two errors. (In all three cases, the incorrect responses were made to the same two phrases: *alone* and *not together*.)

This remarkably accurate performance, given a specific scenario in terms of which the logical connectives could be interpreted, provides rather persuasive evidence that the conceptual relations (presence, absence, conjunction, exclusion, etc.) denoted by these 'little words' could in fact be adequately encoded by the patients and could be accessed from the written or spoken words. What they appeared to find essentially impossible was, given simply one of these words in isolation, to retrieve an appropriate corresponding word-form in another modality from the input. Provided with a specific scenario, on the other hand, the contrasting meanings of these same 'non-specific' words were quite well understood.

Word-concepts and 'concept-nodes'

This observation, and the preceding discussion of 'sensory' and 'non-sensory' semantic systems, prompts us to question two, somewhat intertwined assumptions that often appear, implicitly or explicitly, in discussions of the relationship between words and their cognitive representations. These are the assumptions of what can be called 'word concepts' and (access-and-exit) 'concept nodes'.

Many psychological models of semantic memory postulate a store of discrete functional units or nodes, linked in an associative network. Thus, 'A concept is regarded as a point or node in mental and neural processing, which, when active, makes information about an object or entity available to thought' (Potter, 1979). The significance of such a concept-node is carried solely by its position in a network of other concept-nodes, i.e. by its connections to other nodes and ultimately to sensory and motor inputs and outputs of the system. Quillian (1967) is the prototype of this approach. In Quillian's model there is a type-node, or 'concept-node' for each word in a given language (in this case English); each type-node is in turn linked to a network of token-nodes (with links to *their* type-nodes) constituting a structural representation of the word's dictionary definition. Quillian thus makes two basic assumptions: (i) that 'concepts' stand intrinsically in a one-to-one correspondence with words; and (ii) that access to and from conceptual knowledge is mediated by unitary (access-and-exit) *concept-nodes*. (Specifically, therefore, communication between *words* and conceptual knowledge is necessarily mediated via these hypothetical access-and-exit concept-nodes.)

The same assumptions recur, with small variations, in many different models of language and non-linguistic cognition, including Kintsch (1974), Collins and Loftus (1975), Anderson (1976), Potter (1979), Mackay (1982, this volume), and many others.

As they stand, however, this pair of assumptions is not easily reconciled with our transcoding data. If there existed unique access-and-exit nodes for each 'word-concept' then, whatever other functions they serve, these concept-nodes should surely also serve to mediate in spoken-to-written word transcoding tasks. So long as the access-and-exit node for a given word-concept is functionally intact, together with its links to and from the corresponding word-forms, this should presumably be sufficient for successful spoken-to-written transcoding (even in the absence of graphemic–phonetic or word-form to word-form recoding), without necessarily activating any conceptual information beyond the access-and-exit node itself. Given such an account, it appears problematic, therefore, that the referential *content* of word-meanings (their 'specificity') should massively affect the success or failure of what, *ex hypothesi*, was supposed to be a direct, one-to-one transcoding process.

Even if unique 'word-concepts' are postulated only for the major grammatical categories of nouns, verbs and adjectives, the hypothesis of unique (access-and-exit) concept nodes for each word-concept still needs extensive and apparently *ad hoc* further assumptions — about differential strength of accessibility to, and from, different categories of word-forms in order to begin to account for our results.

It is obvious that words cannot be simply *partitioned* into those having, or not having, specific sensory reference (or into 'imageable' versus 'non-imageable', or 'concrete' versus 'abstract', etc.). Few if any words — not even names of the most concrete or imageable objects and actions — have meanings that are *exclusively* imageable or exclusively non-imageable. If it is proposed that two or more functionally distinct conceptual systems each have their own sets of concept-nodes, this step necessarily concedes that there cannot be one-to-one correspondence between *words* and *concepts* (even for unique word-senses). In such a scheme, any one word-form must have several different concept-nodes in different 'conceptual systems', e.g. one to access the sensory component of its meaning, another in a functionally distinct 'conceptual system' to access its non-sensory meaning, etc. Whatever the postulated concept-nodes represented, therefore, they would not be 'word-concepts'.

It is worth noting that the 'concept-access-node' hypothesis, to which we take exception here, is in certain respects equivalent to the hypothesis of an abstract or modality-independent lexicon (e.g. Forster, 1976), whose empirical adequacy we have questioned on other grounds before (Allport and Funnell, 1981; Allport, 1983). A version of this hypothesis appears also to be proposed by Garrett. ('Each simple surface vocabulary element corresponds to a conceptually simple entity at the message level' Garrett, 1982, p. 26.) However, if such 'conceptually simple entities' (i.e word-specific, amodal, access-and-exit nodes) exist, why could they not be used uniformly by these patients to mediate cross-modal transcoding? The observed gradient of performance, from around zero to around 100% accuracy, as a function of variables that appear to belong wholly within the *non-linguistic, cognitive* domain, presents a serious challenge to such an hypothesis.

In what follows we put forward an alternative, general conception of the relationships between word-forms and cognitive representations.

Modularity and distributed representation in semantic memory

According to the view that we have tried to develop elsewhere (e.g. Allport, 1980; 1985; in press), 'semantic' knowledge — i.e. our general, non-linguistic knowledge of the world — is distributed over a range of different, content-specific or material-specific systems in the brain that specialize in the representation of different domains of attributes (and relationships and actions). Thus the neural representation of a particular object-concept, for example, is provided by a (richly structured) assembly of information, distributed over many, functionally dissociable subsystems. Focal cerebral injury can *selectively* affect knowledge of the characteristic form, *or* the colours of familiar objects, *or* their topographical relationships, or their functional and causal properties, their contextual associations, or their motivational and emotional significance, leaving knowledge in those *other* domains essentially intact.[4]

Information in these different coding domains must of course be intricately co-ordinated and integrated. In current analyses of distributed, associative memory systems (Hinton and Anderson, 1981; Hopfield, 1984; McClelland and Rumelhart, 1985; Rumelhart and McClelland, 1986), a given memory 'item' — an 'engram' — is realized as a pattern of activation distributed over many different coding elements. Such a pattern can come to act as a functional unit, to the extent that its constituent elements are each associatively linked to all (or many) of its other constituent elements. The entire composition of elements is then said to be 'auto-associated'. Activation of a subset of auto-associated elements will tend to recruit the remainder of the pattern, so that the whole, composite pattern comes to behave, to be 'retrieved' or activated, *as a unit*.

At a different level of description, the behaviour of such a strongly unitized engram might be summarized, or symbolized, by the state of a single node (a 'concept-node'). However, that node has no realization other than as a summary description of the collective state of the set of constituent micro-features. Thus one could not (logically) think of anything that affected the microfeatures, but did not also affect the 'concept node', or *vice versa*. This point deserves some emphasis. In contrast to the tradition of semantic memory models that we have been discussing previously, in parallel-distributed-process (PDP) models, mental representations are fundamentally compositional and distributed. That is, they are realized as patterns of activity, where the same coding elements occur in different combinations as constituents of many different representations. There is no *further*, physically separable, or independently identifiable structure (no concept-node or access-node) that uniquely stands for, or points to, or gives access to that representation, other than the assembly of coding elements of which the representation is composed. According to this conception, a theoretical notation that shows 'concept nodes' in turn priming or activating 'conceptual feature nodes', or *vice versa*, simply confuses different levels of description.

There are other, important reasons why 'concept nodes' should not be conceptualized as fixed, indissoluble entities. To cite a specific illustration, when one reads a sentence such as 'The man lifted the piano', one's knowledge of pianos as *heavy* objects becomes salient (or 'primed'); in contrast, reading 'The man tuned the piano' appears to prime a different subset of piano attributes (Barclay, Bransford, Franks, McCarrell and Nitsch, 1974; for related examples see Anderson and Ortony, 1975; Garnham, 1979; Tabossi and Johnson-Laird, 1980; Tabossi, 1985; Tversky, 1977). In a parallel-distributed memory system, different, temporary *coalitions* of active elements (over the same population) encode different engrams. However, the coalitions change (fragment, coalesce with other patterns, etc.) under the constraints imposed by inputs from 'outside', in accordance with the structure of (excitatory and inhibitory) linkages in the entire matrix of interconnections, that sculpts the 'landscape' of possible activity states (Rumelhart, Smolensky, McClelland and Hinton, 1986). Thus different subsets of elements, which together make up (say) the full 'piano-concept', can receive selective enhancement or inhibition, depending on the *activity* state of the other units interacting with them and which together constitute the current context of processing.

Further, high-level cognitive units (PDP coalitions) will vary widely in terms of their degree, or strength, of auto-association, depending on the structure and frequency of past experiences; hence they will vary, correspondingly, in the degree to which they resist fragmentation, or 'capture' by larger coalitions, and in their tendency to show part-to-whole reintegration.

The above, very brief and necessarily impressionistic outline of ideas provides the framework for our interpretation of the main results that we have reported here; namely the continuous gradient of performance shown by our patients in the cross-modal transcoding tasks, ranging from around zero to around 100% accuracy (Table 4). The account which follows concludes our discussion. As is clear, our interpretation is plainly speculative. We put it forward here, not because we suppose the data to compel this interpretation and no other, but because it seems to offer, nonetheless, a relatively simple account that is open to further empirical explanation and falsification.

Conceptual independence, and the stability (and instability) of cognitive representations

The word-sets used in our cross-modal transcoding tasks were rated by 10 independent assessors on a range of measures of 'word-meaning', including one that we called conceptual *Independence*. These different rating measures showed generally extremely high intercorrelations among themselves (Table 10b), so that an attempt to establish empirically which if any of them carried the greatest weight, in accounting for our patients' transcoding data, was plainly not justified. Rather, we are tempted to suppose that each of these three major rating variables (Conceptual Independence, Concreteness, and Imageability) provides an approximate measure of broadly the same underlying dimension. That is, certain classes of words evoke cognitive representations that are themselves relatively autonomous (strongly auto-associated) and therefore form relatively stable cognitive structures. Prototypically these are the names of physically separable, familiar, 'basic-level' objects. Such objects are typically encountered in many different contexts, and can be thought of as relatively independent of any particular context. In comparison, our other nominal (and pronominal) word categories — superordinates ('vehicle'), abstract nouns ('theme'), 'generic' nouns ('thing') and pronouns ('it') — can be communicatively effective as anaphora provided a specific cognitive reference for them has been established already (e.g. Sanford and Garrod, 1981); but in the absence of an appropriate pragmatic context, they can be expected to evoke only rather diffuse — hence weakly activated and unstable — cognitive structures. They can thus provide only a relatively inadequate input to the (damaged) word-finding processes on which our patients had to rely. The categories of 'specific verbs' ('write') and specific adjectives ('loud') presumably evoke comparatively sharply-specified conceptual structures. However, in ordinary experience the action of writing (for example) is invariably performed by some particular agent, using a particular instrument, operating on some particular object to produce a particular result. Similarly (for example) the attribute 'loud' applies normally to a perceived sound having some particular quality, coming from a particular source, etc. In other words the cognitive representations evoked by these classes of words, in isolation, will tend to be linked to a range of other cognitive structures which they will tend to activate. Again, therefore, though for rather different reasons, the pattern of activity evoked is likely to be extended and diffused. Many possible words might be used to name different aspects of this complex cognitive structure and each of them will tend to interfere with retrieval of the original target word.

The argument is similar, again, for the remaining ('non-specific') word-classes, on which the patients obtained even poorer cross-modal transcoding scores. That is, these categories of words (e.g. prepositions, connectives) evoke cognitive codes that are stable only in the context of other, more autonomous cognitive representations, which they may then serve to link together. Given an appropriate, concrete scenario, however, both the patients were able to show that they could discriminate the referential contrasts implicit in these word classes, very nearly without error.

In summary, our interpretation of the cross-modal transcoding data is as follows.

(1) AL and RC are effectively incapable of generating a spoken or written word-form 'directly', from an input in the opposite modality, without semantic mediation. (There may be just sufficient, residual communication in this channel, however, to veto the overt production of cognitively generated 'semantic' errors.)

(2) We have also argued that the data are incompatible with transcoding *via* a word-specific (hence also language-specific) but modality-independent 'word-concept' unit.

(3) We infer that transcoding between modalities, in these patients, depends on word-generation driven by a non-linguistic, cognitive representation.

(4) Finally, we propose, the ease with which a word can be generated from a cognitive, or conceptual base varies with the conceptual *independence*,[5] hence stability and autonomy, of the (auto-associated) cognitive representation elicited, in the transcoding task, by the corresponding stimulus word.

Acknowledgements

We are grateful to Stephen Monsell and David Howard for their searching reviews of a previous version of this chapter, and to Eckart Scheerer for exerting his deft editorial leverage on its rewriting. We also thank Max Coltheart for invaluable advice and support.

Notes

[1] These correlations are not critically dependent on the particular subsets of words sampled from the different word categories (Funnell, 1983), nor upon analysis by category. Similar correlations are obtained when the analysis is based upon individual words (Funnell, in press).

[2] RC's language production improved during the course of this investigation, with the gradual reappearance of some very limited and fragmentary verb constructions, but remained markedly dysfluent and syntactically grossly impaired.

[3] Both AL and RC made transcoding errors indicating confusion among syntactic and other 'non-referential' contrasts of word-meaning: e.g. she → 'her', a → 'the', the → 'a', this → 'now', now → 'this', etc.

[4] The literature providing evidence of this range of functional dissociations in cognitive representation (which makes no claim whatever to comprehensiveness) is both large and fragmented. A review of this literature is quite beyond the scope or purpose of the present chapter (but see, for recent examples, Levine *et al.*, 1985; Rolls, 1981, 1986; Shallice, 1986).

[5] Or Concreteness or Imageability; we have no grounds, in our present data, to differentiate between these rated dimensions.

References

Allport, D. A. (1980). Patterns and actions: Cognitive mechanisms are content-specific; *and* Attention and performance. In G. Claxton (Ed.) *Cognitive Psychology: New Directions*. London: Routledge and Kegan Paul, pp. 26–64, 112–53.

Allport, D. A. (1983). Language and Cognition. In R. Harris (Ed.) *Approaches to Language*. Oxford: Pergamon, pp. 61–94.

Allport, D. A. (1984a). Auditory–verbal short-term memory and conduction aphasia. In H. Bouma and D. G. Bouwhuis (Eds) *Attention and Performance 10: Control of Language Processes* Hillsdale, NJ: Erlbaum, pp. 313–25.

Allport, D. A. (1984b). Speech production and comprehension: One lexicon or two? In W. Prinz and A. F. Sanders (Eds) *Cognition and Motor Processes*. Berlin: Springer, pp. 209–28.

Allport, D. A. (1985). Distributed memory, modular subsystems and dysphasia. In S. Newman and R. Epstein (Eds) *Current Perspectives in Dysphasia*. Edinburgh: Churchill Livingstone, pp. 32–60.

Allport, D. A. (in press). Selection-for-action: Some behavioural and neurophysiological considerations of attention and action. In H. Heuer and A. F. Sanders (Eds) *Perspectives on Perception and Action*. Hillsdale, NJ: Erlbaum.

Allport, D. A. and Funnell, E. (1981). Components of the mental lexicon. *Philosophical Transactions of the Royal Society* (London) **B295**, 397–410.

Anderson, J. R. (1976). *Language, Memory and Thought*. Hillsdale, NJ: Erlbaum.

Anderson, R. C. and Ortony, A. (1975). On putting apples into bottles: A problem of polysemy. *Cognitive Psychology*, 7, 167–80.

Barclay, J. R., Bransford, J. D., Franks, J. J., McCarrell, N. S. and Nitsch, K. (1974). Comprehension and semantic flexibility. *Journal of Verbal Learning and Verbal Behavior*, **13**, 471–81.

Beauvois, M. F. (1982). Optic aphasia: a process of interaction between vision and language. *Philosophical Transactions of the Royal Society (London)*, **B298**, 35–47.

Bub, D. and Kertesz, A. (1982). Deep agraphia. *Brain and Language*, **17**, 146–65.

Caramazza, A. and Berndt, R. S. (1978). Semantic and syntactic processes in aphasia: A review of the literature. *Psychological Bulletin*, **85**, 898–918.

Chomsky, N. and Halle, M. (1968). *The Sound Pattern of English*. New York: Harper and Row.

Collins, A. M. and Loftus, E. F. (1975). A spreading-activation theory of semantic processing. *Psychological Review*, **82**, 407–28.

Coltheart, M. (1980). Deep dyslexia: A review of the syndrome. In M. Coltheart, K. Patterson and J. C. Marshall (Eds) *Deep Dyslexia*. London: Routledge and Kegan Paul, pp. 22–47.

Forster, K. I. (1976). Accessing the mental lexicon. In R. J. Wales and E. Walker (Eds) *New Approaches to Language Mechanisms*. Amsterdam: North-Holland, pp. 257–87.

Funnell, E. (1983). Ideographic Communication and Word-class Differences in Aphasia. Ph.D. Thesis, University of Reading, England.

Funnell, E. (in press). Object concepts and object names: some deductions from acquired disorders of word processing. In G. W. Humphreys and M. J. Riddoch (Eds) *Visual Object Processing: A Cognitive Neuropsychological Approach*, London: Laurence Erlbaum.

Garnham, A. (1979). Instantiation of verbs. *Quarterly Journal of Experimental Psychology*, **31**, 207–14.

Garrett, M. F. (1982). Production of speech: Observations from normal and pathological language use. In A. W. Ellis (Ed.) *Normality and Pathology in Cognitive Functions*. London: Academic Press, pp. 19–26.

Geschwind, N. (1967). The varieties of naming errors. *Cortex*, **3**, 96–112.

Goodglass, H. (1980). Disorders of naming following brain injury. *American Scientist*, **58**, 647–55.

Goodglass, H. and Kaplan, E. (1972). *The Assessment of Aphasia and Related Disorders*. Philadelphia: Lea and Febiger.

Green, E. and Howes, D. H. (1977). The nature of conduction aphasia: A study of anatomic and clinical features and of underlying mechanisms. In H. Whitaker and H. A. Whitaker (Eds) *Studies in Neurolinguistics*. New York: Academic Press, pp. 123–56.

Hart, J., Berndt, R. S. and Caramazza, A. (1985). Category-specific naming deficit following cerebral infarction. *Nature*, **316**, 439–40.

Hinton, G. E. and Anderson, J. A. (1981). (Eds) *Parallel Models of Associative Memory*. Hillsdale, NJ: Erlbaum.

Hopfield, J. J. (1984). Collective processing and neural states. In C. Nicolini (Ed.) *Modeling and Analysis in Biomedicine*. Singapore: World Scientific, pp. 369–89.

Jones, G. V. (1985). Deep dyslexia, imageability, and ease of predication. *Brain and Language*, **24**, 1–19.

Kintsch, W. (1974). *The Representation of Meaning in Memory*. Hillsdale, NJ: Erlbaum.

Lesser, R. (1978). *Linguistic Investigations of Aphasia*. London: Edward Arnold.

Levine, D. N., Warach, J. and Farah, M. (1985). Two visual systems in mental imagery: Dissociation of 'what' and 'where' in imagery disorders due to bilateral posterior cerebral lesions. *Neurology*, **35**, 1010–8.

MacKay, D. G. (1982). The problems of flexibility, fluency and speed-accuracy trade-off in skilled behavior. *Psychological Review*, **89**, 483–506.

McClelland, J. L. and Rumelhart, D. E. (1985). Distributed memory and the representation of general and specific information. *Journal of Experimental Psychology: General*, **114**, 159–88.

Morton, J. and Patterson, K. (1980a). A new attempt at an interpretation, or, an attempt at a new interpretation. In M. Coltheart, K. Patterson and J. C. Marshall (Eds) *Deep Dyslexia*. London: Routledge and Kegan Paul, pp. 91–118.

Morton, J. and Patterson, K. (1980b). 'Little words — No!' In M. Coltheart, K. Patterson and J. C. Marshall (Eds) *Deep Dyslexia*. London: Routledge and Kegan Paul, pp. 270–85.

Paivio, A. (1971). *Imagery and Verbal Processes*. New York: Holt, Rinehart and Winston.

Patterson, K. E. (1981). Neuropsychological approaches to the study of reading. *British Journal of Psychology*, **72**, 15–74.

Potter, M. (1979). Mundane symbolism: The relations among objects, names and ideas. In N. R. Smith and M. B. Franklin (Eds) *Symbolic Functioning in Childhood*. Hillsdale, NJ: Erlbaum.

Quillian, M. R. (1967). Word concepts: a theory and simulation of some basic semantic capabilities. *Behavioral Science*, **12**, 410–30.

Rolls, E. T. (1981). Processing beyond the inferior temporal visual cortex related to feeding, memory, and striatal function. In Y. Katsuki, R. Norgren and M. Sato (Eds) *Brain Mechanisms of Sensation*. New York: Wiley, pp. 241–69.

Rolls, E. T. (1986). Information representation, processing and storage in the brain: analysis at the single neuron level. In J.-P. Changeux and M. Konishi (Eds) *Neural and Molecular Mechanisms of Learning*. Berlin: Springer.

Rosch, E. (1978). Principles of categorization. In E. Rosch and B. B. Lloyd (Eds) *Cognition and Categorization*. Hillsdale, NJ: Erlbaum, pp. 27–48.

Rosch, E., Mervis, C. B., Gray, W. D., Johnson, D. M. and Boyes-Braem, P. (1976). Basic objects in natural categories. *Cognitive Psychology*, **8**, 382–439.

Rumelhart, D. E., Smolensky, P., McClelland, J. L. and Hinton, G. E. (1986). Schemata and sequential thought processes in PDP models. In D. E. Rumelhart and J. L. McClelland (Eds) *Parallel Distributed Processing*. Cambridge, MA: Bradford Books/MIT Press.

Rumelhart, D. E. and McClelland, J. L. (1986). *Parallel Distributed Processing: Explorations in the Microstructure of cognition*. Cambridge, MA: Bradford Books/MIT Press.

Saffran, E. M., Schwartz, M. F. and Marin, O. S. M. (1976). Semantic mechanisms in paralexia. *Brain and Language*, **3**, 255–65.

Sanford, A. J. and Garrod, S. C. (1981). *Understanding Written Language*. Chichester: Wiley.

Shallice, T. (1987). Impairments of semantic processing: Multiple dissociations. In M. Coltheart, R. Job and G. Sartori (Eds) *The Cognitive Neuropsychology of Language*. Hillsdale, NJ: Erlbaum.

Shallice, T., McLeod, P. and Lewis, K. (1985). Isolating cognitive modules with the dual-task paradigm: Are speech perception and production separate processes? *Quarterly Journal of Experimental Psychology*, **37A**, 307–32.

Shallice, T. and Warrington, E. K. (1980). Single and multiple component central dyslexic syndromes. In M. Coltheart, K. Patterson and J. C. Marshall (Eds) *Deep Dyslexia*. London: Routledge and Kegan Paul, pp. 119–45.

Tabossi, P. (1985). Lexical information in sentence comprehension. *Quarterly Journal of Experimental Psychology*, **37A**, 83–94.

Tabossi, P. and Johnson-Laird, P. N. (1980). Linguistic context and the priming of semantic information. *Quarterly Journal of Experimental Psychology*, **32**, 595–603.

Tversky, A. (1977). Features of similarity. *Psychological Review*, **84**, 327–52.

Tulving, E. (1984). *Elements of Episodic Memory*. Oxford: Oxford University Press.

Warrington, E. K. (1975). The selective impairment of semantic memory. *Quarterly Journal of Experimental Psychology*, **27**, 635–57.

Warrington, E. K. and Shallice, T. (1984). Category specific semantic impairments. *Brain*, **107**, 829–54.

Weizenbaum, J. (1966). ELIZA. *Communications of the Association for Computing Machinery* **9**, 36–45.

Section 6

Sequencing and timing in language perception and production

Introduction

Donald G. MacKay

Because Keele (Chap 21) provides a detailed and eloquent analysis of the remaining chapters, along with a paper which was presented at our 1985 conference but did not arrive in time to be published here (Mateer, 1985), I will confine my introduction to a summary of the five main themes in this section: sequencing in production, sequencing in perception, hierarchic processing, timing and modularity, the issue of whether language use shares some of the same underlying mechanisms as other behaviors.

Sequencing in production

Sequence plays an essential part in language use, constituting its very essence according to linguists, and three of the papers in this section examine sequencing in production (Gordon and Meyer (Chap 20), Keele (Chap 21) and MacKay (Chap 18)). Gordon and Meyer use a response priming procedure to test between three general classes of models for describing the sequencing of elementary units, especially syllables, and provide strong support for a hierarchic sequencing model whereby units become sequenced at multiple levels in speech production. MacKay agrees with Gordon and Meyer in rejecting the alternative, element-to-element, and element-to-position sequencing models, and reviews some additional constraints on theories of sequencing at the phrase, word, morpheme, syllable and segment levels of speech production. Included among these constraints are a priming or preparation stage which must precede the sequential activation of speech production units, a special connection between the mechanisms for sequencing and for initiating behavior, and sequential regularities in speech errors, such as the fact that substituted words usually belong to the same sequential class, e.g., noun, verb, adverb. However, MacKay's most interesting point is that sequencing (and timing) must be a distributed process, rather than a stage of processing which occurs at some fixed point in the hierarchy of output specifications.

Sequencing in perception

Two chapters in this section deal with sequential processes in perception (Huttenlocher and Goodman (Chap 19), and MacKay (Chap 18)). MacKay reviews some well known speech perception phenomena (e.g., phonological fusions, phonemic restorations and the perceptual displacement of clicks during sentence perception) which violate the widely held theoretical assumption that perceptual sequences invariably mirror the sequence of external events in the real world. Huttenlocher and Goodman suggest another violation of this 'sequential isomorphism assumption' (see also Cutler, Chap 2) by arguing that identification of spoken words (and nonwords) is not a strictly left-to-right process at the phoneme level.

Hierarchic processing

The hierarchic processing theme emerges experimentally in Gordon and Meyer, and theoretically in Keele and MacKay (1982), who argue that hierarchic processing enables a sequence of established subunits to serve new superordinate control structures, and enables an established superordinate control structure to acquire new subunit sequences (as when someone learning a word in a foreign language produces a new phoneme sequence for an already familiar concept). As Keele points out, this 'hierarchic transportation' plays a fundamental role in the acquisition, transfer and flexibility of perception-production skills, language perception–production being just one highly salient example.

Timing in perception–production

MacKay outlines some general constraints on theories of timing, the most important being the fact that different theoretical mechanisms are required for timing and for sequencing speech production units. Keele and MacKay also review a large body of work indicating that not just speech perception–

production but many diverse perception–production systems seem to share the same timing mechanisms.

Modularity

Keele and MacKay both address the issue of modularity, but from different angles. Many chapters of the present book converge on the hypothesis that language systems for speaking, listening, reading and writing share common mechanisms. Keele argues that other skills share in the most important of these mechanisms, those for sequencing, timing and hierarchic organization. Keele goes further, arguing that hierarchic sequencing in language is 'but an offshoot of an even more fundamental achievement in human evolution, that of being able to rapidly learn and modify complex sequences of activities in many domains'. Under Keele's hypothesis, not just language perception–production, but other quite different perception–production systems are highly interactive from an evolutionary perspective. Is Keele's hypothesis a new twist to the Moebius circle, an 'integrated-but-unequal' alternative to both the separate-and-unequal and the integrated-and-equal approaches? Does Keele's hypothesis challenge the idea of modularity itself, or is there some solution to his modularity-generality issue which resembles the one that MacKay provides for the interaction–encapsulation issue, the fact that modules seem to exist as relatively autonomous processing systems, but nevertheless interact extensively with one another? Interesting questions remain to be answered.

References

MacKay, D. G. (1982). The problems of flexibility, fluency, and speed-accuracy trade-off in skilled behavior. *Psychological Review*, **89**, 483–506.

Mateer, K. (1985). Common sites for oral motor sequencing and phoneme identification: Evidence from electrical stimulation of the language cortex. Paper presented to the conference on 'Common Processes in Listening, Speaking, Reading, and Writing.' held at the Center for interdisciplinary Research (Z.i.F.), University of Bielefeld, July 1–5.

18   Constraints on theories of sequencing and timing in language perception and production

Donald G. MacKay

Abstract

This chapter reviews some fundamental phenomena which theories of sequencing and timing in language perception and production must address. I begin with the problem of sequencing: how do speakers order the words in sentences, and how do they order the morphemes, syllables and segments that make up the words? I address five basic constraints on theories of sequencing.

Preparation for sequencing. Speech errors, reaction time experiments and neurolinguistic disorders indicate that a priming or preparation stage is necessary for the sequential activation of speech production units.

Separate mechanisms for sequence versus content. Evidence from speech errors, word games and simultaneous translation indicate that the units representing words, syllables and speech sounds must be separate from the mechanisms for sequencing these units.

A special relationship between sequencing and the initiation of behavior. Theories of sequencing must explain why it takes longer to initiate a preprogrammed output such as a word when the output consists of a sequence of subcomponents, e.g., syllables, than when it consists of a single subcomponent, all other factors being equal.

The sequential error regularity. Theories of sequencing must explain why substituted and substituting components in speech errors usually belong to the same sequential class; e.g., nouns substitute with other nouns, and not with adverbs; vowels substitute with other vowels, and not with consonants.

Different mechanisms for sequencing and timing. The mechanisms for timing speech production units must be different from the mechanisms for sequencing these units: the same mechanism cannot both time and sequence behavior.

LANGUAGE PERCEPTION AND PRODUCTION
ISBN 0-12-052750-2

I next outline some phenomena which must be explained in theories of sequential perception, but which violate an assumption which has become part of virtually every theory of perception and memory published to date. Under this 'sequential isomorphism assumption', perceptual sequences mirror the sequence of external events which has occurred in the real world. Example violations include click detection, phonological fusions, phonemic restorations, and the fact that subjects can respond to higher level units such as words and syllables before they can respond to lower level units such as segments.

Finally, I outline some general constraints on theories of timing in language production and perception: the distributed nature of timing; the occurrence of periodicity, and its relation to skill or practice; interactions between the timing mechanisms for perception and production, and between the timing mechanisms for different output systems such as speech and finger movement; and phenomena such as constant relative timing which characterize many different skills.

Introduction

Theories of language perception and production must deal with three basic questions: What content units or components represent language perception and production, and how are these units organized? How are the content units activated in proper sequence during everyday language perception and production? And what mechanisms are responsible for timing, or determining when and how rapidly these units become activated?

So far, the chapters of the present book have been dealing in various ways with the first of these problems, the nature and structure of the components, and especially the relation between the components for perceiving and producing speech, whether spoken or spelled. I too have examined this issue in other reports (see MacKay, 1985a, b, 1987), and have concluded that exactly the same units play a role in both perception and production above the distinctive feature level (see also Meyer and Gordon, 1983) and that an entire hierarchy of units is required. Included within the hierarchy are units representing distinctive features, segments, initial consonant groups (syllable onsets), vowel groups (rhymes), final consonant groups, syllables, morphemes, words, phrases and sentences (see MacKay, 1985a, b, 1987).

In this chapter, I examine the two remaining issues: how do shared perception–production components become activated in proper sequence and at the proper time and rate? My goal is to develop a list of fundamental phenomena or constraints that viable theories of sequencing and timing must explain.

I will begin with constraints on theories of sequencing, first in production, and then in perception. I will then examine constraints on theories of timing in both perception and production.

Sequencing in language production

How do we execute sequences of behavior in proper serial order when we do, and in improper order when we make errors? Language production has provided the most extensively studied example of the problem of sequencing. Although other cerebral activities raise similar issues, and may even make use of similar mechanisms (see Lashley, 1951; MacKay, 1985a; Mateer, 1985), sequencing is especially complex and interesting in the case of language. One reason is that the issue of sequencing arises at many different levels at once in language production. How do we produce sentences one after the other in logical order? How do we order the words within sentences? How do we order the morphemes, syllables and segments that make up the words? And finally, how do we order the muscle movements that give rise to the sequence of articulatory gestures making up a segment? Our everyday capacity to organize and to produce such a hierarchy of simultaneous, nested sequences is probably fundamental to our uniquely human ability to use spoken language. Our ability to perceive and produce written language is derivative of this more basic ability: the left-to-right and top-to-bottom spatial arrangement of orthography simply mirrors one or more of the levels of sequencing in spoken language.

Constraints on theories of sequencing

The list of fundamental questions which theories of language sequencing must address is relatively small: Is there a nonsequential or preparatory stage which precedes the sequential activation of language behaviour? How is the sequencing mechanism related to the output units for language production? Can sequencing be accomplished by the mechanisms responsible for timing? What is the relationship between the mechanisms for sequencing and timing in language production? I elaborate on these issues below.

Preparation for sequencing

Lashley (1951) was the first to recognize that a priming or preparation stage is necessary for sequencing: According to Lashley, a set of output units must be primed or simultaneously readied for activation before an independently stored sequencing mechanism can activate and impose order on them. Lashley (1951) outlined three sources of support for his idea that simultaneous priming precedes sequential activation. One was anticipations, where a unit occurs before its time, the most frequently occurring type of speech error. In anticipatory errors, an upcoming or soon-to-be-produced word or speech sound becomes produced before its time, as in, 'We have a laboratory in our . . .' instead of, 'We have a computer in our laboratory.' Anticipations indicate that, prior to actual activation, soon-to-be-produced units are simultaneously pre-excited, primed, or readied for activation. Otherwise, why would an upcoming or about-to-be-produced unit be so much more likely to intrude than any other unit in the speaker's vocabulary?

Another argument for a (simultaneous) preparatory stage prior to (sequential) activation is that, 'a general facilitation, a rise in the dynamic level' seems necessary for the performance of many sequential activities (Lashley, 1951, p. 187). For example, when sufficiently aroused, brain-damaged patients can execute sequences of behavior that under normal circumstances they cannot. For example, an aphasic who is unable to produce the word 'watch' in a laboratory test, may exclaim, 'Give me my watch!', when the experimenter pretends to make off with his watch (Teuber, 1965, personal communication). Such examples suggest that an output sequence cannot become activated unless its units have received sufficient priming: Of course, motivational factors helped to provide the priming in this particular neurolinguistic example, whereas factors associated with the specific word or action being produced normally provide the primary source of priming.

Lashley (1951, p. 189) also noted evidence from studies of reaction time and of word association indicating that a preparatory stage preceding activation can facilitate specific patterns of action. 'Reaction time, in general, is reduced by preliminary warning or by instructions which allow the subject to prepare for the specific act required. In controlled association experiments, the subject is instructed to respond to the stimulus word by a word having a certain type of relation to it, such as the opposite or a part of which the stimulus is the whole: black–white, apple–seed. The result is an attitude or set which causes the particular category to dominate the associative reaction.' It is as if controlled association instructions simultaneously prime or ready-for-activation, a large number of specific responses, thereby short-circuiting the first stage of the prime-then-activate process, so that the response can be produced soon after presentation of the stimulus.

Lashley's third basis for assuming that priming precedes sequential activation during production is that perception exhibits a similar process. To demonstrate perceptual priming, Lashley auditorily presented to his audience the garden path sentence, 'Rapid righting (writing) with his uninjured hand saved from loss the contents of the capsized canoe.' As might be expected, a sudden reinterpretation of the word 'writing' ('righting') took place once the audience heard the last two words of the sentence. On the basis of this demonstration, Lashley argued that the units for comprehending the word 'righting' ('writing') could not become activated until the phrase 'capsized canoe' had occurred, and so must have been held in a state of readiness or partial activation 'for at least 3 to 5 seconds after hearing the word' (p. 193). Thus, priming or readying-for-activation precedes actual activation during comprehension, and by analogy, during production as well, because 'the processes of comprehension and production of speech have too much in common to depend on wholly different mechanisms' (Lashley, 1951, p. 186).

Lashley's distinction between the processes of priming and activation is of course recognized in at least *some* recent theories of language production (e.g., MacKay, 1982, 1985a, b), and can be seen to provide a solution to the interaction-encapsulation issue, one of the main outstanding problems with the concept of modularity. The problem is that modules such as speech perception–production seem to exist as relatively autonomous processing systems but nevertheless interact extensively with one another, so that if modularity requires 'encapsulation of processing' (see Fodor, 1983), there are no modules. However, modules can be both interactive and encapsulated if *priming* is distinguished from *activation* as in MacKay (1982, 1985a, b), because priming is automatic and unencapsulated within modules, whereas activation requires a module-specific activation mechanism (sequence and timing nodes) and is therefore encapsulated or confined within particular modules.

Independence of sequence and content

The mechanism for sequencing behavior must be separate from the units which represent the content or form of the behavioral sequence. And in particular, the basic units making up a sequence of language units must be independent of the mechanism which sequences these units. To see why this is so, consider a set of theories incorporating non-independent sequencing and content mechanisms; chain association theories, the first class of theories discussed in Gordon and Meyer (Chap 20). There is no independent sequencing mechanism in chain association theories: unidirectional links between the units representing the content of behavior provide the representation of sequence. Activating the first content node directly primes, and indirectly causes activation of the second (connected) content node, and so on, until the entire sequence has been produced.

Many variants of this unidirectional bond assumption have been proposed, and the bonds are usually assumed to be excitatory in nature. But not always. For example, Estes (1972) proposed a chain association theory where the bonds are inhibitory rather than excitatory. The first unit inhibits the remaining units, the second inhibits all but the first, the third inhibits all but the first two, and so on. For example, in producing a simple word such as *act*, a superordinate node representing the entire word becomes activated, and primes its three subordinate nodes representing the segments, /a/, /c/, and /t/. Now under the unidirectional bond assumption, the first element, representing /a/, inhibits the other two, and the second element, representing /c/, inhibits the third, representing /t/. Thus, the first element, not being inhibited by any of the others, achieves the greatest degree of priming, and becomes activated under a most-primed-wins principle (see MacKay, 1982). The second, no longer being inhibited by the first, now has the greatest priming, and becomes activated, releasing the third from inhibition, and so on.

Lashley (1951) anticipated the basic problem with this, and other recently proposed chain association theories. The problem is that links between the basic output components will interfere with one another. For example, inhibitory links between the content nodes for the word *act* will interfere with the production of *cat* and *tack*, or any other words containing the same components in a different order. Extrapolating to a normal 50 000 word vocabulary, the conflicting inhibitory connections between the phonological components in this theory would simply prevent speech production altogether.

Theories confounding the sequencing mechanism with the production units therefore fail to explain the production of language sequences *per se*. These theories also predict sequential errors which do not occur, and have difficulty explaining the ones which do occur (see MacKay, 1970). Because they postulate non-independent mechanisms for sequence and content, chain association theories also have difficulty explaining the flexibility observed in sequential behavior. Children's word games, such as Pig Latin, illustrate the nature of this flexibility (see MacKay, 1972, and Treiman, 1983). When playing Pig Latin, children quickly and easily impose a new order on the segments of both never-previously-encountered nonsense syllables, e.g., *snark*, and frequently used words, e.g., *pig*. When children produce the word *pig* as *igpay*, for example, no painful process of unlearning the old habitual sequence is required, as might be expected if the old sequence were built into the output units themselves by means of unidirectional bonds. Instead, the sequencing mechanism appears to operate on the basis of rules which apply to an indefinitely large number of behavioral units, and which can be easily altered so as to produce never-previously-encountered forms such as *arksnay* (see MacKay, 1972).

Lashley noted one final set of phenomena calling for independence of the sequencing mechanism and the content units themselves; the ability to translate freely from one language to another using different word orders. An experienced translator does not have to proceed word by word, but quickly and easily alters the order of the components making up the original idea when translating into a target language with different word order. Such flexibility suggests that sequence is not part of a lexical concept or idea *per se*, but is imposed on the idea by language-specific rules or sequencing mechanisms.

Bilingual sequencing errors likewise suggest that the sequencing mechanism is independent of the words and ideas being sequenced. Sometimes bilinguals inadvertently impose the *wrong* order on words: For example, a native speaker of German may unconsciously adopt aspects of German syntax when attempting to speak rapidly in English, postponing the verb to the end of a frequently encountered English expression. Such errors simply could not occur if the sequencing mechanism consisted of links between the units representing language-specific words.

Sequencing and the initiation of behavior

Theories of sequencing must explain a special and repeatedly demonstrated relationship between sequencing and the initiation of behavior. A large number of recent studies have shown that it takes less time to initiate a preplanned behavior which consists of a single component than one which consists of a sequence of components. This relationship between sequencing and the initiation of behavior is an embarrassment to chain association or horizontal link theories, even ones augmented with vertical links such as Estes (1972) and Wickelgren (1979). It also presents problems for theories incorporating a scanning mechanism, including a long-abandoned theory of my own (MacKay, 1969). In 'scanning' theories, a behavioral sequence is loaded into a memory buffer in preparation for sequencing, and behavior becomes initiated by a scanner which sweeps over the buffer from e.g., left to right. Thus, a subject who is prepared to say the word *paper*, for example, has already loaded the word into the output buffer; following a go signal, the word can then be produced by sweeping the scanner over the buffer, causing activation of the initial /p/, followed by the remaining segments of the word in proper order. This process is of course independent of word length, so that the scanner should trigger the initial /p/ of a one-syllable word such as *paint* no faster than the initial /p/ of a two-syllable word such as *paper*.

Available data do not support this prediction, however, For example, Klapp, Anderson and Berrian (1973) investigated the time required after a go signal to begin to say a large number of one- versus two-syllable words such as *paint* and *paper*. All of the words were five letters long, and began with the same segment. The results showed that response time was significantly longer for two-syllable than one-syllable words, a finding replicated in other studies and for other language behaviors besides speech, e.g.,

Morse code (Klapp and Wyatt, 1976), and typing (Sternberg, Monsell, Knoll, and Wright, 1978).

Errors in sequencing

Theories of sequencing must of course explain how sequential errors occur. Not just the fact that sequential errors occur, but the detailed nature of the regularities that have been observed in these errors. An example is the sequential class phenomenon, one of the most general regularities observed to date. The phenomenon is this: when a speaker inadvertently substitutes one linguistic component for another, the substituted and substituting components almost invariably belong to the same sequential class. Cohen (1966) originally observed this regularity in errors involving interchanged words. An example is the error, 'We have a laboratory in our own computer', where one noun (*laboratory*) interchanges with another (*computer*). As in this example, nouns generally interchange with other nouns, verbs with other verbs and not with, say, nouns or adjectives (Cohen, 1967). Even 'Freudian slips' such as, 'He found her crotch, I mean, watch', adhere to this sequential class rule. Because both *watch* and *crotch* are nouns, this (invented) error obeys the sequential class regularity, even though, as Fromkin (1973) points out, semantic (Freudian) factors may simultaneously contribute to such errors.

The sequential class regularity has also been observed for errors involving (1) morphological components: prefixes interchange with other prefixes, suffixes with other suffixes, and never prefixes with suffixes (MacKay, 1979), (2) syllabic components: initial consonant clusters interchange with other initial clusters, and final with final, but never initial with final (MacKay, 1972), and (3) segmental components: vowels interchange with vowels, consonants with consonants, and never vowels with consonants (MacKay, 1972). In short, the sequential class regularity holds for all levels of speech production, and a viable theory of sequencing must explain this fact.

Exceptions to the sequential class rule. Even though exceptions to the sequential class rule are rare, they must also be explained in theories of sequencing because they display interesting regularities of their own. Consider the following examples from Fromkin (1973): 'She was waiting her husband for' (instead of, 'waiting for her husband'), and 'I don't want to part this book with' (instead of, 'to part with this book'). These regularities pose three questions: Why do these errors violate the sequential class rule (both errors involve a noun phrase changing places with a verb particle)? Why are these errors so rare? And why do these errors result in a sequence (Verb + Noun Phrase + Verb Particle) which is appropriate for other expressions such as 'She called the man up'?

Different mechanisms for sequencing and timing

Another general constraint on theories of sequencing is that the same mechanism cannot both time and sequence language behavior: sequencing cannot be achieved by a timing mechanism, and timing cannot be achieved by a sequencing mechanism (see also Keele, Chap 21). To see why timing and sequencing require different mechanisms, let us examine the two hypothetical alternatives. Consider first the possibility that a timing mechanism is by itself responsible for both sequencing and timing in speech production. This hypothetical timing mechanism is able to generate the sequence of phonemes in a word by specifying their time of production, and sequencing errors arise because phonemes have been improperly timed. The word *cat*, for example, might be misproduced as *act* because the *a* has been produced relatively early, and the *c* produced relatively late. Likewise, at a higher level, the phrase 'in the car', might be misproduced as 'in car the', because the noun is produced relatively early, and the article relatively late.

Unfortunately for this hypothetical account, no such errors occur: proficient speakers never simply misorder components in time. As discussed here, substituted components in actually occurring speech errors do not just exchange places in time, but virtually always belong to the same sequential class. For example, in the error, 'cake the ring of teas' instead of 'take the ring of keys,' the segments /t/ and /k/ exchange temporal positions, but they also belong to the same domain or sequential class, *initial consonant group* (see MacKay, 1972). This sequential regularity would not be expected if a timing mechanism determines sequencing.

Consider now the opposite possibility, that a sequencing mechanism determines both sequencing and timing, an idea proposed by Norman and Rumelhart (1983). Norman and Rumelhart's theory of typing incorporates a sequencing mechanism, but no timing mechanism, and timing of a keystroke in their theory depends on how long it takes to sequence a set of preprogramed keystrokes. Under this view, errors in the timing and sequencing of typestrokes are one and the same: when typestrokes occur out of sequence, one component is being activated especially early, and the other is being activated especially late. No one has proposed a similar hypothesis for speech production, for reasons which should be obvious from an examination of the speech error illustrated above.

However, it is important to stress that the Norman–Rumelhart hypothesis also encounters difficulties in explaining typing. Consider the findings of Grudin (1981) on the timing of keystrokes in transposition errors, e.g., *the* mistyped as *hte*. Grudin's data showed no tendency for one key to come especially early, and the other especially late in a large number of transposition errors produced by skilled typists. Rather, the keys exchanged places both in sequence, and in time, just as in speech errors. For example, assume that a skilled typist normally types the word *the* correctly with about 140 ms. between hitting *space* and *t*, and 75 ms. between hitting *t* and *h*. Grudin found that if this typist produced the transposition error *hte*, timing remained the same; about 140 ms between space and *h*, and 75 ms between *h* and *t*. The wrong components occurred at the right time. This finding indicates that timing is independent of the behavior being timed, and this independence could only occur with separate mechanisms for determining the content, sequencing and timing of behavior.

Grudin's findings also indicate that timing is being 'programmed' in proficient typing, and this is an especially important fact for theories of sequencing and timing, because typing is a skill which does not demand consistent or accurate timing, unlike say, music, Morse code, or speech. Apparently a timing mechanism plays a role in language production even when precise timing is unnecessary.

Constraints on theories of sequencing in perception

I turn now to sequencing in perception, the problem of how we perceive input sequences in proper serial order when we do, and improper order when we make errors. This problem places as many constraints on psychological theories as Lashley's problem of serial order in behavior, but has been largely ignored in psychology: studies of perception over the past 150 years have concentrated mainly on static visual displays, and have devoted relatively little attention to the perception of input sequences.

To illustrate the problem of sequential perception, I begin with the most frequently overlooked constraint on theories of sequential perception: effects of practice. Warren and Warren (1970) noted that we can perceive the serial order of sounds in familiar words such as *sand* at rates of 20 ms per segment, but require over 200 ms per sound for perceiving the order of unfamiliar sound sequences such as a hiss, a vowel, a buzz and a tone (when recycled via a tape loop). One interpretation of these findings attributes this difference to practice or familiarity: sequences of speech sounds are much more familiar than non-speech sequences such as *hiss–vowel–buzz–tone*. Another interpretation focuses on acoustic differences between speech vs. nonspeech sequences (see Bregman and Campbell,

1971). However, this second interpretation will not do for Warren's (1974) experimental demonstration of how practice facilitates the recognition of nonspeech sequences. Subjects in Warren (1974) repeatedly listened to non-speech sounds in sequences which were initially unrecognizable, e.g., *hiss–vowel–buzz–tone*, and after about 800 trials of practice, the subjects became able to identify the order of these sounds with durations of less than 20 ms. per sound. This order-of-magnitude effect of practice on the recognition of auditory sequences is all the more interesting because similar perceptual reversals are observed in the speech perception of children, but not adults. Children often reverse adjacent segments in perceiving a word, misperceiving 'spaghetti' as 'psghetti' or 'snow' as 'nows', for example (Allen, 1981), but adults virtually never make such errors. This developmental difference suggests that effects of practice on the recognition of sequence represent a general constraint on theories of sequential perception.

Violations of sequential isomorphism

Why is the problem of sequencing in perception often considered trivial and uninteresting? One reason seems to lie in an implicit, but fundamental assumption which has become built into virtually every theory of perception and memory published to date. Under this *'sequential isomorphism postulate'*, perceptual sequences invariably mirror the external sequence of events in the real world. If correct, this 'first-in-first-perceived' postulate indeed renders the problem of serial order in perception trivial and uninteresting. In fact, however, whole classes of striking and well-documented phenomena, discussed below, violate sequential isomorphism (see also Cutler, Chap 2; and Huttenlocher and Goodman, Chap 19) and provide strong constraints on theories of sequential perception. Needless to say, however, the fact that sequential isomorphism appears to predominate most of the time in the remainder of our lives provides an additional constraint on theories of sequential perception.

The perceptual precedence of higher level units

Theories of perception must explain why units which end later in an input sequence are sometimes perceived more quickly than units which end sooner. The recognition of segments vs. syllables provides an example: subjects require more time to identify a segment than a syllable within a sequence of nonsense syllables, even though the segment ends sooner than the syllable in the acoustic stimulus. The original experiment by Savin and

Bever (1970) can be used for purposes of illustration because many subsequent studies have replicated their basic findings, and come to the same conclusion (see Massaro, 1979).

Savin and Bever (1970) had subjects listen to a sequence of nonsense syllables with the aim of detecting a target unit as quickly as possible. There were three types of targets: an entire syllable, e.g., *splay*, the vowel within the syllable, i.e., *ay*, and the initial consonant of the syllable, i.e., *s*. The subjects were instructed to press a key as soon as they detected their target, and the surprising result was that reaction times were faster when the target was the entire syllable rather than either the initial consonant or the vowel in the syllable. Theories of perception must therefore explain why higher level units, and in particular, a syllable or word, can be detected before the phonemes making up the syllable or word.

Sequential illusions

Sequential illusions occur whenever the surface units of an input sequence are perceived as coming sooner or later than they actually occur in the real world. I discuss two examples below.

Phonological fusions. Phonological fusions occur when a subject wearing earphones is presented with an acoustic stimulus such as *banket* in one ear, and *lanket* in the other ear: even with a sizeable (e.g., 200 ms) onset lag or temporal asynchrony between the stimuli, subjects often report hearing *blanket*, a fusion of the two inputs (Day, 1968; and Cutting and Day, 1975). If perception accurately represented the input sequence, subjects would perceive the *l* followed by the *b*, because the order of arrival at the acoustic level is *l* followed without overlap by *b*. Some subjects in fact do perceive the input sequence veridically, but there are large individual differences, and most subjects do not: instead they fuse the inputs, and report that the *b* preceded the *l* (see Day, 1968).

As their name suggests, phonological fusions depend on a phonological rather than on an acoustic representation of the input: phonological factors readily influence the probability of fusion, whereas lower level factors within the acoustic analysis system do not. One of these phonological factors is wordhood: fusions sometimes occur when both inputs are words, but they occur much more frequently when both inputs are non-words, such as *banket* and *lanket*. Words are also the most common type of fusion response, regardless of whether the stimuli are words or nonwords (Day, 1968).

Another phonological factor is sequential permissability: fusions always result in phonological sequences which are permissable or actually occurring within the listener's language. Percepts which violate phonological rules (e.g., *lbanket*) never occur, even when nonoccurring sequences represent the only possible fusions. For example, simultaneous presentation of *bad* and *dad* never results in fusions such as *bdad* and *dbad*, because initial *bd* and *db* do not occur in English.

By way of contrast, acoustic factors have little or no effect on the likelihood of fusion: Cutting and Day (1975) found that number of fusions remained constant when the fusion stimuli differed in intensity, in fundamental frequency, and in allophonic characteristics, as when one stimulus contained a trilled /r/ and the other an untrilled /r/. Explaining the detailed nature of phonological fusions, and other sequential illusions, provides a fundamental challenge for theories of perception.

Phonemic restorations. Phonemic restorations represent another sequential illusion. When subjects listen to a sentence containing a word such as *legi*lature*, where the *s* has been masked by a cough (*), they hear the word intact, and are unable to accurately locate the cough within the sequence of phonemes, or tell which phoneme is missing when informed that the cough has physically replaced a single speech sound (Warren and Warren, 1970). This inability to locate the cough in the sequence of phonemes violates sequential isomorphism and must be explained in theories of sequential perception. Click localization studies (see Fodor, Bever, and Garrett, 1974, for a review) provide a similar example.

Constraints on theories of timing in language perception and production

I turn now to the third basic problem, timing in langue perception and production. How do we produce language units of different durations? And how do we produce these units at different rates, and with different rhythms or patterns of durations?

What fundamental phenomena or constraints must theories of timing address? The section on sequencing has already discussed one of these constraints: independence of the mechanisms for timing and sequencing the basic language units. In addition, theories of timing must address six other fundamental issues discussed below: Where in the specification of output components is rate and timing determined? What mechanisms underlie the production of rhythmic outputs? How is periodicity or near-miss periodicity achieved in language skills such as typing, handwriting and speech? What is the relationship between the timing mechanisms for language perception and production? What accounts for the ability to flexibly adjust the rate and timing of behavior? Why do activities with different timing characteristics interact with one another?

The distributed nature of timing and sequencing

The most fundamental constraint on theories of timing is that timing is an 'everywhere' or distributed characteristic. Each and every component in speech production, from the lowest level components controlling muscle movements, to the highest level components representing sentential concepts, must be activated at some rate, and for some duration. Rhythm, rate and timing permeate the entire process of language production, and cannot cannot be tacked on as an independent stage at some point in the theoretical specification of output processes.

To see why timing must be a distributed characteristic, it is only necessary to examine existing 'stage of processing' proposals, including one of my own (MacKay, 1969). These proposals treat rhythm and timing as an 'afterthought', a late stage of processing introduced just before or during the programming of muscle movements. For example, in my (1969) stage-of-processing proposal for timing the producing of speech, the entire syntax, semantics and phonology for producing a sentence are first constructed, and then stored within a simultaneous or nontemporal spatial display. Only following this construction and storage stage are timing characteristics such as speech rate specified as part of the output.

Stage of processing proposals such as this one face many unsolved problems. One is the complexity and reduplication of information which is required for the simultaneous display. Rhythm and timing depend on information associated with units at every level (sentences, phrases, words, syllables and segments), and the proposed spatial display must incorporate all of this information before timing specifications can be added. Because these specifications are also required for constructing the sentence in the first place, adding timing at one particular level in the construction of a sentence complicates the process.

An even more serious problem for stage-of-processing theories of timing is speed-accuracy trade-off, one of the most pervasive phenomena in the study of skilled behavior. For all known skills, increased speed leads to increased errors in the activation of components, whether low-level muscle movement components, or high-level mental components. As an example of speed-accuracy trade-off in the activation of high-level mental components, consider phonological speech errors such as the substitution of 'coat-thrutting' for 'throat-cutting'. Here components within the phonological system have become interchanged, and in a study of experimentally induced speech errors, MacKay (1971) demonstrated that such errors increase as a function of speech rate (see also Dell, 1985). These findings cannot be explained if timing is determined *after* the specification and mispecification of phonology: for rate to influence phonological errors, the phonological components and their rate of output must become specified at the same time. And because rate also influences errors occurring at other levels, both above and below the phonological level, rate and timing must be specified throughout the entire hierarchy of units for producing a sentence, from the lowest level muscle movements to the highest level phrase and lexical concepts (see MacKay, 1987 for details). In short, rate must be a distributed characteristic, specified everywhere, rather than at just one point in the hierarchy of output units.

Monitoring, rate and errors. A possible counterargument in favor of stage-of-processing theories of timing is that errors increase with rate not because rate is a distributed characteristic, but because various output monitoring devices become suspended at faster rates, thereby allowing more errors. To be taken seriously, this explanation of speed-accuracy trade-off requires a great deal more theoretical specification and empirical support. There currently exists no empirical evidence for monitoring devices which are independent of the output mechanisms themselves, and no evidence that hypothetical monitoring devices of this sort are 'suspendable' (see MacKay, 1987). The concept of perceptual monitoring as a final stage in production also has difficulty with the time characteristics of how errors are detected and corrected: error detection and correction is so rapid as to sometimes precede the full-blown appearance of an error in the surface output (see Levelt, 1984). And even if monitoring and production are viewed as parallel rather than serial processes, the monitoring counter-argument has difficulty with the fact that perception can proceed much faster than production at maximal rate (see MacKay, 1985b, 1987): suspending perceptual monitors could not facilitate output rate if perception proceeds in parallel with and faster than production.

The generation of periodicity

Proficient performance of language skills such as speech production, Morse code, typing and handwriting has been shown to exhibit perfect or nearly perfect periodicity in various ways which must be explained in theories of timing. For example, Wing (1978) demonstrated 'near-miss' periodicity in handwriting for the time between successive downstrokes and upstrokes of subjects producing the letters m, n, v and w. The temporal deviations from perfect periodicity were quite small, and tended to alternate with one another, temporal undershoot on one stroke followed by temporal overshoot on the next, and vice-versa. Similar zig–zag alternations in the time between adjacent components have also been observed for speech (in the durations of successive syllables in an utterance; Kozhevnikov and Chistovich, 1965), and for skilled typing (Shaffer, 1978, Wing, 1980). Typestroke periodicity becomes especially obvious when highly skilled typists transcribe specially constructed materials (Shaffer, 1980). These 'alternation passages' contain phrases, such as 'authentic divisors', where normal typing conventions require a different hand on each stroke, so that interactions between successive movements with the same hand cannot occur. In typing these passages, the inter-key intervals of expert typists become nearly equal, and subsequent strokes tend to compensate for deviations from perfect periodicity. That is, an especially fast stroke tends to follow, and make up for, an especially slow one, and vice versa. As Shaffer (1980, p. 116) points out, this 'negative serial covariance' sometimes approaches the theoretical limit that could be expected for a perfectly periodic internal clock. Shaffer's conclusion is especially interesting because neither rhythm nor precise timing is necessary for executing typestrokes. Apparently people not only *can*, but normally *do* generate near-miss periodicity, even when neither rhythm nor precisely timed output is required.

Effects of practice on timing

Effects of practice are everywhere apparent in the timing literature, and must be explained in theories of timing. For example, language skills such as typing only exhibit near-miss periodicity following extensive practice. Genest (1956) found that the interval between typestrokes came closer and closer to perfect periodicity as typists became progressively more proficient, but observed no periodicity whatsoever during the early stages of learning to type (see also Shaffer, 1978, 1980, discussed above).

Interactions between timing mechanisms for perception and production

On-line interactions between perceptual events and the timing of ongoing speech and action have frequently been observed, and suggest that systems of perception and production may share some of the same timing mechanisms (see also Keele, Chap 21; MacKay (1987); and Keele, Pokorny, Corcos, and Ivry, 1985). Lashley (1951) was the first to note such an interaction between a perceptual rhythm (listening to a marching band) and ongoing motoric activities, including walking, breathing and speaking: when someone is listening to a salient rhythm such as a marching band, the perceptual rhythm tends to cause the listener to fall in step, gesture, breathe and even speak in time with the band. Such interactions suggest that identical timing mechanisms govern perceptual processes such as listening to music, and motoric processes such as walking, breathing and speaking.

Prosodic flexibility

Timing in syllable production is flexible rather than built in, and theories of timing must explain our ability to learn and to produce different types of language rhythm. An example is the more varied use of durational information in 'stress-timed' languages such as English as compared to 'syllable-timed' languages such as French (see Cutler, Mehler, Norris and Segui, 1983).

Constant relative timing

As the overall time to produce a behavioral sequence changes due to a voluntary decision to increase rate, the proportion of time required to produce some segments of the sequence often remains constant. This phenomenon, known as constant relative timing, has been observed within limits for many behaviors (e.g., walking, running, typing, handwriting, speech, lever rotation), and can be considered a general law of behavior. As a single example of this general law, Shapiro, Zernick, Gregor and Diestal (1981) had subjects walk at various speeds on a treadmill, and found that the proportion of time required to execute the four basic phases of a step (lift, stride, heel contact and support) remained virtually invariant at the different speeds. If the lift phase required 20% of the duration of a step cycle at a slow rate, it required about 20% at a faster rate. Relative timing only remained constant within a limited range of rates, however: When the treadmill was accelerated beyond a certain point, subjects broke into a jog, and the temporal configuration of the components of their strike changed dramatically. Walking and running clearly have different temporal characteristics, and are controlled by different underlying mechanisms, which both conform to the law of constant relative timing. Handwriting and transcription typing also exhibit constant relative timing. Here changes in overall rate of output have been found to scale the duration of response components in almost perfect proportion, as would occur with a change in rate of a low level internal clock (Shaffer, 1978).

Interestingly, constant relative timing has also been observed for *involuntary* changes in the rate of language production. Components in a sentence speed up involuntarily as a result of practice, and these changes in relative duration sometimes exhibit constant relative timing as well. For example, MacKay and Bowman (1969) had subjects practice producing a sentence as quickly as possible over 12 trials of practice, and found that the maximal speech rate increased systematically with practice (see also MacKay 1974). More importantly, different components of the sentence speeded up proportionally: the relative duration of words and syllables remained constant at the faster speed. The constant relative timing that occurs when behavior speeds up, due either to voluntary rate changes, or to involuntarily effects of practice, places fundamental constraints on theories of timing.

Theories postulating a computational process for calculating the durations of behavioral components have difficulty explaining constant relative timing because the phenomenon appears in the behavior of insects and crustaceans (see Shapiro, Zernick, Gregor, and Diestal 1981), where such computations are unlikely. Constant relative timing also appears immediately after a voluntary decision to change rate, without the lag times which seem necessary for computing the new temporal values. The mechanism for adjusting timing on the basis of rate must instead be automatic and noncomputational in nature.

Deviations from constant relative timing. Constant relative timing cannot be expected for *all* response components. In particular, not all changes in speech rate can be expected to scale proportionally over the durations of vowels versus consonants. With voluntary changes in speaking rate, vowels exhibit much more 'elasticity' than do consonants: vowels can be prolonged almost indefinitely to slow down the rate of speech, but if stop consonants are greatly prolonged, they no longer resemble speech sounds. Such observations suggest that different timing mechanisms may control the production of consonants versus vowels, and consistent with this hypothesis, Tuller, Kelso and Harris (1982) found that at different rates of nonsense syllable production, the durations of consonants remained constant relative to vowels, but only when compared to the interval between vowel onsets. Neither consonant nor vowel duration *per se* remained constant relative to overall utterance duration.

Temporal interactions between different activities

Theories of timing must explain why concurrent activities with different timing characteristics tend to interfere with one another. For example, speech exhibits temporal interactions with finger movement: when subjects attempt to produce a sequence of syllables and a sequence of finger taps at the same time, they experience considerable difficulty if the movements conflict in timing, but little difficulty if the concurrent movements are temporally compatible, or occur at identical or harmonically related times.

Klapp (1981) had subjects press a telegraph key in time with tones presented periodically via headphones to one ear, and simultaneously produce a syllable in time with tones presented to the other ear. The goal was to maximize the temporal overlap of keypresses and syllables with the tone to the corresponding ear. The tones arriving at the two ears were either temporally compatible, or temporally incompatible. In the temporal compatibility condition, the rhythms to the two ears were harmonically related: One series proceeded at twice the rate of the other. In the temporally incompatible condition, the rhythms to the two ears were equally fast on the average, but were desynchronized, or occurred at harmonically unrelated times. The results were straightforward; the average temporal overlap of tone and behavior was greater in the temporally compatible condition than in the temporally incompatible condition, as if the same internal clock was needed for timing both speech and hand movements.

Summary and conclusions

This chapter has reviewed a number of fundamental constraints or characteristics which can be used to evaluate current theories of sequencing and timing in language perception and production. Indeed, I have already used some of these characteristics to illustrate problems with four general classes of theories: stage of processing theories of timing, chain association and scanning theories of sequencing, and monitoring theories of the processing of perceptual feedback. However, a general evaluation of extant theories on the basis of these characteristics remains to be carried out.

The list of characteristics developed here is short, and undoubtably incomplete, and will surely grow as the field progresses. Contained within the list, however, are the *sine qua non* requirements for a viable theory: Theories of sequencing and timing which lack one or more of these characteristics can be considered incomplete or inadaquate. And in addition to providing a standard against which to evaluate current theories, the criteria of this chapter can be used to develop new and more adequate theories. Indeed, I myself hope to use these criteria in developing such a theory (see MacKay, 1987).

What sort of theory will be needed for explaining the fundamental phenomena of sequencing and timing in language perception and production? The theory must postulate a hierarchy of units, including units representing sentences, phrases, words, morphemes, syllables, segments and distinctive features. These units must be separated from the mechanisms for activating them in proper sequence, and the sequential activation of these units must be preceded by a priming or preparation stage in the theory. Moreover, the sequential activating mechanism must operate on classes of units, so as to explain why substituted and susbtituting components in speech errors usually belong to the same sequential class; e.g., verbs substitute with other verbs, and not with pronouns; syllable initial consonants substitute with other syllable initial consonants, and not with final consonants.

On the perceptual side, the theory must somehow allow violations of sequential isomorphism, so that the perceived sequence can differ from the actual sequence for relatively unfamiliar, rapidly presented external or real-world events. And somehow, the theory must also give precedence to higher level units, so that more rapid responses can be generated for higher level units such as words and syllables than for lower level units such as segments.

Timing must employ different mechanisms from sequencing in the theory. And the timing mechanisms must act like an internal clock which is basically periodic in nature and can be sped up to introduce proportional changes in the duration of different output components. The timing mechanisms must also develop with practice, and must operate throughout the entire hierarchy of production units, so as to capture the distributed nature of timing. Finally, language perception and production must have identical or closely interacting timing mechanisms; and so must different output systems such as speech and finger movement.

How general are these characteristics? Do they apply to other skills besides language perception–production? As Keele (Chap 21) points out, timing in language skills may reflect a more fundamental ability which characterizes many other skilled behaviors. And sequencing likewise reflects a fundamental ability with basically similar manifestations in speech and other everyday activities (see Lashley, 1951). The present chapter may therefore provide a rough outline of what a general theory of sequencing and timing in behavior must eventually explain.

Acknowledgements

This paper was prepared in part while the author was a member of the Research Group on Perception and Action at the Center for Interdisciplinary Research (Z.i.F.), University of Bielefeld, and was presented to the conference entitled, 'Common Processes in Speaking, Listening, Reading, and Writing', which was held at the Z.i.F., Bielefeld, July 1–5, 1985. A preliminary version of this chapter appeared as Perception and Action, Report 84, 1985, Zentrum fuer interdiciplinaere Forschung, Universitaet Bielefeld, FRG. The author thanks M. Studdert-Kennedy and an anonymous reviewer for comments on an earlier version of this chapter.

References

Allen, G. D. (1981). Suprasegmental constraints on segmental representation: Research involving speech production. In J. Myers, J. Laver, and J. Anderson (Eds) *The cognitive representation of speech*. Amsterdam: North-Holland.

Bregman, A. S. and Campbell, J. (1971). Primary auditory stream segregation and perception of order in rapid sequences of tones. *Quarterly Journal of Experimental Psychology*, **25**, 22–40.

Cohen, A. (1967). Errors of speech and their implication for understanding the strategy of language users. *Zeitschrift fuer Phonetik*, **21**, 177–81.

Cutting, J. E., and Day, R. S. (1975). The perception of stop-liquid clusters in phonological fusion. *Journal of Phonetics*, **3**, 99–113.

Cutler, A., Mehler, J., Norris, D., and Segui, J. (1983). A language-specific comprehension strategy. *Nature*, **304**, 159–60.

Day, R. S. (1968). *Fusion in dichotic listening*. Unpublished doctoral dissertation, Stanford University.

Dell, G. (1985). Positive feedback in hierarchical connectionist models: Applications to language production. *Cognitive Science*, **9**, 3–23.

Estes, W. K. (1972). An associative basis for coding and organization in memory. In A. W. Melton and E. Martin (Eds). *Coding processes in human memory*. Washington, DC: Winston.

Fodor, J. A. (1983). *The modularity of mind*. Cambridge, MA: MIT Press.

Fodor, J. A., Bever, T. G., and Garrett, M. F. (1974). *The psychology of language*. New York: McGraw-Hill.

Fromkin, V. A. (1973) (Ed). *Speech errors as lingustic evidence*. Paris. Mouton.

Genest, M. (1956). L'analyse temporelle du travail dactylographique. *Bulletin du Centre d'Etudes et Recherches Psychotechniques*, **5**, 183–91.

Grudin, J. (1981). *The organization of serial order in typing*. Unpublished doctoral dissertation, University of California, San Diego.

Keele, S. W., Pokorny, R. A., Corcos, D. M. and Ivry, R. (1985). Do perception and motor production share common timing mechanisms?: A correlational analysis. *Acta Psychologica*, in press.

Klapp, S. T. (1979). Doing two things at once: The role of temporal compatibility. *Memory & Cognition*, **7**, 375–81.

Klapp, S. T. (1981). Temporal compatibility in dual motor tasks II: Simultaneous articulation and hand movements. *Memory & Cognition*, **9**, 398–401.

Klapp, S. T., Anderson, W. G., and Berrian, R. W. (1973). Implicit speech in reading reconsidered. *Journal of Experimental Psychology*, **100**, 368–74.

Klapp, S. T., and Wyatt, E. P. (1976). Motor programming within a sequence of responses. *Journal of Motor Behavior*, **8**, 19–26.

Kozhevnikov, V. A., and Chistovich, L. A. (1965). *Speech articulation and perception*. Washington, DC: Joint Publications Research Service.

Lashley, K. S. (1951). The problem of serial order in behavior. In L. A. Jeffress (Ed.) *Cerebral mechanisms in behavior*. New York: Wiley.

Levelt, W. J. M. (1984). Spontaneous self-repairs in speech: processes and representations. In M. P. R. van den Broecke and A. Cohen (Eds) *Proceedings of the Tenth International Congress of Phonetic Sciences*. Dortrecht: Foris, pp. 105–11.

MacKay, D. G. (1969). Forward and backward masking in motor systems. *Kybernetik*, **6**, 57–64.

MacKay, D. G. (1970). Spoonerisms: The structure of errors in the serial order of speech. *Neuropsychologia*, **8**, 323–50.

MacKay, D. G. (1971). Stress pre-entry in motor systems. *American Journal of Psychology*, **84**, 35–51.

MacKay, D. G. (1972). The structure of words and syllables: evidence from errors in speech. *Cognitive Psychology*, **3**, 201–27.

MacKay, D. G. (1979). Lexical insertion, inflection and derivation: creative processes in word production. *Journal of Psycholinguistic Research*, **8**, 477–98.

MacKay, D. G. (1982). The problem of flexibility, fluency, and speed-accuracy trade-off in skilled behavior. *Psychological Review*, **89**, 483–506.

MacKay, D. G. (1985a). A theory of the representation, organization, and timing of action with implications for sequencing disorders. In E. A. Roy (Ed.) *Neuropsychological studies of apraxia and related disorders*. New York: North-Holland, pp. 267–308.

MacKay, D. G. (1985b). Asymmetries between the perception and production of speech. The Research Group on Perception and Action, Report # 8, ZiF, University of Bielefeld, FRG.

MacKay, D. G. (1987). *The organization of perception and action: A theory for language and other cognitive skills*. New York: Springer.

MacKay, D. G., and Bowman, R. W. (1969). On producing the meaning in sentences. *American Journal of Psychology*, **82**, 23–39.

Mateer, K. (1985). Common sites for oral motor sequencing and phoneme identification: Evidence from electrical stimulation of the language cortex. Paper presented to the conference on 'Common Processes in Listening, Speaking, Reading, and Writing.' held at the ZiF, University of Bielefeld, July 1–5.

Massaro, D. W. (1979). Reading and listening. In P. A. Kolers, M. E. Wrolstad, and H. Bouma (Eds). *Processing of visible language*. New York: Plenum, pp. 331–540.

Meyer, D. E., and Gordon, P. C. (1983). Dependencies between rapid speech production and perception: Evidence for a shared sensory-motor voicing mechanism. In H. Bouma, and D. G. Bouwhuis (Eds) *Attention and Performance X*. Hillsdale, NJ: Erlbaum.

Norman, D. A. and Rumelhart, D. E. (1983). Studies of typing from the LNR research group. In W. E. Cooper (Ed.) *Cognitive aspects of skilled typewriting*. New York: Springer, pp. 45–66.

Savin, H. B., and Bever, T. E. (1970). The nonperceptual reality of the phoneme. *Journal of Verbal Learning & Verbal Behavior*, **9**, 295–302.

Shaffer, L. H. (1978). Timing in the motor programming of typing. *Quarterly Journal of Experimental Psychology*, **30**, 333–45.

Shaffer, L. H. (1980). Analysing piano performance. In G. E. Stelmach, and J. Requin (Eds) *Tutorials in motor behavior*. Amsterdam: North-Holland.

Shapiro, D. C., Zernicke, R. F., Gregory, R. J., and Diestel, J. D. (1981). Evidence for generalized motor programs using gait pattern analysis. *Journal of Motor Behavior*, **13**, 33–47.

Sternberg, S., Monsell, S., Knoll, R. L., and Wright, C. E. (1978). The latency and duration of rapid movement sequences: Comparisons of speech and typewriting. In G. E. Stelmach (Ed.) *Information processing in motor control and learning*. New York: Academic.

Tuller, B., Kelso, J. A. S., and Harris, K. S. (1982). Interarticulator phasing as an index of temporal regularity in speech. *Journal of Experimental Psychology: Human Perception and Performance*, **8**, 460–72.

Treiman, R. (1983). The structure of spoken syllables: Evidence from novel word games. *Cognition*, **15**, 49–74.

Warren, R. M. (1974). Auditory temporal discrimination by trained listeners. *Cognitive Psychology*, **6**, 237–56.

Warren, R. M., and Warren, R. P. (1970). Auditory illusions and confusions. *Scientific American*, **223**, 30–6.

Wickelgren, W. (1979). *Cognitive psychology*. Englewood Cliffs, NJ: Prentice Hall.

Wing, A. M. (1978). Response timing in handwriting. In G. E. Stelmach (Ed.) *Information processing in motor control and learning*. New York: Academic.

Wing, A. M. (1980). The long and short of timing in response sequences. In G. E. Stelmach, and J. Requin (Eds) *Tutorials in motor behavior*. Amsterdam: North-Holland.

19 The time to identify spoken words

Janellen Huttenlocher and Judith Goodman

Abstract

Recently, it has been proposed that spoken word recognition is based on a single left-to-right analysis of the sound pattern. According to the proposed model, that analysis terminates at the phoneme where the word is uniquely specified or, for a nonword stimulus, at the phoneme where the sound pattern deviates from all possible words. In this chapter, we review the arguments and evidence that have been presented in favor of this position. We find that the arguments are underspecified, and that, as a result, the empirical evidence for the proposed model of word recognition is ambiguous. Some of the claims made are less problematic with respect to nonword stimuli. Hence, we carried out two experiments involving nonword decisions. We found that these decisions are not initiated at the phoneme where the sound pattern deviates from all possible words. In our discussion, we consider the structural properties of the lexicon which suggest some of the cues that may be important in recognizing spoken words.

Introduction

Listeners identify spoken words from the acoustic–phonetic patterns produced by speakers. Certain aspects of the process seem clear. First, the identification of words from incoming speech involves both 'bottom-up' processes, i.e. recognition of acoustic–phonetic information, and 'top-down' processes, i.e. integration of information from the syntactic and semantic context. Second, the identification of words occurs 'on-line'; that

LANGUAGE PERCEPTION AND PRODUCTION
ISBN 0-12-052750-2

is, the integration of information is rapid enough to allow listeners to keep pace with continuous speech. Recently a model was proposed to account for the integration of acoustic–phonetic and contextual information, which makes testable predictions concerning the time course of the processes involved (Marslen-Wilson, 1978; Marslen-Wilson and Welsh, 1978; Marslen-Wilson and Tyler, 1980). The model holds that word identification is based on an acoustic–phonetic analysis of only portions of the incoming sound pattern. Initial phonetic information leads to access of a set of candidates (the cohort) and, as more phonetic information is received, candidates incompatible with the input are removed. In addition, syntactic and semantic context interacts with phonetic information, also removing incompatible candidates from the cohort. Identification occurs when only one word remains. Thus, an on-line interaction between bottom-up and top-down information results in word identification during the presentation of a word.

The cohort model makes claims that have important theoretical implications. Below, we examine the model and the evidence reported in support of it, and point out some problems with that evidence. We did two experiments investigating certain claims of the model concerning the time course of nonword decisions. The experimental approach was similar to that in earlier studies cited in support of the model, but included controls not previously used. Our results were not consistent with the cohort model. Following a description of our experiments, we discuss properties of the lexicon which, along with our findings and those of certain earlier studies, suggest that sources of information other than those utilized by the cohort model contribute to word identification.

The original study which led to the cohort model involved a shadowing task where subjects repeated short passages (Marslen-Wilson, 1973). A few subjects (4 out of 65 screened) were 'very close shadowers' who stayed consistently just over one syllable behind the input. Speed itself is not evidence of rapid word identification, since shadowing can be based on a lower-level analysis of input. What was taken as critical was that these fast shadowers sometimes added to or changed words in ways that were appropriate to the context. Marslen-Wilson argued that the subjects' responses were constrained by the preceding context 'up to and including the word immediately before the error.' The data presented do not support such a strong claim; of the two examples given, one could easily reflect syntactic/semantic context earlier than the immediately preceding word, and the other a parsing error independent of the context. The argument made in this initial paper has been pursued more systematically in a series of later studies.

One later experiment (Marslen-Wilson and Welsh, 1978) also involved shadowing. The passages shadowed contained multi-syllabic words which, unknown to the subjects, were mispronounced by a single phoneme in the first or third syllables. (This study included no fast shadowers; subjects were, on average, 1.6 words behind the input.) According to the cohort model, subjects should more often restore (i.e., fail to detect) mispronunciations in the third than first syllable, because the target would already have been identified as a particular word. About half of the mispronunciations were restored, and the predicted effect of syllabic position was significant only when the target was semantically constrained. In addition, the syllabic position effect may not reflect only the postulated processes. Syllable stress was neither manipulated nor controlled in the shadowing experiment. Yet it has been shown that the probability of detecting mispronunciations is much greater in stressed (82%) than in unstressed (47%) syllables independent of syllable position (Cole and Jakimik, 1980). In the shadowing study, the authors note that most of the target words had primary stress on the first or second syllables; this might well contribute to the less frequent detection of third syllable mispronunciations.

Later studies examined two strong predictions of the cohort model. First, when only a single word candidate is compatible with the incoming sound pattern (and context, if present), the word will be identified. Thus, the 'uniqueness point' — the point where input becomes compatible with just one word — is critical. Second, when no word candidates are compatible with the incoming sound pattern, a nonword decision will be made. Thus the 'nonword point' is also critical. These predictions have been assessed in studies of the identification of words and in studies of the detection of nonwords.

Consider first studies of word identification. Marlsen-Wilson and Tyler (1980) used monitoring tasks where subjects listened for a prespecified word, a word from a particular category, or a word which rhymed with a prespecified word. We focus on the condition where subjects listen for a prespecified word since the authors argue that this provides a pure measure of word identification. They found reaction times that were shorter than the word durations both in and out of context, but this result does not provide strong support for the cohort model. The claim of the model is that a word will be recognized at that point, going from left to right, where only one candidate from the initial cohort is compatible with both the acoustic–phonetic information and contextual information. Therefore, the critical issue is whether there is a correspondence between reaction times and uniqueness points for particular words, but this was not examined. Further, it is not clear that the processes used in monitoring for a prespecified word are the same as those used in ordinary word identification, where the incoming sound can be any word consistent with the context. Instead, monitoring for a prespecified word greatly constrains lexical search. Thus even if there were strong evidence that subjects made their decisions at the uniqueness point, which there is not, the findings would not be completely convincing.

Marslen-Wilson (1978) also used a phoneme detection task to evaluate the cohort model. There is evidence that people detect a particular phoneme only after they recognize the word containing it (Cutler and Norris, 1979; Morton and Long, 1976). Marslen-Wilson found that RTs measured from the target phoneme decreased the later in a word that phoneme occurred. In fact, RT decreased linearly as the target phoneme approached the uniqueness point. Marslen-Wilson took these findings as support for the view that words are recognized at the uniqueness point and that phonemes are then detected from one's phonological knowledge of the words. However, the data do not provide strong evidence for this view. First, decreasing RTs to later targets would be expected even if RTs were constant from the beginning of the word, reflecting the later starting point of the measurement (more of the word has been presented before the start of the measurement). Second, there is no reason that RTs should continue to decrease for target phonemes occurring after the uniqueness point: RTs from target phonemes should be a constant after the uniqueness point.

Gating studies of word identification also have been used (Grosjean, 1980; Tyler and Wessels, 1983, 1984). In these tasks, the initial portions of words are presented, with increasing amounts of acoustic information on successive trials. The amount of information needed to identify a word both in and out of context is assessed. Words are identified correctly from part of the sound pattern; e.g. Grosjean found that 83% of the sound pattern was required to identify isolated words. However there are problems in equating the processes in gating tasks with those in normal word identification. First, subjects are required to use partial information to decide what word the target might be, and this is not the case in normal speech when words continue to completion. Second, these decisions are made after incoming speech has ceased, and may be based on a strategic process of considering what words are consistent with the sound and the context. Such a process may be too slow to be used on-line. Even if subjects are instructed to respond rapidly, as in a recent study by Tyler and Wessels (1984), the problems remain — the word is stopped midstream, with an elapse of time not present in normal listening.

Tyler and Wessels (1983) used the gating technique to evaluate the cohort model by determining whether more than one word candidate remained at the point of word identification. However, neither the definition of word identification nor the nature of the mental lexicon from which candidates are drawn were theoretically predetermined. Tyler and Wessels tried two different definitions of word identification and two different sorts of mental lexicon to fit their data to the cohort model. One measure of word identification was the point of correct responding and the other was the point of correct responding with 80% confidence. One mental lexicon proposed to determine the number of candidates remaining at the identification point was an ordinary dictionary; the other a lexicon consisting only of base morphemes. In short, the measures of the uniqueness point and of the nature of the lexicon were not theoretically justified by the model. Rather they were selected *post hoc* to best fit the model.

Further specification of 'uniqueness' points is clearly critical; to argue that a word becomes unique before it ends requires specifying what is meant by uniqueness. Words can take various endings, and in that sense, a target rarely becomes unique until the end. Not only are there plural and tense markings, there are also suffixes (e.g. govern becomes government) and compounding (e.g. scare becomes scarecrow). A dictionary of base morphemes is quite different in size from a dictionary of words. To test the hypothesis that the subject identifies targets at the uniqueness point requires that these issues be resolved, and to resolve them requires information that is not yet available about the nature of the mental lexicon.

Consider now studies of nonword decisions. Marslen-Wilson (1978) tested his claims as to when nonword decisions occur with a lexical decision task. Subjects pressed a key when they detected a nonword. The point when targets became nonwords was systematically varied to test the claim that reaction time, measured from the nonword point, should be a constant, regardless of where that nonword point occurs. However, the following problem must be noted. It is difficult to create an item that becomes a nonword early and yet follows the phonotactic rules of English, and the early nonwords included some nonlegal sound sequences (e.g. Sthoidick, Vleesidence). For nonlegal patterns, nonword decisions can be made without consulting the lexicon. Since no cohort elimination process is needed, the model is not tested if there are differences in the number of such sequences for early and late nonwords.

The experiments

The set of experiments summarized below explored nonword decisions in a lexical decision task. The experiments are reported in detail elsewhere

(Goodman and Huttenlocher, 1985). They evaluate the psychological reality of the nonword point, in particular, the claim that nonwords are detected at the point where they deviate from all words. Because of the problems in establishing the theoretical uniqueness point noted above, we decided that it would not be possible to assess claims concerning the role of a uniqueness point in word identification processes. Nonword targets were constructed from words by substituting one consonant phoneme with a phoneme from a different phonetic class. For each word, two nonwords were constructed, one of which became a nonword early in the sound pattern and the other late. Changing a phoneme in a word need not result in a nonword; the target may become some other word (e.g., changing the 's' in servant to an 'f' leads to fervent). When the change does result in a nonword, it does not necessarily do so at the point of the mispronunciation; it may only become a nonword sometime after that point (e.g., changing the 's' in servant to 'j' results in a nonword, jervant, but only at the 'v'; before that point it might become germ, gerbil, jerk, or jersey). In the present study, all changes did result in pronounceable, phonotactically legal nonwords that differed by one phoneme from existing words.

We constructed nonword targets from a set of 152 words from the phonetic transcription of Webster's pocket dictionary of 20 000 words used by the MIT speech group (Shipman and Zue, 1982). The words were of various form classes — nouns, verbs and adjectives — and varied from 2 to 5 syllables, corresponding to the frequency of those groups in the dictionary. The cohort model predicts that RTs from the nonword point should be constant, regardless of when the nonword point occurs. In order to test this prediction about the nonword point it is critical to know when in the sequence of phonemes a target becomes a nonword. However, the location of the nonword point depends on the size of the lexicon with which the nonword target is compared: the larger the lexicon, the longer a target is likely to remain a word because there will be a greater number of potential words with which the target may be compatible. However, information about the size of people's lexicons is not available. We dealt with the problem of when the targets become nonwords by consulting two dictionaries: the Random House Dictionary (1966) which contains over 200 000 entries, and the Thorndike Barnhardt Intermediate Dictionary (1965) for fourth through seventh graders which contains 58 800 words. While the nonword points were defined using the larger dictionary, we included only targets where the early nonword points occurred at least 2 phonemes earlier than the late nonword points in the smaller dictionary as well. It was not generally possible to create phonotactically legal nonwords very early in the sound pattern, and some of the early nonword points occurred at the start of the second syllable.

The mean overall duration of a target was about 750 ms. The mean time from the start of a word to the early nonword point was 235 ms, and the mean time difference between early and late nonword points was 300 ms. Two examples are shown of a target word from which two nonwords were constructed. The first becomes a nonword relatively early; the second becomes a nonword relatively late. The italicized letter indicates the phoneme at which the string becomes a nonword: harvest (sar*v*est; har-ve*n*t); desire (de*y*ire, desi*l*e).

A context manipulation was included to allow us to examine the possibility that nonwords were detected as mispronunciations of particular words. If nonwords are detected as mispronunciations of particular words, preceding the target with a prime related to the word from which the nonword was created should facilitate response time. Targets were presented in pairs, half of which were preceded by a semantically related prime and half by an unrelated prime. Subjects were presented with 152 pairs, 38 each of four types; related and unrelated word pairs, and related and unrelated word/nonword pairs. For nonwords, the prime was related to the word from which the nonword target was constructed. Half of the nonword targets became nonwords early and half late. The proportion of the mispronunciations occurring on the stressed versus unstressed syllables was controlled for early and late nonword targets because mispronunciations are easier to detect in stressed syllables.

In the first experiment, subjects were told to press a key as soon as a 'nonword' was detected. The critical data are RTs measured from the nonword points, since the cohort model predicts that these should be equal regardless of where the nonword point occurs. Yet as shown in Part A of Table 1, late nonwords are responded to 256 ms faster than early nonwords. The actual time difference between early and late nonword points averages 300 ms. A two-way Anova shows the early/late difference to be highly significant ($F(1,15)=222.40, p<0.0001$). Further, as shown in Part B of Table 1, even within the narrow range of early nonword points, the same picture emerges. That is, when early nonword targets are grouped in thirds by duration from target onset to nonword point, RTs decrease with increasing time to the nonword point. A one-way Anova indicates that these RT differences are significant ($F(2,30)=32.56, p<0.01$). These results are not consistent with the predictions of the cohort model.

In Part C of the table, RTs from target onsets are shown. These RTs are considerably longer than the target durations, which averaged 750 ms, even for targets that become nonwords early. Thus it seems unlikely that nonword decisions were initiated before the targets were completed as the cohort model predicts. When measured from target onset, decisions are faster for targets which become nonwords early than for targets which

Table 1.   Results of experiment 1.

A. RTs (in ms) measured from nonword point.

	Early	Late	RT Difference (from nonword point)
Related	809.72	535.98	273.74
Unrelated	799.25	561.42	237.83

B. RTs from nonword point for early nonwords varying in durations from start to nonword point.

Median length from target onset to nonword point	RT from nonword point
150	842.45
220	799.23
325	737.8

C. Nonword RTs measured from the start of the target.

	Early		Late		Difference
	RT	% error	RT	% error	
Related	1054.09	2.6	1084.42	2.0	30.33
Unrelated	1046.68	4.1	1105.14	0.7	58.46

become nonwords late as predicted by the cohort model. A two-way Anova shows that this difference is significant ($F(1,15)=9.12, p<0.01$), but is not of the predicted magnitude (i.e., it is approximately 45 ms rather than the full 300 ms difference between early and late nonword points). There was not a significant relatedness effect.

In the second experiment, we examined whether nonword decisions are made at the nonword point by comparing RTs to make word versus nonword decisions. The procedure was identical to Experiment 1 except that there were two response keys, and subjects were instructed to press the proper button as soon as they knew if the target was a word or a nonword. It should be noted that word decisions cannot be made until the end of the sound pattern in this task, because a word might become a nonword on the final sound. Thus if nonword decisions are made at the nonword point, then they should be faster than word decisions, especially for early nonwords. Alternatively, if the uniqueness point precedes the nonword point for late nonwords, early nonwords might be detected at the nonword point, while late nonwords might be detected as mispronunciations of the target word. Again, early nonwords should be detected faster than either late nonwords or words, i.e., at the nonword point. Detection times should be similar for words and late nonwords because in both cases, the word can be recognized at the uniqueness point, but the decision must be postponed until either the mispronounced phoneme (for late nonwords) or the end of the sound pattern (for words). In this case, both words and late nonwords would be responded to faster when preceded by a related prime than an unrelated prime, while RTs for early nonwords would be unaffected by a related prime.

Table 2 shows the results. RTs for nonword targets from the nonword point were comparable to those in the first experiment for early and late nonwords. A two-way Anova shows the early/late difference to be highly significant ($F(1,15)=183.27$, $p<0.0001$). Results were also comparable for early nonwords that varied in the time to the nonword point. A one-way

Table 2. Results of experiment 2.

A. RTs (in ms) measured from nonword point.

	Early	Late	RT Difference (from nonword point)
Related	822.12	563.02	259.10
Unrelated	812.36	592.74	219.62

B. RTs from nonword point for early non-words varying in durations from start to nonword point.

Median length from target onset to nonword point	RT from nonword point
150	832.49
220	816.44
325	712.47

C. Nonword RTs measured from the start of the target.

	Nonwords				Words	
	Early		Late			
	RT	% error	RT	% error	RT	% error
Related	1064.64	5.9	1104.88	0.7	1045.2	2.3
Unrelated	1065.56	2.0	1136.38	0.7	1075.75	2.3

Anova indicates the RT differences are significant ($F(2,30)=28.57$, $p<0.001$). Consider now the critical comparison between nonword RTs and word RTs from target onset shown in Part C of Table 2. There are significant effects of target type (words, early nonwords and late nonwords) and relatedness (Target Type: $F(2,30)=9.87$, $p<0.001$). Relatedness: $F(1,15)=8.18$, $p<0.025$). Relatedness effects were small but significant both for words ($p<0.05$ and for late nonwords ($p<0.05$). There was no effect of relatedness for early nonwords.

The fact that early nonwords are not detected faster than words indicates that nonword decisions are not made at the nonword point. The fact that the overall RTs are much longer than the target durations suggests that subjects might first listen to the entire sound pattern. The relatedness interaction suggests that late nonword detections might be based on discrepancy from a word.

Discussion

The experiments summarized above examined whether nonword decisions are made at that phoneme where a target diverges from all the words in a person's lexicon. We used a lexical decision task in which targets containing a mispronounced phoneme resulted in nonwords either early or late in the sound pattern. According to the cohort model, the time to make nonword decisions should be a constant from the nonword point (Marslen-Wilson, 1978). The detection of a mispronunciation — at least if the sound pattern deviates from all possible words before the uniqueness point — is equivalent to recognition that a nonword has been heard. Our data were not consistent with this prediction; when measured from the nonword point, responses to late nonwords were about 250 ms faster than to early nonwords, and for early nonwords, RTs decreased as nonword points came later in the input. Parallel findings are reported by Ottevanger (1981) for the detection of nonwords in Dutch. Using single phoneme mispronunciations, she found steadily decreasing RTs for 5 successively later nonword points, with a 279 ms difference between the earliest and latest nonword points.

In the present experiments, nonword decisions took much longer than total target duration, suggesting that they usually were made on the basis of the entire sound pattern. In addition, word decisions in our task had to be delayed until after the final phoneme occurred, because that phoneme could turn the target into a nonword. Nevertheless, not even early nonword decisions were faster than word decisions. Thus, nonword decisions do not seem to be made at the nonword point.

Our experiments assessed the claim that nonword decisions are made at the nonword point. The other major claim of the cohort model is that words are identified at the uniqueness point. In the introduction we pointed out that the strongest empirical evidence for the psychological validity of the uniqueness point is from gating studies, and the findings are not convincing. Our experiments are not designed to examine the role of the uniqueness point in normal word identification, but there are reasons to question its psychological validity. The first concerns characteristics of the lexicon. Luce (1984) examined the uniqueness points in a 20 000 word lexicon and found that only 39% of words deviate from all other words before they end. Also, Marcus and Frauenfelder (1985) found that after the uniqueness point, words became increasingly different from words in the lexicon, suggesting that the overall deviation of a word from all other words, rather than some particular point, may be what is important in identification.

There are additional reasons to question the cohort model as well. Listeners can identify words even when initial phonemes are deleted (Samuel, 1981a; 1981b). Indeed, they often believe they have heard the deleted phonemes. In such cases, particular phonemes are heard because words are identified from partial information involving phonemes after the point of deletion. Nooteboom (1981) found that subjects can not only identify words on the basis of word-initial fragments (from word onset to uniqueness point), but also on the basis of word-final fragments (from 'right-to-left' uniqueness point to word offset). Also, Salasoo and Pisoni (1985) found subjects were able to identify words in gating studies that incremented the sound pattern, right to left, from the end of the word. According to the cohort model, when initial phonemes are deleted there is no way to activate the set of word candidates that includes the target.

Finally, recent computational studies of structural properties of the lexicon furnish information about what aspects of the sound patterns of words might provide good recognition cues. Shipman and Zue (1982) used a broad phonetic classification involving six categories to classify each phoneme of the acoustic–phonetic sequence of items in a 20 000 word lexicon. On average, only two word candidates fit each sequence. Thus it might be advantageous for a person to analyse the entire sound pattern in terms of such broad classes in the process of identifying a word. In further work with this broad classification, D. Huttenlocher (1984) found that the information in stressed syllables is far more important in constraining word candidates than the information in unstressed syllables, and this difference was maintained in an analysis using phonemes. Thus, it might be advantageous for a person to analyse stressed syllables regardless of where they occur in the process of identifying a word. Further, Carlson *et al.* (1985) found that a phoneme-by-phoneme analysis that proceeded from right to left was even more rapidly constraining than one which proceeded from left to right, and in a comparison of half words involving the phonemes from the first half of a word versus the phonemes from the last half, Pisoni *et al.* (1985) found that the cohorts that remained were roughly equal in size in the two cases. Thus it might be advantageous for a person to take account of the ends as well as the beginnings of sound patterns in the process of identifying a word.

In conclusion, the notion that acoustic–phonetic patterns are detected as nonwords at the particular phoneme where the patterns deviate from all possible words is not supported. In addition, the length of the RTs in deciding that a sound pattern is not a word suggests that subjects listen to the entire pattern before responding. Certain features of the cohort model, however, are supported by the present findings. First, the slight advantage of late nonwords in related pairs over those in unrelated pairs suggests that the target word may have been recognized before the mispronounced phoneme. Second, the small RT advantage of early nonwords over late nonwords (50 ms) when measured from the target onset suggests a left-to-right process which is in some way sensitive to the nonword point. However, further work is clearly necessary to specify the nature and time course of the processes involved in word identification.

Acknowledgements

This research was supported by a grant from the Spencer Foundation to the first author and by a grant from the Harris Center for Development studies to the second author. The authors would like to thank Catalina Danis for her help in preparing stimuli and running subjects.

References

Carlson, R., Elenius, K., Granstrom, B. and Hunnicutt, S. (1985) Phonetic and orthographic properties of the basic vocabulary of five European languages. *Speech Transmission Laboratory Quarterly Progress and Status Reports*. Stockholm: Royal Institute of Technology.

Cole, R. A. and Jakimik, J. (1980) How are syllables used to recognize words? *Journal of the Acoustical Society of America*, **67**, 965–70.

Cutler, A. and Norris, D. (1979) Monitoring sentence comprehension. In W. E. Cooper and E. C. T. Walker (Eds) *Sentence Processing: Studies in Honor of Merrill Garrett*. Cambridge, MA: MIT Press.

Goodman, J. and Huttenlocher, J. (1985) Do We Know How People Identify Spoken Words? Unpublished manuscript.

Grosjean, F. (1980) Spoken word recognition processes and the gating paradigm. *Perception and Psychophysics*, **28**, 267–83.

Huttenlocher, D. (1984) Acoustic–Phonetic and Lexical Constraints to Word Recognition: Lexical access using partial information. M.S. Thesis, MIT, June.

Luce, P. A. (1984) A computational analysis of optimal discrimination points in auditory word recognition. *Research on Speech Perception: Progress Report No. 10*, Indiana University, 345–355.

Marcus, S. M. and Frauenfelder, U. H. (1985) Word recognition — uniqueness or deviation? A theoretical note. *Language and Cognitive Processes*, **1**, 163–169.

Marslen-Wilson, W. (1973) Linguistic structure and speech shadowing at very short latencies. *Nature*, **244**, 522–3.

Marslen-Wilson, W. D. (1978) Sequential decision processes during spoken word recognition. Paper presented at the meeting of the Psychonomic Society, San Antonio, Texas, November, 1978.

Marslen-Wilson, W. D. and Welsh, A. (1978) Processing interactions and lexical access during word recognition in continuous speech. *Cognitive Psychology*, **10**, 29–63.

Marslen-Wilson, W. D. and Tyler, L. K. (1980) The temporal structure of spoken language understanding. *Cognition*, **8**, 1–71.

Morton, J. and Long, J. (1976) Effect of word transitional probability on phoneme identification. *Journal of Verbal Learning and Verbal Behavior*, **15**, 43–51.

Nooteboom, S. G. (1981) Lexical retrieval from fragments of spoken words: beginnings vs. endings. *Journal of Phonetics*, **9**, 407–24.

Ottevanger, I. B. (1981) The function of the recognition point in the perception of isolated mispronounced words. *Progress Report of the Insitute of Phonetics (PRIPU)*, **6**, 54–69.

Pisoni, D. B., Nusbaum, H. C., Luce, P. A., and Slowiaczek, L. M. (1985) Speech perception, word recognition and the structure of the lexicon. *Speech Communication*, **4**, 75–95.

Random House Dictionary of the English Language, (1966) Unabridged Edition, New York: Random House.

Salasoo, A. and Pisoni, D. G. (1985) Interaction of knowledge sources in spoken word identification. *Journal of Memory and Language*, **24**, 210–31.

Samuel, A. G. (1981a) Phonemic restoration: Insights from a new methodology. *Journal of Experimental Psychology: General*, **110**, 474–94.

Samuel, A. G. (1981b) The role of bottom-up confirmation in the phonemic restoration illusion. *Journal of Experimental Psychology: Human Perception and Performance*, **7**, 1124–31.

Shipman, D. W. and Zue, V. W. (1982) 'Properties of large lexicons: Implications for advanced isolated word recognition systems'. *Proceedings of the 1982 IEEE International Conference on Acoustics, Speech and Signal Processing*, Paris, France, April.

Thorndike Barnhardt Junior Dictionary, (4–7), (1965) Sixth Edition, Chicago, IL: Scott Foresman.

Tyler, L. K. and Wessels, J. (1983) Quantifying contextual contributions to word-recognition processes. *Perception and Psychophysics*, **34**, 409–20.

Tyler, L. K. and Wessels, J. (1984) Is gating an on-line task? Evidence from naming latency data (unpublished manuscript).

20   Hierarchical representation of spoken syllable order

Peter C. Gordon and David E. Meyer

Abstract

Three alternative classes of models have been proposed to characterize how the serial order of elementary response units is represented in speech production. Two of these, element-to-element and element-to-position models, assume that serial order is represented by simple linear structures. In contrast, hierarchical models assume a more complex structure with multiple levels of representation. The experiments reported here use a response-priming procedure to test these alternatives for the production of rapidly spoken syllable sequences. The procedure required subjects to produce either a primary or a secondary sequence of syllables after first preparing for the primary sequence. The reaction times, durations and accuracy of the subjects' utterances were measured as a function of different relationships among the serial orders of the primary and secondary syllable sequences. The results provide strongest support for a hierarchical model with binary tree branches for guiding the vocal production of a syllable sequence. This outcome may be related to certain properties of short-term memory grouping and/ or rhythmic patterns of speech.

Introduction

In attempting to understand human activity, cognitive psychologists generally assume that complex responses are composed of elementary units, and that different responses can be produced by combining these units in

LANGUAGE PERCEPTION AND PRODUCTION
ISBN 0-12-052750-2

different ways. One way that this combination occurs is through the simultaneous coordinated movement of different effectors. A second way is through the combination of elementary response units in different ordered sequences. The occurrence of such combinations raises the issue: How do elementary units of behavior, which lack any intrinsic order, get produced in appropriate sequences? This issue is Lashley's famous 'problem of serial order in behavior'. It applies to most types of movement control, and has been considered especially central to the understanding of speech production. In the present chapter, we will consider what kinds of representational structures enable the production of speech to proceed in a systematic serial order.

Our work focuses especially on the production of syllable sequences, since syllables are the smallest units of speech that can be produced in isolation (Stetson, 1951). As such, they can definitely serve as independent units during the production of multisyllabic utterances. While speech production undoubtedly involves a variety of units more complex than syllables, such as sentences, phrases and words, we assume that at some point during the production process, these units must be broken down into their component syllables. This assumption is a common one in psycholinguistic theories, and is supported by a variety of evidence. For example, syllables are related to regularities in patterns of speech errors (Dell, 1984; MacKay, 1972), and they serve as useful variables in predicting the latencies of rapid utterances (Klapp, 1974; Sternberg, Monsell, Knoll and Wright, 1978). Speech production may also involve units smaller than the syllable, such as phonemes (Fromkin, 1971) and phonetic features (Meyer and Gordon, 1985). However, these smaller units undergo substantial phonological recoding within the span of a syllable, and are to a large degree articulated in parallel, rather than sequentially (Liberman, Cooper, Shankweiler, and Studdert-Kennedy, 1967). Consequently, it seems particularly worthwhile to focus on the ordering of syllable sequences.

Current models of speech production can be classified into three groups according to their assumptions about the nature of the order information used to produce response sequences. These groups include element-to-element coding models (Lashley, 1951; Keele, 1975; Wickelgren, 1969), element-to-position coding models (Keele, 1975; Sternberg et al., 1978) and hierarchical coding models (Dell, 1984; Lashley, 1951; MacKay, 1982). The goal of the experiments reported here is to determine which of these three kinds of models provides the best account of the representation of syllable order in short, rapidly spoken utterances. The results suggest that a hierarchical representation of order is used, even when there is no basis in the pattern of a sequence to bias subjects toward adopting such a representation.

Types of models

Element-to-element coding models

These models assume that the order of a response sequence is maintained by direct associations between successive response units. Element-to-element coding models thus incorporate the associative chaining hypothesis considered by Lashley (1951) in his original discussion of serial-order behavior. As is well known, Lashley scorned and rejected this hypothesis because it cannot explain all aspects of creative linguistic performance. Nevertheless, the element-to-element coding models might still provide a viable way of representing serial order in speech production once a short sequence of response elements has been fully prepared for output. Such representations could employ a simple response-chain structure as a way of selecting the motor commands for a forthcoming response unit after the output of an immediately preceding unit (Wickelgren, 1969).

Element-to-position coding models

This type of model employs a second type of order representation. According to element-to-position models, individual response units have their appropriate place in a sequence represented through associations with members of an ordered set. In essence, the latter set provides a collection of slots or 'place holders' with which the response units are temporarily connected, just like the slots of a mail box provide positions for temporarily sorting a group of letters to be delivered in a particular order. This type of model has been prominent in short-term memory research (Conrad, 1965), and has also appeared in some accounts of speech production. For example, Sternberg *et al.* (1978) proposed that uttering a short prepared sequence of words involves storing a set of subprograms in a motor-program buffer. Each subprogram is assumed to have a position tag that designates its ordinal location as part of the sequence. Executing the subprograms supposedly requires a search of the program buffer to find the appropriate tags. Such use of the connections between the subprograms and the position tags is the essence of the element-to-position models.

Hierarchical coding models

A third possible representation for the control of serial order is employed by the class of hierarchical models. Unlike the previous cases, hierarchical models do not rely on a simple linear organization. Instead, they include a number of components at different levels of abstraction. The order of the lower-level response units is represented only with respect to higher-level elements, and not directly with respect to each other or with respect to their absolute positions in an utterance. The purpose of the higher-level elements is to guide the execution processes indirectly to the motor commands for the individual response units at the lowest level.

This sort of model was suggested by Lashley (1951) as an alternative to the associative-chaining hypothesis. Subsequently, a number of investigators, including Dell (1984), Estes (1972), MacKay (1982), Martin (1972) and Rosenbaum, Kenny and Derr (1983) have adopted similar perspectives to characterize various facets of speech production, manual performance and short-term memory. Hierarchical models have a good deal to recommend them. They are consistent with linguistic descriptions of language, and they provide a possible account for the flexibility of skilled performance (MacKay, 1982). However, it is not yet clear to what extent a hierarchical model would apply under circumstances where a large amount of response preparation must be achieved, and where the response units are relatively basic ones like spoken syllables. Under such circumstances, an element-to-element coding model or an element-to-position coding model might be more appropriate, because the simple linear organization in these models could conceivably allow faster selection and output of the response units. Thus, in order to test these various classes of models, we have employed a type of response–priming procedure involving the rapid production of short syllable sequences.

The response–priming procedure

Our response–priming procedure modified and extended one that we have used previously to study the production of phonetic features (Meyer and Gordon, 1985) and short word sequences (Meyer, Sternberg, Knoll and Wright, 1978). At the beginning of each trial, a subject was presented with a primary sequence of syllables (e.g., BEE–BAY–BAH–BOO) and a secondary sequence of syllables (e.g., BAH–BOO–BEE–BAY) on a video display screen. The syllables in these two sequences were the same, but they had different serial orders. The subject was instructed to prepare to say the primary syllable sequence as quickly and clearly as possible in response to a high-pitched response tone. On half of the trials, the high-pitched tone was then presented after the preparation interval, and the subject actually had to produce the prepared utterance. On the other half of the trials, the high-pitched response tone did not occur, and the subject did not have to produce the primary sequence, even though he or she had been instructed to prepare for it. Instead, we presented a low-pitched response tone, signaling the subject to switch and to say the secondary syllable sequence. We rewarded the subject for the speed and accuracy of his or her performance on both the primary and secondary responses; however, the payoff structure was designed to encourage preparation for the primary response (see Meyer and Gordon, 1985, for details). The trials with the two different response signals were mixed randomly, so that the subject did not know beforehand which sequence would have to be produced. Subjects were instructed to place equal stress on the syllables of a sequence. The experimenter, blind to the correct response, coded the syllables in the subject's utterance, and the subject was given negative feedback after trials on which incorrect sequences had been produced.

For dependent variables, we measured the reaction time, duration and accuracy of the subjects' utterances in producing each type of syllable sequence. Reaction time was defined to be the amount of time from the presentation of the response signal (high-or-low-pitched tone) to the acoustic onset of the vocal response, as determined by a computerized voicekey (Meyer and Gordon, 1985). The duration of the utterance was defined to be the amount of time between the acoustic onset of the vocal response and its final offset. Errors were recorded whenever the subject pronounced one of the syllables incorrectly or produced them in a wrong order. The main independent variable was the relationship between the serial orders of the primary and secondary syllable sequences.

Rationale

We assume that the response–priming procedure induces subjects to prepare an utterance plan for rapidly articulating the primary syllable sequence as soon as the high-pitched tone occurs. This plan would include information about the required serial order of the syllables in the primary sequence. However, suppose that the low-pitched tone occurs instead, so that a subject has to switch and produce the secondary syllable sequence. Then the utterance plan associated with the primary sequence may provide an initial basis for preparing and producing the alternative secondary sequence. For example, the original plan might be edited and/or rearranged to generate the needed output for the secondary sequence (cf. Rosenbaum, Inhoff and Gordon, 1984).

The difficulty of making this switch presumably depends on the nature of the serial-order information stored in the utterance plan for the primary syllable sequence, and on how the orders of the primary and secondary sequences are related to each other. If their relationship is congruent with the type of information specifying output order, then the switch from the primary to the secondary sequence should be facilitated relative to cases where the sequences are not congruent with respect to that information. Such facilitation could appear as an effect on the latency, the duration, and/or the accuracy of producing the secondary syllable sequences. Thus, by examining subjects' performance for the secondary sequences with various order relations to the primary sequences, we may test the different models of serial-order coding. (For further discussion of the logic and justification of the response–priming procedure, see Meyer and Gordon, 1985; Meyer et al., 1978; Rosenbaum and Kornblum, 1982.)

Composition of syllable sequences

In the experiments reported here, all of the primary and secondary syllable sequences contained four syllables. We restricted the number of syllables per sequence to this number for two reasons. First, four-syllable sequences have the minimal length sufficient to study the types of serial-order relations that interested us. Secondly, sequences of length four are short enough to fit easily within the usual assumed spans of short-term memory (Conrad, 1965) and motor-program buffers (Sternberg et al., 1978). The latter constraint seemed especially important because it helped ensure that subjects would, indeed, be able to prepare fully for producing the primary syllable sequences, as required by our response–priming procedure.

The syllables used in the sequences had a simple consonant–vowel (CV) structure, beginning with either the consonant 'B' or 'D'. We chose to study the production of such syllables because of their supposedly canonical structure on which all others are based (MacKay, 1972). The selection of such syllables also facilitated the acoustic detection of sequence onsets and offsets by our computerized voicekey (Meyer and Gordon, 1985).

Experiment 1

Experiment 1 was designed to test one particular version of a hierarchical coding model, which is outlined in Figure 1. Here the production of a syllable sequence stems from a hierarchy of control elements with binary branches connecting one level to the next. At the top of the figure is the structure that would control the production of a primary syllable sequence like BEE–DAY–BAH–DOO. Farther down on the left is the structure that would control the production of an alternative secondary sequence like BAH–DOO–BEE–DAY, whose serial order is hierarchically congruent with the above primary sequence. In contrast, on the right is the

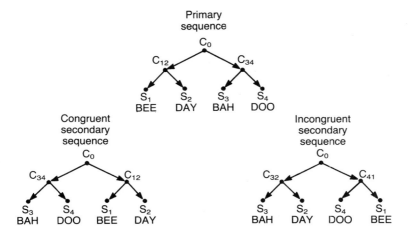

Figure 1. Binary tree structures used by a hierarchical coding model for representing the serial orders of primary and secondary syllable sequences with hierarchical congruence and incongruence.

structure that would control the production of a secondary sequence like BAH–DAY–DOO–BEE, whose serial order is incongruent with the primary sequence. Fewer operations would be required to transform the structure at the top into the bottom left structure than into the bottom right one. For example, one might obtain the bottom left structure from the top structure simply by interchanging its two upper-most branches, whereas such a simple rearrangement could not yield the lower right structure. Consequently, if the kind of hierarchical coding model shown here is valid, then we would expect performance on the congruent secondary sequences to be better in at least some respects than performance on the incongruent secondary sequences.

This particular version of the hierarchical coding model is important to test because it already has some tentative experimental and theoretical support. For example, Rosenbaum *et al.* (1983) proposed binary tree structures to characterize manual performance in the production of sequential keypresses. The applicability of such structures was supported by the latencies of keypress sequences with certain patterns of alternation and repetition. Furthermore, in a well known paper on speech and rhythm, Martin (1972) proposed a binary tree structure to characterize the perception and production of stressed and unstressed syllables. Following these developments, our aim is to determine whether binary tree structures may extend to the level of utterance plans representing the serial order of syllable sequences.

In Experiment 1, we varied two factors concerning the primary and secondary syllable sequences. One of these factors was the relation between the serial orders of the primary and secondary sequences. In some cases, there was a hierarchical congruence between the primary and secondary sequence orders, as shown in Table 1 (also see Figure 1). Given that a primary sequence had the order $S_1S_2S_3S_4$, a secondary sequence with hierarchical congruence had the order $S_3S_4S_1S_2$, where the subscripts indicate what the original serial positions of the syllables were in the primary sequence. For example, when the primary sequence was BEE–DAY–BAH–DOO, the congruent secondary sequence paired with it was BAH–DOO–BEE–DAY. In other cases, the primary and secondary sequences were incongruent. Given that a primary sequence had the order $S_1S_2S_3S_4$, an incongruent secondary sequence had the order $S_3S_2S_4S_1$. For example, when the primary sequence was BEE–DAY–BAH–DOO, the incongruent secondary sequence was BAH–DAY–DOO–BEE. (It should be noted that the hierarchically congruent sequences were also congruent according to an element-to-element model. Experiment 2 will disentangle these alternatives.)

Table 1. Syllable sequences in Experiment 1.

Sequence type	Serial order	Examples	Consonant composition	Order relations
Primary	$S_1S_2S_3S_4$	BEE–DAY–BAH–DOO		
			Heterogeneous	Hierarchical
Secondary	$S_3S_4S_1S_2$	BAH–DOO–BEE–DAY		congruence
Primary	$S_1S_2S_3S_4$	BEE–DAY–BAH–DOO		
			Heterogeneous	Incongruence
Secondary	$S_3S_2S_4S_1$	BAH–DAY–DOO–BEE		
Primary	$S_1S_2S_3S_4$	BEE–BAY–BAH–BOO		
			Homogeneous	Hierarchical
Secondary	$S_3S_4S_1S_2$	BAH–BOO–BEE–BAY		congruence
Primary	$S_1S_2S_3S_4$	BEE–BAY–BAH–BOO		
			Homogeneous	Incongruence
Secondary	$S_3S_2S_4S_1$	BAH–BAY–BOO–BEE		

The second factor varied in Experiment 1 concerned the initial consonants of the syllables. In some cases, the syllables of a sequence contained two different initial consonants, as in the sequence BEE–DAY–BAH–DOO. We refer to these as 'heterogeneous' sequences. In other cases, the different syllables of a sequence all had the same initial consonant, as in the sequence BEE–BAY–BAH–BOO. We refer to these as 'homogeneous' sequences. Our manipulation of this homogeneity factor allowed us to check whether the applicability of the hierarchical model would depend on salient alternation of the syllables' physical features.

Method

The method was similar in many respects to the one used by Meyer and Gordon (1985), and that article should be consulted for more detail.

Seven University of Michigan undergraduates served as paid subjects. Each subject participated for five hour-long sessions, with the first session being considered practice and excluded from the analyses. Half of the trials required producing the primary syllyble sequence, and half the secondary. Table 1 illustrates the various types of syllable sequences whose production we studied. Across blocks of trials, the assignment of individual CV syllables to possible serial positions was randomized.

At the start of each trial, a pair of primary and secondary syllable sequences was presented on the video terminal, with the secondary sequence appearing as a row of syllables directly below another row of syllables for the primary sequence. This display remained visible over a 2 s interval, during which the subject prepared to produce the primary sequence as quickly and accurately as possible. Next, the primary sequence disappeared from the display while the secondary sequence remained visible. Following a 1 s pause, the subject heard three medium pitched (417 Hz) warning tones and then either a high-pitched (833 Hz) or low-pitched (208 Hz tone). Each tone had a 100 ms duration and was separated from the succeeding one by a 400 ms silent interval.

Results and discussion

Table 2 shows the main results of the experiment. It contains the mean reaction times, durations and error rates for primary and secondary syllable sequences for the hierarchically congruent and incongruent relationships. The data are presented separately for the heterogeneous and homogeneous syllable sequences.

The first fact to notice is that subjects performed considerably better on the primary sequences than on the secondary sequences. Their mean reaction times were about 290 ms shorter for the primary sequences than for the secondary sequences; $F(1,6)=40.3$, $p<0.01$. In addition, the durations of the primary sequences were about 70 ms less than those of the secondary sequences; $F(1,6)=16.4$, $p<0.01$. There were only about half as

Table 2. Results of Experiment 1.

	Primary/Secondary Relationship			
	Homogeneous		Heterogeneous	
	Hierarchy	Incongruent	Hierarchy	Incongruent
Reaction time (ms)				
Secondary	588	608	564	593
Primary	287	290	301	309
Duration (ms)				
Secondary	537	559	465	501
Primary	504	508	403	399
Error rate (%)				
Secondary	3.0	9.9	6.7	10.3
Primary	2.8	4.3	2.6	4.6

many errors on the primary sequences as on the secondary sequences; $F(1,6)=8.3$, $p<0.05$. These results are encouraging because they support the assumption that subjects were highly prepared for producing the primary syllable sequences.

Next, consider the effects of serial-order relations with the primary syllable sequences on production of the secondary syllable sequences. On all three measures of performance, subjects did better when the secondary sequences had hierarchically congruent relations with the primary sequences than when they had incongruent relations. Their reaction times were about 24 ms less ($t(6)=3.2$, $p<0.02$), their durations were about 29 ms less ($t(6)=5.2$, $p<0.01$), and their error rates were about 5% less ($t(6)=2.5$, $p<0.05$). These results support the hypothesis that the utterance plan used to govern the serial order of a syllable sequence during speech production relies on a hierarchical coding structure with binary branches. There were no significant interactions between sequence homogeneity/ heterogeneity and primary/secondary sequence relationship on any of the dependent measures ($p>0.10$ in all three cases). This outcome indicates that the effect of hierarchical congruence does not depend on the alternating consonants in the heterogeneous syllable sequences. Thus, it appears that a binary-tree version of the hierarchical coding model has some generality.

However, these results could also be viewed as consistent with a simple element-to-element coding model. In particular, consider the primary syllable sequence $S_1S_2S_3S_4$ and the secondary sequence $S_3S_4S_1S_2$ which we have treated as hierarchically congruent. These two sequences are likewise congruent with respect to direct element-to-element links. The secondary sequence $S_3S_4S_1S_2$ preserves two of the three links between the successive syllables of the primary sequence $S_1S_2S_3S_4$. The secondary sequence could be obtained from the primary sequence merely by breaking the link between S_2 and S_3 and then interchanging the two pieces of the response chain. This easy rearrangement would not be possible for the incongruent secondary sequences. Thus, one might argue that we have actually found evidence in Experiment 1 to support an element-to-element coding model of serial order rather than a hierarchical model (cf. Keele, 1975).

Experiment 2

Experiment 2 was designed to obtain a sharper test of the hierarchical coding model versus the element-to-element coding model. As before, we used the response-priming procedure, but added some further types of primary and secondary syllable sequences with new serial-order relations, which are shown in Table 3. The pairs of sequences again included hierarchically congruent ones along with others whose serial-order relations were incongruent with respect to both the hierarchical and element-to-element coding models. There were also primary and secondary sequences designed specifically to evaluate the element-to-element model. The serial orders of these sequences had 'element-to-element congruence'. For example, when the primary sequence was BEE–BAY–BAH–BOO, the secondary sequence BAY–BAH–BOO–BEE was congruent with it. This element-to-element congruence was achieved by ordering the syllables of the secondary sequence as $S_2S_3S_4S_1$, relative to the primary sequence.

Table 3. Syllable sequences in Experiment 2.

Sequence type	Serial order	Examples	Order relations
Primary	$S_1S_2S_3S_4$	BEE–BAY–BAH–BOO	Hierarchical congruence
Secondary	$S_3S_4S_1S_2$	BAH–BOO–BEE–BAY	
Primary	$S_1S_2S_3S_4$	BEE–BAY–BAH–BOO	Element–element congruence
Secondary	$S_2S_3S_4S_1$	BAY–BAH–BOO–BEE	
Primary	$S_1S_2S_3S_4$	BEE–BAY–BAH–BOO	Incongruence
Secondary	$S_4S_3S_2S_1$	BOO–BAH–BAY–BEE	

The rationale for the sequences with element-to-element congruence is straightforward. They preserve the links between three of the successive response syllables (i.e., $S_2S_3S_4$). If the element-to-element coding model is correct, then the preservation of these links ought to facilitate the production of the secondary syllable sequence. However, the secondary sequences with element-to-element congruence involve substantial disruption of the binary tree structure that represents the order of the primary sequence (cf. Figure 1). Therefore, if the hierarchical coding model is correct, we would not expect to find facilitation in the production of these sequences.

Another feature of Experiment 2 was that all of the primary and secondary sequences had syllables beginning with the same consonants. The consonants did not alternate from one syllable to the next, unlike the heterogeneous sequences of Experiment 1. We included only homogeneous sequences to determine whether the hierarchical coding model could be extended to a situation where none of the salient physical markings in any of the utterances suggest a binary tree structure. This allowed us to check whether hierarchical coding is adopted spontaneously by subjects in dealing with the serial order of syllables. Finally, in Experiment 2 we used a slightly different incongruent syllable sequence from the one used in Experiment 1 (compare Tables 3 and 1). We did this in order to see if the effects we had observed previously were due to the particular incongruent sequence used as a control sequence.

Method

Eleven individuals, none of whom had participated in Experiment 1, served as paid subjects. The apparatus, design and procedure were similar to those of Experiment 1 except for the modifications outlined above (e.g., see Table 3 versus Table 1).

Results and discussion

Some results of the second experiment appear in Table 4. It displays the mean reaction times, durations and error rates of subjects' utterances for the primary and secondary syllable sequences with the various serial-order relations (Table 3). In most respects, the data look similar to what we found in Experiment 1. Performance was faster and more accurate on the primary sequences than on the secondary sequences; for the reaction times, $F(1,10)=86.9$, $p<0.01$; for the durations, $F(1,10)=19.0$, $p<0.01$; for the error rates, $F(1,10)=14.8$, $p<0.01$. As before, this supports our assumption that subjects followed the instructions for the response–priming procedure and prepared to produce the primary sequences upon command. Furthermore, for the secondary sequences, there may have been

Table 4. Results of Experiment 2.

	Primary/Secondary Relationship		
	Hierarchy	Element-to-element	Incongruent
Reaction time (ms)			
Secondary	641	652	662
Primary	298	297	292
Duration (ms)			
Secondary	607	618	619
Primary	520	524	519
Error rate (%)			
Secondary	7.8	10.9	14.6
Primary	4.9	3.7	4.2

some facilitation induced by element-to-element congruence with the serial order of the primary sequence. This facilitation seems clearest in the error rates. However, it did not reach statistical significance ($t(20)=1.4$, $p>0.10$). The most facilitation occurred for the secondary sequences with hierarchical congruence. With respect to the control condition, this condition yielded a marginally significant effect on latency ($t(20)=2.0$, $p=0.06$) and a more robust effect on error rates ($t(20)=2.5$, $p<0.02$). This facilitation due to hierarchical congruence occurred even though there were no salient physical markings in the syllable sequences to induce an alternation among response elements. Consequently, we conclude that for the production of serially ordered syllables, a major source of control is a hierarchical representation of a binary tree structure spontaneously adopted by subjects as part of preparing to speak.

Experiment 3

The conclusions from Experiment 2 are supported by a third experiment that we have done to test the hierarchical coding model against the element-to-position model outlined earlier. As may be recalled, the element-to-position model assumes a coding structure in which response units have direct links with members of an ordered set, corresponding to prearranged slots like those of a mailbox or memory buffer. This assumption may be evaluated with pairs of sequences that have what we call 'element-to-position congruence' (Table 5). We obtained such pairs by using a secondary sequence with the order $S_3S_2S_1S_4$ relative to the primary

Table 5. Syllable sequences in Experiment 3.

Sequence type	Serial order	Examples	Order relations
Primary	$S_1S_2S_3S_4$	BEE–BIH–BAH–BOO	Element–position congruence
Secondary	$S_3S_2S_1S_4$	BAH–BIH–BEE–BOO	
Primary	$S_1S_2S_3S_4$	BEE–BIH–BAH–BOO	Hierarchical congruence
Secondary	$S_3S_4S_1S_2$	BAH–BOO–BEE–BIH	
Primary	$S_1S_2S_3S_4$	BEE–BIH–BAH–BOO	Incongruence
Secondary	$S_3S_1S_4S_2$	BAH–BEE–BOO–BIH	

sequence $S_1S_2S_3S_4$. For example, with the primary sequence BEE–BIH–BAH–BOO, the secondary sequence BAH–BIH–BEE–BOO has element-to-position congruence. The latter arrangement preserves the absolute serial positions of two syllables (i.e., S_2 and S_4). Thus, if an element-to-position coding model were valid, we would expect facilitation to occur in producing the secondary sequences of these new congruent pairs, even though they disrupt all of the links between individual syllables needed to obtain a representation of the secondary sequences from an element-to-element or hierarchical coding structure for the primary sequences (cf. Figure 1 and Table 3). In addition, to check the hierarchical model further, Experiment 3 also included some primary and secondary syllable sequences with hierarchical congruence and with a new type of incongruence.

Method

Thirteen individuals, who had not taken part in the previous experiments, served as paid subjects. Some examples of the syllable sequences used in the experiment appear in Table 5. The apparatus, design, and general procedure were the same as in Experiments 1 and 2.

Results and discussion

Some results of the third experiment appear in Table 6. As in the previous two studies, subjects obeyed the basic instructions of the response-priming procedure. They produced the primary syllable sequences with relatively short reaction times $(F(1,12)=30.0,$ $p<0.01)$, short durations

Table 6. Results of Experiment 3.

	Primary/Secondary Relationship		
	Hierarchy	Element-to-position	Incongruent
Reaction time (ms)			
Secondary	568	583	568
Primary	290	297	297
Duration (ms)			
Secondary	652	655	667
Primary	511	506	506
Error rate (%)			
Secondary	12.8	17.1	23.8
Primary	6.6	6.0	7.4

$(F(1,12)=38.0, p<0.01)$, and low error rates $(F(1,12)=42.0, p<0.01)$. For the secondary sequences, there was some evidence of facilitation when they had element-to-position congruence with the primary sequences. Some facilitation appeared in the error-rate data $(t(24)=2.9, p<0.01)$; however, the reaction times for the secondary sequences were actually longest when they had element-to-position congruence with the primary sequences $(t(24)=1.9, p<0.01)$. This suggests that a speed/accuracy tradeoff may have been responsible for the observed differences between performance on sequences with element-to-position congruence and on incongruent sequences. There was no apparent facilitation revealed by the reaction times for producing the secondary sequences with hierarchical congruence. Nevertheless, the hierarchical congruence of the secondary sequences yielded the most facilitation in the error-rate data $(t(24)=4.9, p<0.01)$. We therefore conclude that the element-to-position coding models, like the element-to-element coding models, may make a small contribution to describing the production of spoken syllable sequences. However, the greatest contributor is probably the hierarchical coding model. Certainly the total weight of evidence from our three experiments tends to favor the hierarchical model over other alternatives.

General discussion

The outcome of these experiments helps to generalize the role of hierarchical coding in various aspects of the speech-production process. Previous theoretical accounts of relatively high-level processes involving abstract semantic, syntactic and lexical transformations have relied extensively on the notion of hierarchical coding (MacKay, 1982). Based on the present results, we have a better foundation for extending this type of model to the level of utterance plans that direct the production of syllable sequences, just as the same type of model may apply to the representations of other outputs (e.g., manual reponses; Rosenbaum *et al.*, 1983).

There are several potential bases for the hierarchical coding of syllable order exhibited in these experiments. One possibility is that the coding structures adopted by the subjects rest on principles of grouping similar to those in short-term memory tasks. Many memory studies have shown that serial recall of items is facilitated by decomposing a sequence of elements into groups (Johnson, 1972). Perhaps the utterance plans that represent syllable order rely on the same sort of general short-term memory mechanisms. If this is the case, then it would point to a common use of processing resources by speech comprehension and production.

Such a possibility can be assessed by using the response-priming procedure to study the production of longer syllable sequences. Studies of short-term memory have shown that longer sequences are optimally broken up into subgroups of three units each (Wickelgren, 1967). If the production of syllable sequences makes use of a general short-term memory, then we would expect the response–priming procedure to yield results for longer syllable sequences consistent with a ternary rather than binary tree structure.

Another possibility is that the hierarchical coding of syllable order stems from the rhythmic organization of speech. Simple rhythmic patterns consist of alternating accented and unaccented elements. Martin (1972) argued that speech rhythms can be described by a tree structure composed of binary branches. Thus, our results perhaps demonstrate the complementarity of ordering mechanisms with those processes that control the temporal organization of an utterance.

Martin also argued that the hierarchical organization of speech rhythms facilitates speech perception by allowing listeners to predict the temporal location of stressed syllables. His general notion has, in fact, been borne out by phoneme-monitoring experiments (Shields, McHugh, and Martin, 1974; Cutler, 1976). Moreover, Cutler (Chap 2) has argued that prosodic structure provides important cues to the location of word boundaries. To the extent that the hierarchical coding of serial order in speech production is bound up with rhythmic organization, certain aspects of articulatory performance may have strong bonds with the perception of speech. This notion is consistent with many proposals (e.g., Liberman *et al.*, 1967; Gordon and Meyer, 1984; Meyer and Gordon, 1984) that speech production and perception rely on common processes.

Acknowledgements

This work was supported by a National Science Foundation grant (BNS 82–06809) to D. E. Meyer and by research funds provided to P. C. Gordon by Harvard University. In addition, during part of the work, P. C. Gordon was supported by a fellowship from the Horace H. Rackham School of Graduate Studies at The University of Michigan. The authors thank S. Keele, D. MacKay, S. Monsell, and D. Rosenbaum for helpful criticisms and suggestions. Appreciation is also expressed to C. Huff, T. Krugler, and I. Yaniv for technical assistance. Requests for reprints should be sent to Peter C. Gordon, Department of Psychology and Social Relations, Harvard University, Cambridge MA, 02138, USA, or to David E. Meyer, Department of Psychology, University of Michigan, Ann Arbor, MI 48019, USA.

References

Conrad, R. (1965). Order errors in immediate recall of sequences. *Journal of Verbal Learning and Verbal Behavior*, **4**, 161–9.

Cutler, A. (1976). Phoneme-monitoring reaction time as a function of preceding intonation contour. *Perception & Psychophysics*, **20**, 55–60.

Dell, G. S. (1984). The representation of serial order in speech: Evidence from the repeated phoneme effect in speech errors. *Journal of Experimental Psychology: Learning, Memory, and Cognition*, **10**, 222–33.

Estes, W. K. (1972). An associative basis for coding and organization in memory. In A. W. Melton and E. Martin (Eds) *Coding processes in human memory*. Washington, DC: Winston.

Fromkin, V. A. (1971). The non-anomalous nature of anomalous utterances. *Language*, **47**, 27–52.

Gordon, P. C., and Meyer, D. E. (1984). Perceptual-motor processing of phonetic features in speech. *Journal of Experimental Psychology: Human Perception and Performance*, **10**, 153–78.

Johnson, N. F. (1972). Organization and the concept of a memory code. In A. W. Melton and E. Martin (Eds), *Coding processes in human memory*. Washington, DC: Winston, pp. 125–59.

Keele, S. W. (1975). The representation of motor programmes. In P. M. A. Rabbit and S. Dornic (Eds) *Attention & Performance V*. New York: Academic.

Klapp, S. T. (1974). Syllable-dependent pronunciation latencies in number naming: A replication. *Journal of Experimental Psychology*, **102**, 1138–40.

Lashley, K. S. (1951). The problem of serial order in behavior. In L. A. Jeffress (Ed) *Cerebral mechanisms in behavior*. New York: Wiley.

Liberman, A. M., Cooper, F. S., Shankweiler, D. P., and Studdert-Kennedy, M. G. (1967). Perception of the speech code. *Psychological Review*, **74**, 431–61.

MacKay, D. G. (1972). The structure of words and syllables: Evidence from errors in speech. *Cognitive Psychology*, **3**, 210–27.

MacKay, D. G. (1982). The problems of flexibility, fluency, and speed-accuracy trade-off in skilled performance. *Psychological Review*, **89**, 483–506.

Martin, J. G. (1972). Rhythmic (hierarchical) versus serial structure in speech and other behavior. *Psychological Review*, **79**, 487–509.

Meyer, D. E., and Gordon, P. C. (1984). Dependencies between rapid speech perception and production: Evidence for a shared sensorimotor voicing mechanism. In H. Bouma and D. G. Bouwhuis (Eds) *Attention & Performance X*. Hillsdale, NJ: Erbaum.

Meyer, D. E., and Gordon, P. C. (1985). Speech production: Motor programming of phonetic features. *Journal of Language and Memory*, **24**, 3–26.

Meyer, D. E., Sternberg, S., Knoll, R. L., and Wright, C. E. (1978). Memory retrieval and motor programming of related word sequences. Paper presented at the meeting of the Midwestern Psychological Association, Chicago.

Rosenbaum, D. A., Inhoff, A. W., and Gordon, A. M. (1984). Choosing between movement sequences: A hierarchical editor model. *Journal of Experimental Psychology: General*, **113**, 372–93.

Rosenbaum, D. A., Kenny, S. B., and Derr, M. (1983). Hierarchical control of rapid movement sequences. *Journal of Experimental Psychology: Human Perception and Performance*, **9**, 86–102.

Rosenbaum, D. A., and Kornblum, S. (1982). A priming method for investigating the selection of motor responses. *Acta Psychologica*, **51**, 223–43.

Shields, J. L., McHugh, A., and Martin, J. G. (1974). Reaction time to phoneme targets as a function of rhythmic cues in continuous speech. *Journal of Experimental Psychology*, **102**, 250–5.

Sternberg, S., Monsell, S., Knoll, R. L., and Wright, C. E. (1978). The latency and duration of rapid movement sequences: Comparisons of speech and typewriting. In G. Stelmach (Ed.) *Information processing in motor control and learning* (pp. 117–52).

Stetson, R. H. (1951) *Motor phonetics*. Amsterdam: North-Holland.

Wickelgren, W. A. (1967). Rehearsal grouping and hierarchical organization of serial position cues in short-time memory. *The Quarterly Journal of Experimental Psychology*, **19**, 97–102.

Wickelgren, W. A. (1969). Context-sensitive coding, associative memory, and serial order in (speech) behavior. *Psychological Review*, **76**, 1–15.

21 Sequencing and timing in skilled perception and action: An overview

Steven W. Keele

Abstract

The chapters in this book section are concerned with sequencing and timing in the production and perception of language. Besides giving an overview of each contribution and relating them to some common themes, the present chapter goes a bit further. It is speculated that not only are processes in common to the various manifestations of language — reading, writing, speaking and listening — but there may be even more general processes that encompass other tasks as well. These general processes include a certain mode of sequence representation, one which is hierarchic in nature, and a general timing mechanism. Hierarchic sequence representation may be the fundamental human achievement in evolution that allows such a remarkable capability to learn new skills and flexibly alter them. Another growing body of literature is beginning to suggest that a timing mechanism, a clock, is in common to diverse motor and perceptual systems. Some of this latter work has been conducted in the present author's laboratory and is summarized in the chapter.

Introduction

Human language is often touted as the prime example of what makes people so astoundingly different from other animals. Yet perhaps it is not far fetched to suggest that language facility is but an offshoot of an even more fundamental achievement in human evolution, that of being able to learn rapidly and to modify complex sequences of activity in many

LANGUAGE PERCEPTION AND PRODUCTION
ISBN 0-12-052750-2

domains. Witness the skilled movements of the woodworker, the pianist, the typist and the gymnast. All of these impressive human skills involve sequencing movements in new ways, feats beyond the capabilities of other animals. It is possible that the evolutionary advances that made them possible also paved the way for a language that involves the ability to arrange words in novel forms.

It is not that many animals do not exhibit extraordinary skill. Rather, humans excel in their extreme flexibility of sequence acquisition, allowing them to acquire arbitrary skills for which evolution had no anticipation. This raises an issue regarding a currently popular approach to both perception and motor control. It is argued by some that skills are best studied by observing natural actions such as reaching for objects, catching balls, or speaking. The argument goes that evolution has invested millions of years in building specialized perceptual and action modules for such actions, and the resultant modules are likely to be narrow in purpose. One should, therefore, study naturally occurring skills if one is to understand skill at all. Very nice examples of this approach are provided by: von Hofsten (1985) for catching movements, who shows that very young infants have the perceptual and motor functions for catching; by Lee, Lishman and Thomson (1983) and McLeod, McLaughlin and Nimmo-Smith (1985), who provide some evidence that the apparent 'timing' of motor movement directed toward a rapidly approaching object is derived from a simple parameter of expansion of the image on the retina; and by Nashner and Woollacott (1979) and Nashner and McCollum (1985), who provide evidence that a variety of complex postural patterns are triggered by differing sensory inputs. A variant of this 'ecological' approach is that many of the dynamic sequential properties of skill are not dictated by higher-order sequential representation (e.g., Kelso and Kay, 1985). Rather, they are a consequence of such things as mechanical properties of the musculo–skeletal system that carries out the action.

Despite these schools of thought that posit very particular perceptual-motor linkages, ability to acquire an unlimited variety of new sequences of activity of arbitrary type suggests a need to investigate general mechanisms of skill not necessarily intrinsic to particular perceptual-motor acts. Indeed, since the human advantage is the learning of arbitrary sequences, it may often be beneficial to study rather novel skills as well as highly practiced ones, such as piano playing or typing, which are foreign to other animals.

The purpose of this chapter is to introduce and provide additional context for the papers in this section on sequencing. The general theme of these conference proceedings is that common processes may underlie speech, reading, writing and listening, all of which are language activities.

The other chapters in this section stick largely with language. However, the argument has just been made that critical mechanisms of sequencing may be even more general than those applying only to language. Aspects of that issue are explored in this paper.

In addition to the act of sequencing, activity in many skills must also be precisely timed and not just put in the proper order. Such is apparent in a skill like piano playing but may also be the case in a skill like typing (e.g., Grudin, 1981) or speech (e.g., Fowler, 1979). It may be the case that a central timing mechanism, a clock if you will, is drawn upon by disparate activities of production and perception of speech and non-speech alike.

The current chapter will focus, therefore, on a discussion of general mechanisms of sequencing and timing. The first main section will concentrate on sequencing with a special emphasis on providing an overview of other chapters in this book section. Another prominent theme in the sequencing section will be the crucial role of hierarchical representation. The second major section will concern timing. Evidence for a general mechanism of timing will be reviewed, and some recent studies from my own laboratory that begin to explore the nature of the timer will be described.

Sequencing

If it is the case that some part or parts of the brain are specialized for sequence control, then there should be a tendency for neuropsychological deficits in sequencing activity in one domain of activity to be accompanied by deficits in another domain. The correlation might be less then perfect, however, because it is possible that different but nearby portions of the same general brain structure would be used by the different domains or that homologous portions on the two sides of the brain would be used. Moreover, as will be developed momentarily, a dominant conception of sequence representation is one of hierarchic structure. Different levels of the hierarchy may be represented in different places of the brain. Only some levels may draw on general mechanisms. At the lower levels of the hierarchy responsible for specific motor activity, disparate brain regions may be involved depending on the specific motor system. Alternatively, it might be that hierarchical representation, once evolved, rapidly proliferated into diverse areas, resulting in common functional representation but disparate anatomical representation. These various possibilities may explain why in a study by Lehmkuhl, Poeck and Willmes (1983) no clear associations were found between disorders of sequencing in speech, that is aphasia, and disorders of non-speech motor sequencing, that is apraxia.

The various aphasic patients did show a tendency toward apraxia, but differing types of aphasics (Wernicke, Broca, Amnesic and Global) did not show differing patterns of apraxia. Since the nature of the apraxic disorder did not covary with the nature of the aphasic disorder, there is no firm basis for relating the two disorders.

Studies by Mateer (1985) raise these issues anew. In one study, she examined fluent and non-fluent aphasics. Fluent aphasics are capable of producing fluent sequences of words but their sentences convey little meaning. Non-fluent aphasics are impaired in the fluency of speech but the choice of words convey appropriate meaning. Mateer tested the patients on both a speech and a non-speech sequencing task. The speech task required an arbitrary sequence of three *syllables* (not words). The gesture task required the subjects to produce three successive oral-facial gestures, such as sticking the tongue out to one side followed by puckering the mouth and then opening the mouth widely. Although there is some overlap between the muscular systems producing speech and those involved in the non-speech sequences, the latter involves a broad set of muscles, grosser movements, and they produce little or no sound. The same pattern of deficits was found for both the speech and gestural tasks. The fluent aphasics were unimpaired on the single gestures but suffered in sequencing a trio of gestures or utterances. The non-fluent aphasics suffered on both aspects.

In Mateer's second line of studies, various tasks were performed by temporal lobe epileptics during the course of neurosurgery. In an attempt to localize the epileptic focal point, many points of the brain were stimulated at the same time that a variety of tasks — sentence comprehension, picture perception, sequencing, etc., — were being performed. The effect of stimulation is to interfere with ongoing tasks, but the nature of interference varies tremendously as a joint function of the portion of the brain being stimulated and the task being performed. However, a central core area in the brain appears to be involved in disruptions of sequencing of either speech or the oral–facial gestures. This central core involves the superior portion of the temporal lobe, the very inferior portion of the parietal lobe and inferior portions of the motor and pre-motor cortex.

Although there is some similarity in the motor systems involved in both the speech and non-speech gestures, Mateer's studies begin to suggest that particular brain areas are particularly adapted to sequence control regardless of the motor system.

A recent and provocative study by Cromer (1983) bears on the issue of whether systems responsible for speech sequencing have more general functions. He examined child receptive and expressive aphasics. Although some of the children could produce and comprehend individual words, they seemed unable to learn to combine words into sentences. Cromer suggested that the deficit involves a failure to use hierarchic structures in guiding activity. To test this idea he showed both the child aphasics and control groups of deaf and of normal children a stick pattern as portrayed in Figure 1. The children were asked to copy the figure with paper and pencil. All groups were able to do a good job of reproduction, but they differed markedly in procedure. The control groups, both deaf and normal children, used a hierarchic strategy in which corresponding portions of the figure on the two sides were drawn in succession. If those children started reproduction at the top, both a left and a right branch would be produced before dropping down a level. The aphasic children, in contrast, tended to produce the figure in linear fashion, starting with a terminal branch and working all the way to the top before beginning another branch. Thus, they showed no tendency to take into account the hierarchic structure involving the encoding of groups and subgroups. Parenthetically, it should be mentioned that since the aphasic children could produce some words, there would appear to be some dissociation of different sequencing systems. Those systems concerned with more global sequencing were affected, leaving at least partially intact more local sequencing systems.

The Cromer study addresses a problem sufficiently different from general sequence control that perhaps one should not make too much of it other than to take it for its heuristic value. The study suggests that sequence problems in one domain, that of organizing words into sequence, may result from a deficit to a fundamental mode of representation in common with other domains. That mode of representation is hierarchic.

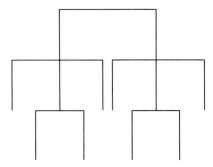

Figure 1.   A line drawing that Cromer (1983) asked children to copy was drawn in hierarchic order by non-aphasic children and in non-hierarchic order by aphasic children. (From Cromer, 1983.)

Hierarchical representation of sequence

A basic point of MacKay's chapter in this section is that a large number of stable, replicable phenomena exist concerning sequentiality, and that any reasonable theory of sequential order must address these phenomena. Some of the phenomena concern sequencing in perception. Very often, the sensory input, on which perception is based, occurs temporally as with speech signals. According to MacKay, some theories either postulate or have implicit a temporal isomorphism between sequential input and perception. That is, it is supposed that perception is sequenced in the same way as the input. MacKay marshals several sources of data against this common assumption.

To the data base which argues against temporal isomorphism should be added the work of Huttenlocher and Goodman presented in this section. A prominent theory of speech perception by Marslen-Wilson (1976) supposes that the speech perception of a word occurs on-line. At any critical point of time in the sequential input of speech at which information becomes available for discriminating between a word and a non-word, the decision is initiated. His own experimental work, in which the temporal position within the speech stream at which the critical information became available was varied, supported his contention. That is, lexical decision reaction time was quicker for non-words that became such at an earlier point in time. However, Huttenlocher and Goodman have pointed out a confounding in some of Marslen-Wilson's examples of non-words that vary in the point at which they become non-words. In particular, non-words which became non-word at an early point appeared to be less phonotactically regular than those non-words that became so at a later point. Phonotatic irregularity would assist the non-word decision, resulting in faster reaction time. In three experiments which attempted to eliminate the confounding, reaction time appeared to be time-locked to the end of an utterance rather than to the point at which it became non-word. This result is consistent with other studies mentioned by MacKay that show a lack of temporal isomorphism between input and perception.

Much of MacKay's presentation is concerned with the data base which must be addressed by theories of sequential action. He argues that a plan that governs action must be prepared before the action occurs. The evidence comes from observations that very often people make anticipatory errors, introducing a part of an upcoming sequence before its time. In addition, upon a signal to respond, preparatory reaction time depends on the number of syllables per word and the number of words that are to follow, as though the utterances are pre-planned (Klapp, Anderson and Berrian, 1973; Sternberg, Monsell, Knoll and Wright, 1978). MacKay observes also that errors are of definite types. In particular, errors are nearly always of the same class as the intended item: nouns substitute for nouns, adverbs substitute for adverbs, syllables substitute for syllables, etc. What does not happen, for example, is that a word substitutes for a syllable.

Preparatory reaction time and the within-class nature of errors argue that sequence representation is hierarchic in nature. Such a concept posits that sequential control passes from general to more specific representations. Reaction time is slightly longer for two-syllable words than for one-syllable words, suggesting that control must pass from a word to a syllabic level before reaching a phonemic level. Likewise, errors indicate that when control is on one level, errors come only from that level. A study that further clarifies this meaning of hierarchical control is provided by Povel and Collard (1982). Subjects in their study produced rapid sequences of key presses. The four figures on one hand rested on keys labeled 1 through 4 from left to right. An example of one of many different sequences performed by subjects is 123321.... Subjects are shown the sequence of numbers, and then they tap the pattern repetitively as rapidly as possible with their fingers, cycling back to the beginning of the sequence after the end. It might be instructive for the reader to tap out the pattern. Another sequence was 332112... and yet another was 233112.... For each of these sequences, the subjective experience is that the successive responses are organized into groups with relatively fast intertap intervals between members of a group and longer intervals separating groups. In fact the data in figure 2a, from Povel and Collard, illustrate exactly this: for

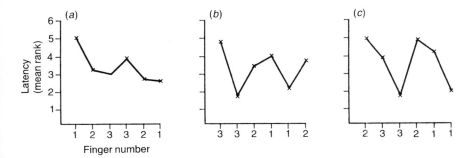

Figure 2. Subjects cyclically tap a six element pattern. The order of finger presses is shown on the abscissa. The mean rank of the intertap interval, averaged over subjects, is shown on the ordinate. (From Povel and Collard, 1982.)

the sequence, 123321.... A relatively long gap occurs after the 123 portion of the sequence and before the 321, and a relatively long pause transpires again after the 321 and before the 123. For the second sequence, 332112.... pauses occur after 332 and after 112 (see figure 2b); for the sequence 233112... pauses occur after 233 and after 112 (figure 2c). Thus, the temporal structure exhibits a grouping.

What may have escaped notice is that the three examples above are exactly the same sequence except for starting position. Despite the fact that the fingers follow one another in the same order in each of the three cases, subjects clearly have differing mental representations for the three which guide the course of action in different ways. The nature of the internal representation determines the intertap pause structure. That representation has a hierarchic structure ranging from general to specific. It is as though the performer first retrieves a group of items, and then from the group a specific movement is retrieved. Within the group, retrieval times of individual elements are relatively fast. When the group is exhausted, a time-consuming retrieval of the next group occurs, and then within the group the first element is chosen. It might be noted that such a temporal structure may be hidden in skills so practiced that their speed is limited by the maximum rate of motor activity rather than by retrieval time.

The utility of the Povel and Collard study is that hierarchic structure is manifest in the on-line production of a sequence, but the essential conclusion of hierarchic representation is also arrived at from the analyses of errors (MacKay, 1982 and the chapter in this book section) and reaction time (Keele, 1986; Rosenbaum, Kenny, and Derr, 1983).

Hierarchical representation and transfer

A reason why hierarchic representation is useful to the organism is that it provides tremendous flexibility in learning new sequences of activity. The flexibility derives from the transportability of subsequences into new arrangements. Upper levels of a hierarchy can be rearranged, making use of already existing lower levels. Thus, it is argued that in human speech, phonemes, or at least low-order segments, are fundamental units that can be rearranged in new ways to form new words. The new words are not constructed from scratch but make use of the sub-units already acquired in other contexts (the fact that errors of word pronunciation often involve segmental substitutions argues for small segments as speech units more fundamental than words: see MacKay, Chap 18). Likewise, words once acquired can be reorganized into new frameworks without the necessity of learning new words.

Chapter 20 by Gordon and Meyer in this section examines the transportability of subunits of speech activity and pits three theories of sequence representation against one another. Subjects learned patterns of speech involving sequences of four consonant–vowel syllables (e.g., Bee–Bay–Bah–Boo). Subjects would prepare to speak one such pattern, but on occasion the signal to begin response would require that a different sequence be produced instead. One possibility is that the sequence string is represented hierarchically. Thus the sequence Bee–Bay–Bah–Boo would be stored at one level as two subgroupings, (Bee–Bay) and (Bah–Boo). Suppose the sequence the subject was prepared to speak was stored in this manner. Then if the response signal required a different sequence, it should be easier for a new sequence like Bah–Boo–Bee–Bay, which preserves the subgroups and simply reverses their order, than for a sequence like Boo–Bee–Bay–Bah, in which adjacent portions of the prepared for sequence largely maintain their adjacency in the unexpectedly required sequence. As predicted by the hypothesis of hierarchic structure, subjects showed greater ease of switch to new arrangements that maintained subunit pairing in the prior sequence than to new arrangements that created different subunits while maintaining adjacency. Moreover, in other situations reported in their chapter, transfer that maintained subunit structure was better than transfer that involved some of the same syllables remaining in the same temporal position of the sequence but with a breakup of the subunit structure.

Gordon and Meyer's study makes two important points. It adds transfer of preparation from one sequence to another to the list of procedures which has yielded evidence favoring hierarchic sequence structure over other forms of sequence structure. It also illustrates why hierarchic representation of sequences is such a powerful mode of representation. Such representation allows subsequences to be transported in their entirety into new sequences without the necessity of a complete relearning of the entire structure, thereby endowing the human learner with enormous flexibility.

Earlier, MacKay and Bowman (1969) had also used a transfer paradigm of a somewhat different sort to provide evidence for hierarchic representations of sequence. Subjects committed novel sentences to memory and then repeated them several times as rapidly as possible. With practice, sentence production became faster, approaching an asymptote by 12 repetitions. All subjects were German–English bilinguals, and after the 12th practice trial they switched to another sentence in the other language. On some occasions the transfer sentence remained the same both in meaning and in basic word order with the only change being from English to German or vice versa. This particular condition resulted in perfect transfer — subjects produced the first four transfer sentences with the same speed that they had attained by the last four practice trials of the preceding utterance. Of course, if the meaning of the sentence as well as the language was changed, speed of utterance slowed down and no transfer resulted.

In another condition, subjects practiced repeating a string of words that did not constitute a sentence. Again, practice speeded production, but in this case, when each word was translated to the other language, no transfer whatsoever occurred.

The interpretation by MacKay (1982) of the MacKay and Bowman results is that the sentence is encoded in hierarchic form. Practice strengthens the connections between hierarchy levels. The structure provides meaning to the sequence of words. Thus, at the highest level below a sentence node, a simple sentence is represented as a noun phrase and a verb phrase. Below that level the noun phrase and the verb phrase are broken into their constituents. These levels are purely conceptual in that the same concepts can be attached either to English or to German words. Since the subjects were experienced bilinguals and were very familiar with all the individual words in the sentences, the practice effects with 12 repetitions presumably were restricted to strengthening the hierarchic sentence structure above the level at which concepts are translated to words. That is, the links between concepts and words were already quite strong because of the past history of learning, and the short practice of 12 repetitions probably had little effect at that level. However, the particular word order is novel, so considerable short-term practice effects would occur at that level of representation. During transfer of the sentence to the other language, the hierarchic superstructure could be transported in its entirety. For a non-meaningful arrangement of words, transfer failed to occur, according to MacKay, because an individual word can take many meanings (think of the number of possible meanings of the word 'right' in English). When a word is embedded in a sentence, the sentence structure pinpoints a particular meaning of the word, making apparent the proper translation. For a meaningless string of words, however, practice strengthens a structure that fails to specify the meaning of individual words, and hence when language is switched, transfer fails to occur.

As with the Gordon and Meyer study, the study by MacKay and Bowman illustrates the enormous flexibility that hierarchic sequence structure provides the learner. In this latter case, the entire upper levels of a hierarchy, not just subunits, can be transferred to a new motor system. To appreciate the power with which hierarchic representation endows the learner, consider an *expert* with two musical instruments, say trumpet and trombone. Suppose the expert practices a new piece of music with one instrument and then transfers to the other instrument. Despite the fact that the motor activity is quite different for the two instruments, one might expect nearly perfect, if not perfect, transfer because what the highly experienced musician learns is not particular finger or arm sequences, but a more abstract structure that dictates what finger or arm movements to make.

A particularly important implication of these various studies that suggest hierarchic representation is that motor control in humans cannot be divorced from abstract, cognitive representations. The argument advanced suggests that the brain systems that directly control movement do not 'learn' motor sequences. Instead the sequence is embedded in hierarchic, perhaps cortical, representation. That representation dictates sequence, and the more motoric brain systems simply accept orders from above. Such a mode of operation may constitute one aspect of the fundamental evolution of human skill capabilities.

Dynamic and synergistic contributions to sequencing

Ultimately if action is to occur, abstract representations of sequence must be interfaced with motor systems to carry out the activity. An issue has been raised whether *all* sequential properties of the movement are represented in the program or neural wiring that directs movement or whether some of the sequential behavior is a result of dynamic properties of the biomechanical motor system itself (e.g., Kelso and Kay, 1985). Consider, for example, pioneering work by Bizzi, Polit and Morasso (1976). Monkeys were trained to make head movements toward a light spot that appeared in an otherwise dark room. As the head began to turn, the spot turned off, removing all visual feedback. Sometimes, via a clutch system attached to the monkey's head, a spring would temporarily retard movement before being released, or weights would be added thereby increasing the rotational inertia of the head. Despite increased inertia, the head reached the target, though more slowly. Once a retarding spring was removed the head moved to the intended target. The crucial observation was that these 'corrective' movements were made without visual feedback, without vestibular feedback (as the monkeys had vestibular senses removed), and without kinesthetic feedback (due to deafferentation). Since no feedback source is available to initiate corrections, it appears that the 'corrections' are simply due to dynamic characteristics of the mechanical system of the monkey's head and muscles.

An analogy can be made between the head with sets of opposing muscles that turn it one way or the other and a cafe door with opposing springs that keep it centered. If one of the opposing door springs is replaced with a stiffer one, the door will immediately begin to move and it will re-center in a new position. Contracting a muscle is analogous to setting its stiffness, and simply resetting stiffness appropriate to a new centering location will cause the head to turn. The temporal properties of the head-turning, like the cafe door, depends on things like mass. Changing the mass will alter movement speed, and may induce oscillation, but will not change centering position. If a retarding spring is added and then removed, the centering location will assume an intial position and then change with removal of the spring. The major point is that details of the temporal behavior are a result of the nature of the mechanical system in response to changes in things like stiffness setting of the muscles. A superordinate program may specify the times at which changes in muscle setting are to occur and the mechanical system's response fills in temporal details.

Not only are some temporal details dependent on mechanical properties rather than being learned and controlled by program, but it also appears that many sequences draw on assemblages of movements as subunits that are more-or-less innate. Such assemblages are called synergies.

To provide a concrete example, Nashner and Woollacott (1979) studied postural responses such as occur when one slips on ice and the feet move forward with respect to the body, thereby rotating the feet relative to the ankles. They simulated such a situation by moving forward or backward a platform on which subjects stood. The response is a patterned array of muscle activity, involving the gastrocnemius, tibialis, hamstring and quadriceps muscles as well as other muscles. Such activity normally helps retain posture. The same pattern is triggered, however, when a platform upon which people stand is rotated. In this case, the perturbation has little direct influence on posture but, nonetheless the same pattern of muscular activities is triggered. Pardoxically, in this case the pattern destabilizes the body. It appears, therefore, that a complex synergy is pre-organized and can be triggered by ankle rotation even when the pattern is inappropriate. One might speculate that such synergies are available to be incorporated into new skills such as when one learns to dance.

Part of the enormous flexibility of humans in building new sequences may depend, therefore, on exploiting both mechanical properties and innate programs. Substantial evidence exists for both of these propositions and is reviewed more thoroughly in Keele (1981, 1986).

Timing

In discussing the sequencing of motor activity, people sometimes fail to distinguish it from the timing of sequential activity. Yet MacKay (Chap 18) points out that timing control must be partly independent of sequence representation. One reason, he claims, is that the same sequence can be conducted at differing rates with near constancy in the relative timing of the different components. For example, Carter and Shapiro (1984) trained subjects to move a handle back-and-forth in an arbitrary temporal pattern in which the duration of the movements bore no correspondence to the metric length of the movements. When subjects were asked to speed up, the relative temporal relationships stayed about the same. Such a result indicates that tempo can be controlled independently of sequence structure.

This book examines processes common to various language activities — reading, writing, speaking and listening. It has been argued that the latter three involve timing beyond mere sequencing. Rhythmic timing in speech production appears to facilitate speech perception (e.g., Martin, 1972); see Cutler, Chap 2). Likewise handwriting would appear to require precise timing (e.g., Wing, 1978). Although each of these tasks require timing, it is not necessarily the case that they share a common timing system. The following sections explore whether a common timer underlies production and perception and begin to delve into the nature of the timing system.

Though there is a large literature concerned with timing, much of it focusses on the subjective experience of time over intervals of seconds, minutes, or even longer periods (see Allan, 1979, for a review). There is no reason for supposing that timing over such long intervals shares any of the same mechanisms with the timing systems involved in relatively fast-paced motor and perceptual activity as occurs, for example, in the production or perception of music. In recent years several investigations have appeared concerning timing of fast-paced motor and perceptual activity. In the following sections, selected work will be reviewed that suggests a timing mechanism common to different activities. Although most of that work is not concerned with language *per se*, it is closely related to the theme of common processes of this volume. In addition, a couple of studies will be mentioned that specifically investigate whether language production draws upon a timer shared with other motor activities. A final section previews some current work that is coming out of our own laboratory that is concerned with the nature of the timing mechanism itself. This brief review leaves out other important topics in timing, particularly of rhythm. The interested reader may consult important papers by Deutsch (1983), Povel (1981, 1984), Essens and Povel (1985), and Vorberg and Hambuch (1984).

The separation of central and peripheral components of timing variability

One important development has involved efforts to differentiate between central and peripheral sources of timing variability. Wing and Kristofferson (1973) showed that if timing variability is affected by two independent sources, clock variability and variability in the duration of the motor processes that implement movement, then these sources can be separated by examining the temporal structure of a sequence. Clock variability and motor variability sum to produce total variability in the timing of successive movements such as a series of taps. However, motor variability also induces a sequential dependency among successive intervals. If by chance motor implementation time is short for one event, that will shorten the interval since the last observable motor event, and assuming the clock ouput is unaltered, lengthen the interval before the next observable motor event. Likewise, a randomly long duration of motor implementation will lengthen the time since the last event and shorten the time before the next. Put another way, randomly varying motor implementation times will induce a negative covariation of the durations of intervals between successive motor events. That negative covariation serves as an estimator of timing variance due to motor processes, and by subtracting that component from total time variance, a residual is left that represents variance of the clock system.

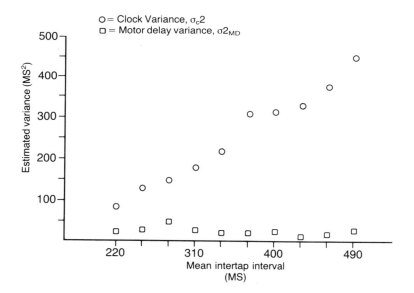

Figure 3. Subjects repetitively tap at mean intervals ranging from 220 ms to 490 ms. The total intertap variance is decomposed into clock variance and motor variance, and such variance is plotted against mean interval. (From Wing, 1980.)

By this model one would expect that the longer the time interval metered out by the clock, the greater would be clock variance. However, the duration for implementing movement should be independent of the interval since the last movement. Wing investigated this prediction in a study in which people attempted to produce a series of even taps at a variety of target intertap intervals. The total timing variance was then parsed into that due to clock and that due to motor processes. The results are shown in Figure 3 (this and other evidence for separable processes are reviewed in Wing, 1980). The fact that clock variance climbs with increasingly long intervals while motor variance remains constant provides striking confirmation of the model.

A model that is different from that of a central timer is one in which timing is governed by the feedback from a preceding movement. For example, in one version (Adams and Creamer, 1962), a decaying proprioceptive trace from one movement serves as the basis for timing another movement. When the trace reaches a target level, the succeeding movement is triggered. Some evidence speaks against feedback-based timing, however. For one thing, a feedback model predicts that since timing of a subsequent movement does not begin until after the receipt of feedback from the preceding movement, whether the preceding interval was randomly shorter or longer than normal would have no influence on the subsequent interval, whose timing is independent of the preceding interval. In contrast, Wing (1980) explains how the clock model predicts negative covariation of adjacent intervals. That is, a short interval tends to be followed by a long one and vice versa (see the earlier discussion of how the negative covariation yields an estimate of motor variability). Since such negative covariation is found, the evidence speaks against a feedback model, which makes no such prediction.

To test more directly a feedback based model of timing, Wing (1977) sometimes slightly altered the timing of a feedback tone resulting from a finger tap of advancing it 10 ms before its normal time of occurrence or delaying it by 30 or 50 ms. These changes were so small that subjects did not notice them. If the time of the next response was dependent on the receipt of the preceding feedback, then alterations in feedback time should be matched by equivalent changes (on the average) in the time before the next response. Such was not the case, leading Wing to reject a feedback model of timing. In a similar study by Conrad and Brooks (1974), monkeys moved a handle back-and-forth between a pair of mechanical stops. Unexpectedly altering the position of the stops caused the movement to strike the stops earlier or later than the expected time thereby advancing or retarding the time of proprioceptive feedback that results from hitting the end. Such alterations did not alter the time at which the monkeys reversed

movement. Such results argue that feedback, either auditory or proprioceptive, does not serve as the basis for timing. Instead, timing seems to be
centrally generated. Of course, when feedback indicates a large departure
from intended time, the timing may be altered. However, it appears that
such feedback is used to adjust a clock but is not itself the clock.

Is the timing mechanism common to perception and production?

Recent work from our own laboratory has begun to ask whether a common
clock underlies both production by different muscular systems and perception of auditory events. Keele, Pokorny, Corcos and Ivry (1985) asked
subjects to tap as regularly as possible with either finger or foot. Variance
of the intertap intervals is correlated between finger and foot about 0.5
(and in unpublished work between finger and forearm about 0.9). In other
words, people that are relatively good at timing with one effector tend to
be good at timing with another. In another task the subjects made judgements about the durations of brief intervals between auditory events. The
acuity of duration judgements also correlated (over 0.5) with the variability
of periodic motor timing. A concern is that the correlations amongst these
timing tasks reflect not a common timing system but some more general
factor such as motivation or general neural noise. A variety of correlations
with other tasks such as force control and motor speed suggest, however,
that the correlation of perceptual timing and motor timing is based on
common timing systems. Timing variability correlates little with force
control (a report is in preparation). Moreover, motor timing correlates
with motor speed but perceptual timing does not. Such an outcome suggests that motor timing is a composite of two separable components, one
related to perceptual timing and the other emerging from the motor system
itself in a way that also constrains speed. In turn, this multicomponent
aspect of motor timing explains why its correlation with perceptual timing
is only about 0.5.

A second approach to the issue of common timing mechanisms examines
the time sharing of tasks. If two different activities both require access to
the same timing mechanism, then their times should interact with each
other. Klapp (1979) has shown, for example, that the simultaneous performance of different temporal patterns by the two hands results in considerable interference. Likewise, subjects have difficulty in simultaneously
producing one temporal pattern with the finger and another temporal
pattern with the voice (Klapp, 1981). In a similar task, Peters (1977) found
large amounts of interference between rhythmic manual tapping and reci-
tation of a nursery rhyme. These studies by Klapp and Peters suggest that

differing motor tasks and motor and speech tasks draw on a common timekeeper. Pokorny (1985), in our laboratory, has extended the time-sharing paradigm to simultaneous motor and perceptual events. While subjects attempted to tap with their fingers a series of even intervals, tones were presented in some of the intertap intervals. One of the tones was longer in duration than the other and one was more intense. Subjects were asked either to identify the loudest tone, or to identify the longest, or to ignore the tones altogether. In a control condition, subjects tapped intervals with no tones present. As it turned out, it made no difference whether people attended to the loudness or to the duration or even whether they attended at all. The mere presence of a tone in an intertap interval lengthened that interval. In additional studies, Pokorny has shown that the amount by which the tone increases the duration of the intertap interval depends on where within the interval the tone occurs. In contrast, variation in intensity of the tone has little or no effect on tap timing.

Pokorny also observed that the effect of the tone on the intertap interval was confined to the interval in which it occurred. The succeeding intervals all maintained normal duration. This is important, for it suggests that the effect of the tone was to temporarily alter a central timer rather than to produce motor interference. If the effect were one of motor interference, leaving central timing unaltered, then the tone would have pushed the *response* back in time. Since the clock would have been unaltered, the following response would have occurred at its intended time. The result would have been a longer than normal interval followed by a shorter than normal interval. Since in actuality the interval following the one in which the tone occurred was unaltered in duration, the interfering effect of the tone would appear to have been on the preceding clock process rather than on the motor process. Thus, along with the correlational evidence that links perceptual and motor timing abilities, the temporal interaction of perceptual events with motoric timing, indicates commonality of the underlying timing mechanism.

Other work from our laboratory (Ivry and Keele, 1985; Keele, Manchester and Rafal, 1985; Wing, Keele and Margolin, 1984), involving neurological patients, has attempted to pinpoint brain structures responsible for timing. One preliminary suggestion (Keele, Manchester and Rafal, 1985) is that several brain structures, including cerebellum and basal ganglia, are involved in timing, and therefore the timing system is best conceived of as a circuit from cortex to cerebellum and basal ganglia and back to the cortex.

Yet a third technique in addition to correlational and time-sharing analyses also suggests a common timekeeper between perception and production, in this case between *speech* perception and production. The technique in general appeals to functional similarities of production and perception to argue for commonality. Fowler (1979) showed that when subjects produce a series of the same word spoken repeatedly, such as the word mad, the interval between successive word onsets is more or less constant. When, however, words like sad and mad alternate over a series, the onset-to-onset interval from sad to mad differs from mad to sad. Fowler produced evidence that the unequal intervals in the alternating word condition are due to differences in onset time of vowel articulation relative to the beginning of the initial consonants of the words. That is, although the intervals between word onsets are unequal, the onset-to-onset intervals measured from beginning to vowel articulation would appear to be equal. The important observation from the present viewpoint is that when listeners *judge* speech rather than produce it, they judge an alternating word sequence to be regular in onset-to-onset times when in fact the time intervals differ in the exact manner of the pronunciation irregularities. This parallelism of perception and production suggests that timing is referred to a common system.

A variety of evidence suggests, therefore, that a common timer mediates not only between different motor tasks but also between perception and production and also across different modes of language and non-language alike.

On the nature of the clock

Besides the question of whether common mechanisms underlie perceptual and motor timing, one may inquire about the basic nature of the timing system. Schulze (1978) has differentiated between two possible timing mechanisms. One is called here a persistent pacemaker or beat-based timer. The idea is that a periodic series of events establishes an internal beat which persists after the events subside. Subsequent events are then timed with respect to the internal beats. The second possibility is an interval timer. By an interval timer is meant that the metering of time to produce an event can begin at any arbitrary point rather than requiring synchrony with an internal beat. A stop watch is an example of an interval timer: the production of a particular interval, say 2 s, can begin at any arbitrary point.

The distinction between a pacemaker and an interval timer becomes blurred if the pacemaker is one which can stop and be restarted at arbitrary times much as can a tuning fork. There are possible tests between such a resettable pacemaker and an interval timer that are currently being developed in our laboratory. However, for the present chapter we will distinguish only between a *persistent* pacemaker, which produces an ongoing series of internal beats after the end of a periodic train of signals and serves as the basis of subsequent time judgements or timed movements, and a resettable timekeeper, which here will be called an interval timer.

In his own research, Schulze produced a series of intervals between tones. In one set of conditions there were six intervals. Sometimes all six were identical in duration. Let us represent that condition as:

t   t   t   t   t   t

where t refers to the 300 ms length of the interval. In other conditions at least one of the intervals was greater or less than t by 10 ms (or 15 ms in some situations). Let us represent a longer interval as t+ and a shorter one as t−. There were three such conditions:

1) t   t   t+   t+   t+   t+
2) t   t   t+   t   t   t
3) t   t   t+   t−   t   t

The task of the subjects was to determine whether all the intervals were the same or not. Given a persistent pacemaker, condition 1 should be the easiest, because the first two intervals should establish an internal beat the persistence of which would become increasingly out of phase with succeeding intervals. Thus, the close of the third interval would deviate from the internal beat by 10 ms; the fourth interval would deviate by 20 ms, the fifth by 30 ms and the sixth by 40 ms. Condition 2 should be more difficult because the one increment interval would put all the following intervals only 10 ms out of synchrony with the internal beat. Condition 3 should be the most difficult, because although the closure of the third interval would be discrepant from the internal beat, the fourth interval would compensate and put events back in synchrony.

Different predictions obtain for an interval timer, depending on how it functions. If successive intervals are compared, condition 1 should be hardest, because a difference of 10 ms at only a single comparison must be discriminated. Condition 2 should be next in ease because it yields two places in which successive intervals differ by 10 ms. Condition 3 should be the easiest, because it yields a difference of adjacent intervals at three spots, two of which differ by 10 ms and one by 20 ms. Thus, the model of successive comparisons makes the opposite predictions to that of the persistent pacemaker timer.

A third model posits that an average of the first two intervals composes a standard which is compared to each of the remaining four intervals (note that subjects were aware that any difference would appear only after the first two intervals). This model predicts condition 1 to be easiest, condition 3 next, and condition 2 the hardest.

The evidence favored a persistent pacemaker in that condition 1 was the easiest to discriminate from a sequence of all equal events followed by condition 2 and then by condition 3. It should be noted, however, that in Schulze's study the advantage of condition 2 over 3 was not statistically significant.

Recently we (Keele, Ivry, Nicoletti and Pokorny) have begun to test Schulze's models with another paradigm, and our evidence, in contrast to Schulze's evidence, appears to favor an interval timer, not a persistent pacemaker. A fuller report with a number of additional experiments will appear elsewhere (some of the additional experiments attempt to distinguish between two versions of an interval timer, a resettable pacemaker and a delay line timer). A subject heard five tones separated by 600 ms in some cases and 650 ms in others. Either 700 or 750 ms following the last tone, the word 'tap' appeared on the oscilloscope screen, and the subject's task was to press a key two times, attempting to reproduce the time interval between the tones. In one condition the subjects were told to initiate the tapping after the tap signal, but there was no emphasis on a fast reaction time. If timing is based on a persistent pacemaker, then the first tap should fall in synchrony with an internal beat established by the series of tones.

Several results at first suggested that some subjects based timing on an internal beat. First, the reaction time between the word 'tap' and the onset of the first tap was shorter for the 750 ms delay between the last tone and the word 'tap' than for the 700 ms delay. Such a result is necessary by the persistent pacemaker theory, because less time remains between the tap signal and the next internal beat the greater the delay of the tap signal. Second, on some occasions the subject didn't initiate the first tap in time for the first of the hypothetical internal beats following the tap signal. In that case the tap should be delayed an additional 600 or 650 ms, depending on the presentation rate of the tones. The result should be a multimodal reaction time distribution with peaks separated by either 600 or 650 ms. Again, some subjects showed such multimodal reaction time distributions. Third, reaction times were longer for the 650 ms pace than for the 600 ms pace. The reason this supports pacemaker timing is that when the tap signal occurs say 700 ms after the last tone, it will be 500 ms until the next internal beat at the 600 ms pace and 600 ms until the next internal beat at the 650 ms pace. Thus, the delay before the first tap should be 100 ms longer for the slower pace, which is what occurred for some subjects.

Despite the apparent support for a persistent pacemaker, we think that it is not a fundamental mode of timing but rather derivative. Not all subjects showed the reaction time patterns as predicted by a persistent pacemaker.

Rather, their reaction times were constant on the average regardless of pace and delay of the tap signal, and they did not show two or more peaks in the reaction time distributions. Second, several manipulations resulted in the disappearance of evidence for pacemaker timing, even for those subjects that showed indications of such timing in the initial condition. For example, when subjects were told to tap out the target interval as soon as possible after the tap signal occurred (a speed emphasis), all the above indicators of synchrony with an internal beat disappeared — i.e., reaction times were constant for different tap rates and tap signal delays, and the multimodality of the reaction time distributions disappeared. Moreover, in another version of the paradigm the subjects heard five tones producing four equal intervals (e.g., 600 ms), followed by a pause and then a final tone. At the final tone, subjects were to make a single tap such that the interval between the last tone and the tap matched the intervals between the initial tones. The accuracy of producing the interval did not depend on whether or not the last tone, which triggered the response, occurred in synchrony with the hypothetical beats established by the initial tones. That is, the accuracy of reproducing the 600 ms interval was the same whether the triggering tone occurred 1150, 1200 or 1250 ms after the last of the five initial tones. Given a persistent pacemaker, timing should have been more accurate when the triggering tone occurred 1200 ms after the initial tones, since the timing would be in synchrony with the hypothetical internal beat.

Altogether our results are not consistent with a persistent pacemaker model of timing. Instead they support the notion that the human timing system is an interval timer that can be started at arbitrary points in time. This raises the issue of why the results are inconsistent with those of Schulze (1979). One possibility is that an interval timer can mimic a persistent pacemaker by recycling after each interval. By this conception, interval timing is the more fundamental mode but it can also operate in a pacemaker mode. This would be in essence a resettable pacemaker in which some kind of neural circuit could hold a memory of the desired interval and be started at will. A second possibility is that a different formal model of interval timing than the two interval models considered by Schulze would be consistent with his results. We are currently exploring a model that we call an 'evidence accumulator'. In this conception, intervals are not compared directly with each other. Rather each actual interval provides evidence to the nervous system for intervals of various lengths. The judgement of interval equality depends on the evidence after all the actual intervals are presented.

A primary theme of this section on timing has been that mechanisms for controlling rate and time are independent of the representation of sequence (see also MacKay, 1985, and Chap 18). There are suggestions — based on individual differences, time sharing, functional similarities, the isolation of a timing component from motor components of production, and the conversion of perceptual to motor time — that there may be common timing systems between production of different effectors and perception. This also appears to be the case for language perception and language production. Exactly what is meant by commonality is not clear, however. Is precisely the same mechanism drawn upon by perception and production? Or is it that different but nearby brain regions are used for different tasks and that correlations and interactions derive from their proximity, such as from similar chemical or neural substrates.

Summary

The view adopted in this chapter is at partial odds with some current conceptions in the literature of cognition, perception, and action. Such conceptions posit tight modules of perception-action organization in which in the course of evolution particular perceptual devices have emerged that provide information for particular actions. While not denying that such modules may be important components of most skills, the noteworthy achievement of humans is their extraordinary ability to acquire new sequences of activity across many domains. The ability to achieve such learning may depend on two kinds of very general mechanisms. One may be a style of sequence representation particularly prominent for humans, and that is hierarchic sequence representation. It may be that the general principle has proliferated throughout many regions of the brain, but some evidence hints that a particular core region of the cortex plays a prominent role in sequence control across both language and non-language domains. In addition at least one childhood disorder of both language and drawing may stem from a common disruption of hierarchic organization. Thus, it may be fruitful to engage in further search for critical brain regions that control sequence acquisition across several domains. The second general mechanism appears to be a timer. Several sources of evidence — correlational, time-sharing results, and functional similarities in production and perception — suggest that either the same clock or at least related and interacting structures support timing across varying domains, including language and non-language tasks. Some evidence is beginning to make a case that the timer is best conceived as an interval timer and not a pacemaker, at least a pacemaker that produces a persistent internal beat after the end of a sequence of periodic events.

Acknowledgements

This paper was written during a stay at the Center for Interdisciplinary Studies (ZIF) at the University of Bielefeld in Germany. I am very appreciative of the opportunities provided by the center and the organizers of the Perception and Action program. Comments by Alan Allport and Don MacKay on this paper are also appreciated. The studies of timing from my laboratory that are reported in this paper were supported by a grant from the U.S. National Science Foundation (BNS8119274) and an Office of Naval Research Contract (N00014–83–K–0601). Richard Ivry, Roberto Nicoletti and Robert Pokorny are collaborators on the work on timing.

References

Adams, J. A. and Creamer, L. R. (1962). Proprioceptive variables as determiners of anticipatory timing behavior. *Human Factors*, **4**, 217–22.

Allan, L. G., (1979). The perception of time. *Perception and Psychophysics*, **26**, 340–54

Bizzi, E., Polit, A. and Morasso, P. (1976). Mechanisms underlying achievement of final head position. *Journal of Neurophysiology*, **39**, 435–44.

Carter, M. C. and Shapiro, D. C. (1984). Control of sequential movements: Evidence for generalized motor programs. *Journal of Neurophysiology*, **52**, 787–96.

Cromer, R. F. (1983). Hierarchical planning disability in the drawings and constructions of a special group of severely aphasic children. *Brain and Cognition*, **2**, 144–64.

Deutsch, D. (1983). The generation of two isochronous sequences in parallel. *Perception and Psychophysics*, **34**, 331–7.

Essens, P. J. and Povel, D.-J. (1985). Metrical and nonmetrical representations of temporal patterns. *Perception and Psychophysics*, **37**, 1–7.

Fowler, C. A., (1979). 'Perceptual centers' in speech production and perception. *Perception and Psychophysics*, **25**, 375–88.

Ivry, R. and Keele, S. W. (1985). Dissociation of the central timekeeper and the peripheral implementation processes in repetitive movements. Technical Report No. 85–7, Cognitive Science Program, University of Oregon, Eugene, Oregon, USA, 1985.

Keele, S. W. (1981). Behavioral analysis of movement. In V. Brooks (Ed.) *Handbook of Physiology: Section I: The Nervous System. Volume II. Motor Control, Part 2.* Baltimore, MD: American Physiological Society (distributed by William & Wilkins).

Keele, S. W. (1986). Motor control. In L. Kaufman, J. Thomas and K. Boff (Eds) *Handbook of Perception and Performance.* New York: Wiley.

Keele, S. W., Manchester, D. L., and Rafal, R. D. (1985). Is the cerebellum involved in motor and perceptual timing: A case study. Technical Report No.

85–4, Cognitive Science Program, University of Oregon, Eugene, Oregon, USA, 1985.

Keele, S. W. Pokorny, R. A., Corcos, D. M. and Ivry, R. (1985) Do perception and motor production share common timing mechanisms: A correlation analysis. *Acta Psychologica*, **60**, 173–91.

Kelso, J. A. S. and Kay, B. A. (1985). Information and control: A macroscopic analysis of perception-action coupling. In H. Heuer and A. F. Sanders (Eds) *Tutorials in Perception and Action*. Amsterdam: North-Holland.

Klapp, S. T. (1979). Doing two things at once: The role of temporal compatibility. *Memory and Cognition*, **7**, 375–81.

Klapp, S. T. (1981). Temporal compatibility in dual motor tasks II: Simultaneous articulation and hand movements. *Memory and Cognition*, **9**, 398–401.

Klapp, S. T., Anderson, W. G., and Berrian, R. W. (1973). Implicit speech in reading, reconsidered. *Journal of Experimental Psychology*, **100**, 368–74.

Lee, D. N., Lishman, J. R., and Thomson, J. A. (1982). Regulation of gait in long jumping. *Journal of Experimental Psychology: Human Perception and Performance*, **8**, 448–59.

Lehmkuhl, G., Poeck, K., and Willmes, K. (1983). Ideomotor apraxia and aphasia: An examination of types and manifestations of apraxic symptoms. *Neuropsychologia*, **21**, 199–212.

MacKay, D. G. (1982). The problem of flexibility and fluency in skilled behavior. *Psychological Review*, 483–405.

MacKay, D. G. (1985). A theory of representational, organization, and timing of action with implications for sequencing disorders. In Roy, E. A. (Ed.) *Neuropsychological Studies of Apraxia and Related Disorders*. Amsterdam: North-Holland.

MacKay, D. G. and Bowman, R. W., Jr. (1969). On producing the meaning in sentences. *American Journal of Psychology*, **82**, 23–39.

Marslen-Wilson, W. D. (1976). Linguistic descriptions and psychological assumptions in the study of sentence perception. In R. J. Wales and E. C. T. Walker (Eds) *New Approaches to the Study of Language*. Amsterdam: North-Holland.

Martin, J. G. (1972). Rhythmic (hierarchical) versus serial structure in speech and other behavior. *Psychological Review*, **79**, 487–509.

McLeod, P., McLaughlin, C., and Nimmo-Smith, I. (1985). Information encapsulation and automaticity: Evidence from the visual control of finely tuned actions. In M. I. Posner and O. S. M. Marin (Eds) *Attention and Performance*. Hillsdale, NJ: Erlbaum.

Nashner, L. M. and Woollacott, M. (1979). The organization of rapid postural adjustments of standing humans: An experimental conceptual model. In R. E. Talbot and D. R. Humphrey (Eds) *Posture and Movement*. New York: Raven Press.

Nashner, L. M. and McCollum, G. (1985). The organization of human postural movement: A formal basis and experimental synthesis. *Behavioral and Brain Sciences*, **8**, 135–72.

Peters, M. (1977). Simultaneous performance of two motor activities: The factor of timing. *Neuropsychologia*, **15**, 461–5.

Pokorny, R. A. (1985). Searching for interaction between timing of motor tasks and timing of perception tasks. Unpublished doctoral dissertation. University of Oregon, Eugene, Oregon, USA, 1985.

Povel, D.-J. (1981). Internal representation of simple temporal patterns. *Journal of Experimental Psychology: Human Perception and Performance*, **7**, 3–18.

Povel, D.-J. (1984). A theoretical framework for rhythm perception. *Psychological Research*, **45**, 315–37.

Povel, D.-J. and Collard, R. (1982). Structural factors in patterned finger tapping. *Acta Psychologica*, **52**, 107–23.

Rosenbaum, D. A., Kenny, S. B., and Derr, M. A. (1983). Hierarchical control of rapid movement sequences. *Journal of Experimental Psychology: Human Perception and Performance*, **9**, 86–102.

Schulze, H.-H. (1978). The detectability of local and global displacements in regular rhythmic patterns. *Psychological Research*, **40**, 173–81.

Sternberg, S. Monsell, S. Knoll, R. L., and Wright, C. E. (1978). The latency and duration of rapid movement sequences: Comparisons of speech and typewriting. In G. E. Stelmach (Ed.) *Information Processing in Motor Control and Learning*. New York: Academic Press.

von Hofsten, C. (1985). Catching. In H. Heuer and A. F. Sanders (Eds) *Tutorials in Perception and Action*. Amsterdam: North-Holland

Vorberg, D. and Hambuch, R. (1984). Timing of two-handed rhythmic performance. In J. Gibbon and L. Allen (Eds) Timing and time perception. *Annals of the New York Academy of Sciences*, **423**, 390–426.

Wing, A. M. (1977). Perturbations of auditory feedback delay and the timing of movement. *Journal of Experimental Psychology: Human Perception and Performance*, **3**, 175–86.

Wing, A. M. (1978). Response timing in handwriting. In G. E. Stelmach (Ed) *Information Processing in Motor Control and Learning*. New York: Academic Press.

Wing, A. M. (1980). The long and short of timing in response sequences. In G. E. Stelmach and J. Requin (Eds) *Tutorials in Motor Behavior*. Amsterdam: North-Holland.

Wing, A. M., Keele, S. W., and Margolin, D. I., (1984). Motor disorder and the timing of repetitive movements. In J. Gibbon and L. Allan (Eds) Timing and time perception. *Annals of the New York Academy of Sciences*, **423**, 183–92.

Wing, A. M. and Kristofferson, A. B. (1973) Response delays and the timing of discrete motor responses. *Perception and Psychophysics*, **14**, 5–12.

Index